Contents

Introduction, *by Joseph Hansen*	6
SECTION I: Marxism vs. Ultraleftism, *by Ernest Germain*	10
A Strange Campaign	10
Caught in the Act	10
The SLL Brought into Its Own Court	13
'Pabloite Revisionism'	15
The Ceylon Example	18
SLL Revision of the Theory of Permanent Revolution —the Case of Cuba	23
An 'Objectivist' Chicken Comes Home to Roost	31
Revision of the Leninist-Trotskyist Concept of the Colonial Revolution	35
Revision of Trotsky's Theory of the Negro Struggle in the USA	40
A Peaceful Road Back to Capitalism in the Soviet Union?	43
The SLL Echoes Third Period Stalinism	50
'Trotskyism in One Country'?	54
Footnotes	57
SECTION II: Healy 'Reconstructs' the Fourth International	62
Sectarianism and Tinpot Despotism—An Example for the Textbooks, *by Joseph Hansen*	62
Letter from G. Healy to Jim Robertson	68
Letter from G. Healy to Tim Wohlforth	69
Letter from A. Nelson to All Locals, Organizing Committees, and Members at Large	69
Letter from Rose J. to the Bay Area Spartacist Committee	70

Letter from G. Healy to Cde. H. Turner and Cde. Sherwood — 71

Letter from Harry Turner to Comrade Healy — 73

Comments on the Letter of Comrade Healy to Comrades Turner and Sherwood on the Third Conference of the International Committee, — 77
by Mark Tishman

Letter from J. Robertson to the Coordinating Committee, American Committee for the Fourth International — 79

Letter from D. Freeman, for the Coordinating Comm., American Comm. for the Fourth Int. to J. Robertson — 79

Letter from J. Robertson, for the REB, to the Coordinating Committee, A. C. F. I. — 80

Letter from Daniel Freeman for the Coordinating Committee, American Committee for the Fourth International to James Robertson, Resident Editorial Board, Spartacist — 80

After the April 1966 Conference which Took as Its Tasks to Reconstruct the Fourth International, — 81
by G. Kaldy

SECTION III: Principled Basis of Trotskyist Reunification — 86

SECTION IV: The Beating of Ernest Tate — 95

Ernest Tate Beaten by Squad at SLL Meeting — 95

SWP National Committee Demands Healy be Expelled — 96

Text of Letter from SWP to Pierre Lambert — 97

Ernest Tate Appeals for Support Against Intimidation by Healyites — 97

The SLL Calls the Cops in Ernest Tate Case — 99

Healy Scores Another 'Triumph' Over Ernest Tate — 102

Wohlforth Tries to Brazen It Out — 103

Wohlforth's Stand on the Ernest Tate Case — 106

SECTION V: Healyites Continue to Flout Workers Democracy — 110

Harry Turner's Complaint to Gerry Healy — 110

Malcolm Kaufman Expresses Doubts on Wohlforth's Devotion to Democracy — 115

SECTION VI: *Healy vs. the Antiwar Movement* — 118

The SLL Yields Again to Imperialist Pressure, — 118
by Joseph Hansen

Once Again—The SLL and Vietnam, — 121
by Joseph Hansen

In Reply to the Slanders in *The Newsletter* — 126

Healy Proves a Point, — 129
by Joseph Hansen

Some Advice to Tariq Ali, — 131
by Joseph Hansen

An Ultraleftist Endorses the Antiwar Movement, — 134
by Les Evans

SECTION VII: *The Struggle in Northern Ireland* — 141

Revolutionary Nationalism, Class Struggle, and Problems of Party Building in Ireland, — 141
by Gerry Foley

Performing Artists on a Flying Trapeze, — 158
by Gerry Foley

SECTION VIII: *The Struggle in Bangladesh* — 172

Healyites in the Camp of Indira Gandhi, — 172
by Joseph Hansen

SECTION IX: *Black Liberation* — 174

Healyites Decide Trotsky Was Wrong on Black Nationalism, — 174
by Joseph Hansen

SECTION X: *Cops as 'Fellow Workers'* — 181

Are New York's Cops 'Workers'?, — 181
by Allen Myers

Healyites in Solidarity with 'Militant Policemen,' — 183
by Allen Myers

SECTION XI: *Women's Liberation* — 187

Where the SLL Goes Wrong on Women's Liberation, — 187
by Caroline Lund

SECTION XII: The SLL Abstains on Krivine,   193
by Joseph Hansen

SECTION XIII: Why the SLL Refuses to Support the Mandel Case,   195
by Pat Jordan and Tariq Ali

SECTION XIV: Healyites Smear Bala Tampoe   200

SECTION XV: Unprincipled 'Unification' with the POR (Lora)   202

  Lambertists Knife Aid for Bolivian Victims,   202
  by Gerry Foley

  Healyites and Lambertists in Strange Company,   203
  by Joseph Hansen

SECTION XVI: Healy Offers to Unify with 'Pabloite Traitors'   206

  Healy's Request to Discuss Unification   206

  Fourth International Reply to New SLL Proposals   207

  SWP Says 'No' to Healyites   210

SECTION XVII: Healy's 'International Committee' Splits Wide Open   212

  Disaster in Bolivia for Healy-Lambert-Wohlforth,   212
  by Gerry Foley

  The Lambertist View of the Bolivian Events (Resolution published in
Sept. 29 issue of *Informations Ouvrières,* paper of the
Organisation Communiste Internationaliste, French component
of the International Committee headed by Pierre Lambert)   221

  Lambertist 'Declaration' on Socialist Labour League
(Leaflet distributed in Paris by the Organisation Communiste
Internationaliste)   224

  The Healyite Case Against the Lambertists
(Statement which appeared in November 5 issue of the *Workers Press*,
newspaper of the Central Committee of the Socialist Labour League
of Great Britain)   226

  Lambertist 'Reply to a Splitting Act' (Statement by the
Central Committee of the Organisation Communiste Internationaliste,
Nov. 21, 1971)   241

  'Construct' or 'Reconstruct' the Fourth International,   258
  by Pierre Frank

SECTION XVIII: Healyite Revision of Marxist Economic Theory 265

Contradictory Nature of the Postwar Prosperity 265
by Dick Roberts

Healyites vs. Karl Marx on Gold and Inflation, 271
by Dick Roberts

Healyites Find That Capitalism Has Dropped Dead, 276
by Dick Roberts

SECTION XIX: Healyite Revision of Dialectical Materialism 282

A Malignant Case of Sectarianism in Philosophy, 282
by George Novack

Healyite Revisionism in the Field of Philosophy, 287
by George Novack

A Travesty of Marxist Method, 292
by George Novack

Facts Are Stubborn Things, 296
by George Novack

Introduction

The contributions to this compilation deal with various aspects of the views of a political grouping organized and led by Gerry Healy, the national secretary of the Socialist Labour League [SLL], a British formation that claims to be Trotskyist.*

Marxism Vs. Ultraleftism, which was published as a pamphlet in 1967, has been out of print for some time. Today most of the members of the sectarian grouping with which it deals have perhaps never heard of it—the turnover in membership of the SLL and the scattered forces in other countries that maintain fraternal relations with it is very high. In addition, it is quite likely that very few of them are acquainted with the articles that have been published in reply to attacks leveled by the SLL and those under its influence against the Fourth International and its sections or sympathizing organizations such as the Socialist Workers Party in the United States. This collection should therefore serve as a convenient reference source for members of the SLL who feel that they really ought to acquaint themselves with the arguments of the other side in the ten-year campaign conducted by their leaders against the Fourth International.

The documents, it is to be hoped, will also provide useful educational material for young people newly recruited to the revolutionary Marxist movement. The disease of sectarianism can represent a hazard, particularly in young and isolated groups lacking knowledge of its causes and symptoms. A study of the ideology and practices of a group like the SLL can serve as an excellent prophylactic.

---

* At a conference held in London on November 4, 1973, the Socialist Labour League changed its name to the "Workers Revolutionary Party." The change in label, however, marked no change in political line, as Healy himself made abundantly clear at the gathering.

The roots of the differences recorded in this collection can be traced back to divisions that appeared in the Fourth International in the early fifties. Some of the views and practices of the secretary of the organization at that time, Michel Pablo, led to a factional struggle that ended in a split. The issues involved conflicting estimates of the probable evolution of the Soviet bureaucracy, conflicting views on the tactics to be followed by the Trotskyists in relation to the Stalinist and Social Democratic parties, and sharp divergences over internal practices in the Fourth International. In opposition to the views and course of Pablo, an international faction, the "International Committee," was organized under the leadership of James P. Cannon, the founder of American Trotskyism. Gerry Healy was a participant in the struggle against the faction headed by Pablo.

By 1956 the key political issues in this dispute had receded. This was shown by the fact that Pablo had apparently retreated from his previous position, and more solidly by the fact that both sides reached similar judgments as to the meaning of Khrushchev's revelations in that year, made similar analyses of the political revolutions that gathered headway in 1956 in Poland and especially in Hungary, and stood together in defending those political revolutions against the efforts of the Kremlin to crush them.

It was the opinion of Cannon and other leaders of the Socialist Workers Party that the common *political* positions reached by the two sides in the Fourth International on such decisive questions made possible a principled reunification and that it was the duty of the responsible leaders on both sides to facilitate such a turn.

The Socialist Workers Party took the initiative in this direction in 1957. Pablo, however, while speaking for reunification, sabotaged its consummation. A few years later it was learned that Healy, too, followed a parallel course, doing everything possible secretly to block steps toward reunification. Healy feared that the attention of the international might be called to his stewardship in Britain. He had good reason for such fears, since he had introduced practices in his organization of the most arbitrary and undemocratic nature. Healy did not indicate his real reasons for opposing reunification; he sought more acceptable reasons for delaying, postponing, and if possible derailing reunification. For example, at one point he publicly advanced the thesis that the differences separating the two sides were not narrowing but widening.

Since there were few facts to substantiate such "reasons," Healy resorted to misrepresentation and outright lying, sometimes of a most brazen nature. Disregard of the facts and doctoring of the truth were to become hallmarks of Healyism, making the press of the Socialist Labour League one of the most unreliable in left circles.

The victory of the Cuban revolution in 1959 was decisive in showing that the International Committee and the International Secretariat of the Fourth International stood on common political positions that made further resistance to reunification highly unprincipled and even politically irrational. The majority on both sides agreed that as an outcome of the revolution a workers state had been established in Cuba which had to be defended as such.

Healy disagreed. In his opinion, there had been no socialist victory in Cuba. "The Castro regime," he said, "did not create a qualitatively new and different type of state from the Batista regime." Healy, it was clear, was incapable of recognizing a revolution when he saw one. Nevertheless, under pressure from the majority of the International Committee, he opened up negotiations with the International Secretariat, and a parity committee was set up to carry out further discussions and to sponsor joint actions. In this way preparations were made for a reunification congress a year later.

When the reunification congress was convened in 1963, a minority of the International Committee headed by Healy and by Pierre Lambert, a French Trotskyist leader, drew back. A principled platform for the reunification, proposed by the Political Committee of the Socialist Workers Party, had been accepted by the majority of the International Committee and the majority of the International Secretariat. Neither Healy nor Lambert took a position on this. They did not propose any modifications. They did not offer a word of criticism of the platform. They even refused to attend the reunification congress as observers. On the side of the International Secretariat, a minority headed by Juan Posadas, an Argentinian, also refused to participate.

After the majority of the International Committee joined in the reunification, Healy and Lambert set up a rump "International Committee." This grouping led an uneasy existence until 1971 when it split wide open. Several articles in this collection deal with this event and its meaning.

Consideration of the arguments of hopeless sectarians may appear to offer little of interest to militants concerned about the realities of the class struggle. The truth is that a study of the politics of a group like the Healyites can lead to a better appreciation of those realities. Sectarians appear bizarre because their answers to problems facing the revolutionary movement correspond to preconceived schemas that are remote from the living struggle. The sectarian nostrums can be assessed correctly, however, only if the issues at stake are analyzed accurately, which means analyzing them on the basis of the Marxist concepts of the class struggle. What emerges from this study, therefore, is a fresh insight into the class struggle even though the point of departure was the sectarian outlook.

Thus the topics covered in this collection include issues of top concern to revolutionists in the past decade—the nature of the Cuban revolution, the importance of the colonial revolution, Black nationalism, women's liberation, the struggle against the imperialist aggression in Vietnam, the monetary crises, etc. Even questions of proletarian morality are included, as in the glaring instance of the beating of Ernie Tate.

That philosophical questions, particularly dialectical materialism, could become involved may seem far-fetched. It is a fact, however, that a thorough understanding of the sectarian pattern of thinking requires a good grasp of Marxist methodology. Curiously enough, the Healyites themselves raised this question, averring that the leading theoreticians of the Fourth International had embraced pragmatism. This was a deliberate concoction inasmuch as figures like George Novack have staunchly defended dialectical materialism for forty years and more. The discrepancy between the amount of ritualistic praise offered by the Healyites to dialectical materialism and their contributions to its defense and advancement could hardly be greater. Nothing else was to be expected, of course, from "philosophers" whose lowest priority is the truth. In demonstrating this in several articles included in this collection, George Novack also brings out the real philosophy behind the positions of the Healyites—it happens to be the most vulgar pragmatism. The lesson he points to—how the dialectic takes its revenge on its abusers—is applicable to much broader areas than the thinking of ossified sectarians.

A similar concoction of the Healyites—that Ernest Mandel invented the term "neocapitalism" and is the chief defender and advocate of that school of thought—is taken up by Dick Roberts. He proves that the Healyite charge is a simple case of slander. More importantly, he examines some economic questions disputed by the Healyites and shows that it is they who are the revisionists. In considering the issues at stake, Roberts provides valuable insights into some complex economic problems.

The Healyites have featured the question of "Pabloism" in their press for the past ten years. Few issues go by without references and even long articles or a series of long articles devoted to it. Evidently they are either immensely afraid of Pabloism as the main danger—or main temptation—faced by their organization, or they consider it to be such a popular issue among the British masses that a broad circulation of their press can be won by concentrating and campaigning on it as they would on mass unemployment. The explanation could, of course, be simpler—Healy is obsessed with the subject. Some ironic aspects of this monomania are worth noting.

First of all, Pablo himself left the Fourth International in 1965, later to affirm some of the positions he held in the early fifties that touched off the factional struggle in those years. Healy hardly noted the event. He paid still less attention to its meaning. The ogre was gone but ogrism remained alive and kicking.

Secondly, throughout this ten-year period Healy has continued to insist over and over on his desire to "discuss" with the Fourth International. One wonders what his real view is of the stream of material he publishes attacking the Fourth International and organizations in sympathy with it like the Socialist Workers Party. Isn't this discussion sufficient? Why doesn't he double the flow? That would undoubtedly be appreciated by the British masses. Perhaps the present compilation of replies to him will serve to convince at least some members of the SLL that a sustained discussion has been carried on.

Thirdly, in April 1970 Healy drew a strange conclusion to his long years of hammering away at the Fourth International. He appealed to the United Secretariat of the Fourth International to open a mutual discussion that might pave the way to unification of the "International Committee" with the Fourth International!

This action, taken at face value, showed how little substance there was to the public attacks he had mounted over the years. In actuality, of course, Healy had not changed his mind. He was merely engaging in a "clever" unity maneuver that he hoped might make it possible to chip away some members from the Fourth International. Healy was turned down by the United Secretariat in view of the unprincipled nature of his maneuver.

Naturally, if the leaders of the Socialist Labour League should ever come to recognize how mistaken their course has been since 1963 in relation to the Fourth International, the United Secretariat would have to take this into consideration and reopen the question of unification. In view of Healy's deadend factionalism, however, the Socialist Labour League is hardly likely to change its orientation on this question in the foreseeable future.

Healy's approach stands in sharp contrast with that of Cannon. Cannon's course was determined by objective political facts. Against Pablo's deviations in 1951–54, Cannon organized an international struggle. But when Pablo retreated, if only temporarily, and it became clear in 1956 that both sides were following similar political lines, Cannon favored recognizing these facts. That called for a corresponding orientation; namely, moving toward reunification and the eventual dissolution of factions. On the other hand, both Pablo and Healy followed narrow factional criteria. For Pablo, reunification would signify loss of his leading role in the international as a whole—a majority would surely vote to replace him as secretary. For Healy, as indicated above, it would have meant condemnation by the international of the bad practices that had developed under his leadership in Britain.

Cannon's approach, based on his experience in the early years of the Communist International under Lenin and Trotsky, his long collaboration with Trotsky in working toward founding the Fourth International, and his efforts to keep the international organization going in the difficult early period, led him to place the interests of the movement as a whole above any narrow partisan concerns. He took a long-range, objective view in the tradition of Leninism.

Healy's subjectivism led him to disregard the objective situation facing the Fourth International; that is, the steady narrowing of political differences between the two factions. He therefore sought to find differences where none existed or to find differences in areas other than the key political issues facing the movement. Thus to demonstrate the supposed incorrigibility of the British followers of the International Secretariat, Healy sought to magnify organizational frictions between the two sides into major scandals. However, with objective observers on the scene, these efforts were deflated. Later Healy was to hunt assiduously for differences in many fields—they form the topics of many of the articles in this compilation.

It was quite true that reunification could not guarantee that new differences over fresh issues would not arise. In fact, it could be counted as certain that they would arise. The reunification, however, would make it much easier to resolve them in the normal process of democratic discussion. Moreover, the reunification would offer the maximum possibility of breaking down the old lines of division, thereby strengthening the international internally.

Instead of participating in this process as a responsible international leader, Healy chose to maintain hardened factional lines, even if his faction was reduced to a small minority of the International Committee. Following this line, he and Lambert split from the International Committee. The British Trotskyist movement had to pay a heavy price for this gross error. The Socialist Labour League stands today as an ingrown sect devoid of internal life. Moreover with the departure of the French sector, the SLL became virtually isolated internationally save for a small group in the United States whose originality consists of mimicking Healy's practices.

As with many other sects and cults that have appeared in the broad socialist movement in the past, the Socialist Labour League may continue for a time as a sideshow never likely to move beyond a small tent. In one respect, however, the SLL has achieved a certain success—as a source of object lessons on the difference between ultraleftism and Marxism. This compilation offers testimony to that.

—*Joseph Hansen*

SECTION I: MARXISM VS. ULTRALEFTISM
by Ernest Germain

1

A STRANGE CAMPAIGN

Since 1963, *The Newsletter*, the official weekly organ of the Central Committee of the Socialist Labour League in England, has been campaigning against the Fourth International as well as the Socialist Workers Party, one of the founding members of the Fourth International although it is barred today by reactionary legislation in the United States from affiliating with the World Party of the Socialist Revolution which it helped Leon Trotsky to launch in 1938.

The SLL campaign is strange enough in itself, coming as it does from a group which claims to espouse the same ideas of revolutionary Marxism and to speak in the name of the same movement as those it subjects to incessant public attack. The campaign is even stranger if one considers the methods which the SLL leaders resort to in almost routine fashion in trying to justify their campaign.

At first sight it might appear rather pointless to give serious consideration to this sect, its bizarre leader and its ultraleft views. To go into detail on the subject would seem to promise nothing positive. What could it be but a barren exercise, a profitless engagement in a dispute of the kind in which no one can tell who is right or wrong and in which it makes little difference anyway? If the reader can manage to follow for a few pages, however, this impression may change. After some thorny opening difficulties, various key problems of the revolutionary Marxist movement begin to emerge, including some of the most vital issues of the day. These are well worth discussing, even within the framework set by the small sect that gets out *The Newsletter*.

We begin, then, by raising the curtain and showing the top leadership of the SLL busy at work.

2

CAUGHT IN THE ACT

The time is the summer of 1964, right after the June 7 conference in Colombo of the Lanka Sama Samaja Party [LSSP] which had constituted the Ceylon section of the Fourth International up until then. At the conference the right wing of the LSSP proposed that the party join the bourgeois Sri Lanka Freedom Party [SLFP] in setting up a coalition government. Against the vehement opposition of the left wing of the LSSP, which remained faithful to the principles of revolutionary Marxism, the right wing, headed by N. M. Perera, succeeded in winning a majority.

In reporting this conference in the June 20, 1964, issue of *The Newsletter*, Gerry Healy, the general secretary of the SLL, put down the following:

> Dr. Colvin de Silva and Leslie Goonewardene, the general secretary of the LSSP, maintained a centre position at the conference.
>
> They were supported by the Pabloite Unified Secretariat in Paris until, at the end of the conference, the former deserted to the right.

What was this "centre position" maintained by Colvin R. de Silva and Leslie Goonewardene? In the same issue of June 20, 1964, the editors reprinted the text of the resolution presented by the two centrist leaders at the conference. The following key sentence provides the substance of their position:

The processes necessary for a progressive solution of the crisis can be inaugurated by a coalition government between the *ULF* [United Left Front] *and the SLFP* on the following conditions . . . (Emphasis added.)

Did the United Secretariat of the Fourth International "support" this proposal for a coalition between the working-class parties in the United Left Front and the bourgeois SLFP, either before, during or after the LSSP conference? It did not. Not for one second! As early as April 23, 1964; i.e., as soon as it heard of the secret negotiations for a coalition being conducted by N.M. Perera and Mrs. Srimavo Bandaranaike, the head of the SLFP, the United Secretariat of the Fourth International spoke out in the firmest and most unambiguous way against *any* coalition with the SLFP. Here are some paragraphs from a letter sent by the United Secretariat to the Central Committee and members of the Lanka Sama Samaja Party on April 23, 1964, that should suffice to show what its stand was:

> As far as the SLFP is concerned, two factors appear to motivate its present course of action: (1) lack of confidence in its ability to continue in office for the rest of its constitutional term; (2) a deep-seated fear of an upsurge in the working-class movement and the real possibility of the emergence of a government of the left. Clearly, it is this latter possibility which drives it today to seek a modus vivendi with the left and attempt a realignment of forces through a coalition with the United Left Front.
>
> Its calculations are fairly obvious. It hopes to gain strength by an infusion from the left. It hopes to disorient the masses by taking on left coloration. It hopes to weaken the threat from the left by splitting the left organizations (since acceptance of a coalition would obviously not be unanimous and would most likely open the most bitter factional struggles). It hopes to associate prominent left figures with its rule and thereby utterly discredit them for the following phase when this one comes to its inevitable end and social forces have reached unendurable tension and polarization.
>
> Its primary immediate aim is to stem the tide of rising mass unrest, contain the parties of the left within its own control and commit them to 'progressive' formulae within the framework of the capitalist structure. It is clear that the 'concessions' proposed by the Prime Minister and reported to the Central Committee meeting remain mere sops insofar as they leave intact the structure of capitalism and in no way touch the essential productive bases of the economy.
>
> It is necessary to declare at this stage, quite categorically, that we oppose our party entering any coalition government wherein decisive control is held by a party that has proved time and again its reluctance to move against the capitalist order, and furthermore has demonstrated in action its essentially antiworking-class character. We do not believe that the character of the SLFP is determined by the declarations of one or another of its individual leaders. Its character has been revealed by its whole history during its years in power. In this sense we see no reason for changing our characterization of it as a party essentially functioning within the framework of capitalism and utilized by certain layers of the bourgeoisie as a possible bulwark against the growing forces of the working class. Any form of coalition with such a party, as long as it remains the dominant majority within such a coalition, can only lead to the immobilization of the left in advance and its becoming itself a target for the growing resentment of the masses.

This letter was distributed at the *beginning* of the LSSP conference; and Pierre Frank, speaking there as the representative of the United Secretariat, followed up by calling for support of the revolutionary wing of the LSSP in its fight against any coalition of any kind with the bourgeois SLFP. It should be noted in passing that Comrade Frank's speech against the coalition was reproduced in the entire daily press in Ceylon; and the papers featured it as of considerable importance in Ceylonese politics that the representative of the Fourth International had clearly and explicitly rejected the proposed coalition. Everyone in Ceylon able to read and interested in the news of the day was aware of the position taken by the Fourth International. Only the readers of *The Newsletter* were kept in the dark about this simple fact and even told the contrary the better to serve Healy's falsification.

Events were to show that this type of reporting was scarcely accidental. In their faction fight against the Fourth International, the SLL leaders decided to proceed without heed to the truth. In the November 7, 1964, *Newsletter*, readers were offered the following "box," printed in black against a background of red ink so as to give it special emphasis:

> On July 1 last year the Unified Secretariat of the Fourth International wrote from the Pabloite centre in Paris to Leslie Goonewardene, Secretary of the Lanka Sama Samaja Party, saying: 'We recognise there is nothing wrong in the principle of negotiations between India and Ceylon on the subject' (the citizenship rights of Tamil workers). The present agreement is a result of the revisionist policies of the Unified Secretariat who have once again betrayed workers in Ceylon. Once again members of the Unified Secretariat stand exposed and condemned as traitors to the working class.

The agreement this slanderous attack refers to is the Shastri-Bandaranaike accord of October 29, 1964, which provided for the forced deportation of 525,000 Indian (Tamil) residents from Ceylon to India within fifteen years. Here again we catch *The Newsletter* in a gross falsification. For what did the July 1, 1963, letter from the United Secretariat of the Fourth International to Leslie Goonewardene really say on the citizenship rights of the Tamil workers? Here is the full passage:

> Concerning point 14 (b) we think that in order to avoid any ambiguity, it must be made clear that the option of deciding the citizenship rights of persons of Indian origin should not be left ultimately to the goodwill of the government of India, but to the people directly concerned, although we recognize that there is nothing wrong in the principle of negotiations between India and Ceylon on the subject.

In other words: whereas *The Newsletter* insinuates that the United Secretariat, by sending the letter quoted above, paved the way for the Shastri-Bandaranaike agreement which meant forced deportation for half a million Tamils, the United Secretariat's letter in fact told the LSSP leadership explicitly, "in order to avoid any ambiguity," *that no agreement which involved deportation or any other solution forced upon the Tamil workers was acceptable*, and that the LSSP should make it clear that the final decision in the question of citizenship should be left up to the Tamil workers themselves!

In order to hide this fact, and launch an unwarranted, slanderous and completely unjustified accusation of "treason" against the United Secretariat, *The Newsletter* is compelled to resort to gross falsification, leaving out the main part of a sentence and converting a subordinate clause into the main subject, even putting a capital "W" on "we" in order to make the frame-up more convincing.

We catch these light-fingered artists at work again in a resolution, "From Revisionism to Opportunism," which they published twice—once in *The Newsletter* of March 28, 1964, and again in their magazine *Labour Review*. (Vol. 1, No. 1 of the new series which Healy, in a piratical operation, renamed *Fourth International*.) The resolution, pretending to be a criticism of the documents adopted at the Reunification Congress of the Fourth International, states:

> And what are the prospects, if any, for the Fourth International? Let us listen to the revisionists:
> 'In the advanced countries, the International can perform crucial services on behalf of revolutions in colonial countries . . . The International can help the fighters of the colonial revolution to remain true internationalists . . . Among the advanced workers, intellectuals and youth of the workers' states, the International can play a special role in helping them to dig through the debris of forty years of falsification . . .'
> Here, in a nutshell is presented the perspective for the International.
> Nowhere in this exposition do the tasks of the movement rise above the level of routine and mundane propaganda.

> Nowhere [!] is there any [!] mention of the party leading struggles against unemployment and the integration of the unions in the state apparatus ... (P. 41.)

The contemptuous sneer at how the International can "help the fighters of the colonial revolution" is very revealing, and we shall have occasion to return to this significant aspect of the Healyite pattern of thought. But let us take up the main contention in the passage quoted from the resolution. Is it true that "nowhere" in the documents adopted at the Reunification Congress is there to be found "any mention" of the necessity of the party leading struggles against unemployment and against the integration of the unions in the state apparatus, that "nowhere in this exposition do the tasks of the movement rise above the level of routine and mundane propaganda"?

This is, of course, the opposite of the truth. Here is what *the very same document*, "The Dynamics of World Revolution Today," from which the authors of the slanderous resolution of the SLL quote, has to say on the subject:

> This increased competition, heightened still further by the constitution of the Common Market in Western Europe, will strengthen the inevitable tendency for the average rate of profit to decline. (In the final analysis this tendency is a consequence of the new technological revolutions; i.e., of the higher organic composition of capital.)
>
> In reaction to these tendencies, the capitalist class will seek periodically to ameliorate its positions in the competitive struggle by slowing down the rate of increase of real wages, by freezing wages, or even by trying to reduce real wages, especially in the imperialist countries where the workers enjoy the highest relative wages. The response of the proletariat to these attacks can lead to great struggles that will tend to move toward pre-revolutionary and even revolutionary situations, provided that the working class, or at least its broad vanguard, has sufficient self-confidence to advance the socialist alternative to the capitalist way of running the economy and the country. This in turn hinges essentially on the activity and influence of a broad left wing in the labor movement that educates the vanguard in the necessity of struggling for this socialist alternative and that builds up self-confidence and an apparatus capable of revolutionary struggle through a series of successful partial struggles.
>
> This is, of course, only a generalized pattern in which various particular variants should be included: the possibility of the working class reacting violently against an attempt to limit or suppress its fundamental political and trade-union rights (against an attempt to impose a "strong" state or against an emergent fascist danger); the possibility of a swift reaction to a sudden financial or political crisis; the possibility of mass opposition against an attempt to launch a new colonial war, or against general preparations for war, etc. *The essential point for revolutionary Marxists is to link up the program of revolutionary socialism with the masses* through a series of transitional demands corresponding to the specific conditions of each country and through intimate ties with the mass movement. *The objective is to stimulate and broaden mass struggles to the utmost and to move as much as possible toward playing a leading role in such struggles*, beginning with the most elementary demands and seeking to develop them in the direction of transitional slogans on the level of government power and the creation of bodies of dual power. [Emphasis added.]

It should also be noted that the Reunification Congress adopted a political resolution, "The International Situation and Our Tasks," which *specifically mentions* the necessity to fight against "an increasing 'integration' of the working class, above all the trade unions, in the bourgeois state"! The slanderer, surely, is in need of visiting an oculist...

3

THE SLL BROUGHT INTO ITS OWN COURT

Thrice we have caught the SLL authors in the very act of cheating, lying, falsifying documents and slandering their opponents in the world Trotskyist movement. Thrice we have found them guilty of the kind of methods used by Stalinism, and Stalinism alone, to try to render impossible real ideological discussions inside the labour movement.

Why do the self-proclaimed "rebuilders" of the Fourth International descend to the kind of methods which the founder of our movement fought against so vehemently all his life? "The revolution is the supreme truth of our epoch," Trotsky said more than once. "It doesn't need lies to defend itself." What is it that compels the SLL leaders to depart from the path that Leon Trotsky laid down for all revolutionists?

The Newsletter of April 3, 1965, has the following to say on this subject:

> The Trotskyist movement's formative years saw a relentless struggle against the systematic campaign of unprincipled lies and distortions projected by Stalin and his faction in the Soviet Union.
>
> *This technique of the big lie is the last resort of all revisionists when they are confronted with a real revolutionary movement.* (Emphasis in the original.)

Here the SLL is pronouncing judgment upon the SLL. Can we thus end our inquiry by concluding that the SLL resorts to lies and slanders and distortions simply because it is "revisionist"? It would be too simple and superficial an explanation.

The key to understanding these unprincipled methods of the SLL lies in understanding the nature of sectarianism and extreme factionalism. Marx himself indicated the basic characteristic of a sect when he wrote in a letter to J. B. Schweitzer:

> You yourself have experienced in your own person the opposition between the movement of a sect and the movement of a class. The sect sees the justification for its existence and its 'point of honour'—not in what it has in *common* with the class movement but in the *particular shibboleth* which distinguishes it from it. (Marx to Schweitzer, 13 October 1868. In *The Selected Correspondence of Karl Marx and Frederick Engels*, International Publishers edition, p. 250. Emphasis in original.)

Here one finds the "secret" of the SLL's polemics, its slanders and systematic stooping to the use of lies and distortions in faction fights with opponents inside the revolutionary movement, explained in a nutshell! For the very nature of a sect *forces* it to distinguish itself constantly from the "real movement" of the world revolution. And where the basis for distinction is insufficient or altogether lacking, it has to *invent* one, either by lies through omission or by outright falsifications.

The same explanation of the secret enables us to understand an extremely striking and revealing aspect of the SLL's activity which appears irrational. Although the SLL has grown in the last period, *The Newsletter* is still a small four-page weekly. A host of economic, social, cultural, national and international political problems need to be explained to the British workers in order to counteract the bourgeois ideology pouring incessantly from the bourgeois daily press, radio, TV, cinema, etc., etc. A host of struggles need guidance and organisation; there are issues to clarify, campaigns to prepare, enemies to denounce, confusion and misunderstandings to straighten out.

The Newsletter is much too weak and small as yet to tackle even a small fraction of these jobs, yet it takes a big proportion of space and resources to attack "Pabloism," "Pabloite revisionism" and "Pabloite capitulation"; i.e., people and ideas that 99.99% of the British workers have never heard of and are not likely to hear of. This practice alone—this obsession with reducing everything to the "particular shibboleth which distinguishes it"—undermines a big part of the sincere and serious efforts of the SLL rank and file to build a strong party, and lends credibility and an appearance of truth to the notion spread by enemies of our movement that the "Trots" are just "loonies," always fighting among themselves over issues which nobody understands who is not initiated into the sect's secret language.

The sect's obsession with its particular shibboleth is pushed to such extremes that even big events in the international class struggle (like the Boumedienne coup d'etat in Algeria) are not at all analysed objectively but simply considered from the point of view of how best to use them against the opponent in the faction fight.

The dangers in such a method are obvious.

Revolutionary Marxism, as an instrument for changing society, revolutionary theory as a guide to revolutionary action, can play their proper role only if they are used to analyse ever-changing reality on an objective level. If theory is degraded until it becomes a mere instrument to justify the existence of a particular sect, the sect loses touch with reality, and its activity, based upon subjective concepts, is doomed to ever increasing sterility.

4

'PABLOITE REVISIONISM'

The key shibboleth, the particular trademark and special commodity which the SLL finds itself bound to peddle to the outside world, is the view that aside from its own organisation and a similar organisation in France, the Fourth International and the world Trotskyist movement have succumbed to a strange disease called "Pabloite revisionism." We call this a strange disease because it refers to a *former* leader of the Fourth International, who insists in a very emphatic and public manner that he has nothing in common with the very people and organisations the SLL calls his followers! In fact, after conducting his own private faction fight against them for many years—a fight in which he combined political opportunism and organisational practices like those characteristic of the SLL—Pablo finally and publicly broke with the Fourth International which he calls "a dead past without a future."

Isn't it at least somewhat ludicrous to call the movement from which Pablo broke publicly and sharply . . . Pabloite?

Revisionism is the ideology which claims to be Marxist but which discards its most vital parts. Historically it is the name given to reformism in the Second International; i.e., the theory of Bernstein who discarded such basic parts of Marxist theory as the inevitability of the downfall of capitalism, the necessity of the socialist revolution for the emancipation of the working class, the necessity of a dictatorship of the proletariat for the overthrow of capitalism, and so on. As an ideology—the ideology of the labor aristocracy and bureaucracy—revisionism was of course false consciousness, but it was quite outspoken and consistent. All the revisions of Marxism indicated above were developed in detail in the writings of Bernstein and his friends.

Stalinist revisionism started with the theory that it was possible to achieve the full construction of socialism in one country, as against the traditional concept of Marx and Lenin that only the victory of the world revolution (at least in the economically decisive countries of the world) could create the necessary basis for a fully developed socialist economy and society. Again, this revisionism, as an ideology of the privileged Soviet bureaucracy, was of course false consciousness, but quite straightforward and outspoken, developed at great length in many articles, speeches and pamphlets by Stalin and his henchmen.

Now, if we are to believe Healy and his specialists in this question, the "revisionism" of the world Trotskyist movement today is a "revisionism" of a special type. It is a "secret," "implicit" revisionism. For, in contrast to Bernstein and Stalin, the leading bodies of the Fourth International (and of the Socialist Workers Party) have not abandoned or revised in writing or in their own consciousness a single one of the basic theoretical tenets of Marxism and Leninism. They still publicly proclaim adherence to all the basic theories. The SLL therefore finds itself in the unfortunate position of having to discover "implicit" revisionism, revisionism by inference, "secret revisionism"—and this is a very difficult matter to prove indeed! And because the SLL is a sect, and sees the justification of its existence and its very point of honour in "proving" that the Fourth International and the Socialist Workers Party are "revisionist," they have to fabricate the "evidence," if need be by falsifying documents, by tearing sentences out of context, or in general by juggling facts and figures and substituting abuse and name-calling for sober objective analysis.

As a matter of fact, when one reads the "theoretical" documents of the SLL—we shall have occasion further on to deal with the dubious offerings of these would-be "developers of theory"—the charge of "revision" of basic Marxist or Leninist theories which they level against the leading comrades of the Fourth International and the Socialist Workers Party involves only one point. They haven't dared to state as yet that the Fourth International has "revised" the labor theory of value, or the Leninist theory of the state, or the theory of permanent revolution. No, the only "revisionism" that our movement is said to be guilty of is our alleged abandonment of building revolutionary parties.

But this, too, is completely untrue. Neither the Fourth International nor the leaders of the Socialist Workers Party have ever abandoned the task or perspective of building revolutionary parties, Trotskyist organisations and sections of the Fourth International. Not only have they not abandoned that perspective, they have carried on that task concretely in an *increasing* number of countries. Today, there are many more organisations affiliated to the Fourth International or sympathetic to it than at any other time in the past, either during the lifetime of Leon Trotsky, or at the end of the second world war, or at the time of the unfortunate split in the world Trotskyist movement in 1954. The total membership of these organisations, notwithstanding a number of splits, is larger than ever before, and so is the influence of the Trotskyist militants and organisations.

This brings us to closer appreciation of the inner nature of the sectarian methods of the SLL. In contrast to the real revisionists of the past and present, the alleged "revisionists" of the Fourth International deny in theory and in practice any "revisionism" or "abandonment" of the task of building revolutionary mass parties. They see this task as their central objective wherever they are active in the world. They say so in their documents. They apply it in action. Thus when the SLL, instead of stating correctly that it has differences with the Fourth International as regards the *way*, the *tactical method* to achieve this objective, brazenly states that the Fourth International has abandoned the objective itself, then it *must* resort to systematic distortions, lies and falsifications in order to maintain its shibboleth, its sectarian raison d'etre. The SLL, in addition, shows itself to be under strong compulsion to reduce everything to the small change of dubious anecdotes about personalities. As Trotsky noted, "For analysis of reality, the sectarian substitutes intrigue, gossip and hysteria." ("Centrism, Sectarianism and the Fourth International," *Against the Stream*, Perspectives Pamphlet, 1965, p. 4.) Consequently the whole discussion takes on a nightmarish character, the SLL polemicists twisting and distorting everything the world Trotskyist movement writes or does, in order to "prove" that it "really" means the opposite of what it appears to mean.

The parallel with the Stalinist campaign of slander against Trotsky and Trotskyism is obvious. Day in and day out, Trotsky fought for the world revolution and against capitalism, defending the Soviet Union against imperialism with all his power. As part of this struggle he attacked the reformist and Stalinist bureaucracies with devastating facts, a thousand times substantiated by sad experience, showing how these bureaucracies paralysed the fight against capitalism and imperialism. The Stalinist polemicists replied by twisting and distorting his writings in order to "prove" that he was "in reality" an agent of counterrevolution and of imperialism.

The world Trotskyist movement is busy day in and day out building revolutionary organisations, fighting for a new revolutionary leadership of the international working class, against the class enemy and the privileged bureaucracies of the labour movement. Healy, Slaughter and their lieutenants see this only as a "cover" for the "real role" of the "Pabloites" which is to sell out the workers to these same bureaucracies![1] The fact that some of the leading spokesmen of the SLL, especially its handful of "red professors," actually were Stalinist hacks slandering Trotsky and the Trotskyist movement with much the same kind of lies and distortions as late as 1956 lends only a specially bitter tinge to this parallel.

In one of the recently published "resolutions of the International Committee in preparation for the international conference in 1966," entitled with that strange brand of dry humour only to be found in Britain, "Rebuilding [!] the Fourth International," we find this type of distortion and bald assertion in very clear form. A good example is the following passage:

> The abandonment of the programme of the Fourth International which had been contained in the earlier theses of Pablo developed into actual support for the Stalinist bureaucracy against the revolutionary workers of East Germany. This constituted proof that the revolutionary organisation founded by Trotsky no longer existed. In 1953, the revi-

sionism contained in Pablo's earlier theses was most sharply expressed in his retreat from the programme of political revolution in Eastern Europe at the time of the East German workers' uprising. The theories of 'centuries of degenerated workers' states', 'mass pressure on the bureaucracy', and the resultant tactic of 'entry *sui generis*', were the revisionist background of this betrayal and later of the Pabloites' similar attitude towards the Hungarian revolution of 1956 . . . (Healy's fake *Fourth International* magazine, Vol. 2, No. 2, August 1965, p. 57.)

The theory of "centuries of degenerated workers' states" was never adopted by any official body of the Fourth International, nor written into any adopted resolution or document. "Mass pressure on the bureaucracy" is not a "theory" but a fact—of which even the SLL from time to time takes cognizance.[2] "Entry sui generis" is not a "theory" either, but a tactic for building revolutionary mass parties, a tactic, by the way, which was first developed by Trotsky himself, and afterwards extensively applied by Gerry Healy in Britain for more than ten years.

But what to think of the brazen statement that the "Pabloites" (in the SLL's quaint sectarian language this means today in fact the entire world Trotskyist movement aside from the SLL!) actually "supported" the Soviet bureaucracy against the revolutionary Hungarian workers, and "betrayed" the Hungarian revolution? To refute this nonsense and to show at the same time what kind of documents the SLL specialists had on their desks when they decided to say what they did, the following extract from a public appeal issued by the International Secretariat of the Fourth International can be offered. It was distributed not only in all the main countries of Europe and the world at that time, but inside Hungary and in Hungarian, under date of October 30, 1956:

> Long Live the Independent and Democratic Republic of Hungarian Workers Councils!
>
> An appeal of the Fourth International to the workers, poor peasants and intellectuals of Hungary.
>
> Comrades,
>
> The Fourth International, which includes in its ranks oppositional Communists in thirty different countries in the world, including the Soviet Union, and which for more than 20 years has conducted a merciless struggle against capitalism and Stalinism, sends its fraternal greetings to the victorious masses of Hungary. . . .
>
> Eternal glory to the martyrs of your great insurrection, which has written a glorious page in the history of the international labor movement!
>
> Hatred and contempt for the rotten clique of bureaucrats who tried to save their regime through the firepower of Russian tanks, passing over the corpses of hundreds of massacred Hungarian workers! This clique has nothing in common with communism, with socialism.
>
> *Your victorious revolution is not finished: it has hardly begun.*
>
> But the deaths of the martyrs of bureaucratic madness must not be in vain.
>
> The power which is today in the hands of the Hungarian people must never again be lost.
>
> The workers and students of Budapest, of Miskolcz, of Debreczen and Zalaegerczegs did not rise in order to see the old masters of Horthy's Hungary, the capitalists and landlords, take the place of the ruling bureaucratic clique . . .
>
> *What you want is a political revolution*, the overthrow of the dictatorship of the bureaucracy, the exercise of power by the toiling people as a whole, and *not a social counterrevolution*, not a return to private capitalism and great landed estates, not an end to planned economy and industrialisation.
>
> This is why we call upon you to show the *greatest vigilance*, and to take the only road which can guarantee the fruits of your victory:
>
> *In each factory, in each neighbourhood and in each town, set up a council of workers, soldiers and students.*
>
> *In each village, set up a council of poor peasants.*
>
> *All legislative and executive power should repose exclusively with these councils, elected in free elections, meeting openly and under the control of*

all the toiling people.

All armed power should be wrested not only from the Stalinist secret police, but also from the old officers; this is why you should call for the dissolution of the police and the permanent army; all weapons should be given to the workers, organised into workers', students' and poor peasants' militia.

Have no confidence in any Parliament which would appeal to the old and new political connivers. All executive and legislative power in the state should be in your hands, victors of October 23. *Demand the immediate convocation in Budapest of a congress of workers councils of all Hungary, which should take power in the whole country . . . (Quatrieme Internationale,* Vol. 14, Nos. 10–12, decembre 1956, pp. 59–60. Emphasis in the original.)

We could continue to quote from this appeal; e.g., its call to set up a Hungarian section of the Fourth International But this should be sufficient to show that in their public appeal, distributed in Hungary at the time, the Fourth Internationalists gave one hundred percent support to the Hungarian revolutionary workers, students and poor peasants against the Stalinist bureaucracy, and tried, despite insufficient means materially, to influence them to set up a democratic republic of workers councils.

Of late, Healy's *Newsletter* has returned to the question and given its slander a new twist. In the November 12, 1966, issue, we read: ". . . the Pabloites, who supported [!] the second Soviet intervention of November 4, 1956 . . . should not be in the Fourth International at all, for they usurped its name and betrayed the struggle of Leon Trotsky."

This is as brazen a lie as the assertion that the Fourth International "betrayed" the Hungarian revolution at any time. In fact, a declaration of the International Secretariat of the Fourth International dated November 5, 1956, denounced the second Soviet intervention in Hungary in the sharpest possible terms, stating that "by crushing in blood the Hungarian workers and again introducing a regime of puppets" the Soviet bureaucracy acted against the fundamental interest of socialism in Hungary, in the Soviet Union and on an international scale. ("Dossier de la Destalinisation," published by *Quatrieme Internationale,* p. 111.)

Anyone who interprets these actions as a "betrayal" of the Hungarian revolution and "support" for the Stalinist bureaucracy against the revolutionary workers of Hungary, is more to be pitied than censured for his sad end as a victim of delirium tremens.[3]

The only alternative, of course, is to conclude that what is involved is deliberate falsification and distortion due to extreme factionalism and organisational sectarianism. This is the basic disease of the SLL, which reduces it to a position where it is often altogether incapable of objective analysis, no event being of interest to it unless it can be turned to use in meeting the insatiable need of the sect to justify its special reason for existence.

5

THE CEYLON EXAMPLE

The impasse into which extreme factionalism, a more and more subjective approach to objective reality, can bring a grouping, is strikingly illustrated by the SLL's reaction towards the events in Ceylon in 1964; i.e., the way they assessed the betrayal committed by the majority of the Lanka Sama Samaja Party leadership in entering a bourgeois coalition government.

This betrayal constitutes a major defeat and a major tragedy in the history of the Fourth International, although the Fourth International itself emerged unstained, inasmuch as it unanimously opposed the opportunist capitulators, and did not hesitate to break with its strongest section in terms of membership and mass influence, once this section had violated a basic principle of revolutionary politics. The establishment of a new, revolutionary LSSP, fully supported by the Fourth International, is further proof of the fact that this defeat suffered by our movement in Ceylon is only temporary, and that Trotskyism will fight again, tomorrow, at the head of the Ceylon masses, stronger than ever before.

It was and is the duty of every serious revolutionist to analyse in detail the roots in theory and practice of the degeneration of the old LSSP leadership, and to critically reexamine the past relationship of this leadership with the Fourth International, in order to determine whether our movement itself might unwittingly have contributed to its degeneration, or failed to recognize it in time or to oppose it effectively. For my part, I undertook to initiate the task in a long article published in the *International Socialist Review,* of which the greater part was published in a French version in *Quatrieme Internationale.*[4] I do not claim that this is the last word required on the question. The Second Congress of the Fourth International since reunification (the eighth since it was founded) had something to say on this matter, and the international discussion on the subject is still continuing.

Up to now, in the course of this critical analysis, we have reached the following conclusions:

(1) The theoretical and practical roots of the degeneration of the old LSSP leadership were:

(a) The concept of "Ceylonese exceptionalism"; i.e., the illusion that for some peculiar reason, Ceylonese revolutionists could conquer power by essentially electoral and parliamentary means (whereas these same leaders rejected such a possibility for the rest of the world).

(b) The inability of the old LSSP leadership to seriously penetrate the countryside and build up a strong organisational base or political following among the village poor (which led it in practice to view the alliance of workers and peasants as an alliance with the Sri Lanka Freedom Party, which the LSSP leaders considered as representing the peasantry).

(c) The weakness of the party as an organisation, the insufficient recruitment of workers into the party, the absence of a full-time leading cadre outside of the parliamentarians, and the excessive involvement of party leaders in their own professions or in electoral activity, as against party building and Marxist educational work.

(2) The International at a very early stage recognized these weaknesses and tried to correct them. But it was seriously hampered in this by:

(a) The insufficient degree of integration of the party membership into the International (e.g., the fact that the big majority of the non-English-speaking members generally were not informed of the International's resolutions and declarations, and were not kept abreast of the work and activities of other sections.

(b) The weakening of the cohesive forces in the world Trotskyist movement, and of the general application of international democratic centralism after the 1954 split, along with the fact that the delay in the reunification made it impossible to catch up with and to counteract the growing centrifugal tendencies in the LSSP in time.

(c) The material weakness of the Fourth International which barred it from sending and maintaining cadres of the world movement on the spot in Ceylon in a permanent way, in order to help counteract the adverse developments and to aid young cadres in building an alternative leadership if the old leadership should show itself to be beyond repair.

It is our conviction that all the basic zigzags of the LSSP leadership in the period 1957–1964 can be explained by the basic causes enumerated above, and that any deepgoing discussion on Ceylon will arrive at the same conclusions.

The SLL leaders, however, look upon the Ceylon question in an entirely different way. They are not interested in analysing objectively the reasons for the old LSSP leadership's betrayal. They are only interested in denouncing the "Pabloites"—which is the self-justification for the existence of their sect. This is why they have discovered entirely different "roots" of the old LSSP leadership's degeneration. According to the SLL, there were two basic roots, the first of which was ". . . the Pablo theory that under the pressure of international events, an irreversible leftward process had begun inside the Soviet bureaucracy. This, it was implied, could lead to a section of the bureaucracy breaking away, assuming the role of a revolutionary leadership . . ." (*The Newsletter,* July 4, 1964). Presumably, the LSSP leadership applied this theory by analogy to Ceylon and to the SLFP. As proof Healy states that Leslie Goonewardene, in "an early 1953 issue" of the LSSP's English weekly *Samasamajist,* designated the SLFP as a "centrist party."

The second root of the old LSSP's degeneration, according to Healy, was that out of factional considerations, the leadership of the International Secretariat first, and the United Secretariat after the reunification, made an unprincipled bloc with the LSSP leadership:

> They gave him [Pablo] support against those Trotskyists organised around the Interna-

tional Committee who wanted a political clarification of international events, whilst he, in turn, praised them to the skies as 'the largest Trotskyist organisation' in the world, thus [!] deliberately covering up for their opportunism. Anyone who attempted to discuss the grave problems facing the movement was denounced as a disrupter and a factionalist by both sides. (*The Newsletter*, July 4, 1964.)

This state of affairs was even aggravated by the Reunification Congress of the Fourth International of 1963, which was "rushed through without a thorough-going political discussion" demanded by Healy and his followers. The rejection of this discussion, they allege, was directly responsible for the old LSSP's betrayal.

This "explanation" of the degeneration of the old LSSP does not hold water. To make Pablo's thesis of 1952 responsible for Perera's or Goonewardene's line of 1964 is ludicrous. . . . if only because of the fact, well known to Healy, that Perera, Goonewardene and Colvin R. de Silva *rejected* Pablo's thesis, and *criticized* the draft thesis for the Fourth World Congress of the Fourth International, "Rise and Decline of Stalinism," *much along the same lines as Healy himself* (see the "Internal Bulletin" of the LSSP of April 1954). In fact, if one regards the 1964 crisis of the LSSP as "directly related" to the split of 1953–54, one could with this sort of logic say that Perera, Goonewardene and Colvin R. de Silva, who started out by approving Healy's brand of "Trotskyism," ended up as allies of capitalism![5] The least one could conclude from this would be that a profession of loyalty to principles is no guarantee against a future betrayal . . .

But in reality, there is no relation whatsoever between Pablo's thesis of 1952, the split in the Fourth International of 1953–54, the documents adopted at the Fourth World Congress of the Fourth International, and Perera's, Colvin R. de Silva's and Leslie Goonewardene's degeneration of 1964. Whether or not Leslie Goonewardene characterized the SLFP as a "centrist party" in 1953 is immaterial. If he did, this could have only been incidental, without any influence on the subsequent political appreciations of the LSSP, not to mention the Fourth International and its leadership. For it is an undeniable fact that the LSSP as well as the Fourth International, in all their official documents and congress resolutions, always characterized the SLFP as a *bourgeois* party and always counterposed the idea of a *workers and peasants* government (either an LSSP government, or a government of a united front of the working-class parties, on an anti-imperialist and anticapitalist platform) to the SLFP government or any coalition with the SLFP.

At its July 20–22, 1962, conference, the LSSP called for a struggle "against the whole policy of the SLFP government" as being a bourgeois policy. And as late as March 21, 1964, Colvin R. de Silva called the masses to fight against that "bankrupt bourgeois government." Innumerable instances can be quoted where the LSSP spoke of the SLFP as a bourgeois party right up until 1964. Speaking about the coalition between the SLFP and Philip Goonewardene's Mahajana Eksath Peramuna (People's United Front), the *Samasamajist* said in its issue of November 28, 1957:

> The broad mass of workers have realised that this is a capitalist government, and that concessions can be gained only through struggle against it.

A week before, in the November 21, 1957, issue of the *Samasamajist*, Colvin R. de Silva wrote:

> Mr. Bandaranaike heads a capitalist government and a cabinet of personal stooges. The renegades from the left, who capitulated to him long ago are capitulating anew.

To deny the fact that the LSSP had considered the SLFP a *bourgeois* party and had constantly criticized Philip Goonewardene and the Communist Party for seeking a coalition with it, is to falsify the history of the LSSP. It is certainly not rendering support to the efforts of the LSSP (Revolutionary Section) to set the record straight!

As for the other allegation, that the International Secretariat first and the United Secretariat after 1964 "kept silent" about the opportunism of the old LSSP leadership in order to maintain an "unprincipled bloc," this is simply untrue. There is a heavy file of correspondence and of documentary proof of the Fourth International's *constant* struggle against the opportunist deviations of Perera (with whom Colvin R. de Silva and Leslie Goonewardene had already split once in 1945 due to this very reason) and against the conciliationist attitude which de Silva and Goonewardene tended to adopt towards these deviations.

It is true that in conformity with the normal rules of democratic centralism and the traditional practice in revolutionary organisations, the leadership of the Fourth International kept these criticisms *internal* as long as the course of the Ceylon leadership did not go beyond certain limits. It did so not only out of concern for organisational principles, but also because the comrades of the left wing of the LSSP, the very comrades of the LSSP (Revolutionary Section) who broke away from the traitors in June 1964 and whom Healy has unsuccessfully wooed ever since, explicitly asked us to do so, because they were afraid—and correctly so!—that given the low degree of real internationalism among the LSSP rank and file, an open appeal of the Fourth International leadership to form a Leninist-type faction inside the LSSP against the Perera group would have *weakened* and not strengthened the left wing!

But if our attitude was wrong, we can ask Healy a simple question: Why didn't he, who presumably knew all about the LSSP's coming degeneration as early as 1953, if not 1945, why didn't he speak out in public and in writing against the LSSP leadership, either between 1945 and 1954 (he was a leading member of the Fourth International in those years) or a least between 1954 and 1960, after he had seen the light on "Pabloite revisionism"? Was it because he still hoped to make an unprincipled factional bloc with Perera and Co.? Was it because of conciliation towards opportunism? Of what worth is his criticism of the "silence" of the leadership of the Fourth International with regard to the LSSP's opportunism, given his own record. . . . which is just a blank page?

In any case, the Fourth International didn't wait for Healy to speak up in public against Perera's opportunist degeneration. It did so openly and clearly after the LSSP's parliamentary fraction voted for Mrs. Bandaranaike's "Throne" Speech in 1960. The Sixth World Congress of the Fourth International adopted in December 1960 the following resolution on Ceylon, which was published in the magazine *Fourth International* (No. 12, page 50):

> The Sixth World Congress, having discussed the situation in Ceylon, states that it disapproves the political line adopted by the LSSP following the election defeat of March 1960.
>
> The Congress condemns more especially the vote of parliamentary support expressed on the occasion of the Speech from the Throne, and the adoption of the budget, by the party's MPs.
>
> The Fourth International does not exclude support for the adoption of progressive measures, even by a national bourgeois or petty-bourgeois government in a colonial or semi-colonial country. But the social nature, composition and general programme of the Bandaranaike government does not justify the support which was accorded to it.
>
> The World Congress appeals to the LSSP for a radical change in its political course in the direction indicated by the document of the leadership of the International.
>
> The Congress is confident that the next National Conference of the LSSP, in whose political preparation the whole International must participate, will know how to adopt all the political and organisational decisions necessary to overcome the crisis which was revealed following the results of the March 1960 election campaign.

This resolution shows what a shameful lie was printed under the name of G. Healy in *The Newsletter* of July 4, 1964, to wit: "The Pabloite International Secretariat endorsed [!], with reservations, the main line of the LSSP in the 1960 elections. . . . Thus Pablo and Co. supplied them with further cover for their capitulation to the SLFP." And when Healy in the same issue of *The Newsletter* attacked the position of the Fourth International that critical support of all effectively anti-imperialist measures of a bourgeois government in a colonial or semicolonial country is entirely permissible from a revolutionary Marxist point of view, he implicitly also attacked Trotsky's critical support of the bourgeois Mexican government's nationalisation of the American and British oil companies in 1938 and Trotsky's critical support of the Chinese bourgeois government's hesitant and self-contradictory defense measures against the invasion of Japanese imperialism in the thirties. In this Healy joins all those ultraleft sectarians whom Trotsky, in those days, characterized as suffering from an infantile disease in their senility!

In the summer of 1963 a widespread movement toward unity in action appeared among the trade unions in Ceylon. One of the promising features of this movement was its adoption of a common platform of "21 demands" which were directed against the government and which aimed at improving the standard of living of the working class, particularly with regard to wages, job security, a shorter workweek and so on. This same encouraging tendency also began to find political expression, giving rise to the formation of a United Left Front of the three parties historically considered as working class parties in Ceylon; i.e., the LSSP, the Communist Party and Philip Goonewardene's Mahajana Eksath Peramuna.

Should this rise in militancy and political consciousness be advanced another step along the road of independent political action by calling for a struggle to put a United Left Front government in power? Healy's answer is that it would be a "betrayal" to even suggest such a thing.

In arguing for his position he counterposes trade-union unity around the 21 demands, which he thinks is good, and the strategy of advancing the concept of a United Left Front government, which he thinks is bad. But if it is a question of displaying "no confidence" in the Communist Party and the MEP (Philip Goonewardene) leaderships, has he forgotten that the unions that adopted the 21 demands were in part led by the very same CP and MEP gentlemen? If it is a question of exposing these gentlemen by demanding that they match their words with deeds, why is it correct to expose them on the trade-union field and not on the political field? If it is a question of forcing the unions onto the road of struggle through the pressure of the masses, why can this pressure be applied on the trade-union field and not on the political field?

But in fact if the 21 demands are examined closely, it is seen immediately that they cannot be realised by mere trade-union struggles. *The question of power is posed*. In a country where the masses remain attached to working-class political parties under petty-bourgeois opportunist leaderships, it is absolutely sectarian and utopian to pose the question of power yet ignore these formations in which the working class still retain confidence. The struggle for the 21 demands *separated from* a government formula—that is syndicalism with all its illusions, and not Leninism. The struggle for the 21 demands *culminating* in the slogan: "A united front of working-class parties and organisations to power, in order to implement the 21 demands and apply a socialist, antiimperialist and anticapitalist programme!"—that is in the spirit of Trotsky's transitional programme correctly applied to the Ceylon scene. That was the political line of the United Secretariat during the whole decisive period of 1963–64 for the Ceylon struggle. And that was the line taken by the Reunification Congress of the Fourth International in 1963 in fraternal collaboration with Comrade Edmund Samarakkody, at that time the leader of the LSSP's left wing and today the secretary of the LSSP (Revolutionary).

The documents of the Reunification Congress and the letter sent by the congress to the LSSP's Central Committee, while stating that the evolution from support to the SLFP government (1960 position) to an extraparliamentary struggle to overthrow that government and put into power a united-front government of working-class parties (1963 position) was a step forward, at the same time criticized the LSSP leadership for capitulating to Philip Goonewardene by excluding the trade union of the Tamil plantation workers from the United Left Front, and called their attention to the fact that the United Left Front could only be progressive if it had an extraparliamentary perspective of struggle for power.

In light of these criticisms, it is another lie when *The Newsletter* states, in its issue of July 4, 1964, that "The unification conference in turn gave full support to the LSSP leadership." And it is as foolish to say that this strategy of a united front of working-class parties, proposed by the United Secretariat, "paved the way" for the coalition with the bourgeois SLFP, as it was of the ultralefts of another day to assert that Lenin's and Trotsky's strategy of the united front "paved the way" for the "Popular Front" betrayals of the Stalinists.

On all these questions, discussions are of course

possible, and would be quite useful and welcome. The publication of my article on the subject in the *International Socialist Review* gave the SLL an excellent opportunity to tear to shreds our theoretical analysis of the reasons for the old LSSP's degeneration—if they had a better explanation to offer. Doesn't the SLL contend that it wants to "develop theory" and to "discuss"? But when *The Newsletter* devoted three lengthy articles (January 9, 23 and 30, 1965) by way of answer, all we were treated to was character assassination, based on vulgar gossip—"Germain the traitor," etc. And the "deep" understanding of Marxist theory displayed by the author can be judged by his conclusion that in considering the theory of Ceylonese exceptionalism I meant that the LSSP leaders should have spent more time in Paris. "Apparently it [the process of degeneration] took place because Colvin de Silva and the other majority leaders preferred to spend most of their time in Ceylon while avoiding direct participation with Germain and the Paris Secretariat."(*The Newsletter*, January 9, 1965.) The editors of *The Newsletter* seem unable to understand, let alone polemicize against, the notion that "Ceylonese exceptionalism" means adhering in theory to Lenin's theory of the state and Trotsky's theory of permanent revolution, but in practice considering Ceylon "an exception," where power can allegedly be conquered through electoral-parliamentary means, without touching the bourgeois state apparatus!

6

SLL REVISION OF THE THEORY OF PERMANENT REVOLUTION— THE CASE OF CUBA

But the logic of subjectivism, of extreme factionalism, is merciless. Having begun on this course out of need to find self-justification for their sectarianism, of need to distinguish themselves at any cost and on all issues from the world Trotskyist movement on which they put the label, "revisionist," and having reduced the Marxist method from an instrument for analysing objective reality in order to be able to change it in a revolutionary way, into an instrument for justifying their own existence, the Healyite leaders of the SLL themselves fell into genuine revision of some of the basic principles of revolutionary Marxism. Their false consciousness became caught up in the dialectics of world reality—and at the end of their journey, the SLL theoreticians landed precisely in the position they wanted to "denounce" no matter what: the position of revisionism, of rejecting some of the basic tenets of Marxist theory and of Trotsky's specific contributions to that theory.

The theory of permanent revolution states that in the epoch of imperialism the two basic problems of the backward countries, the agrarian and national questions—together with all the other classical objectives of the bourgeois-democratic revolution—can be solved only by the proletariat, leading a workers and peasants alliance, conquering power and thereby establishing a dictatorship of the proletariat:

> Under the conditions of the imperialist epoch the national democratic revolution can be carried through to a victorious end only when the social and political relationships of the country are mature for putting the proletariat in power as the leader of the masses of the people. (L. Trotsky: *The Permanent Revolution*. 1962 edition, p. 132.)

But having conquered power, the proletariat cannot stop at solving only the historical tasks of the bourgeois-democratic revolution; it must also *start* to solve the tasks of the socialist revolution:

> The dictatorship of the proletariat which has risen to power as the leader of the democratic revolution is inevitably and very quickly confronted with tasks, the fulfillment of which is bound up with deep inroads into the rights of bourgeois property. The democratic revolution grows over directly into the socialist revolution and thereby becomes a *permanent* revolution. (Ibid., p. 154.)

Having thereby started on the road of socialist revolution, the victorious proletariat of a backward country is confronted with tasks of social and political upheaval and economic construction which cannot be achieved within national boundaries, and which lead to constant explosions of the class struggle, on a national and international scale, which can only be brought to an end by the victory of the proletariat in the most important countries of the world:

> The conquest of power by the proletariat does not complete the revolution, but only opens it. Socialist construction is conceivable only on the foundation of the class struggle, on a national and international scale. This struggle, under the conditions of an overwhelming predominance of capitalist relationships on the world arena, must inevitably lead to explosions, that is, internally to civil wars and externally to revolutionary wars.... The completion of the socialist revolution within national limits is unthinkable.... The socialist revolution begins on the national arena, it unfolds on the international arena, and is completed on the world arena. (Ibid., pp. 154–5.)

This whole process depends in the backward countries upon two basic preconditions, as has been completely confirmed by fifty years of contemporary history; i.e., the inability of the national bourgeoisie of colonial and semicolonial countries to solve either the agrarian or the national questions; that is, to radically eliminate all remnants of semifeudal or imperialist landed property and to achieve genuine national independence.

Now let us look at the balance sheet of the Cuban revolution from this point of view. Two forms of landed property existed in Cuba which had to be ended in order to solve the historical tasks of the bourgeois-democratic revolution: cattle-raising *latifundia*, privately owned since Spanish colonial times, and the sugar plantations, owned almost entirely by U.S. companies or the Cuban bourgeoisie. The Cuban revolution totally destroyed both these forms of ownership of landed estates as early as May 1959. Out of a total of 9,000,000 hectares of disposable land in the country, nearly 4,000,000 hectares became collectively owned (2,800,000 hectares of the old *latifundia* became people's farms; 170,000 hectares expropriated from counterrevolutionaries became state farms; and 900,000 hectares of sugar plantations became sugar plantation workers cooperatives). Since out of the 9,000,000 hectares, 1,200,000 hectares consist of forests in the public domain, *the major part of the land had become collectively owned in Cuba as early as May 1959.*

The first agrarian reform set a limit of 30 *caballerias* (400 hectares) on all land holdings. One should not forget that Cuban agriculture was largely *extensive* (cattle raising was practised on the basis of one animal . . . per hectare!) and that while holdings of 400 hectares appear large in densely populated countries where intensive agriculture is practised, they are quite moderate in countries practising extensive agriculture. But the second agrarian reform of October 3, 1963, further radically limited the private domain. All farms larger than 5 *caballerias* (67 hectares) were nationalized. The private domain is now reduced to 160,000 private farms (with their families, the owners of these farms represent around 10% of the Cuban population!), owning 32% of the arable land. Publicly owned land covers 68% of the arable land, and, taking into account the forests, 72% of the total disposable area for Cuban agriculture.

The sugar plantation workers cooperatives were also transformed into nationalized people's farms. This was a correct solution, since, as Fidel Castro indicated, if cooperatives are a step forward for independent farmers compared to private agriculture, they are a step backward for agricultural wage earners, and 99% of the members of these cooperatives consisted precisely of agricultural wage earners, of landed proletariat! As a result, by the end of 1963, the social structure of Cuban agriculture was *much more advanced than the social structure of Soviet agriculture ten years after the October revolution*, the bulk of the agricultural land in the USSR at that time still being held by individual peasants as private holdings. *And the nationally owned sector of Cuban agriculture is proportionately much bigger than the state sector in Soviet agriculture even today, 49 years after the October revolution*, as the state sector covers some 25% of the total land in the Soviet Union, whereas it covers more than two-thirds of the land in Cuba.

It is true that in contrast to the Soviet Union—but in conformity with a situation which still exists in most of the deformed workers states of Eastern Europe—there is still an important private sector in Cuban agriculture, consisting mainly of small and middle peasants growing sugar cane or vegetables, and of a few rich peasants growing tobacco and coffee. Fidel Castro has given a solemn guarantee that these private peasants will not be deprived of their holdings against their will. Private agriculture is there to stay in Cuba for a rather long period—until the sons or grandsons of the peasants decide to sell their land to the state because they prefer to work as workers, technicians, engineers or doctors instead of remaining peasants, or until the peasants (or their sons or grandsons) voluntarily give up private ownership to go over to cooperative farming, after they have learned from experience that income is higher, work easier and life better in the publicly owned sector of the economy. This is the classical position of Marxism on the question of the attitude of the socialist revolution towards the small and middle peasant, as explained in particular by Engels.

The idea of forced collectivisation of small and middle peasants against their will has always been considered by revolutionary Marxists as a form of bureaucratic despotism and madness, the disastrous effects of which are still felt by the Soviet economy and the Soviet workers to this very day.

But at the same time Fidel Castro has made it crystal clear, and said so publicly (e.g., in his speech of October 21, 1963, published in *Cuba Socialista*, No. 27, p. 60), that private agriculture will disappear one day, although no one can predict whether this will be in 10, 20, 30 or 40 years. The essential problem is of course to understand that this 10% of the Cuban population still represented by private peasants does not involve any *burning social conflict* comparable to that of the Russian peasants during the NEP, or the Polish or Hungarian peasants today, affecting more than half, or nearly half of the country's population.

It is obvious in any case that to close out the private property of the small and middle peasants—or even of kulaks, if it comes to that!—is not at all a historical task of the *bourgeois-democratic* revolution, but a historical task of the *socialist* revolution, and a task which cannot be accomplished completely in any case immediately after the proletariat comes to power. So it is absolutely impermissible to cite the existence of this small private sector in agriculture as proof . . . that the bourgeois-democratic task of carrying out a thoroughgoing reform has not been "completely" achieved in Cuba. The truth is that one can well say that in no revolution of the twentieth century was the agrarian problem solved as radically, as completely and as quickly as in the Cuban revolution under the leadership of Fidel Castro.

As for the national problem, this was solved in just as radical and complete manner. World imperialism—above all U.S. imperialism—does not hold a single plantation, a single power plant or a single factory in all of Cuba. All its properties—together with those of the Cuban bourgeoisie—have been nationalized, including plantations, industry, public utilities, credit, banking and transportation. It has lost its military bases and ties in the country, which it had maintained without interruption since the time Cuba became a formally "independent" country, with the exception of the Guantanamo naval base. It has lost all political, ideological and cultural influence in the country. It has lost the support of Cuban diplomacy in the international field. In fact, in every field of social activity, Cuba, which was to all intents and purposes a colony of U.S. capital for more than half a century, after having been a colony of the Spanish crown, has become a truly independent country, the only country really independent from the U.S. in all of Latin America.

So the record shows beyond a shadow of a doubt that the basic social tasks historically connected with the bourgeois-democratic revolution—the agrarian question, national unity, national independence—have been carried out in Cuba by the revolution led by Fidel Castro. One can add that this revolution has likewise solved in passing the problem of racial equality—a problem linked historically, at least by analogy, to the right of self-determination for national or racial minorities—which Trotsky also classifies among the basic historical tasks of the bourgeois-democratic revolution.

The conclusion is therefore inescapable: either one must characterize Cuba as a workers state and recognize the existence there of a dictatorship of the proletariat, be it in a somewhat distorted form, or one has to admit that the basic historical task of the bourgeois-democratic revolution can be realized today in a backward country under the leadership of other social formations than the proletariat; i.e., either under the leadership of the "national" bourgeoisie or under the leadership of the urban petty bourgeoisie at the head of the peasantry. But to maintain the latter alternative constitutes a revision of a basic thesis of the theory of the permanent revolution.

And this is not all. One must then either consider Fidel Castro to be a representative of the "national" bourgeoisie—and then the Cuban revolution basically confirms the correctness of the Menshevik (and Khrushchevist) line in the semicolonial world, delivering a crushing blow to the main assumption of the theory of the permanent revolution; or it must be held that Fidel Castro is a "petty bourgeois urban leader" coming to power at the crest of a "peasant war"—in which case another basic assumption of the theory of the permanent revolution must be revised: the inability of the petty bourgeoisie not only to lead a successful bourgeois-democratic revolution in a backward country, under conditions of imperialism, but also (and this is especially important) its inability to follow a course independent from that of either a bourgeois or proletarian dictatorship.[6]

The leaders of the SLL, by their purely subjectivist approach to the Cuban revolution, inspired by factional and sectarian motives, have been caught inextricably in a web of revisionism as regards the theory of the permanent revolution. And with each attempt to extricate themselves, the SLL's "theoreticians" become entangled in more contradictions and more and more revisions of Marxism in general and Trotskyism in particular.

The SLL leaders have no clear-cut position on Cuba. Sometimes they characterize Castro's government as a "bonapartist regime resting on capitalist state foundations." ("Trotskyism Betrayed" in the summer 1965 issue of the Healyite magazine *Fourth International*, p. 16.) Sometimes they say that Castro's is a "petty-bourgeois" leadership which "starting from the traditional programme of the democratic revolution ... conquered power." ("Cuba: Marxism and the Revolution," in the SLL's *Fourth international,* August 1965, p. 72.) The SLL "theoreticians" do not seem to see the contradiction between these two positions. We shall return to this later. But let us first of all assume that this nonsense is valid and examine these "characterizations" on their own merits.

". . . Castro's is a Bonapartist regime still resting on bourgeois state foundations," we read in "Opportunism and Empiricism," (SLL's *Fourth International*, summer 1965, p. 28); ". . . the old state machine was not smashed but was staffed with personnel from Castro's own movement, later supplemented by the Stalinist bureaucrats." (Ibid.) The state, Engels used to say, is above all "men in arms." The question of the army is the supreme key to the nature of the state. Is it true that "the old bourgeois army was not smashed," but just "staffed with personnel from Castro's own movement, later supplemented by the Stalinist bureaucrats"? This is completely *untrue*!

The Cuban army of Batista, the Cuban army before the revolution, was a professional standing army. Of that army, not an atom remains today. It was utterly, completely and totally smashed by the revolution. Its reactionary generals and colonels were killed or fled to foreign lands; its cadre was dissolved; its barracks were turned into schools. Not a single one of its representatives can be found today in any position of responsibility in the state apparatus, let alone the army. Those officers who stayed in the country and who were not put on trial for counterrevolutionary crimes have become what many Tsarist officers became after the October revolution: taxi drivers.

On the other hand, the new armed forces which have emerged from the revolution are, first of all, the revolutionary army that grew out of the revolution's combat against Batista's army and state, in which there are no ranks higher than that of comandante (this is the first army since Trotsky's Red Army which has followed such egalitarian norms!), in which there are no insignia, in which the commanders and lower rank officers themselves are completely new, having nothing in common with the old bourgeois army or order, having arisen from the ranks of the revolution, the poor peasants, the workers and the coloured people. Besides the revolutionary army, the armed forces consist of the people's militia (workers and peasants militia) which are composed of the mass of the workers and peasants of the country, which do not have any ranks whatsoever (not even the rank of comandante), where women serve on an equal basis with men, and which controls its own weapons. If the working people in arms is "the old bourgeois state machine" which "was not smashed," then of course the leadership of the SLL has made a valuable contribution to the Marxist-Leninist theory of the state!

Furthermore, in every bourgeois country there exists the state police, gendarmerie, secret police, etc., which supplement the regular army. These formations of "men in arms" have been completely smashed too—with not a few of their members killed because they were the persons most hated by the people, the ones who had committed the foulest crimes against the revolution.

The provincial and district prefects, the municipal councils and all the other organs through which the bourgeoisie controlled the people of the towns and countryside have been dissolved. Outside a few exceptions, all high functionaries, all top bureaucrats, heads of ministerial bureaucracies, heads of central banks and financial state institutions; in other words, all those people who embody the bourgeois character of the state through their "personal union" with the ruling class, have fled the country or are out of their jobs. What remains are the lower echelon petty functionaries of the ministries—and their analogues likewise remained in the Russian state administration after the victory of the October revolution. (Lenin commented on this fact innumerable times.)

So to say that "the old [bourgeois] state machine was not smashed," when precisely its army, its police, its prefects, its municipalities, its Parliament, its high functionaries and its upper rank bureaucrats were smashed, is either to take one's readers for a ride, or to share the crass anarchist confusion about any kind of "state machine" being bourgeois after the victory of the revolution. The fact that the ministries are called "ministries" and not "people's commissariats" is not essential. What is essential is to know who staffs them, in whose class interest they operate. To say that in Cuba they operate in the interests of the Cuban bourgeoisie, which has been completely destroyed, expropriated and physically dispersed as a class, is to replace historical materialism by mythology.

This is indeed the nub of the question. We can agree with the SLL leaders when they say that "nationalisation of the means of production" is in itself not a sufficient criterion to indicate the existence of a workers' state—provided that what is meant is nationalisation of a special kind. Engels visualised the possibility of a bourgeois state nationalising all capitalist property, and transforming the bourgeoisie into a class of state rentiers. This is what has happened, *mutatis mutandis*, in a country like Egypt. But nationalisation of all the means of production, plus destruction of the bourgeoisie as a class (and this through a revolution in which the overwhelming mass of the urban and agricultural proletariat played the leading role), equals a workers state, if one does not want to capitulate to the ludicrous idea of the "state capitalists" that "capitalism" can somehow "survive" the destruction of the whole bourgeois class and become "reembodied" in other social layers, definitively and radically opposed to private property. The least one could say is that this kind of "capitalism" has nothing in common with the capitalism analysed in Marx's *Capital*. And this applies to the kind of "capitalism" which the SLL sees today as "surviving" in Cuba.

"But can we not have a 'bourgeois state without the bourgeoisie'?" ask the SLL leaders. And without batting an eye they refer to Trotsky's formula about the Spanish popular front government in the early days of the July 1936 revolution being an "alliance with the shadow of the bourgeoisie." ("Opportunism and Empiricism," SLL's *Fourth International* summer 1965, p. 27; "A Reply to Joseph Hansen," by Francisco Rodriguez, ibid., pp. 32–33.) This very reference—which by the way throws a significant light upon the SLL's theoretical confusion—permits us once again to clarify the issue.

Only the "shadow of the bourgeoisie" was present in the July 1936 government—because the majority of the bourgeoisie had physically fled into Franco's camp. But what about the factories, the mines, the banks, the property deeds of the great estates behind the lines of the Republican army? We know that the workers and poor peasants spontaneously seized them; but what did the government do with them? Trotsky has a clear answer to the question!

> "No longer representing in the slightest degree the Spanish bourgeoisie, the left Republicans still less represented the workers and the peasants. They represented no one but themselves. However, thanks to their allies the Socialists, Stalinists and Anarchists, these

political phantoms played the decisive role in the revolution. How? Very simply: in the capacity of incarnating the principle of the "democratic revolution," i.e., *the inviolability of private property."* (Trotsky: *The Lesson of Spain*, Spark Syndicate edition, p. 8. Emphasis added.)

Can anyone suppose that if a Spanish government of say November 1936, instead of handing the factories back to the owners, had nationalised them; if the same government had nationalised all the banks and all the landed estates; if, instead of licking the boots of the London City and the Paris Exchange it had cut off all ties with international capitalism, and openly and publicly appealed to the French, Italian and German workers to arm themselves and carry out a revolution against their capitalist rulers—can anyone suppose that such a government would have been called "bourgeois" by Trotsky, especially if, instead of bringing back the old bourgeois officers into the army, it constructed a new army, without ranks, and with commanders exclusively chosen from among the best *milicianos*? The idea that Fidel Castro is following in the footsteps of Azana, Negrin and Miaja, and ruling in Havana in order to . . . bring back the Cuban bourgeoisie through a back door is too ludicrous to be examined. Haven't the SLL leaders yet grasped the simple fact that *contrary* to Azana, Largo Caballero and Negrin, Fidel Castro has not been "incarnating the inviolability of private property," has not given the banks, factories and landed estates back to the bourgeoisie, *but expropriated them instead*?

What kind of "bourgeois" state is it that allegedly governing as a "shadow of the bourgeoisie" expropriates the propertied classes instead of protecting their property? If "Marxism" means an incapacity to understand the slight difference between restoration and destruction of bourgeois power and capitalist property—then we can only sigh with Marx, when he met up with such "disciples." "If that is Marxism, I am not a Marxist."

So much for the key argument of the SLL's "Cuban thesis," that in Cuba is to be found a "bourgeois state machine" which somehow "represents" the smashed bourgeoisie . . . by expropriating them! There remain three other arguments to be disposed of.

The SLL leaders argue at length that Cuba is no workers state . . . because of its peculiar relation to the world market. Cuba is wholly dependent upon the export of sugar. Today the Soviet bureaucracy has replaced the U.S. as main buyer of that sugar. Tomorrow, says Ed Stillwell (*The Newsletter*, July 18, 1964), and John Castle (the SLL's *Fourth International*, August 1965, pp. 65–67), the Soviet bureaucracy could "sell out" Cuba to American imperialism.

> There is every danger that Cuba's withdrawal from direct imperialist domination and her modest economic development plans will be scuttled as the price the USSR would be more than willing to pay for some more direct agreement with the imperialists. (Ibid., p. 67.)

Suppose this is so. What has this to do with the question whether there is a workers state in Cuba? The Soviet bureaucracy has blockaded China, consciously trying to throw that country back towards trade with imperialism. This caused terrible hardships for the Chinese people, coinciding as it did with three years of agricultural shortages. China's trade with imperialist countries significantly increased afterwards. The Kremlin's policy certainly proves its counterrevolutionary role; it doesn't prove that China is not a workers state.

But isn't Cuba much more dependent upon world trade than China? Undoubtedly it is (although the SLL exaggerates the degree of this dependence and seriously underestimates the efforts toward making the country self-sufficient at least in basic foodstuffs). Under these conditions isn't it more vulnerable to Stalinist and/or imperialist blackmail? Certainly! But, again, what does this mean? That revolutionary Cuba, tremendously weakened in case of a combined Moscow-Washington blockade, would become easy prey to a new counterrevolution? In our opinion, this view is exaggeratedly pessimistic. But let us grant the premise; surely the SLL leaders will not argue that only those states that cannot be overthrown any more by a counterrevolution are going to be recognized as workers states?

Doesn't the theory of the permanent revolution specifically state that *after* the victory of the socialist revolution in a backward country, and *after* the establishment of the proletarian dictatorship, a period of continual national and international civil wars opens up? If, due to a betrayal by the Kremlin, the Cuban revolution is defeated tomorrow; i.e., the workers state in Cuba is smashed and power returned to the counterrevolutionists, one would have to say that a proletarian dictatorship was overthrown by a victorious counterrevolution—not that such a dictatorship never existed in Cuba. And the Cuban workers and peasants would see the difference themselves, very clearly indeed.

But now the SLL revisionists are caught in a new trap:

> In Cuba, [states John Castle] it would be possible for the imperialists to reintegrate production of sugar into the world market mechanism [?] without a counter-revolutionary overturn, i.e., through the existing bureaucratic [?] state, against [?] the workers and peasants. [And even more clearly:] Thus Cuba can be completely re-absorbed into the capitalist market without so much as the de-nationalisation of a single industry. (Ibid., p. 66.)

This is indeed remarkable! Since when is trading with capitalist countries a form of "exploiting its own workers and peasants" for a workers state? Are the SLL leaders against such trade? Have they thrown overboard all the teachings of Lenin and Trotsky on the subject? Don't they know the basic difference between exploitation through trade and exploitation through the purchase of labor power in the process of production? Have the imperialists become philanthropists? Haven't even the imperialist countries of Western Europe—not to mention the semicolonial countries!—learned the hard lesson that when you become dependent upon trade with Washington, this also means that Washington starts buying up shares, factories, plants, banks, establishing subsidiaries of its own corporations, buying up newspapers, politicians, radio stations; i.e., "pieces" of political power? And if the imperialists do not do any of these nasty things; if they don't use this economic "dependence" in order to bring their own stooges back into power; in short, if they don't stage any "counterrevolutionary overturn"—in what qualitative way would the Cuban situation then be different from that of the Soviet Union before 1945, a period during which that country also traded only with capitalist countries, for the good reason that no other workers states existed? What has all this to do with Cuba being a workers state?

Comrade Joseph Hansen, in his excellent article "Cuba—the Acid Test"[7] posed a very concrete question to the SLL: What would you do if you were in power in Cuba? John Castle answers that he would institute direct rule by the workers; that he would not rely upon the "perfidious allies" of the so-called nonaligned countries, nor would he trust the Soviet bureaucracy. He would call for a revolution in all countries. (Ibid., p. 69.) So far, so good. But all this evades Hansen's question. Because Hansen asked specifically what the SLL leaders would do *in the field of the economy, of trade, of international commerce.*

Surely, even a soviet in every Cuban home will not change the immediate dependence of Cuba upon selling its sugar on the world market. To whom would a classical democratic workers state in Cuba sell its sugar? The choice would remain: either to the Soviet bureaucracy (the Chinese bureaucracy, the Rumanian bureaucracy, etc.) or to the imperialists, or doing a balancing act between the two camps. An SLL "council of people's commissars" would, in other words, be in exactly the same trade position as Fidel Castro. Of course it would *try* to further world revolution as Lenin and Trotsky did in their days; but, unfortunately, between these attempts and positive results there is always a time lag, as Lenin and Trotsky learned through sad experience. Revolutionary action and propaganda do not guarantee speedy victories; and only speedy victories will create new buyers of sugar. So in itself this activity does not at all modify Cuba's trade situation.

We need only add that judging from the specimen under examination, it can seriously be doubted that the SLL's propaganda for revolution will be more effective than Fidel's—at least in Latin America. So the dilemma would remain—just as much for a revolution headed by the SLL as for one headed by Fidel Castro! "There is no solution purely *within Cuba* to the problems confronting the Cuban revolution," concludes John Castle. (Ibid., p. 69. Emphasis in original.) Either this is a long-range historical statement—and then of course it is true, although rather commonplace and without implications for the question to whom Cuba is to sell its sugar in the coming years. Or, it is meant as an immediate "guide to action"; then it just means running away from the necessity of concretely defending the Cuban revolution, even through trade, towards general face-saving formulas. In that case it amounts to desertion of the revolution, capitulation and liquidationism.

Let us take up the two remaining arguments. The SLL leaders raise a big hue and cry about the deficiencies of proletarian democracy in Cuba. Some of their statements are quite exaggerated; but there is no doubt that various grave shortcomings as regards proletarian democracy do exist in Cuba. There is no reason for us to deny this. The absence of a clear power structure of the workers' state, based upon democratically elected committees of workers and peasants, is the main deficiency. We certainly advocate and are in favor of such committees being established, just as we are in favor of workers self-management in the factories within the framework of a centralized plan. But all this is beside the point. It only proves that Cuba is a workers state with bureaucratic deformations—as incidentally the Soviet Union likewise was even under Lenin and Trotsky. It certainly does not prove that Cuba is . . . a bourgeois state!

But this is precisely what the leadership of the SLL maintains. To try to prove its contention, it has to fall back upon all the stale arguments of the petty-bourgeois revisionists on the Russian question:

> The relation of these nationalized industries to the world economy [?], the nature of the state apparatus, and the role of the working class, are completely ignored in this approach. "Socialism", it appears, is asserting its historical destiny over the heads of and even against the working class! (John Castle, ibid., p. 70).

To drag "socialism" into the picture is completely incongruous; nobody calls Cuba a "socialist" society. To say that the workers state is "asserting its historical destiny over the heads of the working class" is even more incongruous, because the Cuban working class has fought more heroically and more consciously for socialism during the last six years than any other working class during that period with the exception of the Vietnamese proletariat; if there is a workers state today in Cuba, it is thanks to the constant revolutionary mobilization and activity of the Cuban urban and agricultural working class. But to regard it as impossible for a workers state to act against the working class[8]—what does that make of the Soviet state for at least the last thirty-five years?

Isn't that exactly the same argument as the one advanced by the petty-bourgeois revisionist muddleheads concerning the "impossibility of a counterrevolutionary workers state," on which Trotsky poured such sarcasm?

But the difference between the Soviet bureaucracy and "Castro's Bonapartism," shout Slaughter and Co., is that "Stalin's was a bureaucratic regime resting on the proletarian state foundations conquered by the Soviet workers in 1917; Castro's is a Bonapartist regime still resting on bourgeois state foundations." The "bourgeois state foundations" of the Castro regime we have already disposed of. The argument that "Castro's state" was not born, like the Russian, the Yugoslav and the Chinese states, out of a proletarian revolution and the setting up of a proletarian dictatorship with various degrees of bureaucratic deformation, is in complete contradiction both to facts and to the theory of permanent revolution.[9]

But the main weakness of the SLL formula lies somewhere else: and what do you make of Hungary, Poland, Rumania, Bulgaria, not to mention the so-called German Democratic Republic, comrades of the SLL? Where were the "proletarian state foundations" conquered by the workers of these countries? Did any "proletarian revolution" occur in these countries—except the antibureaucratic political revolution of 1956 in Hungary, which was crushed in blood by the bureaucrats? Yet these very same counterrevolutionary bureaucrats are endorsed with the capacity and the ability to set up workers states "behind the backs and even against" the workers of their own country—whereas Fidel Castro, marching at the head of all the toiling masses of his country, mobilising them continually, crushing the bourgeois state machine through class action, arming the workers and peasants and expropriating the bourgeoisie and breaking the grip of world imperialism, is said to be unable to build a workers state . . . because he didn't create soviets!

The contradictions in which the SLL leaders twist and turn become even more striking if we look at their third argument:

> Castro is, in our opinion, a genuine advocate of petty-bourgeois-led peasant rebellion against the backward latifundist regimes in Latin America and elsewhere. He is thus an advocate of the *bourgeois* revolution which has been incomplete in so many of the underdeveloped countries of the world. It is his distinguishing thesis that the bourgeois revolution can be completed and economic development spurred ahead through an essentially peasant struggle which storms the cities from the outside. Castro is not now, nor has he ever been, an advocate of *proletarian revolution*. (John Castle, ibid., p. 67. Emphasis in original.)

We don't know whether the man is ignorant or whether he is just an impudent liar. But here is what Fidel Castro, this archenemy of the proletarian revolution, this "genuine advocate of petty-bourgeois-led peasant rebellion" has to say on the matter himself, in the main theoretical charter the Cuban revolution has given to the world, the *Second Declaration of Havana*:

> The initial struggle of small fighting units is constantly nurtured by new forces; the mass movement begins to grow bold, the old order bit by bit breaks up into a thousand pieces and *that is when the working class and the urban masses decide the battle*. What is it that from the very beginning of the fight makes those units invincible, regardless of the number, strength and resources of their enemies? It is the people's support, and they can count on an ever-increasing mass support.
>
> *But the peasantry is a class which, because of the ignorance in which it lives, requires the revolutionary and political leadership of the working class and the revolutionary intellectuals*. Without that it cannot alone launch the struggle and achieve the victory.
>
> In the present historical conditions of Latin America, the national bourgeoisie cannot lead the anti-feudal and anti-imperialist struggle. . . . The present world relationship of forces and the universal movement to free colonial and dependent peoples establishes the real task of Latin America's working class and revolutionary intellectuals. *It is to place themselves determinedly in the vanguard of the struggle against imperialism and feudalism*. (Emphasis added.)

A strange "peasant leader" indeed who, in the Trotskyist tradition, clearly and unequivocally states the *inability* of the peasantry to lead a victorious revolution against imperialism and the native ruling classes of backward countries. A strange "advocate of the bourgeois revolution" who proclaims the necessity of the proletariat to conquer power. A strange "opponent" of the proletarian revolution—who proclaims the necessity for the proletariat to conquer power in all of Latin America, and who successfully led a proletarian revolution in his own country!

A "bourgeois" state which expropriates the bourgeoisie; a "peasant leader" who accomplishes a proletarian revolution; an "advocate of bourgeois revolution" who proclaims that neither the national bourgeoisie nor the peasantry but only the proletariat can lead the revolution to victory; the "main hope for the re-entry of the bourgeoisie in Cuba"—hated and reviled by that very same bourgeoisie which has emigrated to the USA; and which is locked in mortal combat with him—this is Castro. Isn't it clear that we are in fact confronted with a monstrous hoax which the SLL leaders are seeking to perpetrate under the stolen banner of "Trotskyism"? Aren't their lucubrations only a puerile attempt to distort reality by means of a subjectivist "theory" degraded to the level of a self-serving instrument to justify the existence of a sect trapped in dead-end factionalism? The SLL's picture of Cuba comes under the well-known formula: any resemblance to reality, living or dead, is purely coincidental.

7

AN 'OBJECTIVIST' CHICKEN COMES HOME TO ROOST

But the SLL leaders, having succumbed to revision of the theory of permanent revolution in relation to the Cuban revolution, have not yet done with their contortions. In their twisting and turning to get out of the contradictions of their position, they knot themselves up still further.

The historical tasks of the bourgeois-democratic revolution can only be realised if the revolution in backward countries is led by the proletariat, says Trotsky (and, as we have seen, Fidel Castro). The revolution in Cuba was *not* led by the proletariat, answer Slaughter and Co. But what about the radical agrarian reform, the nationalization of the latifundia, the expropriation of the plantations? Ah, but wait, you have to take into consideration . . . the new objective conditions, reply the SLL leaders. Listen to their embarrassed "explanations":

> Cuba is one of those countries where capitalist development has been almost entirely a function of foreign investment and control. The dependence of the economies of Latin American countries upon a single crop or resource (for Cuba, sugar) has often been described. The national bourgeoisie could never be an independent social force in Cuba. It could function only as a political or commercial executive for U.S. investments. Under these conditions the petty-bourgeois democratic ideologists could not long play their classical role in the bourgeois [!] revolution, that of providing a political leadership tying the workers and peasants first to the bourgeois struggle against absolutism or for independence, and then tying these lower classes to the new regime. In the Russian Revolution the Social Revolutionaries and the Mensheviks attempted to do this. ("Opportunism and Empiricism," SLL's *Fourth International*, summer 1965, p. 26.)

> What has happened then in Cuba? The objective factors [sic] which motivate the theory of the permanent revolution asserted themselves with great force. The ruling circles of the Cuban bourgeoisie were so tied to U.S. capital that they were unable to command any support whatsoever against the peasant war led by the Castro guerrillas. The latter force, starting from the traditional programme of the democratic revolution—land for the peasants, a democratic constitution, and national independence—conquered power. The defeat of the Batista regime and the expulsion of the U.S. imperialists [!] from Cuba immediately posed the question of going beyond these tasks. The struggle against [!] U.S. interests brought the Cuban leaders up sharply against the world counterrevolutionary strategy of U.S. imperialism. . . . This enormous pressure [!] from imperialism forced [!] very rapidly a split among the petty-bourgeois leaders of the Castro movement. The very exigencies [!] of national defence against the military and economic sanctions of Wall Street necessitated a thoroughgoing purge [!] of the Right in the July 26th movement and in government personnel, and all foreign holdings were expropriated. ("Cuba: Marxism and the Revolution," by John Castle, in the SLL's *Fourth International*, August 1965, p. 72.)

The author is guilty of a slight oversight: not only all "foreign holdings," but also all Cuban "national" capitalist enterprises were nationalised. But leaving aside this "small" oversight, we really cannot believe our eyes: *what do we have here but the supposed "Pabloite" theory, substituting "objectivism" for the outlook of dialectical materialism* against which the SLL leaders inveigh week in and week out?

Since when can the "pressure" of objective conditions, including the "pressure" of imperialism bring the petty-bourgeoisie in backward countries to do what it is historically unable to do; i.e., carry out a thoroughgoing and radical land reform, give land to the peasants, expropriate imperialist property and nationalise "national" capitalist property? Strange "orthodox" Trotskyists, indeed, who on the one hand repeat emphatically that the Nkrumahs, the Ben Bellas, the Sukarnos, not to mention the Nehrus; i.e., all the typical bourgeois or petty-bourgeois nationalist leaders, are *unable* to carry out a thoroughgoing radical land reform, are unable finally and definitively to break with imperialism—yet who continue to apply the label "petty-bourgeois peasant leader" to Castro, who after all *did* carry out a radical land reform and *did* expropriate all imperialist property . . . under the "pressure" of "objective circumstances". The refusal to recognize a socialist revolution when it takes place has brought an "objectivist" chicken home to roost! The historical task, which the theory of the permanent revolution leaves only to the alliance of the proletariat and the poor peasantry, is now turned over to . . . petty-bourgeois leaders, thanks to "objective circumstances." These same "objective circumstances" even prevent the "petty-bourgeois democratic ideologues" from playing their classical role of tying the workers and peasants to the bourgeoisie, it now seems! One only wonders why these genuinely revisionist leaders of the SLL do not see any contradiction between the "objective factors" which *brought* Fidel Castro to break with imperialism and the native ruling classes in Cuba, including the bourgeoisie, and the "objective factors" which *prevented* petty-bourgeois nationalist leaders like Ben Bella, Nkrumah and Sukarno from specifically doing the same thing . . .

At the root of the SLL leaders' revision of the theory of the permanent revolution in the case of Cuba is a wrong theory which can be summarized in the SLL's own words:

> Cuba can and will be defined as a workers' state only when a revolutionary party based on the programme of the Fourth International has successfully overthrown the capitalist state . . . (*The Newsletter*, July 18, 1964.)

This is sectarian to the point of being ludicrous. The conception that only card-carrying members of the "International Committee of the Fourth International" can found workers states is certainly one of the most extreme variants of sectarian deviation from Marxism ever to be encountered in the history of the revolutionary movement (which is so rich in strange turns and in quirks of the most variegated kind). It was, incidentally, anticipated by Trotsky himself who squarely opposed all such nonsense. As early as 1931 Trotsky said that it was not excluded that a revolution could win in Germany under a Stalinist leadership:

> In certain cases, victory is possible even with a very bad policy. With the deepening of the crisis, its prolongation, with the subsequent disintegration of the social-democracy, the demoralization of the governments, the victory of the German Communist Party is not excluded, even with the policy of the Thaelmann leadership. (Letter from "Comrade Gourov" to the editorial board of the *Bulletin of the Russian Opposition*, July 28, 1931, under the title: "Some Ideas on the Position and Tasks of the Left Opposition.")

Seven years later, Trotsky returned to the very same concept when, in the Transitional Program adopted at the Founding Conference of the Fourth International, he wrote:

> However, one cannot categorically deny in advance the theoretical possibility that, under the influence of completely exceptional circumstances (war, defeat, financial crash, mass revolutionary pressure, etc.) the petty bourgeois parties [Trotsky is referring to the "petty-bourgeois representatives of the workers and peasants," or the "traditional organizations of the proletariat," two formulas which he uses in the same chapter of the Transitional Program.—E.G.], including the Stalinists may go further than they themselves wish along the road to a break with the bourgeoisie. (*The Founding Conference of the Fourth International*, p. 38.)

Sectarianism, says Trotsky, often results from fear of succumbing to temptation. Why are the sectarian leaders of the SLL so afraid of admitting that Cuba is a workers state? Because, they presumably think, once you admit that a workers state can be established without the prior building of a revolutionary party, then you must conclude that it is no longer necessary to build revolutionary parties anywhere, that revolutions can somehow be victorious without such parties . . . and then the sect (which they identify in their own minds as the revolutionary party) would have lost all justification for its existence!

This is obviously the Marxist method turned upside down: subjectivism elevated to the level of a dogma, instead of an objective scientific analysis of reality. Objective scientific criteria exist by which the class nature of a state can be determined, including the class nature of the Cuban state. We have to start by applying these criteria to the facts. In the case of Cuba, this method—the Marxist method—points to an inescapable conclusion: in Cuba we do, indeed, have a workers state. All this was fully worked out by the Trotskyist movement—and at the very time it happened. Similarly on the next question: is the fact that a workers state was established in Cuba without the prior creation of a revolutionary Marxist party and without that party gaining the leadership of the mass movement, an exception or the rule? If it is an exception it has to be explained as such—and the need to build revolutionary Marxist parties everywhere then stands. If it is the rule, then there remains no alternative but to conclude that the building of revolutionary Marxist parties is no longer necessary to overthrow capitalism, but only to establish real proletarian democracy.

That was the method Marx, Lenin and Trotsky applied to new problems in their lifetime. That was the method Trotsky applied in studying the class nature of the Soviet state and the Soviet bureaucracy. That same method has been applied by us to the problem of the expansion of world revolution in the backward countries since 1945. And our conclusion, summarized in the documents of the Reunification Congress of the Fourth International in 1963, is completely unambiguous: we say that the case of Cuba is *an exception and not the rule*; we explain the exception by the extremely favourable circumstances of near complete decomposition of the ruling classes—and of imperialism being taken by surprise; and we conclude that such an exception will, in general, *not* be repeated, and that the building of revolutionary Marxist parties, and their winning leadership of the masses, is a necessary prerequisite not only for the conquest of socialist democracy, but also for the overthrow of capitalism the world over.

Sectarians refuse to recognize reality, being afraid of succumbing to opportunist temptations; opportunists impermissibly generalize exceptions and draw liquidationist conclusions from the experience of the Cuban revolution. Only the Fourth International has been able at one and the same time to explain and understand the news facets of world reality, including the appearance of the Cuban workers state, without abandoning the Marxist-Leninist theoretical heritage by a single iota.

Castro's scandalous attack against Trotskyism and the Fourth International at the Tricontinental Conference in Havana in January 1966 provided the SLL with new ammunition for its assumption that Cuba is a "capitalist" state; but it also involved the SLL theoreticians in new contradictions. The SLL interpreted these attacks as proof "that Castro has taken the road of liquidation of the Cuban Revolution," (SLL's *Fourth International*, April 1966, p. 99.) and that he "accepts the anti-revolutionary strategy of the Stalinist bureaucracy" (ibid., p. 100). The SLL's American followers have spelled this out more concretely: ". . . the political nature of the Havana-Moscow line for underdeveloped countries" is, according to them, "armed struggle if you must, but collaboration with the bourgeoisie at all costs." (*Bulletin of International Socialism*, February 28, 1966, p. 4.)

Unfortunately for these lucid analysts, Castro, in answering the leader of the Chilean "national" bourgeoisie Frei, *after* the Tricontinental Conference, had the following to say:

> We had discussions with those [Chilean] deputies. And we explained to them that to make a revolution it is first necessary to confront imperialism: that to make a revolution, although it may not be a socialist but a bourgeois-democratic revolution, a nationalist revolution, they had to confront imperialism and they had to confront the national oligarchy.
>
> I told them also that I did not think that conditions in Chile permitted a revolution of that type, and that in the conditions of Chile, if a revolution was desired, it would necessarily have to be a socialist revolution, and I explained why. Because an underdeveloped country, burdened with debts as Chile is, a country where large masses of the population live in the worst conditions, would necessarily have to strike a blow against the interests of imperialism, of the oligarchy, of big industry, of the import-export trade and of the Bank if something was to be done, to give something to the peasant masses and to the masses of workers in the country.
>
> And, also that to wage a battle against the oligarchy and against imperialism, the support of the worker and peasant masses was necessary to confront imperialism; and . . . that the masses of workers and peasants

would not lend support to any bourgeois revolution, because the workers and the peasants would not be willing to collaborate to serve the interests of an exploiting class. (*Granma*, March 20, 1966, reprinted in *World Outlook* April 22, 1966.)

If, as Michael Banda says, "there is little or no difference in the type of *state* set up by Castro or Batista" (*The Newsletter*, June 18, 1966. Emphasis in original.), he would have a tough time finding any precedent for a Batista (!) or any other bourgeois Bonaparte calling on the workers of a whole continent to rise in a *socialist* revolution against imperialism and against the native bourgeoisie as Castro does!

But the SLL's contradictions now stand out in the most glaring way. On the one hand, the SLL spokesmen allege that Fidel Castro and his followers have lined up with the Stalin-Khrushchev followers of the Menshevik theory of "revolution by stages," a theory according to which a bourgeois-democratic revolution and not a permanent revolution is on the order of the day in Latin America, and according to which the proletariat and the poor peasants must subordinate themselves to the "national" bourgeoisie within the framework of that revolution. The American followers of the SLL push this thesis to the extreme in a screaming headline: "Castro Embraces Stalinism." (A strange "proof" for the existence of a "capitalist state" in Cuba, isn't it? Since when do capitalists "embrace Stalinism"? Has the SLL "embraced" the theory of state capitalism in the USSR?) But, on the other hand, in logical consistency with its own absurd concept of a "bourgeois state" in Cuba, the SLL promises to . . . defend Blas Roca against Castro, and even retrospectively defends the miserable bureaucrat Escalante, hated and despised by all the Cuban workers, against being "purged" by Castro![10]

And thus the SLL theoreticians reach the conclusion that it is the duty of a "Trotskyist" of the SLL-type to line up with the "working class" supporters of the Menshevik theory of a "bourgeois-democratic revolution" in Cuba and in Latin America, against the "bourgeois" Castro and the Fidelista current, who fought, not without success, for a socialist revolution in Cuba and who, against the Soviet bureaucracy and its Cuban agents, have maintained their orientation towards a socialist revolution in the rest of Latin America! If a tree is judged by its fruit, this conclusion, drawn by the SLL theoreticians themselves from their theory of a "capitalist state in Cuba" would be enough to condemn the concept as utterly absurd and highly discrediting to Trotskyism![11]

8

REVISION OF THE LENINIST-TROTSKYIST CONCEPT OF THE COLONIAL REVOLUTION

Having lost their grip on theory as an instrument of objective analysis, the necessary prerequisite for theory to become a correct guide to action in changing reality, the leaders of the SLL are now succumbing more and more to the logic of sectarianism. By degrading theory into a mere vehicle of faction fighting against "revisionism," they are compelled step by step to revise essential parts of revolutionary Marxist theory and tradition. Their revision of Trotsky's theory of permanent revolution is but one instance of their departure from Marxism. Another is their basic attitude towards the colonial revolution, the main sector of the world revolution for the past seventeen years.

The attitude of Marxist-Leninists toward the colonial revolution was developed in an extensive way for the first time at the Second Congress of the Communist International in Lenin's *Theses on the National and the Colonial Question*, and in the famous 21 conditions for membership in the Communist International. The key position is the absolute duty of a revolutionary party in an imperialist country to support by propaganda and by action wars of liberation waged by the colonial peoples, no matter what social force happens to be leading the struggle. In that spirit, the Communist parties of the twenties supported the war of liberation fought by the Rif Kabyls under feudal leadership against French imperialism; the world Trotskyist movement supported the war conducted by the Ethiopian people under the leadership of slave owners against Italian imperialism; and Trotsky went out of his way to justify, against his ultraleft critics of those days, his critical support of the butcher Chiang Kai-shek at the head of the Chinese government opposing Japanese imperialism.

So dangerous is the chauvinistic and social-imperialist poisoning of the working class of the West, especially in relation to the liberation movements in the colonial countries, that Lenin established the iron rule that lack of active, material support for such struggles on the part of any party calling itself "Communist" would be enough to exclude it from joining the Communist International.[12] The record of the SLL on the Algerian revolution is so disgraceful that Lenin would have certainly fought for the expulsion of such a group from the Communist International.

The Healy group did not always have such a disgraceful attitude towards the colonial revolution. When it collaborated closely in publishing the *Socialist Outlook*, it gave active support to the struggles of the Ghanaian and Kenyan peoples for independence. Writing in the *Socialist Outlook* of April 30, 1954, A. Banda had the following to say on the Mau Mau war against British imperialism:

> It is now one year and five months since the declaration of the Emergency in Kenya. All attempts to crush the Kenya people have so far failed. The "Mau Mau" have broken through every encirclement and operate as a popular movement—in the rear of the colonialist forces, in the mountains as before, in the reserves and in the towns...
>
> The African Land Army has created its own organization. It is organised into regular military formations with their own staff and committees on a territorial basis. There is a kind of commissariat of supply with its liaison committees with civilian sympathisers. It has a million pair of eyes and ears in its intelligence service, as has every popular uprising. It has its courts with their own emergency laws and regulations. In fact, it is one system of law and order pitted against another system.
>
> The duty of British Labour is to support those forces which are fighting for the freedom of the African in Kenya. Without a betrayal of socialist principles it can neither stand aside nor support the Tory Government and white settlers, who have launched the new terror offensive against the Kenya people.

This position is entirely correct. Provided there is a popular uprising and a real fight against the imperialist butchers, it is the duty of the working-class movement in the imperialist countries to support this uprising, regardless of its leadership, and to give it not only political but also active material support. Any other attitude would in the best case be "neutrality" ("standing aside"), an attitude tantamount to a "betrayal of socialist principles."

Now the example of Kenya is very significant because, obviously, the leadership of the uprising was by no means socialist or working class in nature. As a matter of fact, its main political leader, Jomo Kenyatta, has become the principal neocolonialist stooge in Kenya today. Was it therefore wrong for Banda to take the attitude he did towards the Mau Mau movement in 1954? Certainly not! For in the first place as long as Kenyatta was persecuted by imperialism, he objectively embodied a progressive cause. In the second place, precisely if one foresaw that many petty-bourgeois nationalist leaders would eventually reach compromises with imperialism and sell out the colonial revolution, it was all the more necessary to support the just struggle for national independence. For only if one gave unambiguous and active support to that struggle could a real hearing be gained among their followers at the stage when the "sellout" occurred. In the third place, the colonial revolution viewed as a *process of permanent revolution* is also a process of constant differentiation and splits in the popular uprising's leadership, a process in which the ideas of revolutionary Marxism can gain ground and create the conditions for the appearance of a real revolutionary party, provided the individual revolutionists and the Fourth International as such identify themselves from the beginning, and unambiguously, with the revolution and the uprising.

Now all that applies to Kenya applies even more to Algeria. After all, Algeria, socially and economically, was more advanced than Kenya, although it was still a backward country. Even more than Kenya, the ruling class was identified with the European settlers and its leaders served as direct representatives and stooges of imperialism. Even more than in Kenya, the Front de Liberation Nationale [FLN] operated as a popular movement, with the support of the bulk of the population, with "one system of law and order pitted against another system," with "regular military formations with their own staff and committees on a territorial basis." Even more than in Kenya, consequently, Labour could not stand aside or against the popular uprising for national independence, "without a betrayal of socialist principles."

But the SLL leaders refused to support the Algerian uprising, and for the most sectarian and sophistic of reasons!

They did so in the first place with the excuse that there was a rival movement, the Mouvement National Algerien [MNA] which had adopted a "revolutionary social programme." (*The Newsletter*, March 10, 1962.) So blinded by factionalism were the sectarians of the SLL, that they were not impressed by the fact that this so-called "revolutionary social movement"[13] was allowed to hold legal conferences in France under police protection, whereas the FLN, involved in a bloody war with French imperialism, was undergoing the severest persecution; that this so-called "revolutionary social movement" actually controlled a stretch of territory in Algeria under the command of one Si Bellounis without enacting or putting into effect a single progressive social or economic measure there; that Si Bellounis ended up by making a military deal with the imperialist army against the FLN; that this allegedly "revolutionary social" party centered its propaganda around a nauseating "orthodox" religious appeal to the Muslims; and that it addressed itself internationally to the most reactionary forces of the Muslim world, the governments of Saudi Arabia and Pakistan.

It required the MNA's public approval of de Gaulle's coming to power in 1958 for the Healy group to "recognize" that they "were no longer dealing with the same movement," and to express regrets—"no doubt those who had supported the MNA should have realised sooner" what was going on. (*The Newsletter*, March 10, 1962.)

After they—belatedly—recognized the nature of the MNA, the SLL leaders and their French followers practically withdrew from the Algerian scene. They had nothing to offer but scorn for the FLN while 500,000 imperialist soldiers were thrown against the popular uprising occurring under its leadership. What was this but that very same "standing aside" condemned by Banda in 1954 as a betrayal of socialist principles?

Looking back today, the SLL theoreticians view the various splits and shifts in the FLN, and the limited nature of the petty-bourgeois governments arising in Algeria after political independence was won, as confirming the correctness of their refusal to offer critical support to the FLN against French imperialism. But this excuse is utterly unprincipled!

What should strike any observer of the Algerian scene since 1962 is the fact that all the differentiations have taken place *within* the forces that fought French imperialism from 1954 to 1962 under the banner of the FLN. The agricultural workers who occupied the landed estates of the French settlers and organised them into collective property under self-management; the trade-union leaders of the Union Generale des Travailleurs Algeriens [UGTA] who rose against the various right-wing and centrist FLN leaders to defend stubbornly the rights and autonomy of the Algerian working class; the left-wing theoreticians of the FLN who drafted the "Algiers Charter" with its revolutionary socialist programme and its project for a socialist Algeria; the Boudiaf forces which assembled a small opposition against Ben Bella and Boumedienne and which has the somewhat shamefaced sympathy of the SLL; the organisers of the new underground movement against the Boumedienne regime—all these various left-wing forces which have emerged since 1962 in Algeria have developed out of the FLN.

Isn't it evident that those who, like the sections of the Fourth International, carried out their Leninist duty by giving material support to the FLN between 1954 and 1962, have possibilities of collaborating with these left-wing Algerian forces and convincing them of the necessity to set up a revolutionary Marxist party, possibilities which the SLL leadership and its French followers completely lack as a result of their abstentionist attitude before political independence was won?

To justify that abstentionism because of the compromises which the FLN leaders reached with imperialism *after* the struggle, and because of their hesitating on the road to socialism or turning back is quite wrong. Revolutionary Marxists have no confidence in bourgeois or petty-bourgeois nationalists carrying the struggle against imperialism to its final conclusion, or starting to build socialism. But the absence of illusions does not in the least prevent revolutionary Marxists from giving critical support to such forces in their struggle against imperialism—as long as they fight at the head of the masses. It is the duty of revolutionary Marxists to strive for an independent class organisation of the workers and poor peasants, and to educate them in the spirit of distrust towards the bourgeois and petty-bourgeois leaders of the national movement. In other words, it is the duty of the proletarian revolutionists to struggle for hegemony inside the national movement. But they cannot do this if they do not recognise that this movement is genuinely revolutionary and progressive, and that it must be supported against imperialism.

This *dialectical combination of tasks* is precisely what the SLL leadership cannot understand under the limitations of its primitive sectarian dogmatism. It thus comes to deny any progressive significance whatsoever to the struggle for national independence or to the conquest of national independence, as in the case of Tom Kemp in *The Newsletter* of July 14, 1962. His article on the conquest of national independence by the Algerian masses[14] is significantly entitled "Algeria—situation unchanged [sic]—No gains for workers and peasants"! That the conquest of national political independence leaves the situation "unchanged" and represents "no gain" for the workers and peasants, flies in the face of all the teachings of Lenin and Trotsky on the colonial question. It should be recalled here that Trotsky considered *national independence—even under the leadership of a Chiang Kai-shek—worthy of defence against imperialism:*

> But can Chiang Kai-shek assure the victory? I do not believe so. It is he, however, who began the war and who today directs it. To be able to replace him it is necessary to gain the decisive influence among the proletariat and in the army, and to do this it is necessary, not to remain suspended in the air, but to place oneself in the *military* struggle against the foreign invasion and in the *political* struggle against the weaknesses, the deficiencies, and the internal betrayal. At a certain point, which we cannot fix in advance, this political opposition can and must be transformed into armed conflict, since the civil war, like war generally, is nothing more than the continuation of the political struggle....
>
> We never denied [in 1925–27] that it was the duty of the Communist Party to participate in the war of the bourgeois and petty-bourgeois of the South against the generals of the North, agents of foreign imperialism. We never denied the necessity of a military bloc between the C.P. and the Kuomintang. On the contrary, we were the first to propose it. We demanded, however, that the C.P. maintain its entire political and organizational independence, that is, that during the civil war against the internal agents of imperialism, as in the national war against foreign imperialism, the working class, while remaining in the front lines of the *military* struggle, prepare the *political* overthrow of the bourgeoisie. ("On the Sino-Japanese War" by L. Trotsky, September 23, 1937. See *Internal Bulletin* published by the Organizing Committee for the Socialist Party Convention. Emphasis in original.)

From this dialectical combination of tasks, the SLL (like the ultralefts against whom Trotsky was polemicizing in 1937) hold only to the necessity of political struggle against the bourgeois or petty-bourgeois nationalist leadership, and *precisely because* they refuse to become involved actively in the movement for national liberation, this political "struggle" against the traditional leadership of the nationalist movement remains largely on paper: in actual fact if the attitude of the SLL leadership were to be duplicated by revolutionists in the colonial countries, it could only lead to their abandoning the national movement to these treacherous leaders and helping to consolidate their grip!

The logic of this revisionist position on the colonial revolution leads the SLL so far astray that the very existence of such a revolution and national liberation is denied and the only "reality" of today is proclaimed to be the "proletarian revolution." (David Francis in the SLL's *Fourth International*, April 1966, p. 54.)[15] The fact, stressed a thousand times by Lenin and Trotsky, that there are hundreds of millions of nonproletarian *peasants* in the colonial and semicolonial countries, whom it would be absolutely unprincipled to call "proletarians" and to organise in "proletarian parties," but who nevertheless lead historically progressive struggles against imperialism, which the proletariat must support and in which it can win political leadership only if it supports these struggles—this fact the SLL has completely forgotten.

But now the SLL sectarians, on the basis of their view that without sections of the Fourth International at the head of the masses you can't have a proletarian revolution, and that there is no colonial revolution but only a proletarian revolution, are compelled to make a complete somersault and deny everything they have invoked up to now. For the SLL leadership is caught unexpectedly in a new confrontation between the colonial revolution—led by a bloc composed of the Communist party and petty-bourgeois nationalists—and world imperialism, a confrontation of such fierce violence that it exercises a powerful *attraction upon the SLL's own youthful rank and file*. And so the SLL leaders, *forced* to take sides, end up calling for support to the National Liberation Front's struggle against American imperialism in south Vietnam and *The Newsletter* emphasizes its own somersault with a screaming headline: "Arm the Vietcong." (May 8, 1965.)

What is this if not "capitulation before Pabloite revisionism"? Isn't the "Vietcong" fighting the civil war on the basis of a demand to implement the Geneva agreement—which was a "sellout"? Isn't it fighting for "only" a limited program of national independence and unity and some social reforms, keeping quiet about "socialist revolution"? Isn't the "Vietcong" an agency of the "treacherous Stalinist bureaucracy which has systematically sold out all revolutions in the last thirty years"?

The SLL leaders are caught here in a contradiction between theory and action which they have been utterly unable to resolve. They published a letter by one Webster (*The Newsletter*, April 24, 1965) which states that the Kremlin and the Chinese bureaucracies cannot but betray the Vietnamese revolution, and which labels as "treacherous drivel" the appeal from the Fourth International to all the workers states to come to the aid of the Vietnamese revolution with all the military means at their disposal. But at the same time, they call for arms for the "Vietcong"! Presumably, it is "counterrevolutionary" to demand that the workers states "arm the Vietcong," but it is revolutionary to ask the imperialist state of Britain to do so. The confusion becomes worse confounded when *The Newsletter* plays up Bertrand Russell's appeal to Kosygin to send jet planes to Vietnam. (July 23, 1966 issue.)

To refuse to support Castro's civil war in Cuba (presumably because of its "bourgeois-democratic" programme) but to support the "Vietcong's" civil war notwithstanding its "bourgeois-democratic" programme; to give credit to the revolutionary drive of the Vietnamese poor peasants and workers, while refusing to credit the Algerian workers and peasants with being able to outflank in action the limited programs of their leaders—the SLL has entangled itself in an inextricable net of contradictions due to revising the Trotskyist program on the colonial revolution.

We predicted that the SLL leaders would be called to order on these contradictions by their own ultraleft critics (every ultraleft always finds someone more "to the left" who calls him an "opportunist revisionist").[16] The prediction was borne out in the May–June 1965 issue of *Spartacist* which printed a copy of a letter sent by P. Jen to the editorial board of *The Newsletter* taking that body to task for its opportunism. The following excerpts from this letter (which *The Newsletter* did not see fit to print) indicate the line of criticism:

> The article which appeared in the January 2 *Newsletter* under the title: "Vietnam: workers face 20th year of war" by P. Desai, was deficient in both historical accuracy and Marxist criticism. It refers to the "heroic" struggle of Ho Chi Minh and the Indo-Chinese Communist Party from 1945 to 1954 without mentioning that this "heroism" expressed itself in a consistent policy of betrayal of the revolutionary workers' and peasants' movement which has served only to prolong the war. The article does not refer to the murder of Trotskyists by the Communists, the disarming of the workers and peasants, and the handing over of the population to the Allied occupation forces late in 1945. . . .
>
> Thus, the retreats and betrayals of Stalinism have been a determining factor in the nature and extent of the present war.
>
> And yet another betrayal is being prepared by the Communists in the National Liberation

Front. Their demand for a *neutral* South Vietnam leaves open the possibility of a settlement which will leave basic problems unsolved, *and will thus require further armed struggle*. And this treacherous policy is not criticized in the *Newsletter* article! Nor is there mention of the necessity for building a Marxist party which will lead the struggle not for neutralism, but for a *Vietnamese workers' republic*.

What has happened to the Permanent Revolution? Do we now put our faith in Stalinists and petty-bourgeois nationalists? (Emphasis in original.)

Do we indeed, to the point of calling upon the British workers to collect arms for these traitors preparing another sellout? Alas, it is a sad day when "Pabloite revisionism" worms its way into the editorial board of *The Newsletter* . . .

9

REVISION OF TROTSKY'S THEORY OF THE NEGRO STRUGGLE IN THE USA

In its revision of the Leninist-Trotskyist theory of the colonial revolution, the SLL leadership skirts dangerously close to social-chauvinism; for it is social-chauvinism, according to Lenin, to see no difference between the nationalism of the oppressors and the nationalism of the oppressed.[17] And we find a similar position, bordering on white chauvinism, in the SLL leadership's rank revision of Trotsky's concept of the Negro freedom struggle in the United States.

The Negro proletariat in the United States is victim of *double* exploitation and oppression. It is the worst exploited, the lowest paid sector of the industrial and agricultural working class of wage earners; and it is specially oppressed for racial reasons, as *black* wage earners, submitted to indignities, humiliations and discrimination which no white wage earners have to undergo. As a result of this situation, it is obvious that the Negro freedom struggle has a *double* character; it is a struggle against capitalist exploitation and a struggle against racial discrimination. When we say that the victory of the struggle against capitalist exploitation will historically mean the victory of the struggle against discrimination (which is true) it does not automatically follow at all that the victory in the struggle against discrimination can coincide only with the victory against capitalist exploitation, nor does it follow that it is unnecessary to engage in a special fight against racial discrimination quite apart from the general fight against capitalism.

The problem is even more concrete today. For historical reasons with which we are familiar, the American white working class has been politically quiescent now for more than two decades. The Negro working class on the other hand has awakened, both as a result of the superexploitation it suffers (lower wages, higher rate of unemployment, bad housing conditions, etc.) and in response to the progress of the colonial revolution in Africa and Cuba. It has started to revolt against the terrible inhuman system of racial discrimination it is subjected to. It is the elementary duty of white American revolutionists to support the movement fighting for "freedom now" and "black power" and to understand the objectively progressive and revolutionary nature of Negro nationalism in the United States. To counterpose to this actual *movement* of today the *hope* of future collaboration between the mass of white and black workers, means to follow the road of sectarianism into the blind alley of white chauvinism! For isn't it a position of white chauvinism to equate the "nationalism" of exploited and downtrodden masses with the nationalism of the white imperialist rulers of the United States?

Yet that is exactly the position which the SLL leadership has adopted! When violence against the Negro freedom fighters broke out, *The Newsletter* (October 6, 1962) did not call for the formation of armed defence guards by the Negroes; no, they called for the formation of armed defence guards by the American working class and by the AFL-CIO, completely ignoring the fact that the trade-union bureaucracy which leads the American working class at this stage is in many places of the South one of the mainstays of racial segregation even in the trade unions. When the Watts uprising took place, *The Newsletter* (August 21, 1965) refused to see anything of racial liberation in it, but equated it purely and simply with an uprising of the working class. When Malcolm X formed his nationalist party, *The Newsletter* condemned him as "leading this section of the United States' population into defeat" (April 4, 1964); it again denied the existence of a specific fight against racial discrimination, and stated emphatically: "For the coloured working class this is a fight for socialism side by side with white workers, not for an idealistic one-race society."

And when the SWP courageously and correctly came out in support of Malcolm X, it was chided and criticised by *The Newsletter* (May 30, 1964):

> *No true Marxist can possibly support the kind of nationalism put forward by Malcolm X. To do so is to take part in the selling out [!] of millions of Negro and white workers who are at the moment crying out for a leadership that will take them forward in struggles against American imperialism.* [Emphasis in original.]

Everything is wrong here. In the first place, it is simply not true that millions of white workers are at this moment "crying out for a leadership that will take them forward in struggles against American imperialism." At the present stage, the white working class is dormant and politically conservative. It does *not yet* understand the need to fight for socialism and against U.S. imperialism. This can change very quickly, provided events help and the revolutionary socialists apply a correct policy. But at the present time, such phrasemongering represents mere wishful thinking.

In the second place, millions of Negro workers *are rising* against U.S. imperialism, but they are *not yet* conscious of the fact that this should be a fight for socialism. They believe instead that it is *only* a fight against the terrible system of Jim Crow they are subjected to. If socialists counterpose the fight for socialism to this fight for racial equality and Negro nationalism, most Negroes will answer: "You gentlemen are only defending the rule of white supremacy with more sophisticated arguments"; they will turn their back to this kind of socialists (and rightly so!) and thereby the sway of nationalist leaders or dangerous quacks over the Negro masses will be strengthened.

Under the given conditions in the United States, where the Negro workers are *today* the only part of the proletariat objectively in action against American imperialism, it is the duty of the class-conscious white workers *to support this specific Negro struggle*. It is the necessary precondition for building a united front of Negro and white workers *tomorrow* against bourgeois society in the USA. Any attempt to evade this *concrete* duty of internationalism today in the name of an *abstract* principle of "internationalism" ("immediate unity of Negro and white workers against capitalism") would condemn both the struggle for internationalism and the struggle against capitalism in the United States tomorrow to certain defeat.[18]

On the other hand, if socialists, as is their elementary duty, support the revolt of the Negro masses regardless of its leadership, and tell them: "After the horrible oppression you have suffered at the hands of the white rulers of this country—unfortunately supported by poor whites too!—you have the right to choose for yourself either the objective of racial equality or of separation; we shall support your freedom struggle under any conditions"; in that case the Negro masses will begin to listen to these socialists and will at least believe that they are *genuinely* opposed to white supremacy; and *by the very logic of their progressive nationalist struggle*, they will then *reach*, with the help of the revolutionary socialists, *genuinely revolutionary, internationalist and socialist conclusions*.

This is exactly what the Socialist Workers Party predicted and what happened in the case of Malcolm X. Malcolm X started out as a genuine Negro nationalist. He ended up by saying:

> We are living in an era of revolution, and the revolt of the American Negro is part of the rebellion against the oppression and colonialism which has characterized this era . . .
>
> It is incorrect to classify the revolt of the Negro as simply a racial conflict of black against white, or as a purely American problem. Rather, we are today seeing a global rebellion of the oppressed against the oppressor, the exploited against the exploiter. *Malcolm X Speaks* [Pathfinder, 1965, 1989], pp. 256–257 [2015 printing]

He also said in an interview with the *Young Socialist* magazine (March–April 1965) that in his opinion, capitalism would not survive. (Ibid., p. 215.) He also said:

> I believe that there will ultimately be a clash between the oppressed and those that do the oppressing. I believe that there will be a clash between those who want freedom, justice and equality for everyone and those who want to continue the systems of exploitation. I believe that there will be that kind of clash, but I don't think that it will be based upon the color of the skin, as Elijah Muhammed had taught it. (Ibid., p. 232.)

This evolution from black nationalism to the border line of revolutionary international socialism was possible because the American revolutionary socialists of the Socialist Workers Party had not approached him with the kind of sectarian ultimatism the SLL leadership preaches, but precisely in the spirit Trotsky educated them in.

For Trotsky's positions on Negro nationalism in the United States are well known to the pundits of the SLL leadership. They know that the position of the Socialist Workers Party is in complete conformity with Trotsky's views and in complete contradiction with the views they expound. They conceal Trotsky's opinions on Negro nationalism from the membership of the SLL, because they do not want the rank and file to know that, contrary to their view, Trotsky considered the appearance of Negro nationalism to be progressive through and through as is clearly shown from the following excerpts from his contribution to discussions held on April 4, 1939, on the American Negro question:

> I do not quite understand whether comrade George proposes to eliminate the slogan of self-determination for the Negroes from our program, or is it that we do not say that we are ready to do everything possible for the self-determination of the Negroes if they want it themselves. It is a question for the party as a whole, if we eliminate it or not. We are ready to help them if they want it. As a party we can remain absolutely neutral on this. *We cannot say it will be reactionary. It is not reactionary.* We cannot tell them to set up a state because that will weaken imperialism and so will be good for us, the white workers. That would be against internationalism itself. We cannot say to them: "Stay here, even at the price of economic progress." We can say: "It is for you to decide. If you wish to take a part of the country, it is all right, but we do not wish to make the decision for you."
>
> I believe that the differences between the West Indies, Catalonia, Poland and the situation of the Negroes in the States are not so decisive. . . .
>
> But the black state could enter into a federation. If the American Negroes succeeded in creating their own state, I am sure that after a few years of the satisfaction and pride of independence, they would feel the need of entering into a federation. Even if Catalonia, which is a very industrialized and highly developed province, had realized its independence, it would have been just a step to federation. (*Bulletin of Marxist Studies*, No. 4, "Documents on the Negro Struggle," p. 16. Emphasis added.)

The following dialogue between Trotsky and comrades George and Carlos is even more illuminating in relation to the question now under dispute between the Socialist Workers Party and the SLL:

> *George*: . . . I consider the idea of separating as a step backward so far as a socialist society is concerned. If the white workers extend a hand to the Negro, he will not want self-determination.
>
> *Trotsky*: It is too abstract, because the realization of this slogan can be reached only as the 13 or 14 million Negroes feel that the domination by the whites is terminated. *To fight for the possibility of realizing an independent state is a sign of great moral and political awakening. It would be a tremendous revolutionary step.* This ascendancy would immediately have the best economic consequences.
>
> *Carlos*: I think that an analogy could be made in connection with the collectives and the distribution of large estates. One might consider the breaking up of large estates into small plots as reactionary, but it is not necessarily so. But this question is up to the peasants, whether they want to operate the estates collectively or individually. We advise the

peasants, but we do not force them—it is up to them. Some would say that the breaking up of the large estates into small plots would be economically reactionary, but that is not so.

Trotsky: This was also the position of Rosa Luxemburg. She maintained that self-determination would be as reactionary as the breaking up of the large estates. (Ibid., p. 17. Emphasis added.)

"Black nationalism remains a major obstacle and a dangerous obstacle"; "separatism is the obverse of the segregation policies of the Southern reactionaries." "Those, who, like the SWP leaders, proclaim that black nationalism is progressive . . . are consciously deceiving and betraying the heroic struggles of the Negro workers. They are helping to perpetuate a gigantic fraud," bombastically proclaims *The Newsletter* (February 27, 1965). Black nationalism and separatism ("to fight for the possibility of realizing an independent state") "is a sign of great moral and political awakening. It would be a tremendous revolutionary step," answers Leon Trotsky. Perhaps, comrades of the SLL, Leon Trotsky was also "helping to perpetuate a gigantic fraud," "consciously deceiving and betraying the heroic struggles of the Negro workers"? Or would you rather draw the conclusion that in your sectarian factionalism you have completely lost touch with Marxism and real, concrete internationalism—that you have substituted for it abstract ultraleft phrasemongering?

10

A PEACEFUL ROAD BACK TO CAPITALISM IN THE SOVIET UNION?

A perennial theme in SLL declarations is the need to "develop theory." There can be no quarrel with this truism of Marxism—unless theory is kept up to date, changing reality will outmode it in one respect or another, whereupon a sect can easily convert it into ossified dogma.

Unfortunately, between insisting on the need to develop theory and actually developing it, SLL practice leaves much to be desired. As they see it, the leading cadres of the Fourth International, following Trotsky's death, proved incapable of developing theory. As a result the vanguard of the world proletariat was paralyzed until the SLL leaders stepped in to fill the breach. Cutting all ties with the Socialist Workers Party and the Fourth International, they ploughed ahead in their great work. The resulting achievements, as we have already seen, are indeed wondrous. But the best is yet to come; they did not hesitate to develop a few novelties even on the character of the Soviet Union.

The world Trotskyist movement has an extremely rich legacy of discussions on the nature of the Soviet Union and analyses of its society, economy and state. Indeed, the rest of the world has fed on crumbs from this work. Up to now no other ideological tendency has been able to develop any new interpretation of the complex and contradictory phenomena of Soviet reality which was not previously assayed (and in most cases rejected) by the Trotskyist movement. The SLL's attempts to "develop theory" in the Soviet field without taking all this into consideration have served only to reveal how it combines colossal ignorance with crass revisionism.

This was not always the case. For a time, analysis of Soviet affairs was in the SLL the rather exclusive domain of Tom Kemp who has at least enough knowledge of economics in general and Marxist economics in particular to avoid the worst pitfalls. He limited himself to describing on the one hand the USSR's rapid economic growth (". . . despite the colossal distortions and mistakes of the Stalin period, Russia had become a great and rapidly expanding industrial country." *The Newsletter*, February 15, 1964), and on the other hand the many economic problems which the Soviet bureaucracy, by its very nature, was unable to solve. His weakness was precisely that of *not* "developing theory"; i.e., he repeated over and over again the formulas which Trotsky advanced thirty years ago, instead of proving their *relevance* by a thorough analysis of the *concrete* contradictions of Soviet economy, and their manifestations in the new zigzags of Soviet economic policy and Soviet economic thought.

But Tom Kemp was too mild an opponent of "Pabloite revisionism"; the field had to be worked by more hardened representatives of the sectarian species. And so we were treated in the SLL's *Fourth International* of January 1966 to a special festival on "Soviet economics" sufficient to make a Marxist's hair stand on end.

SLL "theory" in the Soviet field (the economic evolution of the USSR in particular) is developed by one Michel Varga, in the form of a polemic against an article written by E. Mandel in *Les Temps Modernes* on the economic reform in the Soviet Union. Much of the polemic is bombastic wordplay, written in obvious bad faith, and scarcely merits attention.[19] But two theoretical problems posed by Varga (the origin of commodity production in the USSR, and the influence of foreign trade in the economy) involve the whole question of the class nature of the Soviet economy and its dynamics, and are quite revealing with regard to the revisionist direction in which the SLL's pundits are "developing theory."

Varga takes up the question of the survival of the categories "commodities, commodity production, money, etc.," in the USSR. Mandel explained that this survival is due to the insufficient level of development of the productive forces in the Soviet Union; i.e., to a scarcity of *use values*. No, answers Varga: "The products of labour become commodities *independently* of their quantity ... because they are the products of independent private labour ..." (SLL's *Fourth International*, January 1966, p. 28.)

So far, so good. Should we then conclude that in the Soviet Union, "private producers" exchange the "products of their independent private labour"; i.e., that the survival of commodity production proves the existence of a capitalist mode of production, as the representatives of the theory that there is state capitalism in the Soviet Union allege? Varga cannot frankly arrive at such an openly revisionist conclusion (which is, however, clearly in the logic of everything he says) so he squirms around a bit and then discovers that the exchange of "the products of independent private labour" in the Soviet Union means in the first place the exchange of products of the "national division of labour ... based upon different kinds of ownership—state, cooperative and private." (Ibid., p. 28.)

This would mean concretely that there is commodity production because, as Stalin said in his own inimitable way, the kolkhoz peasants are not "willing" to freely distribute the products of their "private labour" but are "demanding" to exchange them against the products of state industry.

But in the first place this is a travesty of the truth, for the kolkhoz peasants were *forced* by the state to "exchange" a large part of the products of their "private labour" at an insignificant fraction of its production cost. In the second place, there is no reason why the kolkhoz peasant, who is after all not a fanatic of "commodity production," would not be perfectly willing to give away freely the products of his "private labour," provided solely that society freely gave him in return all the industrial goods and communal services he needs (and thus we are right back to the problem of the *quantity of use values available*.) In the third place, the very survival of the "cooperative form of ownership" (not to speak of the private plots and husbandry) expresses the insufficient degree of development of the productive forces; for a free distribution of an abundant quantity of consumer goods would certainly not leave a single "defender" of the "cooperative form of ownership" among the kolkhozniks (as a matter of fact, even today, the peasants are quitting the kolkhozes by the millions and prefer to become industrial workers, because the income of the workers is higher than the income of the kolkhozniks). And in the fourth place the whole idea that there exists exchange of "the products of independent private labour" in the Soviet Union, where more than 80 percent of the national income is produced in the sector of state-owned industry, agriculture and trade, is completely ludicrous, standing Marxism on its head: Marx made it crystal clear that when he speaks of "products of independent private labour" he means products which are *private property*,[20] a point which is conveniently, and significantly, skipped over by Varga.

And here the reasons for the survival of commodity production in the USSR, which are cloaked by Varga in a thick tangle of confused abstractions, are easily clarified. For isn't it evident that commodity production; i.e., production for the market—objects produced to be *sold*—necessarily implies *changes in ownership*? You can't sell something to yourself. The Ford Motor Co. can't "sell" motors produced at its plant No. 1 to its plant No. 2 where the frames are produced and the cars assembled (even if this simple transfer of use-values can be covered by bookkeeping transactions which take the *outward form* of "buying" and "selling"; i.e., of exact money calculation and accounting of "inputs" and "outputs"). The Soviet state can't "sell" machine tools to itself. And inasmuch as it is owner of all the means of production in industry, *these means of production are no longer commodities in the USSR* (indeed no "market" exists for them).

How then does commodity production come to survive there? Because of the separate owners of agricultural products? We have already disposed of that argument; suffice it to add that one could very well visualise complete statification of agriculture in countries like Czechoslovakia or the German Democratic Republic but nobody would believe that upon such a decision commodity production would cease to exist.

In order to disclose the roots of commodity production, we must bring to light a form of ownership different from state ownership, not at the periphery but at the very heart of the Soviet system (and of any society in transition between capitalism and socialism, whether bureaucratically degenerated, deformed or simon-pure). And this ownership is of course the *private ownership of labour power*.

The Soviet worker cannot freely give his labour power to society, because society is not able to freely fulfil his needs. He could work in exchange for a certain amount of material goods and services—under a system of rationing. But this would only lead to more injustice and more fleecing of the worker than under the present system, because rationing that does not adequately cover all basic necessities inevitably leads to formation of a black market. So the worker prefers to sell his labour power in exchange for a money wage—as the least unfavourable system of distributing a still too limited amount of consumer goods. And as society is forced to keep an exact accounting of production costs, a money wage automatically implies cost accounting in money terms and in the *form* of "monetary inputs" and "monetary outputs" calculation for all factories, including those which produce means of production. The survival of money wages (an inevitable result of the scarcity of consumer goods) gives to consumer goods the nature of commodities, for they then are exchanged against wages. This is the sole basic root of commodity production in a society in transition from capitalism to socialism. Commodity production withers away with the production of an abundance of consumer goods—given the social ownership of the means of production.

Having mistakenly discovered one of the roots for the survival of commodity production in the Soviet Union to be "different kinds of ownership" of the means of production—thereby following Stalin!—Varga does not stop at this first revision of Marxist theory; he goes on to a second revision: ". . . exchange value would not disappear in the USSR and in the Peoples' Democracies even if one managed to completely liquidate private and group property and to bring about complete industrialization . . ." (SLL's *Fourth International*, January 1966, p. 29.) Why? Because of the world market! The maintenance of exchange values in the Soviet Union "depends far more on the world capitalist market than on the home market. . . . the existence of varied types of ownership and labour in the USSR and in the Peoples' Democracies is dependent not on the dearth or abundance of products but on the influence of the world capitalist market, since the home market is subordinate to it." (Ibid., p.29.) What extraordinary nonsense is spun out in the guise of profound science!

Varga began by recalling that for Marx, commodity production stems from the appearance of independent producers and proprietors of goods produced under conditions of a division of labour. But Marx never said that international trade in commodities automatically produced commodity production in each country participating in it, regardless of the extent of involvement. On the contrary, he explicitly states the opposite: a country whose economy is not based upon commodity production can perfectly well participate in exchange on the world market! Only when and if the results of that international trade have *transformed the internal relations of production* will international commodity exchange thereupon result in internal commodity production. And it is well known that after centuries of such participation in international commodity exchange, countries like India and China continued to be mainly producers of use values (continued to be based essentially on a "natural economy") and not of commodities.[21]

The capacity of the old Asian society to resist commodity production holds a thousand times more for a workers state, provided it is reinforced by the monopoly of foreign trade, a small detail which Varga is scarcely inclined to mention! His confused calculations on the determination of exchange value in the USSR are completely beside the point, for to deal with the amount begs the question: before you can establish the "exchange value" of a Soviet machine tool you must first prove that it is a commodity, how it is the result of "independent private [!] labour," and who is buying and selling it to whom!

Foreign trade has nothing to do with this. One can perfectly well visualise a society in which commodity production has been abolished exchanging three percent of its annual output of physical goods on the world market, at world market prices, without this at all creating "commodity production" or "exchange value" inside the country. Such foreign trade would merely imply that a certain expenditure of labour time and raw materials would not directly produce use values for the needs of the country's population, but would produce goods to be exchanged on the world market for other goods which would then be consumed as use values inside the country. Whether this exchange involved an absolute "loss" or "gain" of labour (an exchange of more labour against less labour, of products of an industry working with less productivity against products of an industry working with more productivity or the opposite) would not have the slightest bearing on the social relations of production in that country, or on the disappearance of commodity production, provided these "gains" or "losses" were of such proportion to the general level of production as not to radically change all the material conditions of production. It would simply add to or reduce by one or two percent the annually distributed amount of use values.

In fact, Varga's pathetic attempt to "explain" the survival of commodity production in the Soviet Union through the influence of foreign trade recalls Stalin's attempt to "explain" the survival of the state through the influence of the "hostile foreign environment." Instead of finding the argument against "socialism in one country" simply in the fact that within the frontiers of the Soviet Union it has been impossible to create plenty, to achieve a level of development of the productive forces capable of advancing towards an abundance of use values, so that *therefore* commodity production survives, proving that socialism is far from being achieved in the USSR, Varga confuses everything by introducing foreign trade, thereby separating the problem of commodity production from that of the mode of production and production relations, and, worse still, implying that foreign trade somehow has the secret and malignant power in and of itself to overthrow socialised property relations in the USSR.

Varga is caught in an inexorable logic. He alleges that the Soviet home market is subordinate to the world market; at the same time he posits that the productivity of labour in Soviet industry is lower than that of the capitalist countries. If you take these two statements together, the conclusion is inescapable: the Soviet Union is condemned to the same process of industrial retrogression, of reverting to production of agricultural and mineral raw materials, to which subordination of their home market to the world market has condemned all backward countries!

This is of course completely untrue. In fact, the Soviet Union has undergone and is still undergoing a breathtaking process of industrialisation. This process was made possible notwithstanding the starting point of backwardness, because, thanks to the monopoly of foreign trade, the home market is *largely independent* of the world market. "Largely independent" of course does not mean "completely independent"; complete isolation and autarky are impossible, and an attempt to impose such autarky only puts a brake on economic growth. But between marginal dependence and "subordination" there is all the difference created by the October revolution, which this fine "developer of theory" for the SLL chooses to ignore.

On the other hand, it is not even true that the productivity of labour in the Soviet Union is lower than that "established internationally." Varga here confuses the international *averages* which determine world market prices—at least in industry—and the international maximum of productivity which enables those nations at that level to realise *surplus profits* from international trade. The Soviet Union's average productivity of labour is undoubtedly still some 40 percent lower than that of the United States; but it is largely equal to or even above that of most other capitalist countries, a fact attested to not only by economics professors in the U. S. but also by the appearance in many capitalist countries of a great number of Soviet "commodities" of average quality at average prices, without this causing any bankruptcy in the Soviet economy; on the contrary.[22]

Varga says that "In the national revenue of the USSR... the part played by foreign trade increases ceaselessly [!], sometimes giddily." (Ibid., p. 25.) This is absolutely untrue. (Just in passing, and to underline once more with what lack of seriousness theory is taken in the SLL, the magazine appearing under the stolen name "Fourth International" publishes this nonsense without a murmur of protest, although Tom Kemp correctly stated in *The Newsletter* as late as March 14, 1964: "Moreover, the rapid growth of the Soviet economy has been accompanied by a big increase in the volume of foreign trade, though its weight in the economy has remained about the same.") Here are the relevant figures (in 1961 gold rubles):

	Imports into USSR (millions)	National Income (millions)	Percentage
1940	245	33,000	0.7
1951	1,792	60,500	2.9
1952	2,255	67,500	3.4
1954	2,864	82,600	3.5
1955	2,754	90,650	3.0
1959	4,566	132,900	3.4
1960	5,066	142,800	3.5
1962	5,805	162,500	3.6
1963	6,853	166,400	4.1
1964	6,963	180,000	3.9

In other words: from 1950 to 1964, the proportion of imports to national income increased by exactly 1%, or an annual average of less than 0.1%. This is indeed a "ceaseless" growth, and one can understand the kind of balance Varga must have to feel "giddy" at traveling at such tremendous speed.

But isn't there a "giddy" increase in foreign trade compared to national income between 1940 and 1950, when the percentage rose from 0.7% to 2.9%? The trouble is that the 1940 figure represents trade with the *capitalist* world, whereas in 1950 there were a few other workers states around; it so happens that trade with the *capitalist* countries (the sector that "dominates" the internal market in the Soviet Union, to believe Varga, and induces commodity production to appear there), involved only 17% of the USSR's total foreign trade in 1950, only 35% in 1959, and some 40% in 1964. So the proportion of capitalist imports in relation to the Soviet Union's national income jumped "giddily" from 0.7% in 1940 to 0.5% in 1950, 1.2% in 1959 and 1.5% in 1964, an increase of far less than 0.1% per year.

But even these figures don't give the whole picture; for a large part of this trade is actually with semicolonial countries, whose average productivity of labour is notoriously *below* the Soviet Union's, and who, far from inducing the growth of commodity production in the USSR, can be said to be exploited by the USSR, as long as trade is conducted on the basis of world market prices. Soviet trade with the advanced capitalist countries covers only 18% of the total import figures in 1959, 20% in 1962 and 19% in 1963; i.e., *it remains constantly under 0.7% of the USSR's national income* (the 1940 percentage). Varga's whole preposterous thesis now stands glaringly exposed: it amounts to the assumption that this 0.7% of the national income of the USSR somehow "dominates" all the rest...

Equally false and preposterous is Varga's assumption that the lag of Soviet industry behind that of the advanced capitalist countries has *increased*; no proof is advanced for this thesis, which flies in the face of all known statistics, both Soviet and Western, which reveal a slow but constantly narrowing difference between the West and the USSR in production and income. There are temporary lags in certain industrial fields (e.g., chemicals and automobiles), but they are compensated for by relative advances in other fields (e.g., machine tools, nuclear industry, space satellite techniques, etc.). What is involved here is simply the law of uneven development which operates among all industrial nations; it is not a specific shortcoming of the Soviet system.

We have spent quite some time and space on what appears to be an abstract theoretical question. But the topic is a basic one, where the real reason for the SLL's floundering in the field of theory is clearly revealed. Trotsky and the Fourth International always attributed the weaknesses and deficiencies of the Soviet economy to the *specific policies of the Soviet bureaucracy*—its conservatism, greed, narrow defence of its own material privileges, its organic inability to harness the creative capacities of the working class to the gradual resolution of the system's disproportions. In place of this, what Varga actually does is adduce *objective, "unalterable" causes*. SLL theory has undergone a complete somersault. They started out to prove, at any cost, that the "Pabloite revisionists capitulate before Stalinism"; they end up advancing positions that in essence *systematically whitewash the Soviet bureaucracy's crimes* against the Soviet economy!

How can one otherwise interpret statements such as: "Soviet industry is incapable [!] of transforming agriculture"; "the permanent crisis of Soviet agriculture and the industrial lag are explained by the pressure of world imperialism"; "The USSR was incapable of harmoniously developing the different branches of its economy because it was isolated from the international division of labour"; etc., etc.? (SLL's *Fourth International*, January 1966, pp. 18–19.) If all these terrible crises are not the result of bureaucratic mismanagement and of the bureaucracy's regime but of objective circumstances such as the rule of "the international division of labour," why then indict Stalin's policy of forced collectivisation of agriculture (which, as we naively thought, was at the bottom of the "permanent crisis of agriculture" in the USSR, and not "the international division of labour")? Why then prepare an alternative economic programme for a regenerated Soviet Union, under Soviet democracy? One should really only say, if Varga is right, "You must wait for the world revolution and until it comes about, it is inevitable that disproportions will grow."

Trotsky was of another opinion. He developed a programme aimed at the gradual reduction of disproportions.[23] The distance between Trotsky's programme and Varga's pseudo-learned mystifications is the distance between revolutionary Marxism and revisionism.

But once you say "A" you must also say "B." Once you admit that foreign trade, and foreign trade alone, is in the last analysis the source of commodity production in the Soviet Union, independent of production relations or the relationship of social forces inside the country, then it logically follows that foreign trade, and foreign trade alone, can also reintroduce capitalism in the Soviet Union; for, after all, commodity production is the natural hotbed of capitalist production, isn't it? And so we read these unbelievable lines in the small bulletin of the SLL's American followers:

> Since Soviet productivity is way below U. S. levels, Soviet workers' production can compete directly in the world market only through reduced Soviet real wages and intensive speed-up in the factories committed to production for capitalists. This is exactly the case in Yugoslavia, where a program of "market prices" and "profit-sharing", advertised as a means of increasing Yugoslav workers' material income, has had exactly the opposite effect.
>
> Worse, as U.S.-Soviet trade increases under such arrangements, the whole [!] production planning cycle and structure of inter-industry commodity flows of the Soviet bloc [remember this trade concerns less than 0.7% of the national income!—E.G.] tends to be brought into line with secular and seasonal cycles prevailing in the Imperialist world market. First, the individual industry gearing its production to capitalist market needs is compelled to regulate its production and inventory cycles according to capitalist-dictated delivery schedules. [Why? Can't a system of compensation be worked out, taking into consideration the needs of the Soviet consumers and economy as well? Can't deliveries to Soviet "purchasers" be automatically increased when capitalist purchases suddenly decline? Why does foreign trade mysteriously imply the disappearance of central planning?—E.G.] Second, since the outputs of these industries require raw and semi-finished materials from non-exporting Soviet industries, the production and marketing cycles prevailing in the Imperialist world tend [Actually *tend* already! And all this because less than 0.7% of the national income is imported from advanced capitalist countries.—E.G.] to penetrate more deeply into the Soviet bloc economy, undermining national economic planning.
>
> As U. S.-Soviet trade increases in this way, quantitative dislocations in the Soviet economy go over to becoming qualitative, *ulti-*

mately [emphasis in original] threatening to bring about *U. S. Imperialist conquest of the Soviet Union without the firing of a single shot* [my emphasis—E.G.] *except* those fired by Soviet Army and militiamen against Soviet workers protesting this hideous treachery. [Unsigned article in February 14, 1966, *Bulletin of International Socialism*, New York, edited by Tim Wohlforth.]

The history of the revision of Marxism started with the concept of a peaceful, gradual road from capitalism to socialism, a concept against which Lenin and Trotsky fought throughout their lives. In their ill-fated sectarian "struggle against revisionism," the SLL leaders have now reached the point where they sing the old reformist tune of revisionism backwards—they believe in the possibility of a peaceful, gradual transition from a workers state to capitalism, "without the firing of a single shot." The hapless adventurers in theory have accepted gradualism and should really give credit, if not to Bernstein, then at least to . . . Stalin!

We say Stalin, for it was the great Stalin himself who first discovered the possibility of a "peaceful transition from socialism to capitalism." He stumbled onto this while analysing the case of Yugoslavia, noting that in some mysterious way, without any changes in its mode of production, it had become transformed from a "socialist" to a "capitalist" country, and a fascist one at that! The great Mao, following in the footsteps of the great Stalin, has now made a similar discovery in the case of the Soviet Union, where Khrushchev and his gang "restored capitalism" without anybody noticing it at the time. And now the not so great, but very studious, Healy, an apt pupil of these two masters, is following in their illustrious path—all for the sake of the "struggle against Pabloite revisionism"! Isn't it remarkable how a sect can offer itself as an object lesson in the dialectical movement of ideas?

What makes this paradoxical turn of events all the more striking is the fact that as late as March 9, 1963, the SLL actually called the Chinese to order for the very same ideas it now pushes—cautiously in its *Fourth International*, shamelessly in the *Bulletin of International Socialism*. *The Newsletter* of that date carries a "Statement by the National Executive Committee of the Socialist Labour League" (dated February 28, 1963) which among other things has this to say on the point in dispute:

> While correctly criticizing many aspects of Yugoslav foreign policy and socialist theory, they fail to see or consciously ignore the enduring achievements of the Yugoslav Revolution in the decentralization of administration, planning of economy and social management of enterprises. The introduction of market relations and the principle of profitability of industry *within the context of state ownership and social management*, does *not* constitute a new form of capitalism as the Chinese suggest. In fact it is a significant and welcome departure from the administrative and bureaucratically centralised system of planning which prevails in the USSR. [Emphasis in original.]

We can substantially agree with this formulation (although we would be somewhat more critical of the excessive "decentralisation" and "market economy" which the Yugoslav bureaucracy introduced *in order to strengthen their own power and privileges*) and would propose that it be applied to the problems of foreign trade: The introduction of increased foreign trade with capitalist countries, within the context of state ownership of the means of production, of a centrally planned economy and the monopoly of foreign trade, does not constitute a source of restoration of capitalism as Messrs. Varga and Wohlforth mistakenly believe. In fact, it is a significant and welcome departure from the utopian and reactionary system of autarky which Stalin introduced, and which, far from being indispensable to socialist planning in the USSR, made it more difficult and slowed down its rate of growth.[24]

Now, comrades of the SLL, you have to choose. Either the authors of the February 28, 1963, statement of the National Executive Committee of the Socialist Labour League were in reality hidden "Pabloite revisionists," in league with the archvillains Frank, Hansen, Maitan, Germain and Moreno, conspiring in hideous treachery to "sell out the world Trotskyist movement" and "prevent the real Trotskyists" like Varga and Wohlforth from "building the Fourth International"; or else

Varga and Wohlforth themselves are simpletons—harmless simpletons, perhaps, but revisionist simpletons in any case. You have to make up your minds, friends; you can't have your cake and eat it, too. Both sides of your self-contradictory "theory" can't be right at one and the same time.

11

THE SLL ECHOES THIRD PERIOD STALINISM

We have found that the SLL's blunders in politics and theory are rooted in its nature as a sect; i.e., the compulsion it feels to justify under any and all conditions its *separation* from the general movement of revolutionary Marxists, its *split* from the Fourth International. Driven by such a motive, its elaboration of theory, of political line, becomes more and more divorced from objective analysis of reality and more and more subordinated to self-justification. Becoming a goal in itself, the sect falls victim to a phenomenon long characteristic of religion which, under capitalism, as Marx noted, became extended into economic and social relations generally, including the political field—this is the phenomenon of *reification*, of *fetishism*. The SLL leaders make a fetish of the "fight against revisionism," develop ideas in accordance with narrow factional aims, and are thereby carried away by the logic of their ideological productions into widening still further the gap between their own needs as a sect and the objective needs of the class struggle. "Every sect is in fact religious," Marx wrote to Schweitzer. (October 13, 1868.) The "fighters against revisionism" thus become, despite the best of intentions, producers of ideas that approach closer and closer to open revisionism. The sect is caught up in a process it does not understand nor even visualise—it moves farther and farther away from its original purposes and objectives. Nowhere is this more clearly visible than in its policy in its own home country, England.

The SLL is largely a product of the original Healy tendency within the British Trotskyist movement. This tendency sought and found distinction (and historical merit) through a constant and consistent fight to break the British Trotskyist movement out of isolation and towards the Labour Party, which in Britain, in distinction from any other country with a Social-Democratic mass movement, still commands the respect and allegiance of the overwhelming majority of the organised British working class, and to a higher degree than ever before in the past. In the course of this fight it established itself as a solid tendency inside the Labour Party, exerting a decisive influence in the weekly *Socialist Outlook* which, when banned by the Labour Party bureaucracy, received the support of more than two million organised British workers.[25]

When the Soviet bureaucracy brutally repressed the Hungarian revolution in 1956, a sizable revolt broke out in the British Communist Party, especially among its intellectuals and students, hundreds of whom joined the Healy tendency. Finally, when the youth became the first sector of the British Labour movement to become radicalised and strongly opposed to Transport House in the early sixties, young militants around the paper *Keep Left*, sympathetic to the SLL, won the leadership of the Young Socialists, and in answer to Transport House reprisals led them away by the hundreds from the Labour Party, towards an independent youth organisation. Healy today quite frankly confirms this break with the Labour Party. Reporting at the eighth national congress of the SLL, he said, according to *The Newsletter* (June 4, 1966), "We have been able to keep the youth and win them away from the Labour Party . . ."

If a balance sheet is drawn up of these developments, two conclusions are inescapable. First, that the Healy tendency during the past ten years undoubtedly faced the greatest opportunities for rapid growth open to European Trotskyism in this period; and, second, that most of these opportunities have been wasted. Of the old cadre of the Healy tendency few remain members of the SLL. Of the hundreds of CP militants won over in 1957, hardly a dozen or so are still around. The original editor of *The Newsletter*, the original editor of *Keep Left*, are not among them. The first chairman of the SLL is now an "honorary anarchist" of Her Majesty's Establishment. The chairman who succeeded him remained a revolutionist but also left the organisation. It is doubtful that the SLL today is as strong as it was in its first year of existence, at the time of the "Assembly of Labour"; it certainly isn't much bigger. Losses by the hundreds have more or less cancelled the gains.[26]

On the other hand, in order to achieve these gains, the SLL leaders had to make a complete somersault, ending up at exactly the opposite pole from the position the Healy tendency fought for over so many years. At the 1965 Labour Party conference, where the fight against the incomes policy, against the subordination of the unions to the state and against Wilson's shameful collaboration in U. S. imperialism's war of aggression against the Vietnamese revolution first started seriously, the voice of the SLL was conspicuously absent; it limited itself to parading a few hundred misguided youths *outside* the conference hall—exactly the same antics Healy had made fun of year after year. In the 1966 conference they had little more than they had in 1965. Their boasts about "getting into the Labour Party in greater numbers" than those expelled have been belied by events. In fact, at the very time when the controversy inside the Labour Party has started to gain momentum, when powerful unions are beginning to be involved, when the seamen's strike created a first issue on which a broader opposition could be assembled, the SLL found itself completely isolated from what is going on inside the Labour Party.

This is due in the first place to its internal regime, which is one of the causes for the continuous loss of leading cadres, of the highest degree of turnover in membership which a party calling itself "Trotskyist" has ever had. We need not dwell at length on this rather unattractive subject. Suffice it to call attention to the antics which went on at the SLL's ill-starred "international conference," which have now been bared and commented on by two groups of participants. (See the pamphlet, *Healy "Reconstructs" the Fourth International*.) No traditional Trotskyist organisation would ever tolerate the bureaucratism and monolithism in which the SLL leaders take pride; the organisational methods of a sect are the symmetrical complement of sectarian politics![27]

But the SLL's growing isolation is due above all to its wrong policies. The Healy tendency started out with a clear-cut conception about the way to build a revolutionary mass left wing in the Labour Party. Today, it has tacitly abandoned this conception, without self-criticism, and without replacing it openly by another one. It shouts all the more stridently about the need to build a revolutionary leadership, the more it appears to ignore the concrete ways and means of building such a leadership.

The absence of any fresh, clearly stated concept of how to build a revolutionary mass party in Britain does not mean, however, that no concept exists around which activity is carried out, activity pragmatically expressing a view that is neither clearly formulated nor fully thought out. In actual fact, the SLL acts as though it were expressing the famous concept of "third period" Stalinism; i.e., that it is possible to build a revolutionary leadership *not from within* the Labour Party but *from without* by systematically intervening from the outside, by participating in working-class struggles and picking up militant workers who have become disillusioned with the official leadership (which is fully justified) and with the official organisation (which is much less justified, as long as 95 percent of the workers continue to adhere to the organisation).

"Third period" Stalinism represented sectarian politics *par excellence* in the Western capitalist countries. That the SLL, transforming itself into a sect, would gravitate towards such politics was quite logical. A case of political regression may also be involved in view of the historical origin of the Healy tendency, which arose within an organisation called The Workers International League, a splitoff from the Communist Party which never really broke with third period politics, simply turning away from Stalinism when the CP leadership shifted from its ultraleft third period tactics to ultra-opportunist "People's Frontism" in 1935. Thus in breaking with the Fourth International Healy tended rather naturally to revert to ultraleft infantilism, a process in which he was actively assisted by some of the "red professors" who joined the SLL in the period following the Twentieth Congress and the suppression of the Hungarian revolution.

Such a policy undoubtedly exercises a temporary attraction for radical youth, especially in the first stages of their revolutionary education and particularly when it is combined, as is the case with the SLL, with a commendably high degree of activism and devotion to the organisation. Engels noted long ago, in his letter to Bebel of June 20, 1873, that each *sect* is necessarily fanatic and through this fanaticism obtains, particularly in regions where it is new . . . much greater momentary successes than the Party, which simply represents the real movement, without any sectarian vagaries. On the other hand, fanaticism does not last long. (*Selected Works*, p. 433, 1951 Moscow edition. Emphasis in original.)

This description fits the SLL like a glove! For, indeed, it does not take the young militants and activists long to discover the fundamentally sterile nature of this activism which is not geared to a correct vision and concept of the building of a revolutionary mass party. The more critical elements will reflect that the "biggest" leap forward which the SLL promises its members—the publication of a Trotskyist daily (still to be realised)—is after all only a repetition, thirty years later, of what the CP did in the old days, without thereby achieving anything to change the reformist leadership of the British labour movement. As for another boastful promise which has not come off ("We shall be 5,000 youth next year"), even if it had proved true that would have been only a fraction of what the Young Communist League had at its peak, without modifying in the least the fundamental relationship of forces inside the British labour movement. In fact, the whole conception of building a revolutionary mass party by starting with a few hundred members and then *individually* recruiting the membership one by one, is ludicrous. Healy used to know this; *what does he think about it today?*

The ultraleft third-period nature of the SLL's policies is very pronounced in many fields. A few examples should suffice to establish this. *The Newsletter* devoted a whole series of full-page articles to the rise of German fascism in the thirties in order to draw certain parallels with the English scene at present (issues of May 2, 1964; May 9, 1964; November 28, 1964; December 12, 1964; February 13, 1965; February 20, 1965). In these articles the mistakes and crimes of the Social Democratic and Stalinist bureaucracies in Germany are more or less correctly analysed. But the illusion is created that a new revolutionary leadership like that of the Young Socialists could "unite the working class," without taking into consideration its organisational allegiance to its traditional party, the Labour Party. Indeed, in the thousands of lines comprising these articles, there is only a single reference—and a very confused one![28]—in a subordinate sentence to the problem of the *United Front* between the Communist Party and the Socialist Party as a necessary prerequisite for victory over fascism, which was the *central* theme of Trotsky's ceaseless political campaign in the fateful years 1930–33. This is not an accident: third-period Stalinism was notoriously opposed to a "united front from above with the Social-Democratic leaders, traitors to the working class."

How far Healy has gone in reverting to "third period" sectarianism can be judged from his article on the Trades Union Congress of 1966 where the deliberations were dominated by the fight between those supporting and those opposing Wilson's wage-freeze measures. Whether Cousins, the leader of the left wing in opposition to the wage freeze, is or is not personally preferable to the right-wing bureaucrats is beside the point. The thing is that by opposing the wage freeze, he expresses in however confused a way the class feelings of millions of British workers and their opposition to Wilson's shameful use of the bourgeois state machine against the working class.

Instead of offering Cousins a united front in the struggle against the wage-freeze measures, Healy wrote: "The Socialist Labour League says that both tendencies help each other in order to avoid the real issues. They both, in fact, betray the working-class." (*The Newsletter*, September 17, 1966.) Far from fighting effectively against the trade-union bureaucracy, Healy only helps Cousins and Co. to maintain their control over the more advanced sectors of the British working class. He thereby unwittingly reveals that he does not understand the ABC's of the united-front tactic, which Trotsky explained as early as 1922 to the French Communists as follows:

> Unity of front consequently presupposes our readiness, within certain limits and on specific issues, to correlate in practice our actions with those of reformist organizations, to the extent to which the latter still express today the will of important sections of the embattled proletariat.
>
> But, after all, didn't we split with them? Yes,

because we disagree with them on fundamental questions of the working-class movement.

And yet we seek agreement with them? Yes, in all those cases where the masses that follow them are ready to engage in joint struggle together with the masses that follow us and when they, the reformists, are to a lesser or greater degree compelled to become an instrument of this struggle. . . .

. . . But it is necessary that the struggling masses should always be given the opportunity of convincing themselves that the non-achievement of unity in action was not due to our formalistic irreconcilability but to the lack of real will to struggle on the part of the reformists. . . .

It is possible to see in this policy a rapprochement with the reformists only from the standpoint of a journalist who believes that he rids himself of reformism by ritualistically criticizing it without ever leaving his editorial office but who is fearful of clashing with the reformists before the eyes of the working masses and giving the latter an opportunity to appraise the Communist and the reformist on the equal plane of the mass struggle. *The First Five Years of the Communist International, Volume 2* [Pathfinder, 1953, 1972], pp. 132–34 [2015 printing]

Trotsky's description of the sectarian fits Healy to a "t"—provided the words "editorial office" are replaced by "printshop."

In an editorial devoted to the then impending general election, *The Newsletter* under a screaming (and contradictory) banner "Labour to Power!," engaged in the following typical third period boasting:

> . . . the right-wing proscribed the [Socialist Labour] League on the day it was founded.
>
> Since that time they have done their best to witch-hunt and expel our members and supporters from the Labour Party.
>
> *Fortunately, they have failed to prevent our organisation from growing stronger and stronger until today it has a decisive* [!] *influence inside the ranks of the labour movement. (The Newsletter,* March 21, 1964. Emphasis in original.)

If the SLL really wielded "decisive" influence in the ranks of the labour movement, it would be criminal folly to seek the victory of a Labour Party under Wilson's treacherous leadership. The right slogan would then be: "The SLL to power!" If the influence of the SLL were as large as *The Newsletter* of March 21, 1964, boasted, one would have to conclude that all the terrible blows struck at the British working class by Transport House since Wilson came to power must to a great extent be the SLL's fault. Fortunately for the SLL, its claims are slightly exaggerated, its influence is small and marginal, and for that reason, it does not really bear any responsibility for the defeats suffered by the British workers at the hands of Wilson.

The smaller headlines sprinkled around the main banner in the same issue emphasize the third-period orientation: "To be with the working class is to build the revolutionary Party—Socialist Labour League Congress call: LABOUR TO POWER! Fight for Socialist policies." Everything here is upside-down in this Alice in Wonderland fantasy of ultraleftism.

What should have been said (and not in a headline) was this: In order to build a revolutionary party, you have to be with the working class, and since the working class is with labour, it is impossible to abstain from calling Labour to Power, however unsocialist the policies of its present leadership may be.

The conclusion of the editorial is even more ultraleft: "The fate of the working class depends upon the building of the Socialist Labour League as the mass revolutionary party of the future." Unfortunately the secret of how this is going to be done while the working class remains with the Labour Party is not revealed.

In the same issue we read such ultraleft nonsense as: "There must be committees for nationalization set up in all the main industries which put clear demands on the Labour government." Where are these "committees" today, two years later? "Tenants' committees and even workers' committees on education will need to investigate the whole [!] network of government finance and relations with private business." Such language, adapted to a prerevolutionary situation, was of course completely out of place in the Britain of 1964, where the overwhelming majority of the working class still had confidence in Wilson, and was not ready to set up such committees inside the Labour Party, not to speak of outside.

It is true that sometimes, remembering part of what they learned in the past, the SLL leaders do call for a fight for a socialist policy and a new socialist leadership *inside* the Labour Party. But this is only all the more contradictory. For how can the advanced British workers believe at one and the same time that it is necessary to build an "alternative leadership" *inside* the Labour Party—and that the only "alternative leadership of the British working class is the Socialist Labour League" outside the Labour Party—as *The Newsletter* so often contends?

It is not a question of being "milder" or "harsher" towards the Labour Party bureaucracy; quite the contrary! It is a question of how to fight effectively against this malignant group of labour lieutenants of the capitalist class, *how to actually break its hold on the British working class*. Today, after 18 months of the new Labour government, we can say that the SLL, as a result of its ultraleft third-period tactics, is missing an historic opportunity to organise and lead hundreds of thousands of unionists and Labour Party members inside their organisation, against Wilson; instead, it contents itself with leading demonstrations of some hundreds of young people, outside the Labour Party.

12

'TROTSKYISM IN ONE COUNTRY'?

At the bottom of the SLL's political and organisational departure from Marxism and degeneration into a sect lies its split with the Fourth International. To justify that split and thereby justify its existence as a sect has become the major preoccupation of the SLL, its essential political interest, overshadowing its concern in the objective needs of the revolutionary movement in Britain and elsewhere. Any balance sheet of the political and organisational evolution of the SLL therefore logically culminates in a balance sheet of its relations with the Fourth International. And nowhere else does its sectarian degeneration appear as clearly as it does around this key question for revolutionary Marxists.

The SLL claims to speak in the name of the "International Committee of the Fourth International." But this is a double fraud. In the first place, the International Committee formed during the 1953–54 factional struggle that led to a split in the Fourth International, decided by a large majority in 1963 to participate in a Reunification Congress together with the forces represented by the International Executive Committee between 1954 and 1962. Of the eight sections which were part of the International Committee, six approved participation in the Reunification Congress of the Fourth International and ratified the documents adopted at that gathering, thereby confirming the fusion which took place at that time and which has become strengthened in the period since then. Only two groups adhering to the International Committee, the British and the French, refused to participate in the Reunification Congress and in the fusion, thereby deliberately splitting from the unified Fourth International. Then the SLL and its French allies set up a rump "International Committee," hoping to profit from the confusion this might create.

But the usurpation of the label is also a political fraud. For the "International Committee of the Fourth International" never ceased acting as a tendency or an organised faction *inside* the world Trotskyist movement from the time it was formed up to the time of the Reunification Congress. It never decided to launch itself as a distinct organisation, separate and apart from the organised Fourth International. It wanted to reunite with the other Trotskyist faction around the International Committee Executive provided certain organisational guarantees were given and certain political conditions were fulfilled. As early as 1957, it stipulated these guarantees and conditions. The leaders of the SLL and their French factional allies have completely reversed this principled course and tried to organise a separate organisation, whose essential activity consists in an obstinate and utterly sectarian struggle *against* the world Trotskyist movement.

The leaders of the SLL refused to participate in the reunification of the Fourth International under the pretext that the congress had not been prepared for by a long and principled political discussion. It pretended that it sought precisely such a discussion, stating ambiguously:

> The purpose of these discussions would be to organise an international conference where the forces of the International Committee and the Pabloites would be able to present their various opinions in a way that would help to clarify the international movement. (*The Newsletter*, August 22, 1964.)

An official statement issued by the Socialist Labour League at its 1964 conference explicitly stated that the League was in favor of "a principled unification of the world Trotskyist movement..." (See Healy's *Fourth International* magazine, Vol. 2, No. 1, summer 1965, p. 39.)

Six months later, when, contrary to the "predictions" of the SLL, the left wing of the Belgian Socialist Party, far from "capitulating to reformism," actually was expelled from that party after a fight to the finish, the editorial board of *The Newsletter* signed in its issue of February 6, 1965, an "Open Letter" addressed to the United Secretariat of the Fourth International, calling upon it not to throw away "a valuable opportunity to arrive at a principled agreement with the Socialist Labour League..."

Yet *at the same time*, while the SLL leaders were *pretending* to look for a "discussion," a common conference, a principled agreement, and even, after a period, a reunification with the world Trotskyist movement, they were dumping abuse and slander on it by the bucket! In the March 28, 1964, issue of *The Newsletter*, they speak about the United Secretariat "and its transatlantic allies" as a "reformist and philistine-liberal . . . sect;" people who have "sold their revolutionary birthright for the sake of a little bit of respectability"; and who "insult the honourable name of 'revolutionary socialism."

The leading members of the Fourth International are characterized as "enemies of the working class [who] aided the betrayal of thousands of Ceylonese and Indian workers and peasants . . ." (*The Newsletter*, August 15, 1964.)

The Socialist Workers Party which is prevented by reactionary legislation from affiliating to the Fourth International, but which is in full political solidarity with the reunified world Trotskyist movement is characterised in the following way:

> The SWP can no longer be considered as a Trotskyist organisation. Its leadership is in fact, just as politically corrupt as that of N. M. Perera and his friends who have now become supporters of imperialism. (*The Newsletter*, August 29, 1964.)

And the August 1965 issue of the magazine appearing under the stolen flag of the *Fourth International* says that the "spurious internationalism of the Pabloite revisionists ends by actively assisting imperialism." (p. 59.)

It is obvious that there is something wrong here. One does not engage in common conferences with "enemies of the working class" in order to consider uniting with them. Orthodox Trotskyists don't seek a principled agreement with a "reformist and philistine-liberal . . . sect." This whole ambivalent posture of the SLL towards the world Trotskyist movement was unprincipled through and through, a manoeuvre aimed at engineering a somewhat bigger split. When the fraud was exposed, when nobody fell into the trap, when it threatened to snare the unprincipled manoeuverers themselves—then they beat a hasty retreat and today the SLL magazine *Fourth International* brazenly proclaims:

> We do not discuss with the revisionists. The programme of the Fourth International and the overall positions and activity of the revisionists are imcompatible. In the class struggle, we are not on the same side of the barricades. This means, among other things, that we feel no need to justify any of our positions in debate with these people. (April 1966, p. 69.)

Their fraudulent "international conference" of 1966 said the same thing.[29] It is perfectly clear that from the beginning their appeal for a "discussion" was just a fraud, and that the *SLL leaders in reality consciously and deliberately sought to split the world Trotskyist movement*. Of what social force is it the unconscious tool? What social force is interested in weakening the Fourth International through unjustified and unprincipled splits?

As for us, we stand on the same principled position as we always did on the question of international unity. All those who consider themselves Trotskyists and who accept the general programme and principles of the movement could and should be united in a single International—on condition that they agree that the International must function as a real *organisation*. The only rules which enable a revolutionary organisation to function efficiently are those of democratic centralism: full freedom of democratic discussion *inside* the movement; full unity of action *outside* the movement, on the basis of majority decisions. Only in this way can an organisation combine freedom of expression for minority tendencies with real united activity in the class struggle. Any other concept of the international organisation debases it to an international letter-box center. And, as Trotsky argued for the last ten years of his life, the difference between these two concepts of the International is today the main dividing line between Bolsheviks and centrists.

Factional groupings that break with the Fourth International in reality express through this action the opinion that their own specific brand of tactics or "particular" analysis is much more important than the building of the movement on the basis of a correct program, which is a *historical* task to be achieved in a whole *historical* period, and which will certainly not depend on this or that particular emphasis in this or that particular country. That's why such behavior is *organisational sectarianism*, blind factionalism, the basic infantile disease diagnosed by Lenin. An understanding of the noxious character of such sectarianism and factionalism must be made part of the basic education of the members and sympathisers of all sections of the International.

We do not like splits. But if splits of this kind are harmful to the world Trotskyist movement, they are fatal to the groups that engage in them. Separated from the International, it is impossible to maintain a correct political orientation, a correct analysis of the evolution of the world situation and of the tasks of the revolutionary Marxists. Only revolutionary action is in the last analysis the testing ground for revolutionary theory, the touchstone of revolutionary truth. Without an international organisation of Trotskyist cadres and militants which in all the main countries of the world have tried and tested in action the essential elements of political analysis, a correct understanding of the international situation and its constant changes becomes more and more difficult. Sterile repetition of stereotyped platitudes, or hastily pasted together newspaper clippings, then inevitably take the place of a real Marxist analysis of the world situation. The sad outcome can be seen in the SLL's "development of theory."

Trotskyism is international socialism at its highest level of expression. The world Trotskyist movement has fought throughout its existence against any form of nationalist deviations. But in the little island of Britain there are people today who call themselves "orthodox Trotskyists" yet who calmly think of "building Trotskyism in one country," with the help of one other organisation in France and a sprinkling of individual followers in two or three other places, in opposition to the organised Trotskyist movement in forty countries! So preposterous is this expectation, born of the insularity and national isolation which has always been one of the basic weaknesses of the British Left, that the SLL must shamefully hide it behind the false front of an "international committee" for "rebuilding" the Fourth International. But the fraudulent "international conference" of April 1966 has now exposed the bluff.[30] You are not "rebuilding" any international movement, comrades of the SLL; you are just busy trying to build "Trotskyism in one country," a project as absurd as that other still-born brain child of your Great Leader: the "crushing" of the Fourth International!

The SLL has not a few young, active and promising militants in its ranks. Generally, after a few years of activism of the highest intensity, they tend to become disillusioned, and to be lost to the movement. Their bad experience with the SLL tends to turn them against Trotskyism in general. There are hundreds of people like that today throughout Britain. It is especially for the education of these comrades that we have written this pamphlet, in order to show them the real face of Trotskyism as opposed to the not very attractive countenance of the SLL.

For them, and much more so for the hundreds of fine young militants who have been misled and miseducated in the SLL in a spirit of blind factionalism and sectarianism that is the opposite of revolutionary Marxism, there remains but one choice: either to continue on the road of a sect, a road leading to more and more pronounced political and organisational degeneration; or to find their way back to the Fourth International!

Footnotes

Chapter 4

1. One should not of course confuse the political struggle against the enemy and the ability to win an immediate victory in this struggle. This depends not only on our ability to fight, but also on many other factors, among which the relationship of forces is not a negligible one. If our "revisionism" is proved by our inability to prevent the defeat of the Hungarian revolution, then it could equally be said that the SLL "betrayed" the workers because of its inability to prevent the Wilson government from backing Johnson's war of aggression against the Vietnam revolution. Similarly it could be said that the French associates of the SLL, the Lambert group, "betrayed" the workers by their inability to prevent de Gaulle from coming to power. Really, the SLL leaders should be very cautious with such "arguments." They have a tendency to boomerang . . .

2. "Khrushchev is forced by working class pressure to open up limited relations [!] between the workers and the bureaucracy." Gerry Healy himself was the author of this "Pabloite drivel"—at least it appeared over his signature in *The Newsletter* December 1, 1962.

3. This is also the case with Stephane Just, who, starting from the fact that we criticised negative factors which undoubtedly existed in the Hungarian revolution of 1956—and Lenin reminded the "purists" a long time ago that he who waits for a "pure" revolution, without "negative factors," will never see one!—has the temerity to conclude that for Germain, the Hungarian revolution was "inopportune," "negative" and shouldn't have been started! Is it a case of bad faith, or the inevitable consequence of going on an ultraleft binge?

It is probably the latter, since this French disciple of Healy devoted 218 pages of the September 1965 issue of a magazine called with ironic derision *La Verite* to the theme that the thousands of Trotskyists in the Fourth International and the Socialist Workers Party carry on their activity, build their sections and parties, hold their congresses and publish their papers and magazines . . . only in order to prevent the "real Trotskyists" of the Healy-Lambert sect from building their movement. The whole world is seen as a conspiracy against a handful of persons. One does not have to have studied medicine to diagnose this as a clear case of paranoia.

Although Just "hates" and "fights" Stalinism, foaming at the mouth, he is not sharp enough to understand how much his "method" resembles that of Stalinism; is, in fact, a pure product of Stalinism. Only Stalinism introduced into the labour movement the poisonous method of fighting ideological differences not on the field of ideas, or by pointing out the social forces whose interests these ideas express, but by charging "conspiracies" and "treason" committed by "arch villains." Stalinism on the ideological field represents to a large extent regression from the theory of the class struggle to the theory of demonology. Healy, Just and Co. come close to that level in their "polemics."

Chapter 5

4. See "From Wavering to Capitulation," by E. Germain in the fall 1964 issue of the *International Socialist Review* and the November 1964 issue of *Quatrieme Internationale*.

5. As late as January 1958, the secretary of the LSSP, Leslie Goonewardene, sent a letter to the International Secretariat of the Fourth International criticising some elements of the theses, "Decline and Fall of Stalinism," along the same lines as Healy's criticism. (See: *Bulletin Interieur du Secretariat International de la IVe Internationale*, "Les travaux du 20e Plenum de C.E.I.," No. 2, February 1958.)

Chapter 6

6. A further consequence would then be the correctness of the Khrushchevist concept of "states of national democracy"—states that are neither bourgeois nor proletarian—being set up in various countries in the wake of the colonial revolution.

7. "Cuba—the Acid Test. A Reply to the Ultraleft Sectarians." *SWP Discussion Bulletin*, Vol. 24, No. 2. January 1963. Published by the Socialist Workers Party, 873 Broadway, New York, N.Y. $.55.

8. "The theory of the Cuban 'workers' state took a blow last August when the press of the Cuban Trotskyists was smashed and the plates of Trotsky's 'Permanent Revolution' destroyed." (Tom Kemp in *The Newsletter*, April 28, 1962.)

9. We might add in passing: our strange "dogmatists" who are so exacting when it comes to Cuba, are much more "lenient" when they consider Yugoslavia and China. There, you see, a workers state can be built without soviets, and without the previous existence of a revolutionary party. But in Cuba it is "impossible." Fidel Castro will be recognized as a conscious proletarian revolutionist only when and if he formally joins the Socialist Labour League; but Josip Tito and Mao Tse-tung, who are not exactly card-carrying members of the "International Committee of the Fourth International," nevertheless headed genuine revolutions, although slightly bureaucratized (and without soviets). Castro's basic mishap was not to have been a member of the Cuban Communist Party, it now seems. But the Cuban CP was *against* the revolution, and Castro could only bring it about precisely because he stood independent of the CP and *to the left of it*. Each step in its "reasoning" involves the SLL in bigger contradictions on the Cuban question.

Chapter 7

10. "Thus, paradoxical as it may seem, the defence of Trotskyism against Stalinist slanders is the first condition

of defence of the whole working class movement of Cuba and, incidentally, of the Stalinists as well, against future reprisals by the capitalist state of Castro." (*The Newsletter*, June 18, 1966.) "Thus every attempt by the working class to assert its political power either independently or through fissures in the Castro government is met immediately by powerful and violent resistance from the capitalist state machine. It is from this point of view, and only [!] this point of view, that the repeated purges within the regime (Salvador David, Escalante, Guevara), and the repressions directed against independent trends such as the pro-Chinese Communists and the Posadas group, acquire any meaning." (Ibid.)

Escalante, that representative of a rotten and materially privileged bureaucracy, seen as an expression of the working class (!) attempting to assert itself, this is a discovery Healy should really be proud of.

11. To complete the record, it should be noted that the Cuban Communist Party leader Blas Roca, an old Stalinist hack, whom Healy would have us "defend" against Castro, sought to "prove" his most recent slanders against Trotskyism by citing the irresponsible position taken by the SLL leaders on the Cuban question. (See *World Outlook*, Vol. 4, No. 16, May 20, 1966.)

Chapter 8

12. "A particularly explicit and clear attitude on the question of the colonial and the oppressed peoples is necessary for the parties in those countries where the bourgeoisie possess colonies and oppress other nations. Every party which wishes to join the Communist International is obliged to expose the tricks and dodges of its' imperialists in the colonies, *to support every colonial liberation movement not merely in words but in deeds*, to demand the expulsion of their own imperialists from these colonies, to inculcate among the workers of their country a genuinely fraternal attitude to the working people of the colonies and the oppressed nations, and to carry on systematic agitation among the troops of their country against any oppression of the colonial people." (Condition No. 8 of the 21 conditions for admission to the Communist International, passed by the Second Congress of the Communist International August 6, 1920. The first draft was prepared by Lenin. Emphasis added.)

See also thesis No. 9 of the *Theses on the National and Colonial Question* adopted on July 28, 1920, at the same congress, in which the following appears: ". . . Communist parties must give *direct support* to the revolutionary movements among the dependent nations and those without equal rights (e.g., in Ireland, and among the American Negroes), and in the colonies. Without this last *particularly important* condition the struggle against the oppression of the dependent nations and colonies, and the recognition of their right to secede as separate states, remains a deceitful pretense, as it is in the parties of the Second International." (Emphasis added.) Both documents cited here are available in *The Communist International 1919–1943 Documents*. Vol. I, Oxford University Press.

13. In fact, this "revolutionary social" programme was nothing but a hoax. In all official proclamations, the MNA—as early as 1955—limited itself strictly to demanding national independence and democratic liberties; there was even no question of a radical land reform! See the MNA's message to the Bandung conference, in the MNA organ *La Voix du Peuple*, April 30, 1955.

14. It is true that the SLL, a perfect example of theoretical confusion confounded on all basic questions, often lets the left hand piously ignore what the right hand writes. Tom Kemp can see "no gain" in national political independence. David Francis, writing in the April 1966 issue of the SLL's *Fourth International* sees just the opposite, speaking about "a revolutionary war forcing [!] French imperialism to abandon its direct rule." (P. 66.)

15. ". . . there is no 'colonial sector' with its own 'colonial revolution' for particular objectives (national independence, industrial development)"! Contrast this with what Trotsky had to say: "With the acute agrarian problem and the intolerable national oppression in the colonial countries, the young and relatively small proletariat can come to power on the basis of a *national democratic* revolution sooner than the proletariat of an advanced country on a purely *socialist* basis." (*The Permanent Revolution*, p. 130. Emphasis in original.)

Of course, the authoritative David Francis, whoever he is, can maintain that this was a revisionist deviation on Trotsky's part. To be consistent, he should go further and point to the same deviation in the Transitional Program itself, Trotsky having declared there: "The central task of the colonial and semi-colonial countries is the *agrarian revolution*, i.e., liquidation of feudal heritages, and *national independence*, i.e., the overthrow of the imperialist yoke. Both tasks are closely linked with one another." (See the *Founding Conference of the Fourth International*, published by the Socialist Workers Party. 1939. p. 40. Emphasis in original.)

16. E. Germain, "From Wavering to Capitulation," in the fall 1964 issue of the *International Socialist Review*.

Chapter 9

17. This has been quite noticeable in *The Newsletter* on several occasions. Here are two examples. In the issue of July 24, 1965, it is argued that "The bourgeois-national leaders of the Kurds, aided by the Iraqi Communist Party, demand a 'reasonable solution, keeping the integrity of Iraqi structure intact.'" Instead of opposing this as an abandonment of the principle of the right of self-determination for the Kurdish people, including their right to separate from the Iraqi state, the SLL author, completely forgetting the Leninist position on the national question, argues that "The future of the Kurdish peasants and workers lies in their unity with the Iraqi workers."

Similarly in *The Newsletter* of December 5, 1964, an article, from which the editorial board never differentiated itself, speaks about "The shooting of helpless white and coloured women and children, in the past week, in the Congo" which "cannot be condoned," and goes so far as to say that "Stalinist tactics stain the hands of the Peking clique, gory with the carnage of helpless children," simply repeating the propaganda of the imperialist press!

18. The historical parallel which leaps to the mind is the present situation in the USA and the situation in Britain in the early seventies. "And most important of all: every industrial and commercial centre in England now possesses a working-class population *divided* into two *hostile* camps, English proletarians and Irish proletarians. The ordinary English worker hates the Irish worker as a competitor who lowers his standard of life . . . His attitude towards him is much the same as that of the "poor whites" to the "niggers" in the former slave states of the U.S.A. The Irishman pays him back with interest in his own coin. He regards the English worker as both sharing in the guilt for the English domination in Ireland and at the same time as serving as its stupid tool." (Letter from Karl Marx to Siegfried Meyer and August Vogt, April 9, 1870. In *Selected Correspondence*, International Publishers, p. 288. Emphasis in original.)

Replace "English domination in Ireland" by "white supremacy," and you have a nearly perfect analogy with the situation in the U.S.A. And how did Marx see the solution of the problem? He *did not* fall into the trap of "abstract internationalism" (which in fact condones national and racial oppression). He *did not* call for the immediate unity of English and Irish workers for a socialist Britain, although he was of the opinion that England was the country where conditions were the ripest for such a revolution. No, he *called upon the English workers to support the struggle for national emancipation of Ireland* as a necessary precondition for a united front between English and Irish workers against capitalism: "The special task of the Central Council [of the First International] in London is to awaken a consciousness in the English workers that for them the *national emancipation of Ireland* is no question of abstract justice or humanitarian sympathy but the first condition for *their own emancipation*." (Ibid., p. 290.)

Chapter 10

19. Just a couple of examples: On page 12 Varga alleges that "throughout the entire length of his article, Mandel carefully avoids mentioning the class struggle or even the classes"; in reality the whole final part of Mandel's article is devoted to an explanation of the Liberman reforms as the result of a *social struggle* between the bureaucracy and the working class.

On page 16 Varga states that for Mandel, the great weakness of the economy of the USSR lies in a gap between the growth in production of production goods and that of consumer goods, whereas, in reality, this is only a secondary aspect, the main aspect being a continual drop in the rate of growth of gross social production. But Mandel mentions explicitly "the constant fall in the annual rates of growth of the national income and industrial production during the last five years" as the main cause generating the economic reforms in the USSR.

On page 12 Varga charges Mandel with basing himself on "idealism" and having "the principle" of planning to fight "the principle" of the market in a society that is in transition from capitalism to socialism. In fact the "opposition" between the market sector and the principle of planning is analysed and taken as the basis of economic policy by Preobrazhensky, the Left Opposition and Trotsky himself, all idealists, soaring "over the earth on a cloud of schemas" like Mandel.

On the same page 12 Varga alleges that "Not for one instant does he 'Mandel' suspect that the system of planning under Stalin . . . reflected the social and political relationships of a degenerated workers' state." But Mandel writes explicitly: "That old system of administration 'under Stalin' corresponded to a precise need and a precise social logic . . . a bureaucratic system closed upon itself . . . a total lack of initiative in behalf of the working class, an extremely hierarchical structure." Mandel continues by saying that the system was "based upon the material interests of the bureaucrats," etc., etc.

Indeed, to polemize with people who display such obvious bad faith, who systematically distort and falsify the positions of their opponents, is largely wasted effort.

20. "In order that these objects may enter into relations with each other as commodities, their guardians must place themselves in relation to one another, as persons whose will resides in those objects . . . They must, therefore, mutually recognize in each other the right of private proprietors." (Marx, *Capital*, Vol. I, Chapt. 2, p. 96. Kerr edition.) In passing, it should be noted that when Varga says that "according to Marx, use-values become commodities because they are the products of independent private labour, i.e., the social production of producers isolated by the division of labour is realised only in the exchange of the products, which have an exchange value because they are products of *private* labour," he mystifies the word "private," making it incomprehensible, separated from the notion of *private property*.

According to Marx, division of labour does not automatically "isolate" producers; it can very well keep them in the status of immediate producers of social labour and of social products, as long as they remain within the framework of a natural economy; e.g., subsistence farming. Only when the producers meet each other at the same time as *private owners* of their products (or when they work for private owners of the means of production who appropriate the product of their labour) does division of labour indeed "isolate" them from each other, and force them to establish the amount of socially necessary labour they produced only indirectly, through the operation of the market. Commodity production therefore does not automatically arise from division of labour; it arises in a society where division of labour is combined with *separate owners of products*.

And we may well ask: where do we find today, in the Soviet Union, the owners of products of "private labour" which Varga prattles about? And in what sense does foreign trade convert the Soviet producers into owners of "products of private labour"? This alone shows that his long reference to Marx's analysis of the origin of commodity production is largely irrelevant to the problem he tries to deal with.

21. According to Marx, a long period of international commodity trade, including trade with the great capitalist powers of the seventeenth and eighteenth centuries, did not succeed in destroying the basic self-sufficiency of the

Indian village. Even the harsh taxation system of the East India Company did not succeed in introducing commodity production in these villages. Only the competition of modern British industry—and the colonial political domination of Britain in India—destroyed the self-sufficient village economy by destroying home industry, thereby beginning the generalization of commodity production in the middle of the nineteenth century. (Cf. Marx's letter to Engels of June 14, 1853, and his article in the *New York Tribune* of June 25, 1853.)

22. For instance oil and watches, as well as certain kinds of equipment like linotype machines. In his book *The Economics of Soviet Planning* (Yale University Press, 1964), the American Prof. Abram Bergson, a hardened opponent of the October revolution and of the Soviet system, admits that around 1955, the Soviet worker had already reached the *per capita* level of consumption of the Italian worker, which would have been impossible without a more or less equivalent level of productivity. (P. 286.)

23. "Only through the interaction of the three elements, State planning, the market, and Soviet democracy, can be realized the correct management of the economy of the transitional epoch, and only thus can be assured—not the complete surmounting of contradictions and disproportions within a few years (this is Utopia!)—but their mitigation, and, through just that, the strengthening of the material bases of the dictatorship of the proletariat until the moment when a new and victorious revolution will widen the arena of socialist planning and will reconstruct the system." (Trotsky, *The Soviet Economy in Danger*, Pioneer Publishers, 1933, p. 32.)

If it was possible to reduce disproportions in the Soviet industry of 1932, when Trotsky wrote these words, why is it "objectively impossible" to do so in the Soviet industry of 1966, which is immeasurably stronger and more variegated, and which, incidentally, has a much larger "arena of socialist planning" thanks to the new and victorious revolutions that followed World War II? Instead of pointing to the reactionary nationalist policies of the Soviet bureaucracy, which have prevented consistent international planning in the "socialist camp," Varga explains away what is due to the bureaucracy as due . . . to the pressure of the capitalist world market!

24. That is why Trotsky proposed more foreign trade and not less. According to Varga's logic, he thereby sought to make the Soviet economy more dependent on the capitalist world market. But perhaps, after all, Trotsky was just serving as an "agent of imperialism" by advancing such a "Pabloite revisionist demand"?

Chapter 11

25. For many years the Belgian Trotskyists applied a similar policy in the Belgian Socialist Party. They came under sharp criticism from the SLL for doing exactly the same thing that Healy advocated and practised for nearly 15 years. When the SP bureaucracy banned the paper *La Gauche*, in which they played an important role, nearly 20 percent of the SP Congress delegates voted against the ban. Yet when *Keep Left*, the Young Socialist paper, was banned by Transport House, no significant support could be won for its defence inside the Labour Party, so greatly had the SLL and its followers alienated the rank and file through their sectarian tactics and language.

26. In view of this record, Healy's obsession with splits in the Fourth International, no matter how small, each of which he describes as a "product of revisionism," looks rather ridiculous, reminding one of the good old biblical story about the mote and the beam.

27. *The Newsletter* offered two grotesque examples of organisational sectarianism. It published a photo of Lenin, with the caption: "He crushed his enemies!" Presumably, to Healy and Co., the victory of the October revolution, the building of the Soviet state, the creation of the Third International, the building of the Bolshevik Party, the writing of *State and Revolution* are all minor achievements compared to that major one: the "crushing" of one's factional enemies.

In 1966 at the annual conference of the SLL, the hall was decorated with the following banner: "LEON TROTSKY'S LAST WORDS: ". . . I AM SURE . . . OF THE VICTORY OF THE FOURTH INTERNATIONAL . . . GO FORWARD. THIS MEANS—FORWARD TO THE DAILY TROTSKYIST NEWSPAPER." In his blind organisational sectarianism, Healy apparently does not see the difference between the world and Britain, and between victory of the proletariat and establishment of a small daily paper such as the British Communist Party has put out for thirty years. It is striking proof of how the Healyites have converted the concept of party building as a *means* for enabling the *working class* to overthrow capitalism into an end in itself. They have fallen victim to reification, the tendency nurtured by commodity production.

28. Peter Arnold writes: "Instead of uniting the working class and the petty-bourgeoisie, and entering into united fronts with the social-democrats to expose the Nazis, they [the Communists] merely contributed to the demoralisation of the class by further dividing it." (*Newsletter*, December 12, 1964.) In reality, the CP could not by itself unite the working class, and certainly not the working class and the petty-bourgeoisie. Its task was not to enter into "united fronts with the social-democrats," but to offer a united front to the Social Democratic Party (this is precisely the *nuance* between third-period Stalinism and Trotskyism!). The goal of such a united front was not merely "to expose the Nazis," but rather to fight them, destroy them and assure, on the basis of that destruction, a working-class upsurge towards a socialist Germany.

Chapter 12

29. "Revisionism, which separates into distinct sectors the revolution in the advanced countries, the 'colonial revolution,' and the political revolution in the workers' states, *is a most important cover for capitalist domination of the workers' movement* and for obstructing the construction of revolutionary parties. This revisionism is expressed particularly in the theory and practice of the self-styled Unified Secretariat of the Fourth International . . ." (SLL's *Fourth International*, August 1966, p. 116. Emphasis added.)

The authors of this resolution forget, rather foolishly, that Trotsky, in the Transitional Program, also worked out a "separate program" for the "distinct sectors" of the imperialist countries, the backward countries and the Soviet Union. The reason for this is simply that the historic tasks confronting these three revolutions are different.

Only people lacking the most elementary understanding of dialectics could maintain that the Fourth International, in following Trotsky's distinction, which still holds true for the world of today, was guilty of "breaking up" the world revolution into distinct "sectors." As the document, "Dynamics of World Revolution Today" (adopted at the 1963 Reunification Congress of the Fourth International) painstakingly explained, the *unity* of the world revolution will result from the proletariat's capacity to solve these *distinct* tasks of the colonial revolution, the political revolution in the degenerated or deformed workers states, and the proletarian revolution in the imperialist countries as these revolutions interact with each other. But Healy and Co. are still at that infantile stage of reasoning where unity combined with diversity is "unthinkable."

30. At that conference, Lambert, Healy's French associate, introduced a motion to the effect that while democratic centralism is necessary in "principle," it cannot yet be applied in practice. The motion was adopted. Even Lambert, Healy's only international ally with any following whatsoever, doesn't want to submit to Healy's discipline . . .

SECTION II: HEALY 'RECONSTRUCTS' THE FOURTH INTERNATIONAL

Sectarianism and Tinpot Despotism— an Example for the Textbooks
By Joseph Hansen

> In their own circles they [the sectarians] customarily carry on a regime of despotism.
> —Leon Trotsky.*

The documents included in this pamphlet deal with a conference sponsored by the so-called "International Committee." Official accounts of the gathering, which was held early in April 1966, are readily available. However, the accounts are far from complete. References to certain happenings remain obscure and puzzling. The documents assembled here make it possible to now fill in these dark areas, at least partially. In view of their educational value, plus the likelihood that they might otherwise be buried in the archives, the Socialist Workers party, which received copies of them by chance, is making them public in this form.

As for the official accounts, their nature can be gathered from the following sentence which appeared in the May 9 *Bulletin of International Socialism*:

> The third International Congress called by the International Committee of the Fourth International, held in London from April 4–8, has been called the most impressive conference of the international Marxist movement since the Founding Conference of the Fourth International in 1938.

The author of these words (Tim Wohlforth?) does not indicate who made this impressive historical judgment. Perhaps it was wise to preserve his anonymity; for the truth is that in the history of the various groups that have proclaimed adherence to Trotskyism, whether justifiably or unjustifiably, it would be difficult to find a conference that opened with such fanfare and ended with such a disaster for its promoters.

The conference, which was guided in its deliberations by Gerry Healy of the Socialist Labour League, did not succeed in one of the main points on its agenda—to unite the two groups in the United States (Wohlforth and Robertson) that have vied in proclaiming political solidarity with the SLL and each other.

In fact, James Robertson, whom the betrayal caught by complete surprise (he came to believe his own propaganda about Healy being a model leader), was summarily thrown out in the most scandalous way, as can be judged from the documents in the following pages.

The delegation of the *Voix Ouvrière* [Worker's Voice] group, representing a bigger organization than the existing French component of the "International Committee" (the *La Verité* [The Truth] group headed by Pierre Lambert), were victims of a comparable sellout. In the middle of the conference Healy suddenly switched the political basis on which they had agreed to participate as observers and served them with an ultimatum to vote for a new line. They walked out.

The conference, anonymously described as the most impressive of its kind since 1938, thus ended up with two splits and what would appear to be a thorough poisoning of relations with the

---

* *The Transitional Program for Socialist Revolution* [Pathfinder, 1973, 1977], p. 193 [2014 printing]

only two formations in the entire international scene, aside from the Wohlforth group and an individual here or there, that have evinced any interest in the politics and perspectives offered by Healy-Lambert.

In one of the documents, Healy contends that he planned this outcome from the very beginning. In response to that boast we can only offer the SLL leader congratulations on his success in organizing the conference in such a way as to make it a completely cut-and-dried affair before it even opened. But was it really necessary to utilize such elaborate means to drive away his closest allies and supporters? It may be, of course, that we should congratulate Healy for no more than an impressive ability to waive aside setbacks and defeats.

Unfortunately no congratulations of any kind to the Robertson and *Voix Ouvrière* groups seem in order. They don't claim to have planned it that way. However, they might seek consolation in the thought that they asked for it. After all, they were well aware of the fraud built into the very foundation of this conference.

In 1963 the majority of the International Committee participated in a Reunification Congress which brought together on a principled basis the overwhelming majority of the world Trotskyist movement after a ten-year split. Of all the organizations in the International Committee, or sympathetic with its aims, only Healy's Socialist Labour League and Lambert's *La Verité* group rejected reunification, refusing to go along with the majority. After the International Committee participated in the reunification of the Fourth International, Healy and Lambert set up a rump "International Committee," representing no one but themselves. It was to a conference sponsored by these splitters that the Robertson and *Voix Ouvrière* groups decided to send observers. What did they expect there? Freedom to voice an opinion? A fair hearing for ideas they wished to advance for consideration? Observance of democratic rights?

They overlooked the undemocratic origin of Healy's "International Committee." It was set up from the very beginning as private property, well posted with "No Trespassing" and "No Hunting" signs—which ought to have been thought of before responding to the notices in the "Discussions Wanted" column of the Healyite press.

The testimony of the Robertson delegation on Healy's undemocratic practices, the main subject matter of the documents included here, is well worth study by all those who are interested in the health of the Socialist Labour League and the good name of Trotskyism in the British labor movement.

An apparently trivial incident occurred at the conference. Robertson was absent from one of the sessions.

In the Socialist Labour League, under National Secretary Healy, something like that is not "trivial." You can be hauled up on charges for it,

That's not all. You must acknowledge your guilt. Moreover, you must admit it in a way to meet some exacting specifications. If you don't, the charges can rapidly escalate.

Thus Robertson found himself, to his consternation, suddenly sinking in quicksand.

(1) He was charged with being absent from a session.

(2) He admitted his guilt.

(3) A motion was passed demanding that he apologize and admit having committed a "petty-bourgeois act."

(4) He apologized in an emphatic way for having been absent but refused to acknowledge that he had committed a "petty-bourgeois act."

(5) The escalation proceeded. Healy, according to Rose J., scored Robertson's absence and his refusal to vote for his condemnation, characterizing it as a "petty-bourgeois, reactionary act expressing the chauvinism of American imperialism, etc."

(6) Robertson was threatened with expulsion if he did not voice approval of the motion branding him with the alleged class nature of his crime.

(7) The dazed man still said, no.

(8) He was expelled.

The incident and the procedures followed in handling it become even more astonishing when examined in detail.

Rose J. reports that Robertson had been sick for three weeks, had spent the night working on a document, and had continued in the morning by presenting his views to the conference. Evidently exhausted, he sought to take a nap. "He mentioned to Comrade Healy that he was going."

Healy states in his letter to H. Turner and Sherwood,

> ... he asked me if it would be all right to leave the meeting to go to bed since he was working all night on a document.... I told him that I would convey his request to the appropriate comrades controlling the congress...

This august body met and "unanimously decided that he be requested to return..."

The necessity for an indisposed person to request permission not to attend a session is in itself a scandal. The proper procedure would have been to accept without the slightest question Robertson's admission that he was exhausted. In fact, if it had been learned that he was feeling ill or exhausted, and he had nevertheless insisted on remaining, he should have been persuaded to at least skip a session and get some rest. The arrangements committee, set up for such purposes in any well-organized gathering, should immediately have seen to it that every facility was made available to the comrade, including prompt medical attention if necessary.

In the evening, again according to Healy, Robertson returned. He was "asked to apologize for not having attended the session."

Robertson, still according to Healy, "refused to do this on the grounds that he did not know the rules. It was pointed out that these rules were implicit in all Bolshevik Congresses, otherwise everyone would do as he pleased."

This set of "implicit" rules for "Bolshevik congresses" is spun out of thin air. Harry Turner is completely in order to demand of Healy, "Can you cite any written precedent in any previous Bolshevik Congress for this rule?" And Turner might well have reminded Healy—which he didn't, unfortunately—that without established written rules, or agreed-upon rules placed in the record at the beginning of the gathering, any petty bureaucrat could do as he pleased.

That's aside from the ludicrous pretension that this was a "Bolshevik congress" or anything remotely resembling one.

Turner states that the acknowledgment demanded of Robertson, in view of the accusations leveled at him, would have signified making a "false confession to a petit-bourgeois outlook, American chauvinism, and capitulation to Black Nationalism."

Rose J. can hardly bring herself to say it—she apologizes for the great man who was steering the conference; it was "a mistake"; it is "almost" a "Stalinist version of democratic-centralism."

No, Comrade Rose J., it was no "mistake"; it was a crime; it is not "almost" a Stalinist version; it *is* a Stalinist version. No epithet is involved—that is the correct label for the way National Secretary Healy ran his conference.

Harry Turner sums it up quite accurately in his letter to Healy:

> Your attacks on Robertson were designed to make him knuckle under and adopt an attitude of humble worship for the omniscient British leadership. You were not interested in creating a movement united on the basis of democratic centralism with strong sections capable of making theoretical contributions to the movement as a whole and of applying Marxist theory creatively to their own national arenas. You wanted an international after the manner of Stalin's Comintern, permeated with servility at one pole and authoritarianism at the other.

Of course, Healyism is not the equivalent of Stalinism—meaning the rule of a parasitic bureaucratic caste wielding power in a workers state without checks or controls. Healyism is simply a case of factionalism and cultism, a not uncommon phenomenon among ingrown sects, as Trotsky observed in his time. Thus, fortunately, Healyism is but a grotesque caricature of Stalinism. After all, the most the tinpot autocrat could do to Robertson was to expel him.

Let us recapitulate. The atmosphere is such that Robertson feels compelled to ask Healy to take up with the "appropriate comrades" in control his need to drop out for a couple of hours. Robertson doesn't simply tell Healy, as would be normal—"he asked me if it would be all right..." Robertson has in fact already both asked permission and apologized. He apologized for being unable to stay on his feet; he asked permission to lie down. Where are we, on a slave plantation?

Thumbs down, comes the response of the "appropriate comrades" in control. They issue an order. Robertson is to stay on his feet. What should we call this? Insensitivity? Rudeness? Brutality? It is at least a good sample of the bureaucratic mind, all the purer because it lacks even the check of a serious sociological base.

Robertson returns to the next session, feeling, let us hope, no longer near collapse. The welcome he gets does not exactly reflect fraternal interest in his health. His comrades constitute themselves into a court and pass sentence. He must make a formal apology to the body as a whole. It is becoming monstrous!

Robertson, attempting to meet this strange situation, does apologize. He is in a foreign land . . . among unusual people given to unusual ways. In fact, of all the organizations he has been in, it can safely be said that he has never seen anything like this. He says he didn't know it was against the rules.

The man has claimed ignorance of the law! The inquisition replies at once to that hoary dodge. The rules, if not written down, are "implicit." It's been that way since the time of the Druids. Therefore the apology is rejected. (Harry Turner reports that Robertson made the apology "in a written statement"—apologies, say these remarkable "implicit" rules, must under no circumstances be left implicit.)

Something more is demanded of the miserable culprit than the squirming half-confession he has offered up to this point. He'd better come clean! But what do they want from him?

The "real political face of Robertson" must be "thoroughly exposed." The "thoroughly reactionary attitude" shown in the written half-confession must be dealt with implacably. The "idealist, pragmatic, petty-bourgeois basis of the Spartacist group" must be brought to light. The inner nature of this two-faced criminal who "retained his greatest venom and hatred for the congress itself" must be exposed before the entire body. (All the phrases in quotation marks appear in Healy's letter to H. Turner and Sherwood.)

Healy and the other "appropriate comrades controlling the congress" dictate an apology for adoption by Robertson. The man must confess that he committed a "petty-bourgeois act"; he must confess the correctness of the charge that he is guilty of "American chauvinism and capitulation to Black Nationalism."

Robertson, however, feels he just can't do it. The response of the judges is swift and merciless. The "Congress," as Healy reports it, "unanimously . . . decided that he should leave."

But the national secretary, who instigated all this, who is obviously a past master at dishing out super "Bolshevism," plays the cat-and-mouse game. "At this point I proposed a motion that he should stay until the end of the session, thus giving him time to reconsider his position."

Instantly the entire body falls into line; instantly the national secretary's motion is approved. They are like seals who have done all this many times before. Only *Voix Ouvrière* abstains, as Healy is careful to note. (He mentions it in his letter to H. Turner and Sherwood.)

After the reprieve is up, the victim is again seated in the dock. "Robertson was then asked," continues Healy, "if he would carry out the unanimous request of the Congress and apologize for his attitude towards the Congress." Robertson "refused to do this and was accordingly asked to leave . . ."

Expelled forthwith! At the end of the same session where he was first confronted with the ultimatum to apologize! In Healy's organization the rope is very short . . .

Is there anyone who knows the first thing about the abominations of Stalinism whose blood doesn't boil on reading about such procedures?

If such things could occur in an international gathering where Healy presumably had his best foot forward, what is the atmosphere like inside the Socialist Labour League?

For years rumors have circulated in the British labor movement about Healy's methods. Generally the sources turned out to be dissidents who walked out or were expelled from the Socialist Labour League. Some of the stories they told sounded to Trotskyists in other countries like gross exaggerations and thus tended to be discounted as due to factionalism. Yet it had to be noted that in the international scene, Healy's organization was the only one claiming to represent Trotskyism that had such an ugly reputation in the labor movement because of continual tales about gross violations of the democratic rights of its own members.

The facts reported by the Robertson delegation are different from anything yet revealed since they come from people who were pathetically loyal to Healy and who could scarcely believe their eyes as they witnessed what was happening. Their report of how Healy expelled Robertson, backed as it is by Healy's own boasts and admissions, is utterly convincing. And all the more so in view of their reiteration, after the event, that they still have no political differences with him—even on Cuba, which Healy holds to be capitalist and which they maintain is a workers state!

One can well appreciate why the Wohlforth group, as shown by one of the documents, is afraid to agree to hold even a debate with another group without first getting approval from Big Brother. What if he should jerk the rug they're standing on! And so Wohlforth, who used to take pride in standing in opposition to no matter whom, ends up as a rubber stamp for a . . . Healy.

But let us move on. With the exception of the article by Georges Kaldy, the documents included here touch on the political issues only incidentally. This, of course, is due to the nature of the material. The authors of the correspondence were dealing with what was really going on at the conference and what was most important to them and the members of their groups. Their political interpretations, which are something else again, can be found in their publications. Unfortunately, with all their studied poses, self-delusion, wrong theories, sectarian attitudes and carelessness about facts, what they write for the public is generally simply boring. Certainly it doesn't compare in educational value with this material in which the real world they live in tends to break through.

Kaldy's article about the famous conference lacks this vitality. Writing for the *Voix Ouvrière* audience, the author is concerned about maintaining a certain public image which apparently can admit to dueling but not to brawling—at least when the weapons are broken beer bottles à la Healy. We have made it available in an English translation as a courtesy inasmuch as it is rather doubtful that this service will be rendered by either Healy, Wohlforth or Robertson.

The most interesting political question is: What brought these groupings to stage an international conference if a face-to-face confrontation would only cause them to fly apart?

It is as easy to find the answer as it is to put the question. Their common opposition to the Fourth International and the Socialist Workers party—which they claim is really opposition to "Pabloism"—brought them together. The uneven development of the different groups in their evolution away from Trotskyism caused them to split, an outcome none of them foresaw.

This becomes completely clear if considered against the background. Among the key issues that led Healy, the main figure at the conference, to separate from the majority of the world Trotskyist movement a few years ago was a difference in appreciation of the colonial revolution, its importance and its course of development. The dispute occurred concretely over the events in Cuba which led to the overthrow of capitalism under the leadership of Fidel Castro.

Healy decided that nothing fundamentally decisive had really happened in Cuba. To this day he maintains that Cuba is capitalist.

A free discussion of several years' duration was held in the Socialist Workers party on the nature and results of the Cuban Revolution. The party ranks almost in their entirety decided that Cuba was a workers state.

This view, which had been reached in parallel fashion by the International Secretariat of the Fourth International, became a strong element in healing the ten-year breach in the world Trotskyist movement.

At the same time, the outcome of the discussion greatly intensified the differences that had already appeared between the Socialist Workers party and the Socialist Labour League. In the Socialist Workers party, Robertson and Wohlforth, who stood in a minority on this question, were drawn politically toward Healy. He in turn decided that the best field of practical activity for them in the United States was to serve as a faction in the SWP run by remote control from London. This brought them into increasing violations of discipline, the upshot of which, after several warnings over a considerable period, was their expulsion.

Despite their common adherence to Healyism, Robertson and Wohlforth had differences with each other, including the tactical side of their struggle against the SWP. Unable to resolve these differences by themselves, they turned to Healy as the arbiter and were thus led into competition for his favor. Healy preferred Wohlforth, the main reasons being that Wohlforth came closer to sharing his ultraleft sectarian views on Cuba and on black nationalism as well as displaying a flattering degree of appreciation for the thought of Healy, particularly on the organizational level. However as can be gathered from the correspondence made available here, Healy's choice of Wohlforth was not generally accepted, particularly among Robertson's followers. To complicate matters, the Wohlforth contingent was outnumbered by the other group. Thus if the two groups were combined, Robertson would exercise a majority. How to get around that without appearing to be against majority rule? A ticklish question!

Healy maneuvered for time, deferring consummation of the projected unification of the two groups, probably in hope that Wohlforth might pick up enough at Robertson's expense to gain a majority.

However, the scheme could not be put across in time for the conference. Healy delayed no longer. As Rose J. reports it in a letter included in this collection, "Mike Banda said the next day—'we decided to make war on you'!" That was when the moment of truth came for Robertson. Or as Rose J. so graphically puts it, that was when "the bull hit the fan."

From a certain point of view, of course, it could be said that it was only a case of destiny utilizing Healy as a blind instrument to mete out poetic justice on Robertson for the way he flouted majority rule in the Socialist Workers party for such a long period. Or, as a Freudian might see it—it was just a case of Robertson demonstrating once again that he is faction prone.

It is not clear from the documents how the *Voix Ouvrière* group really fitted into the strategy, explained rather boastfully by Healy in his letter to H. Turner and Sherwood, which called for inviting them to come to his conference so they could be kicked out of it.

Possibly this was Lambert's contribution to the masterful wheeling and dealing. Healy favored it because he is in sad need of international reinforcements and because, in his general ignorance of things outside Britain, the declamations of the *Voix Ouvrière* group against "Pabloism" sounded very good—good enough to warrant putting them on the list for a ticket to the conference, compliments of the house.

When Healy learned during the conference for the first time what the group really stood for, he was flabbergasted. Some kind of state caps! China, these "theoreticians" maintained, is still *capitalist* although it is obviously a workers state, as all the facts show. What does that make the *Voix Ouvrière* group but state capitalist? Their position on China, in truth, sounded almost indistinguishable from Healy's own position on Cuba. Instead of being the fox, as he had thought, he was in the position of the goose. There were no if's, and's or but's about it; he had to get out of the trap ... fast! With the energy typical of the man, he went to work at once; and, of course, succeeded beautifully. As he himself testifies, that was the plan from the beginning ...

What did the wily politicians of *Voix Ouvrière* see in the conference? Probably a heterogeneous, amusingly ignorant, thoroughly unconscious grouping of British Insulars, American colonials and French syndicalists who stood at the beginning of a familiar enough road, one they themselves had traveled since they split from the Fourth International a quarter of a century ago. Now given an opportunity through a lucky break to play the role of teachers and mentors to a contingent already far enough advanced to be considered fellow travelers, they were only doing their duty in bringing consciousness into the common deliberations. Besides, in the way of immediate practical dividends, they stood a good chance of chipping off something, particularly from Lambert's group.

On the political and theoretical level, the *Voix Ouvrière* delegation was not far wrong in their estimate of the conference. All these groups do stand at different milestones along the same road.

By taking the position that the state in Cuba today is capitalist in character, Healy, for instance, places in question the Trotskyist position that China, North Vietnam, North Korea, Yugoslavia and the other countries in Eastern Europe have overthrown capitalism and established workers states. He does this by virtue of the fact that in all these cases the same basic criteria apply as in Cuba. Healy was challenged on this during the internal discussion in the SWP on the subject; as yet he has not bothered to respond. Probably it is beyond his depth. Nevertheless, the view that all these countries are state capitalist is the logical conclusion to Healy's position on Cuba. Or rather it is a logical stage in the possible evolution of Healy's state capitalist position on Cuba, for by the same reasoning, the Soviet Union is state capitalist and it can even be questioned that it was anything but state capitalist in the time of Lenin and Trotsky.

Such a view is erroneous, of course, so glaringly erroneous that even Healy draws back when a group like *Voix Ouvrière* congratulates him on his progress and beckons him to proceed further.

Last December, while Healy was getting out the publicity for his coming circus, the Fourth International held the Second Congress since Reunification (the eighth since the movement was founded by Leon Trotsky in 1938). There was no attempt at describing it as more than it was, or pulling any bluffs.

Differences of opinion on some points were freely expressed at the congress. This was expected and, in fact, was welcomed as an indication of the democracy and free atmosphere reigning in the internal life of the movement.

It was a serious gathering of delegates and observers from well-established sections and parties in a number of countries. Their main objective was to consolidate the reunification, bring the main political analyses of the movement up to date, and open a new stage of expansion for the world Trotskyist movement.

These aims were accomplished and a period of healthy growth can be expected on the basis of the very solid gains made since the reunification of the movement in 1963. The periodic funeral orations pronounced by its enemies have not succeeded in convincing the Fourth International that it is dead. It is very much alive and its prospects are excellent.

Since the documents included in this pamphlet all emanate from groupings that maintain that the Fourth International is either dead, bankrupt or sadly in need of reconstruction—due, as they explain it, to the influence of Pablo—it is not without interest that they have a significant new recruit to the gloomy view that the International founded by Trotsky must be buried or rebuilt from the ground up. The new recruit is Pablo himself. Pablo split after the Reunification Congress as a result of deepening political differences. He finally came to the conclusion that under its present leadership the Fourth International is finished and he gave up his option under the rules of democratic centralism of trying to win over a majority of the membership to his views.

Will the crepehangers welcome this distinguished newcomer to their ranks? They seem embarrassed. But Pablo's voice, it must be admitted, does blend in rather harmoniously with Healy's. Perhaps Healy should consider the question more closely.

Is it possible that Healy would seek a bloc with Pablo against the Fourth International? I would not venture to reply in the affirmative. On the other hand, Georges Kaldy of *Voix Ouvrière*, after the recent first-hand experience with Healy at the most impressive conference of its kind since 1938, deserves to be listened to attentively. His judgment of Healy and his circle is that "even in denouncing Pabloism, they could not rid themselves of the Pabloist methods of analysis." With "Pabloism" that deeply ingrained in your system, nothing is ruled out, is it?

186a Clapham High Street,
London, S.W.4, England
16th March, 1966

VERY URGENT
AWAITING YOUR REPLY IMMEDIATELY

Jim Robertson
Dear Comrade,

I have heard this afternoon from one of our Central Committee members who has seen Cde. Tishman, that you may not be attending the International Conference which is being held from April 4th–8th.

This will indeed be a big setback to the Conference since we want you as well as representatives of the Wohlforth group to be here. Cde. Tishman cannot under any circumstances be regarded as a representative of yours at this conference. He has no real knowledge of the present situation in the United States and he was not present at the Montreal discussions.

I am therefore asking you urgently to attend

this Conference of the international movement, otherwise there cannot be in my opinion any real settlement of the problems in the United States.

Enclosed is a copy of a letter I have sent to Cde. Wohlforth.

GH/JS
(Copy to Wohlforth)

Yours fraternally,
/s/ G. Healy
National Secretary

186a Clapham High Street,
London, S.W.4, England
16th March, 1966

VERY URGENT
AWAITING YOUR REPLY

Tim Wohlforth
Dear Comrade,

I am enclosing a copy of a letter I am sending to Cde. Robertson. It seems to me absolutely impermissible that neither you nor he should attend the International Conference.

Please understand that you cannot manoeuvre with the international movement. No matter what your difficulties are with your work in the United States, you and he must attend. I will personally take the floor at the conference and oppose both your absences.

Yours fraternally,
G. HEALY
National Secretary

GH/JS
(Copy to Robertson)

—FLASH—

New York
9 April 1966

TO ALL LOCALS, ORGANIZING COMMITTEES, AND MEMBERS AT LARGE:

Word has arrived by phone from our delegation that the SLL and the IC *have broken off unity with Spartacist*! The break came in the form of a full, savage attack on the Spartacist by the SLL that totaled 18 hours. The attack was artificially precipitated by a super-inflated incident. Our delegation arrived late at one of the sessions. Upon arrival they were confronted with an attack from the floor by Healy and the SLL leadership characterizing their absence as an example of "American arrogance and chauvinism" and "petty-bourgeois indiscipline." We were denounced at one point or another as "Pabloites", anti-democratic centralists, being in a bloc with the SWP, etc., etc. These attacks will continue in the pages of the *Newsletter*. The ACFI delegation participated *fully* in the assault. Fred Mazelis did a better job than Slaughter (leading SLL'er) in denouncing us and explaining why we had to be broken or driven from the movement. After the ridiculous incident—coming late to a session without informing the chairman when no prior mention of such a "special rule" had been made—had been so grotesquely inflated, a verbal apology to the IC Conference for our "petty-bourgeois indiscipline" was demanded of Comrades Robertson and our delegation. We of course refused and in a prepared statement stated that this was a violation of Leninist practice and represented singling out of the Spartacist for special "treatment", using fear and intimidation as substitutes for international discipline based on political consciousness, and that to apologize would be to vote for false charges. After attacks and denunciations (with other IC delegates beaten into line by the SLL), we were expelled from the Conference. It was clear that, whatever incident was utilized, the attack on us had been planned before-hand. Michael Banda, editor of *Newsletter*, stated that they had decided to declare war on the "Americans" and the French "Voix Ouvriere" group. The VO group was also driven from the Conference after being similarly attacked.

Remarks made by Healy, as well as examination of previous experience with Healy (1962 and the Northern Conference) indicate that this was an attempt to blackjack us into "submission", figuring that the process of unity had gone too far for us to pull back and that we would have to submit.

There are preliminary indications that a number of the members of ACFI are determined to consummate unity no matter what. We are not hostile to the *members* of ACFI, and remain in *political* solidarity with the International Committee. Whoever rejects this move by the SLL and wishes to solidarize himself with the Spartacist will be welcomed.

[ALL PUBLIC SALES OF THE *NEWSLETTER* AND THE ACFI *BULLETIN* WILL BE DISCONTINUED IMMEDIATELY].

Until further notice this information must be kept *inside our organization*. We will have detailed information upon the arrival of our delegation on Monday.

We must stand firm in the face of this unprincipled attack. Nothing must get in the way of building a revolutionary movement here as part of the rebuilding of the Fourth International. Attempts may be made to "raid" our membership. Any communications or contact from ACFI or IC members should be reported immediately to the REB. A full report of the Conference and the break by the SLL will be mimeographed and sent out as soon as information is received or our delegation returns.

Granite Hardness!!
A. Nelson, National Office

London, 9 April 1966
To the Bay Area Spartacist Committee:
Dear Comrades,

I am sending this letter to you as a member of the Bay Area Spartacist Committee who was also a member of the delegation to the IC conference. As you know, we have been kicked out of the conference on the contrived groups [grounds?] of a breach of democratic centralism.

The immediate circumstances:

Many delegates and observers had been absent from parts of one or another session. Jim, who had been sick for 3 weeks and had spent the night working on a document, and had made a presentation of the Spartacist's views in the morning, went over to take a nap in the afternoon. He mentioned to Comrade Healy that he was going. The next thing we knew, there was an announcement from the chairman that Jim had "requested" to be absent from this session. Then the bull hit the fan. The SLL was very angry because it seems that Comrade Mike Banda had prepared an answer to our views on Cuba. The rest of the delegation might have made it clearer that these views were not a personal contribution but from the Spartacist, and that the delegation had caucused over these points, although I did speak to explain why the charges of black nationalism which were leveled against us were unfounded and ludicrous. There was no basis for singling out Jim from among those who had missed parts of sessions. We were sharply aware of our junior status at the conference and felt that our contribution to the discussion would evoke little response.

All this is beside the point, for the incident was then used by Comrade Healy to open a vitriolic attack against the Spartacist organization. Healy said that Jim's absence from the session, and refusal to state that this absence was a petty-bourgeois act, was deemed an act of contempt—a petty-bourgeois, reactionary act expressing the chauvinism of American Imperialism, etc. Gerry kept saying that he's dealt with arrogant Americans before, Cannon and Hansen, and if there is one thing the Americans have to learn it is to take orders.

It became clear to us at this point that the SLL was using this to attack and exclude the Spartacist from the conference (as Mike Banda said the next day—"we decided to make war on you"!). In hindsight, it was probably a mistake for Jim not to have attended that session, or to have done or said anything which could be misinterpreted, for that matter.

But I'm very saddened and fearful of the kind of mistake which leads the SLL to an almost Stalinist version of democratic-centralism. This concept of obeying the majority will to the extent of declaring oneself a petty-bourgeois expression of American chauvinism is quite dangerous and is part of the "methods" of fake Bolshevik discipline such as that practiced by the SWP to avoid political struggle with factions.

At the conference, there were signs of weakness on the obedience question. The fight they pick with us will enable them to rally their forces around for a while, but their capacity to maintain this kind of obedience won't last. In other words, they're in for some problems.

A very sad effect is that this lets the SWP with their rotten politics and organizational methods off the hook for a time. The SLL, like the SWP, has raised a similar type of "Bolshevik discipline" to a basic political principle, a methodological concept which supposedly differentiates working-class organizations from petty-bourgeois organizations.

So, I guess, in addition to turning outward to educate people on Trotskyism, we will be dealing with a lot of attacks from the SLL and Wohlforth. So, shortly you will be getting the reports and documents from the conference.

We are very much in agreement with the basic principles of the IC. The strongest and best worked out point is on the crisis of leadership, though with the sectarian leadership of the SLL, this necessity of revolutionary leadership has been distorted in three areas: 1) the colonial revolutions, 2) the serious defeats, such as Indonesia, which are seen merely as a reflection of an increasing crisis of capitalism and the bureaucracy, rather than setbacks for the working class in addition, and 3) the inability to assimilate other groups, such as *Voix Ouvrière* and ourselves, which should be a part of the IC.

Well, on to a study of the French IC and the *Voix Ouvrière* groups. I find myself quite curious about them and the rest of the continent. My address in Paris will be in care of the Thomas Cook Travel Agency, 2 Place de la Madeline (mark "Passenger's Mail").

With warm and comradely greetings,
Rose J.

P.S. We have gotten some news from some of the other observers at the conference about what went on after we left. ACFI was the brunt of some attacks, evidently aimed at making clear once again just who is boss. Also a motion was proposed by Lambert, head of the French IC section, and adopted as part of the work of the Commission on rebuilding the F.I. It reads:

> We agree to democratic centralism and intervention in principle, but at present it is impossible. The only method of arriving at decisions that remains possible at present is the principle of unanimity.

This contradicts the excuses which were used to get rid of both the *Voix Ouvrière* group and the Spartacist, since 1) the attack on *Voix Ouvrière* was based on the assertion that the F.I. as an organization has not been destroyed (how can this be squared with the "impossibility" of democratic centralism?) 2) the demand for an apology was justified as the necessity for Spartacist to abide by the majority will through democratic centralism. The observers, from the Ceylonese LSSP(R) and the Danish Trotskyist party, previously sympathetic to the IC, were repelled by Healy and the SLL. They no longer believe that the IC under the leadership of the SLL can rebuild the Fourth International.

London
15th April, 1966.

To: Cde. H. Turner and Cde. Sherwood
Dear Comrades,

We concluded the Third Congress of the International Committee of the Fourth International a week ago.

There were present at this Congress delegates from Japan, Greece, France, Hungary and Britain. Those from the Congo and Nigeria were unable to obtain the necessary papers on time. There were observers from Denmark, Germany, Iraqui students in Great Britain, the French youth section Revolt, Young Socialists in Britain, Ceylon, the *Voix Ouvrière* in France, the American Committee for the F.I. and the Spartacist group from the United States.

The main political resolution and report before the Conference was adopted with only one vote against (Japan), his difference being that he and his group considered China state capitalist.

The main political struggle at the Congress consisted in an attempt by the *Voix Ouvrière* group and supported to some extent by the Hungarian delegate, to declare that the Fourth International had in fact collapsed and would have to be reorganised completely.

Considerable discussion took place on this point which in the opinion of the Congress was an attempt to play down the historical and theoretical struggle of the F.I. and in this way to open up the gates for an anti-theory tendency, especially represented by the syndicalist *Voix Ouvrière*. This trend was decisively repudiated.

As a result, the Congress in a very powerful way vindicated the fight of Trotsky in relation to Marxist theory and opened up the way to reconstitute the Fourth International on a very solid political foundation.

A discussion revealed the connection between the theoretical struggle of the F.I. and party building today. It was in my opinion the most important congress of our movement since the founding congress in 1938.

From the beginning of the Congress it was clear that the Robertson delegation were not at home in a Congress of this description. The English comrades made them as comfortable as possible and treated them with every courtesy due to visiting members from another country. It was clear, however, from the start that the relations within the delegation resembled that of a clique. We had the impression that insofar as Robertson said things that were correct he was in fact attempting to hide his real political opinions.

Things came to a head on the third day of the Congress when he made a report on the United States. He especially disagreed with the main line of the report made on behalf of the I.C. by Cde. Slaughter. He claimed that their role in the United States could only be that of a propaganda group, and in his speech implicitly adopted the Posadas attitude on Cuba, as a deformed workers' state. Immediately after his report Conference broke for lunch and at the end of the meal, he asked me if it would be all right to leave the meeting to go to bed since he was working all night on a document. It should be understood here that Robertson had had at least four months to prepare this document prior to the Congress which he had not done. Instead he brought the anti-Trotskyist Mage into one meeting of the Negotiating Committee which this renegade effectively broke up. I told him that I would convey his request to the appropriate comrades controlling the congress and when the session resumed it was unanimously decided that he be requested to return to the Congress in order to hear the debate on his report. He refused to do this.

A number of delegates, including M. Banda, sharply criticised his report while his delegation remained silent. As soon as he returned to the evening session where the final summing up was to be made by Cde. Slaughter, he was asked to apologise to the Congress for not having attended the session. He refused to do this on the grounds that he did not know the rules. It was pointed out that these rules were implicit in all Bolshevik Congresses, otherwise everyone would do as he pleased. He refused to apologise and the Congress unanimously, including the observers from the *Voix Ouvrière*, decided that he should leave. At this point I proposed a motion that he should stay until the end of the session, thus giving him time to reconsider his position. This was approved with the *Voix Ouvrière* abstaining.

At the end of this session, Robertson while voting for the main amended resolution, abstained on the report of Cde. Slaughter on the grounds that he disagreed with the position in the United States. In relation to the theoretical continuity of the Fourth International he voted for the midway position of Cde. Varga who at this point had proposed an amendment which was unanimously rejected, apart from the vote of the Hungarian delegation. Varga subsequently rejected Robertson's support as unprincipled.

Robertson was then asked if he would carry out the unanimous request of the Congress and apologise for his attitude towards the Congress. He refused to do this and was accordingly asked to leave, with the proviso that the remainder of his delegation could remain and participate in the Congress. The content of Robertson's statement was to the effect that Congress had no right to ask him to do something he did not want to do and this was not a Leninist conception. I need not stress to you comrades the thoroughly reactionary attitude shown in this statement. It confirmed the opinion formed by all the leading comrades in the Congress of the idealist, pragmatic, petty-bourgeois basis of the Spartacist group. The Greek delegate, a comrade 76 years old who had been in the Trotskyist movement since its foundation asked Robertson to apologise and the latter laughed in his face. The decision to remove Robertson was unanimous, delegates and observers alike.

Prior to this episode, the *Voix Ouvrière* group had submitted a statement that if we did not recognise that Trotsky's Fourth International was completely finished and needed to be rebuilt then they could not stay at the Congress. An appeal to them was made to stay and fight for their position but regardless of this they walked out of the Congress. When Robertson was asked as to his attitude to the *Voix Ouvrière* group behaviour, he declared that he thought they were good comrades but misguided. He retained his greatest venom and hatred for the congress itself, which he said had driven them out. In the debate preceding Robertson being asked to leave, many comrades dealt with this unprincipled amalgam and thoroughly exposed the real political face of Robertson. It must be stressed to all who are interested that the Congress was completely unanimous on the Robertson question. There have been far too many experiences of the role of cults and cliques in the Trotskyist movement, from Field in the early 30's to Abern, Johnson and Haston in England. The essential basis of these combinations has always been anti-centralist.

Robertson would have liked a charter for a unified section in the United States with which he could do as he pleased, while strictly excluding the politics of the International except those aspects with which he had particular agreement. To have effected a unification on this basis would have been disastrous and would have strengthened the anti-internationalist trend of the S.W.P.

Some comrades might ask if our Montreal meeting served a useful purpose. We are confident that it did. We knew from the beginning the anti-internationalist attitude of this man and his tendency when they split from the Wohlforth group, but it was necessary to clarify before the entire international movement their real political positions. That is why we postponed the actual unification until after the International Congress. We had to bring him to the Congress the same as *Voix Ouvrière* in order to reveal the nature of these tendencies.

Some comrades might believe that our movement has taken a step back because there will be no unification. This is an entirely superficial activist conception of building the revolutionary party in the United States. Our movement in the United States has been considerably strengthened in a qualitative way. We can now proceed to draw the real lines of political differences between ourselves and Robertson. This group may for a while exist on the basis of renewed hostile activity towards the International Committee. In this, of course, it will find many supporters amongst the American radical petty bourgeois. But it cannot last because it has no political future. We think that the basis for the building of the movement in the United States must be on correct internationalist Trotskyist foundations. That is why we hope you will understand what took place at the Congress. If you have any points which you wish to write to me about I will be very pleased to answer them.

Yours fraternally,
G. Healy

New York, New York
April 30, 1966

Dear Comrade Healy,

Cde. Sherwood and I wish to acknowledge the receipt of your letter of April 15, 1966 in which you present an account of events at the London conference of the International Committee of the Fourth International. We, for our part, wish to acquaint you with our own approach and that of the Spartacist comrades prior to the conference as well as our reaction to the proceedings.

Spartacist recognizes its historic responsibility for the development of a working-class vanguard in the stronghold of world capitalism and the significance of this vanguard for mankind's future. Our members consequently hailed the unity agreement between Spartacist and the American Committee for the Fourth International arrived at in Montreal as an important step in the process of building this revolutionary vanguard and wholeheartedly welcomes the prospect of the reestablishment of an international of revolutionary Marxism.

Meaningful unity, in practical activity and in the progressive elimination of political differences between Spartacist and ACFI, seemed to be developing—toward the SWP, on the Negro Question, and on economic perspectives in the United States. We therefore saw excellent prospects ahead for the rapid growth and influence of the Spartacist

League-to-be. Similarly, we foresaw a reconstructed F.I. gaining in numbers and influence on a world scale, particularly now that the ideological shipwreck of the Pabloist revisionists following events in Algeria, Indonesia, Cuba, and Africa.

The possibility that Cde. Robertson would be expelled or that the *Voix Ouvrière* group would withdraw from the conference was never entertained by any of our members. Extraordinary attention was therefore paid by the New York local membership to the full account of the positions and actions of our delegates and to the conference proceedings presented to them two days before the receipt of your letter. Your account of the conference serves to reenforce the report by Cde. Robertson and makes very clear that the Socialist Labour League leadership which organized and directed the conference, and you in particular, chose to focus on and magnify either secondary theoretical differences or minor procedural disagreements in the spirit of Stalinist monolithism and not in a manner consistent with Trotskyist principle and organizational practice.

Thus, the SLL leadership insisted on the V.O. group giving up the erroneous conception held since 1943 that the F.I. had been both organizationally and politically destroyed, refused to accept Cde. Varga's amendment that the world movement had managed to maintain political continuity, and treated the Spartacist delegation's support to Cde. Varga's amendment as a monstrous deviation. You fulminate about an "unprincipled amalgam". Yet our document, "Toward Rebirth of the Fourth International" written in 1963 and reprinted in our first edition of SPARTACIST in February–March 1964 states that the manifestation of the ". . . theoretical, political, and organizational crisis" of Trotskyism ". . . has been the disappearance of the Fourth International as a meaningful structure.", that "The struggle for the Fourth International is the struggle for a program embodying the working-class revolutionary perspective of Marxism.", and that "The Trotskyists, lineal continuers of the earlier stage, have an indispensable contribution to make to this struggle [the overthrow of the Soviet bureaucracy]: the concept of the international party and of a transitional program required to carry through the political revolution." As can be seen, Spartacist held a position identical with Cde. Varga's amendment for approximately three years. Moreover, you were thoroughly acquainted with this position, or should have been. Had Cde. Varga not presented his amendment to the conference, it would have been completely correct for our delegation to have done so.

You similarly attacked Cde. Robertson's report for reaffirming Spartacist's position on Cuba as a deformed workers' state—a position also held by us for at least three years. You did this despite the existence of complete programmatic agreement between the SLL, ACFI, and Spartacist on this question, e.g., overthrow of the Bonapartist bureaucracy, establishing of workers' power, unconditional defense of the Cuban Revolution, etc. Your letter seems to indicate that our Cuba position came as a surprise to you. Yet our documents, both internal and external, e.g., SPARTACIST Nos. 2 and 3, have been made available to you over the years. Furthermore, you personally engaged in extended debate on just this question with Spartacist comrades in Montreal last winter. You must also have been aware that Spartacist was prepared to subordinate this position, as a democratic centralist organization, to that of the world movement after full discussion and binding vote.

Again you attack Cde. Robertson in your letter for stating that Spartacist sees the immediate tasks of revolutionary Marxists in the U.S. to be the building of a viable propagandist organization. You must be aware that Robertson meant by this what Lenin meant when he wrote of the work of the propagandist who "counts in thousands" and who must "still concentrate on winning the proletariat's vanguard" (*Left-wing Communism*). You must certainly be acquainted with Spartacist's record of involvement in trade-union, anti-war, and Negro rights struggles, and therefore have known that Robertson was not proposing a literary orientation for the movement in the U.S., but merely pointing out that our activity at this time can only have an exemplary quality and cannot pose the question of leading the class.

Your account of the conference is both malicious and dishonest. Thus you do not indicate that Robertson had, in effect, apologized to the conference for missing a session in a written statement which pointed out that he had not been aware of the European rules of procedure and that no discourtesy to the conference had been intended. Neither do you indicate that the apology you had demanded would have been a demeaning and false confession to a petit-bourgeois outlook, American chauvinism, and capitulation to Black Nationalism.

Your statement that from the start ". . . relations within the delegation resembled that of a clique" and that Robertson initially tried to "hide his real political opinions" is contrary to all that is known about Cde. Robertson and the actual relations obtaining within Spartacist. It is because Robertson and the members of our tendency are not trimmers and would not call a centrist swamp a revolutionary organization that a split in the Revolutionary Tendency was engineered by Wohlforth and Muller with your help in 1962. It was precisely the refusal by Robertson and other members of our tendency to hide their real political opinions that enabled Wohlforth and Muller to conspire with the SWP majority to have our tendency expelled. It is just because Robertson and the members of Spartacist do not conceal their views that their positions have been completely consistent and have stood the test of time from 1962 until today—on the Negro, the Russian (China, Cuba) and the American Questions. Compare this record with Wohlforth's gyrations!

As for Cde. Robertson and relations within Spartacist, Robertson owes his position of leadership in our organization to his knowledge of Marxism, his devotion to the revolutionary movement, and to the quality of his leadership. Robertson, more than any other leader of our organization, is responsible for the fact that Spartacist has attempted to function as a model Bolshevik organization. Thus, Spartacist is democratic centralist in character with minorities having the right to publish and express their views within the organization and to representation on higher bodies. The minutes of our local and central committee meetings will show both the dynamic interaction of ideas and the unity in action of a revolutionary Marxist organization.

Your characterization of Shane Mage as an anti-Trotskyist renegade who broke up a session of the negotiations of the Joint Unity Committee after being "brought" into it by Robertson is also spiteful and untrue. Mage has recently and publicly revealed political differences with Spartacist which, in our opinion, effectively removes him from the ranks of revolutionary Marxists. However, he is neither anti-Trotskyist nor a renegade. Mage was a central committee member at that time and, therefore, had every right to attend a session of the JUC. He was "brought" into the session because of his considerable background in economics and before his differences with Spartacist had emerged. It was not Mage who broke up the meeting but Wohlforth! Wohlforth deliberately aborted the perspectives discussion by failing to respond to criticisms raised by Mage and other Spartacist representatives. Your purpose in interjecting Mage's name into your report is clearly an attempt to identify Spartacist's politics with Mage's present outlook. An old trick, Cde. Healy! On this basis, the SLL could be smeared with the present politics of Ken Coates, Peter Fryer, or Brian Behan.

Several other questionable points require answers which were raised either by your letter or at the conference.

You indicate that "implicit" rules of procedure "in all Bolshevik Congresses" prevent a member of a delegation from absenting himself without prior permission from the Congress. Can you cite any written precedent in any previous Bolshevik Congress for this rule?

Do the minutes of the third day of the Congress indicate that *Voix Ouvrière* voted with the Congress to expel Robertson? Did anyone from the V.O. group or observers from other groups witness the incident you recount in which Robertson was supposed to have laughed in the face of the 76 year old Greek delegate who asked him to apologize? I must inform you that a copy of your letter is being sent to the V.O. group and to other delegates for their answers to the above questions.

You state in your letter that you brought the Spartacist delegation to the London conference (at great expenditure of their money and time) only to expose "before the entire international movement their real positions." How can we reconcile this statement with your expressed views in Montreal last winter about the necessity and desirability of unity based upon our agreement with the I.C. perspectives resolution and our agreement with other fundamental documents of Trotskyism, e.g., the transitional program, and the principles embodied in the decisions of the first four congresses of the Communist International? When were you being dishonest, then or now?

Much was made at the conference of Robertson's

supposed American chauvinism. Why does your letter not say a word about this?

A final question, assuming for a moment that Cde. Robertson is the individual you say he is, when in the history of revolutionary Marxism has the personality and attitudes of an individual rather than the politics and program of a movement been the basis for a decision on unity? Can you offer a single precedent?

You indicate that Spartacist "may for a while exist on the basis of renewed hostile activity toward the International Committee." This concept is also completely erroneous. We have never initiated hostile activity toward the I.C. and do not contemplate it now. We intend to maintain a correct attitude toward the I.C. indicating that we share with them the same spectrum of political views. We consider ourselves to be a part of international revolutionary Marxism. We will defend ourselves from public attack, but it is not our desire to advertise the unprincipled attacks on Cde. Robertson and Spartacist by the SLL leadership. We will, of course, reserve the right to disagree publicly with the SLL when we do so in principle.

We cannot help feeling bitter about the temporary setback to the world movement and to our prospects in the U.S. We hold the SLL leadership responsible for this and for the resultant aid and comfort given to the SWP and to Pabloist revisionists internationally. You have also given delight to Stalinists of all varieties who have for years attacked Trotskyists as unprincipled splitters.

The reason for the behavior of the SLL leadership toward the Spartacist delegation is not hard to find. You obviously wish to create a Trotskyist movement in the U.S. which would be completely subservient to the SLL leadership. Your attacks on Robertson were designed to make him knuckle under and adopt an attitude of humble worship for the omniscient British leadership. You were not interested in creating a movement united on the basis of democratic centralism with strong sections capable of making theoretical contributions to the movement as a whole and of applying Marxist theory creatively to their own national arenas. You wanted an international after the manner of Stalin's Comintern, permeated with servility at one pole and authoritarianism at the other. You are attempting to fashion an international modeled after the internal regime of the SLL and currently in vogue in your youth movement.

The question is why such a profoundly anti-Leninist organizational approach should exist. Your origin from a bureaucratically degenerated Communist movement and your carry-over of organizational practices obtaining there may be a factor as may traditional petit-bourgeoise British insularity acting to produce a caricature of internationalism. An adequate answer will have to be sought in the historical development of an SLL leadership molded under the pressures of social classes. "Any serious fight in the party is always in the final analysis a reflection of the class struggle," said Trotsky.

The bureaucratic practices of the SLL leadership would seem to relate to the theoretical incapacity shown by the followers of Trotsky after the second World War with the development of deformed workers' states in Eastern Europe and China. Under conditions of pronounced isolation of the world movement from the working class, the revisionists abandoned a working-class revolutionary perspective for an orientation toward petit-bourgeois formations such as Stalinist bureaucrats, social-democratic labor bureaucrats, and the nationalist leaderships of the colonial countries. The British Trotskyists while having correctly and necessarily attacked the revisionists for their capitulations, have similarly demonstrated an incapacity to creatively develop Marxism, as witness their current position on Cuba as a capitalist state. The British leaders seem to have responded to the "theoretical, political, and organizational crisis" of Trotskyism by retreating into "orthodoxy." Their reaction to revisionism seems to have been that of high priests entrusted with the protection of holy writ; thus the emergence of an iron-fisted, authoritarian leadership.

Bureaucratic centralism is also an abandonment of the working class in its own way. The bureaucratic centralism of the SLL, in separating the top leadership from the party ranks, acts to reinforce the isolation of the movement from the working class and from validation of the party's tactics and program. Certain sectarian and ultra-left approaches by the SLL in the recent past are explainable on this basis: for example your bragging that at the Morecambe Young Socialist conference, your youth tore up the leaflets of the Young Communist League distributors and "sent them packing." A contradiction has now developed between the organizational methods which were possible under conditions of deep isolation from the working class of a numerically weak movement and the present position and potential of the British workers under conditions whereby decaying British capitalism is attempting a solution to its problems on the backs of these same workers. The prospects for British Trotskyism are bright with the SLL currently the largest party of Trotskyism in the world and having a large base among British youth.

For these bright prospects to be realized, it is essential that the SLL abandon the organizational methods now prevalent under the regime of Healy and Banda. These methods will act as a brake on the future development of the movement and prevent the SLL from meeting its responsibility, now being placed on the historical agenda, to root itself in the working class and give it leadership.

The desire to manipulate and dictate to other national sections is a negation of internationalism. Unfortunately, some of our new, young cadres and potential recruits may take the bureaucratic behavior of the SLL leadership for good internationalist coin and thereby be drawn toward a narrow, ingrown nationalism. We shall do everything in our power to guard against such a development. We well know that the abandonment of internationalism leads to the political death of revolutionists. It is our hope that future developments will soon enable Trotskyists to unite to provide the international working class with the vanguard movement without which world capitalism, the enemy of mankind, cannot be vanquished.

This response to your letter was formulated by both Cde. Sherwood and myself. We would be pleased to receive your reaction to it.

Fraternally yours,
Harry Turner

Comments on the Letter of Comrade Healy to Comrades Turner and Sherwood on the Third Conference of the International Committee

Healy's discussion on the debate over the state of the Fourth International is rather unsatisfactory. As a matter of fact, the debate on that issue at the Conference itself was extremely confused, largely because of the vague and often incantatory way in which the I.C. delegates used the term "Fourth International". To pose the question, "Is the Fourth International dead or alive?" full-stop, is simply meaningless. On the one hand, the Fourth International can be regarded as simply the fundamental tenets of Trotskyism, which includes the idea that a world revolutionary party is a necessary prerequisite to successful socialist revolution. In this minimal sense, the Fourth International is synonymous with Trotskyism and is obviously very much alive. At the other end of the spectrum one can regard the Fourth International as a full-bodied international revolutionary party, whose ultimate validity will not be secure until it has led the working class to power on a world scale. In this sense, the Fourth International is not only dead, but has never existed. Between these two extremes, exists a wide spectrum of organizational forms, and programmatic and theoretical concepts, which can be considered as representing the Fourth International or not, depending upon how one uses that term.

However, it should be clearly stated that the discussion was not really about the definition of the term "Fourth International", or still less about the historical and theoretical continuity of the Trotskyist movement. That was simply a thin rationale to disguise the real issue, which was whether the present International Committee, in which the Socialist Labour League is far and away the most important national section, constitutes the *sole organized successor* to the Trotskyist movement. That this is the case was indicated by the S.L.L. delegates at the Conference and also in Healy's present letter, particularly the section discussing the relationship between "Robertson's group" and "the International". In fact, the whole business was a crude semantic ploy to identify the S.L.L. leadership with the Fourth International and the Fourth International with Trotskyism, so that any criticism of the leadership of the S.L.L. would appear to be a criticism of Trotskyism.

The assertion in paragraph No. 5, that *Voix Ouvrière*'s opposition to the amendment was based on their "anti-theory" position (another meaningless phrase—evaluation and organization of thought is a necessary part of the cognitive process) is incorrect. V.O.'s position that the Fourth International is dead seems to stem from a well-documented historical interpretation of the Trotskyist movement, the substance of which is that the main organs of the F.I. have been Pabloite since 1940. One may accept or reject this interpretation, but it does not reflect "anti-theory syndicalism".

Comrade Healy's astute observations of our delegation's behavior at the Conference are not worth commenting upon.

On paragraph No. 10—Comrade Robertson did not "implicitly adopt a deformed workers' state position on Cuba", he explicitly stated it, although his analysis was quite different from that of Posadas.

On paragraph No. 11—The statement that the Spartacist delegation remained silent during criticism of our positions, with the implication that we were unable to answer the trenchant criticisms of our position, is almost the exact opposite of the truth. A speakers' list had been prepared the previous day and no more Spartacists were listed. Comrade Jersawitz attempted to get on the list, was refused permission and finally was allowed permission to speak for five minutes, during which time she carefully explained that we were not supporters of Black Nationalism. This is a good example of the appositeness of Comrade Banda's criticism.

On paragraph No. 13—Comrade Robertson *did not* say "that the Conference had no right to ask him to do something he did not want to do". He said that neither the Conference, nor anyone else, for that matter, had the right to make him say something he didn't believe to be true—i.e., to apologize for something he did not think was wrong—although he said, had he known of this rule (a rule which apparently applied to no one else), he would have followed it.

The logical process by which Healy derived from this single statement the conclusion that it "confirmed" (?—and what is the other evidence?) . . . "the idealist, pragmatic, petit-bourgeois basis of the Spartacist group." (An organization of over 80 members and a three-year history), is beyond my meager understanding. It should be noted that the S.L.L. is a group which prides itself on its "anti-impressionism".

Paragraph No. 14, on V.O.'s leaving the Conference, is a pack of lies. V.O. did not leave the Conference because the Conference refused to accept their position on the state of the F.I. Nor did they submit any requests that the Conference do so. They left because during the discussion on the subject numerous personal attacks were made upon them; they were called petit-bourgeois enemies of Trotskyism. At one point, Healy claimed that if he had known their real position, he never would have invited them to the Conference. Their criticisms of the main resolution were published a month before the Conference. At this point, it should be emphasized that the statement saying "the Fourth International was dead and had to be rebuilt" was a statement in the main I.C. resolution, the basic document of the Conference and the one on which groups were invited to the Conference and agreed to come. The controversy arose when the I.C. leadership attempted to amend their *own* major document, with an amendment which said, in effect, "the Fourth International is alive, and We're it".

Paragraph No. 15 dealing with the Spartacist and supposed political differences with the I.C. is interesting. Unless one regards "the International" as a kind of sacred document, which one accepts or rejects *en toto*, differences between the Spartacist and the majority of the I.C. have nothing to do with the Spartacist's "internationalism", but simply represent differences between two political organizations, which should be resolved by the usual democratic processes, designated for that purpose. It is strange that methods of settling political differences within I.C. or the organization of the I.C. in general was one topic not discussed at the Conference. It is even stranger when one considers that, had the unity taken place, the Spartacist and its present leadership would have constituted the majority faction of the second or third largest national section of the I.C., which now has six national sections, three of them very small indeed. To be fair to Healy on this point, it should be noted that he never intended to go through with the unity agreement anyway, so possibly he regarded it as an unimportant point.

Paragraph No. 16 speaks all too eloquently for itself.

Paragraph. No. 13 again, Comrade Robertson did not laugh in the face of Comrade Raktos.

In closing, I would again like to remind the comrades that Comrade Healy is a liar.

received
7 May 1966

Mark Tishman
Alternate Delegate
Spartacist League
to the 1966 International
Committee Conference

19 April 1966

Coordinating Committee,
American Committee for
the Fourth International

Dear Comrades,

Two weeks have passed since the spokesman for the Spartacist delegation was expelled from the London Conference. This action was taken upon the initiative of G. Healy of the British Socialist Labour League despite the exhibition by Spartacist of its clear-cut political solidarity with the International Committee even under conditions of extreme provocation. This exclusion of our organization, supported by your delegation, effectively disrupted the projected fusion of our two groups.

As a pre-condition for a responsible outcome to the present situation, we believe that the membership of our two organizations should have the opportunity to hear and compare conference reports by participants in the two delegations.

Therefore we ask for a joint New York membership meeting to be scheduled at the earliest convenient date to hear the delegates and discuss fully and freely the alternatives open before us now.

We also ask that a Spartacist delegate to the IC Conference speak to your Minneapolis local, either along with an ACFI reporter or separately as you wish. If this is acceptable we would readily grant the same privilege to your organization to speak before our San Francisco Bay Area group and in any case would seek to bring our entire East Coast membership into the NYC joint meeting where they could hear and discuss reports on the Conference and resulting situation facing us.

We make these proposals because we continue to believe firmly that a fusion in the U.S. of the principled Leninist type projected in the Montreal agreement remains a political responsibility for genuine Trotskyists.

Fraternally,
J. Robertson,
for the Spartacist National Office.

April 22, 1966

J. Robertson
Spartacist National Office
New York, N.Y.

Dear Comrade Robertson,

In reply to your letter of April 19 the Coordinating Committee of the American Committee for the Fourth International states as follows:

The American Committee for the Fourth International concurs completely with the actions of the International Committee on Spartacist. It is our opinion that your organization has broken politically in an unprincipled manner with the world Trotskyist movement. Since we maintain our political solidarity with the International Committee we view your organization as an opponent organization and must conduct ourselves accordingly. Unification between the two groups is out of the question.

Under such conditions a joint membership meeting along the lines of the one held prior to the IC conference is of course out of the question. Your proposal assumes a relationship between our two groups completely apart from solidarity with the International movement. However, if you wish to organize a formal debate to explain the positions of the two organizations before the memberships in New York this would be acceptable to us.

If we are able to work out debate arrangements in New York City it should be simple to organize similar debates elsewhere. The next issue of the Bulletin will explain our position more fully.

*Fraternally,
D. Freeman,
for the Coordinating Comm.,
American Comm. For the Fourth Int.*

2 May 1966

Coordinating Committee,
A.C.F.I.

Dear Comrades,

We are in receipt of your letter of 22 April responding to our request for joint membership meetings to hear and discuss the reports of our two delegations to the London Conference.

We regret your absurdly false accusation that we have "broken politically . . . with the world Trotskyist movement" and your willfully hostile self-characterization as an "opponent organization" to us.

Nonetheless we believe the complete and sudden somersault on reunification of our two groups and the resulting confusion makes it mandatory for us to seek whatever discussion and clarification we can. Therefore we are willing to settle for the formal debate between our groups which you make clear is the only form of oral discussion between us you would accept.

As regards the debate in New York City we propose that it be held on Saturday evening, the 21st of May. Because many of our comrades will drive long distances to attend, a Saturday evening meeting would maximize our participation and avoid compelling comrades to drive all night. We cannot propose an earlier date because the preceding Saturday will be the occasion for mass picketing of the student draft deferment tests and many of our comrades will be involved. And to set a later date would again cut deeply into the attendance of student comrades because of the scheduling of school final examinations.

In line with the usual practices for such events we propose holding the meeting in a neutral, rented hall with either an agreed, acceptable outside chairman or failing that two chairmen, one from each group, with one presiding over the first half and the other over the second half of the debate. We accept the standard arrangements for formal debates of this sort: that the speaking order be set by the toss of a coin; that floor discussion be held tightly to one round of three minutes each; and that summaries be reversed. We suggest that the speaking times be: presentations by each reporter—1½ hours each; summaries—½ hour each; that total speaking time for each reporter be held rigidly to within the set amount of time by the chairman, but that small shifts of time between presentation and summary be permitted if desired by the speaker.

We further propose that all other details be explicitly worked out in advance by consultation between our two NYC organizer.

We request that you inform us as soon as possible when it would be convenient for you to schedule a similar debate in the Twin Cities.

*Fraternally,
J. Robertson,
for the REB.*

May 5, 1966

James Robertson
Resident Editorial Board
Spartacist

Dear Comrades,

We are in receipt of your letter dated May 2nd on the matter of a debate between our two organizations over the Third World Congress of the International Committee of the Fourth International.

We are referring this letter, as we have our past correspondence, to the International Committee for its opinion.

As soon as we receive a reply from the IC, we will get in touch with you.

*Yours fraternally,
Daniel Freeman
for the Coordinating Committee,
American Committee
for the Fourth International*

After the April 1966 Conference which took as its task to Reconstruct the Fourth International

By Georges Kaldy

The following article has been translated from the May 2, 1966 *Voix Ouvrière*, semimonthly newspaper of a group in France that stands "For the construction of a Revolutionary Workers party." Subheadings appear in the original.

Today, as much as in the past, every individual revolutionary and every revolutionary organization feels the cruel lack of a revolutionary international which would be able to analyze the experience of the class struggle on a world scale and establish an organizational and political link between the revolutionary vanguards of the industrialized countries, the underdeveloped countries and the countries ruled by the bureaucracy.

The Fourth International founded by Leon Trotsky in 1938 has been the only international organization whose program was compatible with revolutionary activity, but it was never able to play a leading role in the class struggle. After the death of its founder, the Fourth International ended by foundering on the shoals of petty-bourgeois opportunism and gave birth to what is known today as Pabloism, which amounts to the abandonment of Marxism, both organizationally and politically.

There is no International today even in the formal sense. Four fragments of it survive, each claiming that it alone continues the Fourth International of Trotsky's time.

—The so-called official Fourth International led by Frank and Germain.

—The Latin-American Bureau of Posadas.

—The so-called "Marxist-Revolutionary" tendency of Pablo.

—And the International Committee.

Until recently, the latter, which bases itself on the 1952 split, was the only one of these groups which demonstrated an entirely relative modesty by not calling itself "The Fourth International." It was this group which recently called an International Conference with the aim of reconstructing the Fourth International. (We have dealt with this conference and our attitude toward it and the groups that called it on several occasions, in nos. 53, 55, 56 and 57 of our paper.)

Our participation

We decided to take part in this congress. First of all, we cannot stand aside from any attempt to recreate an international revolutionary organization. And secondly, because we found three positive elements in the draft document of the I.C. and in the attitude of the host organizations:

1. A sharp, definitive critique of Pabloism, of both its organizational and political principles.

2. MOST IMPORTANTLY—the Fourth International is DEAD and therefore it MUST BE RECONSTRUCTED IN ITS ENTIRETY and there can be no question of simple adherence to any of the existing shops, including that of the I. C., as the document recognized.

3. The I. C. appeared to disavow the antidemocratic organizational concepts of the Fourth International in the years 1943–52.

We proposed to participate on a CRITICAL basis and we made that clear in advance. For we had no political illusions about the organizations that make up the International Committee, either before or after the conference. Their past both in the Fourth International and after the split, has been an aggregate of monumental political mistakes, beginning with their nationalism during the war, and continuing with their analyses of Yugoslavia, of the Peoples Democracies, of China, and more recently of the MNA [Mouvement National Algérien].

Their document itself proved that even in denouncing Pabloism, they could not rid themselves of the Pabloist methods of analysis. We made all these criticisms prior to the conference. We said that the most serious fault in their document was that although they condemned Pabloism vigorously, they were unable to explain HOW and WHY it appeared and how to fight against the causes of such a phenomenon.

Nevertheless, we participated in the conference, because, even if its organizers were unable to analyse the causes of Pabloism, in breaking with Pabloism and in stating that the International no longer exists, the I. C. had laid the necessary foundations for such an analysis. From there a serious discussion on the causes of the failure of the Fourth International, and thus on the methods by which to reconstruct it, could be initiated.

In contrast to the other fragments who content themselves with a fictitious International (or Internationals), which exists only in their own minds, and to which they can give no reality, and with which they are perfectly content, one group originating in the International had the courage to half-open its eyes to the sad reality. To be sure, that was very little, all the more since they were men who, in the face of the enormity of the task, might well quickly close their eyes again and return to their ever so much more comforting and, above all, more convenient illusions.

It was very little but it was a chance that had to be taken.

Obvious lack of seriousness

Unfortunately, our expectations were confirmed during the conference, as our predictions in 1943 have been confirmed with the elapse of time.

We found ourselves confronted with organizations which were incapable of discussing the real problems, the methods and the tasks of the construction of a world revolutionary organization. We found people who made a pretense of analysis by playing with words. We were confronted with people who, instead of making an attempt to explain the reason for the failure of the International spent their time in congratulating themselves on the past, which, as one of them said, "gives us no cause to blush."

We certainly did not go there to make anyone blush and, certainly, we had no idea that we could do it. But, all things considered, if thirty years after its founding, the International does not exist otherwise than in the program left by Trotsky; if the balance sheet of the organizations that make up the Fourth International comes to nothing or almost nothing, after twenty years; if the Trotskyist organizations have never been able to compete for the leadership of the proletariat with the reformist and Stalinist machines, anywhere or at any time; isn't there some reason for it?

Did we go there to discuss, or to learn what would make each other blush?

We were confronted with people whose internationalism scarcely went beyond the limits of the conference hall. Not that declarations and speeches were lacking! But it would seem that a necessary, if not sufficient precondition for engaging in an international discussion with other groups would be a knowledge of their political positions.

But there were leading delegates there who meted out their advice and their thunderbolts, with an admirable self-sufficiency, to groups of which they knew nothing at all except that they existed!

Thus the major speaker for the principal host organization stated on the third day of the conference that he had learned with amazement about our position on China only that morning and by chance!

Let us leave aside the fact that it could amaze a Trotskyist to define as bourgeois a state which was established without the participation of the proletariat and in opposition to it. We must bless the happy chance that gave the comrade in question the opportunity to learn of our position on a vital question.

We might note, all the same, that there are many other ways besides happy chance through which an international leader can learn the position of a group which he proposes to advise, one of them being through reading their press!

Is this just an anecdote?

Yes, but it reveals the lack of seriousness with which they dealt with questions which were serious.

Reconstruct or rebuild?

In this conference where the length of the speeches could scarcely make up for the emptiness of the remarks, we were treated like troublemakers when we tried to initiate discussion on the real problems. Indeed, there was no discussion. Just like the International in 1943, its present day fragment refused discussion, and in a way which was quite characteristic.

If, in taking the floor, we did not convince the I.C., at least they got a better understanding of their own draft document. They came to understand what we hoped they had understood—namely; that stating that the Fourth International no longer exists carries with it the obligation to analyze the causes for its failure. They understood, in a word, that what they had written contained the kernel of our criticism and implied our analysis.

But we can only believe that they are incapable of making this analysis. In fact, in the very middle of the conference, rather than undertake this analysis, they chose to revise their own document! By means of an amendment added to a secondary phrase, they completely changed the spirit of their own draft resolution. Here is the original phrase:

> Petty-bourgeois opportunism, in the shape of a hardened revisionist tendency penetrating all sections of the Trotskyist movement, has destroyed the Fourth International as an organization founded on the Transitional Programme and now necessitates a complete break from the theoretical, political and organisational methods of the revisionists.

The amendment proposed to modify this sentence by beginning with:

> The Fourth International defended itself against and won a victory over petty-bourgeois opportunism which . . . etc.

While the original edition said that the International had been destroyed, according to the amendment the same International was not only very much alive but had won a victory!

We had to tell them that if this amendment was voted, the ENTIRE meaning of the document would be changed, including the conclusion where it says:

"The Fourth International founded by Leon Trotsky no longer exists," and including the title which speaks of the "reconstruction of the Fourth International."

It is true that one of the zealous supporters of the amendment, the editor of *La Verité*, realized that it was hardly logical to speak of the reconstruction of something that had never been destroyed. With a fine eye for delicate shades of meaning, he proposed to replace the word, "reconstruct," now considered to be inadequate, with the word, "rebuild" [rebâtir].

We were not the only ones to lose our way in these subtleties. The translator—no pun intended—also got lost. Although up to then he had translated the French word, "reconstruction," with the English word, "rebuilding," he now resolved the difficulty brilliantly by translating the word "rebâtir" [rebuild] with the Gallicism, "reconstruction."

At a congress which had been called originally to discuss the task of the RECONSTRUCTION of the International, we learned that this International had not been destroyed, and that thanks to the I.C. the continuity of the International had been safeguarded!

And what is more, before continuing, or more exactly, really beginning the discussion, it was demanded that we vote on a document according to which the Fourth International continues to exist and that it is none other than the International Committee. Naturally, we refused. And since our participation in the conference had lost its point, we left the hall.

It is easy to offer quotations where those who identified the Fourth International with the International Committee during the conference, developed a diametrically opposite idea.

The draft resolution itself from beginning to end dealt with the question of an International which had been "destroyed" or no longer existed, etc.

We will add some quotations from the preparatory documents of the French section:

The pamphlet published by *La Verité* on this subject (p. 4) referred to the destruction of the Fourth International "as a coherent political whole." In the French preparatory document, it is stated that "the development of the class struggle has confirmed the program of the Fourth International but it has DESTROYED the International."

Elsewhere, one reads:

"The I.C. is NOT the Fourth International . . . ," etc.

We could quote more abundantly; there is quite a choice. But we know that a few contradictions will not bother the I.C. No doubt, they will even find a way of claiming that there is no contradiction there and that the terms, the destroyed International and the living International, which is identified with the I.C., mean the same thing. No doubt, they will add also that anyone who doesn't understand this understands nothing about dialectics!

We will be delighted to read in the next number of *La Verité* how these comrades explain the positions they took in the I.C., in view of what they wrote in the two previous issues of *La Verité*.

Unless they think (as is their habit) that their readers deserve no explanation for the change in their political attitude.

Lenin said that you can't trap an opportunist with quotations. And we don't want to trap the I.C. in this way.

We know the organizations of the I.C. too well to be surprised at the ease with which they tear up the evening's documents the following morning.

Nonetheless, it must be said that they made a choice when they voted for the amendment. The former draft resolution contained an ambiguity which our remarks brought into the open.

The Pabloist continuity

Anyone who says that the International has been destroyed must analyze the causes of its destruction; this, however, would force the I.C. to submit its own past to a severe and painful criticism. The I.C. has chosen the second path. Since it is incapable of analyzing the reason for this failure, it ended by denying that there was a failure.

The decision made by the I.C. is more than erroneous. It proves in reality the inability of the organizations which compose it to analyze and criticize the political and organizational methods which were at the origin of Pabloism and consequently their inability to break with it. It proves that the causes that engendered Pabloism in the majority of the International mortally infected the minority which broke, formally, with Pabloism.

We will not make a point of our numerical size with respect to the *La Verité* group, but it is certainly this incapacity of theirs which causes them to vegetate and to fail to develop, whereas in 1945 they had an organization that was able to get some tens of thousands of votes in the elections.

The decision made by the I.C. also proves that this organization, like the other fragments of the International contents itself in reality with illusions and grandiloquent phrases, and that it refuses even to discuss with those willing to seriously take up the task at hand.

The incapacity of the I.C.

We left the conference with no regrets. But in leaving it, we did not break with the organizations in the International Committee. We break definitively with no one.

On the contrary, we will show these comrades that if they follow the same path they followed during and after the war, if they use the same methods, if they hold to the same attitudes, if they pursue the same policies; they will give up any chance of participating in building a real International which would play a leading role in the class struggle.

They would have their international conferences, perhaps. Their so-called "International," so quickly reconstructed in two days, would doubtless grow from conference to conference, at least in words; in the same way that this meeting called to construct the International was transformed on the second day into the third conference of the International Committee.

And since reality will not yield to their desires, they will brush reality aside.

During our stay, we read an article in a recent issue of the *Newsletter*, the weekly paper of the English section of the I.C., devoted to the student strike against the Fouchet reform.

We read the following report: "Led by Trotskyists, 70 percent of the 23,000 students (from the Faculty of Law) went on strike on Wednesday [Thursday?], March 17." There was something to pick up the morale of the English comrades. It is too bad that these 16,000 law students led by the Trotskyists exist only in the pages of the *Newsletter*, and not in the Faculty of Law in Paris!

Doubtless, they think that by brushing reality aside this will make their International stronger every day. But a revolutionary organization cannot be built on bluff. And you can't build it with people who are satisfied with bluff.

It is not sufficient to proclaim yourself to be an heir of Trotsky to immediately achieve the stature of a great revolutionary.

Before any group proclaims itself to be an International in the tradition of Lenin and Trotsky, it must prove that it has the right to do that and prove it politically. If Trotsky's writings educated an entire generation of militants, the same cannot be said for the stack of theses, documents, resolutions, proclamations and speeches published since 1945 by the organizations that call themselves the Fourth International. Furthermore, even for them, these documents are useless, if not superfluous and embarrassing. In any case they appear to pay little attention to them.

The I.C. can entertain illusions about itself, but other organizations are taken in much less than they think.

We know that the I.C., as such, is incapable of leading the necessary work of reconstructing the Fourth International. We have no confidence in the International Committee.

But we have great confidence in the Trotskyist movement.

For a genuine new course

We make no claim that we will reconstruct the International. But we know that it will be reconstructed and that we will have a role to play in this work.

We will play our role, and it is up to the I.C. to choose whether it will play a positive or merely an ineffectual role. It is beyond its strength to play a negative one.

We went to the conference to begin discussion on the tasks of reconstructing the Fourth International. Those that we found there were not ready to engage in this discussion. But it is our custom to do what we say we will do. Therefore, we will pursue this discussion, outside of the framework set by the I.C. certainly, but we will pursue it because it is vital for the future of the revolutionary movement.

Furthermore, we are certain to find favorable echoes inside the organizations of the I.C. themselves.

Because superficial unity based on documents which mean nothing and can bind no one since they can be disavowed three days later, shouldn't fool anyone. Quite a few members of the delegations represented at the congress were not far from sharing our opinion on the nature of the tasks to be undertaken in order to do something else than reenact for the nth time the same play which has already proved a fiasco a number of times.

What we want, what we are fighting for, is that the Trotskyist organizations which exist nearly everywhere in the world should take on this task, without hiding their weaknesses, without bluffing, without disrespect for their own ideas or for the ideas of others. We know that much effort and many struggles are necessary before an international revolutionary organization can be brought into being. But the effort required does not frighten us nor the distance which separates us from the goal.

And we will not abandon tomorrow's reality for today's illusions.

SECTION III: PRINCIPLED BASIS OF TROTSKYIST REUNIFICATION IN 1963

A Note on Healy's Current Slanders
By Joseph Hansen

In the past months, the leadership of the Socialist Labour League, a British sectarian grouping that calls itself "Trotskyist," has been campaigning against the United Secretariat of the Fourth International and the Socialist Workers party of the United States, which is in fraternal solidarity with the world organization of the Trotskyist movement although barred by reactionary legislation from maintaining organizational ties with it.

The occasion for the campaign is an internal discussion that was begun by the sections of the Fourth International and the Socialist Workers party in preparation for the third world congress of the Fourth International since reunification (held in April 1969) and that is being continued in literary form.

In the morgue-like atmosphere maintained by National Secretary Gerry Healy in the Socialist Labour League, such a free discussion would amount to a scandalous situation if not a "betrayal." And the SLL leaders, of course, judge such discussions in other organizations by their own anti-Leninist and anti-Trotskyist standards. Recently—as if they were making an extraordinary exposé, they published several documents (with "necessary deletions") and extracts from others that came into their hands.

Shocking as it may seem to a good many members of the SLL that such a free discussion could be held, others may begin to wonder about the monolithism in their own organization. Unexpectedly to Healy, some good may thus come of his efforts to "expose" the discussion occurring in the world Trotskyist movement.

In his list of further documents to be "exposed," we should like to suggest that Healy give top priority to the one reprinted below. It should be of special interest to members of the SLL since it can safely be asserted that 99.9 percent have never heard of it and the remaining 0.1 percent probably had to turn their numbered copies back in to Healy personally.

The document is of decisive importance in judging the basis of the reunification of the Trotskyist movement in 1963. Healy has attacked the reunification as "unprincipled." This is his main contention in his current campaign. The fraudulent nature of the contention can be judged from the fact that neither Healy nor any of his lieutenants has ever taken up this document publicly.

Under the title "For Early Reunification of the World Trotskyist Movement," the document was submitted by the Political Committee of the Socialist Workers party to the International Committee and the International Secretariat, the leading bodies of the two factions in the Fourth International at that time. It was accepted by an overwhelming majority on each side and thus became the statement of principles on which the two sides carried out a fusion at the subsequent Reunification Congress in 1963.

What did Healy object to in this document? He has never stated his objections but they are hardly any secret.

In my considered opinion, Healy was motivated primarily by dead-end factionalism. He sought, however, to find a "high level" on which to express his opposition. The points to which he objected,

---

Intercontinental Press, May 11, 1970.

as indicated by all his subsequent propaganda, concerned (1) the designation of Cuba as a workers state, (2) the recognition of the role played by the colonial revolution in the postwar period, and (3) the acknowledgment that at a certain point in the revolutionary struggle in some countries, guerrilla warfare can serve as a useful tactic.

In the years since the Reunification Congress, Healy has covered up his differences on these points with an immense amount of verbiage about the importance of theory. The word "about" is accurate. I doubt that any sect anywhere has written more *about* the importance of theory while contributing less to developing it.

Eleven years after the victory of the Cuban revolution, Healy still holds that Cuba's economy is state capitalist and that Castro is another "Batista." This is his dogma. He has, of course, a democratic right to live with it and to enjoy it insofar as this is possible. Nonetheless it is sad that a person who shouts so much about the importance of theory should have found so little time to attempt to make at least a small contribution to the economic theory of state capitalism in Cuba and the political theory of Castroism as a synonym for "Batistaism."

There are good theoretical reasons for Healy's impotence. He has refused to recognize that the Cuban revolution led to the establishment of a workers state because of the fact that the leadership there was not exercised by a political party that measured up to the norms of Leninism. This is the empirical basis of his position.

By the same criterion, he should have refused to recognize that the Chinese revolution led there to the establishment of a workers state (however deformed by Maoism). But in this instance, Healy bowed to the empirical fact that a workers state had been established in China, no matter how much its leadership had departed from the norms of Leninism.

Healy did the same in the case of the East European workers states, recognizing the empirical fact of their establishment even under a leadership (Stalin himself!) that departed so far from the norms of Leninism that it had to be designated as *counterrevolutionary*.

It is this profound contradiction in Healy's theory—the inconsistency between his position on Cuba and his position on China and the East European workers states—that has deprived him of all capacity to offer even the most meager contribution in the area that he selected to mark his separation in theory from the world Trotskyist movement.

The Reunification Congress did not exclude Healy or his cothinkers because of their views on this or any other question. In the past, the Fourth International has included in its ranks revolutionists who maintained that the economy of the Soviet Union is state capitalist. Repeated debates were held over the years with such comrades and they were never expelled for such views. It was Healy who decided that his position on Cuba made it impossible for him to participate in the reunification of the world Trotskyist movement.

It was Healy who decided that his position on Cuba and the related questions of the colonial revolution as a whole, including guerrilla warfare, were more important than all the other points in the statement of principles on which the reunification was based.

Because of his bizarre position on Cuba, Healy until recently was unable to gain a single recruit, to anyone's knowledge, throughout Latin America. However, last fall he finally succeeded in making a breakthrough. He formed a bloc with the Guillermo Lora grouping in Bolivia.

The first public indication of this alliance was an attack in the press of Healy's French followers (the Lambertists) against Hugo González, a leader of the Partido Obrero Revolucionario, the Bolivian section of the Fourth International.

Hugo González was the object of a nationwide police hunt because of his revolutionary activities. This was the moment chosen by the Lora grouping to slander González with the allegation: "Serious suspicions exist today that Mr. González Moscoso in person is working in the pay of the Bolivian government."

Commenting on this in the December 15, 1969, issue of *Intercontinental Press*, Gerry Foley said:

> It is to be hoped that the nature of the relationship between the Lora group and the Lambertists will be clarified. Does this alliance rest on a principled agreement? Does Lora, like the Socialist Labour League and

Lambert, believe that the Cuban revolution was not socialist, giving rise only to state capitalism? Does he hold with them that Fidel Castro is another "Batista"? Does he approve of the slanders that appeared in the Socialist Labour League press (before it became known that Che Guevara was in Bolivia) that Castro had liquidated his comrade in arms?

Neither Healy nor Lambert answered this challenge. Instead, they repeated the slandering of Hugo González. The Healyite press did this in a particularly unctuous way, modifying the English-language translation of the slander so that it made nonsense.

Lora joined in personally with a statement that he solidarized completely with the original slander. He added that members of the POR, many of whom had been arrested, were "adventurers who have turned revolutionary involvement into a business proposition designed to satisfy their personal needs."

In reply to this, I sought in the March 2, 1970, issue of *Intercontinental Press* to show precisely how the English translation of the slander of González had been fixed up in the January 17 issue of the Healyite paper *Workers Press*. I repeated the challenge made by Gerry Foley as to the basis in principle of the bloc with Lora and added:

> Neither Healy, Lambert, nor Lora have answered these questions. To this day they have not made public the basis in principle of their political combination.
>
> Or have they? Take another look at the slanders repeated by Lora, besmirching the Bolivian Trotskyists in the prison cells and torture dungeons of the Bolivian political police.
>
> There's genuine Healyism at its purest and finest!

Healy finally replied in an "Open Letter to Joseph Hansen" (left unsigned as is habitual among writers of poison-pen letters). The letter was hardly a short one. It took up more than one-quarter of two issues (No. 144 and No. 145) of *Workers Press*.

Despite its length, it must be admitted that the author did an admirable job of sustaining Healy Thought at its purest and finest. Not a word of apology is to be found in it about the slandering of Hugo González and the jailed Bolivian Trotskyists. That topic has been buried! Nor is there a single word in reply to the repeated challenge to clarify the basis of the united front with the slanderer Guillermo Lora.

Instead the masked marvel professes to find a difference between me and Hugo Blanco on the Latin-American revolution!

This is coupled with strings of quotations torn out of articles I or other members of the Socialist Workers party have written about Cuba since the victory of the revolution. For all his diligence, the writer sedulously avoids quoting a single item that would require going into the theory of the Cuban revolution. In this area the SLL has not advanced a millimeter since Healy first discovered where Cuba is on the map.

In Healy Thought, this method of replying is known as Squid Karate—swoosh back in a cloud of ink.*

What is Healy trying to hide concerning the basis of his bloc with Lora? It would appear justifiable to conclude that we have before us an instance of *unprincipled combinationism*—all that Lora and Healy have in common is an agreement to join in attacking the "Pabloites" (the label they pin on the members of the Fourth International), even if this means running with the police as in the case of their slander of the Bolivian Trotskyists.

Before coming to this conclusion, however, it is best to wait to hear from Lora. If Lora today agrees with Healy that no revolution occurred in Cuba, that all that happened was that another "Batista" installed "state capitalism," then the bloc would not be unprincipled. It would be instructive, however, to see what achievements Lora might boast of in Bolivia and the rest of Latin America in applying such a theory.

While Lora is expounding to what degree he has

---

* For documentation casting a most revealing light on the methods that have gained notoriety for the SLL, see *Healy "Reconstructs" the Fourth International* (40 pages, 35 cents). A good discussion of the key issues in Healy's challenge to the Fourth International is to be found in *Marxism Vs. Ultraleftism* by Ernest Germain (97 pages, $1). Both pamphlets are available from Pathfinder Press, 873 Broadway, New York, N.Y. 10003.

accepted Healy Thought, he might also examine the basis of the 1963 reunification of the Fourth International, as stated in the document below, and tell us wherein he disagrees with it.

Or has he agreed to keep his mouth shut like Healy on anything that might bring up the question of what principles, if any, they followed in constituting their bloc?

'For Early Reunification of the World Trotskyist Movement'

The world Trotskyist movement has been split since 1954. Various efforts in the past to heal the rupture proved unsuccessful. On both sides, however, it has been felt for some time that a new and more vigorous effort for reunification should be made in view of the encouraging opportunities that now exist to further the growth and influence of the Fourth International, the World Party of Socialist Revolution.

The Socialist Workers party has stressed that a principled basis exists for uniting the main currents of the world Trotskyist movement. During the past year the International Secretariat took the initiative in urging the necessity and practicality of ending the split. For its side the International Committee proposed that a Parity Committee be set up. Although some of the comrades in the IC viewed this as involving no more than a practical step to facilitate common discussion and united work in areas of mutual interest, the majority, it appears clear, welcomed the formation of the committee as an important step toward early reunification.

While substantial differences still remain, especially over the causes of the 1954 split, the area of disagreement appears of secondary importance in view of the common basic program and common analysis of major current events in world developments which unite the two sides. With good will it should be possible to contain the recognized remaining differences within a united organization, subject to further discussion and clarification, thus making possible the great advantages that would come through combining the forces, skills, and resources of all those now adhering to one side or the other.

The main fact is that the majority on both sides are now in solid agreement on the fundamental positions of the world Trotskyist movement. As briefly as possible we will indicate the points of common outlook:

1. The present agonizing world crisis reflects at bottom a prolonged crisis in revolutionary leadership. The development of the productive forces on a global scale has made the world overripe for socialism. Only a socialist planned world economy can rapidly overcome the economic underdevelopment of the colonial and semicolonial countries, deliver mankind from the threat of nuclear extinction, and assure a world society of enduring peace, of boundless plenty, the unlimited expansion of culture and the achievement of full freedom for all. Without the international victory of socialism, decaying capitalism will continue to waste enormous resources, to hold two-thirds of the earth's population in abject poverty, to maintain social and racial inequality, and to support dictatorial regimes. To complete this grim perspective of hunger, insecurity, inequality and oppressive rule, capitalism offers the permanent threat of nuclear destruction.

2. The delay of the world socialist revolution beyond the expectations of all the great Marxists before our time is due basically to the lack of capacity of the traditional leaderships of the working-class movement and to their cynical service as labor lieutenants of the capitalist class or the Kremlin bureaucracy. They are responsible for preventing the main revolutionary postwar crises of 1918–23 and of 1943–47, as well as the lesser crisis of 1932–37, from ending as they should have ended with the proletariat coming to power in the advanced capitalist countries.

3. Only by building new revolutionary Marxist mass parties capable of leading the working

class and working farmers to power can the world crisis be met successfully and a third world war prevented. To build such parties is the aim and purpose of the world Trotskyist movement. A program of transitional slogans and measures plays a key role in party-building work inasmuch as the principal problem in overcoming the crisis of leadership is to bridge the gap between the present consciousness of the masses—which is centered around immediate problems and preoccupations—and the level of consciousness required to meet the objective necessity of overthrowing capitalism and building workers states based upon democratically elected and democratically functioning councils of the working people. Leninist methods must be used to construct revolutionary-socialist parties. These include patient, persistent recruitment of workers to the nuclei of revolutionary socialist parties already established; but also, where necessity or opportunity dictates, flexible advances toward various tendencies in mass organizations which may eventually be brought to the program of revolutionary Marxism. Individual recruitment and tactical moves of wide scope are complementary ways of party construction, but each carries its own problems and special dangers. In the one instance a tendency toward sectarianism can arise out of converting enforced isolation into a virtue; in the other, adaptation to a reformist environment can lead to rightist opportunism. In the tactic known as "entryism," where unusually difficult and complicated situations can occur, it should be the norm for those engaging in it to maintain a sector of open public work, including their own Trotskyist publication. Departure from this norm must be weighed with full consciousness of the heavy risks involved.

4. The Fourth International as an international organization, and its sections as national parties, must adhere to the principles of democratic centralism. Both theory and historic experience have demonstrated the correctness of these principles. Democratic centralism corresponds to the need for quick, disciplined action in meeting revolutionary tasks while at the same time assuring the freedom of discussion and the right to form tendencies without which genuine political life is denied to the ranks. In its adherence to internal democracy, the world Trotskyist movement stands at the opposite pole from the stifling regimes imposed on working-class organizations controlled by bureaucrats trained in the schools of Stalinism, the Social Democracy or reformist unionism.

5. The bureaucratic reformist and Stalinist machines do not use the organized strength of the working class to overthrow capitalism where this is possible. They are primarily interested in their own privileges and power instead of the long-range interests of the working class. Because of inertia, an antisocialist outlook, or recognition that an upsurge can sweep over their heads, they undertake struggles in the interests of the proletariat only with great reluctance and under great pressure. While condemning and opposing the twin evils of reformism and Stalinism, Trotskyists refuse to identify the genuinely socialist or Communist workers of these mass organizations with their treacherous leaderships. The Trotskyist movement recognizes that the main task is not simply to wage literary war on reformism and Stalinism, but to actually win these socialist- and Communist-minded workers to the program and organization of revolutionary Marxism. Under the pressure of long years of prosperity in the advanced capitalist countries and in reaction to the crimes of Stalinism, petty-bourgeois intellectuals have opened a wide assault on the fundamentals of Marxism. It is necessary to wage a firm ideological struggle against this revisionist current.

6. The Soviet Union is still a workers state despite the usurpation of power by a privileged bureaucracy. The mode of production is noncapitalist, having emerged from the destruction of capitalism by the socialist October Revolution; and, whatever its deficiencies, lapses and even evils, it is progressive compared to capitalism. The tremendous expansion of Soviet productive forces through a colossal industrial and cultural revolution transformed a backward peasant country into the second industrial power of the world, actually challenging imperialism's lead in many fields of technology. This great new fact of world history bears witness to the mighty force inherent in planned economy and demonstrates the correctness of the Trotskyist position of unconditional defense of the degenerated workers state against imperialism.

7. In the wake of World War II, the Soviet bu-

reaucracy was able to extend its power and its parasitism into the so-called "people's democracies" of Eastern Europe and North Korea. But to maintain its position of special privilege, it had to destroy capitalism in these countries, doing so by bureaucratic-military means. That such means could succeed was due to the abnormal circumstances of temporary collapse of the local capitalist-landlord rule coupled with extreme weakness of the working class following the carnage of war and occupation. In this way deformed workers states came into existence. These are defended by the Trotskyist movement against imperialist attempts to reintroduce capitalism.

8. In the workers states where proletarian democracy was smashed by Stalinism, or where it never came into existence because of Stalinist influence, it is necessary to struggle for its restoration or construction, for democratic administration of the state and of the planned economy by the toiling masses. Through a political counterrevolution, Stalin destroyed the proletarian democracy of the time of Lenin and Trotsky. The Leninist forces are therefore faced with the need to organize revolutionary Marxist parties to provide leadership for the working class in exercising its right to overthrow the dictatorial rule of the bureaucratic caste and to replace it with forms of proletarian democracy. This signifies a political revolution. With the rebirth of proletarian democracy on a higher level, the workers states—the Soviet Union above all—will regain the attractive power enjoyed before the days of Stalin, and this will give fresh impetus to the struggle for socialism in the advanced capitalist countries.

9. The appearance of a workers state in Cuba—the exact form of which is yet to be settled—is of special interest since the revolution there was carried out under a leadership completely independent from the school of Stalinism. In its evolution toward revolutionary Marxism, the July 26 Movement set a pattern that now stands as an example for a number of other countries.

10. As a result of the new upsurge of the world revolution, above all the tremendous victory in China which changed the relationship of class forces on an international scale, the Soviet proletariat—already strengthened and made self-confident through the victory over German imperialism in World War II and the great economic, technological and cultural progress of the Soviet Union—has exerted increasingly strong pressure on the bureaucratic dictatorship, especially since Stalin's death. In hope of easing this pressure, the ruling caste has granted concessions of considerable scope, abolishing the extreme forms of police dictatorship (dissolution of the forced labor camps and modification of Stalin's brutal labor code, destroying the cult of Stalin, rehabilitating many victims of Stalin's purges, granting a significant rise in the standard of living of the people, even easing the strictures against freedom of thought and discussion in various fields). The Khrushchev regime has no intention of dismantling the bureaucratic dictatorship a piece at a time; its aim is not "self-reform" but maintenance of the rule of the caste in face of mounting popular pressures. But the masses accept the concessions as partial payment on what is due and seek to convert the gains into new points of support in pressing for the ultimate objective of restoring democratic proletarian controls over the economy and the state. This slow but solid strengthening of the position of the proletariat in the European workers states is one of the basic causes of the world crisis of Stalinism.

11. The differences which finally shattered the monolithic structure of Stalinism began in a spectacular way with ideological and political conflict between the Yugoslav and Soviet Communist party leaderships. This conflict was widened by the attempted political revolution undertaken by the Hungarian workers. The Cuban Revolution deepened the crisis still further. With the Chinese-Soviet rift it has become one of the most important questions of world politics. While expressing in an immediate sense the conflict of interests among the various national bureaucratic groups, and between the Soviet bureaucracy and the working classes of countries under its influence, the crisis reflects fundamentally the incompatibility of Stalinism with living victorious revolutions in which the militant vanguard seeks a return to the doctrines of Lenin. The crisis is thus highly progressive in character, marking an important stage in the rebuilding of a revolutionary Marxist world mass movement.

12. In conjunction with the world crisis of Stalinism, the colonial revolution is now playing a key role in the world revolutionary process. Within

little more than a decade, it has forced imperialism to abolish direct colonial rule almost completely and to turn to indirect rule as a substitute; i.e., form a new "partnership" with the colonial bourgeoisie, even though this bourgeoisie in some places may be only embryonic. But this attempt to prevent the countries awakened by the colonial revolution from breaking out of the world capitalist system runs into an insuperable obstacle. It is impossible in these countries to solve the historic problems of social, economic, and cultural liberation and development without overthrowing capitalism as well as breaking the grip of imperialism. The colonial revolution therefore tends to flow into the channel of permanent revolution, beginning with a radical agrarian reform and heading toward the expropriation of imperialist holdings and "national" capitalist property, the establishment of a workers state and a planned economy.

13. Along the road of a revolution beginning with simple democratic demands and ending in the rupture of capitalist property relations, guerrilla warfare conducted by landless peasant and semiproletarian forces, under a leadership that becomes committed to carrying the revolution through to a conclusion, can play a decisive role in undermining and precipitating the downfall of a colonial or semicolonial power. This is one of the main lessons to be drawn from experience since the second world war. It must be consciously incorporated into the strategy of building revolutionary Marxist parties in colonial countries.

14. Capitalism succeeded in winning temporary stability again in Western Europe after the second world war. This setback for the working class was due primarily to the treacherous role played by the Stalinist and Social-Democratic leaderships, which prevented the masses from taking the road of socialist revolution during the big postwar revolutionary crisis. However, this temporary stabilization of capitalism and the subsequent upsurge of productive forces gave rise to more extensive, and ultimately more explosive, contradictions. These involve the other imperialist powers, above all the USA and Japan. They include sharpening competition in a geographically contracting world market; increasing incompatibility between the need to fight inflation and the need to transform potential major economic crises into more limited recessions; mounting conflict between the desirability of maintaining "social peace" and the necessity to attack the workers' standard of living, job conditions, and employment opportunities in order to strengthen competitive efficiency. These contradictions point to increasingly fierce class battles which could become lifted from the economic to the political level in acute form and, under favorable conditions of leadership, arouse the labor movement to a new upsurge in the imperialist countries, challenging capitalism in its last citadels.

15. Socialist victory in the advanced capitalist countries constitutes the only certain guarantee of enduring peace. Since the close of World War II, imperialism has methodically prepared for another conflict, one in which the capitalist world as a whole would be mobilized against the workers states, with the Soviet Union as the main target. Rearmament has become the principal permanent prop of capitalist economy today, an economic necessity that dovetails with the political aims of the American capitalist class at the head of the world alliance of capitalism. American imperialism has stationed counterrevolutionary forces in a vast perimeter around China and the Soviet Union. Its first reaction to new liberating struggles is to seek to drown them in blood. Its armed interventions have become increasingly dangerous. In the crisis over Cuba's efforts to strengthen its military defense, the billionaire capitalist families who rule America demonstrated that they were prepared to launch a nuclear attack against the Soviet Union and even risk the very existence of civilization and of mankind. This unimaginable destructive power can be torn from the madmen of Wall Street only by the American working class. The European socialist revolution will play a decisive role in helping to bring the American proletariat up to the level of the great historic task which it faces—responsibility for the final and decisive victory of world socialism.

16. While participating wholeheartedly in all popular mass movements for unilateral nuclear disarmament, while fighting for an immediate end to all nuclear tests, the world Trotskyist movement everywhere clearly emphasizes the fundamental dilemma facing humanity: world socialism or nuclear annihilation. A clear understanding of this dilemma does not demoralize the masses. On

the contrary, it constitutes the strongest incentive to end capitalism and build socialism. It is a suicidal illusion to believe that peace can be assured through "peaceful coexistence" without ending capitalism. Above all in America. The best way to fight against the threat of nuclear war is to fight for socialism through class-struggle means.

In view of the agreement on these basic positions, the world Trotskyist movement is duty bound to press for reunification. It is unprincipled to seek to maintain the split. Reunification has also become an urgent practical question. On all sides, opportunities for growth are opening up for the revolutionary movement. The Cuban Revolution dealt a blow to the class-collaborationist policy of Stalinism in Latin America and other colonial countries. New currents, developing under the influence of the victory in Cuba, are groping their way to revolutionary socialism and seeking to apply the main lessons of the colonial revolution to their own situation. The Algerian Revolution has had a similar effect on the vanguard of the African revolutionary nationalist movement. To meet these leftward-moving currents, to work with them, even to combine with them without giving up any principles, has become an imperious necessity. Reunification will greatly facilitate success in this task by strengthening our own forces and bringing the attractiveness of Trotskyism into sharp organizational focus. The immediate corollaries will be increased effectiveness of our defense of the colonial revolutions within the imperialist countries and the added weight which the principled program of Trotskyism will gain among all serious revolutionists who seek the fundamental economic, social and political transformation of their countries. On the other hand, it is self-evident that the continued division of the world Trotskyist movement in factions wrangling over obscure issues will vitiate its capacity to attract these new forces on a considerable scale.

Similarly, the crisis of Stalinism, which has led to the great differentiation visible in the Chinese-Soviet rift, has unlocked tremendous forces within the Communist parties throughout the world. Attracted by our Leninist program and traditions, by the vindication of our decades of struggle against Stalinism, and by our insistence on internal democracy, many militants are puzzled and repelled by our lack of unity, by our seeming incapacity to mobilize our forces into a single cohesive organization. The reunification of the world Trotskyist movement would contribute powerfully towards reeducating Communist militants in the genuine spirit of Leninism, its real tradition of international solidarity and proletarian democracy. Obviously a united world Trotskyist movement would prove much more attractive to all those forces within the world Communist movement who are increasingly critical of Stalinism and its offshoots, and who are ready to examine the views of a movement which appears serious not only in its theory but in its organizational capacity.

Finally, we should consider with utmost attentiveness the problem of appealing to the youth, both workers and students, who are playing an increasingly decisive role in demonstrations, uprisings, and the leadership of revolutionary upheavals. The Cuban Revolution was essentially fought by the youth. Similar young people overthrew the corrupt dictatorial regimes of Menderes in Turkey and Syngman Rhee in South Korea. In the struggle for Negro equality in the USA, for solidarity with the Algerian Revolution in France, against rearmament in Japan and Western Germany and against unemployment in Britain, the shock forces are provided by the youth. Youth stand in the forefront of the fight to deepen and extend de-Stalinization in the USSR and the East European workers states. Throughout the world they are the banner bearers of the struggles for unilateral nuclear disarmament. We can attract the best layers of this new generation of rebels by our bold program, our fighting spirit and militant activity; we can only repel them by refusing to close ranks because of differences over past disputes of little interest to young revolutionists of action, who are primarily concerned about the great political issues and burning problems of today.

Early reunification, in short, has become a necessity for the world Trotskyist movement. Naturally, difficult problems will remain in various countries where the faction fight has been long and bitter. But these problems, too, can best be worked out under the conditions of general international reunification, so that it is possible for the outstanding leaders of both sides to begin the job of establishing a new comradely atmosphere and of removing fears which have no real basis in the situation in the world Trotskyist movement today. After a period of common fraternal activity in an increasing number of areas, we are convinced that what may appear at the outset to be insuperable local problems will be solved by the comrades themselves through democratic means.

We think that it should also be possible for a reunified organization to bring in recommendations for subsequent consideration and adoption which, without breaching the centralist side of democratic centralism, would remove any doubts that might still remain as to the guarantee of democratic rights contained in the statutes.

Our movement is faced with a responsibility as great and grave as the one it faced at the founding of the Fourth International in 1938. We ask both sides to decide at their international gatherings in the next months that the time has come to reunify the world Trotskyist movement, and that they will do this at a World Congress of Reunification to be held as rapidly as possible after these gatherings.

MARCH 1, 1963.

SECTION IV: THE BEATING OF ERNEST TATE

Ernest Tate beaten by squad at SLL meeting

London

An attempt to revive the methods made notorious by Stalinism in the thirties appears to be underway in England. This time it is being done by the leadership of the Socialist Labour League, an ultraleft sectarian organization that makes the fraudulent claim of being "Trotskyist."

The latest incident was the brutal beating of Ernest Tate, an internationally known Trotskyist who has been active in London in the work of the Vietnam Solidarity Campaign and the International War Crimes Tribunal initiated by Bertrand Russell. He is the manager of Pioneer Book Service, the major supplier of Trotskyist literature in England.

Ernest Tate was distributing literature in front of a meeting sponsored by the Socialist Labour League at Caxton Hall November 17. The items he was selling included the *International Socialist Review* and a pamphlet *Healy "Reconstructs" the Fourth International*.

Six young toughs jumped Tate, smashing his glasses and bringing him down to the pavement. In commando fashion they continued to kick him, aiming at his genitals, kidneys and head, until pulled off by horrified spectators. Tate had to be hospitalized.

Witnesses stated that they recognized the assailants as members of the Socialist Labour League. Thomas Gerard Healy, the general secretary of the organization, appeared to be supervising the action personally.

Nothing like this has been seen in the radical movement in England since the thirties when Stalinists physically assaulted Trotskyists to prevent them from speaking their views and selling their newspapers. In those days, the Stalinists tried to rationalize their gangster attacks by slandering the Trotskyists as counterrevolutionaries.

The attempt to revive Stalinist methods was preceded by comparable slander in the Healyite press aimed at prejudicing members of the Socialist Labour League so as to prevent them from reading material such as that provided by the Socialist Workers Party and the United Secretariat of the Fourth International.

A particular target has been the pamphlet *Healy "Reconstructs" the Fourth International*, which includes a series of documents exposing the dictatorial methods employed by Healy in running the Socialist Labour League.

In denouncing the pamphlet in the August 20 *Newsletter*, the Political Committee of the Socialist Labour League included the following open threat: "We shall not hesitate to deal appropriately with the handful of United Secretariat agents who hawk it around the cynical fake-left in England."

The news of the shameful and cowardly attack spread swiftly in left circles in London. Messages began coming in very quickly from many politically left circles and trade unions. A conference is being called at an early date to consider what steps can be taken to block any further development of such cancerous methods threatening the democratic rights of all radicals.

World Outlook, December 2, 1966.

SWP National Committee demands Healy be expelled

*National Committee,
Socialist Labour League
186 Clapham High St.,
London, S.W.4, England*

November 21, 1966

Dear Comrades,

We call your attention to an exceedingly grave occurrence that will forever disgrace the Socialist Labour League unless you undertake the most rapid and energetic action.

On November 17, Ernest Tate, an internationally known Trotskyist who has been active in furthering the work of the Vietnam Solidarity Campaign and the International War Crimes Tribunal initiated by Bertrand Russell, was set upon by a gang at the entrance of your public meeting on that date at Caxton Hall. He was seriously beaten by six young toughs and had to be hospitalized.

All the evidence shows that these assailants were not would-be fascists attracted to your meeting but members of your organization and that they were acting under the direct personal supervision of your general secretary Thomas Gerard Healy.

The six who overpowered Comrade Tate and kicked him in the head, kidneys and genitals used this way of preventing him from selling literature to people entering the hall.

This literature included copies of the *International Socialist Review* and a pamphlet, *Healy "Reconstructs" the Fourth International*.

We ask you to do four things:

(1) To at once place your general secretary on trial for sponsoring such methods. The least that can be said of the employment of physical violence in this way is that it is reminiscent of the tactics employed by the Stalinists against their political opponents in the workers movement, particularly against Trotskyists, in the worst period of the thirties.

(2) To publicly and forthrightly condemn these hoodlum tactics sponsored by your general secretary against a member of a workers organization holding different political views from yours.

(3) To expel all those involved for engaging in an act that dishonors the labor and socialist movement.

(4) To immediately assure all workers organizations in Britain, through a prominently placed notice in your journal, *The Newsletter*, that you have undertaken measures to prevent any repetition of such criminal assaults on workers holding political views differing from your own and that you will guarantee protection of the democratic right of all opponent groups to offer their literature at the entrance to your meetings.

*Fraternally,
National Committee
Socialist Workers Party
Farrell Dobbs, National Secretary*

World Outlook, December 2, 1966.

Text of letter from SWP to Pierre Lambert

Pierre Lambert
Informations Ouvrières
39, rue du Faubourg du Temple
Paris 10, France

November 21, 1966

Dear Comrade Lambert,

We are enclosing copies of various communications concerning a matter that holds the gravest implications for the organization you head, as you will no doubt quickly see.

The principal one is a letter from the National Committee of the Socialist Workers Party to the National Committee of the Socialist Labour League. It concerns the serious beating inflicted on Ernest Tate by six assailants who, from all the evidence, were acting under the direct personal supervision of Thomas Gerard Healy, the general secretary of the Socialist Labour League.

Since you are in complete political agreement with Healy, judging from the declarations of your group as well as your joining Healy in recently sponsoring an international conference to advance your joint aims, it is clear that your political reputation has been compromised by the assault perpetrated on Comrade Tate.

We expect that you will join us in demanding that the Socialist Labour League immediately place Healy on trial, publicly condemn the hoodlum tactics he sponsored, expel all those members of the Socialist Labour League involved in the attack, and issue assurances that the Socialist Labour League has undertaken measures to prevent any repetition of such methods smacking of Stalinism at its worst period.

We call your attention in particular to the statement in the August 20 issue of *The Newsletter* in which the Political Committee of the Socialist Labour League denounced the pamphlet, *Healy "Reconstructs" the Fourth International*, and gave the following notice: "We shall not hesitate to deal appropriately with the handful of United Secretariat agents who hawk it around the cynical fake-left in England."

In view of your own long record of vigorously advocating the practice of democracy in workers organizations, we naturally count on your issuing a public statement at once making your own stand in this matter crystal clear.

Fraternally,
Farrell Dobbs, National Secretary

World Outlook, December 2, 1966.

Ernest Tate appeals for support against intimidation by Healyites

In a letter which he sent to the press of the labor movement November 20, Ernest Tate provides further details of the circumstances in which he was set upon by a gang of young toughs at the entrance to a Socialist Labour League meeting in London at Caxton Hall on November 17. [See *World Outlook*, December 2.]

The meeting, he reports, had been scheduled by the SLL to commemorate the tenth anniversary of the uprising of the Hungarian workers against bureaucratic misrule. He arrived early in order to offer Trotskyist literature for sale at the entrance. The two items which he thought would prove of particular interest were the *International Socialist Review* and a pamphlet, *Healy "Reconstructs" the Fourth International*. Others were also present at the entrance selling various publications. These included a group of Irish Communists and a partisan of the English *Militant*.

Tate found himself singled out for special atten-

World Outlook, December 9, 1966.

tion by supporters of the SLL and was subjected to some heckling. He did not mind this, however, as no one sought to prevent him from continuing to hawk his literature.

About one-half hour later, Gerry Healy, the general secretary of the SLL, accompanied by Michael Banda another top leader of the SLL arrived. They went inside.

A few moments later, Healy appeared at the entrance.

As if they had been given a signal, six or seven individuals known by Tate to be supporters of the SLL, attacked him in gang fashion.

> My literature was knocked from my hands, [he writes] I was punched and thrown to the ground, my glasses were smashed, and as I lay on the ground I was kicked repeatedly in the groin and stomach.
>
> After the attack I had to attend the casualty department of the Middlesex Hospital and I was forced to stay in bed for the greater part of the next day. At the moment of writing I am still badly bruised.

As to the reason for the attack, Ernest Tate offers the following opinion:

The issue is a simple one. The Socialist Labour League leadership hope by their actions to prevent me selling my literature outside their meetings. They hope to take away my freedom of speech. This attack comes after a number of threats against me and my friends by members and supporters of the Socialist Labour League. At Brighton during the Labour Party Conference, my comrades were physically threatened and prevented from selling our literature. The same was true at the recent antiwar demonstration in Liège, Belgium, where I was threatened.

Tate ends his letter by declaring that he refuses to be intimidated.

> Neither a fascist Mosley nor an ultraleft sectarian Gerry Healy, who imagines himself to be a Trotskyist should be allowed to curtail our democratic rights. I intend to be present at the next public meeting of the Socialist Labour League to sell my literature. I ask for full support from all people on the left to ensure I do it without interference from the misguided followers of Gerry Healy.

The SLL calls the cops in Ernest Tate case

The following letters concerning the latest developments in the Ernest Tate case were made public by Farrell Dobbs, national secretary of the Socialist Workers Party. For more information on the case see *World Outlook*, December 2, 9 and 16.

December 15, 1966

National Committee
Socialist Labour League
186 Clapham High St.
London, S.W.4, England

Dear Comrades,

As yet we have not received a reply from you to the November 21 letter of our National Committee asking you to place on trial all those in your organization responsible for the beating inflicted on Ernest Tate in front of your public meeting at Caxton Hall on November 17, and, specifically to expel your general secretary, Thomas Gerard Healy, for his role in this shocking assault upon a member of the revolutionary socialist movement.

Instead, it would appear that the victimization of Comrade Tate is being compounded by a move on the part of the top officers of your organization to resort to bourgeois law and the bourgeois courts.

We call your attention to the following items which should sufficiently indicate the emerging pattern:

(1) In response to the pamphlet *Healy "Reconstructs" the Fourth International*, which made public a number of documents exposing the antidemocratic practices that featured the April 4–8 international conference sponsored by the SLL, your Political Committee issued a statement which was published in the August 20 issue of *The Newsletter*. This statement contained the following clear indication of the course of action decided upon with regard to the pamphlet *Healy "Reconstructs" the Fourth International*:

"We shall not hesitate to deal appropriately with the handful of United Secretariat agents who hawk it around the cynical fake-left in England."

What was this if not a confession of incapacity to give any kind of effective answer, political or otherwise, to the exposure contained in the pamphlet? What was it if not a public threat directed against individuals designated by your Political Committee as "United Secretariat agents," specifically those who might "hawk" the pamphlet in England?

(2) At a meeting in Paris November 4 at which your general secretary, Thomas Gerard Healy, was the featured speaker, members of the audience who asked to take the floor to answer accusations made by the speaker were set upon by the sergeants at arms.

The November 29 issue of *Voix Ouvrière* reported that the sergeants at arms "beat and threw out a member of the JCR who wanted to take the floor because his organization had been attacked and reviled throughout the meeting."

The same issue of *Voix Ouvrière* reported in addition: "The sergeants at arms also set upon distributors of *Voix Ouvrière*."

The incidents at the Paris meeting were reported in the November 12 issue of *The Newsletter* as follows:

> The Pabloites and *Voix Ouvrière* . . . attempted to provoke incidents at the meeting. These, fortunately, did not get very far. They demanded the right to speak at 11:30, when the meeting was closed. The chairman refused them.

It is clear from the account in *The Newsletter* itself that the "provocation" consisted of asking for the "right to speak." *The Newsletter* left out what happened to the comrades who asked for the democratic right to answer a public attack. But the entire working-class vanguard in France knows what happened. At least one revolutionist was beaten and thrown out at a meeting where your general secretary was the featured speaker. Other revolutionists were attacked.

World Outlook, December 23, 1966.

The most shameful and reprehensible aspect of this is that *The Newsletter* did not denounce the attacks. Instead it approved! And *The Newsletter* went so far as to accuse the victims of attempting to "provoke" what happened.

That sounds like the standard formula used by the cops when they work someone over. The victim, it is well known, always "provokes" the beating he receives; and the cops are always merely defending themselves and acting in the line of duty.

(3) On November 17, some two weeks after the "incidents" at the Paris meeting, Ernest Tate, a "United Secretariat agent," was in front of a meeting sponsored by the Socialist Labour League at Caxton Hall in London.

This "agent" was there exercising his democratic right to "hawk" the pamphlet *Healy "Reconstructs" the Fourth International* and copies of the magazine *International Socialist Review*.

He was not alone. Representatives of other socialist groups were likewise there to hawk socialist newspapers, magazines or pamphlets.

Comrade Tate was on the pavement in front of the hall. He was not inside the hall. He was not guilty of the provocative crime of demanding the right to take the floor at 11:30.

But at a certain moment, it appears, Thomas Gerard Healy came from inside the hall to the entrance.

We have no way of divining what was going on in his head. We do not know what duties you as the National Committee might have assigned to your general secretary that required him to come from inside the hall to the entrance at that precise moment. We do not even know if it had any connection with carrying out the line laid down in your Political Committee statement published in *The Newsletter* of August 20:

"We shall not hesitate to deal appropriately with the handful of United Secretariat agents who hawk it around the cynical fake-left in England."

Thomas Gerard Healy would best be able to answer, we would suggest, whether his appearance was purely coincidental or in line with obscure official duties pertaining to the highest post in your organization.

We understand that he has averred that what he was engaged in was giving directions to members of the SLL on clearing the pavement so that people arriving in coaches could walk directly into the meeting without any inconvenient obstructions. If this report is wrong—and it does seem incredible that you would assign your general secretary to the task of regulating the flow of traffic in front of a meeting sponsored by the SLL—perhaps you may have a correction to offer.

The fact remains that at that precise moment, Comrade Tate, the only one hawking *Healy "Reconstructs" the Fourth International* was set upon by a gang. Nowhere have we seen any denial that they were members of the SLL. Indeed, they appear to have been acting directly under your general secretary in whatever functions they were engaged in.

This gang beat Comrade Tate. They beat him severely, knocking him down and kicking him in the head, kidneys and genitals. He had to be hospitalized.

Let it be noted well—the beating occurred in the very presence of the general secretary of the SLL, as if the gang felt that what they did would meet with no censure. Perhaps they had good reason to believe that it would even meet with approbation, as was the case with the sergeants at arms at the meeting in Paris, and that was why they went to such lengths even after their victim had been knocked down!

It may be contended that this is perfectly normal procedure in the SLL; that this is the way the SLL always clears the pavement in front of its meetings in order to facilitate the coming and going of coaches.

Comrades! The Political Committee of a *Trotskyist* party would have placed charges at once against every single member involved in such an assault; and, in face of the evidence, would have expelled them forthwith—no matter what their posts.

Still more, comrades, the Political Committee of a *Trotskyist* party would at once have instituted the most searching examination of the organizational pattern that had made such an occurrence even conceivable.

The Political Committee of a *Trotskyist* party would have taken the severest measures against all the key officers responsible for such degeneration of the organization.

And, if the Political Committee defaulted in its obvious duties, the National Committee of a Trotskyist party would have called an emergency meeting to consider the grave situation and to undertake the appropriate measures.

So far as we are aware, you have not followed this course. Instead, something still worse followed.

(4) It was decided to resort to the bourgeois courts in a legal action against Comrade Tate!

The legal basis sought for this action, it appears, is a phrase or two in a letter which Comrade Tate wrote to the labor and socialist press describing what happened to him in front of your meeting as he witnessed it.

Despite the great injury done to him at the time of the beating, he did not call the cops. Despite the gross violation of his democratic right to hawk socialist literature on the pavement in front of an SLL meeting, he did not go to any representatives or institutions of the class enemy. Instead, he appealed to the labor and socialist movement.

Why did not your top officers follow that principled example if they disagreed with Comrade Tate's account of the circumstances under which he was beaten by a gang in front of an SLL meeting while he was selling socialist literature?

The answer would seem self-evident. In a court of working-class opinion, before an impartial body of unionists, Labour Party members, socialists or partisans of proletarian democracy, the SLL executive officers reached the conclusion that they had a losing case.

On the other hand, if a sharp lawyer could be hired to comb through the open letter of this working-class militant beaten up by a gang in front of an SLL meeting, phrases might be found that could be presented in such a way in a bourgeois court that a sympathetic bourgeois judge would hand down a decision in favor of the SLL and against the victim. What a triumph that would be for the SLL!

(5) This course does, naturally, offer the top leaders of your organization the vision of an immediate gain of the most opportunistic character. Perhaps this was sufficient to sway the balance in their calculations. By instituting legal proceedings against the victim of the beating administered in front of an SLL meeting, a plausible pretext was provided for not reporting the assault in the columns of *The Newsletter*. It has now become a legal matter, you know. And the following sentence actually appears in the December 3 issue of *The Newsletter*:

> The issues raised in the Nov. 21st letter by Farrell Dobbs, Secretary of the Socialist Workers Party, about what happened at Caxton Hall on the night of November 17th, we cannot discuss at this stage for legal reasons.

In addition, by bringing in bourgeois "law and order," other publications may be intimidated into saying nothing about the beating inflicted on a well-known Trotskyist in front of an SLL meeting.

This has the same happy effect as a conspiracy of silence in the bourgeois press—workers are kept in ignorance of an important development. Above all the members and followers of the SLL are kept in ignorance of the scandal.

That the news about the beating inflicted on Comrade Tate is known to the entire vanguard in all other countries where a Trotskyist movement exists is of small importance to the top leaders of the SLL. They are not internationalists. They are nationally minded. They are concerned about their own bailiwick.

In this way, they unexpectedly reveal once again how far they have departed from the principles of Trotskyism.

(6) Comrades, please consider more closely what is revealed by this action:

(a) Your executive officers either did not think of appealing to working-class opinion or ruled it out. They decided to appeal to the class enemy. What then is the inescapable conclusion as to their class instincts? What does this say in turn about the nature of the class pressures to which your top leaders are responding? They have more confidence in pettifogging lawyers, shyster lawsuits and bourgeois courts than in a working-class court of honor. It is more natural for them to appeal to the bourgeoisie than to the workers. It is in accord with their principles—strange principles!—to ask the class enemy to deal with a working-class political opponent.

(b) From the moral point of view, the SLL ends up in an even worse light. The open letter of a working-class victim of a beating inflicted by a gang in front of a public meeting of the SLL, the open letter of a revolutionary socialist who tells how he was set upon and who his assailants were, is studied from the viewpoint of bourgeois law to see in what way it can be turned against the victim in order to damage him still further; and especially to block him from voicing his outrage.

Even more, the open letter appears to have been studied to see if it could not be utilized in the bourgeois courts so as, with a favorable ruling from a sympathetic bourgeois judge, to bring down a curtain on the whole matter and even prevent any further hawking of literature damaging to the pretension of the SLL leaders that they are authentic spokesmen for Trotskyism in Britain.

Doesn't this call for the addition of a chapter to Trotsky's *Their Morals and Ours*—a chapter on the morals sometimes to be found in ultraleft sectarian groups as they degenerate?

(c) Note the background against which this action occurs. As the heroic Trotskyist Hugo Blanco faces a possible death sentence in Peru under the workings of bourgeois law and the bourgeois courts, the SLL leaders set in motion an appeal to the British bourgeois cousins of the Peruvian dispensers of class justice—and the action is directed against one of Hugo Blanco's most ardent defenders in England, a "United Secretariat agent" like Hugo Blanco himself.

What infamy your top leaders have brought upon the SLL!

(7) Finally, we ask you to consider what this course of action signifies as to the sincerity of the headlines to be read with monotonous frequency in *The Newsletter* about organizations or figures in the labor movement with whom you have differences who are charged with "calling the cops."

In the light of what happened at the Paris meeting on November 4 and in front of the SLL meeting at Caxton Hall on November 17, what conclusion can be drawn except that the editors of *The Newsletter* are guilty of the most disgusting hypocrisy. The SLL itself calls the cops!

A suspicion arises. If the leaders of the SLL can with such singular lack of compunction and in such gross violation of their professed principles resort to calling the cops themselves, can it be possible that they are guilty of the very crime they have charged against the comrades at the Paris meeting; i.e., "provoking" incidents leading to fisticuffs? Is it a pattern now for the SLL to "attempt to provoke incidents," as *The Newsletter* put it, that will cause inexperienced political opponents to call the cops?

We would not like to believe this of the SLL, comrades; but we are duty bound to call your attention to the fact that such conclusions may well be drawn by wide circles of the vanguard in light of the course of action being followed by your top leaders.

We hope that you will again read the November 21 letter which our National Committee sent to you and that you will act on its recommendations at once without further damaging delay.

Fraternally,
Political Committee
Socialist Workers Party
Farrell Dobbs, National Secretary

Healy scores another 'triumph' over Ernest Tate

In previous issues we have reported how Ernest Tate, a Trotskyist, was beaten up in front of a Socialist Labour League meeting held at Caxton Hall in London on November 17. We have also reported how Ernest Tate refused to call the cops, preferring to register his protest with organizations in the socialist and labor movement. For instance, he wrote a circular letter in which he gave his impression of what happened in front of Caxton Hall and fixed the responsibility on Healy.

Healy's reply to this was to go over the letter in hope of finding formulations that could be utilized in the bourgeois courts in a shyster lawsuit. He hired attorneys to open proceedings. Solicitors'

World Outlook, January 6, 1967.

letters were sent to Tate and to two working-class newspapers that had published Tate's letter, the *Socialist Leader* and *Peace News.*

The two working-class papers, which have no large sums at hand to fight shyster lawsuits in the bourgeois courts, felt it best to print formal retractions and pay the "costs" demanded by Healy—10 guineas in each case.

We now come to Healy's latest "triumph" over Ernest Tate. In the December 17 *Newsletter*, under the heading "Apologies," Healy reprinted the two formal retractions. Almost identical in text, they obviously show the fine touch of the SLL's great legal brain. First they refer to having published a letter by Ernest Tate in which he accused

> Mr. Gerry Healy, National Secretary of the Socialist Labour League, of having instigated several of his supporters to assault and prevent him from selling literature outside Caxton Hall, where an SLL meeting was being held.

Then the two formal retractions, which are really choice examples of such instances in the bourgeois system of jurisprudence, print the alibi provided by the SLL's wily expert in this field:

> We have been informed that Mr. Healy asked a steward to clear the pavement in front of the entrance of the Hall so that passengers alighting from coaches would not be delayed in getting to the meeting; that he did nothing to prevent Mr. Tate or anyone else from selling literature; and that others were selling literature at each side of the entrance without interference.' [Both retractions then] 'sincerely apologise to Mr. Healy for having published the suggestion that he employs violence or seeks to curtail freedom of expression.

And the beating inflicted on Ernest Tate? Not a word outside of the reference in these two formal retractions. Not a whisper yet in *The Newsletter*! Like resorting to the bourgeois courts, you see, clearing the pavement in front of a meeting is routine for the SLL. Particularly clearing the pavement of the one person among "others" selling literature who happens to be offering the pamphlet, *Healy "Reconstructs" the Fourth International*. That pamphlet really obstructs traffic . . .

Wohlforth tries to brazen it out
Some comments on a curious way of defending Healy in the Tate case
By Joseph Hansen

Last November 17, Ernest Tate, an internationally known Trotskyist active at present in furthering the work of the Vietnam Solidarity Campaign and the International War Crimes Tribunal, was set upon by a gang at the entrance of a public meeting sponsored in London by the Socialist Labour League, an ultraleft British organization that claims to be Trotskyist. Ernest Tate was so severely beaten that he had to be hospitalized. The beating was administered by stewards belonging to the SLL and took place in the presence of the national secretary of the group, Thomas Gerard Healy. The beating was administered to prevent Tate from offering socialist literature to persons entering the hall. The literature included copies of the *International Socialist Review* and a pamphlet, *Healy "Reconstructs" the Fourth International*.

The National Committee of the Socialist Workers party sent a protest November 21 to the National Committee of the SLL, demanding that they at once place their national secretary on trial for his part in employing physical violence against a political opponent in the socialist movement, that they publicly condemn such hoodlum tactics,

World Outlook, February 24, 1967.

expel all those involved, and immediately assure all workers organizations in Britain that measures had been undertaken to prevent any repetition of such criminal assaults on workers holding political views differing from those of the SLL.

Farrell Dobbs, national secretary of the Socialist Workers party, sent copies of this letter to the organizations sharing the political views of the SLL and asked them to make public statements indicating their positions in this matter. The request was addressed to Pierre Lambert of *Informations Ouvrières* in Paris, Tim Wohlforth of the American Committee for the Fourth International in New York, and James Robertson of the Spartacist League in New York.

Instead of responding, all four organizations remained silent. Healy then compounded the outrageous scandal of the beating inflicted on Ernest Tate. He opened legal proceedings against his victim and against two working-class newspapers that published a letter from Tate describing the circumstances of his being beaten by the SLL stewards and charging Healy with responsibility for the attack.

The Newsletter, the organ of the Central Committee of the SLL, then sought to bring down a curtain of silence on this unsavory business by publishing the following notice in its December 3 issue:

> The issues raised in the Nov. 21st letter by Farrell Dobbs, Secretary of the Socialist Workers Party, about what happened at Caxton Hall on the night of November 17th, we cannot discuss at this stage for legal reasons.

The notice was remarkable for its modesty in the usually flamboyant *Newsletter*. The seven-line notice appeared at the bottom of page 3 and did not even have a headline.

The Political Committee of the Socialist Workers party again wrote to the National Committee of the SLL, calling their attention to Healy's second violation of the most elementary norms of conduct in the labor movement; i.e., in effect calling the cops against the very victim of the beating inflicted by the stewards of the SLL in the presence of the national secretary of the organization. [See *World Outlook*, December 23, 1966, for the text of this letter.] The Political Committee of the Socialist Workers party appealed to the SLL National Committee to act on the recommendations already submitted to them concerning bringing Healy up on charges and expelling all those involved in utilizing physical violence against workers holding political differences with the SLL.

As in the previous instance, Farrell Dobbs sent copies of this letter to Pierre Lambert, to Tim Wohlforth and to James Robertson, asking them to take a public stand on the issues involved.

Spartacist, which is edited by James Robertson, responded in its January–February issue. It took an honorable stand, denouncing the use of physical violence against other currents in the labor movement. The statement included a reaffirmation of the "political similarity between the Spartacist League and the SLL" and the group's political differences with the Socialist Workers party. Of special interest was the inclusion of fresh testimony as to the antidemocratic nature of the SLL. The statement ended by calling for a "workers' inquiry" to expose Healy, "this fraud who disorients and corrupts the Trotskyist movement by posing as a revolutionary leader." [See *World Outlook*, February 3, for the text.]

Tim Wohlforth has now responded to the two letters addressed to him by Farrell Dobbs. The February 13 issue of the *Bulletin*, edited by Wohlforth, carries a statement issued by the "Political Committee Workers League." [See page 216 of this issue of *World Outlook* for the full text.]

The statement represents a decided shift from the previous position of the *Bulletin*, indicated by a box in the December 19, 1966, issue which read:

> The issues raised in the Nov. 21st letter by Farrell Dobbs, Secretary of the Socialist Workers Party, about what happened at Caxton Hall on the night of November 17th, we cannot discuss at this stage for legal reasons. —Dec. 3 Newsletter

Alert readers will note that the stand taken by the *Bulletin* was not widely divergent from the one taken by the *Newsletter*. The *Bulletin* was, however, somewhat bolder. Instead of page 3, it put the notice on page 1. It placed a heavy border around the box and it used a somewhat sensationalistic headline: "LEGAL REASONS."

Just why "legal reasons" prevented the bold and fearless editor of the *Bulletin* from reporting the beating inflicted on Ernest Tate was left unexplained at the time and it still remains unexplained in the statement. Equally baffling is the reasoning that led Wohlforth to conclude that after all no legal reasons actually prevent him from taking a stand in this case. Perhaps he came to the conclusion that the American colonies are no longer subject to the British courts. Or it may be that Healy decided that evasion of the issues was not paying off and that Wohlforth's brains were needed to get him and *Informations Ouvrières* off the hook.

Wohlforth, it is clear, thought the whole thing through and saw where Healy had pulled some real boners. The statement is designed to rectify things. Healy's denial of guilt in indicating to his stewards that they should beat up Ernest Tate is an instance of this. When Tate publicly charged that Healy *was* guilty, Healy utilized this as the legal pretext for running to the courts of Her Majesty the Queen. The letters sent out by the solicitors hired by Healy cited Tate's testimony as the basis for legal proceedings, and it was because Healy appealed to bourgeois jurisprudence on this count that two newspapers which had published Ernest Tate's charges made the formal retractions demanded by Healy and paid the legal costs he also demanded. Wohlforth brushes aside the fumbling course taken by Healy. Not only does Wohlforth concede Healy's guilt, he defends in principle Healy's "right" to have his political opponents in the labor movement beaten up whenever he feels such action is called for!

As a defense of the use of physical violence in answering arguments advanced by other tendencies in the labor movement, Wohlforth's statement is probably unique aside from the precedents to be found in the Stalinist movement when the GPU sought to justify the use of violence against "Trotskyites" and other political dissidents.

As outlined by Wohlforth, the criteria to be used in deciding who should be victimized follows the same grim precedent. These criteria exist solely in the warped mind of the head of the cult, in this case the warped mind of the tinpot despot who serves as the national secretary of the badly degenerated SLL.

Perhaps the strangest twist in Wohlforth's statement is that even after going so far as to defend and advocate the use of violence in polemics with other tendencies in the labor movement, the author cannot quite screw up enough brazenness to defend Healy on resorting to the bourgeois courts. It is too gross for even this boneless political contortionist to swallow in one gulp. And so his statement breathes not a word about Healy's monstrous action of rushing to the class enemy for help against Ernest Tate. However, Wohlforth indicates that he will eventually manage to down this, too, for he approvingly cites the fruits of the solicitors' letters served by Healy; namely, the formal retractions printed by two working-class newspapers (although he does not mention the cash fines levied by Healy).

As a final curiosity, it should be noted that Wohlforth, embarrassed at indicating that his statement is in response to two letters sent him by Farrell Dobbs, gives his statement the form of a denunciation of James Robertson for taking a public stand on the issues involved in the Ernest Tate Case, hence the bizarre title of Wohlforth's statement: "Spartacist Joins Revisionists Against Fourth International."

Robertson, we should imagine, must feel grateful to Wohlforth for this small assistance in the rather sticky job of trying to remove the loathsome taint of "political similarity" between the Spartacist group and an outfit that so clearly echoes the abominations of "third period" Stalinism.

Wohlforth's stand on the Ernest Tate case

Below we publish the full text of a statement on the Ernest Tate Case which appeared in the February 13 issue of the *Bulletin* edited by Tim Wohlforth. The original title of the statement is "Spartacist Joins Revisionists Against Fourth International" and it is claimed to be "by political committee workers league." The subheads appear as shown in the original. We have taken the liberty of correcting some obvious typographical errors. Joseph Hansen has supplied footnotes to help clarify the more obscure or contradictory points. These are identified in each instance. The emphasis appears as shown in the original.

✍

On November 21st, 1966, Farrell Dobbs, National Secretary of the Socialist Workers Party, wrote to James Robertson, National Chairman of the Spartacist League about the so-called "Tate Affair."

> We trust that you will clarify your stand—and its relation to your expression of political solidarity with Healy—in an adequate way and as rapidly as possible [Dobbs demanded].

Robertson hastened to oblige Dobbs, the man who sent condolences to Kennedy's widow. And so the lead editorial of Spartacist #9 is entitled: "Oust Healy!" This is the real political relationship between Spartacist and the SWP. This is the concrete meaning of the statement in our Perspectives Resolution: "The Spartacist must be understood as a 'left' expression of the nationalism and revisionism of the SWP."

Let us now take a look at the Tate Affair. Our purpose is not so much to pass judgement on the facts of the case, about which we know little,[1] but rather to discuss how such a question should be approached. It seems that there was an altercation between stewards at a large meeting in London, sponsored by the Socialist Labour League and Ernest Tate who was selling literature in front of this meeting. Tate claims he was beaten because he was selling literature critical of the SLL and of Gerry Healy, national secretary of the SLL.

World Outlook, February 24, 1967.

However, as previously reported in the Bulletin, two papers which printed Tate's charges issued apologies to Comrade Healy stating in part:

> We have since been informed that Mr. Healy asked a steward to clear the pavement in front of the entrance of the Hall so that passengers alighting from coaches would not be delayed in getting to the meeting, that he certainly did nothing to prevent the writer of the letter from selling literature; and others were selling literature on each side of the entrance without any interference.[2]

These are the basic facts as known to us and as known to Spartacist.

First task

Our first task is to put this incident within the context of the class struggle. Trotsky deals with this question with great thoroughness in his "Their Morals and Ours." When attacked for having hostages during the Russian Civil War Trotsky responded:

---

1. It is odd, in view of this professed ignorance and the extreme seriousness of the case, that Wohlforth does not join Robertson in demanding a workers' commission of inquiry.—J.H.

2. The two papers were *Peace News* and the *Socialist Leader*. They published legal retractions that were almost identical in text. They referred first to having published a letter by Ernest Tate in which he accused "Mr. Gerry Healy, National Secretary of the Socialist Labour League, of having instigated several of his supporters to assault and prevent him from selling literature outside Caxton Hall, where an SLL meeting was being held." Then came the alibi provided by the distinguished client of the solicitors: "We have been informed that Mr. Healy asked a steward to clear the pavement in front of the entrance of the Hall so that passengers alighting from coaches would not be delayed in getting to the meeting; that he did nothing to prevent Mr. Tate or anyone else from selling literature; and that others were selling literature at each side of the entrance without interference." Both retractions then "sincerely apologise to Mr. Healy for having published the suggestion that he employs violence or seeks to curtail freedom of expression."

It is particularly instructive that Wohlforth omitted quoting the sentence including the actual apology. It goes counter to his defense of Healy's "right" to use violence against workers who disagree with the SLL.—J.H.

The petty-bourgeois moralist thinks episodically, in fragments, in clumps, being incapable of approaching phenomena in their internal connection. Artificially set apart, the question of hostages for him is a particular moral problem, independent of those general conditions which engender armed conflict between classes.

This is Spartacist's method. The SWP raises this incident and the Spartacist judges it *without* exploring its context! the politics of the forces involved in the incident, the relation of these forces to the class struggle. On the basis of its moral evaluation of this isolated incident the Spartacist concluded: "Oust Healy."[3]

We are reminded of two recent incidents within the trade union movement which may help illustrate this point. During the New York City Welfare strike conducted by the SSEU a person turned up in front of a strike meeting distributing a piece of literature entitled: "Strike? An Obsolete Weapon." The leaflet turned out to be an open appeal for *scabbing* against the strike. It ended up by urging welfare workers to get in touch with the Socialist Labor Party, a sectarian group opposed to working in legitimate unions.

One SSEU militant, stumbling to the meeting after 8 hours on the picket line in bitterly cold weather, took one look at this leaflet and began to work over the person distributing it. As far as this militant was concerned this "socialist" gentleman was as much a scab as somebody crossing the picket line.[4]

Earlier this fall a group of thugs descended upon James Morrissey, the leader of a rank and file opposition within the National Maritime Union, and beat him up with lead pipes. Morrissey's crime, no doubt, was distributing literature critical of NMU President Joe Curran. How do we judge these two incidents? Are they of equal weight? Are they really identical? We hold that despite a formal identity they are in reality opposites in content. In the case of Morrissey violence was being used to terrorize the rank and file workers who were struggling to make their union a more effective weapon for fighting the bosses. In the case of our "socialist scab," violence was being used to terrorize those who would break the unity of the working class against the bosses, those who act as the agents of the class enemy.

A strike without some sort of intimidation and terror, yes terror, against those who seek to break the unity of the class is not serious.[5] An unserious strike is a blow against the working class. Violence used to terrorize workers when they seek to battle the bosses and the bosses' agents, the union bureaucracy, is unforgivable, criminal, intolerable.

---

3. *Spartacist* maintained that the incident was not isolated. *Spartacist* cited its own experiences with Healy, offered to submit fresh evidence to a bona fide workers' investigating commission, and pointed to the *two* incidents in the current scandal—the beating inflicted on Ernest Tate and Healy's appealing to the bourgeois courts. Wohlforth's argument that the beating was an "isolated incident" stands, of course, in contradiction to his view that it was morally justified. In fact, in the very next paragraph, trying to put up a case for Healy, Wohlforth seeks to show empirically that it is quite customary in the labor movement to reply to political arguments with physical violence and that this often warrants applause.—J.H.

4. If this alleged incident is not simply a concoction, the worker obviously reflected the notorious political backwardness of the American proletariat and was sadly in need of attending a class where he could learn about working-class democracy and elementary morality in the conduct of political disputes within the labor movement as well as gain a correct understanding of the views held by a leaflet distributor willing to brave "bitterly cold weather" to bring what he thought (if mistakenly) was a socialist message to striking workers. The Socialist Labor party is well known in the American radical movement as an ossified sect with no influence in the unions, fanatically devoted to the program and memory of Daniel De Leon, one of the pioneers of American socialism. The fact remains that the American working class can still learn much from De Leon's writings although he has been superseded in the field of theory by the contributions of the Russians who led the October Revolution. It is sad that one of the members of this completely uninfluential group should have been beaten and still sadder that Wohlforth should feel under compulsion to hail the beating and even label it as morally good.—J.H.

5. In the days of the Stalinist terror against working-class political opponents, the standard excuse advanced by Stalin's hatchetmen for using physical violence to stamp out dissidence, was that their opponents, particularly the "Trotskyites," were breaking the "unity" of the working class. Wohlforth at one time understood the falseness of this argument to perfection. As a newly converted "conditional" supporter of Mao, he appears to have undergone a "cultural revolution" on this as well as some other important items.—J.H.

The only way we could thus make a decision as to who was right or wrong in the above cases was to go beyond the act of violence itself to get at the politics of the participants. There is no other way for Marxists to proceed.

Classic position

The first question then is who is Ernest Tate: what are his politics; how does he fit into the class struggle? Tate is the representative in England of the Socialist Workers Party. His specific task is to peddle SWP literature throughout England and to work together with the SWP's political co-thinkers in Europe—the Pabloite revisionists like Germain, Frank and the little British Pabloite grouplets.

The SWP and its international friends have become the agents of capitalism within the working class movement.[6] This is the classic centrist role they are playing all the more clearly and openly as every day passes. Can there be any doubt about this?

What is the position of the SLL? This too is crystal clear. The SLL is the only organization in England to battle consistently and unceasingly for the interests of the working class. As the SLL sums up its relations with the SWP: "It is a fight between the working class and the servants of the class enemy." (See SLL declaration "Course of the Socialist Workers Party" in Jan. 2nd Bulletin.)[7]

The relationship between these two international forces—the Fourth International and the Pabloite Revisionists—is symbolized by this confrontation with Tate. Less than two weeks before the meeting in question, the Young Socialists and the French Revoltes youth has sought to defend the Hungarian Revolution during the international demonstration at Liege. Tate's political collaborators sought to prevent the SLL and YS members from carrying a banner supporting the Hungarian Revolution. These finks even went so far as to seek police help in preventing our comrades from carrying this banner.[8] Tate then shows up in front of the SLL meeting also organized to defend the Hungarian Revolution to peddle a pamphlet containing scandal which, interestingly enough, originates with Spartacist.[9]

When the SLL and YS raise a banner defending the Hungarian Revolution in Liege Tate's political allies bloc with the Belgian Stalinists and call the cops. When the SLL holds Hungarian memorial meeting in London Tate turns up to sell his political smut.[10] These are the politics of the contending forces in front of Caxton Hall.

Political scabs

Tate and his political allies represent political scabs of the worst sort. These gentlemen have been instrumental in aiding the right wing of the British Labour Party in expelling our comrades. These gentlemen have a habit of calling the cops against our comrades. These gentlemen bloc with the Stalinists everywhere—in Belgium, France, England, U.S.—against the interests of the working class.[11]

On the other hand the SLL has consistently cham-

---

6. Wohlforth comes late to the field. This charge was invented decades ago by the Stalinists. Its age does not improve its flavor.—J.H.

7. In other words, Healy serves as prosecuting attorney; Healy serves as judge; Healy's stewards carry out the sentence; and Healy's altar boy Wohlforth pipes the moral sermons. An efficient system! Credit for perfecting, if not inventing this megalomaniac way of drawing the class line properly belongs, however, to Stalin.—J.H.

8. Wohlforth appears to be counting on the ignorance of readers of the *Bulletin*. The slander which he repeats here first appeared in *The Newsletter*. It was exposed in detail by Henri Valin in an article "The Healy School of Falsification." See *World Outlook* January 27, p. 104.

9. The unmentionable pamphlet, *Healy "Reconstructs" the Fourth International*, contains documents originating from all three of the tendencies that attended a conference of the "International Committee" in London last April. An introduction, "Sectarianism and Tinpot Despotism—An Example for the Textbooks," attempts to draw some of the main political lessons. A copy of the pamphlet can be obtained by sending $.35 to the Socialist Workers Party, 873 Broadway, New York, N.Y. 10003.—J.H.

10. "Smut." In this obscure way Wohlforth may be referring to the letters written by Healy which were a prominent part of the documents in the pamphlet, *Healy "Reconstructs" the Fourth International*. It is true that these letters need to be read to be believed. However Healy has not denied their authenticity, and the internal evidence shows them to be genuine.—J.H.

11. Wohlforth's capacity to testify on the occurrence of unspecified alleged incidents in many countries may appear surprising in view of his professed ignorance about the facts of the Ernest Tate Case. The enigma is easily resolved. Wohlforth is simply displaying in his own fashion his familiarity with the area of London known as Billingsgate.—J.H.

pioned the interests of the working class. It has fought in every corner of England exposing the role of Wilson as a servant of capitalism. It has exposed the fake lefts who refuse to fight Wilson seriously. It has reached out to the young workers of Britain and built a strong working class youth movement.

The SWP comes along and writes us a letter accusing the SLL of "the poisonous methods that were the hallmark of Stalinism in its worst period." We cannot help but view this "moral indignation" in the same light as we would that of a supporter of Joseph Curran who attacked SSEU militants for reviving trade union hooliganism.[12]

The truth is that the SWP is presently in a political bloc with the Stalinists. As we pointed out in the last issue of the Bulletin the SWP is collaborating with the CP to limit the struggle against the Vietnam War to politics acceptable to pacifist Muste. Today the SLL and its comrades in the International Committee throughout the world consistently expose this political bloc of the revisionists with the Kremlin's agents and call for the military victory of the National Liberation Front.

Spartacist

Where does Spartacist stand in this *principled* political struggle? The Spartacist views itself as a "supporter of the IC." It speaks of "the political similarity between the Spartacist League and the SLL." On the other hand an earlier issue of the Spartacist characterizes the SWP as moving "from centrism to reformism."

Spartacist is very broad minded about it all. They are very happy to overlook their proclaimed political solidarity with the SLL and supposed political antipathy with the SWP. Everything is to be subordinated to a *clear stand*—on an incident in front of Caxton Hall, taken out of context, distorted by the revisionists and used by them in a *war* against principled Trotskyists.

The Spartacist's role in this affair is even more reprehensible than that of the SWP. The SWP makes no bones about it. They are the political opponents of the SLL and the Tate affair is just one weapon—admittedly a slimy one—to use in this war.

But Spartacist claims political solidarity with those it slanders and attacks. These "moral" people find nothing immoral in exchanging slander and scuttlebut with the revisionists and uniting with them in a common organizational struggle against Healy. Dobbs asks Robertson where he stands. Robertson gets up and yells: "Oust Healy." First the SWP peddles Spartacist's organizational criticisms of the IC. Now Spartacist peddles SWP's organizational criticisms of the IC.

Common front

The relationship is clear. The real politics of the SWP and Spartacist require a *common front* against the *common enemy*. The difference between reform and revolution must be subordinated to the mutual hostility to the revolutionary camp.

We state that this organizational bloc of the political smut peddlers is the politics of the Spartacist while its supposed adherence to "revolutionary principles" is an artificial formal declaration unrelated to Spartacist politics-in-action.

We warn Spartacist: There is presently a *war* going on between revolutionary Trotskyists represented by the International Committee and revisionist agents of capital represented by the SWP-Germain-Frank Pabloite formation. You are on the other side in this war. Henceforth we will have no relations with you.

---

12. And what about Wohlforth's silence concerning Healy's hiring solicitors and bringing the full majesty of the law of the class enemy down upon a working-class political opponent and two working-class newspapers because they sought to publicize a beating that Wohlforth approves? This spectacular silence provides a convincing measure of the worth of *his* "moral indignation."—J.H.

SECTION V: HEALYITES CONTINUE TO FLOUT WORKERS DEMOCRACY

Harry Turner's complaint to Gerry Healy

One of the duties of the staff of *Intercontinental Press* is to keep up to date, insofar as it is possible, with happenings among the so-called splinter groups in the left. Politically these formations range from devout followers of Mao Tsetung, Enver Hoxha, and Kim Il Sung to self-proclaimed "Trotskyists." They are generally—but not always—ultraleft sectarians. In size the groups range from half a dozen persons or less to organizations of some pretensions.

We faithfully read their publications—that is, all those we receive. (Some groups consider it unprincipled to put us on their mailing list.) We follow their disputations with interest—after all, they want to be revolutionists—and we acknowledge a certain enlightenment that would otherwise not have been ours on many a fine hairline in doctrine and dogma. Occasionally we run across an item that strikes us as deserving the attention of a broader audience than the narrow one aimed at by the author. The letter reprinted below is an example.

The letter appeared in the March issue of the *Vanguard Newsletter*, a well-mimeographed fourteen- to sixteen-page monthly published in New York. Signed by one of the editors, Harry Turner, it is addressed to Gerry Healy, the national secretary of the Socialist Labour League.

Healy has as yet not publicly acknowledged the letter. Rather than accuse him of not deigning to reply, we leave open the possibility that he never received it. If that happens to be the case, he will no doubt appreciate our making it available to him through the columns of *Intercontinental Press*.

A few words on the political background so as to make some of the references in the letter more comprehensible: The world Trotskyist movement underwent a split in 1953–54, two factions being formed—one under the leadership of the International Secretariat, headed at the time by Michel Pablo, and the other under the International Committee, which, in the United States, was supported by the Socialist Workers party.

By 1963 it became possible to reunite the movement on a principled basis, and this was achieved at a Reunification Congress. In token of the healing of the old rupture, the top executive body of the Fourth International was named the "United Secretariat." (For the text of the document stating the principles on which the two sides agreed, see *Intercontinental Press*, May 11, 1970, pp. 442–45.)

A minority faction in the International Secretariat refused to participate in the reunification. This faction, headed by Juan Posadas, held that a worldwide nuclear war is inevitable; and, since it is inevitable, the sooner the better. Today the Posadist group is considerably reduced in size but still has some forces, principally in Uruguay, where they are currently practicing class-collaborationism as one of the sponsors of the recently formed popular front. Posadas claims to have "reorganized" the Fourth International and to be its true and only leader.

A minority of the International Committee likewise refused to participate in the reunification. This group was headed by Gerry Healy in Britain and by Pierre Lambert in France. Their principal point of difference was over the Cuban revolution, which they held had not been victorious. Healy in particular maintained that Fidel Castro was just another "Batista," a view he still insists on. Healy and Lambert continued to use the name "International Committee," although they and their followers constituted only a rump of that formation. Their goal, they have repeatedly proclaimed for the past eight years, is to "reconstruct" the Fourth International.

Within the Socialist Workers party, which was barred by reactionary legislation in the United States from

Intercontinental Press, May 17, 1971.

maintaining its affiliation with the Fourth International, the world party of socialist revolution founded by Leon Trotsky in 1938, a small tendency joined Healy in opposing the 1963 reunification. This tendency was headed by James Robertson and Tim Wohlforth, both of whom were originally followers of Max Shachtman, one of the leaders of a split from the Fourth International in 1939–40.

Robertson and Wohlforth later parted company. Robertson wound up as the leader of the "Spartacist League" and Wohlforth as leader of the competing "Workers League."

Harry Turner was aligned with Robertson, but eventually moved into an orbit of his own. The group he belongs to at present apparently calls itself only by the name of its monthly publication.

We have tried to reproduce the text of Turner's letter exactly as it appeared in the *Vanguard Newsletter*, but have taken the liberty of adding three footnotes.

March 12, 1971

Dear Comrade Healy,

You will, of course, wish to be informed about a meeting on January 20, 1971, in which Hugh Fredricks, Harold Robins, Mark Berns and I met as delegates of VANGUARD NEWSLETTER with Tim Wohlforth, Fred Mueller, Pat Connolly and Denis O'Casey of the Workers League.

We considered that a discussion with the WL was again in order upon noting its partial return to Trotsky's and our own position on the Negro question, e.g., the recognition that the Blacks are, "the most dynamic section of the working class", who, therefore, "can and will play an important role . . . in the construction of a vanguard leadership for the class as a whole", that the real "content" of the Black movement, is one of militant struggle against all oppression, which tends to break through the Black nationalist "form" in which it is often initially expressed.

In arranging with Wohlforth for the meeting at the WL's headquarters, I made clear our reason for requesting it, namely, to explore the implications of the shift in the WL's line on the Negro question, to determine whether a sufficient basis now existed for a cooperative working relationship in which differences would be narrowed, and which, therefore, might lead to an eventual unity.

Wohlforth agreed to the meeting, while also stating his belief that the "real" difference was not on the Negro question, but rather on "internationalism". Despite our feeling that this response was not too promising, we decided to follow through on our overture.

I opened the meeting with a twenty minute presentation of our positions. We welcomed the WL's return to some of Trotsky's positions on the Negro question, and then presented our arguments. We re-stated our belief that our disagreement on this question was the essential barrier to our unity. We requested information as to whether the WL had also reconsidered its position denying that the Black and Spanish-speaking minorities were subject to a special oppression, manifested in the workplace as super-exploitation. We again informed them that we believed the recognition of this condition to be a potentially powerful lever with which to raise the political class consciousness of Black and white workers in the process of uniting them in a struggle for their immediate and fundamental interests. We contrasted our approach, in which the struggle against special oppression was united to the transitional program, to theirs, in which a *concrete* program of struggle against racism was absent.

We also posed our positions for a united front approach to existing Black caucuses, support to the *right* of the Black masses to a section of the US for a separate state, should they wish it, and to the *right* of the Quebecois to independence, as rooted in the Leninist position of the right of nations to self-determination, which seeks to unite the workers of oppressor and oppressed nations for the socialist revolution.

We praised their work in publishing a regular weekly paper, and their concentration in the trade union movement, and concluded with the hope that the discussion would prove fruitful in further narrowing existing political differences.

Wohlforth responded by informing us that, in his opinion, the fundamental question was our recognition that the International Committee's struggle against Pabloism[1] represented the conti-

---

1. In January 1964, Michel Pablo launched a personal magazine called *Sous le Drapeau du Socialisme*. In the May 1965 issue, he published a statement indicating that he would

nuity of the struggle for the Fourth International, and that the Negro question was subordinate to the "program of the WL and IC". According to Wohlforth, our decision not to join their organization was "historically wrong". Their shift of position on the Negro question proved that we could have influenced the course of the WL from within, instead of opposing it from without.

Even had they arrived at full agreement with us on the Negro question, they "could not care less", as they were not interested in "episodic agreements". It was a question of "Marxist method". Until we reconsidered our attitude toward the "fundamental question" of "internationalism", on which they had become "even more fanatical", acknowledged that we had adopted "Robertson's position" toward the IC, and repudiated our incorrect course, there was "nothing to discuss". This accusation and demand for our recantation were echoed by Pat Connolly.

Furthermore, said Wohlforth, they were still in basic disagreement with Trotsky's position on the Negro question, although they now "understood more clearly" those "parts" concerning the "relationship of the Black vanguard to the working class as a whole". They still held to their criticism of Trotsky, made in the pamphlet on Black nationalism and in Lucy St. John's articles.[2]

---

not abide by the decisions of the projected world congress of the Fourth International. For a translation of this statement and a declaration of the United Secretariat on it, "Pablo Announces His Break with the Fourth International," see *World Outlook* (the former name of *Intercontinental Press*), May 28, 1965, pages 31–40. Pablo is at present the leader of Tendance Marxiste Revolutionnaire, which continues to publish *Sous le Drapeau du Socialisme* as its "central organ." Aside from this quarterly, which is printed in Paris, we do not know of any other publication put out by this grouping.

The Healyites dismissed Pablo's departure from the Fourth International as meaningless. Of the various currents that pay homage to either Healy or Lambert, not one has ever analyzed the political significance of the split led by Pablo in 1965. To do so would bring into question their first article of faith, namely, the dire menace of "Pabloism."—*IP*

2. The Healyites believe that Trotsky was ignorant on the question of the Black liberation struggle in the United States. Because of this presumed ignorance, Trotsky was led, they believe, into a "revisionist" position—that is, supporting Black nationalism a number of decades before it appeared. For an analysis of the Healyite position referred to in the letter above, see "The Healyites Begin to Unravel Their

In an attempt at provoking a discussion, Cde. Fredricks questioned Wohlforth as to the motivation for the changes which the WL had made on this question. However, Wohlforth's reply was evasive. Throughout the meeting, he refused to argue the merits of their position on this question, but simply made assertions. He insisted that they "were not blind followers of Trotsky", that he had made a number of mistakes, that he was "wrong", not only on this question, but also on the Jewish question. He had referred to the "Jewish nation". "Wrong!"

Wohlforth also falsely charged Cde. Robins with being a "Zionist", and informed him that he would not be permitted in their organization under any circumstances. It was, however, his reaction to Cde. Robins' contribution to the discussion, which completely revealed Wohlforth's real political "method".

Cde. Robins criticized the account of the politics in the "International Report" by Wohlforth to the WL's convention which had appeared in the Jan. 11, 1971 "Bulletin", as lacking in the most fundamental premises and methodology which one would expect from a Trotskyist. It did not contain an analysis of the international and domestic economic situation, the spiraling inflation throughout the world, or conclusions as to its effect on the working class movement in the US. It said nothing about the US imperialist war in Indochina, the present split in the ruling class, the role of Stalinism and petty-bourgeois pacifism, and the morale of the army, and presented no comprehensive military policy toward the war. The report also reflected the WL's abandonment of the Trotskyist policy of uniting the Black and white workers in struggle against job and other forms of racial discrimination. For a period of developing crisis, Wohlforth simply dwelt on the need to study philosophy. "What kind of Trotskyism is that", asked Cde. Robins?

At this point, Wohlforth interrupted, refused to allow him to finish his remarks, and then justified this conduct on the basis that at *their* headquarters, *they* made the rules governing discussion!

He then broke up the meeting by demanding that Cde. Robins immediately vacate their prem-

---

'Trotskyism'" by Joseph Hansen, in *Intercontinental Press*, February 24, 1969, pages 190–95.—*IP*

ises, by calling him a "deserter from Trotskyism", and by threatening, at some distance and in the language of the gutter, that he would have his nose broken if he ever returned there. This, to a man who is more than twenty years his senior, was a founding member of the Trotskyist movement and an active Trotskyist for more than forty years, and who continues to function prominently and openly as a Trotskyist in his trade union and as a member of our organization!

Assuming that Wohlforth's behavior has a rational explanation, what could he have hoped to gain by so gross a rejection of our well-intentioned overture? Fear that a cooperative relationship might expose his members to our ideas, might cause his "flock" to stray? Perhaps. He may have felt that our small numbers permitted him to act in so arrogant a fashion. If so, his miscalculation was as gross as his behavior.

We do not bluff about our size, as do some other radical groups. Our newsletter, however, is read by most political tendencies on the "left" in this country, as well as by a number of organizations abroad. His "method" in "discussions" with other tendencies will, unfortunately, discredit, not only the WL but also, the other organizations of the IC with which it is in solidarity. Wohlforth's conduct will, undoubtedly, provide grist to the mills of the Pabloist United Secretariat, who may even use it to justify their rejection of your own recent proposals for discussion with them.

As to the criticism by Wohlforth which alone deserves a response—that we have not "broken" from Robertson's "method", in rejecting "internationalism" for such "subordinate" considerations as the Negro question—we welcome the opportunity of again making our position clear.

Hugh Fredricks and I informed the WL, in refusing Wohlforth's invitation to join it, of our belief that a section of an international Leninist and Trotskyist working class vanguard party *could not be built* in the racially divided US on the basis of its program of passive adaptation to white chauvinism, and that it would have been an abrogation of principle unworthy of Trotskyists to have joined an organization whose program, we believed, *insured* the failure of our common perspective.

In addition, and as I stated in my letter to Robert Sherwood, at the time, in informing him of the events which had transpired at the last WL meeting which we attended:

> . . . the forms of membership would be emptied of content, under the circumstances, in that we would have to either mutely radiate our differences on a question touching almost every aspect of practical activity, or would, by constantly raising our differences, constantly disrupt the work of the organization . . . the relationship of the individual to the collective could not be maintained, where programmatic differences were so serious, without doing violence to one, the other or both . . .
>
> Until we can reach sufficient programmatic agreement with the WL, it is as wrong for it to pose membership to us, as it would be wrong for us to accept it. What kind of members could we be under circumstances where we were, in effect, debarred from making *political* contributions on basic questions? It was not our subordination to the WL that was posed, but, in reality, our political obliteration.

The WL responded, as you know, by passing Wohlforth's motion that, "the Turner group" is an "alien petty-bourgeois tendency", and "breaking off all political relations with it". We believe, however, that our position was and is principled and in excellent agreement with Trotsky's conception, as stated in his article on the centrism of the ILP, "In the Middle of the Road", that:

"The International is first of all a program, and a system of *strategic, tactical and organizational* methods that flow from it." (Trotsky's emphasis)

We are small, but, in our modest way, we are also trying to build the Fourth International. We do this, however, not by subordinating program to the *fetish* of "internationalism", as does Wohlforth, but by fighting for a program which we believe can build a real, living section of such an international in the US, the heartland of world capitalism and imperialism. We believe this to be the greatest service we can provide an international.

Robertson's split from the IC in 1962 and 1966,[3]

---

3. At an international conference of the Healyites held in April 1966, Robertson, as well as others who had been invited to attend, was thrown out. For documents and comments

was motivated, as we have shown, by petty egotistical considerations. Programmatic disagreements were *entirely subordinate*. By lumping our serious political differences with Robertson's unprincipled behavior, Wohlforth only reveals his own unprincipled attitude toward program. Having rejected Trotsky's position on the Negro question, the heart of the American question, he really demands that we behave as Robertson did, to ignore our program, to discard it to worship, along with Wohlforth and company, at the empty shrine of an abstract "internationalism" without program.

Under the fetish of "internationalism", Wohlforth is, obviously, building a *personal* organization, and not the "Fourth International", as he claims. We believe that he cannot tolerate an organization which unites "under its banner the most audacious iconoclasts, fighters and insurgents . . .", in Trotsky's choice descriptive phrase of Lenin's Bolshevik Party in *The Revolution Betrayed*. We had noted two years ago, and had so informed the WL's members at the last meeting which we attended, that their meetings resembled a "chicken-pecking order", and not a real collective. Wohlforth "pecks" all others, but no one dares reply to the criticism or to criticize him. The other "leaders", in their turn, criticize lesser "lights", also without fear of a rejoinder. The same technique is utilized by Robertson, who was also trained in these methods in the same Shachtmanite school.

It is possible that Wohlforth believes that this sort of "leadership" can produce a mass party. We do not agree. He is able to draw together a few dependent souls by utilizing the banners of the IC in a mystical fashion. We have noted not a few individuals in the WL's ranks whose approach to the organization resembled that of "true believers". As you well know, utilizing the banners of October, the Stalinized Communist parties were able to recruit and even retain thousands of very devoted and subjectively revolutionary members, not only in the ultra-left period, but also in the overtly counter-revolutionary "popular front" period, i.e., regardless of program. We do not believe that the IC's banners can be utilized in this manner to build a mass party. Even if such a fantasy could be realized, such a party would be entirely incapable of leading the working class to power.

We have never denied that the IC, in fighting Pabloist revisionism, was conducting a struggle for the continuity of revolutionary Marxism, for the Fourth International. It is because of that struggle and because of our own struggle along the same lines, that our tendency stands politically closest to you. We share a common heritage, outlook and goal. However, we do not have sufficient programmatic agreement to enable us to join you in one organization.

Our differences on China seem to have vanished along with your critical support to Mao Tse Tung and his "Cultural Revolution". However, we still differ on Cuba. We do not see it as capitalist, but rather, as a deformed workers' state, not qualitatively differing from those in Eastern Europe, China or the Soviet Union. We cannot see the "Arab Revolution" in the peasant-guerrilla struggles of the fedayeen as you do. You share this position with the Pabloists, the Stalinists and a number of other opportunist organizations. We consider your long diplomatic silence on the Stalinist *program* of betrayal of the Indochinese struggle, which you have covered over with the slogan of "Victory to the NLF", to be a serious disservice to the "struggle for the Fourth International". Finally and decisively, we believe that your co-thinkers in the WL are still following policies which make impossible the construction of a viable section of the Fourth International in the US.

We do not believe that the WL's present eclectic political patchwork, which it presents as having been derived by Marxist "METHOD", can produce anything but what it already has produced, confusion. Nor do we believe that personal vituperation, slander, spite and willfulness have anything in common with Leninist hardness. The hardness of the Bolsheviks was founded in theoretical clarity, in a clear understanding of the road which the working class must take to the socialist revolution.

Wohlforth seems eager to call attention to the "number", usually unspecified, of Trotsky's "mistakes" to justify the WL's faulty politics, and to present himself as the superior "theoretician". And what was Trotsky's "mistake" on the Jewish

---

on the fiasco of this conference, see the pamphlet *Healy "Reconstructs" the Fourth International*. Available for $.35 from Pathfinder Press, 873 Broadway, New York, N.Y. 10003.—*IP*

question? Trotsky was incapable of conceptualizing eternal, immutable categories, and saw every phenomenon, *including the national*, in motion, in development, in the process of becoming or disappearing, unlike the master of "METHOD", Wohlforth. Trotsky had pointed out, early in 1937, that the anti-semitic policies of "decaying capitalism" was helping keep alive Yiddish culture in Europe, and bringing into being a "Jewish nation", which would "maintain itself for an entire epoch to come", and which would, therefore, seek a "common territory". While Zionism was "incapable of resolving the Jewish question", socialism would enable "the dispersed Jews", other "scattered nations" such as the Arabs and "parts of nationalities" to be "reassembled" in a community of their own choice.

We believe that the process of building the Fourth International will eventually bring us together in one organization. We look forward to the narrowing of our political differences. We believe that this unity can only come about as a result of our contending ideas, acted on and tested in the crucible of the objective process. To the extent that our political differences diminish, we will seek to further the process of unity. We do not allow personality to outweigh program.

We are confident that you will find objectionable Wohlforth's assertion that his petty-bourgeois property rights determine the norms for discussion or the rules of conduct for meetings of socialists or for any civilized group, for that matter. The WL's adoption of neo-Stalinist methods should be a matter of concern to revolutionary socialists, and certainly to his co-thinkers abroad.

Fraternally,
Harry Turner

Malcolm Kaufman expresses doubts on Tim Wohlforth's devotion to democracy

Under the title "The Stalinist-Gangster Tactics of the Workers League," the letter reproduced below was first printed in the April issue of *Vanguard Newsletter*, a mimeographed monthly published in New York. Dated April 2, the letter was addressed to Tim Wohlforth, national secretary of the Workers League, and was signed by Malcolm L. Kaufman for the Committee for Rank and File Caucuses (CRFC).

The Workers League is in political solidarity with the Socialist Labour League (SLL) in England. Its March 29 demonstration, described in the letter, was called against "unemployment, budget cuts and repression."

The CRFC is described by *Vanguard Newsletter* as "a united front of workers' organizations and working class militants concerned to build rank-and-file caucuses in the trade unions." The "presently participating organizations" are listed as New York Revolutionary Committee, *Socialist Forum*, and *Vanguard Newsletter*.

Readers of *Intercontinental Press* may recall that this is not the first time that *Vanguard Newsletter* has felt it necessary to criticize the Workers League's attitude toward workers' democracy. The March 1971 issue of *Vanguard Newsletter* charged that a fraternal discussion between delegates of that publication and the Workers League had ended with Tim Wohlforth threatening to break the nose of a *Vanguard Newsletter* supporter. (See *Intercontinental Press*, May 17, 1971, p. 461.)

In its introduction to Kaufman's letter, *Vanguard Newsletter* writes that the March 29 incident was foreshadowed by the Workers League's use of the term "rat groups" to describe certain of its political opponents. It also suggests that the Workers League's conduct in this incident is at least partially due to imitation of the SLL and the French Organisation Communiste Internationaliste (OCI—Internationalist Communist Organization). Until their differences became public last fall, the SLL and OCI were jointly engaged in "reconstructing" the Fourth International.

Vanguard Newsletter suggests that two incidents may have served as a model for the Workers League:

Intercontinental Press, May 8, 1972.

the beating of British Trotskyist Ernie Tate by SLL goons in London in November 1966; and an "international youth conference" in Essen, Germany, last July during which marshals physically assaulted members of the German section of the Fourth International who were attempting to distribute a leaflet (See *Intercontinental Press*, September 20, 1971, p. 799.)

At this writing, the Workers League has not yet responded publicly to Kaufman's letter. It would probably be a mistake to conclude from this that Wohlforth has privately communicated the apology requested by Kaufman.

✣

Dear Comrade:

The absolutely barbaric and uncalled-for behavior exercised by your organization against members of the Committee for Rank and File Caucuses at your Foley Square demonstration last Wednesday, March 29th, requires on my part an expression of the strongest possible objection.

The CRFC supported the general goals of your demonstration and participated in the march. When we sought to distribute copies of the leaflet "Youth and the Labor Movement" in a peaceful and non-disruptive manner, a WL marshal, on your instructions, harassed and physically intimidated Comrade Thomas Lowy. Other members of the CRFC were similarly menaced and were told that they were barred from the demonstration. This, in spite of the fact several of those threatened belonged to Social Service Employees Union local 371 and had accepted an open invitation made by Ronold Roberts, a member of your organization, at a membership meeting of that union on March 23rd.

This type of political crime demonstrates the sheerest hypocrisy. Following serious assaults on several of your members by the MPI (Puerto-Rican Pro-Independence Movement) last year, you wrote the following in an open letter dated 12 April and addressed to all "working class, minority, and youth organizations,"

> The Workers League proposes . . . that all organizations reject and denounce all physical attacks on other tendencies in the working class movement; that we specifically affirm the right of all tendencies to freely present their views and to sell their literature; that we oppose all government or hooligan attacks on these rights.

In my capacity as corresponding secretary of the then New York Branch No. 2 of the Socialist Reconstruction I responded to your open letter, commenting in part,

> We stand with you in the belief that all working class organizations must have the right to openly espouse their views, sell and distribute their literature, and conduct any number of forms of agitational activity. Only open discussion and dialogue can lead to the development of theory and program that can take the working class to victory over the moribund capitalist system.

Unlike yourself, however, Comrade Wohlforth, we mean what we say. We do not support workers' democracy for cheap organizational advantage. We support it as a matter of principle. The same cannot be said for the Workers League; otherwise the organization would not have engaged in criminal acts similar to those it condemned less than a year earlier.

In the same letter quoted above, I discussed the origins of political hooliganism,

> It is hardly accidental that most of the groups engaging in gangsterism are dominated by Stalinist ideology. The Stalinists' theoretical bankruptcy and their history of betrayal of the international working class leaves them with a position that cannot be defended through argumentation but instead only through physical intimidation. Needless to say, there is no better proof of the shallowness of Stalinist politics than their refusal to participate in political discussion and their frequent resort to violence as a substitute.

If you object to portions of our leaflet then the principled thing to do would have been to criticize us publicly in your press or to have at least engaged us in a private conversation that afternoon. But your actions can lead us only to the same conclusion drawn when you were attacked by the Stalinist-influenced MPI. Hooliganism can mean only one thing—confession of political bankruptcy.

It is up to you, then, to clear your record and remove any doubts as to the integrity and character of your organization. An immediate apology would demonstrate a return to the principles outlined by the WL in 1971. We await that apology.

For workers' democracy,
Malcolm L. Kaufman
Secy-Treas

SECTION VI: HEALY VS. THE ANTIWAR MOVEMENT

The SLL yields again to imperialist pressure
By Joseph Hansen

To most of the world, the crisis over Vietnam appears to be one of the most dangerous humanity has faced since the end of World War II. It may be the beginning of a chain reaction leading to a nuclear holocaust. The key to the entire international situation, it has led to the sharpest differences at the moment in the Sino-Soviet dispute; it has brought the Cuban revolutionary leaders to a new level in emphasizing their independent position; it has precipitated a crisis in ruling circles in the United States; it has touched off a great wave of protests in all countries, not least of all among the American people. Revolutionists everywhere have sought to rise to the occasion, voicing and mobilizing the most effective possible opposition to the warmongering course of American imperialism.

There is one rather singular exception to this universal reaction to Johnson's "escalation" of the war in Southeast Asia—the leadership of the British Socialist Labour League. Although their policies are generally quite ultraleftist, in this case they have displayed none of their usual frenetic excitement. In fact they are models of phlegmatism.

Their first reaction, when President Johnson ordered American planes to undertake "reprisal" bombings in North Vietnam February 7 and 8, offered promise of a reasonable facsimile of the revolutionary socialism which they claim to adhere to.

In *The Newsletter* of February 13, for instance, an article of a column and a half by Cliff Slaughter appeared under the attractive title "Hands off Vietnam!" It could be argued that it was a serious editorial mistake to shove this to one side of the front page, giving it only secondary importance,* but at least it was a beginning in the right direction.

The slogans recommended by Slaughter were "No Secret Diplomacy! Demonstrate to Stop the U.S. Bombing Attacks! Stop the Labour Government's Support for the War in Vietnam! Withdraw all British and American Troops from Southeast Asia! Hands Off the People of Vietnam!" These were correct, although one might wonder at the reasons for placing "No Secret Diplomacy!" at the head of the list in view of the actual situation at the time.

An additional article by Sarath Kumar appeared on page three. We will return to this.

In the February 20 issue of *The Newsletter*, the space devoted to the Vietnam crisis was much reduced, which is perhaps understandable from the viewpoint of routine journalism since the single article dealing with the subject was nothing but a report of a speech given by Cliff Slaughter in which he repeated what he had written in the previous issue.

In the February 27 issue, the editors of *The Newsletter* pushed the Vietnam crisis farther down the front page into a third- or fourth-rate position. The readers were offered a statement by the "International Committee," a joint organism of the Socialist Labour League and the French *Verité*

World Outlook, February 26, 1965.

---

* The main headline read "CONSPIRACY OF SILENCE." This referred to the failure of the capitalist press to report a lobbying demonstration of 1,000 aged persons and members of the Young Socialists for an immediate rise and backdating of old-age pensions.

group.* This statement, which is brief but not too bad, ends up with the following slogans: "Hands Off the Vietnam Revolution! Withdraw All U.S. and British Troops, Warships and Military Aircraft from Southeast Asia Immediately! Stop Bombing of North Vietnam! End the British Labour Government's Support for U.S. Imperialism! No Secret Diplomacy! All Support to the Revolution in South Vietnam!"

These slogans, again, are good ones; the removal of "No Secret Diplomacy!" from first place being a commendable change. It is to be wondered why the half of the "International Committee" represented by the Verité group have not yet seen fit to publish the statement. Perhaps they were not in agreement with shifting the rank of the slogan "No Secret Diplomacy!" Or it could be that they decided to publish nothing until the whole crisis is over, when it can be analyzed in an atmosphere more conducive to calm, judicious and scholarly thought.

We now come to something truly scandalous. The March 6 issue of *The Newsletter* does not carry any article whatsoever on Vietnam on the front page. And no articles on page two, or page three or four (which are all there are in the weekly organ of the SLL).

What happened? Did the meeting of the "International Committee" prove paralyzing to everyone on the editorial staff and the whole top leadership of the SLL? Or was this a consequence of directives issued by the "International Committee"? It is noteworthy that one of the slogans recommended by Cliff Slaughter, "Demonstrate to Stop the U.S. Bombing Attacks!" did not appear in the list of official slogans issued by the "International Committee."

But this was the week U.S. imperialism dropped its mask about "reprisal" bombings and launched war on North Vietnam. The SLL leadership had nothing to say about the open move by the White House to start another Korea, a move aimed squarely at the Vietnamese revolution, the People's Republic of China and the Soviet Union!

The scandalous silence was continued in the next issue. This was the week the U.S. ended all pretense about only limited involvement in South Vietnam. The SLL leadership, these ultralefts who boast about their "Leninism," had nothing to say about the landing of the first contingents of U.S. Marines in South Vietnam!

In the current (March 20) issue of *The Newsletter*, a feeble twitching on the subject is observable. A routine article attacks the "Sham fight by 'lefts' on Vietnam." This is not about the shameful silence of the SLL leadership but about the weak opposition displayed by such figures as Sidney Silverman. The article ends with a paragraph repeating the slogans issued by the "International Committee." The author, Robert James, is to be congratulated for his diligence in getting them in the same order as the official statement.

Thus it must be recorded that the most militant and timely statement to come out of Britain on the crisis in Vietnam, the most ably presented denunciation of the betrayal of the Wilson government in its policy in the Congo and Vietnam, was made by Bertrand Russell in a speech February 15—and this despite Russell's well-known adherence to the nostrums of pacifism. [See *World Outlook* March 12.] *The Newsletter* did not even mention Russell's fighting declaration, still less offer extracts or the complete text. Let not the pages of the ultraleft *Newsletter* be sullied by anything like that!

It is obvious that for all their ultraleftism, the leadership of the Socialist Labour League have conceded to the imperialist pressure in one of the gravest crises of the post World War II period.

How is this seeming contradiction to be explained?

It is simple. In their own way, the leadership of the SLL are reflecting the attitude of the Wilson government.

In foreign policy, Wilson chose to act the crawling lickspittle of the Pentagon and the White House. He has publicly given his stamp of approval to Johnson's course in Vietnam. But to make his betrayal appear plausible to the British workers, Wilson is compelled to do two things: (1) argue that the Pentagon is merely defending itself from the

---

* The majority of the International Committee of the Fourth International joined with the International Secretariat in 1963 at a Reunification Congress that brought the majority of the world Trotskyist movement together after a ten-year split. The SLL and the *Verité* group rejected an invitation to participate, refusing to even send observers. They alleged that outside of themselves most of the international Trotskyist movement had gone "centrist." They then set up a rump "International Committee."

"attack" of North Vietnam; (2) spread the impression that the danger is not very grave and that he is taking "secret" steps to fix things up through diplomatic channels. He must try to keep the British workers from waking up to the danger.

While he has not succeeded very well in putting over his brazen defense of Johnson's "escalation" of war, he has scored with the second part of his line. The mass media in Britain have collaborated wholeheartedly in the monstrous conspiracy. They play down the danger; they play up the "secret negotiations." To read the British papers or to listen to the British radio, you would never know that Johnson is taking the world along the brink of nuclear war.

Instead of trying to break through this conspiracy, *The Newsletter* is participating in it.

The source of the pressure on the editors of *The Newsletter* could not be clearer. In the little they have written in a perfunctory way on the Vietnam crisis, if they mention the danger of another world war, of a nuclear holocaust, at all, they never single it out, never explain it, still less develop it, not to speak of lifting it to the level of a campaign.

In the only analysis worthy of the name offered up to this late date by *The Newsletter*, the article by Sarath Kumar in the February 13 issue, the danger of a nuclear war even appears to be dismissed.

Kumar's article, which makes some correct points about the policies of the Soviet and Chinese bureaucracies, appears to envision that the most likely outcome of the Vietnam crisis is a sell-out by Peking and Moscow which the U.S. will pick up, thus ending the matter. The perspective Kumar sees is: "The stage is set for some bribe-giving and taking."

What this far-from-Marxist analysis leaves out—aside from the real aims of U.S. imperialism—is the colonial revolution. Even if it is granted that *both* Moscow and Peking are equally willing to sell out the Vietnamese revolution, including seeing North Vietnam smashed militarily, do they actually have control over the Vietnamese revolution? And what about the repercussions of such a raw betrayal throughout the colonial world?

Here we come to one of the great flaws in the international position of the SLL leadership. They downgrade the colonial revolution. They are so convinced of their estimates on this question that they even made it a key issue in splitting from the majority of the former International Committee, holding that the recognition accorded by the majority of the world Trotskyist movement to the importance of the colonial revolution is a sign of "centrism."

We have now been provided with an instructive example of the consequences of the SLL position. By depreciating the colonial revolution, they are led to concede greater possibilities than are open to Peking and Moscow in meeting the demands of American imperialism. By believing it possible for the two bureaucracies to get away with a crass sell-out in Vietnam—and that this will satisfy the ravenous appetite of U.S. imperialism!—they come to the position that the danger of a chain reaction in Vietnam, leading to another world war, is not too great. In brief, their course of action shows that they accept Wilson's view of the reality as not inaccurate, whatever they may think of his policies, and that they therefore believe the whole question of American aggression in Vietnam is not as important as, say, the struggle for immediate higher, back-dated old-age pensions in Britain. Ultraleftism thus displays its opposite side, opportunism.

This is not the first time the SLL leadership have conceded to imperialist pressure since they split from the majority of the International Committee and isolated themselves from the world Trotskyist movement. A flagrant instance occurred during the Congo crisis. One of *The Newsletter's* featured writers echoed the imperialist propaganda about the Congo freedom fighters shooting "helpless white and coloured women and children."

When Ernest Germain called attention to this despicable buckling to imperialist pressure [see *World Outlook* January 8 or *The Militant* January 18, 1965], the editorial staff of *The Newsletter* reacted in characteristic fashion. A letter was published from a reader, W. Hunter, noting correctly that to talk as the author had about the Congolese revolutions was "to yield to imperialism." This was followed by a note from the guilty author confessing his error. And with that the unpleasant subject, like other things filed under the rug at SLL headquarters, was mentioned no more. As for Ernest Germain! He was singled out for what easily rates as the most energetic campaign undertaken by *The*

Newsletter in the recent period. The main danger faced by the British workers today, clearly, is the "centrism" of this "treacherous" figure.

Left unanswered is the question of how it was possible for the editor of *The Newsletter* not to notice that one of his main contributors, dealing with no less an important subject than the American-Belgian-British aggression in the Congo, had yielded to imperialism. Apparently the National Secretary of the Socialist Labour League thought it was sufficient to offer up a small scapegoat, the guilty author, and let the much more guilty editor go scot-free.

There is not the slightest indication that a serious examination of SLL positions was undertaken to determine how such yielding to imperialist pressure in the official organ of the Socialist Labour League could have occurred. No lessons were drawn about the dialectical interrelationship of theory and practice and how a gross error in practice is a certain indication of something decidedly rotten in theory. The unspeakable method of singling out a scapegoat was sufficient, it appears, to meet the norms of the SLL.

The consequence was that within weeks another and even worse case of yielding to imperialist pressure occurred. *The Newsletter* followed up its buckling in the Congo crisis by buckling in the crisis over Vietnam.

It is to be hoped that readers of *The Newsletter* as alert as W. Hunter will now write to the editors, demanding a change in course. We hope that this occurs and that the pressure will have some influence on the leaders of the SLL. Even at this late date, we should be most happy to see them open up a campaign against American aggression in North Vietnam, with particular attention to the real role of the Wilson government.

But it would also seem to be high time that members of the SLL began inquiring as to what is wrong in the positions of their leaders that can bring them into the parade behind Wilson, shuffling along in a paralytic way with their bedraggled ultraleft banners.

Once again—the SLL and Vietnam
By Joseph Hansen

In a previous article [see *World Outlook* March 26], I called attention to the sluggish way in which the leadership of the Socialist Labour League reacted to the opening of the war on North Vietnam by U.S. imperialism, and suggested that this was a second case in recent months of the SLL yielding to imperialist pressure. One of the leaders of this generally ultraleftist British organization, Cliff Slaughter,* has attempted an answer in the April 3 issue of *The Newsletter*.

The reply is of abysmal mediocrity. The author makes no attempt to consider the issues. He seeks, instead, to evade them, to cover up the facts and to deafen the audience by shouting "outrageous lies and slanders." He even entitled his article, "HANSEN'S BIG LIE."

World Outlook, April 16, 1965.

To begin with, let me recall that I expressed the hope that under criticism the leaders of the SLL would correct their course. I stated:

> Even at this late date, we should be most happy to see them open up a campaign against American aggression in North Viet-

---

* A brief biography of Slaughter appeared in the January 2, 1965, *Newsletter* under the headline, "Cliff Slaughter to work full-time for SLL." We are told that besides remaining in the Communist party from an early age until after the Hungarian events of 1956, when he began to move in the direction of Trotskyism, he is a Cambridge man who became a Leeds University lecturer, a post he is now leaving. We utilize the occasion to offer our congratulations to Slaughter for his decision to join the ranks of full-time revolutionists, although we must say that the headline about it in *The Newsletter* is something of a journalistic curiosity like: "48-YEAR-0LD MAID GETS MARRIED."

nam, with particular attention to the real role of the Wilson government.

They appear now to be making the effort. In the March 26 issue, *The Newsletter* elevated the U.S. war against North Vietnam from a routine minor place to a central position in the news of the week. The April 3 issue announced that they succeeded in getting together "over 300 Young Socialists" from "London, the Midlands, Yorkshire and South Wales" to join "2,000 members of the Indian Workers Association" who were marching in London against the jailing of Communists in India and in favor of "the restoration of civil rights" in that country. After participating in the march of the Indians and attending a meeting protesting the violation of civil liberties in India, the Young Socialists went to an SLL meeting to protest the imperialist aggression in Vietnam. While the report in *The Newsletter* indicates that the parade of 2,000 members of the Indian Workers Association was aimed at pressuring the Congress government in India to release the more than 1,000 political prisoners in dungeons there, the headline over the article reads, "3,000 MARCH AGAINST VIETNAM WAR and imprisonment of Indian Communists." (The difference in type face appears in the original.)

What led the leaders of the SLL to decide to try to break out of their rut and have *The Newsletter* give the Vietnam events the special prominence they deserve is not clear, since if any self-criticism was made, they have kept it to themselves. Perhaps the use of gas by the Pentagon shocked them, as it did others in Britain, to realization of the importance of the situation; or perhaps they suddenly became concerned over the possibility of being outflanked from the left on this issue by figures like Bertrand Russell, who saw the need to speak out and go into action; or, in their own way, they may have responded to criticism from some source or other. Whatever the reasons, we repeat that we are glad to see the SLL make an attempt to join the rest of the international socialist and radical movement in placing the struggle against American aggression in North Vietnam at the top of the agenda where it belongs. Let us hope that this is not a mere spasmodic action. There is every reason to close ranks in face of the common enemy in this grave crisis.

The qualitative turn in Vietnam

Let us turn now to Slaughter's apologia. It was the position of the Fourth International from the time it happened that the bombings of North Vietnam, carried out February 7 and 8 under orders from President Johnson, marked a qualitative turn in the long, bloody intervention of American imperialism in the civil war in South Vietnam. This conclusion was reached by many others who saw that the American move toward the north was aimed not only at the Democratic Republic of Vietnam but at the People's Republic of China, the Soviet Union, Cuba, and, indeed, the freedom struggle throughout the world; and that it posed the clear threat of ending in the catastrophe of nuclear war.

The SLL leaders, however, gave no evidence of a similar assessment. They continued *as if they had failed to recognize a qualitative change in the situation.*

What little they did print in their press about the war in Vietnam was not basically wrong—there was no conscious betrayal. But the articles on this topic declined and even vanished from the official organ of the SLL precisely as the American bombers extended and increased their forays, the "escalation" rose, and the world crisis deepened. This sag and collapse in propaganda constituted *a grave default in leadership, occurring as it did at a crucial time.* It was this that I called attention to and sought to explain as due to acceptance of Wilson's estimate of the lack of gravity of the situation despite the SLL's opposition to Wilson's policies.*

---

* Slaughter shows little restraint in distorting what I said. On this particular point the distortion is particularly bad. "Our readers," says Slaughter, "will be amazed to learn that *The Newsletter* and the Socialist Labour League have capitulated to imperialism over the war in Vietnam, and that, in particular, we 'accept Wilson's view of the reality as not inaccurate . . .'" The phrase ascribed to me is torn from the following: "By depreciating the colonial revolution, they are led to concede greater possibilities than are open to Peking and Moscow in meeting the demands of American imperialism. By believing it is possible for the two bureaucracies to get away with a crass sell-out in Vietnam—and that this will satisfy the ravenous appetite of U.S. imperialism!—they come to the position that the danger of a chain reaction in Vietnam, leading to another world war, is not too great. In brief, their course of action shows that they accept Wilson's view of the reality as not inaccurate, whatever they may think of his policies, and that they therefore believe the whole question of American aggression in Vietnam is not as important as,

Didn't omit 'all mention'

In trying to answer, Slaughter follows a curious procedure. He goes down the list of facts I cited from successive issues of *The Newsletter*, showing the way the handling of Vietnam was subordinated to other topics and the way the world crisis was played down, and displays astonishment that there should be any criticism. In the March 6 and 13 issues, where not a single *article* on the Vietnam crisis appeared, Slaughter seeks to apologize by pointing to the fact that *mention* of Vietnam could be found by carefully searching other articles. (He says it is a "lie that we omitted all mention of the struggle in Vietnam"; but I didn't say "mention." I called attention to the absence of *articles*.) In other words, instead of admitting how wrong *The Newsletter* was in losing its usually strident voice in face of the flare-up of perhaps the greatest crisis since the end of World War II, he finds nothing wrong with the judgment of the editors in curtailing their handling of the war in Vietnam and tries to brazen it out by shouting, "Liar!" at their critic.[*]

Slaughter inadvertently reveals that he is perfectly aware of the lapse of the SLL press in the Vietnam situation:

> We understand very well that the kind of politics engaged in by Hansen and his friends measures everything in terms of column inches; but we must inform him that The *Newsletter* is not just a weekly commentary, it is an organiser of thousands of workers and it will be judged by the success of that active movement.

Slaughter says again: "His [Hansen's] 'fight' on Vietnam is entirely a question of writing articles, but for us it is above all a question of building the real movement to smash the imperialist governments which carry through the colonial wars."

In plain language, *The Newsletter* did not have many column inches or many articles on Vietnam in the most crucial weeks; this topic was admittedly pushed out of the center of attention and even reduced to merely passing *mention*; but this default was all right because *The Newsletter*, you see, is "an organiser of thousands of workers"! It is only peculiar to the "kind of politics engaged in by Hansen and his friends" to expect something better.

Pigeonhole thinking

Slaughter thus drives a wedge between propaganda and organization, and downgrades revolutionary-socialist propaganda as if it were in contradiction to organizing workers. This may be what Slaughter learned in practical experience at Leeds University, at Cambridge and in his formative years in the Communist party before 1956. But such a vulgar empiricist concept has nothing in common with the school of Trotskyism. Slaughter, unfortunately, still displays all too many vestiges of his training under bad teachers.

It is true that in our times we have seen instances where revolutionary movements have moved ahead and even won power *despite* propaganda that was in contradiction to the inherent logic and ultimate aims of the mass struggle. The victories in Yugoslavia and China are outstanding examples. The latest one, a most impressive instance, is Cuba although this case is considerably different since the leadership was an honest one and moved toward revolutionary-socialist positions during the course of the revolution itself. But it is a gross departure from the concepts of revolutionary socialism to either advocate or justify conducting propaganda in contradiction to revolutionary action.

The reason for this is the enormous role which

---

say, the struggle for immediate higher, back-dated old-age pensions in Britain. Ultraleftism thus displays its opposite side, opportunism."

Instead of attempting to answer this argumentation based on the hard evidence of what had (and had not) appeared in *The Newsletter*, Slaughter chose to distort what I said, tearing a single phrase out of context and making me appear to accuse the SLL leaders of committing something worse than is indicated in my carefully weighed statement. He did not learn such methods in the school of Trotskyism!

[*] In another instance, Slaughter says that Hansen "omits to mention that this same front-page article [in the March 20 issue of *The Newsletter*] puts the same demands which he called 'correct' a month earlier." Slaughter is blinded by his eagerness to prove me a liar. I not only stated specifically that "The article ends with a paragraph repeating the slogans issued by the 'International Committee'"; I added that "The author, Robert James, is to be congratulated for his diligence in getting them in the same order as the official statement." Is Slaughter as careless as this about the facts in all his writings, or was his misrepresentation deliberate?

political consciousness plays in a socialist revolution. The higher the level of consciousness among the revolutionists and the vanguard of the working masses, the easier becomes the revolutionary victory. The written and spoken word are intimately linked with organization and action, the two sides of the process being bound up with the aims established in successive stages of the revolutionary process.

That is why Trotsky, for one, put such stress on correct and effective propaganda, particularly at crucial turns in the world situation. He taught us that a few days at a moment like the opening of a war can outweigh years of ordinary events in the life and development of a revolutionary party. Such moments test the capacities of a revolutionary leadership, above all its independence and its ability to judge reality correctly in the heat of the class struggle.

Is it so difficult to understand what is involved? Let us take a case. It is Slaughter's boast that *The Newsletter* is "the organiser of thousands of workers." Good. On what issues is it organizing these thousands of workers? On the issues featured in the columns of *The Newsletter*. The editors, if they are to live up to revolutionary socialist principles, have no choice but to single out those issues that are of crucial importance to the working class.

It is true that considerable flexibility is demanded to meet the current level of consciousness of the workers—on this the Trotskyist movement has much to offer, as is evidenced by the Transition Program and its development. Nevertheless, the duty to speak out and campaign in appropriate form on the substance of the crucial issues remains.

The opening of the U.S. war on North Vietnam was such an issue. It was an imperialist aggression against a colonial country; it was an imperialist attack aimed at the workers states; it offered the clear threat of escalating into a nuclear war, thereby involving the fate of all of humanity in the most literal sense. To this should be added the fear, horror, revulsion and indignation that swept the world, making the task of mobilizing the opposition easier. Even in Britain a cry of alarm was raised by such figures as Bertrand Russell. Yet in the face of this, *The Newsletter* acted as if it were paralyzed, incapable of responding to the events.

Obviously it was time for someone to build a fire under the editor's chair.

Lots of inches, well displayed

Having sought to justify giving only passing mention to Vietnam while the rest of the world shuddered at the prospect of going over the brink into a nuclear catastrophe, our newly fledged full-time leader of the SLL offers us a variant. *The Newsletter* was a bit short in column inches and articles for five crucial weeks? So what! You should see the March 27 issue "with its front page almost entirely devoted to the Vietnam war and notice of a public rally on the question in London."

To this we respond, as indicated above: Excellent! A most welcome change! We congratulate the editors, including Slaughter, for giving signs of life; and now that they are awake we hope they stay awake, although their erratic behavior leaves room for doubt that this will be the case. But what then becomes of the previous argument? Is the number of column inches and the number of articles and the way they are featured of importance after all? Then why the nonsense about its being a mark of a different "kind of politics" to judge the quantity of material and its placement as indicative of how a leadership sizes up a situation? Has Slaughter suddenly switched and gone over to that kind of politics? Or is it simply that any argument is good, no matter how contradictory, so long as Slaughter is the one who runs it through his typewriter?

The new argument about the lots of inches, well displayed, does not save the day for this attorney. He has simply escalated himself into new difficulties. In case he hasn't noticed, we call Slaughter's attention to the fact that once again the point of qualitative change rears its ugly head. What caused the editors of *The Newsletter* to suddenly switch and decide to give central place to the war in Vietnam after giving it merely passing mention? *When did the qualitative point of change in the war occur that is reflected in this qualitative change in the amount and placement of propaganda?*

Was it when the Pentagon began bombing North Vietnam; or, say, when the U.S. admitted using gas; or when Bertrand Russell made his eloquent denunciation of the Wilson government; or, perhaps, when the editor discovered flames arising around the seat of his chair?

If the qualitative point was February 7, then *The Newsletter* was wrong in the way it handled its propaganda at the outbreak of the crisis. This could only be due to an incorrect estimate of the situation, which must then be explained. If it was some other date, then the SLL leaders are guilty of failing to offer the revolutionary-socialist movement the correct date. They are guilty at the same time of failing to make public the analysis through which they arrived at that date, although the analysis is all the more important in view of the widespread conclusion, particularly outside of Britain, that it was the earlier date of February 7.

Now we come to the most devastating argument of all. Only a man with a Cambridge degree and much experience as a university lecturer could have thought it up. In response to our criticisms, he says, "You're another!"

Against our analysis of the reasons behind *The Newsletter's* yielding to imperialist pressure, Slaughter refers to accusations levelled by the SLL leaders against the Socialist Workers party which, he claims, show that it has "betrayed." The accusations really reflect the ultraleft position of the SLL leadership; but let us suppose that there were substance to them—does this then justify the SLL yielding to imperialist pressure? It would seem wiser, and certainly much closer to Leninism, for the SLL leaders to seek the source of their own error in order to avoid repeating it again, instead of responding with a high-pitched scream: "So what, you're another!"

The error in the Congo crisis

As I indicated in my previous article, the SLL was guilty only a short time ago of yielding to imperialist pressure on a different occasion—when the American and Belgian imperialists, with the aid of the Wilson government, attacked Stanleyville. An article in *The Newsletter* echoed the imperialist propaganda about the Congo freedom fighters shooting "helpless white and coloured women and children."

Ernest Germain drew attention to this shameful yielding to imperialist pressure. A small rectification then appeared in *The Newsletter*, blame for the error being pinned on the hapless author of the offending article. But no lessons were drawn on how it was possible for something as monstrous as that to have appeared in *The Newsletter*. It was simply swept under the rug; and a campaign was hastily opened against Germain. And, of course, since Germain is regarded as a main enemy of some concern from the ultraleft viewpoint of the SLL leaders, who look at the outside world as a reactionary mass with little to distinguish one part from another, they spared neither articles nor column inches on this foe even though much else of importance to the British working class had to go by the board.

When a second error occurred, this time in relation to Vietnam, another colonial area under attack from imperialism, it was legitimate to ask if there were not some relationship between the two errors. In the final analysis they would seem to have a common origin in the basic SLL position of minimizing the importance of the colonial revolution, the position that led them to split from the International Committee, to set up a rump committee composed of two sections of the International Committee, and to refuse to join in unifying the world Trotskyist movement. Is this right or wrong? Slaughter does not take up the question.

In fact, far from discussing the relation between the two errors, he denies there was any error in *The Newsletter's* handling of Vietnam and remains tight-lipped about the SLL yielding to imperialist pressure during the Congo crisis. By shouting about unrelated matters, he no doubt hopes to divert attention from the unsavory lapse that occurred during the Congo events. A full-time official in the SLL has his share of pettifogging duties it seems.

And the other half of the 'International Committee'?

The SLL leadership, as we have seen, finally came around to the conclusion that it would be costly to continue relegating the war in Vietnam to such a low place in priorities as merely passing mention. But the SLL constitutes only half of the rump "International Committee," the other half being the *Verité* group in France.

In my previous article, I called attention to the strange silence of this half of the "International Committee" on the war in Vietnam. Does this group agree with the declaration on this subject published in the February 27 issue of *The Newsletter* under the name of the "International Committee"? Do they disagree? Why don't they translate it and print it in France? Are they ashamed of it?

Perhaps the French half of the "International Committee" is publishing hundreds of column centimeters, or distributing leaflets, or organizing rallies and making speeches about the situation in Vietnam. If so, why didn't Slaughter include this information among his boasts? Is he ashamed of what they're writing or saying or doing?

Unfortunately, there may be good reason for Slaughter's silence. He may not be hiding anything. He may just have nothing to report. Out of interest in the subject, we initiated inquiries but were unable to locate a single item on Vietnam produced by the French half of the "International Committee" since February 7, not even a translation of the passing "mention" featured in *The Newsletter*.

We would like very much to see these colleagues and collaborators of the SLL also come to life, even if still more belatedly than their British co-thinkers, and join in actively opposing the dirty colonial war being waged by American imperialism in Vietnam.

Can the British half of the "International Committee" get its French half slapped awake around this issue? We hope so, as it would be strange indeed if a paper that is "an organiser of thousands of workers" and which is "rapidly becoming the recognised spokesman of revolutionary Marxism in the international Trotskyist movement," as Slaughter boasts, could not even prod its colleagues across the Channel to stand up and mumble something in face of the threat of nuclear war.

We are waiting, Slaughter, for your report on this. Just give us the facts about the activities of the *Verité* group; no embellishments, please, about "outrageous lies and slanders." The subject is not without interest, for if the British half of the "International Committee" is able to organize thousands of workers by failing to recognize the importance of a world crisis until it is necessary to run to catch up with the crowd, the French half, by maintaining a graveyard silence, may be organizing them by the tens of thousands. Shouldn't a tactical discovery as revolutionary as this be passed on, even if it has to be demeaned by being put in the form of an article, thereby becoming subject to measurement in column inches?

In reply to the slanders of 'The Newsletter'

The following statement was issued in London September 6 by the International Marxist Group in reply to assertions printed in *The Newsletter*, a publication of the Socialist Labour League.

Readers of *The Newsletter* will be familiar with the incessant sniping that paper indulges in against "Pabloites," "Revisionists," and with the numerous other epithets which are used to describe the supporters of the United Secretariat of the Fourth International. When our group is described as "tiny" and "discredited," they might well wonder what all the fuss is about. This reply will attempt to answer that question.

Intercontinental Press, September 23, 1968.

In two consecutive issues (August 27 and 31), *The Newsletter* has criticised the role our group played in the two mass left-wing demonstrations against the Soviet invasion of Czechoslovakia, in articles entitled, "Revisionists and anticommunists unite on Czech crisis" and "Capitalist Press praise Anti-Communists."

First of all, let us say that this is not an honest polemic—this is so easily demonstrated that it is tempting merely to go through these articles and refute them point by point, but we consider it more important to expose the reason for this dishonesty, because these articles are an attempt to cover up the basically mistaken attitude of the Socialist Labour League [SLL] towards the massive radicalisation of youth over the Vietnam question.

The most perverse charges against us are that

we demonstrated alongside anti-Communist and reactionary elements in anti-Soviet demonstrations; that we have abandoned the slogan, "Victory to the N.L.F.," as a capitulation to the Communist Party in order to involve them in the forthcoming October mobilisation; and that we have thus gained the favour of the capitalist press.

To back up the first charge we are told:

> The most noticeable feature of the recent anti-Soviet demonstrations was the unity established between the various political groups.
>
> Alongside *Young Conservatives* (our emphasis) and Liberals eager for an anti-Communist orgy, shouted anarchists and pacifists.
>
> With them came the "International Socialism" group who are accustomed to condemning "Russian imperialism."

Another feature of the demonstrations it seems was

> applause for Dubcek, the leader of one wing of Czech Stalinism, the *burning of red flags* (our emphasis), placards saying "Down with Russian Imperialism!" and the shout "Stalinism out, democracy in!"

This technique is a familiar one; by taking a number of stray facts, distorted reports, and direct lies, an amalgam is made by which you can "prove" the most slanderous and contradictory charges. It is a technique which Stalinism developed to a fine art and has no place in the pages of a professedly Trotskyist publication.

The slogans of the demonstration were "Withdraw Soviet troops from Czechoslovakia; withdraw U.S. troops from Vietnam." The August 27 *Newsletter* carries the headline, "WITHDRAW SOVIET TROOPS NOW!" So we presume that the S.L.L. does not object to the first slogan, and we doubt if they oppose the second, so what principles are violated by Trotskyists participating? Of course, a number of groups and individuals carried slogans which were the result of a mistaken concept of the class nature of the Soviet Union, but it is a principle on these mobilisations that each tendency has the right to carry its own slogans. Thus to impute responsibility for such slogans to the I.M.G. [International Marxist Group] is dishonest. In fact, our group fought against such concepts in the preparations for the demonstration, and in its statements, publications, and speeches and on its own banner stated "The Soviet Bureaucracy—aggressive in Czechoslovakia—passive in Vietnam."

But the main feature of the demonstration was not at all "anti-Communism," it was a sea of red banners; not only did it denounce the invasion, but it aggressively took up the question of the Soviet bureaucracy's betrayal of the Vietnamese struggle, and exposed the hypocrisy of those who have protested about Czechoslovakia, but have backed up U.S. aggression in Vietnam.

What place was there then for the Young Conservatives and the burning of red flags? The first is a direct lie: the young Tories were not part of the united front. Three or four of them did turn up, and when one of them tried to speak he received pretty rough treatment, was shouted down, and the microphone was hauled from his hands. The red-flag burning is taken from a garbled account in the *Guardian* of the Wednesday evening demonstration at the Earls Court Exhibition, when a provocateur on the fringes of the crowd set fire to two of the red flags which were being carried. *The Newsletter* has a touching faith in the accuracy of the capitalist press.

This faith really fouls them up over the charge that we have abandoned the slogan, "Victory to the N.L.F." Taking up another garbled story in the *Guardian*, they repeat the story that a recent meeting of the October Ad Hoc Committee broke up in disorder over the refusal to accept this slogan. This is what the small Maoist group which organised this happening would like to spread around as the truth, but the fact is that they packed the meeting in order to attempt to impose a string of slogans on the committee, and broke it up when they were prevented from diverting the meeting onto whether or not "Long Live Ho Chi Minh" was a better slogan than "Victory to the Vietnamese Revolution."

As for our "honeymoon" with the capitalist press—well, it was back to normal four days after the second *Newsletter* article, with the papers coming out with a scare story about petrol bombs being prepared for the October mobilisation, and M.P.s demanding a ban on the March. Incidentally, this looks like building up into quite a witch-hunt; we would have no objection to *The Newsletter* giving some space to combating the capitalist press lies.

Can we interpolate a comment on the attitude taken towards Tariq Ali? Firstly, we are told that the S.L.L. "is of course hated, and rightly so by Tariq Ali . . ." So far as we know Tariq has never made any statement of any kind about the S.L.L.; he has political differences, obviously, but to interpret this as "hatred" and to go on to say, "It's time Tariq Ali was told to shut his mouth," leaves a very nasty taste that we are sure most workers would not find pleasant. In other words it smacks of a Stalinist attitude towards political opponents.

But why does *The Newsletter* feel obliged to return again and again to attacking us? It would seem from scanning its columns that we have done little else for the past few years but capitulate, liquidate ourselves, collapse, betray, etc., etc. The truth is of course that as we have shown, any similarity between the facts about our activity and *The Newsletter* reports is purely coincidental.

But that the most vicious and slanderous attack to date should come at this particular time is significant. The reason is contained in the last paragraph of the August 27 *Newsletter* article:

> VSC and its hangers-on are enemies of Marxist principles. Their "October" campaign will be directed, not towards aiding the defeat of US imperialism, but towards confusing and misleading those who are seeking a road to revolutionary principles and a revolutionary leadership.

All of the extremely complex charges are directed towards proving the above, and justifying the S.L.L.'s opposition to the forthcoming October Mobilisation, and to the whole struggle which the I.M.G. has carried out to build a mass movement against the U.S. imperialist aggression in Vietnam.

The S.L.L. some years ago set out to build a mass revolutionary youth movement. For this purpose it split away a section of the Young Socialists from the Labour Party. Despite all their statements to the contrary they never achieved more than very modest success with this perspective, and in recent years the "Keep Left Y.S." has stagnated if not declined. But to their horror the struggle in solidarity with the Vietnamese Revolution has drawn into activity, particularly around V.S.C. [Vietnam Solidarity Campaign], thousands of youth, both students and young workers, who, despite many elements of mistaken ideas, adventurist tendencies, etc., are eager for a showdown with capitalism. And not only can the S.L.L. not reach them, but they are bypassing the S.L.L. *on the left*. It is from these youth that the core of a new revolutionary party will be built; therefore for Trotskyists to be unable to influence them is a very serious matter. The S.L.L. does not present it in this way of course; by slander techniques it tries to dub this movement as "petty bourgeois," etc., and to denounce the various groups involved in V.S.C., but even if these groups were pure shit, they do not amount to more than a few hundred people, while the mass mobilisations activate thousands of youth. I.M.G. is confident of the strength of the ideas of Trotskyism; that is why we are eager to participate in this movement—we are eager to prove the superiority of our theories *in action*.

This is why we set so much store on mass actions against the Vietnam War. Experience in every part of the world confirms our contention that this war is the *central* problem of world imperialism, and that movements against this war very rapidly develop consciousness of the nature of imperialism, and how the war is linked to the problems of the day-to-day life of young workers and students. In fact the experience of France shows that young workers and students involved together in a struggle against imperialism can become a very socially explosive mixture.

But to involve the maximum number of youth, a correct approach to building the movement must be taken. This is why we fought for the line of unity on *one issue* between all of the groups which agreed with the struggle for solidarity with the N.L.F. It is very foolish to counterpose to this the argument that Lenin and Trotsky carried out a different tactic in a different epoch, for different purposes, and under different circumstances, merely because our present tactic is loosely called by the same name—"united front."

The lesson of the last two years is that once the factional wrangling between the various Marxist and Left tendencies is broken through, and joint action carried out on vital issues, real progress can be made, and the differences can be fruitfully discussed in the light of this experience.

We note that *The Newsletter* is campaigning for an "All Trade Union Alliance," to fight against the government's attacks on the workers. We find this interesting: what is the basis of a trade unionist participating in this campaign? Does he need first to denounce the Communist Party? Does he require to have a correct theory of the nature of the Soviet state? We rather think not. But if no principle is betrayed in such an organisation, what is the difference with the Vietnam struggle? And if a sectarian attitude is held toward the Vietnam struggle, will this not affect adversely the building of unity amongst trade unionists?

The International Marxist Group therefore rejects the slanders of *The Newsletter*. We will not diverge from the course of fruitful work in which we are engaged, and we give notice to the S.L.L. that it will not for long be able to pose its sectarian attitudes and slanderous methods as genuine Trotskyism.

Long live solidarity with the NLF!
Long live the revolutionary youth!
Long live the Fourth International!

Healy proves a point
By Joseph Hansen

An almost perfect example of the polemical methods used by Gerry Healy's Socialist Labour League, a group in Britain that claims to be "Trotskyist," is to be found in the September 14 issue of their official newspaper, *The Newsletter*.

The sect happens to be confronted with a difficulty. The British bourgeois press has opened a witch-hunt against a mass mobilization scheduled by the Vietnam Solidarity Campaign for October 27 to protest the imperialist aggression in Vietnam and to express solidarity with the heroic resistance of the Vietnamese people.

The Healyites oppose the demonstration inasmuch as it was called by people they disapprove of politically. In accordance with their sectarian views, they refuse to join in the demonstration even though they have the right to carry their own banners in it.

That's hard enough for them to explain. Still worse is the witch-hunt in the bourgeois press. If the Socialist Labour League should rally in any genuine way in defense of the Vietnam Solidarity Campaign, what happens to the dyed-in-the-wool differences with that group? But if you abstain and say little or nothing, how do you explain that?

Intercontinental Press, September 30, 1968.

Fortunately, from the point of view of the Socialist Labour League, one of the bourgeois papers made it possible to turn the uncomfortable situation into its opposite.

The Guardian, making a show of the "fairness" that is worn almost like a national costume by the hypocritical British bourgeois press, noted that the October 27 demonstration will carry twin slogans, "Russians out of Czechoslovakia—Americans out of Vietnam." Therefore it would not be right to charge that the organizers of the demonstration are agents of Moscow, unmindful of the crimes of Stalinism.

The September 14 issue of Healy's *Newsletter* finds a deep lesson in this.

> These "twin slogans" represent exactly the class position of the "left" groups now being attended to by *The Guardian*. They represent a political horizon beyond which the middle class cannot go.

Thus, to believe *The Newsletter*,

> no matter how "left" the Vietnam Solidarity Campaign and International Socialism *think* they are, they come out politically precisely

in such a way as to channel all "protest" back into the "democratic" capitalist camp.

To bolster this assertion, the anonymous author (could it be Healy who is something of a specialist in this field?) refers his readers to the American political scene.

> As in the USA this camp—the "liberal" wing of the Democratic Party—will endorse both "twin demands" of the October 27 demonstration.

This argument is hardly strengthened by the fact that it is presented in the form of a prediction. But let it go. The prophetic powers of this polemicist will receive the acid test soon enough.

The argument continues:

> That is why we warned the Socialist Workers' Party (USA) that its antiwar campaigning, if deprived of the *class* content of a fight to organize the workers' movement against imperialist war and to build a Labour Party in the United States, would lead back into the Democratic camp.
>
> And this was *exactly* confirmed: The SWP's *Militant* carried the twin slogans, against Russian troops in Czechoslovakia, US troops in Vietnam, on August 30, week of the Democratic Convention! [Emphasis in original.]

! !

As usual with *The Newsletter*, its reporting was not *exactly* what ought to be called exact. The August 30 issue of *The Militant* carried the following headline: "Soviet troops, go home! U.S., get out of Vietnam!"

This was the headline over a statement by Fred Halstead, presidential candidate of the Socialist Workers party, issued exactly on August 21, which was exactly the day following the Soviet invasion of Czechoslovakia.

It is true that this issue of *The Militant* was sold in Chicago that week, as it is every week in the year, and not only in Chicago but other cities in the U.S. and abroad. The Chicago supporters of *The Militant*, however, did *not* sell it at the Democratic convention—who would have bought it there even if the police, national guard, and federal troops had let them through the barbed wire?

They sold *The Militant*, besides other places, among those demonstrating *against* the Democratic convention and its support of the Vietnam war and its pleasure over Moscow's invasion of Czechoslovakia which was such a windfall to the Democratic machine in its apologies for Johnson's escalation of the war in Vietnam. The sales of *The Militant*, we may add, were brisk.

Now we come to what Healy himself will no doubt concede is the "payoff."

The August 27 issue of *The Newsletter* ("the week of the Democratic Convention!"), carried the following headline: "WITHDRAW SOVIET TROOPS NOW!"

Not a "twin" headline, but a "single" headline.

What is this supposed to confirm *exactly*? That the Socialist Labour League has given up its opposition to the war in Vietnam completely? Or that it just went soft for that one week in order to improve sales at the Democratic convention in Chicago?

Drawing the moral to it all, our anonymous SLL spokesman says: "This is an invaluable experience for the Marxist movement."

We can agree. Stalinist methods of polemic can destroy those that resort to them.

Some advice to Tariq Ali
By Joseph Hansen

The Vietnam Solidarity Campaign, the organization to be credited for taking the initiative in projecting and preparing the October 27 antiwar demonstration in London, has been singled out for singularly vicious red-baiting in the capitalist press. The police, Scotland Yard, and ultrarightist provocateurs have collaborated in this, seeking to provide "evidence" for the charge that the VSC is seeking to precipitate "violence."

Thus Scotland Yard raided the headquarters of the *Black Dwarf*, the newspaper edited by Tariq Ali, one of the main figures in the Vietnam Solidarity Campaign. After ransacking the place, they found a diagram and instructions crudely scribbled in crayon on a wall telling how to make a Molotov cocktail. This was given sensational treatment in the press.

The most recent sensations consist of an anonymous leaflet giving "instructions" on carrying out violent actions on October 27, and anonymous "information" that the fire in the Imperial War Museum was deliberately set to provide advance "publicity" for the October 27 march.

The purpose of this red-baiting is all too clear. Besides trying to frighten people into staying away, the guardians of "law and order" are seeking to provide a pretext for either banning the demonstration or for using police violence against it.

This is not all that the Vietnam Solidarity Campaign has had to contend with in its efforts to bring together the maximum forces in a demonstration of solidarity with the Vietnamese people and opposition to Harold Wilson's policy of aiding and abetting the U.S. imperialist aggression in Vietnam.

A group in the ultraleft fringe—the Socialist Labour League—has been conducting its own campaign against the October 27 march, against the Vietnam Solidarity Campaign, and specifically against Tariq Ali.

No attention need be paid this popgun echo to the heavy artillery of the capitalist press were it not for the fact that in relation to their opponents in the labor movement, the leaders of the Socialist Labour League do not always confine themselves to purely verbalistic excesses. Those who know the SLL well., took particular note of the following sentence in an article by Cliff Slaughter, an authoritative voice of the central leader Gerry Healy, in the August 31 *Newsletter*:

"It's time Tariq Ali was told to shut his mouth."

This was not merely a display of ugly subjectivism. In the same paragraph Slaughter said of Ali: "He is deliberately used by the capitalist press to build up in the working class a picture of what is supposed to exist anywhere to the left of the Communist Party." In other words, Slaughter charges Ali with being utilized by the capitalist press.

Slaughter continues in the next paragraph:

> Political playboys are an expensive joke so far as the real Marxist movement is concerned. At critical times like the invasion of Czechoslovakia they become the spearhead of all the middle-class "democratic" rubbish around the left, which is never so united as in their opposition to the Soviet Union and to Trotskyism.

By "Trotskyism," Slaughter means the sectarian views of Healy.

A "political playboy," an "expensive joke," a "spearhead" of middle-class democratic rubbish, a convenience for the capitalist press—in Healy's school no alternative exists. It's time—high time—Tariq Ali was told to "shut his mouth." But who is to tell him? And by what means is he to be made to shut his mouth?

A precedent exists by which to judge what Slaughter has in mind.

In June, 1966, the Socialist Workers party published a pamphlet in New York, *Healy "Reconstructs" the Fourth International*. This consisted principally of letters written by Healy and some of his followers providing irrefutable evidence of the kind of regime that exists in the SLL and the Stalinist

---

Intercontinental Press, October 28, 1968.

methods employed by its leaders.

The pamphlet, sold by adherents of the United Secretariat of the Fourth International in Britain, enjoyed lively sales.

The Central Committee of the SLL responded by issuing an official statement, printed in the August 20, 1966, *Newsletter*, denouncing the pamphlet.

Among other things, the committee said that the Socialist Workers party had "capitulated to imperialism," had "sold out the anti-war movement," and had come to play the role of "finger-men for the State Department." The pamphlet was a "provocation" that "constitutes a complete and irreversible departure even from revisionism."

The statement carried the following threat: "We shall not hesitate to deal appropriately with the handful of United Secretariat agents who hawk it around the cynical fake-left in England."

Healy himself further motivated this in an article published in the November 5, 1966, *Newsletter*. The United Secretariat of the Fourth International, he said, "now emerges as the 'left cover' for bureaucracy and imperialism." The Socialist Workers party, he declared, "is initiating a sly stage-by-stage orientation towards the Democratic Party itself." Accusing the Socialist Workers party of adapting to Stalinism, he issued a declaration of war: "Any revisionist tendencies which in one form or another adapt themselves politically to the Stalinists are, in our opinion, mortal enemies."

A case of apoplexy? It soon turned out that more was involved.

On November 17, not two weeks after Healy's article was printed, Ernest Tate, today a prominent figure in the Vietnam Solidarity Campaign together with Tariq Ali, was selling the famous pamphlet on the sidewalk in front of Caxton Hall where the Socialist Labour League had scheduled a public meeting. He was subjected to some heckling by members of the SLL but he paid no attention to them.

Suddenly Gerry Healy appeared at the door. As if they had been given a signal, six or seven members of the SLL attacked Tate in gang fashion.

"My literature was knocked from my hands," Tate testified. "I was punched and thrown to the ground, my glasses were smashed, and as I lay on the ground I was kicked repeatedly in the groin and stomach."

The victim of the SLL punch-up boys had to be hospitalized.

The sequel was, if possible, even more scandalous than this reversion to the methods used by the Stalinists in Britain in the early thirties.

Healy was named specifically by Ernest Tate in an open letter to the radical press describing what had happened. Healy's response to this was to resort at once to the bourgeois courts. He sought to do still further damage to the victim of a beating at the hands of members of the SLL by making him the target of a libel suit based on a technicality (the difficulty of proving to the satisfaction of a bourgeois court that Healy's signal was actually intended to start a punch-up). Healy indicated that he was exploring utilizing the courts of the class enemy to bar further sales of the pamphlet.

The *Socialist Leader* and *Peace News*, rather than fight a shyster lawsuit, met Healy's demand for ten guineas and a retraction for the "crime" of having published Tate's letter.

> We have been informed, they said in formal statements, that Mr. Healy asked a steward to clear the pavement in front of the entrance of the Hall so that passengers alighting from coaches would not be delayed in getting to the meeting; that he did nothing to prevent Mr. Tate or anyone else from selling literature; and that others were selling literature at each side of the entrance without interference.

The two publications, in the form demanded by bourgeois law, said they "sincerely apologise to Mr. Healy for having published the suggestion that he employs violence or seeks to curtail freedom of expression.

Ernest Tate, standing firmly on the principles of revolutionary socialism, countered efforts to have a capitalist court decide on the merits of the case. Tate sought instead to have a working-class tribunal weigh the evidence. This, naturally, met with no response from Healy, a firm adherent to the justice of Her Majesty the Queen.

The tone adopted by the SLL in its current campaign against Tariq Ali and the Vietnam Solidarity Campaign is reminiscent of the tone employed against Ernest Tate before he was beaten. Thus Cliff Slaughter's attack did not pass unnoticed.

The International Marxist Group, to which both Ernest Tate and Tariq Ali belong, issued a leaflet September 6 replying to the slanders. [See *Intercontinental Press*, September 23, p. 794.] Noting Slaughter's sentence, "It's time Tariq Ali was told to shut his mouth," the authors of the leaflet observed that this "leaves a very nasty taste that we are sure most workers would not find pleasant. In other words it smacks of a Stalinist attitude towards political opponents."

This was put about as mildly as it could be, in view of the SLL's record.

Cliff Slaughter's answer, "*The Newsletter* draws blood," in the October 8 issue of the SLL's official organ, may have been intended to allay the apprehensions he had aroused. If so, he had better try again. His tone remains the same. Thus he tells his audience that the International Marxist Group is "squealing" and "we in the Socialist Labour League are going to make them squeal still more."

It is pointless to take up Slaughter's arguments, spread over an entire page in the second of two articles on the subject. They are devoid of the slightest interest, designed as they are merely to "prove" Healy's thesis that the United Secretariat of the Fourth International, the Socialist Workers party, and their cothinkers internationally (all of whom he labels as "Pabloites") have "capitulated" to "imperialism" and the "Stalinist bureaucracy." We will follow Slaughter only on the matter of concern—shutting Tariq Ali's mouth.

> But we are criticized especially, [says Slaughter] for saying (August 31), "It's time Tariq Ali was told to shut his mouth". This, says the leaflet, "leaves a very nasty taste that we are sure most workers would not find pleasant. In other words it smacks of a Stalinist attitude towards political opponents".
>
> Let us put the record straight, and reply to this snide attack.

Here is how Slaughter puts the record straight:

> Everybody in the labour movement knows that we have always fought for the right of all tendencies to be heard. We tell Jordan, Tate and the Pabloites of the "International Marxist Group" straight that, while we will always defend *their* right to speak against repressions from the capitalist state or the Labour Party and trade union bureaucracy, we do not forget that they the Pabloites, joined with the "state capitalists" to *help* Transport House to suppress "Keep Left" and the Young Socialists.

Everybody in the labour movement knows! The truth is that everybody in the labour movement knows just the contrary. For instance, the facts about the beating of Ernest Tate and Healy's rushing to the capitalist courts are well known in the British labour movement. The stifling, undemocratic regime in the SLL, proved by the documents in the pamphlet *Healy "Reconstructs" the Fourth International*, is just as well known to everybody in the labour movement. Everybody in the labour movement has likewise known for years that the charge repeated in the last part of Slaughter's paragraph is a slander. So much for Slaughter's sophistry in the way he appeals to the record. Yes, sophistry.

Our red professor, who unfortunately still exhibits traces of his years of training in the Stalinist movement, continues:

"We say categorically, we did not propose or encourage any suppression of Tariq Ali or anyone else."

Does he not protest too much? The facts in the case of Ernest Tate speak categorically otherwise.

But what then did Slaughter intend to propose or encourage by pointing to Tariq Ali in the invidious way he did and commenting, "It's time Tariq Ali was told to shut his mouth"?

He did not indicate it then; now he has suddenly decided what he meant: "And we offer again [!] some advice to those close to Tariq Ali; tell him to shut up for a while and read and think before he opens his mouth."

In short, Slaughter, motivated by benevolent intentions, was only suggesting to the International Marxist Group that they would do well to imitate what is practiced every day inside the Socialist Labour League. There, under a tinpot despot, a monolithic regime dismisses democracy as so much rubbish. People are told to shut up, or else . . .

Slaughter's disinterested advice to Tariq Ali's friends hardly squares with the Healyite thesis that these friends are nothing but tools of "imperialism" and the "Stalinist bureaucracy"—"mortal enemies" as Healy put it just twelve days before Ernest Tate was beaten by an SLL punch-up squad. Since when has Slaughter come to the position that the SLL should offer friendly advice to "mortal enemies"?

Slaughter has not changed his views as to the nature of Tariq Ali's friends. After his lame explanation about what he really meant by saying, "It's time Tariq Ali was told to shut his mouth," he repeats: "The Pabloites are ideological representatives of the middle class subservient to imperialism."

Lest anyone still mistake his real views because of his backing water on proposing or encouraging that Tariq Ali should be induced to shut his mouth, he reiterates: "Their role in diverting people from the road of Marxist leadership and revolution is their major role, and it is for this that we do principally attack them." (Emphasis in original.)

With diversionists, subservient to imperialism and blocking the road of Marxist leadership and revolution, isn't it permissible to put up a small smoke screen if they happen to have been alerted by something you proposed or encouraged a bit too obviously?

Our advice to Tariq Ali is to remain on guard, particularly if he happens to be on the pavement in front of a meeting of the SLL where either Healy or Slaughter are featured as speakers.

Healy changes his line
An ultraleftist endorses the antiwar movement
By Les Evans

Gerry Healy, the head of the Socialist Labour League in Britain, has just offered his followers and well-wishers a pleasant surprise. The October 18 issue of the SLL's newspaper, the *Workers Press*, signaled a switch in line on a very important question. For the first time since the beginning of the Vietnam war, the sectarians of the SLL decided to endorse a major antiwar demonstration. True, they endorsed the action after it was over; they did not participate in it; and they expressed reservations—but endorse it they did.

Under the headline, "Workers march against war," the *Workers Press* told its readers about the October 15 antiwar Moratorium in the United States. Noting the participation of groups of trade unionists in the demonstrations, the anonymous author of the article declared: "That is why it would be a fatal mistake to dismiss the 'moratorium' as just another, if bigger, 'day of protest'. . . .

"At last the fight of the US working class against unemployment, speed-up, racialism and mass poverty is developing an international, anti-imperialist character."

In a later comment, on October 21, the *Workers Press* was even more enthusiastic, in accordance with the flowering of the new line:

"After the vast demonstrations of 'Moratorium Day' US imperialism finds itself faced, as the revolt in the army itself develops, with a war on three fronts."

And on October 25: "The 'Vietnam Moratorium' hit Nixon really hard and forced those sections of the ruling class opposed to a continuation of the war to speak out more loudly than they have ever done before."

The editor of the *Workers Press* is to be congratulated. What a refreshing contrast to the old line! Who, other than a Trotskyist of the outmoded orthodox school would even think of asking for an explanation of the reasons for the 180-degree switch?

For years, *The Newsletter* (which was just recently renamed *Workers Press*) has denounced the antiwar movement in the most ringing language.

The August 12 *Newsletter*, for example, carried a piece by John Crawford polemicizing against an article on the united-front tactic written by Tom Kerry, a leader of the U. S. Socialist Workers party,

---

Intercontinental Press, November 17, 1969.

in the revolutionary-socialist weekly *The Militant* published in New York.

> Anti-war campaigns and ad hoc committees were formed as substitutes for Marxism, Crawford argued.
>
> For example, Kerry's friend, Ernest Tate [a leader of the International Marxist Group, the British section of the Fourth International], tried to persuade us that the Vietnam Solidarity Campaign was a united front and that we were therefore prohibited from warning its members about the dangers of Stalinism betraying the Vietnamese revolution. . . .
>
> In pretending that working in such organizations, or even leading them, would somehow contribute towards the overthrow of imperialism, the revisionists were only echoing the Stalinist traditions from the late 1920s onwards.

Two months later, this line perished. While few will mourn its demise, perhaps some would appreciate a report from Crawford on how it happened that the movement denounced as a "Stalinist" popular front suddenly came to display an "anti-imperialist character." A dialectician might explain that the antiwar movement had this potential from the beginning. The SLL leaders claim to adhere to the dialectical method. Why then did they stand on the sidelines all these years and condemn the antiwar movement—do everything in their power, in fact, to stab it in the back?

If this question were limited to the SLL alone, it might be of small interest. But the attitude of the SLL on this question is not much different from that of various ultraleft sectarian groups in several countries. These include the Maoist Progressive Labor party and the Students for a Democratic Society in the United States, who have refused to support the antiwar movement on the grounds that it does not raise "anti-imperialist" demands.

Wars and revolutions offer decisive tests for revolutionists. The SLL claims that it is a "Trotskyist" organization, and its leaders justify splitting from the world Trotskyist movement by claiming that the Fourth International founded by Leon Trotsky degenerated and became "revisionist." But the Healyites must explain how it happened that in the midst of an imperialist war against a colonial country, they sought up until October 18 to destroy the very movement which they then suddenly decided to praise. As they finally had to admit, the mass movement against the war reached such depth that it "hit Nixon really hard."

Will they now follow the logic of their new line and admit that they were wrong in the past? This is hardly likely, for it would be tantamount to admitting that the "revisionists" of the Socialist Workers party and of the United Secretariat of the Fourth International were consistent builders of the antiwar movement from the beginning and played a central role in promoting the mass actions in the streets which are having such praiseworthy impact in the United States today.

Has the antiwar movement 'changed'?
If we examine Healy's sudden change of line more closely, we will discover a few flaws.

The October 18 *Workers Press* report on the Moratorium is quite inaccurate. A White House "official" is supposed to have admitted that "at least 30 million people were involved." No source is given for this, but it would be good news for the antiwar movement if it were so.

A real whopper is the following: "For the first time ever, groups of workers marched behind their trade union banners, not as individual 'protesters', *but as contingents of their class*." (Emphasis in original.) And: "Workers from the motor, transport and chemical industries were to the fore in the rallies."

Why did the Healyites print these fantasies? The reason is simple. According to their schema, it is a betrayal to support an action that is not proletarian in character. They want to switch their line on the antiwar demonstrations in the U. S.: Therefore, they find it necessary to locate a proletarian character that was previously missing, according to their theory. The Healyites, in short, required a pragmatic basis to enable them to make the shift.

The truth is that there were few mass marches on October 15. The antiwar outpouring took the form of rallies, school boycotts, and in some cases work stoppages. Because of this, virtually no "groups of workers marched behind their trade union banners," as *Workers Press* has it.

Undoubtedly there were more trade unionists involved than ever before, but it was precisely as "individual 'protesters'" that most of them participated. As to the three industries mentioned, there is not a single report from a major city of official banners being carried by any of these unions or of any official contingents showing up at any rally.

What actually happened is that the Alliance for Labor Action put an advertisement in the October 14 *New York Times* endorsing the action. This was the first time that a major union organization had given official sanction to an antiwar protest. As such it was an important indication of the pressure the mass antiwar movement is placing on the union bureaucrats to join the protests.

Undoubtedly the ALA—an alliance of the United Automobile Workers, the Teamsters, and the International Chemical Workers unions—was acting under pressure from the rank and file as well.

But it should be pointed out that the ALA endorsement came *after* some seventeen U. S. senators and forty-seven congressmen, including many top leaders of the Democratic and Republican parties, had come out for the Moratorium. The *Workers Press*, it should likewise be pointed out, refrained from reporting this fact.

It must also be said that the ALA did not organize any union contingents. (This does not mean that they will not do so in the future: An ALA representative is slated to speak at the rally following the November 15 march on Washington called by the New Mobilization and the Student Mobilization committees, and union contingents are expected to take part in that demonstration.)

The Healyite newspaper is also inaccurate in saying that the antiwar movement has never involved the organized working class before. In the April 15, 1967, demonstrations in New York and San Francisco, there were large official delegations from such unions as the longshoremen, clerks, teachers, social-service employees, hospital workers, etc.

The most curious item of all in the October 18 *Workers Press* article—perhaps it is also the most instructive item—is the fact that the author confused the working class with the trade-union bureaucracy. (Even in their last-minute endorsement, the ALA spokesmen were careful to cover their right flank by denouncing "every form of totalitarianism, whether communist, fascist or military dictatorship," and by deploring "the reprehensible activities of a small minority who burn the American flag and equate anti-Americanism with antiwar . . .")

The *Workers Press* conveniently fails to report the red-baiting statement of the Reutherite bureaucrats. Instead it hails their decision as proving the proletarian character of the demonstration. Upon these bureaucrats finally being prodded into giving official approval to an action organized by others, Healy decided he was now free to give his official approval—after the demonstration. Could a more perfect example be asked of an ultraleft phrasemonger tail-ending opportunist trade-union bureaucrats?

'Repelled by . . . middle-class protest'

In their October 18 report on the Moratorium, the Healyites indicate what impelled them to "proletarianize" the antiwar movement before they would deign to support it:

"The working class," we are informed, "by the very nature of its struggle, is repelled by all forms of middle-class protest, however genuine the feelings supporters of such movements may have."

What an absurd idea! Two paragraphs further on the article declares: "It is, of course, true that the 'moratorium' was largely led by religious, Democratic, Republican and 'liberal' figures." If this is so, and the working class is "by the very nature of its struggle" repelled from such people, how did all those workers come to show up on October 15?

The fact is that the antiwar movement has from the beginning consisted of a coalition of various tendencies, ranging from the revolutionary socialists in the SWP and Young Socialist Alliance, to "liberals" of many sorts. The anti-imperialist character of the movement has been determined by three slogans, for which the SWP has been the main champion:

1. *For the immediate withdrawal of U.S. troops from Vietnam.* As the central axis of the movement, this slogan stands in the way of any defenders of imperialist policy, liberal or otherwise, who would like to divert the struggle into a compromise that would permit the imperialists to continue their aggression. There have been bitter fights in the anti-

war movement as various tendencies have tried to replace this slogan by "more reasonable" ones such as "negotiations," "peace" in the abstract, "cease-fire," etc. The slogan "Bring the Troops Home Now!" is, of course, a popular expression of the principle of self-determination for the Vietnamese and hands off the Vietnamese revolution.

2. *For mass mobilizations in the streets.* In the absence of any mass working-class political party in the U. S., the only means to express independent political action today is through mass street demonstrations. The SWP has opposed every attempt to substitute actions by small groups for the masses or to abandon demonstrations for other kinds of actions such as petition campaigns.

3. *For a "single-issue" movement.* Precisely because the movement includes large groups of middle-class people, who do not have a working-class perspective, the SWP has opposed introducing other issues that would ostensibly give the antiwar movement a "full program." At this stage, such a program would inevitably be reformist; and, instead of a mass revolutionary movement, what would result would be a popular front of the notorious Stalinist variety. It is only by a strict agreement to fight for the specific aim of immediate withdrawal of the troops that the anti-imperialist thrust of the antiwar movement can be maintained.

It was on the basis of this three-point platform that the antiwar activists built a force that finally reached such proportions as to begin to draw in sectors of the organized labor movement despite the decades of political quiescence on the part of the American working class. And it is precisely this systematic construction of a mass movement against an imperialist war that Healy still dismisses as "platonic breast-beating about Vietnam" (October 23 *Workers Press*).

Healy's American disciples, the Workers League, a split-off from the Socialist Workers party, go even further in making a "principle" of rejecting common action with liberals, and using this as a pretext for abstaining from the struggle against the war. In the November 3 issue of their paper the *Bulletin* they declare:

> The liberal capitalist politicians behind the Moratorium Committee are the enemies of every worker in this country. They want to extricate themselves from Vietnam only to [in?] order to attack us further. They want to make sure the protest remains just that: a middle class protest and a plea for reforms. We will have nothing to do with these spokesmen for the bosses.
>
> The New Mobilization Committee including representatives of the Communist Party and the Socialist Workers Party, collaborates with these same enemies of the working class. They act as a transmission belt for capitalist politics. The Communist Party does this openly, carrying forward the Popular Front policies of the 1930s, arguing that it is necessary for the workers to ally themselves with the progressive bosses on the basis of the bosses' program.
>
> Now the Socialist Workers Party plays the same role as the Communist Party. No matter how they may squirm and maneuver, no matter how much they may talk about immediate withdrawal and mass demonstrations, nothing can disguise the fact that these leaders have gone over completely to the policy of the Popular Front, of working with the bosses.

What this amounts to is providing a "left" cover for strikebreaking in the struggle against the imperialist war in Vietnam.

To describe the demand for immediate withdrawal of U.S. troops from Vietnam as a "plea for reforms" is ultraleft phrasemongering. According to this school of thought (if "thought" it can be called), any struggle short of the seizure of power is a "plea for reforms."

The fact that liberals can be drawn into supporting such struggles is not a decisive criterion. The tactics of revolutionists are determined by the potential for mass confrontation with the capitalist state, not by what allies are won in the course of such a struggle, however dubious their credentials may be.

What was wrong with the popular front was not that Marxists found themselves momentarily in an "alliance" with liberals, but something quite different.

First of all, the so-called Marxists were not Marxists; they were *Stalinists* serving as a border guard for the Kremlin which in turn was interested in maintaining the status quo. The popular-front tactic cooked up by Stalin was a rehash of the Social Democratic policy of class collaboration. Through it, Stalin hoped to divert revolutionary struggles into safe channels and to receive in payment from the Western bourgeoisie agreements not to invade the Soviet Union. Thus the Stalinist popular front involved a program committing its adherents to preserve capitalism.

In correctly rejecting the popular front, the Healyites, and other ultralefts, went a shade too far. They threw out Leninism.

Revolutionary Marxists have always made "alliances" with liberals on certain specific issues such as defense of the victims of the class struggle, support for strikes, the defense of civil liberties, and even striking together against fascists and other ultrareactionaries. And if the Healyites are unable to see the obvious reasons for such a policy in relation to the living struggle against the Vietnam war, let them go back to the books. They will discover that it is their leaders who are guilty of revising Marxism on this elementary question.

Lenin on 'alliances'

In Lenin's classic work on revolutionary tactics, *What Is To Be Done?*, written in 1902, he discusses the bloc with the "legal Marxists," who helped smuggle Marxist ideas past the czarist censor in the 1890s:

> It is no secret that the brief period in which Marxism blossomed on the surface of our literature was called forth by an alliance between people of extreme and of very moderate views. In point of fact, the latter were *bourgeois democrats* [emphasis added]; this conclusion (so markedly confirmed by their subsequent "critical" development) suggested itself to some even when the "alliance" was still intact.
>
> That being the case, are not the revolutionary Social-Democrats who entered into the alliance with the future "Critics" mainly responsible for the subsequent "confusion"? This question, together with a reply in the affirmative, is sometimes heard from people with too rigid a view. But such people are entirely in the wrong. *Only those who are not sure of themselves can fear to enter into temporary alliances even with unreliable people; not a single political party could exist without such alliances.* (*What Is To Be Done?*, Lenin's *Collected Works*, Volume 5, page 361–362, Moscow, 1961. Emphasis added.)

Lenin goes even further in justifying this bloc:

> The rupture, of course, did not occur because the "allies" proved to be bourgeois democrats. On the contrary, the representatives of the latter trend are natural and desirable allies of Social-Democracy insofar as its democratic tasks, brought to the fore by the prevailing situation in Russia are concerned. (Ibid., page 362.)

The one condition Lenin places on such an alliance for limited aims is that the socialists have full opportunity "to reveal to the working class that its interests are diametrically opposed to the interests of the bourgeoisie."

Compare the condition insisted upon by Lenin with the way the American antiwar movement, particularly its left wing in the Student Mobilization Committee, has functioned since the SWP entered it in 1965. The condition has been observed as the principle of "nonexclusion." This is the right of all tendencies that oppose the war to participate, no matter what their views are or what they think of the programs of the other participants. They have the right to advocate their revolutionary ideas and to criticize other tendencies in the coalition.

The interests of the antiwar movement were served in another way by insisting upon "nonexclusion." It blocked the witch-hunters, who would have liked to revive the red-baiting practices that played such havoc in the American labor movement in the McCarthyite period. It assured a *democratic* process in deciding on given actions. Observing "nonexclusion" as a principle in the antiwar movement also meant opposing any attempts by ultraleftists to bar liberals because they were not socialists, or anti-imperialists, or proletarians.

But more is involved than the mere permissibility of temporary blocs with liberals in the course of working-class struggles as such. In fact, blocs with liberals are permissible, according to Lenin, in struggles for purely democratic demands that involve only petty-bourgeois or even bourgeois layers. Lenin is quite explicit on this. To show how far present-day sectarians have retreated from Bolshevik politics, it is worth citing a few more lines from Lenin:

> In a word, every trade-union secretary conducts and helps to conduct "the economic struggle against the employers and the government". It cannot be too strongly maintained that *this is still not* Social-Democracy, that the Social-Democrat's ideal should not be the trade-union secretary, but *the tribune of the people*, who is able to react to every manifestation of tyranny and oppression, no matter where it appears, no matter what stratum or class of the people it affects; who is able to generalise all these manifestations and produce a single picture of police violence and capitalist exploitation; who is able to take advantage of every event, however small, in order to set forth *before all* his socialist convictions and his democratic demands, in order to clarify for *all* and everyone the world-historic significance of the struggle for the emancipation of the proletariat. (Ibid., page 423. Emphasis in original.)

Lenin insists that this is not simply a propagandistic intervention on behalf of the workers, but that revolutionists should be leaders of democratic struggles:

> We must also find ways and means of calling meetings of representatives of all social classes that desire to listen to *a democrat*, for he is no Social-Democrat who forgets in practice that "the Communists support every revolutionary movement", that we are obliged for that reason to expound and emphasize *general democratic tasks before the whole people*, without for a moment concealing our socialist convictions. He is no Social-Democrat who forgets in practice his obligation to be *ahead of all* in raising, accentuating, and solving *every* general democratic question. . . .
>
> *We* must train our Social-Democratic practical workers to become political leaders, able to guide all the manifestations of this all-round struggle, able at the right time to "dictate a positive programme of action" for the aroused students, the discontented Zemstvo people, the incensed religious sects, the offended elementary schoolteachers, etc., etc. (Ibid., pages 425–428. Emphasis in original.)

The fight against the war in Vietnam is perhaps the most serious and vital of all the struggles involving democratic rights in the world at the moment. At issue is the democratic right of a people to self-determination in face of the violation of that right by the mightiest imperialist power on earth. Because of the democratic issue at stake, it necessarily involves those elements among the bourgeoisie who genuinely believe in democracy. The only condition placed on their joining the antiwar movement is that they support the demand for immediate withdrawal of U.S. troops and that no political confidence be placed in them, since they will do everything they can (as the record shows) to divert the movement into supporting bourgeois politicians or parties.

The sharpest struggles within the antiwar movement have occurred precisely over the efforts of certain tendencies to divert the coalition from the path it has followed as a giant lever of independent mass action.

The SLL and the Workers League, it must be stated, have not participated in this struggle either. They have abstained from the antiwar movement, contenting themselves with watching—and kibitzing—from the grandstand during the five years in which U.S. imperialism has continued to pour death and destruction on the people of Vietnam. They have acted as if they were completely indifferent to the struggle *within* the antiwar movement. Their attitude was, let the liberal bourgeoisie divert it!

Now that they have belatedly recognized that a struggle of great historical significance has been going on, what can we expect from these strategists of the typewriter and the ballpoint pen? Can we hope to see them participate in building the next wave of antiwar actions on November 15? Will they now undertake a self-reform?

Skepticism is in order. And yet it may be that a

miracle is about to occur. The October 21 issue of the *Workers Press* expresses the greatest concern about bringing up the level of the antiwar movement. This, they assert, requires exposure of the leadership of the antiwar movement. These leaders, it seems, have been aiding imperialism!

"The role of the liberals, the Stalinists and the revisionists in containing the anti-war movement at a protest level is a real aid to imperialism at this juncture," the *Workers Press* declaims, "and must be exposed as such."

Perhaps it would be of greater service to the antiwar movement if Healy would kindly explain just who he was really aiding by abstaining up until October 18 from participating in the struggle for immediate withdrawal of U.S. troops from Vietnam—that is, if he believes anyone is interested in his explanation.

SECTION VII: THE STRUGGLE IN NORTHERN IRELAND

Revolutionary Nationalism, Class Struggle, and Problems of Party Building in Ireland
By Gerry Foley

> Gerry Foley's analysis of the 1972 Official Sinn Fein Ard Fheis (conference) is nothing more or less than a eulogy of nationalism as a solution to Ireland's economic and social problems.
>
> Writing in two issues of the Pabloite Unified [sic] Secretariat's "Intercontinental Press", he argues for a new unity between Officials, Provisionals and civil righters in a revolutionary party using mass action on the streets as its number one tactic.

This was the assessment of my three articles on the Official Sinn Fein *ard fheis*[1] made by Ian Yeats, the Irish expert of the Socialist Labour League, an English sectarian formation headed by Gerry Healy. Yeats's review appeared in the March 22 issue of *Workers Press*, the organ of the SLL.

Dogmatic denunciation of opponents of the SLL is one of the distinguishing features of the *Workers Press*. Denunciation, in fact, is such a prime consideration that it often overrides the need to keep in touch with reality. An example from Yeats's article is his explanation of the source of division among Ulster workers:

> ... if Ulster workers are divided it is precisely because revisionists like Foley, and indeed all those organizations affiliated to the Unified [sic] Secretariat, have actively applauded and fostered sectarian demands and movements as a substitute for building a Marxist revolutionary consciousness and organization capable of uniting them.

Since the Trotskyist groups are the most immediate competitors of the SLL (which claims to be Trotskyist), they are obviously to blame for any setbacks in revolutionary upsurges around the world. From the Healyite point of view they must be agents of the capitalist system. And, of course, the capitalists are interested in fostering these alleged agents. Thus when the British government felt compelled to concede the right to demonstrate, after it had tried for months to end active mass protest in Northern Ireland, the SLL interpreted this as follows:

> It seems the authorities were keen to allow yesterday's protest against internment to enable "left" and "radical" leaders to regain some credibility with the Catholic community. (*Workers Press*, January 3, 1971.)

In other words, the concession gained through mass struggle (in which the SLL did not participate) were part of a plot to keep the masses away from the SLL and its program.

Yeats's attack, while hewing to the usual Healyite requirements, has several unusual features. The most important is that his real target was not that bête noire of the SLL, the "Pabloites," and his purpose was not simply to reassure the faithful.

Intercontinental Press, May 28, 1973.

1. See *Intercontinental Press,* January 22, February 5, and February 12, 1973.

Yeats had in mind a political process taking place in another organization.

The Healyite reporter evidently wanted to impress the most dogmatic and workerist fringe of the Official republican movement, whose attempt to build a mass revolutionary party in Ireland has tended to get bogged down in various types of sectarianism. The fact that he indicated this interest in the Officials confirms the nature of some of the problems this group has been experiencing.

Because of their unique historical advantages, the fact that their organization is known and respected for its heroic past and includes among its activists most of the politically conscious vanguard of the Irish people, the Official republicans tend to think that they cannot fall victim to deviations of the kind affecting some of the smaller left groups. Unfortunately, as the last year in particular has shown, this is not true. In fact, as a result of the all-inclusive political character of the Official republican movement, the disputes of the far-left tendencies have been reflected in its ranks. This process will inevitably continue and deepen as it has in similar organizations elsewhere.

The smaller left groups promulgate various conceptions of party building and revolutionary action. They tend to carry these ideas to their logical conclusion and can thus serve to some extent as laboratory specimens. It would be especially useful for the republicans to study these examples, because if they are to build a revolutionary party as they hope, a party that by necessity will be built on a political program, on ideas, they will have to accustom themselves to thinking in terms of the long-range implications of certain concepts and the way these can become distorted in the complexities of real struggle. However absurd the smaller groups may be, and the SLL certainly ranks high in absurdity, objective processes have produced them; and real political problems, usually very difficult ones to solve, lie at their root.

Moreover, it is not only small organizations that can act in extremely sectarian ways. In its ultraleft phase of 1927–33, the German Communist party, which had a following of millions, displayed aberrations that would put even the strangest of British sects in the shade. The result of this sectarianism was a world-historic tragedy, the victory of Nazism. On the other hand, the British far-left groups have a certain value in that they represent a wide range of errors to avoid in trying to build a revolutionary alternative to the reformist parties.

The Official republicans have learned to some extent how difficult this is. The Communist party's history as a semioutlaw in Irish Catholic society has not made it revolutionary. Nor has the revolutionary daring of the republicans made them proof against the reformist ideas of the CP and the varieties of Stalinism. In fact, as their political situation has worsened, it has become apparent that the Officials, however unwillingly, have been drawn more and more into the train of these reformist concepts—moreover at the very time they are seeing how useless the CP apparatus is for any revolutionary purpose. In fact, reformist ideas are deeply rooted in capitalist society and in the mentality of broad layers of workers under capitalism.

It is also true that the pressures of capitalist society tend to turn ideas and political groups into their opposites. Thus, many Irish rebels of 1916–21 become counterrevolutionists in 1922. The dynamics of this process are illustrated not only by the small groups but also by the disputes that now seem to be developing in the Official republican movement. The fact that the SLL, which claims to be the paragon of Trotskyist orthodoxy, ends up, as we shall see, echoing the arguments of the Irish Stalinists is an example of such an outcome. Another is that, despite an evidently growing antagonism, the basic approach of the workerist ultralefts in the republican movement tends to coincide for all practical purposes with that of the Stalinist-trained reformists.

So, it seems useful to take up Yeats's article in detail, since it illustrates not only the level of the SLL's degeneration but the problems facing the Official republican leaders and some dangerous errors they have made in trying to deal with them.

The problem of party building

As the historic revolutionary organization of the Irish people, the republican movement could pride itself on being a significant factor in the politics of the country, deeply rooted in the society and possessing leaders who had proved their courage, cool-headedness, and devotion in the most difficult situations—eminently practical men and women. But building a revolutionary political party with a consistent program and practice, a party that can challenge the basic structures of imperialism in Ireland, was to all intents and purposes a completely new concept in Irish politics. There was very little in the republican tradition that could serve as a guide for building a party based on a consistent and thoroughgoing critique of society. This is a very different task from building a broad nationalist formation on a program simply of organizing guerrilla struggle against a foreign oppressor and the surface manifestations of colonial subservience.

The style of leadership that has grown up out of nationalist experience is to seek consensus, to avoid sharp political debates, to conciliate and balance off different groupings and individuals with fundamentally different ideas of the kind of Ireland they want. There is little understanding of the need to struggle to clarify political principles and develop tactics in accordance with these principles.

Thus, the inevitable tendency has been to attempt to maintain a politically heterogeneous coalition around a kind of minimum program. For most of modern Irish history, this minimum program in effect has been to prepare a military uprising against foreign rule. Within this framework, revolutionists like James Stephens could work together, however uneasily, with conservatives like Thomas Clarke Luby and even monarchists like John O'Leary.

A revolutionary party also must strive to achieve the broadest possible unity behind democratic and revolutionary-socialist goals. But its method of accomplishing this is completely different from that of vaguely defined formations.

A revolutionary party is built on two foundations: clear political principles, and a constructive and objective approach of working with other groups and tendencies capable to some extent, despite their backwardness and confusion, of participating in the struggle for national and social liberation. United fronts in action with such reformist or eclectic groups are fundamentally a means of reaching out to those layers of the people and the working class that do not yet understand the need for a socialist revolution and must be convinced in practice that socialists are the best fighters for their objectives and that Marxism offers the best practical guide for their struggle.

Trying to put together broad organizational combinations by avoiding or fuzzing over key questions of program is fatal in the long run to both principle and unity. This approach makes it impossible to educate either the vanguard or the masses in any consistent way. Inevitably, policy is decided by back-room compromises. It is neither discussed fully nor tested in action. The result is a tendency toward competition of organizations and personalities instead of programs and methods of work. Rival combinations try to build themselves at the expense of the mass movement, rather than strive to lead it by winning the masses to their ideas and example.

This law seems to be at the root of many of the basic problems the Official republican movement has encountered over the past nine months in particular. Instead of trying to win the Provisionals over to their political program by seeking to work with them on common objectives, the Officials have tried to anathematize them. They have tended, moreover, to develop the idea that it was possible to participate in united-front work without trying to involve the Provisionals. As a result, among other things, the Civil Rights Association, of which the Officials are the major component, has become more and more sectarian and less and less able to mobilize large numbers of people.

At the same time, apparently in order to hold on to their only allies in the North, the Communist party, the Officials accepted a right-wing program at the NICRA convention in February that called for an "impartial peacekeeping force" and a calling in of "illegal weapons." By implicitly offering confidence to a liberal capitalist and Unionist regime, these planks contradicted fundamental republican as well as revolutionary Marxist principles.

The civil rights struggle

The effect of such positions, if they become the program of the movement in practice, will be to transform the Civil Rights Association into the opposite of what it was during the mass marches. At that time the struggle developed around slogans that struck at the essence of the partition and the counterrevolutionary settlement of the Irish war of national liberation, and at the same time seemed immediate and reasonable demands to the masses of the oppressed Catholic population, who were not ready to fight for a united Ireland as such. It is quite unlikely in fact that any large section of the population will take up a fight against an entire system as such. Revolutions generally begin as struggles for concrete demands that the system cannot meet.

Because of its revolutionary dynamic, the civil-rights struggle united large masses of the oppressed population in action behind radical opponents of the partition and the imperialist system. In this context, concessions granted under the pressure of direct action by the people only lent more momentum and raised the aspirations of the masses.

However, if the civil-rights movement now takes the approach of saying right from the start that the government and the ruling class have nothing to worry about, that it will keep its followers from going too far, that it is really the best defender of bourgeois-democratic "law and order," the authorities have no reason to make any concessions. The masses of the oppressed population, whose hatred of the system is constantly fired by the intimidation and brutality of the British troops, have no reason to follow it. And what is worse, calls by a respected organization like NICRA for "impartial peacekeepers" and disarming the people strengthen illusions that the government can play a legitimate role as peacemaker, which not only weakens the resistance of the masses to the inevitable attempts to beat them back into passivity but also makes it more difficult to focus international public opinion against the British and proimperialist repressive forces.

Whereas in the period of the big marches the civil-rights movement had a radical democratic impact, encouraging the masses of the oppressed population to act directly to press their demands, an explicitly reformist civil-rights organization will inevitably tend to shift its focus toward lobbying, becoming incorporated into the game of bourgeois politics that demobilizes and divides the people. In this way, "unity of the left" on a reformist program results in disunity of the really important forces, the forces that can make a revolution.

Role of Stalinism

As for the Stalinists in particular, it is not sufficient to regard them simply as "part of the left." Because of the twists and turns of the Soviet and Chinese bureaucracies to which they are bound and because of the general interest of these privileged groupings in preserving the world status quo, the Communist parties can find themselves in positions to the right of bourgeois and petty-bourgeois democrats and nationalists.

This was the case, for example, in Argentina during and immediately following the second world war when, in the name of unity between the Soviet Union and the West in the war against the Axis, the Communist party opposed the anti-imperialist movement led by Perón. As usually happens when a Communist party is forced to go against the current because of larger opportunistic aims of the bureaucracy, the Argentine CP adopted a sectarian position opposing the driving force of what at the time was the greatest popular movement in the history of the country. As a result it was not only isolated by the Peronist leadership and rendered unable to do anything to wrest control of the movement from the national-bourgeois leadership but it itself divided and weakened the workers movement and the anti-imperialist forces.

In Northern Ireland also the Communist party cut itself off from the main anti-imperialist current owing to the needs of the Soviet alliance with Britain and the United States in the second world war. It remains isolated from the nationalist-minded population because of its integration into the Unionist and British patriotic left and its fear of any violent upset in the heart of the imperialist "sphere of influence." Thus, in the long run an alliance with the Communist party on a reformist and Unionist program means putting "unity of the left" in place of unity of the nationalist-minded population, which is far more important and has revolutionary potential. Subjective reactions to nationalist groups using violence against the left in their own community should not be permitted to obscure this. It should be recalled that where they have had the strength, the Stalinists' record on this score has been far worse than anything alleged against the right-wing Provisionals.

Yeats puts in his oar

The Healyite reporter Yeats seems completely oblivious of the real problems of Official republican strategy in the civil-rights movement. For instance, he writes:

The Ard Fheis was distinguished by an almost complete move away from backing the on-the-streets reformist militancy of the Northern Ireland Civil Rights Movement and the Communist Party of Ireland to the concept of building a new revolutionary nationalist party.

The real problem is the "off-the-streets" reformism of the Communist party. Although the NICRA convention was held in February, Yeats does not mention in his March 22 article that while Official representation on the executive board was reinforced, the program of the organization shifted to the right. This was the fruit of the "move away from backing the . . . reformist militancy of the Northern Ireland Civil Rights Movement and the Communist Party of Ireland." Moreover, the new executive board included republicans whose courage and militancy are unimpeachable.

How were these leaders, who daily risk their lives and liberties for their convictions, cajoled into compromising their principles by taking responsibility for a probourgeois law-and-order program? The most likely explanation is that they were misled by ultraleft and workerist notions that the civil-rights movement was not important, that it was reformist by nature and that revolutionary politics belonged to another sphere. For example, one of the members of the NICRA executive elected in the last convention, Malachy McGurran, told me in an interview December 26, 1972:

> The Civil Rights Association is quite clearly not the mass movement of the people that it once was, the movement that mobilized primarily large sections of the Catholic people. Its impetus as a mass movement is on the wane. As a strong pressure group with a fairly large membership, it is still reasonably effective. But there are other forces in the field, which have to be taken into consideration. The forces of sectarianism, for example, negate an awful lot of the potential of the civil-rights movement.[2]

---

2. "Under the British Occupation," *Intercontinental Press*, January 15, 1973, p. 25.

There can be no question about McGurran's revolutionary ideals, his dedication, or his dislike of Stalinist reformism. But at the same time it is clear that his perspective for the Civil Rights Association parallels that of the Stalinists; that is, he views it essentially as a liberal lobby.

This correspondence between the approach of subjectively revolutionary but non-Marxist republicans and that of the Stalinists and Stalinist-trained reformists and centrists is precisely the most dangerous tendency in the Official movement. I explained this in my article in the February 5 issue of *Intercontinental Press*:

> The civil-rights question is the acid test for Irish political organizations. Not only does it remain the central issue in the North, but the fight against repression has become the key to the political situation in the South. Because of the *political* and *social* mechanisms of imperialist control in Ireland, and because of the revolutionary traditions of the Irish people, the struggle against repression and discrimination is the cutting edge of the fight against imperialism. In fact, the civil-rights movement is an anti-imperialist movement in essence, and this is becoming clearer and clearer as the British army assumes a more and more active role in repressing the nationalist people. Economic issues underlie this struggle, and as it develops, its economic implications will become even clearer. But the *political* issues of democracy and an end to discrimination are the focus.
>
> Nonetheless, there are historical tendencies in the Official republican movement that could deflect it from concentrating on this issue. Furthermore, both ultraleftists and opportunists are anxious to divert revolutionary republicans from this task. From the standpoint of workerist ultralefts, the civil-rights movement has never been "revolutionary" enough because it does not unite Protestant and Catholic workers and explicitly challenge capitalist productive relations. . . .
>
> At the same time the Communist party and its supporters would be happy to see the republicans leave the "civil-rights side of things" to "cooler heads," or "more po-

litically experienced" people, as they picture themselves.

I also referred to this problem in the preceding article on the Official *ard fheis* in the January 22 issue of *Intercontinental Press*, in connection with the attitude of the Officials toward more conservative and traditional nationalists:

> The Official leadership has seen how harmful the growth of dogmatism can be, as manifested by, among other things, the reaction of its own members to the excesses that appeared for a while in the *United Irishman* [under the editorship of a romantic young Stalinoid]. Whatever the role of individuals or groups in fostering dogmatism, it was facilitated by the atmosphere of hysteria created, in essence, by the Officials' failure to deal politically with the problem of the Provisionals.
>
> One of the most ominous aspects of this problem was the tendency of a de facto combination to develop between young republicans influenced by ultraleft currents, opposed in principle to any cooperation with "middle-class nationalists," and romanticizers of the "tough" methods of Stalinism, whose concept of political struggle consisted of issuing denunciations and lurid threats. The Stalinoid romantic posturing in particular was unpleasantly reminiscent of the attitude of the German Communist party in its ultraleft period, when it threatened to "liquidate" the Social Democratic workers at the very time the fascists were preparing in fact to liquidate both the CP and the Social Democrats.

'Utterly non-Marxist'

This analysis stirred my Healyite critic to say the following:

> Not only is Foley's approach to nationalism utterly non-Marxist, but so, too, is his approach to class. Indeed, in his second article [it was actually my first], slating those who foster "dogmatism", Foley condemns "the tendency of a *de facto* combination to develop between young Republicans influenced by ultra-left currents, opposed in principle to any co-operation with 'middle-class nationalists'. . .".
>
> He goes on, quite wrongly, to say the Stalinists adopt the same line and concludes even more outrageously wrongly that such opposition is "unpleasantly reminiscent of the attitude of the German Communist Party in its ultra-left period when it threatened to liquidate the Social Democratic workers at the very time the fascists were preparing in fact to liquidate both the CP and the Social Democrats."
>
> It hardly needs saying that the German Social Democrats have nothing in common with the bourgeois-nationalists of Sinn Fein.

This "righteous" denunciation skates over the fact that the editor of the *United Irishman* responsible for the hysterical attacks on the Provisionals is a self-proclaimed "Stalinist" and tried to use his diatribes against the Officials' rivals as a means of anathematizing Trotskyism in general. Of course, his version of Stalinism is highly romanticized, and it is not clear how consistently he reflects the views of any Stalinist formation. Nonetheless, a very dogmatic "stages" theory was also pushed in the notorious "Provo/Trot" articles, and so it seems evident that he is at least a purveyor of some key Stalinist concepts and methods.

Moreover, in the *ard fheis*, Desmond O'Hagan, now the educational director of Official Sinn Féin, called the Provisionals a "worse enemy than the British troops." O'Hagan has reasons to resent the traditionalist nationalists and can rightly claim that their policies of random bombings and shootings have been disastrous for the national and left movement. But the fact remains that the Provisionals lead the largest section of militant anti-imperialists in the North. Thus, such a statement has a pernicious logic. Of course, it might not have been more considered than other remarks O'Hagan made at the *ard fheis*. But it must be taken seriously since it would be a reasonable conclusion from the line of the *United Irishman* for a whole period.

Moreover, while O'Hagan has taken an extremely rigid attitude toward the traditional nationalists, he has taken quite a moderate tone in other circumstances. For example, he was one of the speakers at a peace conference in Northern

Ireland on March 3 that was convened by the Irish Congress of Trade Unions. The meeting was described by the March 5 *Irish Times* as

> probably the most representative of its kind to be held in the North since the outbreak of the present conflict. About 400 representatives from over 100 trade unions, community associations, statutory bodies, the churches, moderate pressure groups and political parties, attended the conference.
>
> Telegrams of support were received from the Northern Ireland Secretary, Mr. Whitelaw, the British Labour and Liberal parties and the Trade Union Congress.
>
> The new committee, Citizens United for Reconciliation and Equality (C. U. R. E.), met the Minister of State, Lord Windlesham later on Saturday.

The Provisionals were not represented at the conference but O'Hagan referred to them indirectly:

> I don't think I should reject this society, nor be lumped on the side of the bombers and wreckers and those who are trying to bring down formal social institutions.

Of course, the "peace" conference was called by the trade-union movement and had the aim of achieving "unity" between the two communities. Thus, it seems quite likely that from O'Hagan's standpoint these remarks were in line with the highest revolutionary principles.

The Officials' director of education laid out his approach quite clearly in his speech April 22 at the Easter rising commemoration in Dublin: O'Hagan called on his audience to dispense with

> a current myth which states that a national liberation struggle is in progress, and that therefore the need of the hour is to build an all-class alliance to complete that struggle.

O'Hagan went on to say:

> In a relatively urbanised and proletarianised society, it is nonsense to talk of a national liberation struggle in which the working class is not playing the leading and dominating role through their party and kindred organisations.
>
> It is dangerous nonsense to suggest that the Republican Movement should ally itself with those who have been, and still are, the enemies of the Republic, or who fail to see that the primary struggle in the North is for democracy and against sectarianism.
>
> The role of the British Army is clearly one of oppression, and must be resisted by the mobilisation of the people in every way possible. But we republicans would be betraying our class, our principles and our goal, if we were to surrender our movement to the Taca men and their friends in the North.[3]
>
> Those who have misguidedly followed the Provisional Alliance, and are suffering in Long Kesh and Crumlin Road, along with our own comrades, will soon see how the hack politicians will sell them out on the question of internment and Special Powers . . . as they rush to divide the spoils and take their seats in the new Assembly.
>
> An all-class alliance is a return to the "Labour must wait" position of 1919, and the Irish proletariat have suffered ever since; the Republican Movement cannot and will not ignore the lessons of our history, nor will we betray the class we represent.
>
> In spite of repression in the North and the denial of fundamental human rights in the South, we must seek to build a unity of the Left, a unity of all organisations which accept that the Republican programme is the programme for national liberation, and the reconquest of Ireland.

O'Hagan said that

> abroad we must follow in the honourable international tradition of Tone, Connolly, and Frank Ryan [who fought in the Spanish civil

---

3. Taca is the fund-raising organization for Fianna Fail, the historically more nationalistic of the two bourgeois parties, and has been blamed for splitting the republican movement by feeding money to the Provisionals.

war], in solidarity with those who fight against imperialism, and seeking support from those socialist countries which have won the battle. For these and only these can be our allies.

So, there can be no doubt that O'Hagan also says some revolutionary-sounding things and makes some points that are quite correct. But what is the overall effect of this contradictory mélange?

Theory of permanent revolution

It is clear, first of all, that he divides the struggle for "civil rights" from the fight for national liberation. The unity of these movements is the main "myth" he polemicizes against. Surely this should alert the Healyites, who claim to be the chief repositories of the Trotskyist program, that something is fishy here. In fact, the right of national self-determination is part of the historic democratic program. The whole system of repression in the northern statelet was erected to thwart the Irish national revolution. Thus, the mobilization of the oppressed Catholic minority for democratic rights, regardless of the consciousness of the participants, has clearly had an anti-imperialist and nationalist thrust.

The entire history of the Northern Irish struggle has confirmed the theory of the permanent revolution, that is, that in the age of imperialism mass struggles for democratic rights take on a revolutionary dynamic, since they cannot succeed without overturning the capitalist system itself.

Whatever democratic concessions can be won in the context of an increasingly reactionary world capitalist system are temporary by nature and essentially the by-products of confrontations that challenge the essential underpinnings of bourgeois rule in this period. The importance of such concessions is that they stimulate the hopes of the masses and instill in them the confidence that they have the power to change society.

Unless the leaderships of such struggles are politically prepared to face revolutionary battles, they will become paralyzed in the face of the unforeseen violence of the confrontations, allowing the mass movement to become disoriented and impotent. In order to maintain their advance, mass democratic movements more and more must attack the bases of capitalism and bourgeois society as such and at a certain point must make a decisive turn to transform the society as a whole, becoming the basis of a new kind of state and social order.

It is this process that O'Hagan is most anxious to deny, and it is clear that there is a "stages" concept underlying his remarks. The only difference from the usual schema is that instead of the customary two stages—national liberation first and then socialist revolution—a third stage has been added, the stage of winning civil rights. This conforms to the program of the Communist party of Ireland, which has created a third stage to avoid the revolutionary dynamic of Irish nationalism and to preserve its positions in the British patriotic trade-union movement.

The 'workerist' point of view

Similarly, workerists who can see only the economic side of the class struggle—the fight over jobs, wages, and conditions—also deny the national struggle in Northern Ireland.

Both the Protestant and Catholic communities are poor and exploited. And since the only real struggle is supposed to be on economic or "class" issues, the workerist assumes that the one actually taking place must be a product of false consciousness, a fundamentally perverted and sterile conflict. Unlike the Stalinists, who rule out revolution in the foreseeable future, the workerists often have revolutionary aspirations. They tend to think that they can unite the Protestant and Catholic workers through socialist propaganda that avoids the national issues dividing the two communities.

The problem is that the workerist positions tend to converge in actual practice with the Stalinists' outlook. The workerists also regard the threat of clashes between the nationalist and proimperialist popular strata as the ultimate disaster that must be avoided at all costs. As a result, they tend toward a conservative and pessimistic attitude regarding the process going on. And, in making working-class unity their immediate focus, they tend also to try to redirect the nationalist-minded population into the train of the proimperialist trade-union movement.

The workerists and O'Hagan have pointed to some important features in the Irish situation, namely that Ireland is much more integrated into the economy of the imperialist metropolis than the nationally oppressed countries where liberation struggles have taken place in the postwar period. Moreover, the Twenty-Six County state is an old neocolonialist regime, and disillusionment with formal political independence is quite widespread among the working class in particular.

There are various conclusions that must be drawn from this. The most obvious is that the notions of some neo-Maoist dilettantes in the Dublin Official Sinn Féin that there can be a national liberation struggle in Ireland (in a future "stage" of course) like the one in Vietnam are completely divorced from reality. The most important conclusion is that the success of any mass combat in Ireland will be largely dependent on effective support from the international left and working-class movement. O'Hagan's claim that the "only allies" of the Irish people are a vaguely defined category of anti-imperialists and the "socialist" countries who have "won the battle" against imperialism is not only false; it is directly damaging to the Irish revolutionary movement.

By and large, the organized Irish working class has a standard of living closer to that of the workers in the imperialist centers than to that of the workers and peasants of the colonial world. The conditions in the Stalinized workers states have little or no attraction for them. The unqualified claim that these countries have "won the battle" against imperialism does nothing to make the prospect of revolution appealing to the Irish people and a great deal to make it repellent.

It is hard to see how anything less than the hope of revolution in the advanced capitalist countries—where the chances are better for avoiding bureaucratic degeneration and for achieving direct workers democracy that could guarantee efficient administration of the economy, maximum benefits for the most disadvantaged, and more rather than less personal freedom—can inspire the exertions and sacrifices needed to start up a struggle against the worldwide imperialist system on their small, divided island.

Furthermore, unless the Irish revolution aroused broad support in the advanced countries themselves, it would be doomed to collapse in short order. It seems extremely unlikely in view of the evidence of decades that any of the bureaucratized workers states would defend a revolution in the heart of the capitalist world against the determined attempts of the imperialists to destroy it. Even in Vietnam, on the outermost perimeter of world capitalism, where one of the belligerents is an actual member of the "socialist" bloc, the Soviet Union has doled out aid with an eyedropper. And it has forced the Vietnamese, in return for this, to compromise with Nixon. Moreover, it has given more aid to capitalist Egypt, which does not threaten the fundamental interests of world imperialism, than it has to the Vietnamese revolutionists.

The Soviet policy of aiding regimes in the underdeveloped world is part of its policy of peaceful coexistence. The objective is to build a neutral buffer. Even the aid to Cuba was begun with this aim in mind. Supporting a revolutionary regime is quite another matter. The Cuban process took both Moscow and Washington by surprise. We are not likely to see a duplicate. Furthermore, the Irish economy is far more complex than Cuba's. Far more would be needed to sustain it. As for China, its policy is at least as opportunistic as the Soviet Union's. For example, it supports Common Market integration as a counterweight to U.S. imperialism.

An explosive combination

On the other hand, it is equally clear that the driving force of radicalization in Ireland is the national issue, which at its peak has tended to go over into extremely advanced forms of economic struggle, such as the general strike after the Bloody Sunday massacre. Although there has been significant economic unrest in Ireland, one of the episodes involved has touched off a general crisis. The greatest explosions in the recent period, however, have resulted from a combination of national and economic aspirations—for example, the demand for a fair allotment of housing that sparked the first civil-rights march. In every case, it has been the national question fundamentally that has given these upsurges their revolutionary force.

So, while it is essential to get the British working class to oppose the repression that its imperialist government is carrying out in Ireland, to make the Irish struggle subordinate to British trade unionism would mean sacrificing the fundamental revolutionary dynamic. If the support of the British unions for the democratic demands of the Irish people is made conditional on toning down the national struggle or on the "good" behavior of the nationalists, it is worthless. If the struggle in Ireland were brought down to the level of British trade-unionism in order to "unite" British and Irish workers, this would eliminate one of the main factors undermining the stability of British capitalism and preparing the way for a working-class radicalization that could effectively aid the Irish people.

Furthermore, conditional support for "democracy" in Ireland does nothing to educate the British workers to respect the Irish people's right of self-determination. Only a campaign demanding unconditional recognition of the right of the Irish people to determine their own destiny can make inroads into the social chauvinism of the British trade-union movement.

The concept of conditional support for the victims of imperialist repression is also fatal in Ireland. In his Easter commemoration speech, O'Hagan made a strong point warning the imprisoned Provisionals that the conservative elements among their ranks and supporters would betray them if they got a chance to make an advantageous deal with British imperialism. But the fact that the Civil Rights Association (CRA), of which the Officials are the major component, seems to be taking a turn that at least borders on betrayal of the fighters is likely to obscure this lesson for the traditional nationalists.

> The C. R. A. has subtly altered its views on internment, meanwhile [the *Irish Times* reported April 12], and although still opposed to it on principle, recognises that there is no longer a massive outcry from the minority population. In consequence, Mrs. Edwina Stewart [of the Communist party], the C. R. A. honorary chairman, said at a press conference yesterday that for a successful anti-internment campaign to be mounted the Provisional I. R. A. would have to call off its campaign of violence.

No matter how you interpret this, unless the *Irish Times* fabricated its report—which is unlikely—such an attitude means placing partial blame for the repression on the Provisionals. The tactical errors of misguided combatants can, of course, make it easier for a capitalist government to carry out a program of repression. But when a people have been as oppressed as the nationalist people of Northern Ireland, and for as long, it is inevitable that there will be irrational outbursts. It is impossible to defend the oppressed people effectively without making it absolutely clear that the entire blame for the violence rests with the system and those who support and maintain it. The only way the setbacks caused by the wrong tactics of the Provisionals can be overcome is by offering an effective alternative. But the new NICRA policy tends in the direction of surrender.

Furthermore, there is no way any self-proclaimed revolutionary leadership can get the most militant strata of the nationalist-minded population to follow in the train of British trade-unionism. Only the vanguard, the most politically advanced sections of the population, dazzled by abstractions about "working-class unity," can be diverted by such a concept, with serious results both for the left and for the struggle as a whole.

The Bloody Sunday commemoration in Derry was an example of this. Before the event, the British Labour left was congratulating the Official republicans with unwonted fulsomeness for its determination to avoid any "sectarian incidents." The fact that the Civil Rights Association had been able to persuade British trade-union and liberal figures to come to Derry to show their support for democracy, it was confidently declared, had thrown the Provisionals into consternation.

But what happened was that the NICRA action turned into a kind of humanitarian prayer meeting that met with general indifference, a certain amount of amusement, and some hostility from the local population. On the other hand, the Provisionals' march to demand the end of imperialist repression drew a crowd estimated as high as 20,000 persons, a number comparing favorably with the largest civil-rights demonstrations.

Danger of reformist orientation

The tendency of the Official leadership to think that the struggle in progress is entirely the wrong kind of fight has apparently led them in a more and more reformist direction. The natural outcome of this kind of thinking is that the only thing the movement can do is try to outlast the Provisionals' terrorist campaign. When the adventurists become discredited, which is supposed to be inevitable, then the Officials can resume their economic agitations. Since the main thing is just to survive, the arguments of the reformists seem more and more practical, as revolutionary perspectives appear more and more remote and unreal.

This process, moreover, tends to become self-accelerating. While the Provisionals' reliance on forms of struggle carried out by small armed units divorced from the masses has led to increasing isolation of the militants and to a fading of international support for the struggle of the oppressed people, it is also true that the mass civil-rights movement produced such a deepgoing upheaval that spontaneous outbursts of violence can persist for a long time and continue to inspire substantial sympathy from the most oppressed strata of the population. These disorganizing forms of activity may, in fact, continue as long as none of the groups present offers a mass revolutionary alternative. And this is precisely what Stalinist and ultraleft workerist influences have hindered the Official republicans from doing.

Instead of showing how socialist ideas could point the way forward to victory for the national struggle, the Officials have more and more counterposed general socialist slogans to the real fight. They have invoked socialist ideas to convince the people that nothing fundamental could be won in the present "stage."

Not only is it impossible to win the masses of people to socialism by such a method, it is impossible to educate revolutionary militants or build a revolutionary organization in this way. Pessimism, resignation, pacifism, and reformism are the inevitable result of such a course. The organization settles into a rut of routine and repetitive propaganda, becoming less and less able to see beyond a few narrow preconceptions, unable to readjust to a changing reality, or to intervene in a bold and decisive way in the class struggle as new opportunities arise.

In the last stage of degeneration, principles become mere abstractions and daily practice is guided in fact by petty opportunistic considerations. This is the stage reached by the SLL. And it seems to be the development of such sectarian tendencies on the part of elements in the Official republican movement that has attracted the attention of the Healyite "raiders."

The SLL view vs. reality

Just as the Official leaders have clung to their abstract concept of "working-class unity" for almost four years, despite all the blows of reality, the SLL leaders began by believing that they were defending vitally important principles against a whole array of enemies and betrayers. They did in fact argue for some fundamentally correct and crucial concepts, such as the principle that only a revolution can solve the problems of the working class and only a revolutionary party can lead the workers to victory.

But the revolutionary process did not proceed as expected. The working class in the advanced countries was pacified for a whole period by the postwar boom. The axis of the world revolution shifted at the same time to the underdeveloped countries where it combined with the national revolution in unforeseen forms. The reaction of the Healyites was to deny both aspects of the historic detour. Every scattered spark of working-class militancy was puffed up into a revolutionary upsurge, every recession into an impending cataclysm. This tendency reached its ultimate absurdity when they refused to recognize that a revolution had taken place in Cuba because there was no revolutionary party. Following this concept, moreover, they supported the Stalinist Aníbal Escalante against the Castro-Guevara leadership. Escalante, after all, represented a "workers party" while Castro and company were "petty-bourgeois nationalists."

The Healyite reporter Yeats seems to be following the same line of reasoning in his denigration of Séamus Costello, the only one of the Official leaders, to my knowledge, who has openly opposed the Communist party on a basic political point in front of the entire republican cadre:

> With this responsibility upon him [that is, dividing the Northern Irish working class], Foley can still describe his mysterious resolution [on a new orientation to the civil-rights movement] as "symptomatic of a lot of new thinking going on in the Republican leadership".
>
> Foley's quotation continues: "Correct or not, but the feeling is abroad that a lot of people

in the country and many of our members have the idea that we are not in favour of the 'National Struggle' or the ending of this 'Struggle'.

"This is one reason why the Provos are still a force today and why they will not fade away for a long time yet.

"We must begin to show people and demonstrate clearly to all that our objectives are National Unity and Independence and the Socialist Republic."

Yeats commented:

> This is a frank and blatant appeal for unity between the Officials and the Provisionals.
>
> The device used to bring this about is to suggest that the Provisionals can be divided into a left and right wing, permitting him to argue the prospect of an alliance between the anti-bomb-and-bullet followers of Kevin Street [the Provisionals] and the Officials' right wing, led by Costello.

The need for a united front

The dishonesty and destructive intent of this argument are apparent to anyone not blinded by dogma or fear. In the first place there is no reference whatever to "unity" between the Provisionals and Officials. This passage simply points out that errors on the national question have prevented the Officials from meeting the challenge of the Provisionals effectively, and it suggests a readjustment to improve the position of the authors' organization.

Furthermore, in my article I did not advocate "unity" in the sense of fusion but only a united front on specific issues and an end to the political sectarianism that had been growing in the Officials, affecting not just their relations with the Provisionals but all of their work. The need for this, moreover, is felt not just by the "Costello right wing" but by many Official leaders. For example, Malachy McGurran said in his December 26 interview:

> In regard to united fronts with the Provisionals, we would have to define the meaning of the word "front" very carefully. In the Twenty-Six Counties we are faced with open, naked repression, with laws that go beyond even Franco or Salazar. The fact that they have not been used widely so far is only an indication of the Dublin government's cautious strategy of repression. Within this context I could see a united front not in the terms of burying one's own identity and one's own principles and one's own policies, but unity in terms of opposing and exposing the repression, even the injustice of the arrest and farce of a trial of Seán Mac Stiofáin. . . .
>
> . . . On these issues, and on these issues alone, there could be areas of joint action and joint activity with the Provisionals, with the Communist party of Ireland, with the Irish section of the Fourth International, with other radical, progressive, and even liberal forces.

McGurran, a veteran republican, seems to understand the concrete tactic of the united front, a vital part of the strategy of the revolutionary party, better than the Healyite defenders of the abstract concept.

Furthermore, according to Yeats, who is suggesting unity between sections of the Officials and Provisionals? Yeats's slippery prose makes this completely unclear.

The reason for this slipperiness seems evident. Yeats wants to kill two birds with one stone. He wants to suggest that the supporters of the United Secretariat are "Provisional lovers" and he wants the SLL to benefit from the hysteria whipped up by the "Provo/Trot" amalgam of the Stalinoid ex-editor of the *United Irishman*. More significantly, he wants to attract some ultraleft and sectarian members of the Officials who have come to fear that any letup in the denunciations of the Provisionals might mean an abandonment of "socialist principles."

Yeats at work in Derry

Yeats has been trying his hand at this technique for some time. Over the summer and fall of 1972, he did a series of interviews with figures in Northern Ireland, using them as foils for his organization's dogmatic arguments. He showed a special interest in Derry, which has had a more complex political history than other sections of the republican movement. The local Officials group has its own nationally circulated paper, the *Starry Plough,* a monthly that has been by far the most effective propaganda weapon of the Official republican movement. Although it did not go beyond the sectarianism of the Officials on the national question, it at least published good general socialist propaganda in contrast to the *United Irishman* in the "Provo/Trot" period, which appealed neither to any genuine nationalist feelings of the Irish people nor to the socialist aspirations of the young activists.

Yeats talked to the editor and the leading reporter of the *Starry Plough* and then wrote an article in the December 8, 1972, *Workers Press,* which said, among other things:

> Catholics always knew that the Provos had nothing to offer but the gun. But since "Operation Motorman" [the British occupation of the Derry ghettos] they have been driven to the understandable conclusion that the craven reformism of the official IRA is a blind alley too. . . .
>
> Joe Sweeny and Jackie Ward who edit the paper reflect a wide layer of local opinion when they talk of breaking from the Officials and using the Republican Clubs as the basis for a new revolutionary organization.

It was an open secret that pro-Stalinist elements in the Official IRA wanted to make an "example" of the Derry group, as a precedent for curbing all forms of "leftism." Yeats thus had every reason to think that he could provoke a dispute by reporting that the Derry "Trotskyites" were planning a split. It is hard to imagine how he could have more blatantly abused the tolerance of the individuals who agreed to talk to him.

The "happy" result of such a provocation, we must assume, would have been to fan bitterness and suspicion that would have enabled the SLL to pick up a few people on the rebound.

This way of recruiting is part and parcel of the SLL's unprincipled and opportunistic way of relating to other organizations. It is particularly criminal in the case of the Official IRA.

Because of the absence of mass revolutionary parties, centrist organizations have sprung up in many countries. Some have sought to move in a revolutionary direction. The Official republican movement has been one of the best of these. Among other things, it has a historic revolutionary achievement to its credit: the development of the Northern Irish civil-rights struggle. Faced with dramatic pressures, it ran into serious problems. With the development of the crisis in Northern Ireland, the republican movement underwent a politically confused and debilitating split. A political debate was touched off. Although some very fundamental questions of revolutionary organization and action are involved, the debate has been unclear. There is a strong antagonism between the pro-Stalinists and the ultraleft workerists. The "Trotskyist" workerists oppose the civil-rights movement on the grounds that it is neither a specifically working-class nor a socialist movement. The pro-Stalinists furiously denounce the workerists as sectarians, while they themselves propose limiting the civil-rights movement to such a narrow framework that it would in fact become an impotent sectarian front organization.

There is no important practical difference between the two lines. Correct points and abysmal errors are hopelessly tangled. There is, however, an underlying difference in attitude. The best of the workerists reflect revolutionary moods. The Stalinist-trained types have generally been inoculated against all real revolutionary processes. Their instinct is to clamp down on anything that does not fit the "stage" as they define it or is not tightly controlled by some kind of "Marxist" mandarinate. The tragedy of such a debate is that the workerists have no real alternative to the pro-Stalinists. In fact, they are led by their economism to converge with the pro-Stalinists in all practical respects, and so the natural tendency is to try to differentiate themselves by demanding more "radical" slogans and actions while staying in the same general framework. Thus, they simply look impractical, idealistic, and adventurist. The Stalinists, on the other hand, who base themselves on the resignation and cynicism of the conservatized sections of the workers' vanguard, seem nothing if not "practical," and "realistic."

Healyite 'clarification'

The first duty of a revolutionary Marxist is to help sort out the real issues in this debate. In particular, revolutionists in other countries could offer some of the experience of the international socialist struggle to a movement that has suffered unduly from national isolation. The Healyite reporter does the opposite. In fact, his opportunistic twistings and turnings seem designed to avoid reaching definite political conclusions. His December 19, 1972, article on the *ard fheis* was entitled "Official IRA Continues Its Rightward Turn." In his March 22 article, he says:

> The Ard Fheis was distinguished by an almost complete move away from backing the on-the-streets reformist militancy of the Northern Ireland Civil Rights Movement and the Communist Party of Ireland to a concept of building a new revolutionary nationalist party.

Was this part of the "rightward turn" or not? If it was, why does Yeats approve of it, since he says also in the March 22 article:

> But since direct rule the Officials have been working towards the realization that there is no future in a policy of "back to the streets". Their present turn of parliamentary politics and local elections illustrates this.
>
> They also realize that in the north civil rights demands for the "nationalist population" are sectarian, undermining all prospect of the triumph of Republicanism.

Even more explicitly, Yeats says:

> Casting around for a whipping boy, Foley slates "workerist ultra-lefts" for distracting the Officials' attention from the importance of civil rights. He blames them for characterizing the movement as sectarian and as one which failed to "explicitly challenge capitalist productive relations".
>
> Yet everything that has happened since direct rule, including the growth of Protestant organizations and the decline of all reformist and terrorist groups, suggests the critics were right.

If the republicans were "realizing" one of the Healyites' main contentions, why not give them credit for making some progress toward the SLL line, which Yeats apparently thinks is located in a far leftward direction? Otherwise, surely some explanation is needed as to how the republicans can be moving in a "rightward" direction and at the same time be "realizing" what the SLL sees as a key point.

What, moreover, did the turn to the right entail? Yeats mentioned in the December 19, 1972, *Workers Press* the exclusion from the conference of Bernadette Devlin, which he held was "consistent with the leadership's new anti-'left' line." But no adult could claim that this by itself necessarily represented a profound programmatic shift. In fact, in stressing this confused incident, Yeats seemed merely to be fishing in troubled waters.

The main thing, Yeats said, was that ". . . There has been no formal break with the Civil Rights movement but the Ard Feish [sic] passed almost unanimously an amendment shifting the emphasis firmly back to traditional Irish nationalism." Was this the rightward turn? If so, Yeats should have discussed it.

Even in his March 22 article he does nothing more than repeat some broad general principles, quoting Trotsky to the effect that "the completion of the socialist revolution within nationalist limits is impossible." This is a concept that in principle would not be disputed by either the pro-Stalinists or the "Trotskyist" ultralefts in the Officials. The question is, What is the role of the national question in the process that is going on now?

Moreover, how could Yeats analyze the "traditional nationalism" of the republicans when he cannot even honestly take up what I said about the role of the national question in Ireland? He claims, for instance, that my article was "nothing more or less than a eulogy of nationalism as a solution to Ireland's economic and social problems."

If Yeats is serious about this accusation and it is not intended simply to impress the ignorant, it would certainly be very important to prove it. That would constitute final confirmation of the unregenerate "Pabloism," and worse, of the nefarious Foley. But the truth is something of an obstacle to him. For example, in my pamphlet *Ireland in Rebellion*, published in October 1971, I said:

> The history of modern Ireland shows that the Irish nation cannot be finally restored

except within the context of a totally different world order in which the great economic forces serve humanity instead of dominating it. Whatever the subjective political beliefs of the martyrs of Irish freedom, their vision of an Irish Ireland can only be fulfilled within the framework of a world socialist revolution (p. 19).

This pamphlet is sold by the Official republican book service and has circulated rather widely in their milieu.

In the February 5 article, which Yeats specifically referred to, I wrote:

> To win real national freedom and destroy the direct and indirect influence of foreign business and financial interests, a deepgoing social revolution is required in Ireland. A struggle capable of defeating the political, military, and economic power of British imperialism and its allies requires international ties to be successful.

How does this differ fundamentally from the second and third paragraphs of Yeats's quotation from Trotsky:

> The socialist revolution begins on the national arena, it unfolds on the international arena and it is completed on the world arena.
>
> Socialist construction is conceivable only on the foundations of the class struggle, on a national and international scale.

Characteristically, the Healyite reporter seems to have forgotten where the revolution is supposed to "begin," because it has become a mere abstraction for him, divorced from all the real processes. Or perhaps his concept of the "national arena" is different from mine. He says, for instance, at the end of his March 22 article:

"The first step in the fight back is to forge unity between British and Irish workers in the campaign to force the Tories to resign. . . ."

If the Healyites believe that Britain and Ireland form one national whole, however, they should explain this, since the implications for the Irish struggle would not be unimportant.

But maybe the return to "traditional nationalism" was not the main thing in the "rightward turn" at the *ard fheis*. In his March 22 article, Yeats discovered something else.

> The one "step forward" at the December Ard Fheis which went completely over Foley's head was the decisive trend to regard elections as the new revolutionary weapon—a trend verified by the appearance of Sinn Fein candidates in the Eire[sic][4] nomination lists.
>
> This is how the Officials' leadership already sees the new revolutionary party working and how sections of the Provisionals may come to see it too, in time.

This "step forward" must have gone over Yeats's head initially, since he did not mention it in his December 19 article on the *ard fheis*. But now he draws rather drastic conclusions from the fact that I did not take up the question of the Officials' electoral orientation in my articles on the same event.

"Foley sets out to cover up this descent into the worst kind of reformism."

The charge of reformism, let alone the "worst kind," is a serious indictment. The Official republicans include many individuals and leaders who have proved their devotion to their own conception of revolutionary principles by great personal sacrifices. Even those influenced by Stalinism are not yet generally hopelessly hardened reformists. If these dedicated fighters are falling into reformism, it is certainly the duty of Marxists to point out precisely where they are going wrong. There is no other way to do this than to analyze specific cases, showing concretely what reformism leads to. But the Healyite expert makes general denunciations that in the context of Irish politics today are most likely to be interpreted as branding electoral activity per se as reformist.

Why not fight in electoral arena, too?

Yeats even introduces the argument in a dishonest way. Why attribute so much importance, for exam-

---

4. Eire is the Gaelic word for all of Ireland but is used by some chauvinistic English to refer to the Twenty-Six Counties alone.

ple, to my not taking up the electoral orientation put forward at the *ard fheis*? If participating in elections is by nature reformist, Yeats could have "exposed" my position much more effectively by quoting articles where I specifically recommend entering the electoral arena. An example can be cited from my pamphlet *Problems of the Irish Revolution:*

> In particular, challenging the ban on political activity in the North and gaining recognition as a legal party in the South offer the possibility for effective revolutionary propaganda campaigns. By demanding the right to engage in legal political activity, the republicans can defend themselves in the most effective way against repression and at the same time consolidate solid gains. This, of course, does not mean that a "democratic phase" is opening up. All democratic freedoms are precarious in this epoch and especially so in Ireland. But the system can be forced to grant a certain room for maneuver at times, which must be used to advantage....
>
> Elaborate schemes for reforming local government, education, etc., are not very useful for revolutionary agitation, especially given the resources of the republican movement. A few simple themes are needed on which all the propaganda of the movement can be focused, that is, transitional demands. Such demands should seem reasonable to the people they are intended to appeal to and at the same time should expose the contradictions of the system. In a period of general crisis, moreover, local and piecemeal economic agitation stand in secondary place for a revolutionary party. The most important thing is to give political direction and to wage a concentrated campaign against the enemy class, which itself is highly centralized and conscious of its general interests.

Since there has long been confusion in Ireland over the question of revolutionists participating in elections, this is a subject that must be discussed as concretely as possible. As a result of using a fundamentally nonmaterialist method, Irish republicans have traditionally considered that to engage in parliamentary politics is unprincipled. The effects of this stand have been anything but revolutionary.

The inevitable outcome was that the republicans ended up in fact giving unofficial support to bourgeois politicians such as De Valera. In fact, a sort of symbiotic relationship grew up between what was in reality a kind of armed pressure group and bourgeois parliamentary nationalists. As long as the republicans made it a principle not to challenge the politicians in the generally accepted political arena, questions of program simply did not arise.

In this sense, the move of the Official republicans toward a materialistic view of the relation between tactics and principle was a fundamental advance. Once out of the straitjacket of traditionalism, the Officials can of course move in a "normal" reformist direction. If such an evolution becomes definitively established, the result will be to reinforce the sterile old attitudes. The Officials as a whole, and even the leadership, are still a long way from Marxism. There seems on occasion even to be some truth in the Provisionals' claims that when the Officials cast off the bounds of traditionalism, they were left without any firm principles whatsoever. The deeper truth is probably that they have so far replaced one set of abstract principles for another only slightly less abstract set. But the only way the Marxist concept of principle can be explained is by relating principles concretely to the actual problems of political work, pointing the way toward achieving real unity of theory and action. It is hard to do this from three thousand miles away. The Healyites are in a much better geographical position to make concrete criticisms of the Officials' electoral work. But evidently they are not interested in this.

Instead, these sectarians seem to have in mind only a petty raiding maneuver. After the split, sufficient abstentionist sentiment still remained in the Official republican organization to serve as a pole for an opposition grouping. Such a banner could attract serious militants repelled by real reformist mistakes and reformist concepts held by some elements of the leadership. It could also rally ultraleftists and traditionalist adventurers. It could not serve as the basis for developing a Marxist tendency. The only result of a fight over abstention as a principle would be to perpetuate confusion and to waste valuable revolutionary forces. In the process, of course, the SLL could probably pick up a few recruits by raising the banner of abstract principle higher than anybody else. There are after all few restraints on the "ascent" of a purely propagandistic sect.

The way to win sincerely revolutionary republicans to Marxism is the opposite of the SLL's method. The most important thing is to instill the concept that principles are a guide to practical revolutionary activity. The test of principle is the real effect of a policy—whether it advances or retards the process of the masses learning the real nature of society so that they can transform it in accordance with their own real interests. For materialists, moreover, experience is a vital aspect of learning. Whenever principle becomes divorced from reality, even if the letter is kept sacrosanct, the actual result is opportunism in practice. The history of Irish republicanism shows this. The history of the SLL also confirms it. In fact the SLL's formal adherence to Marxist doctrine makes it an excellent example of what happens when principles first become separated from reality and then start to replace it. For this reason primarily, it is worth following the ins and outs of the Healyite line on the Irish struggle.

In the tradition of Lenin and Trotsky

But first the question of principle in electoral policy should be made clear. While boycotting elections and parliament is a possible tactic in specific cases, the leaders of the Russian revolution fought a decisive battle to convince ultraleftists that intervening in elections and parliamentary struggles is essential for a revolutionary party. One of Lenin's major works, *'Left-Wing' Communism, an Infantile Disorder*, was largely devoted to this. Trotsky also set forth the revolutionary Marxist position on this again and again and in particular in a speech to the Executive Committee of the Communist International on November 24, 1920:

> Comrade Gorter thinks that if he keeps a kilometer away from the buildings of parliament that thereby the workers' slavish worship of parliamentarianism will be weakened or destroyed. Such a tactic rests on idealistic superstitions and not on realities. The Communist point of view approaches parliamentarianism in its connection with all other political relations, without turning parliamentarianism into a fetish either in a positive or negative sense. The parliament is the instrumentality whereby the masses are politically deceived and benumbed, whereby prejudices are spread and illusions of political democracy maintained, and so on and so forth. No one disputes all this. But does the parliament stand secluded by itself in this respect? Isn't petty-bourgeois poison being spread by the columns of the daily newspapers, and, first and foremost, by the Social-Democratic dailies? And oughtn't we perhaps on this account refrain from utilizing the press as an instrument of extending Communist influence among the masses? Or does the mere fact that Comrade Gorter's group turns its back upon the parliament suffice to discredit parliamentarianism? Were this the case it would signify that the idea of the Communist revolution, as represented by Comrade Gorter's group, is cherished by the masses above everything else. But in that case the proletariat would naturally disperse the parliament without much ado and take power into its own hands. But such is not the case. Comrade Gorter himself, far from denying, on the contrary grotesquely exaggerates the masses' respect and slavish worship of parliamentarianism. Yet what conclusion does he draw? That it is necessary to preserve the 'purity' of his own group, *i.e.*, sect. In the final analysis Comrade Gorter's arguments against parliamentarianism can be leveled against all forms and methods of the proletarian class struggle, inasmuch as all of these forms and methods have been deeply infected with opportunism, reformism and nationalism.[5]

(To be continued.)

---

5. *The First Five Years of the Communist International, Volume 2* [Pathfinder, 1945, 1972], pp. 192–93 [2014 printing]

Performing Artists on a Flying Trapeze
By Gerry Foley

II

If the leaders of the Official republican movement are to fulfill their aspiration of building a "revolutionary party of the Irish people," two elements are essential: (1) a consistent revolutionary program; (2) a strategy enabling the revolutionary political nucleus to reach out to broader and broader layers of the Irish population and working class and involve them in effective united action against British imperialism and the dependent capitalist system in Ireland.

On both key questions, although they have not been slow to offer advice, the various British sectarian groups have proved unable to point the way forward. One such group, however—the Socialist Labour League (SLL), led by Thomas Gerard Healy—has provided examples of major pitfalls to avoid. In particular, the SLL's apparent attempt to influence the sectarian fringe of the Official republican movement offers some useful lessons.

In the first place, the methods and arguments used reveal a great deal about the SLL and its claims to be a Trotskyist organization. For a group that purports to have maintained intact all of the principles and experience of revolutionary Marxism, the development of an acute crisis almost next door, in the neighboring island, should have been an excellent opportunity to demonstrate the relevance and usefulness of this heritage.

In a situation dominated by a number of groups with vague and unfinished political programs, an organization that claimed to have all of the answers should have been able at least to lay out a consistent strategy for the fighters and show by example some of the techniques of revolutionary organization. It could be expected, moreover, that a principled revolutionary ally in Britain would have been much appreciated by the Irish fighters, who have not seen a great deal of helpful solidarity from the British left and labor movement.

Moreover, one of the main forces in the situation was a recently radicalized and, in many respects, strikingly capable and seasoned leadership—the leaders of the Irish Republican Army and later the Official republican movement. Despite heavy doses of Stalinist influence from various sources, the minds of the key republican leaders were still generally open and receptive to revolutionary ideas. They were eager to make a start toward overcoming the poverty of ideas that had long afflicted the Irish revolutionary movement. Nor was the republican movement the only promising factor in the situation. A whole generation of fighters was displaying high revolutionary qualities in a series of groups and actions.

Thus, if the SLL were really the sole heir of uncorrupted living Marxism—Trotskyism—as claimed, it now had an exceptional opportunity to educate some of the best revolutionary material that has appeared in recent decades.

An important resolution

The history of the SLL's twists and turns on the Irish question in the four years that have passed since the start of the mass civil-rights movement is complicated. The only constant has been the SLL's abstract, propagandists attitude. Nonetheless, the SLL's approach was presented rather well in Ian Yeats's article in the March 22 issue of *Workers Press*, "Marxist Phrases Hide Backing for Nationalists." The "Marxist phrases" were attributed to my articles on the December 15–16, 1972, Official republican convention.

In the first place, it is interesting to see how Yeats reacted to the signs of a political discussion taking place in the Official republican movement. His approach was indicative of the SLL's method. For example, he wrote:

> Foley quotes at length and approvingly from the preamble to a resolution on the north not on the Clar (agenda) but which he claims was circulating among delegates.
>
> A spokesman for Gardner [sic] Place confirmed that no such resolution was on the Clar or put to the Ard Fheis.

Intercontinental Press, June 4, 1973.

In view of an apparent attempt by Yeats to provoke a split in the Derry republican group (see Part I of this article. *Intercontinental Press*, May 28, p. 637), Yeats's discussion with a "spokesman for Gardner [sic] Place" is likely to have been a short one. But he could have read the newspapers. The resolution he was referring to was clearly identified. In my January 22 article I referred to it as the "resolution redefining policy on the Northern question." In the February 5 article I wrote:

> At the *ard fheis* a major resolution on the civil-rights movement was introduced which clarified the policy of the Official republican movement on some issues: "The Republican Movement could not under any circumstances call for the reestablishment of a 6 County parliament. To do so would mean total recognition of Britain's right to impose a Partitionist assembly on the Irish people, and would be in complete conflict with the Republican and Separatist tradition." This resolution made it clear that although the Official republican movement favored demanding democratic rights from the British government and Northern Irish authorities, it did not accept the context of a Northern statelet. In effect, this resolution rejected the 'stages' concept earlier held on one level or another by some of the republican leadership, a concept that envisaged 'democratization' of the Six-County state as a precondition for struggling for national liberation.
>
> In particular, the preamble to this resolution represented a major step forward in republican thinking toward a consistent revolutionary perspective. Unfortunately this document was not distributed; but many of those present seemed to be familiar with its contents. The main objection to making it public seemed to be that it contained a characterization of the Communist party as reformist, which was repeated in the open debate by the resolution's sponsor, Seamus Costello.

What were Yeats's sources?

The debate over this resolution was the most important political discussion at the convention and was referred to in all the press reports. Furthermore, there have been publications and statements of the Official republican movement since the *ard fheis* that reflect this change in policy, which was also expressed by Malachy McGurran in his December 26 interview:

> Our movement both nationally and locally is going through a period of coming to realize the need for reorganization and reeducation, of developing a clearer perspective of its role in relation to the national question and the social question, of how to combine these two main issues and achieve a oneness of the struggle. ("Under the British Occupation," *Intercontinental Press*, January 15, 1973, p. 25.)

Furthermore, Yeats himself, later on in his March 22 article, refers to the very same supposedly "mysterious" resolution.

> The resolution put to the Ard Fheis by rightwing Bray delegate Seamus Costello, which more than any other summed up the Officials' new course, laid down that in future civil rights was to be seen as part of the overall programme and struggle of the revolutionary party.

Is it possible that the Healyite reporter was not sure what resolution I was referring to? But later on he writes:

> Foley argues that the Officials are in danger of abandoning civil rights altogether and that the reason for this is their failure to analyse where the role of the Communist Party helped the movement go wrong.
>
> But as the preamble to Costello's resolution, in which he took the CP to task for their reformism, clearly showed, this analysis had been made.

This preamble, however, was not only not distributed; no report of it, to my knowledge, has appeared in the Irish press. There are only two ways Yeats could have known about it. He either saw a copy or based himself on what I wrote in my article. The indications are that the latter is the case.

Yeats writes that I quoted "at length" from the preamble. In fact, I only quoted a short paragraph or two to indicate its main political point. Virtually all this is requoted in the Healyite reporter's article. I did not, however, directly quote the most politically sensitive section, the part attacking the Communist party. It is notable that Yeats does not quote this passage either, although it would seem to be the most important from his point of view. He really should have quoted it, for example, to prove his contention that the Officials have analyzed "where the role of the Communist Party helped the movement go wrong."

Unfortunately, this claim was grossly overoptimistic, as shown most notably by the parasitic "role" the Officials still allow the tiny Communist party of Ireland to play in the civil-rights movement. The preamble to Costello's resolution was only a first step toward developing a critique of the reformist position on the relationship between the civil-rights struggle and the fight for national independence. This same reformist position, by the way, is not only put forward by the Communist party of Ireland but by some Maoist-tinged and presumably independent Stalinists and Stalinoids, who are not altogether without influence in the Official movement.

Moreover, so far, the new line seems to have had only the most minimal effect on the practical activity of the movement. One of the ways this has been shown is by the Bloody Sunday commemoration fiasco in Derry (see Part I of this article), where the timid reformist policy of the NICRA leadership resulted in a stinging defeat for its major component, the Official republicans.

The Communist party is so small that it has little to lose if the civil-rights movement stagnates. It can even hope to recruit from a narrowing but more committed circle of "democratic" activists. But the decline of the civil-rights movement is a matter of life and death for the Officials, because it leaves them without a mass alternative to the Provisional guerrilla campaign. They would not accept such defeats if they were not to some extent still under the influence of Stalinist reformism.

What was the reason then for all Yeats's pretense about the "mysterious" "preamble to a resolution on the north not on the Clar (agenda), but which he [Foley] claims was circulating among delegates."

The reason is all too obvious, especially after Yeats's Derry operation. He was trying to create a scandal over the document, to arouse fears that its authors represented a trend toward conciliation with the Provisionals. His objective was to stampede a few insecure dogmatists toward the safe harbor of the SLL, where there would never be a thought of "conciliation" with anybody.

The Official leaders did make a mistake, in my opinion, in not distributing the document in question. Failing to inform the membership fully of important discussions among the leadership encourages intrigue of all kinds. Still, to the credit of the republicans, it must be said that this document has now been rather widely circulated. Rank-and-filers who had not gotten copies in December had them in February. And it was evident that the republican leaders intended to distribute it, since the various persons who gave me copies did not regard it as secret but only wanted to restrict distribution in order to avoid arousing untimely speculation in the capitalist press, which does pay a fair amount of attention to rumors about the internal life of the movement.

But producing this document was to the credit of the republican movement in a far deeper and more important sense. It showed that the Officials were still a living political movement able to discuss the political situation in the country objectively and to reevaluate their positions. Is there any such evidence of internal political life in the SLL? In ten years at least there has not been a whiff of real discussion in that organization.

If the SLL were a Trotskyist organization, its reaction to the development of a political discussion in one of the major Irish organizations would have been completely different from Yeats's small-time political skulduggery.

The voice of Chairman Mao

In the first place, one of the most important principles of Leninism is the need for collective democratic discussion of elaborate effective tactics and strategy. Even the Stalinist parties pay lip service to this concept. In an article on building the revolutionary party that appeared in issue No. 3 of the Official theoretical magazine *Teoiric*, an anonymous author was able to cite Chairman Mao as the advocate of internal democracy:

It is through its internal work that a party evolves its theory, applies that theory to decide its practice, learns from its practice to test its theory—evolving better theory for better practice. Correct ideas are not to be found on trees, but are the result of clear, logical thinking and scientific analysis of actual events. Correct ideas cannot be worked out in isolation and then presented to an astounded populace. They must be tested in the crucible of practice. Mao Tse Tung, in his essay "Where Do Correct Ideas Come From?" expresses this perfectly when he says: *"Where do correct ideas come from? Do they drop from the skies? No. Are they innate in the mind? No. They come from social practice and from it alone; they come from three kinds of social practice: the struggle for production, the class struggle and scientific experiment."* In other words theory begets practice which begets theory which begets more practice. For it is experience which teaches lessons, and rationality and logic which puts them into a pattern. The first aspect of internal work, therefore, and the first task of those who wish to build a revolutionary party, is to ensure that the organization is geared for discussion. This depends on the principle of criticism—self-criticism.

Criticism—self-criticism is the principle by which correct theory is evolved. Correct theory is essential for any revolutionary party for otherwise it can never give correct leadership and smash the power of the capitalist and imperialist state. Only conscious action can do that. As Marx said: "Man determines history on the basis of pre-existing conditions." In other words if a situation is correctly analyzed, a balance of forces can be developed favourable to progressive advance. This phrase of Marx is often distorted.... For Marx did not say, as the ultraleft imagine, that it is man's actions alone which determine history regardless of the objective conditions in the situation. It is this type of woolly thinking which leads many sincere people to argue that *socialism* should be the slogan at this stage of our struggle, despite the fact that the working class is viciously divided and overwhelmingly under reactionary influence both in the south, where Fianna Fail is more secure than ever, and amongst the Northern Protestant workers, who still support fascist-type Unionism.

The author goes on to say that the opposite of voluntarism is the "Economist approach to 'revolution,'" whose advocates "argue that Marx meant that objective conditions change the world regardless of man's actual participation." He calls for overcoming these two deviations "through the interaction of practice and theory; and this interaction cannot be achieved unless there is open discussion."

Any reader not dazzled by the wisdom of these Little Red Book aphorisms could legitimately ask what the results of "self-criticism" and "open discussion" have been in the Great Helmsman's own country. Hasn't one previously infallible leader after another been suddenly exposed as a "secret enemy"? Hasn't one disastrous bureaucratic fantasy after another, from the Great Leap Forward to the cultural revolution, prevailed without the slightest voice of criticism being raised against it—that is, not until the worst damage was done and all the blame was suddenly loaded onto one individual bureaucrat or group of bureaucrats? How does this differ from the 180-degree shifts in line that became typical of the Communist International as internal democracy and open discussion were crushed by the Stalinist bureaucratic machine? No matter what the line was, it was always justified by the same sort of ponderous pronouncements indulged in by the author or authors of the *Teoiric* article, which could be given a different concrete meaning to fit each situation.

The role of leadership

The fact that this type of thinking apparently passes for good coin in at least some quarters in the Official movement is, of course, an indication that there may be possibilities there for the SLL, which also supported the Red Guards in the "cultural revolution" on the basis of the abstract rhetoric and "red revolutionary" generalities of Chairman Mao. But this fact also indicates that in order to foster a leftward development in the Official movement, revolutionists must encourage concrete discussions of the fundamental problems the republicans are facing. This involves not only helping to clarify the issues and enrich the debate but explaining how to organize and conduct discussions in a constructive way.

Part of this, too, is making clear the role of leaders in a revolutionary party. Policy is not formulated through some anonymous process. The ranks do not make decisions in a vacuum. Leaders have to take clear and consistent stands and assume responsibility for them. Persons who accept a wrong policy or concept without fighting against it disqualify themselves for leadership.

These principles are crucial for the Official republicans at this point in their development. They cannot go forward unless a leadership emerges that has a consistent revolutionary program and unless the ranks are educated in clear and democratic discussions.

Instead of trying to encourage political discussion in the Official movement, however, Yeats tries, by his pretense about "mysterious" preambles, to turn the very existence of such a debate into a petty scandal. Moreover, he crudely distorts the actual political points of the document in question (see Part I of this article). Instead of commending the leaders who came forward with relatively clear political positions, he tries to rouse unsubstantiated suspicions about them. What is it, for example, that makes Seamus Costello "right wing," and who precisely qualifies as being to the "left" of him and why?

In short, Yeats shows either no understanding or no interest in the process of political development going on in the republican movement. His attitude is basically that of a political parasite.

Yeats, of course, has already written off the possibility of any positive development in the Official movement. In his March 22 article he said:

> A new, "democratic centralist" structure is to be given the party to make sure that in future the leadership's writ runs in unchallenged uniformity.

It is, in fact, not unlikely that there are some in the Official movement who look toward a tighter structure as a means of clamping down on various political elements. It is obvious that there are a number of Stalinist-trained activists who conceive a revolutionary party as being a kind of mystical "Marxist" mandarinate, or church. They seem to have more traditionalist conservative allies. However, Yeats apparently does not take into consideration the effect of the actual experience of the republican leaders in trying to lead a politically heterogeneous formation in a situation characterized by the sharpest tensions. In such conditions, responsible and sincerely revolutionary figures have naturally come to look to the Bolshevik example as an answer to their difficulties.

Why is Yeats so quick to assume that there can be nothing positive in the aspiration of the Official leaders to build a democratic centralist organization? Ordinary sectarianism is one obvious answer. But there also seems to be something more subtle. For the SLL, concrete experience apparently never leads in the direction of revolutionary consciousness but only to "reformism" and "impressionism." The only thing you can learn from experience is that you must renounce your sins and join the true church of Healyism.

One result of this concept is that the SLL tends to recruit individuals disillusioned with all concrete struggles, who are basically looking for the reassurance of routinist activity and airtight ideological certainties. In fact, the SLL's sudden interest in a polemic on Ireland seems to be related to the fact that the struggle has reached a fairly low ebb and there is a considerable amount of demoralization in and around the main Irish organizations. This would appear to be one reason the SLL decided to open up an attack on *Intercontinental Press* at this particular time.

They can turn it on or turn it off

There is, of course, a fundamental difference between the revolutionary-Marxists and the Healyites on the revolutionary dynamic of the national struggle in Ireland. This difference has been clear from the very start of the recent crisis. In article after article over the past four years, I have analyzed the dynamic of Irish national aspirations. In the October 27, 1969, issue of *Intercontinental Press*, for instance, I took up the Healyite position in some detail. None of this provoked any response from the SLL.

It was notable, in fact, that by late 1970, when it was apparent that the crisis in Ireland would be quite prolonged and would have a major impact on the British left, the SLL seemed to lose its taste for polemics somewhat, concentrating more on less ambitious articles exposing the evils to be found in the Six Counties.

As the struggle declined beginning about April 1972, the urge to do political battle on the question seems paradoxically to have revived in the *Workers Press* offices. But the predictions of final betrayal by the major Irish groups have so far at least proved premature. And it can be expected that new flare-ups and turns will soon discredit the SLL's dogmatic generalities, as they have so often in the past.

At various times since the start of the mass civil-rights movement in Ireland, the SLL has argued, of course, in favor of three correct and vitally important principles: the need for arming the masses, distrust of the British army, and opposition to terrorism as a method. But these arguments have always been raised in a way calculated to maintain the SLL's image of unassailable "revolutionary" and "Marxist" virtue without committing the organization to involvement in any real struggle.

The Healyite call to arms

When the first civil-rights marches were being organized, the tactic used by the leaders was to defend the participants politically by stressing the nonviolent and legal character of the actions. The support of international public opinion prevented the fanatical Orange groups and the special police of the imperialist fortress state in the North from immediately suppressing these protests as they had previous ones.

The Healyites were critical. When a student march was attacked in the middle of an Orange area, the *Newsletter*, the predecessor of *Workers Press*, wrote in its January 14, 1969, issue:

> Farrell and the other leaders thus led their marchers, including many young girls, into a conflict with Bunting's thugs bereft of any weapons save their undeniable courage. . . .
> *Workers' defence guards should be formed in every area, and there must be no more unarmed marches. Fight for the repeal of the Special Powers Act and against all bans on marches.* (Emphasis in original.)

The Healyites did not have to worry about the result of "armed marches" in those days because there was no danger of any one taking their call seriously.

When massive fighting and real "workers' defence guards" sprang up in August 1969, the Healyites quickly changed their tune. At first they call for "pure" workers defense guards made up of both Protestant and Catholic workers, a safely unachievable demand.

In the September 20, 1969, *Newsletter*, the "dialectician" in charge, Cliff Slaughter, wrote:

> The Newsletter has called for the *labour movement* to organize workers' defence guards as the only guarantee against the armed right-wing thugs and has denounced the armed intervention as well as Callaghan's visit as a cover for Paisleyism. . . .
> It does not occur to Treacy [the Irish expert of the International Socialists] that insofar as Catholic workers are dominated in their politics by the Catholic hierarchy, their consciousness is reactionary and must be fought against and that those who proceed to support them as "more progressive" are helping precisely the efforts of the Irish capitalists to prevent working-class unity at all costs.

This pious rejoinder came only a month after Catholics in the ghettos of Belfast and Derry were being attacked, shot at, and burned out in the name of their religion.

Then, in the *Workers Press* of October 3, 1969, Slaughter wrote:

> After many months of a disastrous reliance on the middle-class civil rights leadership, the Catholic workers find themselves isolated from their Protestant brothers in the barricaded slum areas.
> Whatever the problems of "law and order" for the capitalists, this situation is *politically a good one for them*. . . . [Emphasis in the original.]
> *All the talk about arms is adventurist rubbish at this stage.* (My emphasis.)

This line had several advantages for an opportunist sect like the SLL. By a neat left feint, it enabled the Healyites to avoid the pressure on them to help defend the embattled Catholics against the regular and irregular repressive forces of British imperialism. Invoking working-class unity that was unachievable in the concrete circumstances sounded much more "Marxist" than defending the "prisoners of a reactionary ideology" in the Catholic ghettos. It also corresponded to the tendency of British left and liberal opinion to dismiss the Irish fighters as "hopelessly backward," and not worth worrying about.

Down the barricades and up again
At its most pious, the SLL has in fact shown a dismaying tendency to slip into imperious attitudes toward Irish revolutionists, as for example when it attacked the Official Sinn Féin organizer Seán Garland in the June 20, 1972, issue of *Workers Press*: "Garland is no ordinary bog-trotting Republican. He prides himself on being some kind of 'Marxist'...."

But vague and hackneyed calls for working-class unity were not entirely sufficient even for the SLL. In order to maintain its claims of offering a revolutionary alternative, it needed to be able to point to concrete betrayals by the forces leading the struggle. Therefore, the SLL switched its position on the barricades that were supposed to be separating the Catholic workers from their "Protestant brothers." The SLL transformed these formerly unfortunate barriers into sacred arks of the revolution. When the barricades were taken down in 1969, the SLL suggested betrayal.

When again, in the summer of 1972, some barricades were taken down in the course of a confrontation between the British army and the people of the "no-go areas," the July 1 *Workers Press* proclaimed:

> What Whitelaw thinks today, the Social Democratic and Labour Party says tomorrow—and the Republicans the day after that.
> So it was with the ceasefire. So it is with the barricades—the last remaining symbol of defiance to British military occupation.
> It only needed a hint from the Ulster Defense Association-Vanguard group that "selective" barricades were going up this weekend for the SDLP—in the person of Bogsider John Hume MP—to immediately launch an appeal for the removal of the barricades....

> Synchronously with this appeal came the announcement from Republican sources that three barricades would come down because they were "rat infested".
> The barricades, of course, have only a symbolic and provisional significance since the IRA agreed to bury their arms together with the cause for which they fought—namely a united Ireland....
> So, thanks to the SDLP collusion and the IRA (Official and Provisional) capitulation, and only a few hours after the SDLP meeting, the Londonderry [sic]¹ Commission bulldozer knocked a 12-foot path through the Little Diamond Barricade to the paradoxical cheers of the local inhabitants.

The UDA did more than hint that barricades were going up. It went on a campaign of building barricades in an attempt to give the imperialists an excuse for attacking the ghetto areas in the guise of impartial peacekeepers. It also threatened to go in and "clean out" the Derry ghetto if the British troops did not do the job.

With the Catholic community divided in the aftermath of a series of political disasters in the spring and early summer, the ghetto defenders were in an extremely difficult position. The objective problems of the Official IRA were made even worse by their ideological weaknesses, including the idea that a confrontation with the "Protestant workers" would be the ultimate catastrophe.

This, of course, was the same line the SLL had been trumpeting since 1969, but the Official republicans, whose skins were really at stake, unfortunately took this dogma seriously and followed it rather consistently, at the risk of finding themselves and their followers ideologically disarmed in the face of new pogroms.

Protestants battling the British!
That the SLL's doctrine of "working-class unity" was only a propaganda pose is clearly shown by

---

1. Derry is the native name. The "London" was added when the London corporation acquired title to the land as a result of English conquest. Since the Irish name also has the advantage of shortness, only proimperialist chauvinists and those most respectful of "her majesty's" municipal nomenclature continue to use the form introduced by the conquerors.

the gyrations on the question of the reactionary Protestant popular organizations and militias.

In its October 7, 1969, issue *Workers Press* hailed the riots touched off in Protestant areas by the moves leading up to the dissolution of the B-Specials, the reactionary militia of the Protestant ascendancy. These outbreaks, according to the Healyites, heralded the approach of working-class unity. British imperialism had proven unable to maintain the division of the class.

> But the game is up! Because capitalism can provide no future for either the Protestant or the Catholic worker; and because these workers sense the strength and offensive power of their class throughout the world, their need to fight will not and cannot be contained within the old religious "sectarian" framework.
>
> Within only a week or two of the clashes between the forces of the state and groups of Catholic workers in August this year, a remarkable change took place in the situation.
>
> Protestant workers, for half a century used as a pillar of support for the "British connection", found themselves in street battles against the British Army!

The republicans (still not formally split) also saw grounds for hope in this clash between Protestant workers and British troops. The November 1969 issue of their paper, the *United Irishman*, carried "An Open Letter to the Poor Protestants of Ulster," which said, among other things:

> Fifty years of religious and political loyalty to the Crown and what do you get but a kick in the stomach. Or worse.
>
> You who have fought so fearlessly for the connection with England have been rewarded by English bullets, English bayonets and English tear-gas. . . .
>
> The main reality is the economic reality; and if worker stands against worker because deluded by the boss that he should do so for some snobbish silly reason ("we're better than they are"), the only one to suffer will be the worker, all workers.
>
> Most of us workers are joined already in a trade union which fights the boss, Orange or Papist, for better wages and conditions.
>
> Isn't it time we got together politically to do away with all bosses and their hypocrisies?

In contrast to the "Marxists" of the SLL, who were so quick to see a linkup coming between Catholic workers fighting the repressive forces of British imperialism and Protestant workers protesting the disbandment of the most ill-famed terrorist force of the state, the republican statement was not outside the bounds of reality. It was correct to take the opportunity to try to explain to Protestant workers that Britain was not really concerned with defending their interests.

But a false conception was embedded in the republican appeal. The flattery of the Loyalists who were supposed to have "fought so fearlessly to maintain the connection with England" (Against whom did they fight? They were armed to the teeth by British imperialism and fought against half-armed and outnumbered nationalists) was indicative of illusions that were to have serious results.

Voices were raised in Official circles suggesting that the next time the British troops and Protestants had a go, it might be a good idea to stage diversionary attacks on the imperialist troops to divert them from attacking "our brother Irishmen." Since the main clashes occurred when Protestant mobs were on their way toward Catholic ghettos, it could be predicted that this idea would be hard to defend to the nationalist-minded people. It was apparently dropped.

The primacy of politics

The same concept showed up in an article entitled "Taobhú leis na Protastúin" ["Side with the Protestants"] in the October 1969 issue of *An Phoblacht*, the monthly paper reflecting the views of Provisional Sinn Féin.

> If a section of the Protestants start a fight against the forces of the crown in the Six Counties, what should we in the republican movement do? If a group of Protestants rise up against Westminster, London, what should we do?
>
> That is how the question was put to me recently. I have only one answer to the two

questions; take the side of the Protestants against the army that has its boot on the stomach of Irishmen in the six counties of the Northeast.

But are these people fascists? . . .

It doesn't matter if they are fascists; they are Irishmen and we are Irishmen and England is the enemy. [Is cuma faisístí nó eile iad nó is Eireannaigh atá iontu agus is Eireannaigh muide agus is ea Sasana an namhad.]

At least this writer was more consistent than the SLL "Marxists." He was able to dismiss and not ignore the political ideology guiding the Protestants who clashed with the British troops. Furthermore, the Irish writer shared the SLL's evaluation of the need for fighting the influence of the Catholic church:

> The Presbyterians never cared much for kings and princes or aristocrats in general. They didn't need bishops. They understood what democracy was.
>
> I must remind those who are dubious about the role of the Protestants in the new Ireland that the Catholic church has worked hard against republicanism with the strongest weapon it could use against believing Catholics—excommunication.

It is not surprising that republicans armed only with moralistic ideas and unanalyzed (but rationalized) tradition should make errors about the dynamic of the Northern struggle, which is certainly extremely complex. This is clearly a case where Marxists can make the best demonstration of the superiority of their method.

The first thing a Marxist would have to explain is the primacy of politics: that as long as the Protestants mobilize in opposition to the movement of the Catholics for national liberation, they can only move in a reactionary direction. It is understandable that populist republicans think that all of the poor, the "people," or the working class can be rallied by appeals to a general common interest. There is no excuse for Marxists making this mistake; they have a rich heritage of analyzing differences in the working class and mobilizations of popular strata for reactionary interests.

But not only did the SLL not offer an objective and scientific analysis of the Protestant behavior; it did not even have the courage of its "convictions."

The republicans, operating in accordance with the romanticized view of the Protestants bequeathed by petty-bourgeois nationalists like Eoin Mac Neil, not only drew the same optimistic conclusions as the SLL about the cases of Protestants clashing with British troops; they tried to act on the basis of this view. They sought contacts and dialogue with leaders of the Protestant militants such as Ian Paisley and the UDA leaders, who were often at sharp variance with the British authorities and the established leaders of Unionism, at times even being subjected to jail terms and other forms of repression.

This policy was a logical conclusion of the SLL's view of the Catholics and the Protestants converging in struggle. But when the republicans actually tried to do something about it, the SLL took this as another chance to raise the cry of betrayal. When Paisley carried out some tactical maneuvers in the fall of 1971, opposing internment (in favor of regular prison sentences for IRA "terrorists") and talking vaguely about a deal with the South, if the theocratic features of the Free State were removed, most nationalist opinion was disoriented. Both the Officials and Provisionals, as well as other nationalist organizations and personalities made overtures to the "activist" proimperialist groups.

In its December 6, 1971, issue, *Workers Press* seized on one such overture by David O'Connell:

> A leading member of the IRA has issued a statement calling on the Rev Ian Paisley to build branches of his extreme right-wing party in Catholic working-class areas.
>
> This reactionary appeal is a damning indictment of the treacherous forces inside the IRA leadership.

It is possible, of course, that the SLL writer was unaware of the circumstances around this appeal; one stray newspaper clipping might have triggered a conditioned reflex. It is also possible that this journalist did not draw any consistent conclusions from the SLL's pronouncement. There is not much real consistency in the SLL's attitude over the last four years. But what was unforgivable was the implication that the Provisionals and the Protestant rightists were both equally reactionary. This was pandering to the worst chauvinist prejudices of the British working class.

On the question of terrorism

Another example of inconsistency on the part of the SLL raises even more serious questions about its understanding of principle. *Workers Press* has continually repeated the classical Marxist criticisms of terrorism as a method of revolutionary struggle, opposing both the republicans and the young British ultraleft. On occasion, these criticisms coincided with the Official IRA's critique of the Provisional campaign. For example, the September 13, 1971, *Workers Press* said:

> The use of "terror" in a negative, one-sided fashion is doing considerable damage to the building of unity between the Catholic and Protestant workers.

After the political disaster the Official IRA suffered in May 1972 in Derry as the result of executing a local youth on leave from the British army, the May 26 *Workers Press* had some friendly advice for the Officials:

> We call upon the official IRA to consider seriously political changes in its policies which will mean the abandonment of terrorism and its replacement with revolutionary policies which unite the Irish with the English working class against their common enemy the Tory government.

But when the Officials called a halt to "offensive action" a few days later, the May 31, 1972, *Workers Press* trumpeted:

> For the second time in ten years the Official IRA leaders in Gardiner Place, Dublin, have sold out the heroic struggle of the Catholic Irish workers in the North.
> No amount of Republican rhetoric and no amount of evocation of sectarian violence can hide this....
> Calling off the military campaign will not lessen the sectarian hatreds, but will only strengthen the demands of the "Vanguard" gorillas. William Craig dismissed the IRA "initiative" as "unimportant" and designed "only to gain favour in Londonderry".
> The Orange reactionaries predictably view this capitulation with contempt and are encouraged in their campaign to put more pressure on the army to take the Creggan and other "no-go" areas by storm.

The Officials' retreat from terrorism was now seen as betraying the forces still engaged in such activity.

> This is exactly British strategy in Ulster: split the Officials from the Provisionals [now who's talking about unity with the Provos?], neutralize the former, isolate the latter, and hit the Provos hard.
> With leaders like the Gardiner Place reformists who needs the British army? Beaten by Lynch's referendum in the South and bewildered by direct rule in the North, these petty-bourgeois imposters are now crawling unashamedly before imperialism.
> Nobody should be surprised if yesterday's inmates of Long Kesh and the wanted men on the RUC's list should soon be seen serving on Whitelaw's wretched advisory commission.
> Is it any accident that Whitelaw's nominee on the Commission, Tom Conaty from the Central Citizen's Defence Committee and his mouthpiece in the SDLP, Gerry Fitt, have unreservedly welcomed the Officials' statement?
> The stage is now set to go from direct rule to direct collaboration.

From the safety of its London offices, *Workers Press* dismissed the danger of the Irish fighters becoming isolated from the nationalist community, where for the first time in months the moderates felt strong enough to launch a "peace offensive."

> While it is true that the indiscriminate bombing of the Provisional IRA has outraged Protestants and incensed many Catholics, this does not give the Officials any political justification to kowtow to Whitelaw or his stooges.

Workers Press, which has criticized in the past and will continue to do so in the present and future, the Provisionals' political bankruptcy and sectarianism, denounces this act of the Officials.

It is unprincipled and traitorous. As the Provisional leaders stated: "We look upon this surrender as a gigantic confidence trick aimed at giving firmer control to the Official wing of their undisciplined members."

The SLL's principles are thus so elastic as to make it possible to have your cake and eat it too. Its "orthodox Marxist" condemnation of terrorism did not stand in the way of appealing to the romantic ultraleftists getting vicarious thrills from the "armed struggle" in Ulster. Out of the wreck of the Irish cause, the SLL could hope to emerge as the only uncompromised guardian of "revolutionary principle," in other words, a church where a few of the survivors might want to seek sanctuary and spiritual solace.

Unfortunately, this sectarian project needed a long period of relative stagnation to be successful, and the Irish struggle was still to experience some dramatic shifts.

When the Provisionals were also forced to declare a truce few weeks after the Officials, the June 24 *Workers Press* wrote that the betrayal of the "nationalists" was now complete and only the "Marxists," represented by the SLL, were still in the field.

> "Peace" says Harold Wilson—three years after dispatching the troops who started the war in Ulster. "Peace" shout the disparate group of People's Democracy, Official Republicans, Women's peace corps and last but not least, Miss Bernadette Devlin, MP, as they crawl behind the SDLP.
>
> And "peace" says the two-faced Lynch as he jails more Republicans to prove it.
>
> "Peace" grunts the paratrooper as he slips another round into the breach of his SLR [self-loading rifle].
>
> And now comes the echoing cry of "peace" from the Provisionals as they bury their arms—and probably some of their comrades who opposed the cease-fire. . . .

If 1922 was a tragedy, then this is history repeating itself as a grotesque farce. The Irish petty-bourgeois Republicans—in alliance with the revisionists—have once again led the Catholic working class into the cul-de-sac of sectarian terror only in order to recoil from their folly and prostrate themselves at the feet of imperialism in the end.

Our line's been changed again

But less than three weeks later, when the Provisionals ended their truce and resumed their bombing campaign, the SLL had to revise its claims about the betrayal being complete. It even began to refer to the Provisionals as "the IRA":

> . . . the IRA had every right to reject the truce and fight back—however tardily. Workers Press, while criticizing the policies of the IRA which led to the "truce", nevertheless supports unreservedly, the disruption by the IRA of the cynical and fraudulent "truce" of imperialism. We also support critically [?] the withdrawal of troops (not in 1975, but now) and the release of internees and political prisoners in Ulster and Britain.
>
> For the same reason we condemn categorically the unprincipled and cravenly middle-class reformist attitude of the Official IRA and the "Morning Star" to the breaking of the "truce".
>
> The Official Sinn Fein in Dublin have "regretted" the Provisionals' decision to resume fighting. Their statement alleges that "the resumption of offensive action will take the pressure off Mr. Whitelaw . . ." Having made their peace with imperialism, these reformist-nationalists have no desire to make Whitelaw's job any more difficult—or to embarrass Generals Ford and Tuzo.
>
> Whilst correctly reproving the Provisionals for having secret talks with Whitelaw and accusing the British army of employing *agents provocateurs* to kill innocent people and inflame sectarian passions, the Officials conclude by the most pathetic display of capitulationism:
>
> "The close co-operation between the British army and the UDA over the last week surely

should have warned the anti-Unionist forces against the position of confrontation."

At least 16,500 British troops, aided by the most brutal police force in the British Isles, stand menacingly over the Irish workers and the Official Sinn Fein says "Don't fight!" (*Workers Press*, July 12, 1972.)

Once again the Healyites took the opportunity to morally condemn the Officials' policy without bothering to analyze it. This was a grave dereliction of duty on the part of a group that claims to be Marxist, because there was, in fact, a serious danger that the Officials' incorrect ideas would disarm them in the face of British repression and Orange terror.

The Officials were only following the logic of the position, put forward with such a show of dogmatic "conviction" by the SLL, that the same dynamic was present in the Protestant differences with the British army and the mobilizations of the nationalist-minded population. Therefore, their basic strategy was to split the Protestant militant groups away from the imperialist and proimperialist establishment and draw them into unity with their Catholic counterparts.

As a result, the healing of the split between the UDA and the British army in the period around Operation Motorman was seen as the ultimate disaster. In point of fact, it was extremely dangerous. Because what it represented was division in the ghettos and international isolation of the nationalist-minded people, which enabled Whitehall to take the "tough" policy against the nationalist ghettos that the UDA demanded. The imperialists and the various proimperialist factions, no longer faced with unity of the anti-imperialist population and the widespread sympathy abroad for their cause, were able to overcome serious divisions over how to handle the threat presented by the protests and demands of the oppressed people.

Nonetheless, the policy of the Officials was the exact opposite of what was needed to stave off attacks on the nationalist people. By flattering the Protestant "activists" and blaming their fanaticism on the actions of the Provisionals, the Officials made it more difficult to arouse international public opinion to defend the beleaguered Catholics. This line in fact coincided with the position of the capitalist press that both sides were equally irrational and reactionary. Still worse, by portraying as the ultimate catastrophe the head-on collision with the Protestant militant groups that is virtually inevitable at some stage if the struggle for national liberation is to be carried through to victory, they paralyzed the will of the most conscious revolutionists in the Catholic ghettos. At the same time, by fostering the illusion that staving off counterrevolutionary pogroms depended on moderation by the Catholics, they fell into reformism.

There is no doubt that political errors by nationalist forces have made it easier for the rightists to rally larger sections of the Protestant community behind them. But the basic fact is that as long as the Protestants remain under the influence of reactionary ideology, that is, in the last analysis, under bourgeois political domination, their actions are dictated fundamentally by the policy of the bourgeoisie, or the sections of it that stand closest to the Protestant community. As four years of conflict have shown, the interests of these strata of the bourgeoisie lie in breaking the spirit of the Catholic population. The "moderation" of the Catholic people and the pessimism of its best leaders could have the precise effect of inviting more determined attempts to intimidate the oppressed population.

Moreover, while criticizing the Officials for "giving up the struggle" in the North, the Healyites commended the very rationale for doing so. In its November 30, 1972, issue, *Workers Press* said:

> By this summer, although they had learned nothing, some Officials at least saw the reality of the position. Commenting on the resistance in the North, Sean Garland said: "We are not on the brink of victory, but on the brink of sectarian disaster and sell out."

It is no wonder that the few Irish Healyites who get their direction from *Workers Press* seem to do nothing but engage in rambling and contradictory denunciations of every group and prominent individual involved in the struggle. What kind of guide does this offer? If you are against terrorism and for working-class unity at any cost, *Workers Press* is even more so than anyone else. No one can possibly be as virtuous as the Healyites on this. If on the other hand you favor striking out immediately at the repressive system at any cost and resorting to bombings and other forms of terrorism, you can't approach the SLL in revolutionism, and if your throwing arm gets tired you face the certainty of being condemned as a "traitor." The only consistent thread in the SLL's attitude is its striving to remain "above" the real struggle and its duties. The SLL's course resembles the flight of a hot-air balloon that rises as the ground heats up.

Need to campaign for troop withdrawal

The Healyites' calling for immediate withdrawal of British troops is a good example of their technique. This demand is probably the one raised most consistently by the Healyites. It is the demand that most sets them off from the bulk of the British left, which also spends most of its time trying to convince Irish republicans of the need for "working-class unity" based on "industrial action"—and in terms that (aside from the inimitable Healyite tone) must seem to an outsider almost indistinguishable from the SLL arguments.

There is no doubt that the demand is a hard one to put across. It is hard to explain its importance to the masses in the Catholic ghettos, who fear the fanatical assaults of the Protestant extremist gangs more acutely than the more drawn-out repression of the army. It is true that the British government is more sensitive to public opinion and more inclined to make concessions to the oppressed population than are the local clients of imperialism.

It is not so obvious that since the entire system of repression, including the Orange gangs, depends in the last analysis on British power, any suggestion that the troops can play even a limited or temporary positive role in the situation strengthens the hand both of the Unionist fanatics and the imperialist regime, which can maneuver to divide the communities and at the same time disarm the oppressed population and prepare the way for still more devastating pogroms whenever it suits Whitehall's interests. Naturally, the masses of the people feel the immediate threat of Orange outrages more acutely than the larger-scale dangers inherent in the operation of the imperialist system of control. Only a well-established and trusted revolutionary leadership could convince the people that they must rely on their own strength against both the British army and the proimperialist terrorists.

A small British group cannot do this. Among other things, it would be too easy to counter that while such a call might sound revolutionary, those who raise it in Britain do not face the same dangers as nationalists in Northern Ireland; or that they do not even really understand these dangers. But a British revolutionary group could help spread an understanding in Ireland of the need to demand immediate withdrawal of the troops if it patiently explained this need to the most conscious elements of the Irish movement. The SLL, however, is uninterested in doing this. Its approach is shown by the statement of the "International Committee of the Fourth International" (the Healyite "international" rubric) in the June 28, 1972, issue of *Workers Press*. Characteristically, it begins:

> Only the Socialist Labour League and the International Committee opposed direct rule from a class standpoint. [The declaration goes on to say:]
>
> Only the International Committee and its sections came out unequivocally against the intervention of British troops in Ireland from the very first minute. Against every other tendency we asserted that this was a basic question of principle: the forces of the capitalist state were there to enforce the protection of property and bourgeois order and on no account could they act in the interests of the working class.

The Healyites had no interest in educating the Irish vanguard, but simply in scoring debater's points in British sectarian circles. If they were seriously interested in getting the Irish people to understand the need for fighting the repressive system as a whole, why didn't they do something in Britain to show the Irish that they were not alone in their struggle against terror and systematic violence?

There is not the slightest indication that in the last four years the SLL has done anything whatever to defend the Irish people except to offer some purely propagandistic support through articles in its paper.

Moreover, while *Workers Press* blossoms with

denunciations of every Irish tendency when explosions or dramatic turns of events occur in Ireland, it has never chronicled any attempts by the SLL to win support for the Irish struggle in Britain. The "Trotskyist daily" has called at various times for "armed" workers defense groups in Ireland and for immediate withdrawal of the British army, but it has never written anything aimed at the British soldiers themselves. It has never done anything to blunt the main instrument of imperialist repression, the army of its own country.

The SLL has organized no demonstrations calling for the withdrawal of British troops. It has not sought to create sentiment in the British troops to get out of Ireland. But in the September 30, 1969, issue of *Workers Press*, one of the first issues of the "first Trotskyist daily," published only a few weeks after the first troops were dispatched to Northern Ireland the following large action by the SLL was featured:

> "Workers' Press in! Wilson out!" Brighton's narrow streets rang with slogans like these on Sunday afternoon as 1,500 members and supporters of the Socialist Labour League, the Young Socialists and the All Trades Unions Alliance marched proudly through the town to celebrate the launching of our paper.
>
> Headed by the Socialist Labour League Central Committee, followed by a sea of red banners, contingents from all over Britain demonstrated behind the lead banner: "Socialist Labour League. Forward with Workers' Press. First Trotskyist daily paper".
>
> Leading trade unionists from many areas marched in step with young workers and students.
>
> The enormous potential of Workers' Press was expressed in the marchers' determination and the magnificent collection at the meeting which followed the demonstration.

In the almost four years since that time there has not been one demonstration or one campaign by the SLL in support of the struggle in Ireland!

It is true that the SLL at one time or another had published all the correct slogans (as well as a series of incorrect ones) for the struggle in Ireland. It is clear at the same time that these slogans were neither consistently followed nor advanced as a guide to action. The SLL's policy in fact is distinguished by repeated 180-degree turns designed to give the group the most "revolutionary" appearance possible.

Not only could such propaganda educate no one, but many of the formally correct statements of the SLL condemn their authors most effectively, such as this incontrovertible observation in the September 13, 1971, issue of *Workers Press*: "Impressionism is the hallmark of idealistic thinking. In practice it leads to empirical and improvised adaptation to events."

SECTION VIII: THE STRUGGLE IN BANGLADESH

Healyites in the Camp of Indira Gandhi
By Joseph Hansen

The position taken by the Healyites on the war between India and Pakistan will hardly come as a surprise to those familiar with the saying, "Scratch an ultraleft and you'll find an opportunist."

The Healyites, who have long been notorious in Britain for their ultraleft sectarianism, decided to offer their support to the bourgeois government of Indira Gandhi.

The official Healyite statement was published in the December 6, 1971, issue of *Workers Press*, the organ of the Central Committee of the Socialist Labour League. Listed as a "statement by the International Committee of the Fourth International," it was entitled "Defeat imperialist conspiracy against Bangla Desh." [See full text on page 24.]

> US imperialism [according to the authors] is determined to utilize the Indo-Pakistan conflict to weaken the Indian economy, as its decision to cut off arms supplies shows.
>
> It wants to facilitate the unlimited penetration of US finance capital into India and the installation of a more docile regime in New Delhi.

In the opinion of the authors of the document, Indian entry into the struggle as a defensive move against the conspiracy of American imperialism was highly progressive:

> Bengali resistance to the barbaric Yahya Khan regime and the heritage of imperialist partition in India has entered a decisive stage with the intervention of Indian armed forces.

The authors are understandably responsive to the heartening action taken by the rulers of India at this decisive stage:

> We critically support the decision of the Indian bourgeois government to give military and economic aid to Bangla Desh.

Bowing in the direction of Trotskyism, to which the Healyites profess to adhere, the authors include correct generalizations concerning the nature of the Bengali and Hindu bourgeoisie, their ulterior aims in the conflict, and the need to oppose them. But these generalizations all speak against supporting the New Delhi regime.

Why then did the Healyites decide to line up with Indira Gandhi ("critically," of course)?

The reason is to be found in Britain. Since last March when Yahya Khan turned his guns on the masses in East Pakistan, the Socialist Labour League has been seeking to make an impression on the Bengali immigrants and exiles who are fervent supporters of the Bangladesh liberation movement.

The news that India had intervened in the conflict with her armies was received with joy among the majority of these Bangladesh patriots. It was an unthinking reaction based on lack of knowledge of the real aims of the Gandhi regime. These, of course, were to take over from the failing Pakistani occupation the task of saving capitalism in Bangladesh.

Intercontinental Press, January 10, 1972.

The Healyites simply adapted in the most opportunistic way to this mood among the Bengalis in Britain.

The Lambertists, who up until recently formed a tight bloc with the Healyites in the "International Committee," felt constrained to publicly denounce the SLL betrayal. They did this in two articles in the December 15 and December 22 issues of *Informations Ouvrières*, the weekly newspaper they publish in Paris.

An editorial note introducing the first article stated: "The SLL fraudulently attributes the position it has taken on the Indo-Pakistan war to the International Committee, whereas the latter has not met."

This "gross usurpation," as the editors put it, "cannot mask the real problems involved. The statement of the SLL . . . offers support to the government of Indira Gandhi whom it raises to the rank of defender of the interests of the Bengali people."

The unidentified authors of the two articles (the Central Committee of the Lambertist grouping, the Organisation Communiste Internationaliste?) do not explain how they happen to know that the "International Committee" has not met. Probably they have in mind their membership in the committee and the proviso that members must be notified in advance of meetings.

Skipping such details, they go to the heart of the matter, as they view it, and prove quite convincingly that the SLL position amounts to rejection of Trotsky's theory of the permanent revolution and adoption of Stalin's theory of "revolution by stages." In this instance, they add, "a 'stage' of the counterrevolution."

If the Indian bourgeoisie are capable of playing a progressive role in a "decisive stage" of the revolution in Bangladesh—which is the position taken by the Healyites—then it follows that Trotsky turned out to be wrong in maintaining that the bourgeoisie in the colonial world in general (as elsewhere) are incapable of playing such a role.

But the Indian bourgeoisie and their regime in New Delhi have no intention of playing a progressive role. On the contrary, their aims are completely reactionary. It is the leaders of the SLL who entertain illusions in the operation, certainly not the Indian bourgeois political strategists or the generals they placed in charge of carrying it out.

Thus Trotsky's theory of permanent revolution stands confirmed once again, while the leaders of the SLL stand condemned.

Curiously, the Lambertist authors never mention the pragmatic reasons for the SLL position. They argue as if the SLL leaders were simply of low theoretical level, do not really understand Trotsky's theory of permanent revolution, and thereby stumbled inadvertently into their betrayal of revolutionary Marxism after depriving themselves of the theoretical wisdom and capacities of the Lambertists.

Perhaps the oversight is intentional—the Lambertists are not invulnerable to finger-wagging from the Healyites on certain opportunistic sins and peccadilloes committed in France.

As for the moral outrage over Healy's usurpation of the name of the "International Committee," this is all for the innocents. Healy, the secretary of the SLL, is merely repeating what he did in 1963 when the majority of the original International Committee joined in a reunification congress that ended a ten-year split in the world Trotskyist movement.

At that time Healy refused to participate in the reunification. Instead, he set up a rump "International Committee" of his own—with Lambert aiding and abetting in the fraud.

Healy is only asserting his property rights against the claims of Lambert to possession of this rump body.

Lambert, consequently, finds himself faced with the problem of deciding what to do about SLL betrayals bearing the official stamp of the "International Committee." An embarrassing situation! But then what did he expect?

SECTION IX: BLACK LIBERATION

Healyites Decide Trotsky Was Wrong on Black Nationalism
By Joseph Hansen

For specialists in such questions, it may be of interest to note that the Healyites* have begun to admit that they have their differences with Leon Trotsky. Previously they had exempted him from open criticism and held him up as a shield against their opponents. Much of their writing is devoted to "exposing" all others who claim adherence to Trotskyism as being nothing but fake Trotskyists.

The issue on which the Healyites have decided to take their distance from Leon Trotsky is Black Power.

The Healyites have opposed this rallying cry of wide sectors of the working class and other layers of the oppressed masses since it first arose in the struggle for black liberation. In the Healyite lexicon, those who support Black Power are fake lefts, betrayers, and class enemies.

A special target of the Healyites on this question has been the Socialist Workers party, the *first* grouping in the radical movement in the United States to call attention to the political significance of the upsurge of black nationalist sentiments and to point out the progressive nature and revolutionary implications of these sentiments in the struggle against capitalism and for socialism.

The SWP was able to do this because of the clarity of its theory on this question, a theory that was worked out in its fundamentals with the direct collaboration of Leon Trotsky.

While the Healyites have vociferously denounced the SWP for hailing the rise of black nationalism as a revolutionary development in the United States, they remained silent until just recently about Trotsky's views on this subject.

Their hesitation about attacking Trotsky's position is understandable, if not exactly commendable.

It now appears that they—or some of them—have screwed up sufficient courage to begin to say publicly what they have been whispering among themselves privately.

Trotsky attacked as source of SWP 'Adaptation'

The first sally was not taken by the top command in London, although they most likely inspired it. Healy's American disciples held a conference of the "Workers League" in New York on November 22–24, 1968, where the question of Black Power was put on the agenda. Thus the December 16 issue of the *Bulletin*, which they publish, said in an editorial note:

> An extensive discussion was also held on the Negro question—particularly in relation to the misconceptions put forward by Trotsky in his 1939 discussions and the attempts of the SWP to turn these misconceptions into a reactionary adaptation to black nationalism. The article on this page by Lucy St. John reflects this discussion and marks the begin-

---

Intercontinental Press, February 24, 1969.

* Gerry Healy of the Socialist Labour League [SLL], an ultraleft sectarian British grouping which claims to be "Trotskyist" although it is bitterly hostile to the Fourth International founded by Leon Trotsky. Internationally, the tendency has adherents in France ("Organisation Communiste Internationaliste") and in the U.S. (the "Workers League").

ning of our theoretical work on this critical question.

Lucy St. John argues that the

> Negroes today do not exist in relation to the capitalist class as a separate nation but rather as a part of the class society, doubly burdened not only with class oppression but racial discrimination so that they share more proportionally in unemployment, unskilled jobs, etc.

This is revealed, Miss St. John argues,

> in the struggles of the Negro people not historically for a separate nation but for political, economic and social equality. The nationalist movements in this country beginning with Garvey have never been supported by the Negro working class and are not today. The petty bourgeoisie have been the mentors of the demand for a separate nation.

She then gets down to Leon Trotsky and his position:

> We say that the demand for self determination for the Negro people is a reactionary demand—that it legitimizes the racial divisions, the "ghetto" and aids the bourgeoisie in maintaining racism, that it divides the working class.
>
> It is within the context of the discussions of the national question within the Marxist movement and the historical political conditions of the United States and from the standpoint of the class struggle, that we approach Trotsky's discussion on the Negro question. The Workers League contends today that Trotsky's conclusions in this discussion were basically incorrect. Trotsky was indeed a genius but not a god.
>
> Trotsky in this discussion contended that the SWP should support the demand for self determination "if the Negroes themselves want it." At the same time he stated that the Negroes are "a race and not a nation." He said the SWP should "not obligate the Negroes to become a nation; if they are, then that is a question of their consciousness, that is what they desire and what they strive for." He saw the demand for a black state as a "sign of moral and political awakening" and as a "tremendous revolutionary step." In his approach to the question of whether the Negroes are a nation, Trotsky appears to be relying on a totally subjective and psychological basis of analysis as he puts it "their feelings and their impulses", rather than an objective analysis.
>
> Trotsky at the time admitted that he had very little information on the Negro in the United States. His statements are far from definitive on the question and often contradictory. Trotsky at the time was concerned primarily with turning the SWP around and forcing it to take up the struggle for the Negro people which they had literally ignored. Trotsky's conclusions appear to be based solely on the need for the SWP to turn to the Negro masses without a clear analysis of the historical, political, and social role of the Negro in the U.S.
>
> We believe that Trotsky was wrong in seeing this demand as a revolutionary step; in that period as well as today it meant the dividing of the working class. Trotsky realized that the demand could have this effect if black and white workers had been united in struggle. Nowhere, nowhere, we repeat, does Trotsky call for black nationalism or in any way advocate cultural nationalism.

Miss St. John contends that the SWP has developed Trotsky's error into something truly monstrous:

> Today the SWP has taken every ambiguity and incorrect conclusion in this pamphlet* and is

---

* The reference is to *Leon Trotsky on Black Nationalism and Self-Determination*, a pamphlet containing transcripts of discussions with Trotsky in Prinkipo and Coyoacan, plus two resolutions adopted by the Socialist Workers party in 1939 and excerpts from writings by Trotsky in which he touches on the question of national oppression and the struggle of the colored races for emancipation. The pamphlet is available from Merit Publishers, 873 Broadway, New York 10003, for $.95. In Britain, it can be obtained from Pioneer Book Service, 8 Toynbee St., London, E.l.—J.H.

using it to give a cover to the most reactionary ideas which serve one purpose and one purpose only and that is to divide the working class and thus aid the capitalist class.

Do Healyites today know better than Trotsky?

As was to be expected, one of Miss St. John's stronger arguments is drawn on the level of the most vulgar empiricism. Trotsky "admitted that he had very little information on the Negro in the United States." The Healyite "Workers League," on the other hand, being in the USA in 1968 knows all about it.

Trotsky customarily made such remarks in discussing tactical questions raised by comrades who came to visit him from various parts of the world. This was an invitation to such comrades to contribute factual material to make the discussion more concrete. Miss St. John avoids saying anything about the knowledge of the other participants in the discussion.

But we can leave such points aside. Whatever his store of information—and theoretical capacity to assess that information—it is not hard to show that Trotsky thirty years ago saw the potentialities of the American scene more clearly than some self-proclaimed "Trotskyists" of today, who, while modestly conceding that they are not up to the level of correcting "a god," do claim to have what it takes to cut "a genius" down to size.

On another point, Miss St. John is simply in error. "Trotsky at the time," she says, "was concerned primarily with turning the SWP around and forcing it to take up the struggle for the Negro people which they had literally ignored."

She offers no explanation as to what connection this presumed concern of his at the time could conceivably have with the possibility of a rise of black nationalism at some future time.

Not the first to 'correct' Trotsky

Trotsky in 1938 and the early part of 1939, insofar as the matter came up, was concerned about the social composition and political and theoretical level of a certain sector of the membership of the SWP. In relation to the number of proletarian cadres, who constituted the stable core of the American Trotskyist movement, he saw a danger in the large proportion of petty-bourgeois youth who had recently been won away from the Social Democracy. They were well-intentioned—say, like the petty-bourgeois members of the "Workers League" today—but he feared that, unless they became integrated into the working class, unless they seriously studied the history of the movement and its theory, they could become lost.

Trotsky's fears about this sector were, unfortunately, later borne out. Under the political banners of Shachtman and Burnham, many of the youth from the Social Democracy, whom the party had not yet had time to assimilate, set out to "correct" Trotsky's "misconceptions" on such items as the validity and usefulness of dialectical materialism, the class nature of the degenerated workers state, and the need to defend the Soviet Union against imperialist attack. They ended up with Shachtman and Burnham, splitting from the SWP in 1940.

Some of them drifted out of politics; some followed Shachtman in the retrogression that finally put him in the camp of the Social Democracy. (If Miss St. John would like more details about this, she has a ready source of information available in her leader Tim Wohlforth, who was recruited by the Shachtmanites, and who never recovered from the basic training he received from them. For those who like dishes with a gamey flavor, Wohlforth's versions of the history of American Trotskyism should be put on the "must try" list.)

Neither original, fresh, nor timely

But let us return to Lucy St. John's attempt to "correct" Trotsky's "misconceptions" on the question which the Healyites find especially vexing.

The editors of the *Bulletin* say that her article "marks the beginning of our theoretical work on this critical question."

If beginnings were to be judged by originality, freshness, or timeliness, this one would take few prizes.

The best that can be said for the theoretical kernel to be found inside the factional husk is that it is essentially nothing more than the position held by the American Trotskyist movement *before 1939*; i.e., before Trotsky called attention to a possibly more complex development of the anticapitalist struggle in the United States than had been anticipated in the party's outlook.

Up to 1939, in addressing itself to what was then

called the Negro struggle, the Trotskyist movement had simply presented the long-range historic goal of a world brotherhood, a classless society of complete equality, in which racism and a series of other evils of increasing virulence under capitalism would be completely eliminated.

In accordance with this world outlook, the American Trotskyist movement had stressed the need for unity regardless of race, color, sex, or nationality as absolutely requisite in the struggle to achieve this goal. The party itself must be constructed in accordance with these principles.

It was clearly recognized that the black community had many special problems but these would be handled through the widening influence and power of the anti-capitalist movement and the revolutionary-socialist party and would be eventually solved when the workers had won power and established a planned economy and a socialist society. No especially difficult tactical problems were envisaged. The slogan of integration made things relatively simple.

What Trotsky actually proposed

Trotsky did not propose to change any of the basic revolutionary-socialist concepts at all. He insisted on these principles as he always had.

What he did raise was the possibility of a rise of nationalist feelings among the black people in the United States in a situation beyond the control of the revolutionary-socialist party, a complex situation that would demand great tactical flexibility.

He suggested that the SWP should not be dogmatic or sectarian in considering this but should leave open the possibility of such a turn of events. Should this occur, the correct way to meet the problems that would arise could be worked out under the general concept of the right of an oppressed people to self-determination, a democratic demand contained in every Marxist-Leninist program, although Miss St. John, we see, considers it to be "reactionary."

The majority of the SWP thought that Trotsky's advice was good and this was registered in the official party positions in 1939.

It should be added that a minority in the SWP remained dubious. Those who held these doubts argued with increasing conviction that events had proved Trotsky to be wrong. The course of the struggle itself showed that the black community, they contended, had closed the door on any alternative other than integration.

For some twenty-five years the question came up at virtually every convention as this minority grouping—which consisted of very good comrades—sought to have the SWP take a public position excluding the possibility of any rise of nationalism among the black people in the United States. The party resolutely refused to shut the door in a dogmatic manner against this variant of development.

This perennial difference was finally settled in practice by the rise of the Black Muslims, the development of a wing that began to turn toward political action under the leadership of Malcolm X, the development of Malcolm X's own thinking in a revolutionary-socialist direction, and ultimately the explosive development of the current Black Power movement with its strong anticapitalist bent.

It would seem impossible to deny that Trotsky's political prescience was given extraordinary confirmation. But people can be found, it must be admitted, who do find it possible to deny it.

Where Healy was during the discussion

Healy himself was not in the Fourth International when the *Transitional Program* and the possibility of the rise of black nationalism in the United States was under intensive discussion. His first political experiences were in the Communist party in its ultraleft "third period" phase. He was further shaped by some years in a small group which proclaimed itself to be Trotskyist but which was ridden with poisonous factionalism. After he joined the Fourth International, he never questioned Trotsky's contribution in this area. Not once. Not even by a whisper in the corridors.

Now that Trotsky's view has been confirmed, however, Healy has apparently decided it is time to "correct" Trotsky. Eventually this will no doubt become part of his rationalization for refusing to go along with the majority in the world Trotskyist movement in 1963 in healing a split that had occurred some ten years before.

What to look for in studying Trotsky

The Healyite editors of the *Bulletin* say that Miss St. John's attack on Trotsky's position on black nationalism is only the beginning and they promise more "theoretical work on this critical question."

It is to be hoped that they will do their utmost to deliver on their courageous promise. To facilitate the task, I should like to suggest a line of inquiry that might save them needless floundering and bring them directly to the heart of the question.

Trotsky was a dialectician. He did not take up subjects as if each of them was sealed off from everything else. He looked for processes and for the connections between processes. Thus, unless we are to maintain that on this question Trotsky was no dialectician but only a bungler and dogmatist, like the leaders of the SLL, then it would be fruitful to examine his approach on other closely related questions at the time.

It does not require much research to turn up something that ought to make the heart of every Healyite beat quicker.

Trotsky suggested the advisability of taking a flexible attitude toward the potential forms of the black liberation struggle in February 1939. This was less than a year after his conversations with the American Trotskyists that led to his working out the *Transitional Program*. And it was during the period immediately following the adoption of the *Transitional Program*, when sections of the Fourth International everywhere were trying to apply it concretely and to work out new variants on slogans.

Could it be that, in discussing the possibility of the appearance of black nationalism and what attitude to take toward it, Trotsky had in mind the same method to be found at the heart of the *Transitional Program*?

What is this method, the method that has made the *Transitional Program* of such extraordinary importance in the world Trotskyist movement? It is to continually try to find *bridges* between the program of revolutionary socialism and whatever the current level of political understanding of the oppressed and exploited masses may be.

Consider the way in which Trotsky expressed his concern about a correct approach to the oppressed black people in the United States. What Trotsky said in essence to the revolutionary socialists was, Watch the development of the consciousness of the black people as it actually occurs—and not as you may preconceive it or prefer it to be. Then find a way of meeting that development with a positive tactic. Especially, he warned, do not make the sectarian mistake of rejecting the development of black nationalism. In the United States its appearance would be a "tremendous revolutionary step."

In reality, as the context shows, the discussion with Trotsky on this subject was an extension of his previous discussions on such subjects as the trade unions, the youth, women, military training, and so on, covered in the *Transitional Program*. If the topic is not included in the *Transitional Program*, this is mainly because it remained to be seen what would develop in this field.

The method to be followed in meeting such a contingency was provided for in the general approach of the *Transitional Program*. It need only be applied in a concrete way—which was what the SWP did, without paying any attention to the fluttering this caused in the Healyite dovecote.

Black power and a labor party—two interrelated slogans

Trotsky's approach on the possibility that the black people in the United States might go through a phase of revolutionary nationalism is not at all different in principle from his approach on the possibility of a great rise in political consciousness among the American workers before the revolutionary-socialist party achieves a mass base, which led him to suggest advocating a labor party as a transitional slogan.

Trotsky's stand on the labor party slogan also met with doubts and opposition in 1938 and 1939 among some of his followers; and, of course, cries of "betrayal" from such dyed-in-the-wool sectarians as the followers of Daniel De Leon. But there was considerable empirical justification for that slogan owing to the widespread sentiment in those years among the militants in the American labor movement who favored breaking with the Democratic machine and organizing labor's own party. The experience in Britain could also be cited as a precedent.

It is because of this empirical background to the question that the Healyites have found the labor party slogan acceptable and, in fact, have converted it into their central slogan in the United States.

Indeed, Trotsky's proposal for a labor party based on the unions in the United States, which is endorsed by Healy's followers, is symmetrical with the idea put forward by the Socialist Workers party for an independent black political party, which they condemn. The grounds for both political proposals are similar. They would provide a vehicle to detach the workers in the one case and the Afro-Americans in the other from subservience to the capitalist parties and to promote their mobilization for struggle in their own interests.

As George Breitman has indicated in numerous articles and pamphlets, the formation of a political party by the black masses would shake and shatter the established structure of capitalist rule in the U.S.A. and even set an example of independent political organization that the organized workers might follow. Thus the emergence of a labor party itself could be stimulated by the political initiative of the most progressive black nationalists.*

Analysis of mass moods is required, too

Lucy St. John, who, naturally propagandizes for a labor party in the United States, struggles to understand what might have been going on in Trotsky's mind to cause him to commit such a bad error with regard to the black people organizing along independent lines! "In his approach to the question of whether the Negroes are a nation, Trotsky appears to be relying on a totally subjective and psychological basis of analysis . . ."

She rejects such subjectivism. How could Trotsky have fallen into such an erroneous pattern of thought—such a departure from the dialectical method as she conceives and practices it? She offers a subjective and psychological explanation: Trotsky was "no god." He was capable of errors every bit as bad as those committed any day of the week by the geniuses who hold high the great red banner of Healy's thought.

It does not occur to her that she fails to understand Trotsky politically. Still less does it occur to her that by her failure she shows that she does not understand the political thinking in the *Transitional Program*.

Trotsky's approach on the tactical level is precisely to determine the current subjective and psychological level of the masses and try to meet that level by raising slogans that *objectively* (because they correspond to the objective needs of the masses) lead them toward socialism, the only system that can actually satisfy their needs. The party avoids opportunism by advancing slogans that correspond with its program—they can be realized only under socialism. It avoids sectarianism by breaking them into transitional steps that gear into the current subjective and psychological level of the masses.

The *Transitional Program* offers a superb example of the use of the dialectical method in the political field. Analysis of the changing and fluctuating mood of the masses is counterposed to the long-range historical objectives of the proletariat as embodied in the program of socialism. This makes possible a dynamic synthesis in the form of a transitional slogan, or, on the organizational level, a transitional measure, that opens the way to a still higher synthesis and higher level of struggle along the road of revolution and the winning of state power.

While we are on the point, it is worth noting that the Healyites provide a good example of how sectarians fail to grasp the dialectical method and confine their politics to parrot-like repetition of statements on basic principles. Opportunists, it should be added, reveal the same methodological defect by pushing basic principles aside and adapting themselves to passing phases of the mass mood.

Because the methodological flaw is the same in both instances—a one-sided mechanical categorizing that is incapable of bridging the phases in a process—sectarians not infrequently become opportunists. And cases can be found of the opposite, where opportunists become sectarians, even of the ultraleft variety.

After the first olive the rest comes easy

If Lucy St. John and the editors of the *Bulletin* and Trotsky's challengers in London are to be consistent, they have no choice. Having rejected Trotsky's approach in the black liberation struggle, logically they must reject his entire approach in the *Transitional Program*.

Of course, they may prefer to be illogical. Many

---

* For a consideration of this question by a writer who agrees with Trotsky and who has followed the Afro-American struggle for more than three decades, see *How a Minority Can Change Society* by George Breitman. Available for $.35 from Merit Publishers in New York and Pioneer Book Service in London.

precedents and examples of this can be cited in the record of the SLL and its two satellites.

Not the least of these is the fact that in practice they do reject Trotsky's approach in the *Transitional Program*. This is one of the main sources of their ultraleft sectarianism.

But as yet they have not reached the point of recognizing that their approach really has little in common with Trotsky's. They have achieved this measure of self-understanding only in the particular question of black nationalism.

Give them time. When they have finished "correcting" Trotsky's "misconceptions" on the importance of an upsurge of black nationalism in the United States, they may feel bold enough to correct him on other critical issues of the day.

It's like prying olives out of a bottle. After the first one, the rest come easy.

SECTION X: COPS AS 'FELLOW WORKERS'

Are New York's Cops 'Workers'?
By Allen Myers

The national secretary of the Workers League (the American cothinkers of the ultraleft Socialist Labour League led by Gerry Healy in England) has confirmed that, as far as the U. S. Healyites are concerned, cops are just one more group of exploited workers.

In the February 15 issue of the organization's newspaper the *Bulletin*, Tim Wohlforth defended the cops and attacked Black nationalism—an indication of the priorities of the Workers League. As though to emphasize his confusion, Wohlforth entitled his article "In Defense of the Working Class."

To be sure, Wohlforth proclaimed it a "slander" to suggest, as I did in the February 8 *Intercontinental Press*, that the Workers League sees cops as class "brothers." Unfortunately, Wohlforth devoted his article to contradicting his own assertion.

"Are we to see only the side of police as the repressive arm of the state but at the same time not understand that the police are also employees of that state?" Wohlforth asked.

Being an employee of the state, however, does not automatically convert a person into a "worker." The CIA agents in Laos are also employees of

LAURA GRAY
Employee of the state.

the state. If they were to demand more money for their dirty work, would Wohlforth thereupon proclaim them to be workers and offer them the *Bulletin*'s editorial support?

It is necessary to look beyond the fact that cops are listed by the capitalist state as "employees" and see their role in class society. Wohlforth attempted to do this—and failed:

"No, they [police] are not the same as other workers because it is their job to repress other workers."

Very simple, you see: some workers produce steel, some workers wait on tables or teach children, and some workers repress other workers. It's all just part of the social division of labor.

But [he continued] under certain conditions those whom the bourgeoisie relies upon to suppress the working class themselves go out in strike against the bourgeoisie. Such an act does not change their fundamental nature as the repressive arm of the state. However, it does definitely create problems for the bourgeoisie.

Wohlforth, who likes to boast of his appreciation of "dialectics," provides us here with reason-

---

Intercontinental Press, March 1, 1971.

ing that can only be rated as sophistry. Cops are workers because when they demand more money and greater latitude in suppressing workers, they "create problems for the bourgeoisie"!

One wonders what Wohlforth's analysis of the recent oil-price negotiations must be. Is the shah of Iran a "worker" because his demand for a bigger share of the loot created "problems for the bourgeoisie"?

"If our stand is with the working class," Wohlforth went on, "then we can only be happy to see the repressive arm of our enemy in struggle against our enemy."

In the first place, Wohlforth here completely falsified the character of the New York cops' strike. These mercenaries were in no way rejecting their role as agents of repression against the working class. Their "struggle" was not "against our enemy" but against the working class: They were demanding greater freedom in carrying out their repressive assignment and more money for doing it.

Secondly, what makes Wohlforth "happy" is beside the point; the question is whether a demand by the cops for more money transforms them into part of the working-class movement. Wohlforth, unfortunately, answers yes:

> The significance of all this [a recapitulation of the 1919 strike by Boston cops] is the importance of placing the recent New York police strike within the framework of the general movement of the working class and at the same time seeking to understand what underlies this movement of the class.

The Healyite theoretician even defended in his own way the extravagant contention of an earlier *Bulletin* article that the action by the cops had brought New York City to "the verge of civil war":

> Yes, Mr. Myers, we have entered into a period when troops can face strikers, when a general strike could take place, when two arms of the repressive state itself could shoot it out.

Wohlforth's methodology is instructive. He carefully avoided the *Bulletin*'s original claim that a cops' strike in New York City in January 1971 nearly touched off civil war. Instead, we are given two deliberately vague generalities: "troops can face strikers" (which strikers?) and "a general strike could take place" (called by the cops?).

These abstract strikers then become a springboard for a dive into civil war mounted by the cops against the ruling class. I expect Wohlforth will tell us that this is getting away from "impressionism" and engaging in "dialectical" leaps.

Wohlforth continued:

> The significance of the police strike is broader than the police itself, for like the growing insurrectionary situation in the army, it signifies that we are now entering on an international scale a period which Prime Minister Heath has characterized as "one not of wars between nations but civil war." And furthermore, that the United States will not be exempt from such struggle but the deepest, most violent battles of all can break out here, and soon.

It may come as a shock to Wohlforth, but the fact that the laws of the class struggle apply to the United States was discovered neither by the New York cops, by Edward Heath, nor by Tim Wohlforth. The contribution on the subject by the U. S. Healyite theoreticians is confined to the hypothesis that in the class struggle, which in an acute stage reaches the point of civil war, the cops can be allies of the working class, brothers in the labor movement, and even workers themselves.

Wohlforth neglected to answer directly the question whether the Workers League now plans to conduct a recruiting drive among police "proletarians" and similar "workers" such as FBI agents. But his one allusion to the question is far from reassuring:

> We for one [sic] . . . enjoyed thoroughly the strike of the police and wished only it had been 100% effective instead of 85% effective and was permanent rather than for a few days. In answer to Myers we would be even happier if the FBI went on strike.

It sounds as though Wohlforth is ready to roll out the welcome mat.

Healyites in Solidarity with 'Militant Policemen'
By Allen Myers

Since the strike of 200,000 postal employees in March 1970, there has been a rising level of unrest among American workers, with those on state and city government payrolls in the forefront. Many factors are involved in this increased militancy: spiraling inflation, growing unemployment, the war in Vietnam, and the influence of the deepgoing youth radicalization that has already affected the campuses of the United States so profoundly.

The youth radicalization has influenced the working class. Hundreds of thousands of young Black and Chicano militants, antiwar activists, and participants in the women's liberation movement, who have joined the labor force in the last five years, have brought a new mood into the unions contrasting with the conservatism of the middle-aged workers who dominated the labor movement in the 1950s.

At the same time, the new labor militancy has been expressed almost exclusively in strike struggles over wage demands and has not yet taken a political form—there are still no mass workers parties in the United States, nor even large-scale participation of the union movement as such in the mass struggles that are being waged around the war and other questions.

This lack of political differentiation has induced serious errors among sectors of the left toward actions taken by government employees. They overlook the fact that "government employees" covers a very heterogeneous group, from workers whose employer happens to be the state—such as firemen, clerks, postal employees, etc.—to components of the repressive apparatus—such as cops. Left groups that fail to see this can misjudge an internal dispute between the ruling class and its watchdogs.

A series of actions in New York City in December and January included walkouts by telephone workers, taxi drivers, longshoremen, and teamsters; a firemen's slowdown; and threats of strikes by sanitation men and social-service workers.

Another category of persons paid by the city government also staged a work stoppage in New York for six days in, mid-January: the police. The bourgeois press was quick to include the cops as just dissatisfied proletarians. Unfortunately, a sector of the left, eager to demonstrate its solidarity with the "workers," accepted this judgment and backed the cops in their action.

The chief demand made by the cops—was more pay for their foul occupation—specifically a contract that would give them $16,000 a year after three years.

There were additional issues not officially part of the dispute. These concerned the officers' dissatisfaction with what they considered interference with their normal duties of protecting private property, breaking strikes, attacking demonstrations, keeping oppressed minorities "in their place," and lining their own pockets. Murray Schumach reported in the January 20 *New York Times*:

> Interviews with policemen produced the following complaints:
> • Other unions of city employees . . . went out on strike and, far from being punished, won fat contracts.
> • Despite years of insults such as 'pig' from radicals at campus outbreaks and other demonstrations, policemen who tried to maintain law and order won little support. . . .
> • Lenient court decisions and the behavior of some judges undermined the police and sometimes humiliated them.
> • The mass media has been unfair, distorting the corruption of a small number of policemen and ignoring the good work of the vast majority.

In short, the cops demanded that the city government step up countermeasures against the present radicalization and, failing that, pay them more for trying to contain it.

The February 1 issue of *Newsweek* noted that

Intercontinental Press, February 8, 1971.

"more than half" of New York's 31,700 police do not even live in the city but commute from comfortable suburban homes. "And when he comes into the city to earn his pay," the magazine commented, "his attitude perforce approaches that of the Hessian soldiers sent to quiet the colonists."

Despite frequent—and remarkably unsuccessful—campaigns to recruit cops from minority groups, the New York police force remains 92.5 percent white.

No demand raised during the work stoppage, no spokesman for the cops—official or unofficial—suggested that the walkout in any way implied dissatisfaction with their role as armed—and very often sadistic—defenders of the ruling class.

Among the most uncritical applauders of this proruling-class "strike" were the members of the Workers League, the American cothinkers of the ultraleft Socialist Labour League led by Gerry Healy in England. Their rationale is worth examining to see how the most simon-pure sectarians can talk themselves into ending up on the same side of the fence as the most reactionary defenders of the status quo.

The *Bulletin*, the "Weekly Organ of the Workers League," which has long denounced the attempt to build a united front against the Vietnam war as a "sellout," in its January 25 issue endorsed the walkout of New York's police force as a legitimate proletarian struggle.

Under a banner headline, "New York Labor Begins Showdown," the *Bulletin* featured a photograph of striking cops. As a caption for the stirring photograph, the editors declared: "Militant policemen march for parity during strike which was supported by 85%."

The author of the article, editor of the *Bulletin* Lucy St. John, wrote:

> While [Mayor John] Lindsay, [Governor Nelson] Rockefeller and city officials were preparing to mobilize the National Guard yesterday, striking patrolmen reluctantly returned to work.
>
> The situation facing the city—*which can only be described as on the verge of civil war*—was sharply posed by a leader of the dissident cops the night before. Speaking to NBC-TV, in relation to the troop threat, he said that the cops did not want "another Kent State" but that they would fight to stay out until their demands were met. (Emphasis added.)

Lucy St. John, it is clear, has been entranced by "New York's finest." She places them in the vanguard of the class struggle. These "dissident" proletarians have brought New York City to "the verge of civil war"!

The editor of the *Bulletin* reached this conclusion on the basis, apparently, that the mayor and the governor were readying the national guard against squads of uniformed men who are armed themselves—and notoriously trigger-happy.

No doubt Lucy St. John is sufficiently aware of the teachings of Marxism to know that in a real class war of major scope, one of the central problems facing the working class is to disarm the cops, who can be counted on to act as the most inveterate and ruthless opponents of any militant mass struggle.

But St. John, in accordance with her training in the school of Healyism, appears to feel that exceptions can occur. A goodly sector of "New York's finest" seem to have engaged in a political revolt against their masters:

> Lindsay and the entire capitalist class must very well be asking themselves what they face if those they pay to break strikes are themselves striking, if those who advocate and defend "law and order" now defy it.

In fact, however, there was nothing in the situation that was not perfectly comprehensible to Lindsay. His cops were not striking against capitalist "law and order." They were putting the squeeze on for more elbow room in defending "law and order." And like mercenaries in the Congo or Indochina, they wanted to be paid in accordance with the risks.

The editor of the *Bulletin* seems to have been taken in by the fact that the cops' walkout was illegal under New York's Taylor Law. But committing illegal actions is nothing new for New York's racist-minded cops.

Few days pass without run-of-the-mill accounts of police graft, payoffs, bribery, not to mention innumerable violations of civil liberties, the brutalization and outright murder of members of oppressed minorities.

The Taylor Law is, of course, a reactionary piece of legislation. But Lindsay's cops were not concerned with that. They will enforce that reactionary law to the hilt in the future as in the past, if they are so ordered, while they continue to break laws involving the rights of workers and the minorities.

St. John, a top leader of the Healyite Workers League, has suddenly forgotten all this. To win a bigger allotment of dog food, New York's cops bared their teeth at their masters. That made them proletarians!

This is not the first time that appearances have led the American Healyites to cross class lines. In 1968 they supported the New York teachers' racist strike—it was a strike, wasn't it!—against the right of the Black community in New York to control its own schools.

The rationale used by the Workers League in 1968 was that the teachers were a legitimate part of the working class and were led in their action by a bona fide union organization. But revolutionists have never given uncritical support to any and all actions of the trade-union bureaucracy. Strikes by construction workers to prevent the hiring of Blacks, for example, are thoroughly reactionary and must be opposed as such.

In fitting the 1968 excuse to the 1971 police strike, the editor of the *Bulletin* found it necessary to stretch things a bit.

The semifascist Patrolmen's Benevolent Association that led the action is pictured by St. John as a genuine trade union.

"Any concessions made to the cops on the question of wages will only raise the fight *by the rest of the unions* whose contracts expired on December 31." (Emphasis added.)

So the fraternal organization of the cops, the Patrolmen's Benevolent Association [PBA], becomes just one more labor organization among "the rest of the unions." But police "unions" in general and the PBA in particular are first and foremost rightwing *political* associations, not collective bargaining agents. The PBA is no more a union than is the American Legion, the West Point Officers Club, or the Ku Klux Klan.

Newsweek, which supports cops if not cop strikes, gave this description of the Patrolmen's Benevolent Association in its February 1 issue:

> Begun in 1894 as a paper organization, the PBA won rights as bargaining agent for the department in 1963 and since then has developed into a formidable empire unto itself—complete with an annual flow of at least $10 million from dues and pension contributions. Until 1969 when a scandal broke involving misuse of union [sic] funds, the men had been hard put to find a financial statement in five years, and when all the figures came out, they found their officers living the life of Mafia capos.

The editor of the Healyite *Bulletin* took a stand to the right even of the *Daily World,* which reflects the views of the Stalinist U. S. Communist party. The *Daily World* wrote in a January 16 editorial:

> ... municipal workers, like all other workers, need the support of the entire working class to defend and advance their living standards. That is obvious in the present struggles of New York's sanitationmen, policemen, social workers, and uniformed firemen.

But the Stalinists, who make no secret of their reformist perspective, tried to cover their right-wing position with a few qualifications:

> The racist currents in the police department, the brutality of many policemen, the anti-black and anti-Puerto Rican attitude of the officialdom of the Patrolmen's Benevolent Association do not win allies, even for justified wage demands.

The Workers League expressed no reservations. Having placed the cops in the vanguard of the class struggle and having devoted more than half her article on "New York labor" to them, St. John apparently felt the need to cite some "objective" results to justify her stand:

> Objectively this action [the police "strike"] supported by transit and housing authority police has triggered a whole fight on the part

of the city labor movement against the attacks on wages, jobs, and working conditions.

Here St. John postulates something not yet seen in the objective world: a "cause" that comes *after* its effect.

The cops' walkout began on the night of January 14–15. It is therefore impossible for it to have "triggered" the phone workers' strike, which began January 11; the firemen's slowdown, which began December 31; or the cab drivers' strike, which *ended* in December. The only strike to follow the cops' action was that of the Teamsters, and there is no reason to regard it as "triggered" by the police walkout.

The "militant policemen," discovered by a top leader of the Workers League, did not "trigger" anything in the labor movement. On the contrary, one day before their own walkout, "militant policemen" attacked a demonstration of striking telephone employees, and six persons—workers, not cops—were "militantly" arrested.

This is rather peculiar behavior on the part of forces alleged to be leading the working class to the "verge of civil war."

St. John's position on the cops' strike necessarily leads to further contradictions. An editorial in the same issue of the *Bulletin* declared:

> . . . the working class is moving forward in such a way that the government, for all its intentions to crush it, is forced into an extremely difficult position. In New York City the police strike continues despite every threat, pressure and the Taylor Law itself, while the phone men defy immense fines and produce truck drivers go out on strike.

Presumably the sentence that immediately followed was intended not to be a logical contradiction but a dialectical unity:

"What this means is that the repression of the courts *and the police* can be beaten back IF the defense of the victims is rooted in the movement of the class." (Emphasis added.)

All clear now? The working class, including the police, is "moving forward." But the working class is also under attack by the courts and the police—who, we have been informed, are part of the working class. This repression of the workers by the workers can be defeated if the class, including the cops, continues moving "in such a way that the government . . . is forced into an extremely difficult position."

The "difficult position" would seem to be greater for the editor of the *Bulletin* than the head of "New York's finest."

But then the Workers League might work its way out of its difficult position through a recruiting drive in the newly discovered sector of the working class. (Police of course have been joining working-class organizations for more than a century, but until now it was done without mentioning who their employers were; and when they were discovered, they were called stool pigeons or provocateurs.)

Another possibility opens up. A distinction between "militant policemen" who are city "workers" and their counterparts who are federal employees would be rather arbitrary. Does an FBI militant, disgruntled over less than $16,000 a year, now meet the proletarian membership standards of the Workers League? Can he at least count on the editorial support of the *Bulletin*?

SECTION XI: WOMEN'S LIBERATION

Where the SLL Goes Wrong on Women's Liberation
By Caroline Lund

The March 14, 1970, issue of the *Workers Press* carried an exchange of opinion on the women's liberation struggle of unusual interest.

Janet Williams, Hazel Twort, and Ann Bahcheli, in behalf of the Peckham Rye Branch of the Women's Liberation Workshop, wrote a letter of protest to the editor of the *Workers Press*, which is the official newspaper of the Socialist Labour League (SLL), a British sectarian organization that claims to represent Trotskyism.

> Your TV and film critics are devoting a lot of words currently to the question of Women's Liberation [wrote the joint authors]. As members of the Women's Liberation Workshop and regular readers of Workers Press we would like to make some comments.

They agreed that the contradictions of being a woman under capitalism flow from the class nature of the system itself. They agreed that women will not be liberated until the defeat of capitalism by the workers' revolution.

> But we can't go along with the completely barren perspective your critics suggest in terms of concrete action. What it amounts to is telling women of all classes NOT TO DO ANYTHING until after the revolution: then everything will be lovely.

Several similar points were scored by the authors, including the following very pertinent observation:

Intercontinental Press, July 27, 1970.

> The road to a workers' revolution goes via women fighting for their liberation. The idea of a workers' revolution made by men workers, who would then presumably "give" the women "their freedom", is mere idealist fantasy. It has its origins in self-deluding male chauvinism, and must be exposed as such.

They closed by saying:

> Objectively, your critics want women to stay on the sidelines. Mr Cartwright implies that women should not work, and he sneers at the perspective of an obliteration of all "role" differences between men and women. We've heard that kind of stuff so often from frank reactionaries. We're surprised to find it in Workers Press.

The SLL leaders assigned Mark Ruskin, who is apparently their expert in the field of women's liberation, to draw up a reply. This was published in the same issue as the letter of protest. In view of the length of this reply and the absence of anything more official, it can be assumed to be a faithful reflection of the views of the leaders of the SLL on this important question.

Mark Ruskin argues that the ruling class tries to divide the working class by means of "racialism, sectionalism, regionalism, nationalism and feminism."

He maintains that revolutionaries must be for "unity" of the class, and for the "mobilization of the [working] class as a class to defeat and overthrow capitalism."

He says further:

> If we are devoting a lot of words currently to the question of women's liberation, it is for the sole reason of warning against the divisive tactic of separating out "the problem of women" from the real class questions, of warning against reformist cul de sacs and defeats.

Ruskin criticizes the women authors of the letter for implying that "what we need is to change and improve things *now* for women, concrete action." This, he contends, is a reformist outlook. According to him, nothing can be done to alleviate the status of women before a socialist revolution:

> Unless the economic and political forms are transformed the social and cultural ones which reflect these forms cannot be. . . . we have to insist that the family is a bourgeois institution, that its transformation depends entirely on the overthrow of bourgeois property relations and capitalist modes of production.

Some comments are in order from the Trotskyist point of view. First of all let's consider the question of "class unity." The SLL expert says he is for class unity, and that sounds very good, of course. But the question raised by the women's liberation movement is not whether the working class should be unified, but *on what program* it should be unified.

Many trade-union bureaucrats would agree with the SLL that working-class unity is highly desirable, but they oppose working-class unity in defense of the rights of the most oppressed workers: women workers, Black workers, foreign workers, and young workers. The Marxist position is for class unity in solidarity with the struggles of women, Black people, and all layers of the most oppressed workers. The SLL stands for "class unity" in the abstract in order to cover up its chauvinist position that the demands of women, and of women workers, *as women*, should be ignored and not be fought for.

When this authoritative spokesman of the SLL contends that it is divisive to separate out women's problems from the "real class questions," and that the only Marxist perspective is "the mobilization of the class as a class," he leaves out of account the two other basic forms of class oppression under capitalism: national oppression and sexual oppression.

In an article written in 1939 supporting the struggle of the Ukrainians for national self-determination, Trotsky pointed out:

> The sectarian simply ignores the fact that the national struggle, one of the most labyrinthine and complex but at the same time extremely important *forms of the class struggle*, cannot be suspended by bare references to the future world revolution. (Emphasis added.)

In the same article Trotsky drew a parallel between the attitude of revolutionists to the struggles of oppressed national minorities and of women. He emphasized the necessity for revolutionary Marxists to support those struggles wholeheartedly, not only under capitalism but also after a socialist revolution, as in the USSR. He wrote:

> The Kremlin bureaucracy tells the Soviet woman: Inasmuch as there is socialism in our country, you must be happy and you must give up abortions (or suffer the penalty). To the Ukrainian they say: Inasmuch as the socialist revolution has solved the national question, it is your duty to be happy in the USSR and to renounce all thought of separation (or face the firing squad).
>
> What does a revolutionist say to the woman? "You will decide yourself whether you want a child: I will defend your right to abortion against the Kremlin police." To the Ukrainian people he says: "Of importance to me is your attitude toward your national destiny and not the 'socialistic' sophistries of the Kremlin police; I will support your struggle for independence with all my might."

Like those sectarians Trotsky was arguing against, the SLL tries to ignore and belittle the just grievances of women and of oppressed national minorities "by bare references to the future world revolution."

Marxists have always been for fighting against *all* forms of oppression in order to promote the liberation of *all* layers of the oppressed people. Marxists must be in the forefront of the struggles of women, of the unemployed, of youth, soldiers, peasants, and oppressed national minorities.

If the SLL leaders doubt that this is the position of the revolutionary socialist movement, they should consult Trotsky's pamphlet *The Death Agony of Capitalism and the Tasks of the Fourth International*, also known as the *Transitional Program*, which was adopted in 1938 as the basic program of the Fourth International. In this pamphlet Trotsky outlines the approach of the revolutionary movement toward the struggles of all layers of the oppressed. Demands are formulated for the struggles of youth, women, farmers, peasants, and the petty bourgeoisie.

The fact that Marxists want to build and encourage struggles of all the oppressed is further illustrated by the institution of soviets, which arose during the 1905 and 1917 Russian revolutions. The Russian soviets were not only organs of the working class, but of all the exploited. In the *Transitional Program* Trotsky explained how the soviets could unite all layers fighting against capitalism:

> . . . the deepening of the social crisis will increase not only the sufferings of the masses but also their impatience, persistence, and pressure. Ever new layers of the oppressed will raise their heads and come forward with their demands . . . The unemployed will join the movement. The agricultural workers, the ruined and semi-ruined farmers, the oppressed of the cities, the women workers, housewives, proletarianized layers of the intelligentsia—all of these will seek unity and leadership.

Paralleling the SLL's denigration of the women's liberation movement and nationalist movements, the sectarian leaders of this organization are also against building a mass antiwar movement in the United States and internationally. The *Workers Press* has repeatedly attacked the Young Socialist Alliance and the Socialist Workers party in the United States for "opportunist adaptations to the antiwar movement, student power, and now 'women's liberation.'"

A strong, independent women's liberation movement, just like the Black nationalist and antiwar movements, has to be seen as an ally of the working-class struggle, because it is fighting against the capitalist system. In the present period, when women have won through struggle many formal, democratic rights, the women's liberation movement is turning its fire against the capitalist state. Its effect is to undermine the family system, one of the main instruments of oppression of women. The major issues so far raised by this movement are the right of women to control their own bodies; complete equality of opportunities in education and employment; and for social responsibility for the care of children, in order to release women from their position as domestic slaves. These issues, along with the remaining issues of legal equality for women, all have their thrust against the family institution.

The main theme of Frederick Engels's book *The Origin of the Family, Private Property and the State* was that the family institution arose out of the class needs of private proprietors and the state. Women have been oppressed through the institution of the family during the periods of slavery and feudalism, not only during the relatively recent period of capitalism.

The women's liberation movement is raising a series of demands that say society should take responsibility for the home and family chores traditionally assigned to women. These are all transitional demands, demands which can lead to consciousness of the need for socialism and the overthrow of the capitalist state.

The demand for free, twenty-four-hour child-care centers controlled by those who use them, for instance, is a transitional demand. The responsibility for child care should be taken off the backs of individual women and individual families. To give the best possible care to *all* children, this task should be socialized, taken over by society as a whole.

The demand for free and legal abortions and birth-control information on demand implies that *all* medical services should be nationalized. Demands for free or low-cost laundry and food services, to relieve women in each family of this responsibility, also raise the question of the need to nationalize all industries, and run them in the interests of people's welfare rather than profit.

The awakening of women of all classes makes it easier for them to understand and become involved in other forms of the class struggle. At the same time, the emergence of a strong women's liberation movement will help stimulate women on the job to struggle for their interests as women workers. This awakening of women to struggle on their own account against the capitalist state can only aid the struggle of the working class as a whole.

The SLL's expert on the women's liberation struggle includes a glaring contradiction in his reply to the women critics of the *Workers Press*. He says that the demand for equal pay for women is a good demand. But he also says that "women's problems" should not be separated from the "real class questions." If the demand of equal pay for women can be raised, why should women not fight against all the other inequalities they face as well? Why shouldn't they fight against *all* the inequalities they face on the job, inequalities in education, inequalities within the family, and inequalities they face owing to being penalized for bearing children? Are these inequalities any less urgent to women than their lack of equal pay?

But, the *Workers Press* argues, the condition of women can't be changed without a socialist revolution, and therefore it is reformist to struggle for these concrete demands. Lenin had quite a bit to say about this attitude in his conversations with Clara Zetkin, a communist women's leader in Germany. Lenin explained why it was absolutely necessary for the communist parties to organize special party commissions or bureaus to conduct work among women. He said,

> The Communist women's movement must itself be a mass movement, a part of the general mass movement. Not only of the proletariat, but of all the exploited and oppressed, all the victims of capitalism or any other mastery.... There can be no real mass movement without women.

After pointing out the necessity for arousing women and winning them to follow the leadership of the Communist party, Lenin continued:

> I am thinking not only of proletarian women, whether they work in the factory or at home. The poor peasant women, the petty bourgeois—they too are the prey of capitalism, and more so than ever since the war....
>
> That is why it is right for us to put forward demands favorable to women. This is not a recognition that we believe in the eternal character, or even in the long duration of the rule of the bourgeoisie and their state. It is not an attempt to appease women by reforms and to divert them from the path of revolutionary struggle. It is not that or any other reformist swindle. Our demands are practical conclusions which we have drawn from the burning need, the shameful humiliation of women in bourgeois society, defenseless and without rights. We demonstrate thereby that we recognize these needs and are aware of the humiliation of the woman, the privileges of the man. That we hate, yes, hate everything, and will abolish everything which tortures and oppresses the woman worker, the housewife, the peasant woman, the wife of the petty trader, yes, and in many cases the women of the possessing classes. The rights and social regulations which we demand for women from bourgeois society show that we understand the position and interests of women and will have consideration for them under the proletarian dictatorship. Not, of course, as the reformists do, lulling them to inaction and keeping them on leading strings. No, of course not; but as revolutionaries who call upon the women to work as equals in transforming the old economy and ideology.
>
> Every such struggle brings us in opposition to respectable bourgeois relationships, and to their not less respectable reformist admirers whom it compels, either to fight together with us under our leadership—which they don't want to do—or to be shown up in their true colors. That is, the struggle clearly brings out the differences between us and other parties, brings out our communism. It wins us the confidence of the masses of women who feel themselves exploited, enslaved, suppressed, by the domination of the man, by the power of the employer, by the whole of bourgeois society. Betrayed and deserted by all, the working women will recognize that they must fight together with us.

The women's liberation movement certainly does bring out the differences between a revolutionary socialist organization and sectarians. The SLL's answer to women who are coming to an understanding of their oppression as women is: Just accept your status, women, and wait and hope until the revolution comes.

Meanwhile, the only thing women can do, according to the SLL, is to join the SLL:

> The decisive task internationally is the building of the Fourth International, in Britain the Socialist Labour League.
>
> You can duck that, deny that, refuse that, you can talk in your groups about emancipation till time immemorial, but outside of that perspective you remain a reformist claque of do-gooders, an obstacle in the revolutionary road.

But, as Lenin pointed out, why should any woman join an organization that gives no assurances whatsoever in its daily practice that it will fight for the interests of women?

In dismissing women's liberation as not a "real class issue," the SLL ignores the fact that the majority of women are either wage workers themselves or wives of workers. The best way to mobilize these women is not only on "working class demands" but on *all* the forms of oppression they suffer.

Working-class women suffer oppression *as women* even more than other women. They have the lowest paying, most demeaning jobs, and then come home to the work of caring for children and keeping the house. They are often subjected to physical brutality from their husbands. They rarely have any free time away from their children or job. They are denied birth-control information and cannot afford an abortion to prevent unwanted children. For these reasons, the women's liberation movement has the potential of uniting working-class women with women of all other layers in common struggles which can severely weaken capitalism.

Mark Ruskin makes another point which clearly indicates that the SLL has capitulated to the general chauvinist attitudes toward women. He says that the demand for equal work opportunities for women is "an irrelevance." He maintains that "To many working class women, marriage means a liberation from this work," and that it is the ruling class which wants women to enter the work force in order to exploit them more.

A film review by Frank Cartwright in the February 3, 1970, *Workers Press* says:

> The capitalist state is being forced to supply some facilities for this process [hiring more women workers] to continue and the oppressive outcome is being further guaranteed by the radical ladies whose perspectives end with obliteration of all "role" differences between men and women.

In the first place, marriage is anything but "liberation from work." If women don't get a paying job, they still have their work as domestic slaves in the home. The argument that women have it easier working in the home, so why should they complain, is analogous to one justification offered for slavery of Black people. People said that slaves actually were happy because they didn't have any serious responsibilities and were "suited" to that type of labor.

Women should not only be given "equal" job opportunities. Marxists must demand *preferential hiring* of women in all fields of employment where they have hitherto been discriminated against.

Not to support preferential hiring to achieve equal opportunities for women in employment is to support their being kept within the bounds of the family and shoved into domestic drudgery and into serving as a doubly exploited reserve army of labor. The women's liberation movement has never maintained that women should be *forced* to work. It has supported women's right to choose. And if they choose to work, they should be able to enter any field of work without discrimination because of their sex.

The refusal of the SLL to support this demand amounts to telling women that the nearest they can come to "liberation" under capitalism is to get married so that they can be financially dependent on their husbands and concern themselves solely with the dreary and petty work within the four walls of their home. This is completely contrary to the Marxist position that discrimination against women in the sphere of production and their relegation to the position of domestic slaves is at the very foundation of their oppression under capitalism.

Rather than tell women they are better off staying in their homes, revolutionists, along with the women's liberation movement, should demand steps to free women from work in the home, such as free, twenty-four-hour, publicly financed, community-controlled child-care centers.

The attacks made by the SLL on the new and growing women's liberation movement are another proof of the sectarian and non-Marxist views held by the leaders of this organization. The women's liberation movement is a potentially anticapitalist movement which is spreading with uneven pace all over the capitalist world. Women, especially young women, are throwing off their oppressed mentality and entering into struggle.

The reaction of the SLL to this movement is to try to squash it, and crush this spirit of protest and indignation at oppression. This attitude has nothing to do with Marxism; in fact, it is the antithesis of Marxism. It must be exposed by revolutionists if women's liberation activists are to be won to the realization that building a revolutionary party to lead a socialist revolution, in addition to building an independent, mass women's liberation movement, is the road to the liberation of women.

SECTION XII:

The SLL Abstains On Krivine
By Joseph Hansen

The position of Gerry Healy's Socialist Labour League on the French elections is worth noting. Despite the claim of this British group and their French allies to stand on the program of Trotskyism, they found it impossible to offer even critical support to Alain Krivine, the presidential candidate of the Communist League (French section of the Fourth International).

As explained by Tom Kemp in the June 7 issue of *The Newsletter*, the reasons for taking this sectarian position were as follows:

The interests of the French working class would have been "best served by the presentation of a single united-front candidate supported by the workers' parties and trade unions."

Tom Kemp does not say so, but we assume that he would be willing to add that the interests of the French working class would have been best served if this single united-front candidate also stood on a program of revolutionary socialism.

Unfortunately the French Socialist party hastened to put its own candidate in the field, Gaston Defferre. The Communist party "followed suit with the wily but ageing Jacques Duclos."

That eliminated the possibility of a single united-front candidate supported by the trade unions and mass working-class parties. But there still remained the candidacies of Michel Rocard of the United Socialist party and the Trotskyist Alain Krivine.

It was correct to refuse to support Rocard. His program was "left" Social Democratic. He had no mass following.

Intercontinental Press, June 23, 1969.

But what about Krivine? Kemp could not support him either. Krivine's platform was not revolutionary enough!

> For all its revolutionary phraseology, this current can be regarded as a petty-bourgeois centrist trend [said the ultraleft Kemp].
>
> Its main support comes from sections of the students and a kind of beatnik fringe. It has never carried out serious and sustained work in the working class in France.
>
> Its policy has been characterized by a complete lack of consistency and principle.
>
> Krivine's candidature can thus only contribute to further confusion and division.

Among the "proofs" of his contentions, Kemp cited the fact that the Communist League had to obtain at least 100 names of elected officials to get on the ballot.

> It is obvious that since no Communist or Socialist representatives would sign up for Krivine, he had to secure the signatures of bourgeois politicians, many, no doubt, hoping that he would split the opposition vote.

This argument is hardly different from the one made by *l'Humanité* against Krivine. And Kemp, in fact, in the very next paragraph indicates his awareness of what the Stalinist daily was saying: "*L'Humanité* made the best of this and has published the names of two Gaullist deputies who signed Krivine's petition."

Kemp refrained from specifying the two names

published by *l'Humanité*. It is unfortunate that the editor of *The Newsletter* did not call his attention to this oversight. Thoughtfulness in making it easier for others to check assertions based on Stalinist sources is always appreciated.

So far as I know, *l'Humanité* published the name of only one Gaullist deputy in trying to throw mud at the Krivine campaign.

Alain Krivine promptly answered this reversion to the old Stalinist practice of seeking to amalgamate Trotskyism with reaction. He wrote *l'Humanité* an open letter dated May 23, extracts of which were quoted in the May 24 issue of *Le Monde*. [See *Intercontinental Press*, June 9, p. 563.]

The Communist League did not solicit the signature of Jacques Moron. Krivine told the editors of *l'Humanité* that upon learning that Moron was a Gaullist deputy, they did not include his name in the nominating petition "because it seemed to offer an opportunity for provocations by political primitives."

Kemp does not report how the French Trotskyists exposed the Stalinist attempt at a smear job and turned it into a public scandal against its authors. Could it be that Tom Kemp finds it in the best interest of his sectarian line to make a united front with . . . Duclos?

Thus, in the absence of a "united front" candidate fitting their ideal, the SLL, echoing their French allies, could not even unite behind a Trotskyist candidate for the presidency.

In this way they proved that at least in the matter of supporting Trotskyist candidates they stand at a more primitive level politically than their allies in the U.S. The American Healyites, organized in the Workers League headed by Tim Wohlforth, supported the Trotskyist ticket in the U.S. in 1968—naturally very critically.

Here is what the Political Committee of the Workers League said in a statement published in the July 22, 1968, issue of the *Bulletin*:

> It is with this perspective [relentless struggle against those political tendencies which seek to turn the mass movement back into capitalist politics] that we welcome the electoral initiative of the Socialist Workers Party in running Fred Halstead and Paul Boutelle for president and vice president in 1968. This campaign poses a socialist alternative to the capitalist parties and thus offers to socialists and militant workers an opportunity to cast a ballot against our oppressors.

As for the SWP platform, Wohlforth was satisfied with a single plank:

> The 1968 election platform of the Socialist Workers Party calls for the formation of a labor party in America and it is this position in particular which gives the campaign relevancy today.

It remains to be seen what stand Wohlforth will announce concerning the candidacy of Alain Krivine. After all, there is the unpleasant business of Healy's discipline to face. Besides, that's French territory. And fortunately the election is over.

SECTION XIII:

Why the SLL Refuses to Support the Mandel Case
By Pat Jordan and Tariq Ali

On February 28, 1972, Comrade Ernest Mandel was forbidden by the West German immigration officials at Frankfort airport from entering West Germany, and was deported back to Belgium. Questioned by a left socialist MP in the Bonn parliament about the incident, the bourgeois minister of the interior, Mr. Genscher, stated that Mandel was forbidden to enter Germany for an unlimited period, "until he changes his revolutionary views."

Genscher tried to make the subtle distinction between the "Marxist economist," who was supposed to be welcome, and the "active revolutionist," leading member of the Fourth International, whose activities were directed at the overthrow of the state and the social order in West Germany and who should therefore be banned from that country.

Specifically Mr. Genscher referred to the Fourth International's programme of wanting to install a workers republic based upon workers councils in Germany, and declared this to be unconstitutional. Before him, the West Berlin Senate had argued along similar lines when it refused to nominate Ernest Mandel to the post of professor for political economy at the Free (!) University of West Berlin, for which he had been chosen by a nearly unanimous vote of students, assistant professors, and professors.

The repressive measures of Minister Genscher and of the West Berlin Senate have provoked a storm of protest in all left-wing circles of the German labor movement and of the German students and intellectuals. This protest is still going on and spreading internationally.

Intercontinental Press, June 5, 1972.

While we are writing this article, thousands of students strike against Mandel being banned at the West Berlin university itself; several faculties have been occupied for more than a week. The University of Heidelberg officially joined the protest of the Free University of West Berlin. Student government bodies are doing likewise in many other universities. Mass meetings have taken place on this subject in half a dozen towns. In Berlin itself a congress convened for the purpose of fighting against this and similar measures of repression assembled more than 3,000 students. Important trade-union officials, several local trade-union bodies, as well as numerous left socialists, the national leadership of the West German Young Socialists, and half a dozen Social-Democratic MPs have come out against the ban.

From the beginning, Comrade Mandel has based his principled fight against the ban on two key issues. First, he never denied holding the programme of replacing bourgeois parliamentary democracy by soviet democracy, by the democracy of workers councils, but strongly insisted on the basic political freedom for all working-class tendencies to defend their full programme in West Germany. Second, he warned the West German trade unionists, Social Democrats, socialists, students, and intellectuals that this ban was only a new stage in a campaign of increased repression not only against the left-wing tendencies in the labor movement, but against the labor movement as such and against the democratic rights of all workers, students, and intellectuals.

He warned that the exclusion of Marxists from professorships would lead to the exclusion of left socialists and members of the "ruling" SPD [Sozialdemokratische Partei Deutschlands] itself, that the ban against free movement of cadres of revolutionary organizations would soon lead to a ban against movement of trade unionists too. Against all these repressive measures it was necessary to build a united front of all working-class tendencies, without any exclusion or divisive tactics, defending the democratic freedom of the whole movement. Otherwise, these freedoms would be chopped away bit by bit from everybody.

These warnings of Comrade Mandel soon became confirmed. The West German tory party of Barzel and Strauss—the Christian Democrats—has started a vicious pogrom campaign against the Young Socialists and left Social Democrats (accused, among other things, of having defended the dangerous revolutionary Ernest Mandel). The French Pompidou regime, which had banned Mandel from France too, thereupon banned a delegation of British Labour MPs and trade unionists from entering that country in order to consult with French trade unionists during the recent referendum campaign in France on the subject of Britain's joining the Common Market.

It is clear that the case of Ernest Mandel is rapidly becoming a symbol of the type of capitalist Europe Big Capital is trying to build at present—a Europe where free circulation is guaranteed only to big entrepreneurs, bankers, capitalist riffraff and speculators, bourgeois politicians, NATO generals and admirals and other underworld characters, but where this freedom of movement is being limited or denied to revolutionists, to socialists, to trade unionists and to "foreign workers," who are not satisfied with being "freely" exploited abroad but also want to be free to defend themselves. If the labor movement allows this kind of discrimination to be generally accepted, this can only mean that its own position becomes further weakened in the Common Market and Capital's position strengthened. So this question of the right to circulate freely without political discrimination has become an issue in the international class struggle itself.

Most people on both sides of the barricades have understood this perfectly—the capitalists by insisting upon their right to stop the activities of "foreign" revolutionists; wide circles of the international labor movement, including those that strongly disagree with Ernest Mandel's views, by insisting on the necessity of lifting the German ban. This has become a source of major embarrassment for the Stalinists, to begin with the Communist party in West Germany and West Berlin, and the ruling SED [Sozialistische Einheitspartei Deutschlands—Socialist Unity party of Germany].

These organizations had stepped up their anti-Trotskyist campaign since the international conference of Communist parties convened a year ago in Moscow to discuss the specific question of how to fight Trotskyism. Comrade Mandel had been singled out by the CP publications the world over as "a professional anti-Soviet agitator" and a "ferocious anti-communist." But now suddenly this notorious "anti-Communist" is expelled from West Germany because he is "guilty" of spreading Communist propaganda, and this "professional anti-Soviet agitator" is being accused by the imperialists of wanting to build a Soviet Republic in Germany! This type of propaganda—as engaged in by Mandel before and after the ban—in favor of soviet democracy, of a republic of workers councils, hadn't been heard in Germany for nearly forty years; and in addition he defends the CP victims of the bourgeois repression and discriminatory measures in West Germany, too . . .

The embarrassment of the CP bureaucrats is all the greater as Comrade Mandel's statements were not only spread on millions of copies by popular weekly magazines like *Der Spiegel, Die Zeit, Der Stern, Pardon,* the organ of the West Berlin Social-Democratic party, the organ of the Young Socialists, etc.; they were also widely publicized on radio and television, which reach millions of workers, intellectuals, and students in East Germany. Most of these people got through these statements their first contact with Trotskyism—and it wouldn't be an unsympathetic contact either. Here you had a revolutionist viciously attacked by the rulers of both West and East Germany—and who stood for the democracy of workers councils.

The CP leaders tried to wriggle out of their plight by advancing a typically Stalinist line. The imperialists, they said, had deliberately selected Comrade Mandel as their main target in order to "force" the left to solidarize itself with a Trotskyist—thereby strengthening this diversionist and "anti-Communist" tendency. In other words:

oppression is really a conspiracy between the oppressors and the victim, in order to make the victim more sympathetic in the eyes of the masses!

With the same "logic" the French Stalinists had already "denounced" the "conspiracy" between the murdered Maoist worker Pierre Overney and the bourgeois private police at the Renault factory in Paris, the objective "proof" of the conspiracy consisting in the fact that the latter had killed the former.

One should add that the German CP has created strong dissension within its own ranks as a result of this unprincipled attitude on the question of solidarity with victims of imperialist repression. Many local youth and student groups have joined united-front actions in favor of lifting the ban against Ernest Mandel. We can only welcome this as a significant break with Stalinist opportunism.

But the Stalinists are not the only ones to cling to this type of "logic." Some sects are confronted with a difficulty similar to the one that faces the CP, be it on a much more modest and limited level, and they try to solve it by an analogous method.

The sectarian leaders of the Socialist Labour League, who refused to take part in the reunification of the Fourth International in 1963 and ever since then have hysterically tried to justify their existence separate and apart from the world Trotskyist movement by inventing all kinds of "accusations" against the Fourth International founded by Leon Trotsky, have for several years made of Comrade Ernest Mandel their target No. 1. He is the "arch-revisionist." He is the "darling of the middle classes," the "centrist *par excellence*," who "objectively" helps imperialism to disorient leftward moving workers. He is "moving rapidly towards bankrupt reformism."

One can only wonder why the imperialists don't share these estimates of Messrs. Healy, Slaughter, Banda, and Co., and put less obstacles on Mandel's activities around the world. On the contrary, these class-conscious and rather clever gentlemen totally disagree with the SLL's judgment of Comrade Mandel. They consider him not a "bankrupt reformist" (whom they would help) but a dangerous revolutionist whom they have to restrict in his activities. And their repression directed against him has been stepped up constantly for four years.

How does the SLL leadership react to this embarrassing situation? Cliff Slaughter, in *Workers Press* of April 12, 1972, engaged in a series of unprincipled manoeuvers which, basically, amount to scabbing on the struggle now being conducted on an international scale against restrictions of democratic freedom for all tendencies of the labor movement.

First he tries to minimize the repressive measures which Comrade Mandel has been subjected to by the bourgeois government of Western Germany. He writes:

> Further, they [the "Pabloites," whatever that may mean—PJ & TA] are campaigning against the action of the W German authorities in refusing Mandel permission even to enter W Berlin when he recently tried to attend a "teach-in" there.

Slaughter knows very well that Mandel, as a Belgian citizen, needs no "permission" to enter West Berlin. He knows very well that what occurred was not a one-time action of the Bonn regime to prevent Mandel from being present at a West Berlin teach-in (this is, in fact, the excuse dished out by the advocates of the bourgeois repressive measures), but a general ban from entering West Germany. And he also knows that this ban has been justified by the government with reference to Mandel's revolutionary activities as one of the leaders of the Fourth International. It therefore constitutes an attempt to illegalize not only the visits of other members of the Fourth International into West Germany, but of all revolutionists as well.

All this Slaughter hides from his readers, thereby helping to whitewash the imperialist repression. The whitewashing job is further amplified by nasty innuendos of this kind:

"He [Mandel] appears at innumerable international seminars and colloquia . . .

"Indeed, Mandel's political identity is nowadays entirely a matter of his impact as some sort of celebrity descending on various capital cities and university campuses."

Just imagine how shameless this revisionist Mandel has become. He has the nerve to "descend on various capital cities," whereas, as everybody knows, the real duty of a real internationalist is to stick to one's own cozy little island and let world revolution elsewhere take care of itself. Isn't such "revisionism" justly punished after all by the bourgeoisie?

Thirdly, Slaughter makes a clumsy attempt to deny that this whole matter of Mandel's being banned from West Germany and four other imperialist countries has anything to do with the interests of the international labor movement as a whole; for him it is only a small matter of the Fourth International itself: "Pabloites everywhere are campaigning against a decision by the W Berlin Senate . . ." This again amounts to an attempt at whitewashing the imperialist culprits.

No, the ban is not a matter of interest to the "Pabloites" only. It is the whole left wing of the international labor movement that has started to "campaign" on this issue. And only blind factionalists can close their eyes to the obvious matter of common interest to all socialists and revolutionists which is involved here.

But then comes the explanation we have been waiting for, of why the imperialists should really have any interest at all to stop the activities of an "arch-revisionist" and of a "bankrupt reformist" (generally, as is well known, such persons are not stopped by imperialist governments under conditions of decaying bourgeois democracy, but rather rewarded with cabinet minister jobs):

> As imperialism . . . moves rapidly into its worst-ever economic and political crisis, it must desperately suck away these middle-class elements to some *centrist* political force to deal with that phase of the crisis when new masses are thrown into political struggle.
>
> Such centrist forces cannot be sucked out of nothing as it were. Mandel is hatching out the kind of politics to fit the bill. Of course, imperialism uses the centrists in this way only as a short step on the road to the eventual fascist and dictatorial repression. [Emphasis in original.]

Here we have Slaughter swallowing the Stalinist position hook, line, and sinker! If there is international repression against Ernest Mandel and the Fourth International, this is not, as naive persons might think, because the increasing strength and influence of the Fourth International in organizing a revolutionary vanguard on a worldwide scale increasingly becomes a threat to the capitalist regime.

Not at all. If the German capitalists and their right-wing Social-Democratic stooges treat Mandel not like "some sort of a celebrity descending" on their cities, but as a revolutionist who wants to overthrow capitalism and establish a soviet republic of workers councils; if they express the fear that he might strengthen a revolutionary organization of students and workers—especially of workers, that's what they are really afraid of!—this is all only make-believe to disorient the gullible, lead them to centrism, and prevent millions from rallying around the shining beacons of revolutionary thought and action ablaze on Clapham High Street.

No, if there is stepped-up repression against Ernest Mandel and the Fourth International, this is because the imperialists want to . . . use them against Cliff Slaughter! The victim is in a conspiracy with the victimizers, against the pure defenders of the faith, who are ignored precisely because they are the really dangerous people. It is difficult to find a more nauseating imitation of the Stalinist logic, produced by a sect which, out of habit, still calls itself Trotskyist, one wonders why.

But Slaughter has some principles left. Don't think he is in active support of imperialist repression. Perish the thought! To prove the contrary, we are treated to the following weighty piece of cant:

> Now, of course, [of course!—PJ & TA], the Socialist Labour League is for the defence of the rights of all persons to travel without restriction, and against all arbitrary actions by the authorities in excluding individuals from universities. But we attack these infringements of elementary democratic rights by mobilizing the working class, behind whom the support of other elements can be rallied.

A bit dour, perhaps, but in essence, excellent! But then, why aren't you busy "mobilizing the working class" in defence of Comrade Mandel, Comrade Slaughter? After all, the very terms which the West German government has used to ban Mandel could be used to ban Slaughter, Healy, and all their followers from entering Germany, too. So it is not only a matter of the elementary principle of international working-class solidarity. It is even a simple matter of self-defence. But instead of lifting one little finger to "mobilize" his own members and sympathizers—let's not speak about the working class, among whom the SLL's influence is negligible if not nil—to defend Comrade Mandel's democratic rights, Slaughter only attacks Mandel, not the West German government and its right-wing Social-Democratic props. Slaughter is so blinded by sectarian factionalism that he cannot understand any more such elementary questions as the need for class solidarity against imperialist repression.

When Sacco and Vanzetti were arrested, the Communist International started a defence campaign for the two anarchist martyrs, not a campaign of denouncing the sins of anarchism. When repression hits a leading member of the Fourth International, and through him threatens to hit anybody calling himself a Trotskyist, Slaughter is only eager to step up his campaign of "denouncing Pabloism." The need for a defence campaign against imperialist repression doesn't reach his cold shoulder . . .

The political content of his denunciation is of the same caliber and the same origin as his political method of approach. It has nothing to do with a principled discussion of the real political and organizational differences between the SLL and the Fourth International—which are plentiful. It is just an attempt to slander and falsify an opponent's position.

The fact that Slaughter uses these tools of slander and distortion in a brazen and cynical way, by printing side by side with his own comments the very text that he tries to falsify, only shows the typical bureaucrat's contempt of his own followers and readers. He believes them to be so stupid or so fanatical that they become unable to distinguish black from white.

One example will be sufficient to illustrate the Slaughter school of systematic slander. Answering the question of a journalist from the magazine *Der Spiegel* as to what kind of activities revolutionists undertake to bring down the bourgeois order in an imperialist country, Mandel answers that revolutions cannot be fabricated out of the blue sky by a small band of conspirators, but that they are the result of a deep-going social crisis in existing society, which pushes millions of people onto the road of revolutionary actions. He then adds ironically: "Unless neo-capitalist society is crisis-free." But in that case why worry about revolutionary propaganda? Instead of answering this question, the journalist of *Der Spiegel* sidesteps towards another track and asks: But in that case (when no great revolutionary upheavals can take place because society is crisis-free) there would be no difference between a revolutionary and a reformist. Mandel answers: Even in that case, revolutionists would still keep up the struggle for a fundamental change of society, in the far future.

Now Slaughter isolates this last sentence from the whole context, in order to have his readers believe that Mandel really thinks neo-capitalist society to be crisis-free. This is, of course, a shameless lie. *In the very next sentence* to the one Slaughter quotes, Mandel refers to revolutionary crises with revolutionary working-class actions, occurring not in a far future, but here and now: in May 1968 in France; in autumn 1969 in Italy. He explains that under such conditions, revolutionists try to bring workers to elect soviets and to fight for a conquest of power. But Cliff Slaughter, who limits his political propaganda day-in day-out to calling for new elections for a bourgeois parliament "in order to kick out the Tories"; who doesn't say a word in this propaganda about soviets or workers councils or the overthrow of the parliamentary system; who never makes propaganda for the dictatorship of the proletariat in his proud daily paper—except when polemicizing against the "Pabloites"—has the nerve to add:

> Here we have the true content of the Pabloite attack on Trotskyism. General lip-service is paid to the idea of a workers' revolution and socialist solutions, but there can be no question [!] of the working class today having any revolutionary significance.

Slaughter's thought and method; his refusal to campaign for the democratic rights of political opponents in the labor movement victimized by imperialism; his systematic use of slander and falsification to replace real political debate and struggle, do not stem from the school of Marx, Engels, Lenin, and Trotsky. They had nothing to do with such methods and rejected them out of hand. These methods were concocted by the famous alchemists called Stalin, Vyshinsky, and Beria. We doubt whether they become more palatable by adding a sniff of English insularity and cant.

MAY 5, 1972

SECTION XIV:

Healyites Smear Bala Tampoe

The following statement was issued October 29 by the United Secretariat of the Fourth International.

The October 21, 1972, issue of the *Workers Press*, the official organ of the Central Committee of the Socialist Labour League, carried a slanderous attack on Bala Tampoe, the general secretary of the Ceylon Mercantile Union. The author of the article, one Jack Gale, asserts that Tampoe is "known to have associated with the CIA."

Why should the imperialist spy agency want to associate with Bala Tampoe? Washington is certainly not preparing to overthrow the Bandaranaike regime—at least from the left. Gale offers no explanation. Nor does he explain what interest Bala Tampoe, who opposes both imperialism and the Bandaranaike regime, could conceivably have in associating with the CIA.

The author of the article indicates as his source of information only Edmund Samarakkody, a former factional opponent of Tampoe. An investigation undertaken by us in 1969 showed that the slander was cooked up and put into circulation originally by the former Trotskyists in Ceylon who betrayed the movement and accepted posts offered them by Bandaranaike, and who were under heavy fire for this from Bala Tampoe.

How did this bit of ancient garbage happen to finally end up gracing the pages of the *Workers Press*, which makes a great show of its repugnance for the former Trotskyists in Ceylon and all their works?

First of all because the technique of the "big lie" has been utilized with increasing frequency in recent years by the leaders of the SLL under the guidance of their general secretary, Gerry Healy, and this item looked particularly suitable for such use.

The smearing of Bala Tampoe, a leading Ceylonese Trotskyist, in this way is on par with the beating that stewards of the SLL inflicted on Ernest Tate, a leading British Trotskyist, while Healy looked on. Tate was "guilty" of hawking Trotskyist literature in front of an SLL public meeting. Tampoe scorned inducements to line up with the SLL.

These are signs, among others, of the deep degeneration of the SLL. Incapable of meeting criticism with reasoned arguments, the leaders of the SLL borrow from the arsenal of Stalinism—which also calls for labeling political opponents as "spies" and "agents" of foreign powers and subjecting them to physical assault.

The timing of the attack on Bala Tampoe is worth noting. Tampoe is one of the main attorneys for the defense of the young revolutionists of the Janatha Vimukthi Peramuna, who are now being processed in the courts by the repressive Bandaranaike regime. Coinciding with this defense, various unions (among them the Ceylon Mercantile Union) initiated the first big action by the toiling masses of Sri Lanka since the "state of emergency" was decreed by Bandaranaike a year ago. This action was a nationwide, twenty-four-hour hunger strike. And the bank workers, in defense of their wage standards, called a strike in defiance of the coalition government composed of the bourgeois Sri Lanka Freedom party, the reformist Lanka Sama Samaja party, and the pro-Moscow Communist party.

Intercontinental Press, November 20, 1972.

All the reactionary supporters of the treacherous coalition regime rallied in support of its efforts to railroad the JVP revolutionists to long terms in prison, to smash the bank workers' strike, and to keep the masses cowed.

This was when the Healyites found it necessary to make their contribution. They did not solidarize with the Trotskyist-led bank workers' strike. They did not solidarize with the legal defense of the young revolutionists of the JVP against the frame-up charges of the coalition regime. They did not solidarize with the hunger strike taken as a step toward arousing mass resistance to the abrogation of democratic rights in Sri Lanka.

Instead, the Healyites singled out the "main enemy" for their bucket of mud.

What does Healy hope to gain from this? Something of great importance to him. In view of the latest developments in Sri Lanka, curiosity in the ranks of the SLL over his real reasons for splitting from the world Trotskyist movement might become troublesome. A fast prophylaxis was required. Hence the poisonous article against Bala Tampoe and the Fourth International.

SECTION XV: UNPRINCIPLED 'UNIFICATION' WITH THE POR(LORA)

Lambertists Knife Aid for Bolivian Victims

By Gerry Foley

An ultraleft grouping in France known as the "Lambertists" has reacted in a most bizarre way to an appeal issued early in November by the French section of the Fourth International, the Ligue Communiste [Communist League], for solidarity with the victims of the political repression in Bolivia.

In a special supplement to No. 37 of their weekly paper, *Rouge*, the Ligue Communiste described the police raids last July against several nuclei of the ELN [Ejército de Liberación Nacional—National Liberation Army], the guerrilla force initiated by Che Guevara.

The Bolivian section of the Fourth International, the Partido Obrero Revolucionario [POR—Revolutionary Workers party] supports the guerrilla movement in Bolivia, and a number of its members fell victim to the raids. The *Rouge* supplement listed the imprisoned Trotskyists and appealed for funds to aid them.

Shortly after this appeal was published, the weekly *Informations Ouvrières* printed a letter from a group led by a former POR leader, Guillermo Lora, denouncing the solidarity campaign as "an operation with all the signs of a fraud."

The letter made an even graver charge, if that is possible: "Serious suspicions exist today that Mr. González Moscoso [the leader of the POR] in person is working in the pay of the Bolivian government."

The truth is that Moscoso has been the object of a manhunt since the July raids, and the police have harassed and mistreated his family.

Informations Ouvrières is the organ of the Fédération des Comités d'Alliance Ouvrière [Federation of Workers Alliance Committees], a French ultraleft sectarian group headed by Pierre Lambert and allied with the Socialist Labour League of Great Britain. Lambert's followers, who claim to be Trotskyists, distinguished themselves by denouncing the battles that touched off the May–June upsurge in France as "adventurist."

Informations Ouvrières gave its full endorsement to the slander issued by the Lora group. The Lambertist paper called this group, which styles itself the POR, "the Trotskyist organization in Bolivia." It described the letter as a "correction by the secretariat of the POR regarding the material published by the Ligue Communiste calling for political and financial aid for Hugo *González Moscoso*, who was presented as the leader of the POR. As the correction indicates, this was a gross deception."

The Lambertists also published some political statements issued by the Lora group on the situation in Bolivia.

The present Lora grouping has developed rather recently. There was a long-standing division in the Bolivian Trotskyist movement between the tendency led by González Moscoso and that led by the brothers Guillermo and César Lora.

In May, 1965, as the army moved in to occupy the mines, César Lora, a popular leader of the miners, attempted to organize guerrilla resistance. He was captured in the northern part of the province of Potosi by the army on July 20, 1965, and executed on the spot.

On February 17, 1966, the two tendencies in the Bolivian Trotskyist movement united. Guillermo Lora, who is a well-known parliamentary figure,

---

Intercontinental Press, December 15, 1969.

approved the unification although he was out of the country. When he returned, however, he refused to work in the united organization. He formed a personal grouping which eventually called itself by the same name as the organization it split from.

The declarations published by *Informations Ouvrières* indicate that Lora has adopted a sectarian line: "The Bolivian POR [Lora's "POR"] is not an advocate of guerrilla warfare of the Castroist type and considers this a typical adventure stemming from petty-bourgeois despair."

Differences are possible among revolutionists over the tactic of guerrilla warfare; but no genuine revolutionist would fail to solidarize with guerrillas as victims of a repression. But Lora fails, as do his newly found French allies, to solidarize with such victims. Still more reprehensible, this bloc slanders the victims in the face of a full-scale anti-Cuban and antiguerrilla witch-hunt, and stabs them in the back by advancing the most poisonous kind of charges against a campaign to raise funds to help them.

Some of the Lora group's charges against the POR tend to echo the major themes of the government propaganda: "Today it is the political intervention and the writings of Castroism that this group of profiteers [the POR] is trying to exploit in order to carry on their shady dealings with the help of the revolutionists' money."

It seems strange that the Lambertists should give unreserved endorsement to such a dubious document from a faraway country, isolated not only by its geographical position but by a repression. Perhaps the Lambertists felt that this was an opportunity to show, for the first time since the Cuban revolution, that they have at least one contact in Latin America.

It is to be hoped that the nature of the relationship between the Lora group and the Lambertists will be clarified. Does this alliance rest on a principled agreement? Does Lora, like the Socialist Labour League and Lambert, believe that the Cuban revolution was not socialist, giving rise only to state capitalism? Does he hold with them that Fidel Castro is another "Batista"? Does he approve of the slanders that appeared in the Socialist Labour League press (before it became known that Che Guevara was in Bolivia) that Castro had liquidated his comrade in arms?

Healyites and Lambertists in Strange Company
By Joseph Hansen

In his informative report on recent developments in the Bolivian guerrilla movement, which is summarized elsewhere in this issue, Carlos Maria Gutiérrez of the Montevideo weekly *Marcha* mentions rumors in La Paz that the Trotskyists who participated in the armed forces led by Inti Peredo may have provided a channel through which the intelligence services "possibly infiltrated the guerrilla movement."

It is not known specifically who started these foul rumors. The intelligence services themselves are the most likely. They have an obvious interest in diverting attention from their stool pigeons and in sowing suspicion among the revolutionary forces so as to make it more difficult for them to hold together in face of the repression.

Another possible source is the Stalinists, since the rumors smack of the ancient slanders cooked up by Stalin's secret police and used in the Moscow frame-up trials.

The most shameless purveyors of the slanders, however, have been the leaders of the Guillermo Lora tendency in Bolivia and some new allies they have found in Great Britain and France, the Healyites of the Socialist Labour League and the Lambertists of the *Fédération des Comités d'Alliance Ouvrière*. It may have been from these tainted sources that María Gutiérrez heard the rumors he

---

Intercontinental Press, March 2, 1970.

mentions in his article.

It will be recalled that nationwide raids were staged by the dictatorial Bolivian regime last summer. Prominent among those thrown into prison and tortured were the Trotskyists who had participated in the guerrilla movement headed by Inti Peredo. The leader of these Trotskyists, Hugo González Moscoso, was the object of an intensive police hunt. His home was raided, and the police sought to terrorize his family.

An international campaign was launched to help these victims of the witch-hunt. In Europe and elsewhere money was collected to help the Bolivian guerrillas recover from the blow dealt their struggle. This was the moment chosen by the Lora tendency to attack the victims, whom they call "Pabloites" instead of Trotskyists.

In a press release dated November 8, 1969, Alberto Saenz, a leader of the Lora group, asserted that the solidarity campaign was a "fraud."

This statement, so far as can be ascertained, was first published outside of Bolivia in the November 19–26, 1969, issue of *Informations Ouvrières*, the Paris publication of the Lambert group.

Among Saenz's assertions was the following:

> 2) The Bolivian Pabloites in any case do not possess any organization because they dissolved it in order to enter the ALN (Army of National Liberation) individually. The latter moreover has denounced some of them as informers and confidants of the Ministry of the Interior. Serious suspicions exist today that Mr. Gonzáles [sic] Moscoso in person is working in the pay of the Bolivian government.
>
> [2] *Les pablistes de Bolivie ne possèdent en tout état de cause pas d'organisation car ils l'ont dissoute pour entrer individuellement dans l'A. L. N. (Armée de Libération Nationale). Celle-ci en a dénoncé d'autre part certains comme informateurs et confidents du Ministre de l'Intérieur. Il existe aujourd'hui de sérieux soupçons sur le fait que le sieur GONZALES MOSCOSO en personne travaillerait pour le compte du gouvernement bolivien.*}

The Paris weekly *Rouge*, the organ of the *Ligue Communiste*, the French section of the Fourth International, in its issue of December 1, 1969, denounced this libelous statement as "garbage."

Guillermo Lora thereupon issued a statement which appeared in the December 10–17 issue of *Informations Ouvrières*. The nature of this statement can be judged from the first point:

> 1. I solidarize completely with the communiqué that was written by my party in order to unmask the adventurers who have turned revolutionary involvement into a business proposition designed to satisfy their personal needs.

The Healyites in London utilized this priceless windfall for feature material in the current campaign they are waging against the Fourth International (which, like the Lora tendency, they call "Pabloite").

They retreated a bit only on the libelous statement concerning Hugo González Moscoso when it was challenged by Pat Jordan of the International Marxist Group, the British section of the Fourth International.

Mike Banda, the "Assistant National Secretary" of the Socialist Labour League, said in the January 17 issue of *Workers Press* that the particularly libelous slander of González quoted by *Intercontinental Press*[1] had been mistranslated.

Banda offered as a correct translation: "Today it is seriously suspected that Mr Gonzales [sic] himself *would work* on behalf of the Bolivian government." [Banda's emphasis.]

In order to inject some kind of meaning into this nonsensical English, Banda added: "Our interpretation of the text leads us to believe that political collaboration between Moscoso [sic] and a bourgeois government *in the future* is quite possible. You don't have to be a police agent to work for a bourgeois government." [Banda's emphasis.]

Two observations can be made on this squirming.

1. Banda did not supply the original Spanish so that his English version could be checked.[2] He did

---

1. See "Lambertists Knife Aid for Bolivian Victims," by Gerry Foley in *Intercontinental Press*, December 15, 1969, page 1119.

2. We have only seen the French version, which we have quoted above.

not even cite the French.

(As an authority in linguistics—like Stalin—Mike Banda ought to put the Paris daily *Le Monde* right on the way the conditional mood is translated in certain articles in its weekly English edition. Here is a current example of this standard usage:

(A sentence in the January 28 *Le Monde*, page 8, column 5, reads: *"Le commandant en chef aurait invité le président Ongania à révoquer l'ambassadeur"* This appears in the February 4 "Weekly Selection," page 8, column 6, as: "The ambassador's dismissal was reportedly pressed on the President by General Lanusse."

(In the Mike Banda school of languages this comes out: "It is seriously suspected that the ambassador's dismissal *would be* pressed *in the future*, it is quite possible . . . you don't have to be a police agent . . .")

2. Mike Banda did not refer to the sentence preceding the one with which he went into his twisting act. That sentence reads, as can be checked above: "The latter moreover has denounced some of them as informers and confidants of the Ministry of the Interior."

The words used are "informers" and "confidants"—not in some distant future but in Bolivia last summer and right now.

This is the garbage that the Healyites found so much to their taste they even put out a pamphlet on it for the delectation of their members.

If one wonders why ultraleft sectarians like these should be found running with the hounds in Bolivia, the explanation is simple. The quarry hunted by the police happens to be a "Pabloite."

We should like to close by asking Healy to please explain the basis in principle of the bloc he and Lambert have formed with Lora. We do not ask Lambert because he is tongue-tied.

> Does Lora, like the Socialist Labour League and Lambert, believe that the Cuban revolution was not socialist, giving rise only to state capitalism? Does he hold with them that Fidel Castro is another 'Batista'? Does he approve of the slanders that appeared in the Socialist Labour League press (before it became known that Che Guevara was in Bolivia) that Castro had liquidated his comrade in arms?

These questions were asked by Gerry Foley in the December 15, 1969, issue of *Intercontinental Press*.

Neither Healy, Lambert, nor Lora have answered these questions. To this day they have not made public the basis in principle of their political combination.

Or have they? Take another look at the slanders repeated by Lora, besmirching the Bolivian Trotskyists in the prison cells and torture dungeons of the Bolivian political police.

There's genuine Healyism at its purest and finest!

SECTION XVI: HEALY OFFERS TO UNIFY WITH 'PABLOITE TRAITORS'

Healy's Request to Discuss Unification

The following statement was issued July 5 by the United Secretariat of the Fourth International, the World Party of Socialist Revolution founded by Leon Trotsky in 1938.

At the end of April, Gerry Healy, the national secretary of the Socialist Labour League, asked to talk with Pierre Frank, a member of the United Secretariat of the Fourth International.

In the following weeks, two conversations were held which included other members of the two organizations.

Comrade Healy raised the question of organizing a mutual discussion that might open the way to the Socialist Labour League and its French sister organization, the Organisation Trotskyste, unifying with the Fourth International.

It should be noted that this move by Comrade Healy stands in strong contrast with the slanderous attacks that have constantly appeared in the press of the SLL and the OT against outstanding figures of the Fourth International, with the systematic refusal to engage in common actions in Britain and France, even in defending victims of repression by imperialism or Stalinism, and with the claim to be "reorganizing" the Fourth International.

In addition to this, it should be noted that on a whole series of political issues the SLL and OT have not modified the very sharp differences they have expressed for years in opposition to the Fourth International.

Under these circumstances, unification is not a realistic perspective.

The Fourth International is, of course, in favor of unifying revolutionary forces wherever possible on a principled basis. We are therefore prepared to reexamine the question of the SLL and OT unifying with the Fourth International if objective evidence should show that this is feasible.

The SLL and OT might well begin this process by beginning to discuss their political and theoretical differences with us in a frank and comradely way, without the use of slander or falsifying the positions we hold, and by beginning to engage in common actions on such elementary questions as the defense of victims of the class struggle.

Intercontinental Press, July 27, 1970.

Fourth International Reply to New SLL Proposals

The Socialist Labour League of London and a group of its sympathizers in the United States have recently made several proposals that on the surface would imply a desire to seek unification with the Fourth International and its cothinkers.

The following statement concerning these moves was issued September 19 by the United Secretariat of the Fourth International.

In a statement issued July 5, 1970, we reported that Gerry Healy, the national secretary of the Socialist Labour League, speaking on behalf of the International Committee, had asked to meet with Pierre Frank, a member of the United Secretariat of the Fourth International. In two conversations that were held, Comrade Healy "raised the question of organizing a mutual discussion that might open the way to the Socialist Labour League and its French sister organization, the Organisation Trotskyste, unifying with the Fourth International."

In its statement, the United Secretariat did not reject in principle the possibility of a unification some time in the future. But we noted the following items:

> 1. [That] this move by Comrade Healy stands in strong contrast with the slanderous attacks that have constantly appeared in the press of the SLL and the OT against outstanding figures of the Fourth International, with the systematic refusal to engage in common actions in Britain and France, even in defending victims of repression by imperialism or Stalinism, and with the claim to be "reorganizing" the Fourth International.
> 2. [That] on a whole series of political issues the SLL and OT have not modified the very sharp differences they have expressed for years in opposition to the Fourth International.

"Under these circumstances," we concluded,

Intercontinental Press, October 5, 1970.

"unification is not a realistic perspective."

Since then, two new developments have been called to our attention.

In the United States, the Workers League, a group sympathetic to the views of the International Committee, addressed a letter signed by Tim Wohlforth and dated August 18, 1970, to our cothinkers of the Socialist Workers party proposing a "joint meeting" in commemoration of the death of Leon Trotsky.

In England, the *Workers Press* of September 8 published a statement signed by Gerry Healy. In this statement, Comrade Healy specified that in his two meetings with Pierre Frank, which included other members of the United Secretariat and the International Committee, "At no time did I or anyone else from the International Committee make proposals as such for unity to the United Secretariat."

What he did do was to make an "approach." This, he pointed out, was clarified in the July 7 *Workers Press* as follows:

> As part of this preparation the Committee requested G. Healy, the national secretary of the Socialist Labour League, to contact representatives of the Unified [United] Secretariat for informal talks around the possibility of joint discussion centered on outstanding political differences and directed towards the holding of a joint international conference.

Comrade Healy made two other significant points:

1. "Factional manoeuvring over 'unity' as such would convince no one, and we have no intention of engaging in this."

2. To facilitate "a comradely approach" to the discussion desired by the International Committee, "we are prepared to enter into mutual agreement that this be *no longer* conducted in our public press, but internally within our respective organizations."

Both the initiative taken by the Workers League toward the SWP and Comrade Healy's latest proposals to the United Secretariat appear to us to disregard the key question; that is, the depth of the political and theoretical differences separating us and whether these have been lessening or growing greater.

The differences involve two interrelated areas: (1) Characterization of the two sides from a class standpoint; (2) specific political and theoretical issues. In our opinion the differences in both areas have been growing greater since 1963 when the SLL and the OT held them to be so deep as to preclude participating in the Reunification Congress of the Fourth International.

We will defer consideration of the political and theoretical differences for another time and confine ourselves here to some items of public record that will serve to illustrate how the Socialist Labour League and its cothinkers have characterized the United Secretariat of the Fourth International and its cothinkers of the Socialist Workers party of the United States.

In the August 20, 1966, *Newsletter* (now the *Workers Press*), the Political Committee of the SLL charged the SWP with having "capitulated to imperialism" and with having "sold out the anti-war movement." The pamphlet published by us, *Healy "Reconstructs" the Fourth International,* which contained documentary evidence, including letters by Healy, showing the sectarian and antidemocratic character of the Socialist Labour League, was called a "provocation" that "constitutes a complete and irreversible departure even from revisionism. . . ."

The SLL Political Committee stated further: "We shall not hesitate to deal appropriately with the handful of United Secretariat agents who hawk it around the cynical fake-left in England."

In an article published in the September 3, 1966, issue of *The Newsletter,* Gerry Healy made the following allegations concerning James P. Cannon, one of the founders of the world Trotskyist movement: "He [Cannon] had decided to sell out to the Stalinist bureaucracy and the imperialists."

In the same article, Healy made his attitude unmistakably clear:

> The Socialist Labour League is out to destroy Pabloism and its SWP accomplices. There can be [sic] and, we repeat, there never will be a compromise on these questions—the fight will go on until we destroy the Pabloites and the revisionist SWP.

A declaration passed by a special conference of the SLL and published in the December 3, 1966, issue of *The Newsletter* stated: "No longer a proletarian tendency, they [the SWP] are the left wing of the radical middle class."

In the same vein, the declaration continued:

> It is *this* to which the SWP is really orientated: the firmer tying of the US working class to the two-party system and the capitalist establishment, despite the propaganda protestations to the contrary.

The SLL declaration made the following assertion concerning the SWP: "Your political actions have placed you outside the camp of Trotskyism and of the working class."

In line with this slander, the authors of the declaration concluded by saying: "Henceforth we have no relations with the SWP: it is a fight between the working class and the servants of the class enemy."

This pronouncement was echoed by Tim Wohlforth, who is regarded by the International Committee as its leading cothinker and exponent of its views in the United States. In the February 13, 1967, issue of the *Bulletin,* in an attack on James Robertson, the national chairman of the Spartacist League, Wohlforth ended by saying:

> We warn Spartacist: There is presently a *war* going on between revolutionary Trotskyists represented by the International Committee and revisionist agents of capital represented by the SWP-Germain-Frank-Pabloite formation. You are on the other side in this war. Henceforth we will have no relations with you.

In our opinion, such assertions are not mere epithets. They express considered conclusions which Comrade Healy and his cothinkers have drawn as to the class nature of our political views, our political course, and the social composition of our organizations and sympathizing groups.

This is the basic explanation for actions directed against us that otherwise remain inexplicable if not irrational. It is sufficient to cite two cases to illustrate the point.

The first is the assault on Ernest Tate on November 17, 1966, committed by six stewards of the SLL in the presence of Gerry Healy. Comrade Tate, a militant of the United Secretariat of the Fourth International, was attacked while selling the pamphlet *Healy "Reconstructs" the Fourth International* in front of Caxton Hall in London where a public meeting of the SLL was being held.

The second case is the slandering of Hugo González M., a leader of the Bolivian section of the Fourth International. During a savage witch-hunt in which many members of the Bolivian section were arrested and tortured and the entire police network was searching for Comrade González, the November 19–26, 1969, issue of *Informations Ouvrières*, the Paris publication of the French cothinkers of the Socialist Labour League, asserted: "Serious suspicions exist today that Mr. Gonzáles [sic] Moscoso in person is working in the pay of the Bolivian government."

In following such practices, the International Committee is acting in accordance with its theory concerning the alleged "degeneration" of the Fourth International and the Socialist Workers party. As Wohlforth expressed it in defending Gerry Healy in the Tate case: "Ernest Tate and his political allies represent political scabs of the worst sort." In accordance with the "class" position he was taking, Wohlforth stated that the relationship between the SWP and its cothinkers on the one hand and the SLL and its cothinkers on the other "is symbolized by this confrontation with Tate."

To summarize: The International Committee has characterized the United Secretariat of the Fourth International and the Socialist Workers party as "servants of the class enemy," who "decided to sell out to the Stalinist bureaucracy and the imperialists," whose actions have placed them "outside the camp of Trotskyism and of the working class," and who must be dealt with as "political scabs of the worst sort."

No other conclusion is possible: Either (1) in making advances towards us, the leaders of the International Committee have decided to sell out to the Stalinist bureaucracy and the imperialists, and are following a course that will place them outside the camp of Trotskyism and of the working class; or, (2) the leaders of the International Committee have begun to recognize how wrong they have been in their characterization of the United Secretariat of the Fourth International and its cothinkers in other countries but do not want to acknowledge their grievous errors, still less engage in public self-criticism.

If the leaders of the International Committee have changed their opinion, then it is their duty to make public their political reasons for changing. On what specific political issues have they altered their views? We await their explanations with interest.

Of course another possibility exists—that Comrade Healy's "approach" to the United Secretariat of the Fourth International, and along with it Comrade Wohlforth's "approach" to the Socialist Workers party, are only part of a "unity" maneuver in the *"war"* being conducted by the leaders of the Socialist Labour League against the Fourth International and the organizations sympathetic to its views.

This would seem to be the most likely possibility were it not for the fact that Comrade Healy has expressly issued a public assurance that he has "no intention" of engaging in "factional manoeuvring" over unity "as such."

Comrade Healy's public avowal that no unity maneuver is involved makes it all the more imperative that the International Committee publicly clarify its stand on the alternative indicated above.

SWP Says 'No' to Healyites

The following letters, which are self-explanatory, have been made public by the Socialist Workers party.

New York, N.Y.
October 5, 1973

Jack Barnes
National Secretary
Socialist Workers Party
15 Charles Lane
New York, New York

Dear Comrade Barnes,

As you know, I have been seeking to meet with a representative of the Socialist Workers Party. I have made several phone calls to this effect making it clear that I was taking this initiative on behalf of the International Committee, with which the Workers League is in political solidarity, as well as on behalf of the Workers League.

The purpose of this initiative is to seek the support of the Socialist Workers Party in urging upon the United Secretariat, with which it is in political solidarity, a discussion as outlined in the International Committee statement "For A Discussion on The Problems of the Fourth International." This statement appeared in the Wednesday, August 29 issue of the Workers Press and the September 24 issue of the Bulletin.

We continue to be interested in holding a discussion with you or any other representative of the Socialist Workers Party to see if a way can be found to bring about such a genuine discussion as outlined in the above mentioned statement.

We are hoping to hear from you in the near future.

Yours fraternally
Tim Wohlforth
National Secretary
Workers League

cc: G. Healy

Intercontinental Press, November 12, 1973.

New York, N.Y.
October 20, 1973

Dear Comrade Wohlforth,

I have attached the September 19, 1970, United Secretariat statement on the "unity" discussions then being sought by Gerry Healy in behalf of the "International Committee." It closed as follows:

> To summarize: The International Committee has characterized the United Secretariat of the Fourth International and the Socialist Workers party as "servants of the class enemy," who "decided to sell out to the Stalinist bureaucracy and the imperialists," whose actions have placed them "outside the camp of Trotskyism and of the working class," and who must be dealt with as "political scabs of the worst sort."

> No other conclusion is possible: Either (1) in making advances towards us, the leaders of the International Committee have decided to sell out to the Stalinist bureaucracy and the imperialists, and are following a course that will place them outside the camp of Trotskyism and of the working class; or, (2) the leaders of the International Committee have begun to recognize how wrong they have been in their characterization of the United Secretariat of the Fourth International and its cothinkers in other countries but do not want to acknowledge their grievous errors, still less engage in public self-criticism.

> If the leaders of the International Committee have changed their opinion, then it is their duty to make public their political reasons for changing. On what specific political issues have they altered their views? We await their explanations with interest.

> Of course another possibility exists—that Comrade Healy's "approach" to the United Secretariat of the Fourth International, and along with it Comrade Wohlforth's "approach" to the Socialist Workers party, are only part of a "unity" maneuver in the "war" being conducted by the leaders of the Socialist Labour

League against the Fourth International and the organizations sympathetic to its views.

This would seem to be the most likely possibility were it not for the fact that Comrade Healy has expressly issued a public assurance that he has "no intention" of engaging in "factional manoeuvring" over unity "as such."

Comrade Healy's public avowal that no unity maneuver is involved makes it all the more imperative that the International Committee publicly clarify its stand on the alternatives indicated above.

Since that time neither in their actions nor their press have the Socialist Labour League or the Workers League indicated any reconsideration of their characterizations of the United Secretariat and the Socialist Workers Party. In fact, the very public statement by the "International Committee," which you now advance as a basis for "discussion," characterizes the United Secretariat and the Socialist Workers Party as "revisionists" totally unable "to return to the basic principles of Trotskyism." The Socialist Workers Party is slandered as having "opportunistically degenerated even further in the last ten years"; that is, further than being "servants of the class enemy," deciding "to sell out to the Stalinist bureaucracy and the imperialists," and engaging in actions placing the party "outside the camp of Trotskyism and of the working class."

In view of your failure to respond to the United Secretariat statement of September 19, 1970, your failure to indicate by any other means that you have modified your views of the United Secretariat of the Fourth International and the Socialist Workers Party, and your persistence in continuing up to this moment to publicly misrepresent and lie about our political positions, we see no reason for altering our previous refusal to engage in private parleys with representatives of the "International Committee."

Fraternally,
Jack Barnes
National Secretary
Socialist Workers Party

cc: United Secretariat
Gerry Healy

SECTION XVII: HEALY'S 'INTERNATIONAL COMMITTEE' SPLITS WIDE OPEN

Disaster in Bolivia for Healy-Lambert-Wohlforth
By Gerry Foley

An article entitled "Bitter Lessons of a Defeat" in the weekly paper of a small sectarian group in New York has provided a curious footnote to the tragedy of the right-wing take-over in Bolivia.

In the August 30 issue of the *Bulletin*, Tim Wohlforth, leader of the ultraleft Workers League, responded to the Bolivian events with a broad denunciation of one of the most prominent personalities in the Bolivian left:

> The key figure of Bolivian Trotskyism has been Guillermo Lora. Lora, who lost his own brother under Barrientos and whose whereabouts at this moment is not known, must share a responsibility in the recent rightist coup.
>
> Lora, in collaboration with the Bolivian Stalinists and with the agreement of the Bolivian and international Pabloites, failed to fight at any point for the overthrow of the Torres military regime. Thus he, along with the rest of the Popular Assembly, acted as a left cover for Torres while the right wing elements in Torres' own army prepared and finally executed their coup.
>
> In so doing Lora was carrying forward a political course begun over a decade ago, from which he has consistently refused to veer. At every point this course has received support within the Fourth International or [from?] forces claiming to represent the Fourth International. Though less known than the evolution of the LSSP [Lanka Sama Samaja party—the former Ceylonese section of the Fourth International, which was expelled in 1964 for entering a bourgeois cabinet] in Ceylon, the role of Lora and the POR [Partido Obrero Revolucionario—Revolutionary Workers party] has been no less treacherous and important.

The average reader of the *Bulletin* might not notice anything unusual about such instant analysis or about the condemnation of yet another "Pabloite renegade." The *Bulletin*'s response to defeats of mass struggles has been, after all, rather standard. Its rule of thumb was set forth clearly in this same article: "In every country of Latin America it can be said that capitalism rules only because of the paralysis and confusion of those elements which call themselves Trotskyists."

It is to be hoped, however, that the name Guillermo Lora rang a bell in the minds of some *Bulletin* readers. Because there was something notable about this article. It was not, in fact, without a certain interest and instructiveness.

A minor but vivid lesson of the Bolivian defeat, it seems, is to be its illustration of the logic and rewards of unprincipled factionalism. Until sufficient information is available to make a judgment about the main questions involved in the rightist victory in Bolivia, it may be worth dwelling a bit on this lesson. It concerns some elementary rules of building a revolutionary movement nationally and internationally, about which a reminder is always useful.

This lesson is apt to be a bitter one for some small groups. We can only hope that they will take

Intercontinental Press, September 27, 1971.

it to heart. They were warned well in advance on where their course was leading them.

However, Wohlforth's article gives little grounds for optimism on this score. If he had learned anything from his Bolivian experience, he really should have admitted frankly that one of the groups "claiming to represent the Fourth International" that supported Lora was the combination to which the Workers League adheres, the so-called International Committee (IC). In fact, Wohlforth's failure to say this openly may lead some to believe that his article represented, among other things, a veiled attack on one or another of his remaining allies, either Gerry Healy in England or Pierre Lambert in France. In view of the speed and roughness with which Wohlforth dumped Lora, who is hardly in a position to defend himself, the rest of the "International Committee" might have reason to be concerned.

Wohlforth does note that Lora had a certain acquaintance with the "IC." He writes

> . . . Lora established contact with the International Committee announcing his agreement with the IC's international perspectives, especially its position on the centrality of the struggles of the working class in all countries. But Lora never made any serious attempt to assess his own history and on this basis to make a fundamental development towards a break with his own past.

What Wohlforth fails to mention is that the Lora group was recognized as the Bolivian section of the International Committee, in fact, was regarded as the key to the future in the colonial world. In issue No. 1 of *La Correspondance Internationale* (the issue was dated May 1971 and issue No. 2 does not yet seem to have appeared), an international bulletin published by the Lambertists, Marc-Etienne Laurent wrote:

> For the OCI [Organisation Communiste Internationaliste—Internationalist Communist Organization, the Lambertist group], it is a fact of the highest importance that—notably through the POR, which is a member of the IC; and through *Politica Obrera* [Workers Politics—an independent sectarian grouping in Argentina] which is working more and more closely with us—the International Committee is present in the revolutionary process under way in Bolivia and now starting in Argentina. No one in the ranks of the IC should fail to recognize the implications of this fact.

This last sentence raises the question whether the OCI's allies fully shared its enthusiasm about the IC's first serious contact in the colonial world since the Cuban revolution. In case anyone missed the point, Laurent stressed:

> Conversely, the links that have begun to form [with the Lora POR] are of an extreme importance for the 'European' organizations of the IC. They will contribute strongly to the political progress of these organizations as such. At the same time every advance on the road marked out must lead to a considerable reinforcement of the IC. Together with the work done in Eastern Europe and in Spain and the work done in building the IRJ [Revolutionary Youth International], such advances must make possible a qualitative leap forward in reconstructing the Fourth International.

In a letter to the Lora POR dated July 30, 1970, and published in the October issue of the Lambertist theoretical journal *La Verité* the OCI Political Committee wrote:

> The first thing for us is that the Bolivian POR is the only organization in Latin America claiming to be loyal to the Transitional Program of the Fourth International that has real roots in the working class and the masses of its country. Thus, the POR is destined to be the organization around which the process of reconstructing the Fourth International in that part of the world will take place.

In view of the importance accorded the Lora group, by his French ally at least, it seems strange that Wohlforth condemned the Bolivian personality, now in the underground, so summarily. After all, Lora was associated with the IC, to all appearances, for more than a year, and one of the most critical years in the history of the Andean republic at that. Surely the *Bulletin*'s readers would be interested in the record of the international discussions in which, we must assume, the fate of the Bolivian proletariat was decided.

One possible reason for Wohlforth's silence on this question is suggested by his statement that Lora "never made any serious attempt to assess his own history and on this basis to make a fundamental development towards a break with his own past." How then could Lora have become a member of the IC, an organization that supposedly demands rigorous public avowal of all past deviations? What, in view of this position, could be more embarrassing than having to admit that Lora was welcomed into the ranks of the Healy-Lambert-Wohlforth combination without any serious inquiry into his political past or even into his present political positions?

When the overwhelming majority of the world Trotskyist movement reunited in 1963, Healy and Lambert justified their refusal to accept the majority decision by claiming that the reunification was "unprincipled." Their argument was that the groups that had decided to work together on the basis of agreement on present tasks had not discussed and settled the question of their past differences. In fact, this justification was reiterated at the beginning of this year in "An Open Letter to Joseph Hansen in Six Parts," which filled long pages of the Healyite organ *Workers Press* and was given emphasis by many dramatic photographs. In part two of this series, Robert Black wrote:

> We never opposed unity with forces outside the IC [that is, one of the two main groupings that reunited in 1963].[1] We simply insisted:
> "Organizational unity must follow political clarification, and we insist on a thorough settlement of all revisionism whatever its source before any organizational fusions can take place."
> That remains our position today. (*Workers Press*, January 19, 1971.)

In 1963 and since then, most Trotskyists have supposed that it was the dead-end factionalism and authoritarian internal regimes of the OCI and the Healyite Socialist Labour League (SLL) that made it impossible for them to participate in a democratic and vital world movement. Such suppositions could only be confirmed by evidence that the Lora group was accepted into the Healy-Lambert-Wohlforth combination without being subjected to the tests these groupings sought to impose on a large section of the world Trotskyist movement.

The next question logically is: On what basis did Healy and Lambert welcome Lora into their camp? I asked this question at the end of 1969 when the Lambert group first publicly associated itself with Lora.

> It is to be hoped that the nature of the relationship between the Lora group and the Lambertists will be clarified. Does this alliance rest on a principled agreement? Does Lora, like the Socialist Labour League and Lambert, believe that the Cuban revolution was not socialist, giving rise only to state capitalism? Does he hold with them that Fidel Castro is another 'Batista'? Does he approve of the slanders that appeared in the Socialist Labour League press (before it became known that Che Guevara was in Bolivia) that Castro had liquidated his comrade-in-arms?[2]

These questions were repeated in the March 2, 1970, issue of *Intercontinental Press* by Joseph Hansen. Neither Healy, Lambert, or Wohlforth ever attempted to give an answer.

The question of the principled basis for Healy-Lambert-Wohlforth's support of Lora was posed very acutely by the way in which this bloc materialized. The first indication that the so-called IC grouping had any interest in Lora came when the Lambertist organ *Informations Ouvrières* published a communiqué from the Lora-POR in its November 19, 1969, issue. The statement entitled "Correction," was not on a very high political level. The "POR of Bolivia," it said,

---

1. The Lambert and Healy groups formed a minority in the International Committee, whose name they appropriated after the majority of this formation participated in the reunification of the Fourth International in 1963.

2. See "Lambertists Knife Aid for Bolivian Victims," by Gerry Foley in *Intercontinental Press*, December 15, 1969, page 1119.

found itself obliged to issue a warning about a fund-raising campaign that has just begun. This is an operation possessing all the characteristics of a swindle set up by a discredited political group headed by an individual named Hugo Gonzáles [González] Moscoso, a person who represents nothing in Bolivia.

This is not the first time that such a thing has happened. On several occasions in the past, these people have already represented themselves abroad—as they would not dare to do in Bolivia—as the inspirers of all the work accomplished by our party, as the authors of all its political documents and writings, as the leaders of its intervention in the class struggle. They have even gone so far as to try to appropriate our martyrs. And they have done this with the aim of collecting funds which only go to fatten the purse of Mr. Gonzáles Moscoso.

Let us point out, in fact, both to those who are unaware of it and those who pretend to be unaware of it, that this group has not published any material for many years and more than four years ago even ceased publishing its organ *Lucha Obrera*. This is the swindle we are exposing.

Today it is the political activities and writings of Castroism that this group of profiteers is trying to cash in on so that it can carry on its crooked dealings with the help of the comrades' money.

In view of the propaganda that the epigones of Pablo are disseminating abroad on behalf of this defunct group, we feel obligated to point out to the comrades some of the grossest misrepresentations contained in this material.

1. The Bolivian POR [that is, the Lora group] is not an advocate of guerrilla warfare of the Castroist type. It considers this activity as an adventure typical of petty-bourgeois despair.

2. The Bolivian Pabloites [i.e., the POR led by González] do not in any case have an organization because they dissolved it to enter the ELN [Ejército de Liberación Nacional—National Liberation Army, the guerrilla force led in 1967 by Che Guevara] as individuals.

The ELN, moreover, has denounced some of them as informers and confidants working for the Ministry of the Interior. There are in fact serious suspicions today that Mr. Gonzáles Moscoso in person is working on behalf of the Bolivian government.

3. It is false to claim that any of these people are in any way leaders of the guerrilla struggle (to which, let us repeat, the POR is completely opposed). Because of their extreme numerical and political weakness they have offered it an entirely secondary sort of help. None of them has joined the guerrillas or fired one shot. The ELN has used them in its quartermaster department. In particular, they have spent their time making knapsacks.

4. Elio Vásquez has never been a workers' leader in the mines and has never been involved with the mass struggles in which the workers have engaged. He was released a few days after being arrested, in return for revealing the plans of the ELN.

5. Berta Porcel is a woman known for her left views who is not active in any party. She was arrested and held for a few hours (on the basis of informing by Gonzáles's own followers) for buying a fund-raising bond with Che Guevara's picture on it.

6. Gabriel Guzmán is not a railroad workers' leader. In fact, he has found himself far removed from all trade-union or political activity.

7. F. Melgar has never left the PRIN [Partido Revolucionario de la Izquierda Nacionalista—Revolutionary party of the Nationalist Left] and has never had anything to do with the POR.

We could continue indefinitely listing similar errors.

The statement was signed by Alberto Saenz, as "press secretary of the POR." It was dated La Paz, November 8, 1969.

In the December 10–17, 1969, issue of *Informations Ouvrières*, Lora personally endorsed these charges. He wrote:

> 1. I solidarize completely with the communiqué that was written by my party in order

to unmask the adventurers who have turned revolutionary involvement into a business proposition designed to satisfy their personal needs.

These attacks were made in response to a campaign by the European sections of the Fourth International on behalf of the Bolivian revolutionary movement, which was hard hit by police raids in July 1969. Many revolutionists and their sympathizers were arrested, some were killed. The organizations involved suffered heavy material losses.

In the September 22, 1969, issue of *Intercontinental Press* ("Guerrilla Fighters Seized in Nationwide Raids," p. 820) we listed the following POR members as having been arrested:

> Tomás Chambi, an Aymara peasant leader from Camacho province; Anselmo Herrera López, a Huanuni youth leader; Gabriel Guzmán Illanes, a leader of the railway workers, whose health is very poor; Cecilio Alcón and Victor Alcón, students who are charged with setting up a 'special laboratory' for preparing time bombs, fire bombs, and other explosives.

The same article described the response in Bolivia and internationally to these raids:

> The student federations in La Paz, Oruro, and Cochabamba have condemned the tortures inflicted on the persons arrested and have demanded their release. They have also demanded that any trials be conducted in the regular courts. The same position has been taken by the Committee for the Defense of Human Rights, which seeks to organize a worldwide campaign.
>
> The ELN and the POR have made no official statement on the arrests. According to very widespread reports, the Trotskyists of the POR have begun to reorganize among the workers, peasants, and students, above all with the aim of starting up a campaign of solidarity with those imprisoned. Given the party's international connections, this campaign should acquire the scope of the campaigns on behalf of Hugo Blanco and Régis Debray.

Thus, if the Lambertists had taken a principled attitude, they would have asked themselves a few questions right away. Why did Lora challenge only a few names on this list? Did he accept the fact that the others were members of the POR led by González? What was his attitude to the antiguerrilla and anti-Cuban witch-hunt and the persecution of these revolutionists by the military dictatorship?

In particular, what about the Aymara leader Tomás Chambi? This question takes on a new importance now. Chambi died in La Paz fighting the Banzer coup. Was he a "swindler"? Were those who sought to build a campaign in his defense in 1969 "swindlers"? What do Lambert-Healy-Wohlforth think about such charges today?

Then, the question arises, why were the publications of this sectarian combination so quick to pick up and spread such poisonous charges against revolutionists in a remote country isolated from the world by geography and by a ferocious repression? What attempts did they make to verify these accusations? It seems strange that they did not wonder about Lora's charge that the POR led by González was not publishing anything. Were they so ignorant of the real conditions in Bolivia that they did not know about the severity of the repression? During the Torres period, when the repression was relaxed, the POR did not fail to publish substantial material. Some of it has been translated and reprinted in *Intercontinental Press*. Did this inspire any doubts in Lambert-Healy-Wohlforth about the truthfulness of their Bolivian ally?

In fact, the resemblance of Lora's charges to Stalinist-type slanders seems to have embarrassed at least the Healyites. When the Fourth Internationalists in Britain challenged the SLL to defend these charges, especially the claim that González was a police agent, the response was not very reassuring. In the January 17, 1970, issue of *Workers Press*, "Assistant National Secretary" of the SLL Mike Banda argued that it was all a matter of mistranslation. The passage in question, he claimed, should read: "Today it is seriously suspected that Mr. Gonzales [sic] himself *would work* on behalf of the Bolivian government" [Banda's emphasis].

This was not the first time, of course, that an SLL "theoretician" sought a way out of his difficulties by resorting to gibberish. In fact, this approach is rather typical of the Healyites' much celebrated "method." But in this case the transparency of the tactic—to say nothing of the illiterate disregarding of the idiomatic use of the French conditional mood—seemed to indicate more than usual discomfiture.

That the Healyites did not expect much more from the Lora affair than a chance to fling a few wild charges against the Fourth International was indicated by the subsequent scarcity of references in their press to their new-found Latin American ally. In the world of the British far left—which has been rather isolated from the international revolutionary movement and severely afflicted by sectarianism—Healy could hope to raise some doubts and reinforce some suspicions about the Trotskyist movement in the rest of the world. In this way, he could divert attention from the national narrowness of his own organization. Thus, presumably, from Healy's standpoint, Lora had only limited uses.

Under the pressure of a much better informed and much more internationally oriented left, Healy's French allies seem to have placed a much greater value on their Bolivian contact. In addition to the article in *La Correspondance Internationale* quoted above, many reports on the positions of the Lora group appeared in *Informations Ouvrières*. A good number of articles from Lora's paper *Masas* were translated and reprinted. The July 9, 1971, issue of *Jeune Révolutionnaire*, the organ of the Lambertist AJS [Alliance des Jeunes pour le Socialisme—Alliance of Youth for Socialism] carried an interview with the Lora group's youth leader Victor Sossa. In its July 7, 1971, issue, *Informations Ouvrières* printed another interview with him.

Although the Lambertists seem to have had no second thoughts about supporting Lora's slanders of imprisoned Bolivian fighters, they apparently quickly became alarmed by what they viewed as a dangerous sloppiness in programmatic formulations. This concern developed to the point that the OCI began a public polemic with Lora. In the October 1970 issue of its theoretical journal *La Verité*, it published the letter, already mentioned, to the Lora group dated July 30, 1970, and signed by its Political Committee.

What upset the OCI leadership were several imprecise or incomplete formulations, as well as the absence of some important theoretical points from the *Teses* of the COB [Central Obrera Boliviana—Bolivian Workers' Federation], a contradictory document reflecting the pressures of the various tendencies in the labor movement.

The OCI granted that some bad passages might be owing to Stalinist influences but blamed the Lora group for voting for the document as a whole. The argument was long and complex but the main criticism seemed to be that the document was not sufficiently internationalist.

The OCI letter noted:

> In the theses of the COB, we read:
> "History teaches us that in the present stage, which is marked by the disintegration of imperialism, the backward countries will achieve their goal of civilization—complete and harmonious development of their economies—only by the road of socialism."
>
> That is an incomplete formulation, which, if taken further, would become a false position. Not just the backward countries but also the advanced ones cannot achieve complete and harmonious development of their economies except by socialism. And in the case of both, experience has shown that it is impossible to envisage this goal as achievable by *any* country acting in *isolation*.

The same issue of *La Vérité* printed an article listed as taken from the August 25, 1970, issue of *Masas*, which replied to the OCI criticisms. It said, among other things:

> The comrades will understand very well that a trade-union document is one thing and a party document another.
>
> It is clear that the most revolutionary union has many limitations by comparison with a revolutionary party. It is sufficient, in this regard, to note that a union has the character of a united front of various tendencies operating and living in the working class.
>
> We believe that we are correct when we describe as ultimatists those who try to impose—by reprehensible methods totally alien to the revolutionary arsenal—the totality of their party program on trade-union organiza-

tions. In Bolivia we have had a long experience in this regard. When the so-called Pulacayo theses were adopted by the miners, we saw a proliferation of critics—including many people who called themselves Trotskyists and ended up later by capitulating to nationalist and even imperialist tendencies—who were astonished that in this document we had not raised all the questions that arise in a revolutionary party (the nature of the vanguard, of the future government, etc.). It is true that there were also in this document confused passages and many gaps on important questions. At the time an underestimation or ignorance of the international question could already have been noted.

Still the facts later demonstrated that this document, which was indisputably limited and imperfect in many points, served as the axis for one of the most powerful revolutionary mobilizations ever known in this country. This was possible because on the crucial aspects of the Bolivian political situation the document contained clear answers.

In defense of the COB document, *Masas* wrote:

> The most vital political problem at present is to give a clear answer to the nationalist, that is capitalist, reforms the military chiefs now in power are trying to carry out.
>
> The Trotskyists have given an answer by restating the central thesis of the theory of permanent revolution in the best possible form. The attempt of the bourgeois nationalists to carry through the democratic tasks is condemned to failure. This objective can only be achieved if the proletariat can assume the leadership in the process and take power in order to achieve the democratic tasks fully and transform them into socialist ones.
>
> The theses of the COB open the perspective of a struggle for socialism not in a distant and vague future but at present, as the result of the political process that we are experiencing. This idea constitutes the backbone of the entire document. And this is the way in which all our enemies have understood it. That is why the government, as well as the industrialists and a whole gamut of imperialist agents, have roused themselves for a furious battle against the document adopted by the workers' congresses.

It would be encouraging if Lora succeeded in convincing the OCI leaders to be less formal in their approach. Despite the poor basis on which they came together, this would be a good result of their bloc. Unfortunately, we know nothing about their further discussions.

Criticism also came from Lora's British ally. But not until after the coup, when Lora was, at least temporarily, *hors de combat*. But if the Healyites waited a bit long before voicing their objections to the course Lora was following, they did not let any time pass after this decisive event.

The attack came in the August 24 issue of *Workers Press* [WP] in an article entitled "Laying blame for defeat in Bolivia." It could not, thus, have been written later than one day after the coup was completed. In fact, since it is signed by a *"Workers Press* correspondent," should we assume that it was written the day of the take-over itself?

There is a certain vagueness in the analysis, which does not, however, seem to be a result of haste. "Responsibility for this defeat rests squarely at the door of Castroism and Stalinism," the "correspondent" wrote. But there are at least two Stalinist parties in Bolivia and a number of groupings influenced by the Cuban revolution. Who were the specific culprits? The "correspondent" gives us a discreet hint:

> *Granma*, indeed, said that there might be a coup—but then again there might not! In the words of Filemon Escobar:
>
> "If there isn't any coup, we will work for political objectives that help radicalize the present process—for example, worker-participation in COMIBOL (Bolivian Mining Corporation). These measures haven't been put into effect as yet (!) but they . . . are all demands of the Assembly."

The main task, then, was not to arm the workers militarily and politically to defeat counter-revolution and carry through a revolution, but—again in the words of Escobar—"that the people at the grassroots level be made aware of the resolutions of the assembly in order to continue making progress along the road to revolution."

In this way, by sowing illusions in powerless Assemblies and "worker-participation" instead of arming the masses; by unswerving support for "left" military regimes; Stalinism and Castroism prepares [sic] the way for ever more defeats in Latin America.

But the *"Workers Press* correspondent" does not tell us specifically just what organization this reprehensible Escobar spoke for. He does say that Escobar was one of a "Bolivian delegation to the celebrations of the 18th anniversary of the Cuban Revolution." Was he condemned implicitly as a "Castroist" just for attending the celebration of the anniversary of revolution? Or was it because he was one of the signers of the statement of this delegation which said the following?

> We would like to inform the revolutionary people of Cuba and their Revolutionary Government about one of the most important agreements made by the Bolivian workers' power.
> The People's Assembly has decided to launch an all-out struggle to obtain immediate diplomatic, commercial and cultural relations with our brothers in Cuba, Chile and the People's Republic of China.
> With this declaration, the People's Assembly pays tribute to Ernesto Che Guevara, Major of the Americas, who died fighting for the revolutionary unity of Latin America. In this way we express our concept of proletarian internationalism in an objectively revolutionary manner.

Was it because of this statement that the *Workers Press* "correspondent" failed to note that Escobar is a leading member of the Lora group? In any case, we seem, finally, to have an answer to the question of whether Lora shared the Healy-Lambert position that Cuba is a capitalist state. How could you "express proletarian internationalism" by paying tribute to the representative of a bourgeois regime or at best a petty-bourgeois adventurer?

This statement must have been especially jarring to the Healyites, since early this year *Workers Press* ran a multiple-part series on Cuba, calling, among other things, for a revolution against Fidel Castro. Under the subheading "Overthrow," another *WP* correspondent with the colorful name of "Rumi Yajuar" ["Rock Blood" in Quechua] wrote:

> The realization of a workers' state in Cuba implies necessarily the revolutionary overthrow of Fidel Castro, its [sic] petty-bourgeois entourage and its Stalinist stooges.
> This task can only be realized by the working class. The emancipation of the working class can be realized by the working class itself and only under the leadership of its own conscious advanced guard: the revolutionary Marxist party.
> This is true in Cuba, in Syria, in England or anywhere else in this planet. As revolutionary Marxists, as Bolsheviks, as Leninists, as Trotskyists, this is our task!
> Long live the forces of the International Committee of the Fourth International! [*Workers Press*, June 22, 1971.]

It is understandable, thus, that the Healyites would be reluctant to admit that the forces of the IC in Bolivia may not have shared their position on the Cuban regime.

Such an admission could be expected to be all the more embarrassing since in the six-part letter to Joseph Hansen, already cited, Robert Black singled out the support given by the American Trotskyists to the Cuban revolution as proof of their incorrigible revisionism. The series ended, in fact, on this stirring note:

> The time has now come to make a political, theoretical and historical accounting of ten years of Castroism.
> As its main publicist within the SWP [Socialist Workers party], you have acted as a conduit for relaying petty-bourgeois ideology into your own party.
> Castro's individualism found a ready response in your own native American pragmatism, against which Trotsky warned so many times in his period of political collaboration with the SWP.

You have betrayed the heritage of Trotskyism, and served as the mouthpiece for the enemies of the Latin American socialist revolution.

Not only the Socialist Labour League, but the entire international movement will indict you for this treachery. [*Workers Press*, February 2, 1971.]

Another reason the *WP* correspondent may have failed to note that Escobar was a representative of the Lora group, and thus, theoretically, of the same organization to which he himself belongs, the IC, was that the Healyites did not make the same assessment of Lora's role in the upsurge in the period preceding the rightist coup as their French allies did.

In his article in the August 24 issue of *WP*, "correspondent" wrote:

> According to *Granma*, the goals of the revolutionary masses in Bolivia were being reflected through the People's Assembly.
>
> As we pointed out in yesterday's *Workers Press*, this was granted by Torres *only as an advisory body*, in order to syphon off the demands of the masses. [Emphasis in original.]

The role played by the People's Assembly in the Bolivian process was, in fact, a vital one. But on this crucial question the Lambertists held a position diametrically opposite to that of their British cothinkers.

In its June 30–July 7, 1971, issue, next to a long report on a lecture given to the AJS by "Comrade Gerry Healy," *Informations Ouvrières* wrote that "very tentatively" at least it was "possible to make the following assessment of the situation" in Bolivia.

> 1. A new stage in the development of the revolutionary process has victoriously begun. The threat of a military coup by the right grouped around the officer corps has been crushed. The People's Assembly has met and deliberated under the protection of the armed workers' and peasants' militia.
>
> The reactionary forces have been unable to prevent the People's Assembly from meeting. Thus, they have suffered a defeat all the more important politically because they had announced previously their intention of overthrowing Torres and blocking the Assembly from meeting. Of the greatest political importance also is the fact that the workers, peasants, and students have risen up, arms in hand, to protect their delegates and assure that they could meet without obstacles being placed in their path.
>
> 2. The meeting of the People's Assembly and the nature of the first decisions it has taken have laid the foundations of a situation of dual power. . . .

As for Healy-Lambert-Wohlforth's cothinkers in Argentina, the *Politica Obrera* grouping, they described this [nefarious, according to Healy] assembly as virtually an invention of the Lora POR. In the August 24, 1971, issue of their publication, they wrote:

> In May and early July nobody outside of the POR thought that the People's Assembly would meet and function effectively. This attitude persisted even in July, that is, the doubt persisted that the masses would begin to mobilize through the opening provided by the People's Assembly.

Perhaps it was such basic differences over the question of the People's Assembly that led to the total confusion on this question in the September 8 issue of *Workers Press*, which reprinted Wohlforth's "Bitter Lessons" article in full. In an introductory note, the editors say: "In May he [Torres] set up the 'Peoples' [sic] Assembly' to act as a safety valve for the masses."

On the very same page as this editorial note and "Bitter Lessons," a dispatch allegedly written by "a Latin American correspondent J. Gomez" says:

> The People's Councils ('Assambleas [sic] Populares') which appeared recently in Bolivia were a new working-class organization—new, that is, for Latin America.
>
> But for the weakness of working-class leadership, these councils could have acquired the characteristics of soviets, such as the ones that led to the conquest of political power by the

working class in Russia in 1917.

But even if they were not actual soviets, a dual power situation existed in Bolivia. The 'Assambleas [sic] Populares' had constituted themselves in a working body without permission from the bourgeois state.

The working class, represented by all the trade unions and by the working-class parties, held by statutory decision at least 60 per cent of the votes.

The 'Assambleas [sic] Populares' sat and worked in the former legislative palace and in the provinces in state-owned buildings without asking anyone's authorization.

The decisions taken there did not only concern the policies of the working class, but also actual governmental decisions, disputing the prerogatives of the bourgeois state.

The comment by the editors in the September 8 *WP* ends on a high note: "Despite the treachery of the Stalinists and revisionists the Bolivian workers will succeed in assimilating the lessons of August and build a mass revolutionary leadership on Trotskyist foundations." Despite the pompous language in which it is expressed, this is a commendable sentiment.

But the entire history of the Wohlforth-Lambert-Healy combination's relationship with its Bolivian cothinkers indicates that this unprincipled sectarian bloc can make no contribution whatever to achieving such a result. Dead-end factionalism, which is such a striking feature of the combination, led them not only to become accomplices in crimes against the Bolivian revolutionary fighters, but ultimately to complete political incoherence. We can expect with some confidence that the Bolivian workers and revolutionists will learn the lessons of August. The outlook for the Wohlforth-Lambert-Healy group is more dubious. But we can only hope that their Bolivian experience has taught them something.

The Lambertist View of the Bolivian Events

The defeat suffered by the Bolivian workers in the military coup of August 18–22 has raised again a number of basic questions of revolutionary strategy and tactics. In this, some negative lessons have been provided by the sectarian combination that entitles itself the "International Committee for the Reconstruction of the Fourth International."

This group was affected by the Bolivian coup because it includes the POR headed by Guillermo Lora, a well-known figure in Bolivia who played a role in the events leading up to the right-wing take-over. The inclusion of Lora in the International Committee was a marriage of factional convenience.[1]

It should be mentioned that there are two parties in Bolivia named the POR (Partido Obrero Revolucionario—Revolutionary Workers party). In opposition to the POR headed by Lora is the POR headed by Hugo González Moscoso. This is the Bolivian section of the Fourth International. The two groupings united following the Reunification Congress of the Fourth International in 1963. Lora, however, soon organized a split.

The coup in Bolivia led to some striking differences in opinion among the components of the International Committee. For instance, Tim Wohlforth, expressing his personal views in the August 30 issue of the *Bulletin*, weekly organ of the Workers League, attacked Lora in these terms:

> Lora, in collaboration with the Bolivian Stalinists and with the agreement of the Bolivian and international Pabloites, failed to fight at any point for the overthrow of the Torres military regime. Thus he, along with the rest of the Popular Assembly, acted as a left cover for Torres while the right wing elements in Torres' own army prepared and finally executed their coup.

Intercontinental Press, October 18, 1971.

1. See "Disaster in Bolivia for Healy-Lambert-Wohlforth," in *Intercontinental Press*, September 27, p. 816, for a history of this unprincipled bloc.—*IP*

The Workers League is an American satellite of the British-based Socialist Labour League, headed by Gerry Healy; and the September 8 issue of the SLL organ, *Workers Press*, reprinted this attack.

In what appears to be a public reply, the Organisation Communiste Internationaliste (Internationalist Communist Organization), the French-based component of the IC headed by Pierre Lambert, published the following resolution on Bolivia in the September 29 issue of its paper, *Informations Ouvrières*. This was not signed by Lambert but was passed as a formal statement by the Central Committee of the OCI.

Up to now the International Committee itself has made no comment on the events in Bolivia, and its point of view is not known. Since the IC is obviously deeply divided over this issue, it is to be hoped that it has organized a discussion among its warring cliques as to what is to be done about the situation.

For our part, we invite the *Bulletin* and the *Workers Press* to reprint our translation of the OCI resolution so as to bring their supporters up to date on the views of their French comrades.

❦

Having studied the Bolivian situation on the basis of all the available documentation—in particular the report on the development of the revolutionary struggle written by Comrade Guillermo Lora, secretary of the Revolutionary Workers party of Bolivia—the Central Committee of the Organisation Communiste Internationaliste, section of the International Committee for the Reconstruction of the Fourth International, emphatically declares its total solidarity with the POR—which is also a Trotskyist party and a member of the International Committee for the Reconstruction of the Fourth International—in the struggle it is leading in Bolivia for a workers and peasants' government and a state based on soviets.

The Central Committee of the OCI notes that the International Committee has characterized the period opened by the May–June 1968 general strike [in France] and the process of political revolution in Czechoslovakia, as a period of the imminence of the revolution, that is, a period in which class confrontations challenge the state power. It declares that the process of the class struggle in Bolivia fits perfectly into this perspective. In fact, in their struggle against the domination of Yankee imperialism and the wretched Bolivian bourgeoisie, the worker and peasant masses in Bolivia rallied around an organ of the soviet type. As in the case of the Irbid soviet in Palestine and the workers' councils in the Polish Baltic ports, the creation of the People's Assembly expressed the fundamental tendency of this period, i.e., the determination of the workers and the peasant masses to launch a struggle for a government of their own.

The CC of the OCI, member of the International Committee, hails the heroic struggle waged by the Bolivian POR in a situation where all of the forces of imperialism have been concentrating on crushing this profound aspiration of the Bolivian masses to destroy the bourgeois state and capitalist productive and property relations and create a workers' government.

In the coup d'etat organized by the CIA and the military dictatorships of Brazil and Argentina, and facilitated by the Torres government, the CC of the OCI sees proof that the policy followed by the POR was in fundamental harmony with the interests of the workers of Bolivia and of the entire world. The facts agree. At every stage in the process, the political fight waged by the POR has enabled the masses to preserve their class independence vis-à-vis Torres and to frustrate the maneuvers aimed at subordinating them once again to bourgeois and petty-bourgeois nationalism.

It was the POR's policy that made it possible to maintain to the end a class united-front of the proletariat and all its political and trade-union organizations at the government level represented by the People's Assembly. It was this unity in and around the People's Assembly, an organ of dual power, that, under the leadership of the Trotskyist party, the POR, marked the entirety of the revolutionary process before and after the clashes of August 20–23.

The Moscow bureaucracy was not far wrong when it condemned its Bolivian party in its press for capitulating to the POR.

To all of the petty-bourgeois currents, the POR gave an example of armed struggle based on workers' militias and fully integrated into the movement of workers struggling for their liberation.

Yankee imperialism saw things clearly when, on the first day of the fascist uprising in Santa Cruz, it said through the columns of the *Washington Post* that the Bolivian situation was far graver than the one in Chile, that it confronted the United States with a more dangerous state of things even than the Cuban revolution in 1959, inasmuch as the Bolivian masses had begun to struggle for a "workers' government."

The CC of the OCI declares that the Bolivian revolution meshes with the East Berlin uprising of 1953, with the revolution of the Hungarian workers' councils, with the movements for political revolution of the Czechoslovak people, with the struggle of the Polish workers, with the May–June 1968 general strike in France, with the struggles of the English proletariat against the Conservative government, with the strike against General Motors in the U. S. A., with the struggles of the Spanish proletariat against Franco, with the struggle of the Argentinian proletariat against military dictatorship, with the struggle of the world working class to end the domination of imperialism and that of the Stalinist bureaucracy, which has entered into alliance with it. This fact is what caused the imperialist intervention, and it explains the hatred of the Bolivian revolution by the entire international bourgeoisie, the Moscow bureaucracy and its Stalinist parties, as well as by all the petty-bourgeois parties.

The CC of the OCI, member of the International Committee, declares that those who attack the Bolivian POR are attacking the party which has been the inspirer and driving force of the People's Assembly, i.e., the organ that incarnated the struggle of the Bolivian people to create their own government and which was opening the way toward a dictatorship of the proletariat in Bolivia. In attacking the POR, these elements mark themselves as enemies of the dictatorship of the proletariat. They take the side of imperialism and Stalinism. They assume the role of agents of the counterrevolution and are conscious or unconscious enemies of the Fourth International.

The CC of the OCI, member of the International Committee, notes that the elements that are attacking the POR and displaying their total incapacity to understand the meaning of the struggle of the Bolivian masses are the same elements that gave the tide of "revolutionist" to Ho Chi Minh, the man who covered up the murder of the Trotskyist leader Ta Thu Tau, the same elements that accommodated to Nasser and then to the petty-bourgeois leaders of the Palestinian resistance, the elements that have tried to justify the Kremlin's intervention in Czechoslovakia by claiming the existence of counterrevolutionary threats. All these elements take their rightful place in the camp of the slanderers of the heroic struggle of the POR, a number of whose leaders fell in the civil war, paying the heavy price of the struggle for the international proletarian revolution.

The CC of the OCI, which in 1951–52 began the struggle to safeguard the continuity of the Fourth International, i.e., the link with the struggle of Lenin, Trotsky, and Bolshevism, against those who followed Pablo in his attempt to liquidate the Fourth International by capitulating to the Stalinist bureaucracy, notes that the Pabloite United Secretariat has once again come out against the POR and the Fourth International[2] and taken the side of the Stalinist bureaucracy, as it did in 1953 at the time of the East Berlin uprising and the French general strike, as it did at the time of the second intervention in Hungary in 1956, and as it has at every crucial moment in the class struggle.

Today when all the perspectives on which Leon Trotsky based his struggle are taking clearer and more concrete form, in step with the acceleration of the joint crisis of imperialism and the bureaucracy, and when confrontations posing the question of power are increasing, the CC of the OCI states that it will pursue with all necessary firmness the struggle it began twenty years ago. For this is a struggle for the victory of the proletarian world revolution, for a worldwide government of soviets, for building revolutionary parties, sections of the Fourth International in every country, and for reconstructing the Fourth International, the indispensable instrument of victory.

SEPTEMBER 17, 1971

---

2. The Lambertists are referring, of course, to the POR of Lora and the "Fourth International" that Lora is helping Healy, Lambert, and Wohlforth to "reconstruct." For a contrasting view, see the quotation, cited in our editorial note, in which Wohlforth accuses Lora of acting "with the agreement of the Bolivian and international Pabloites."—*IP*

Lambertist 'Declaration' on Socialist Labour League

The following is a translation by *Intercontinental Press* of an open *"Déclaration"* that has been printed as a leaflet and distributed by the thousands in Paris by the Organisation Communiste Internationaliste (OCI—Internationalist Communist Organization).

The declaration makes a number of obscure references. To appreciate these, a bit of background is required.

In 1963, the majority of the International Committee and the International Secretariat, two factions within the Fourth International, decided to participate in an effort to reunite the world Trotskyist movement, which had been split for almost a decade. A minority of the International Committee headed by Gerry Healy of the British-based Socialist Labour League and Pierre Lambert of the OCI rejected this course and set up a rump "International Committee" for the purpose of "reconstructing" the Fourth International.

In the opinion of this grouping, the majority of the International Committee, including the leadership of the Socialist Workers party in the United States, had "sold out" to the International Secretariat (referred to in the open "Declaration" below as the "Pabloites"—although the adherents of the "International Committee" now use the term as an epithet designating any grouping outside of their own that considers itself to be Trotskyist).

In the light of this background, the main interest in the "Declaration" lies in the sharp public attack leveled against what constitutes a sizeable minority, if not the majority, of the rump "International Committee," that is, the Socialist Labour League and its American satellite grouping, the Workers League.

The tone of the declaration indicates that the disarray in this unprincipled bloc is such as to make "reconstruction" of the "International Committee" a hardly promising enterprise.

For further material on the background, as well as the differences over the Bolivian events referred to in the open declaration, see "Disaster in Bolivia for Healy-Lambert-Wohlforth," in *Intercontinental Press*, September 27, p. 816, and "The Lambertist View of the Bolivian Events," in *Intercontinental Press*, October 18, p. 894.

The delegations of the Political Bureau of the OCI, French section of the International Committee for the reconstruction of the Fourth International; of the POR [Partido Obrero Revolucionario], Bolivian section of the International Committee; and of the Committee for Organization of the Communists (Trotskyists) of the countries of the East have discussed some questions of common interest raised by the combat led by the POR, the significance of which is stated as follows:

Since the General Strike in France and the process of the Political Revolution in Czechoslovakia, the question of the working class taking political power has stood at the heart of every struggle of the workers and the youth throughout the world. In face of decomposing imperialism which offers them misery, unemployment, fascist barbarism, and wars of extermination; in face of the bureaucracy which threatens to destroy the conquests of the glorious October 1917 Revolution, and which holds back and breaks up their struggles, all the demands and the will to resist of the workers, their whole desire to live, require a direct and immediate struggle to seize power, in order to set up a workers' government.

Never has the conquest of power by the proletariat appeared as such a clear task, so realizable, so urgent!

The creation of the Irbid soviet by the oppressed Palestinian masses, the committees and councils formed by the Polish working class, the Bolivian People's Assembly materialized the convergence of the struggles toward this immediate aim, although they proceeded through different stages and forms toward the Universal Soviet Republic.

It was in BOLIVIA that this forward march of the working class toward its own power reached its highest level, rich in experiences, expressing and realizing the most profound aspiration of the international working class as a whole. At the head of the Bolivian workers stood the Revolutionary Workers Party, armed with the Program of the Fourth International, tempered by decades of tenacious struggle for the proletarian revolution against nationalism, against Stalinism, against Pabloite revisionism, and against all varieties of the petty bourgeoisie, such as guerrillaism, solidly

Intercontinental Press, November 1, 1971.

rooted in the most militant sections of the Bolivian proletariat. Because this Party had prepared this combat, it was prepared for it; it knew how to seize the occasion and, at each step of the revolutionary process, bring to maturity the conditions for the working class to take power. In the process of the Bolivian revolution were concentrated not only the aspiration of the workers throughout the world to have their own government, but also and above all, the lessons and experiences on the means and methods to obtain this. The realization of class unity through the Workers United Front, driving power of the Anti-imperialist United Front, was embodied in the People's Assembly, the organ of power. It was for this unity, assembling the indispensable conditions for the assault on power, that the Revolutionary Workers Party of Bolivia, member of the International Committee for the Reconstruction of the Fourth International, worked.

This experience of struggling for a worker-peasant government, by a Trotskyist Party and under its leadership, a vital experience for the international working class, revives the universal lessons of the October 1917 Revolution. This constitutes the most worthy commemoration of it on the eve of its next anniversary. It is thus the positive response to the Councils of the Hungarian Revolution which, fifteen years ago, vainly sought for an organized political leadership. It is the Trotskyist demonstration of a combat to provide an organized and centralized force to the struggle of the proletariat as a whole marching toward power against the French Stalinists who betrayed and broke up the 1968 General Strike, battling the efforts of the OCI in behalf of such an organized centralization.

Today, the PCF [Parti Communiste Français] is conducting a campaign of slanders against the POR with the aim of diverting the proletariat from accomplishing its revolutionary tasks. The international apparatus of the Kremlin finds, in this work, the most real support in the campaign of the Pabloites of all kinds (Ligue Communiste, Lutte Ouvrière, etc.) against the POR engaged in struggle.

No one mistakes the target. All the hidden and open enemies of the dictatorship of the proletariat and its Party are heaping mountains of lies and slanders today against the Revolutionary Workers Party of Bolivia. The Stalinists who, on an international scale and under all circumstances battle against class independence such as was realized in the People's Assembly and firmly maintained thanks to the POR, are glorifying class collaboration in CHILE, condemning not only the POR but the Bolivian CP which, in the People's Assembly, was constrained to accept the United Front. All the petty-bourgeois currents are spitting their hate against the Revolutionary Workers Party of Bolivia because it vigorously resisted the adventures of the sects, firmly guiding the combat of the popular masses towards a workers' government. Particularly active in the Petty-bourgeois Front against the POR are to be found the Pabloites of all shadings from "Lutte Ouvrière," from the so-called "Communist" League, and from the United Secretariat of renegades from the Fourth International. The very ones who have been glorifying the petty-bourgeois leaders—from Stalinists like Gomulka to Yassir Arafat—who reached an unprincipled agreement with the representatives of the bourgeoisie in the "Vietnam Committees." These same petty-bourgeois are attacking the POR which knew how to express the revolutionary process in Bolivia. They are capitulating in Latin America, as in France and everywhere to the so-called spontanéist currents of the petty bourgeoisie in order to participate in the Stalinist barrage against the revolutionary upsurge of the masses which, in every country, places at stake the dictatorship of the proletariat, the democracy of Councils.

It is precisely because the events in Bolivia condense to the highest degree the march of the international working class toward power, bringing to the fore all the decisive problems of the conquest of power as well as the activity of the Trotskyist Party in the heart of this world process, in an epoch of overturns and sharp turns, that the unresolved problems stemming from the crisis of the Fourth International which Pablo, Mandel, Frank, etc., sought to destroy in 1950, are finding their expression, including within the International Committee.

Only petty-bourgeois elements find any reason for surprise in this.

The history of the Fourth International, since its foundation by Leon Trotsky in 1938, has consisted of a difficult combat to maintain it against immense forces in league to destroy it. Only the Fourth International, through its Program and its tireless struggles, has always battled for the class independence of the proletariat, for the world proletarian revolution against imperialism and class-collaborationist Stalinism. That is why it was, is still, the target of the ferocious attacks of all the enemies of the proletariat. The Fourth International constitutes the real stake in the whole world class struggle, because it is the continuator of Bolshevism, of the October Revolution. The Trotskyists who, since 1950, have resisted the policy of capitulating before the bureaucracy which constitutes the very substance of Pabloism, the Trotskyist organizations which, in 1953, constituted the International Committee, have alone assured the continuity of the Fourth International and thus preserved the conditions indispensable for the construction in each country of the guiding Revolutionary Workers Party, national section of the Fourth International.

What is more natural than that all the difficult problems of the whole international class struggle should be reflected and concentrated within it? What is more natural than that the stake in a gigantic world combat should be translated into the crises of the Fourth International as it is translated into the crisis of all the organizations of the working class?

Today, the leadership of certain organizations of the International Committee, like the Socialist Labour League and the Workers League, lacking the necessary clarity with regard to the strategy for the conquest of power and the reconstruction of the Fourth International, have given way to the enormous pressures by attacking the POR.

The three delegations, meeting in Paris, while holding that a discussion is legitimate, both between the sections adhering to the IC as well as within each of the sections, condemns the method utilized by the Workers League and the SLL which, without even having studied the reports issued by the leadership of the POR, have undertaken to publicly condemn the Bolivian section of the IC.

That is why the delegations of the OCI and of the Committee for the Organization of the countries [sic] of the East approves the demand made by Comrade G. Lora, insisting that the IC be convened in a plenary session in the shortest possible time in order to take a stand on the report on the Bolivian Revolution and the tasks of reconstructing the Fourth International which the leadership of the POR has prepared.

PARIS, OCTOBER 12, 1971

Guillermo Lora, Secretary of the POR of Bolivia, member of the International Committee for the reconstruction of the Fourth International.

Pierre Lambert, of the CC of the OCI, French section of the International Committee for the reconstruction of the Fourth International.

Balazs Nagy, Responsable [leader] of the Ligue des Revolutionnaires Socialistes de Hongrie [League of Socialist Revolutionists of Hungary], member of the International Committee for the reconstruction of the Fourth International, Responsable of the Committee for the Organization of the Communists (Trotskyists) of the countries of the East.

The Healyite Case Against the Lambertists

In our November 1 issue, we published a translation of an open declaration, dated October 12 and signed by Guillermo Lora of the Partido Obrero Revolucionario (POR—Revolutionary Workers party, a Bolivian grouping), Pierre Lambert of the Organisation Communiste Internationaliste (OCI—Internationalist Communist Orga-

Intercontinental Press, November 22, 1971.

nization, the French section of the "International Committee"), and Balazs Nagy, a Hungarian leader of the International Committee. The open declaration, which was widely distributed in Paris by the OCI, attacked other members of the International Committee, namely, the Socialist Labour League (SLL) of Great Britain and the Workers League (WL) of the United States.

The SLL and the WL have responded in kind. In a

release entitled "Statement by the International Committee of the Fourth International (Majority) October 24, 1971," they announce that the International Committee has split wide open. By way of explanation, the authors have made public for the first time some of the issues over which the two sides have been warring.

The statement is of considerable interest to those who follow developments among the groupings claiming adherence to Trotskyism. We are therefore reproducing it in its entirety, including the subheads, utilizing the text published in the November 5 issue of the *Workers Press*, the newspaper of the Central Committee of the SLL. We have sought to follow copy exactly as published in the *Workers Press* except for obvious typographical errors.

Since the document is not without obscure references, we have provided footnotes to help clarify various points. These have been prepared by Joseph Hansen, the editor of *Intercontinental Press*. For further material on the background and immediate issues that precipitated the split, see the September 27, October 18, and November 1 issues of *Intercontinental Press*.

We would suggest that our readers suspend judgment on the merits of the arguments until both sides have had full opportunity to explain their points of view. No doubt Lambert, Lora, and Nagy will soon reply to the claims and assertions of their factional opponents. As the polemic develops, new facts can be expected to be revealed that should be taken into account in drawing a final balance sheet on the dispute.

✍

1. A new period for the Trotskyist movement

• The Fourth International, founded by Leon Trotsky in 1938, now faces the greatest change and the greatest challenge in its history. Capitalism's international economic crisis entered a completely new stage on August 15, 1971, when President Nixon administered the death blow to all the economic and political relations imposed by the ruling class, assisted by the Stalinist bureaucracy, in 1944–1945.

In the new conditions, the working class is everywhere driven into struggles for power, and the Trotskyist movement has now unprecedented opportunities for assembling and training the revolutionary working-class leadership. The conditions of defeat in which the movement was founded, the war which followed, and then the long years of post-war boom, means that the fight for the continuity of revolutionary Marxism was a fight against Stalinist repression, against isolation and under conditions unfavourable for the development of Marxist theory.

Trotskyism suffered from revisionist attempts to liquidate the Fourth International, and since 1953, when Pablo and his group split from the Fourth International only the International Committee of the Fourth International has fought for the continuity of Trotskyism.[1] Now the International Committee

---

1. This statement is inaccurate. In 1953 a sharp factional struggle broke out in the world Trotskyist movement. Michel Pablo, the secretary of the Fourth International at the time, headed one faction. The other was led by James P. Cannon, the present national chairman of the Socialist Workers party. At Cannon's suggestion, this faction set up a coordinating body, the International Committee. The other side was led by the International Secretariat. Prominent among those adhering to the International Committee were Gerry Healy, currently the secretary of the Socialist Labour League, and Pierre Lambert, the present main leader of the Organisation Communiste Internationaliste.

By 1957, the main political differences separating the International Committee and the International Secretariat had been overcome; but a reunification was deliberately blocked by both Healy and Pablo. The continuation of the split, however, became more and more difficult to justify, and the two sides finally united on a principled basis at a reunification congress held in 1963. (For the statement of principles on which the two sides agreed, see the May 11, 1970, issue of *Intercontinental Press*.)

A minority of the International Committee headed by Healy and Lambert refused to participate in the reunification. They set up the rump "International Committee" which has now ended in an irretrievable split. On the side of the International Secretariat, a group headed by Juan Posadas likewise refused to participate.

Pablo at first greeted the reunification of the world Trotskyist movement. However, maintaining a faction of his own, he soon took a split course that brought him and his group outside of the Fourth International by 1965. This group is still in existence.

While proclaiming adherence to Trotskyism, Pablo today stands on such concepts as "centuries of degenerated workers states" and the possibility of Communist parties "reforming" themselves, which he advanced some two decades ago and which helped precipitate the factional struggle and split of that time. From about 1955 until 1965, he retreated publicly from these positions. Upon setting up shop as an independent formation, he proclaimed them publicly.

The United Secretariat of the Fourth International, formed by the fusion of the International Secretariat and the International Committee, does not agree with Pablo's views and has attacked them at various times. Healy and Lambert have disregarded all this and have continued to argue as if Pablo were still the secretary of the Fourth International and as if

has the task of building parties in every country capable of leading the struggle for power.

The leap in consciousness, the development of revolutionary theory and practice, necessary to meet this responsibility, involves an ideological struggle within the IC itself.

On October 12, 1971, a minority of the IC, i.e., two sections: The Hungarian LSH[2] and the French OCI, published a declaration denouncing the Socialist Labour League, the British section, and the Workers League USA (in political solidarity with the IC) for their criticisms of the Bolivian POR.

One of the signatories of the declaration is Guillermo Lora, Secretary of the POR, which is not a section of the International Committee. Its application for affiliation was to be considered at the next IC Conference (Fourth). The IC consists of British, Greek, Ceylonese, Hungarian, French and Canadian sections, together with the Irish and Mexican (LOM)[3] sections admitted at the 1970 pre-Conference of the IC.

Lambert (OCI) and Nagy (Hungary) do not speak for the IC, and this present document is the reply to their minority statement by the IC majority.[4]

The calling of a meeting in Paris advertising as Chairman, Stephen Just, 'Secretary of the IC for the reconstruction of the Fourth International', shows that the OCI has arrogated to itself the functions of the IC, rejected the IC, and nominated its own 'secretary' as opposed to the elected secretary.[5]

This is a split from the IC and its politics. It is a split by a minority.

On September 22, the OCI issued a public declaration denouncing as 'enemies of the dictatorship of the proletariat, agents of counter-revolution and enemies, conscious or unconscious, of the Fourth International, all those who attack the POR (Bolivian)'.[6] They refer to the SLL and the Workers League.

There is the International Committee of the Fourth International, resting on the foundation laid down by Trotsky in 1938, the first four Congresses of the Third International, and all the work of the IC since 1953, particularly the decisions of the 1966 Conference. And there is the bogus 'IC for the reconstruction of the Fourth International', represented by the OCI and the Hungarian section, who want to regroup with centrists *against* the Fourth International. This split, and not the Bolivian revolution and the Bolivian POR is the basic issue.[7]

2. The split at Essen

• This became crystal-clear at the Essen Youth Rally in July 1971.[8] There, representatives of the

---

his special views had been adopted by all the Trotskyists outside of their own "International Committee." Hence their use of the label "Pabloite" as an epithet that has nothing to do with current realities in the international Trotskyist movement.—J.H.

2. "Hungarian LSH." In the open declaration issued October 12, 1971, by the Lambertists, the group is listed as "Ligue des Revolutionnaires Socialistes de Hongrie" (League of Socialist Revolutionaries of Hungary). The correct initials would thus seem to be LSRH. Perhaps the Healyites are not too familiar with the organization and its activities.—J.H.

3. "LOM." The reference is to the Liga Obrera Marxista, a small group in Mexico whose main activity has been to supply occasional articles for the *Workers Press.*—J.H.

4. The authors of the statement fail to indicate whether their claim to represent the "majority" of the International Committee is based on the division of the membership as a whole or on the division among the component organizations, some of which consist of only a handful of individuals.—J.H.

5. The name of the "elected secretary" is not given. Thus the implications of advertising Stephen Just as "Secretary of the IC for the reconstruction of the Fourth International" remain unclear. Was the post regarded as a low-level job not requiring a publicly identifiable figure? Apparently so. At least the "elected secretary," presumably a member of the "majority," has not come forward as yet to denounce the usurper.—J.H.

6. For the text of the OCI public declaration, see the October 18, 1971, issue of *Intercontinental Press.*—J.H.

7. The International Committee headed by Lambert, Lora, Nagy, and Stephen Just is "bogus"? What about the rump "International Committee" set up by Healy and Lambert in 1963? It was just as bogus. The original International Committee was dissolved as a faction in the Fourth International following its participation in the 1963 Reunification Congress.—J.H.

8. This was a conference held in Essen, West Germany, July 3–4, 1971. According to the Lambertist paper *Informations Ouvrieres*, some 5,000 youth attended, including representatives or observers from nineteen organizations on five continents.

One ugly incident went unreported by *Informations Ou-*

OCI, the Hungarian section and the Mexican LOM, voted along with centrists and even right-wing organizations against the amendment to the main resolution put by the representative of the SLL and supported by representatives of a majority of the IC sections (Ceylon, Ireland, Canada, Greece, SLL).[9]

The issue was clear: the OCI and its associates voted against amendments stating that the only revolutionary international and revolutionary parties are the *Fourth* International. In their opposition they naturally received the support of the POUM (Spain)[10] and other centrists, as well as of the right-wing American National Students' Association. NSA is a right-wing student organization directly tied to the bourgeois establishment, even to the extent, under a previous leadership, of admittedly receiving funds from the CIA.[11] Its spokesman used the Essen rally as a platform for the Stalinist-supported 'People's Peace Treaty in Vietnam' campaign. Such are the dangers involved in the OCI's movement to centrism and centrist methods.

The OCI and its associates opposed and voted down the following amendment (presented by the SLL and supported by the majority of the IC sections: Greece, Canada, Ceylon, Ireland):

> There can be no revolutionary party without revolutionary theory. Behind every opportunist development in the history of the workers' movement, and especially of Stalinism, has been the revision of Marxist theory. The continuity of the struggle for revolutionary Marxist theory in the past, the struggle of the Fourth International and the International Committee, was the only basis for the initiatives which led to this rally and for the struggle to build the international revolutionary youth movement. Revolutionary youth everywhere must devote themselves above all to the task of developing Marxist

---

vrieres. Members of the Fourth International sought to pass out leaflets to the gathering. Monitors of the OCI used physical force against the leafleters. One was beaten and kicked. Others were driven away. (See "German Trotskyists Protest Assault by Ultralefts" in the September 20, 1971, issue of *Intercontinental Press.*)—J.H.

9. "Ceylon, Ireland, Canada, Greece, SLL." What country does "SLL" stand for? No country. The authors merely wanted to emphasize the very special position of the Healyite group in the "International Committee."—J.H.

10. The July 7, 1971, issue of *Informations Ouvrieres*, which offers considerable reportage on the Essen conference, does not list the POUM among the participating organizations.

During the Spanish Civil War, Leon Trotsky was of the opinion that the Partido Obrero de Unificacion Marxista (Workers Party of Marxist Unification) held the key to a socialist victory but threw it away because of centrist policies.

In the third of a century that has passed since then, both the leadership and membership of the POUM have changed. The Trotskyists of today, while bearing in mind the record of the previous generation, must be guided by an analysis of the current composition, program, and direction of movement of the POUM in determining their attitude toward it. Is it on this concrete analysis that the Healyites and Lambertists disagree? The statement is silent on the subject.—J.H.

11. According to *Informations Ouvrieres* (July 7, 1971), one observer from the NSA was present at the Essen conference. This was sufficient, however, for the authors of the statement to drag in the CIA. The saving phrase "under a previous leadership" should be noted. This presumably enables the authors to deny a deliberate attempt to smear the present leadership of the NSA (and their own Lambertist comrades) with the tarbrush of the CIA.

The NSA was only one of hundreds of organizations infiltrated by the CIA. In most instances the leaderships of the organizations caught up in the web did not know of the CIA involvement, since the CIA converted only selected individual leaders into pawns and undercover agents.

The highly secret campus activities of the spy agency were exposed by *Ramparts* magazine in February 1967. The scandal rocked public opinion in the United States and gave new impetus to the radicalization of the campus.

The press picked up the leads revealed by *Ramparts* and soon showed that the CIA had similarly penetrated any number of other organizations, including some very prominent trade unions in the United States, among them the United Automobile Workers (Walter Reuther himself was accused of taking funds from the CIA). The scandal went right up to the top bureaucrat of the AFL-CIO, George Meany, and his international lieutenant, Irving Brown.

Magazines, book publishers, radio and TV stations, cultural institutions, churches, youth groups, literally hundreds of different kinds of bodies were involved.

Among institutions in other countries, the French trade-union federation Force Ouvriere was named.

(For more about the revelations, see the March 3, March 17, and May 26, 1967, issues of *World Outlook*—the former name of *Intercontinental Press.*)

Out of the broad array of organizations victimized by the CIA, why did the authors of the statement single out the NSA? One imagines that the Lambertists will have something to say on this. Their comments should make instructive reading.—J.H.

theory through the struggle against bourgeois ideology in all the forms it takes in the workers' movement. This is the only basis for combating the dangers of adventurism, activism and "pure" militancy with which revisionists and Maoists mislead the youth, and which can only lead to historic defeats for the working class.[12]

This was already a split, the real split. They do not want the FI built on the foundations of dialectical materialism and the politics of Lenin and Trotsky, but they want a centrist amalgam of all those who want to disarm the masses by talk about 'revolutionary united fronts' and 'expressing the will of the masses'. Their 'IC for the reconstruction of the FI' is their fraudulent attempt to use the revolutionary name of the IC of the FI for their own opportunist aims. They will never succeed in doing this.

The majority of the IC rejected their unprincipled manoeuvre at Essen. Now they have chosen to stake everything on the issue of Bolivia, as a smokescreen for the real issues which they will not discuss.

Running away from the real theoretical and practical questions of building the FI, they propose to intimidate the movement with shouting about solidarity with the POR of Bolivia. This was the old trick used by the SWP on Cuba in 1963: no theoretical discussion and no criticism of Cuba; they are involved in a revolution.[13] Similarly Pablo excluded political discussion with his theory of the imminent Third World War.[14] And it must never be forgotten that the suppression of discussion on Cuba and Ceylon, used to effect the 'unification' of 1963, had as its direct consequence the entry of the Lanka Sama Samaja Party (LSSP), while still a section of the Pabloite Secretariat, into the bourgeois coalition of Mrs Bandaranaike.[15]

The vote of the OCI and the Hungarian section at Essen against the IC majority was carried out in front of an observer of the American Spartacist group of Robertson. This has an historical significance which cannot be overstated.

At the Third Conference of the IC in 1966, the French and Hungarian sections voted with the rest of the IC delegations for resolutions affirming the revolutionary continuity of the Fourth International. Opposing this were two groups invited as observers to the Conference, Robertson's Spartacists and the French 'Voix Ouvrière' (now 'Lutte Ouvrière'). As opportunists and pragmatists they denounced the IC's struggle for continuity against revisionism.

After the Conference, Robertson collaborated with Hansen and the revisionist Socialist Workers Party (SWP) in wholesale slander of the SLL and

---

12. This is typical of the abstract generalizations the leaders of the SLL are fond of. Why they insisted on its being put to a vote at the Essen conference—they in fact made it a splitting issue—and why, in face of the ultimatum, the Lambertists decided to vote it down, still remain to be explained concretely.—J.H.

13. The authors depart from the truth. The Socialist Workers party conducted a thoroughgoing internal discussion on the meaning of the Cuban revolution and its relation to the Chinese revolution and the overturn of capitalist property relations in Eastern Europe. The sharpest point of difference with Healy and his followers in the SWP came over his view that no revolution had occurred in Cuba and that Fidel Castro was another "Batista." Such a view, revealing absolute blindness to reality, would have made it impossible to defend the Cuban revolution had it been adopted.

For an analysis of Healy's position, see the chapter "SLL Revision of the Theory of the Permanent Revolution—the Case of Cuba" in Ernest Germain's booklet *Marxism vs.*

Ultraleftism—Key Issues in Healy's Challenge to the Fourth International.—J.H.

14. At the beginning of the 1950s, Pablo held that World War III could break out within several years. He did not exclude discussion on this question. The fact was that few were of an opposing opinion at the time. If Healy was among them, he certainly did not put it on record in a clear way.

On the basis of this wrong premise, Pablo drew a number of conclusions: (1) that there would not be sufficient time to build *mass* revolutionary parties; (2) that the labor bureaucracies, particularly those linked to Moscow or subject to the pressure of Moscow, would be impelled to engage in far-reaching actions against the war involving the masses; (3) that to exercise effective influence in these coming events, the cadres of the Fourth International had to engage wherever possible in the tactic of "entryism sui generis." (That is, enter the Communist and Social Democratic parties as rank-and-filers and seek to build a revolutionary wing within them while still maintaining a public Trotskyist organization and press.)—J.H.

15. The entry of the LSSP into the Bandaranaike coalition did not come as a "direct consequence" of the 1963 reunification of the world Trotskyist movement but *in spite of it*. See footnote No. 28 for more on this.—J.H.

the IC.[16] In its resolution at the 1966 Conference, the IC, including the OCI, unanimously stated:

> ... The IC not only dissociates itself from the activities and publications of the Spartacists (Robertson) group but insists that a Marxist party can be built only in opposition to it.

Robertson's politics since then have been opportunist on every question, and his group has worked in complete opposition to the International Committee. To admit Robertson's group as observers at Essen at this stage is in effect to junk the whole struggle for principles upon which the IC is based.

The OCI will reply that the invitation was issued on individual initiative by Comrade Berg, secretary of the AJS,[17] and that they have condemned it. On July 9, after Essen, the OCI Political Bureau carried unanimously the following resolution:

> The Political Bureau regrets that the Robertson "Spartacist" group was invited as observer to Essen, without this decision being taken responsibly. The PB considers this individual initiative to be wrong and condemns it.

This leaves unanswered the point that the OCI leadership is itself politically responsible for the opportunist politics of Berg.

Is it accidental that the OCI at Essen returned to an alliance, against Trotskyism, with a tendency such as the POUM, hostile to the very foundation of the Fourth International, and prepared to collaborate with the OCI *only* on the basis of *abandoning* the struggle for its foundation and continuity? Precisely at the point in the world crisis where everything depends on the conscious creation, on the basis of Marxist theory and programme, of revolutionary parties, where the struggle against liquidationism and against the revision of dialectical materialism comes to a head, at this point comes the split! The OCI runs clean away from this historic struggle and, in the name of 'expressing' spontaneous movements of the masses, joins sworn opponents of the FI, collaborates with the centrist riffraff against the IC.

3. The fight for dialectical materialism

• When the French delegation at Essen opposed the SLL amendment on the struggle for Marxist theory, they set the seal on an opposition to dialectical materialism which was not at all new. One year earlier, in June 1970, at the international pre-Conference of the IC, these differences became explicit. And for very good reasons objectively founded in the struggle. Anticipating the profound worsening of the economic crisis and the struggle provoked by it, the SLL delegates stressed the urgency of the basic training of the youth in dialectical thinking.

What was most essential in the preparation of the sections was to develop dialectical materialism in a struggle to understand and to transform the consciousness of the working class in the changing objective conditions. This means the understanding and development of dialectical materialism as the theory of knowledge of Marxism.[18]

---

16. The reference is to the pamphlet *Healy "Reconstructs" the Fourth International—Documents and Comments by Participants in a Fiasco*. The "fiasco" was the 1966 conference of the "International Committee" that ended with some of the participants being ejected, including the unfortunate Robertson, who is prone to such mishaps. Aside from an introduction by me, the pamphlet consists mostly of letters, including three signed by Healy, that were circulated internally in the Robertson group. To obtain copies, the Socialist Workers party did not require the "collaboration" of Robertson.

The pamphlet created such a furor in the SLL that a well-known Trotskyist militant, Ernie Tate, was set upon and beaten by a squad of SLL stewards for attempting to sell it in front of an SLL meeting. When Tate, in an open letter, protested the beating, Healy immediately went to the bourgeois courts to lodge a complaint of "slander." He compelled two publications to pay up for having printed the letter. Tate had committed the crime of mentioning in an unlegalistic way that it was his impression that the squad had acted on a signal from Healy, while Healy contended that his intention was to intervene in Tate's behalf.

The documents included in *Healy "Reconstructs" the Fourth International* offer incontrovertible evidence on the undemocratic practices of the Healyite leadership.—J.H.

17. "AJS." Alliance des Jeunes pour le Socialisme (Youth Alliance for Socialism), the Lambertist youth organization.—J.H.

18. For an organization that talks so incessantly about dialectical materialism, the SLL has produced singularly little in the way of theoretical contributions to Marxism. This is because the leaders of the SLL are not really interested in the

Reflecting the attacks on dialectical materialism by the petty-bourgeois intelligentsia of the advanced capitalist countries, especially France and Germany, and of E Europe, the OCI and Hungarian delegations declared that dialectical materialism was not a theory of knowledge and took up the position that only programme was the basis of the building of parties. Here is the very essence of revisionism which prepares the way for liquidating the party into centrism.

We insist once more, with all our force: only a basic struggle for dialectical materialism against all enemies of Marxism and carried forward in struggle *against* the spontaneous consciousness of the working class, can equip the youth for the building of the Fourth International.

In the polemic with Burnham and Shachtman (1939–1940), Trotsky wrote:

> In the United States ... where the bourgeoisie systematically instills vulgar empiricism in the workers, more than anywhere else, it is necessary to speed the elevation of the movement to a proper theoretical level.

The theoretical struggle at this basic level is essential for every section of the Fourth International. And against those who refuse to 'acquire and develop dialectical materialism', Trotsky wrote: 'This is nothing else than a renunciation of Marxism, of scientific method in general, a wretched capitulation to empiricism.'

4. The OCI and the French working class

- This opposition to the basic theoretical struggle for the revolutionary youth has roots in the orientation of the OCI towards the French proletariat. At no time has the OCI been able consistently to put forward a policy and programme to bring it close to the mass of the French workers who vote for the Stalinists and are organized around the Stalinist-led CGT. Instead they have orientated towards those sections still supporting the social-democrats, primarily in the older industries.

They sought support outside of the orbit of the Stalinists instead of fighting for policies which would break the main body of workers from their mass party. One of the consequences is that the rapidly accumulating effects of the world crisis find the OCI paralysed in its political work in the French working class. Their hysterical outbursts on Bolivia, their frantic desire to find an issue to separate from the SLL and the IC—these are the reactions to the deepening crisis of a petty-bourgeois group which falls back on revolutionary shouting, not of a party which goes deeper into the masses to fight for a development of theory. This characteristic resort to radical phrasemongering is, again, connected with the failure of the OCI to struggle on every level for dialectical materialism against the dominant forms of bourgeois philosophy, in this case French rationalism and its twin, pseudo-revolutionary rhetoric.

The Essen rally itself was conceived and carried through by the OCI as a diversion from the unresolved problems of their work in the French working class. An artificial formula was constructed which made W Germany the focal point of the workers' struggle in Europe, and then the OCI led their youth movement to a rally where less than 200 German youth participated, and real political work to build sections of the FI was replaced by demagogy and showmanship.

It could not and did not have the slightest effect on the workers of France or of Germany. The SLL participated reluctantly, and only on the understanding that we received the preparatory document in time. It was received untranslated, only a few hours before our delegation left for Essen. The SLL and the majority of the IC sections, having moved their amendment, voted for the general resolution despite differences, only in order to preserve public unity of the IC during the period of preparation of the International Fourth Conference, at which the disputed questions would be discussed.

May–June 1968, with the French workers on

---

subject. They appeal to dialectical materialism as a dogma for the precise purpose of stifling critical thinking, particularly thinking that is critical of the SLL leadership.

A striking proof of this is the incapacity of the Lambertists to understand the Healyite position on dialectical materialism. On the other hand, they may understand it only too well.

Of interest would be an explanation from both sides as to why they could remain in such a tight bloc for such a long time in view of their profound differences all these years over the most important issue of all—a correct grasp of dialectical materialism.—J.H.

General Strike, themselves striving for an alternative government, was the greatest testing time for the OCI. But what did the strike reveal?

It revealed the theoretical bankruptcy and political impotence of the OCI whose leadership—guided by a superficial impressionist analysis of de Gaulle's coup in 1958—had exaggerated the strength and viability of the Fifth Republic, abandoned its revolutionary perspective and written off the revolutionary capacities of the French working class.

This defeatist conception, which extended even to the Vietnam war, was summed up in the rationalization of Lambert that the French working class was 'decisively defeated in 1958'. This pessimistic and essentially middle-class outlook expressed itself in all the organizational and agitational work of the OCI and the AJS before and after 1968. It is an undeniable fact that at no time during the General Strike did the OCI leadership advance a socialist programme. Nor did it attempt to undermine the political credibility of the Stalinist leadership by critically supporting the demand of the Renault workers for a 'popular government' by advancing the demand of a CP-CGT government.[19] Instead, the OCI leaders tail-ended the working class and restricted the political scope of the strike by demanding a central strike committee. This was a complete evasion of the *political* responsibilities of revolutionary leadership.

Is it necessary to remind the OCI leaders that one of the chief reasons for the definitive split with the Pabloites was their refusal to address political demands to the trade union bureaucracy and fight for a CP-CGT government in the French General Strike of 1953? Revolutionists do not abstain on basic political questions—only centrists and syndicalists do.

The Socialist Labour League had warned the French section of the dangers *before* 1968:

May 15, 1967:

Now the radicalization of the workers in W Europe is proceeding rapidly, particularly in France. The election results there, the threat of a return to the political instability of the ruling class in the Fourth Republic, the mounting strike struggles, the taking of emergency powers—all these place a premium on revolutionary preparation. There is *always* a danger at such a stage of development that a revolutionary party responds to the situation in the working class not in a revolutionary way, but by adaptation to the level of struggle to which the workers are restricted by their own experience under the old leaderships, i.e., to the inevitable initial confusion. Such revisions of the fight for the independent party and the Transitional Programme are usually dressed up in the disguise of getting closer to the working class, unity with all those in struggle, not posing ultimatums, abandoning dogmatism, etc. (Reply to the OCI.)[20]

Even from this 1968 experience the lessons were not learned. In fact the abstentionist methods and omissions of the General Strike period were continued into the presidential elections of 1969.

In the referendum in March of the same year, the OCI had correctly campaigned for a vote against de Gaulle, in contrast to the abstentionism of the Pabloites. However, the gains from this correct turn were lost in the presidential elections, the class character of which was ignored by the OCI. Basing themselves on their fraudulent theory of the 'United Class Front', the OCI leaders used the failure of the CP and Socialist Party to agree on a single candidate as a pretext for not supporting the CP candidate, Duclos, against Pompidou.

The task of revolutionaries was to raise the consciousness of Stalinist rank and file by critically supporting Duclos and pointing out that the main enemy was Pompidou. The OCI should have campaigned throughout the labour movement to demand that the CP candidate be pledged to a so-

---

19. "CP-CGT government." The proposal was to advocate that the leaderships of the Communist party and the Confederation Generale du Travail (General Confederation of Labor) oust the bourgeois government and take power. Refusal to follow such a course, in face of broad sentiment favoring it, would expose these leaderships in the eyes of the workers and thereby help remove them as obstacles to the building of a mass revolutionary party.—J.H.

20. Where can the document from which this paragraph has been taken be obtained? Both it and the document it answers have been circulated only internally by the Healyites and Lambertists. It is to be hoped that they will now be made public so that this intriguing extract can be studied in the proper context.—J.H.

cialist policy against the banks and monopolies. To carry forward this fight, while calling for a massive vote for Duclos, was the best way to exposing the Stalinists and their programme of 'advanced democracy' and fighting for alternative revolutionary leadership. Any other course leaves the Stalinist control undisturbed. It was also necessary to expose the SP candidate whose party refused to vote for Duclos in the second ballot and supported the bourgeois candidate, Poher.[21]

The OCI leaders did none of these things. Some members voted for Duclos, others for Deferre (SP) and others, including comrade Lambert, abstained. What was worse, the OCI attacked the Stalinists for having dared to stand a candidate in the elections despite the fact that the Stalinists in the previous presidential elections in 1965 did not do so and instead supported Mitterand,[22] a bourgeois politician.

In 1965, the OCI did not even intervene: thus in France, as in Bolivia, the policy of the 'united class front' and the 'united workers' front' has become a means for disorienting the workers and strengthening the grip of the Stalinists and petty-bourgeois nationalists over the mass movement. The sectarian absence of any policy towards the Stalinists in France easily turns into opportunism, so that the OCI now writes in *Informations Ouvrières* about the Clyde struggle in Britain without any criticism of its Stalinist shop steward leaders—in the same issue as their denunciation of the Socialist Labour League and Workers League as agents, of counter-revolution!

5. The capitulation to spontaneity

• Just as the difference over dialectical materialism at the IC's pre-Conference was the necessary and conscious anticipation of the essential theoretical problems to be overcome in the impending revolutionary crisis, so Essen was the anticipation of the open split which these problems would produce on the International Committee.

The real split was already effected at Essen, when the OCI lined up with anti-Trotskyists in a public vote against the majority of the IC. They ran away from the principled questions raised at Essen. They raise the question of Bolivia in a totally unprincipled way in order to keep around them their middle-class allies. We will never accept this running to the centrists, and we will oppose to the end the OCI and anyone else who does it. As the Secretary of the SLL wrote to comrade Lambert of the OCI on July 14, 1971, in reference to Essen:

> We have not spent all our lives fighting centrism to suddenly decide to capitulate to it on the eve of the greatest class struggles in history.[23]

It is necessary to make one other major point on the split pronounced by the OCI. They carry out this split while a Congress of the IC is in preparation and due to be held before the end of 1971. Even though the events at Essen created conditions where day-to-day collaboration with the OCI became impossible, nevertheless it was agreed to proceed with the preparation of documents and arrange the Conference, as the only way of dealing with the differences. These documents are now

---

21. Another alternative would have been to run a candidate of the OCI. Why was this alternative rejected? The lack of explanation makes quite a gap in the statement.

If the OCI was too weak to participate in the presidential elections, as may well have been the case, a practical solution would have been to support—however critically—the presidential candidacy of Alain Krivine, who was nominated by the Ligue Communiste, the French section of the Fourth International. Krivine's campaign drew a favorable response not only in France but in other countries. It did much to publicize the program of revolutionary socialism. Support from the OCI would have strengthened Krivine's campaign. And, among other benefits, it would have brought a certain credit to the OCI by demonstrating its capacity to place principles above factional considerations.

But this alternative was likewise rejected by the OCI—and with the full approval of the SLL. (See "The SLL Abstains on Krivine" in the June 23, 1969, issue of *Intercontinental Press*.)—J.H.

22. Francois Mitterrand (not Mitterand) is meant. For a good analysis of Mitterrand's candidacy in 1965, see the article by Pierre Frank, "Mitterrand—the New Miracle Man of French Politics," in the October 1, 1965, issue of *World Outlook*.—J.H.

23. The name of the author of such a memorable quotation ought really to be preserved for posterity. The indication that it was written by the Secretary of the SLL gives us a clue. Have we guessed right that it is Gerry Healy? Perhaps there are other memorable quotations in the same letter. Let us hope that we do not have to wait for posthumous publication of a correspondence that contains such gems.—J.H.

prepared. But the OCI and the Hungarian sections have chosen to split before the Conference. They act in the same tradition as the SWP, which in 1963 avoided the Conference of the IC and effected its 'unification' with the Pabloites.[24]

At the very heart of the attacks of revisionism has been the attempt to liquidate the party into spontaneous and so-called 'objective' processes. This is the expression of an anti-dialectical method which denies the role of revolutionary consciousness in changing the material struggle itself under specific conditions. Thus Pablo held that given a changed world balance of forces in the post-war period a 'new reality' existed whereby the 'revolutionary process' would force the Stalinist Parties, the social democratic bureaucracies and the petty-bourgeois nationalists in a 'rough way' to make the revolution.[25]

---

24. "Same tradition as the SWP." The authors display admirable skill at compressing the record and drawing false analogies. The process of unifying with the "Pabloites" was actually initiated by Healy with his proposal for a Parity Commission in which both sides participated for more than a year before the Reunification Congress of 1963.

The question of reunification was thoroughly discussed among the members of the International Committee, which was a loose factional formation, and each organization belonging to the committee reached its own decision—as was proper—on whether to participate in the reunification. After the successful experience of the Parity Commission, the proposal of the Political Committee of the Socialist Workers party for early reunification of the world Trotskyist movement on a principled basis was ratified by an overwhelming majority, the only holdouts being the Healyites and Lambertists. To this day neither Healy nor Lambert have explained what they considered to be unprincipled in the statement of the basis for reunification. A silence of nine years!—*J.H.*

25. This is a gross simplification of Pablo's views. More importantly, the authors evade the very real problem that faced the world Trotskyist movement in accounting theoretically for the emergence of a series of workers states following World War II without the direct leadership of revolutionary socialist parties.

Not a single leader in either the Healyite or Lambertist camps played any positive role in the search for a solution to the problem. They agreed with the analyses made by others—including Pablo—that workers states had been formed in Eastern Europe, whether under the sponsorship of Tito or Stalin. They likewise agreed that a similar outcome was to be seen in China under Mao. They boggled only when it came to the revolution led by the Castro team in Cuba. How could a *non-Stalinist* group lead a revolution!

Upon deciding that Cuba remained capitalist, they were necessarily required in view of their declared adherence to

We now find this method developed once again by the OCI. We are told we are in a period of 'imminent revolution'. Within this period there is a 'revolutionary process'. Parties and leaderships then 'correspond' to this 'process'. We are even told of an overall process occasionally 'concretized' in something like the Popular Assembly in Bolivia, which proceeds 'through different stages and different forms towards the Universal Republic of Soviets'. The revolutionary party's task is to 'express these processes'.

This is nothing more than idealism in the form of French rationalism gone mad. We repeat what Lenin said: 'The truth is always concrete.' Only through a detailed and specific analysis of the actual development of the class struggle under the specific conditions of the capitalist crisis can we begin to relate our strategy to the actual changes in the consciousness and life of workers. This requires of us a conscious development of dialectical materialism as we struggle within the workers' movement. This struggle is at all times the struggle to construct Trotskyist parties independent of centrism and Stalinism. Such parties and only such parties can lead the revolution. They can only lead the revolution in the bitterest of struggles against the counter-revolutionary Stalinist and social democratic betrayers.

Within this framework the OCI's position on the 'united class front' becomes a complete liquidation of the party and its subordination to the Stalinist and social democratic parties and union apparatus. Lenin and Trotsky saw the united front as a *tactic* and not a strategy as the OCI claim. They saw it as a relationship between mass workers' parties of a temporary character for the purpose of winning the masses to the Communist Party. The OCI has transformed this into an overall 'unity' of the class achieved on the basis of its present leadership,

---

the dialectical method to review the stands they had taken on the Chinese and East European workers states. They refused to do this. Thereby they proved that they did not really follow the dialectical method.

The consequence of their rejection in practice of dialectical materialism is the combination displayed here of pious incantations to dialectical materialism in the abstract coupled with absolute sterility of thought and outright misrepresentation of the most difficult theoretical problem the Fourth International has had to face since the death of Trotsky.—*J.H.*

without the participation in the united front of our party. This 'united class front' more and more, in their theorizing and practice, takes over the role of the revolutionary party itself.

In the October 12 statement we find reference to 'the achievement of the unity of the class through the workers' United Front, motive force of the anti-imperialist United Front . . .'. This carries the liquidation one step further dissolving even the *workers'* united front into a broader 'anti-imperialist' one— broad enough, no doubt, to include the bourgeoisie or at least its petty-bourgeois representatives.

In the 1950s, the OCI made an identical mistake in their policy in Algeria. The bourgeois-nationalist MNA of Messali Hadj was elevated to a revolutionary party not only in Algeria, but in France itself. The Pabloites supported one wing of the nationalist bourgeoisie, the FLN, and the OCI supported the other, the MNA. In Britain, the SLL had given critical support to the MNA, but broke off all relations with their representatives in Britain when the MNA approached the United Nations for intervention in Algeria.[26]

The OCI continued its relations with Messali Hadj even until the open collaboration of Messali with de Gaulle. The OCI's position today on the 'united class front' and 'anti-imperialist' front, even after the defeat in Bolivia, shows that their 'correction' of the Algerian adventure has been purely formal, and that its theoretical roots remain firmly implanted in the OCI.

Related to this has been the OCI's position that it is not a party, and that the Fourth International does not really exist.[27] It sees the national and international party in quantitative terms rather than from the point of view of the development of Marxist theory. This in turn led it, on the eve of the May–June 1968 events, to not even have the post of secretary of its organization, so far had the capitulation to spontaneity developed.

On the question of the struggle in the colonial and excolonial countries, the anti-Marxist method of the OCI has had the obvious results, and not only on Algeria.

The OCI refused to campaign in support of a victory for the National Liberation Front, because of its Stalinist leadership, and called instead for the 'victory of the Vietnamese workers and peasants'. This led to a situation on the eve of the 1968 Tet offensive where comrade Berg openly stated an abstentionist position on Vietnam.

And now, after years of refusal to support the struggle of the Palestinian people for self-determination, and inability to take the side of the Arab revolution against Zionism and US imperialism, the OCI welcomes the Irbid 'Soviet' as some manifestation of a world process towards the Universal Republic of Workers' Councils! Inability to fight against the Stalinists and petty-bourgeois nationalists in a real fight for independent leadership in the anti-imperialist struggle, and at the same time an abstract demagogy about the victory of the workers and peasants and the international striving for Soviets.

6. The Bolivian revolution

- Bolivia is being used as a smokescreen to cover up the bloc with centrism against the International Committee. As if this were not criminal enough, in proceeding in this fashion, the OCI turns against the most fundamental lessons of our movement on the question of political principle and at the same time covers up for the worst sort of opportunism in Latin America.

---

26. Messali Hadj was one of the founders of the Algerian liberation movement. On paper the program of his Mouvement National Algerien was more radical than that of the Front de Liberation Nationale. It was this radical program that attracted Lambert and Healy and caused them to downgrade the FLN.

The Algerian masses, however, went with the FLN, and this should have proved decisive for revolutionary Marxists.

The correct course was to become involved in the mass movement regardless of the program under which it was marching at the moment. This did not mean that the revolutionary Marxists should give up their own program. On the contrary it was their duty to advance it, doing it in such a way (through transitional slogans and democratic demands in the beginning) as to make it attractive to the masses and bring them ultimately to accept it as a whole.

Pablo understood this and won considerable recognition among the Algerian vanguard. Where he failed was in building a cadre organization, and for this he was severely criticized by the Fourth International.—*J.H.*

27. "The Fourth International does not exist." The Healyite meaning is that the OCI does not recognize that the Fourth International really exists in the form of the SLL and the thought of its secretary, Gerry Healy.—*J.H.*

We take back nothing from our criticisms of Lora and his role in the defeat of the Bolivian working class. How could we have proceeded otherwise than with an open attack? The road to coalition government in Ceylon was paved by such cover-ups time and again on the part of the Pabloite leadership. How could we draw the lessons we do from their betrayal in Ceylon and practise the same politics in relation to someone on the periphery of the International Committee? We cover over nothing. We build the Fourth International on the basis of political principle and complete honesty.[28]

It was in fact the OCI which first publicly criticized the politics of Lora and the POR. The October 1970 issue of *La Vérité* carried a lengthy criticism of the thesis passed at the April 1970 Congress of the COB (Bolivian trade union federation).[29] This thesis was the product of the joint collaboration of the POR and the Stalinist Bolivian CP. It was voted for by both parties and the Popular Assembly was later to base itself politically on this document. The OCI wrote:

> . . . We are dealing with a text which after having made certain concessions to the idea of constructing socialism in Bolivia alone, takes on the one hand, a Stalinist type view of the Ovando regime, and introduces in the chapter on proletarian internationalism, a Stalinist analysis. We have found in the COB thesis on the one hand passages of direct Stalinist inspiration, and on the other a serious omission concerning Czechoslovakia.

The OCI concludes:

> Comrades, we tell you without evasion, moved by a profound and even anguished conviction, that if this really became the charter of the Bolivian workers' movement and represented its orientation and if the POR was to adopt it (or even for a long time keep silent on the fact that it is the result of a compromise and only has a very circumstantial value) then the thesis of the COB can constitute a noose around the neck of the Bolivian proletariat for it encloses it within the framework of Bolivia.

Was the OCI at that time giving in 'to enormous pressures' as the OCI now says of the SLL and the Workers League? Was the OCI in making those criticisms identifying itself 'as enemies of the dictatorship of the proletariat' and placing itself 'on the side of imperialism and Stalinism'?

The truth is that in 1967 the OCI held the position that revolutions could not be made in the underdeveloped countries until such time as mass revolutionary parties were created in the advanced countries. So distant was the struggle in the underdeveloped countries from the thinking and perspectives of the OCI leadership until very recently that the basic resolution around which it wished the Fourth Conference to be organized 'For the Reconstruction of the Fourth International'

---

28. The authors protest too much. A sharp public criticism of the LSSP's turn toward opportunism was voiced by *The Militant* in an editorial "LSSP Policy in Ceylon" in the October 3, 1960, issue. This expressed the views of the SWP. A similar criticism was publicly stated in a resolution passed at the Sixth World Congress in December 1960, when Pablo was still secretary of the Fourth International. These statements were made almost three years before the Reunification Congress. What were Healy and Lambert doing at the time? Covering up the LSSP by their silence? Or agreeing with the criticism made by the SWP?

The International Secretariat engaged, in addition, in extensive correspondence with the Ceylonese, seeking to convince them of the incorrectness of their course and the need to change it. This is reported in the chapter "The Ceylon Example" in Germain's *Marxism vs. Ultraleftism*.

The truth of the matter is that the deterioration of the Trotskyist movement in Ceylon was taken by most responsible leaders of the world Trotskyist movement as a grave warning that extraordinary measures would be required to rectify the situation, and that these could be undertaken only if a principled reunification could be achieved.

By blocking and slowing down the reunification, both Healy and Pablo were responsible for a bad, and, as it turned out, fatal delay in effectively countering the rot that had been spreading in the Ceylon section.

As for what happened in Bolivia, the authors draw a false analogy. All of the leaders of the rump "International Committee" bear heavy responsibility if what they say about Lora is true.

They not only made an unprincipled bloc with Lora, they remained silent until after the coup and then they sought to make a scapegoat out of Lora without acknowledging their own political responsibility.—J.H.

29. "COB." Central Obrera Boliviana. The theses (not thesis) were adopted by the mine workers' convention in April 1970 and by the COB in May 1970. For a translation of the text see the July 13, 1970, issue of *Intercontinental Press*.—J.H.

hardly mentions Latin America and does not mention Bolivia at all. And yet the Bolivian question is now made the pretext for a split from the International Committee.

We cannot educate a new generation of cadres as revolutionaries with such factional and dishonest methods. We cannot allow the question of Bolivia to be *used* rather than assessed for the purpose of actually developing theoretically a new leadership in the underdeveloped countries.

We restate what we said about the history of the Lora group. Lora was the major supporter of Pablo in Latin America in 1952. With Pablo's help he gave critical support to the bourgeois MNR[30] Paz government. Here is how a member of his party reported the POR's position in the Fourth International at the time.

> The POR began by justifiably granting critical support to the MNR government. That is, it desisted from issuing the slogan 'down with the government'; it gave the government critical support against attacks of imperialism and reaction, and it supported all progressive measures.

This is just the way the LSSP began its move towards openly joining the Ceylonese coalition government.

The POR broke with Pablo, but it turned its back on the International Committee, refusing to take up a fight for the IC in Latin America though urged to do so. Lora from then on played only a national role. This is the history as we printed it in the *Workers Press* and *'Bulletin'*. The OCI does not deny this.

We can add to this some more. Understanding the past background of Lora, a background of Pabloism, nationalism and opportunism, the Socialist Labour League refused to put up any money towards his fare and collaboration in bringing him to the 1966 International Conference as the OCI had proposed. When he appeared in Europe in 1970, the Socialist Labour League made it quite plain it would not favour his admission into the IC unless a full discussion was held on his whole history and an understanding reached on this basis. We do not have one policy for the LSSP and the Pabloites and another for Lora.

In our public statement we made this fundamental assessment of Lora's role in the Bolivian events:

> Lora, in collaboration with the Bolivian Stalinists and with the agreement of the Bolivian and international Pabloites, failed to fight at any point for the overthrow of the Torres military regime. Thus he, along with the rest of the Popular Assembly, acted as a left cover for Torres while the right-wing elements in Torres' own army prepared and finally executed their coup.

Then, after writing this, we received Lora's own account of the Bolivian events which we published in the *Workers Press* and in the *'Bulletin'*. The OCI has yet to publish this account. Lora himself in this account states:

> At the same time everybody thought—including we Marxists—that the arms would be given by the governing military team, which would consider that only through resting on the masses and giving them adequate firepower could they at least neutralize the *gorila* right.

---

30. "MNR." Movimiento Nacionalista Revolucionario (Revolutionary Nationalist Movement). The argument developed against Lora is a telling one. The OCI reply will be read with attention.

Perhaps answers will also be provided to the following questions raised by Gerry Foley in the December 15, 1969, issue of *Intercontinental Press*:

> It is to be hoped that the nature of the relationship between the Lora group and the Lambertists will be clarified. Does this alliance rest on a principled agreement? Does Lora, like the Socialist Labour League and Lambert, believe that the Cuban revolution was not socialist, giving rise only to state capitalism? Does he hold with them that Fidel Castro is another "Batista"? Does he approve of the slanders that appeared in the Socialist Labour League press (before it became known that Che Guevara was in Bolivia) that Castro had liquidated his comrade-in-arms?

If the leaders of the OCI are reluctant to take up these questions, perhaps they will at least give us their opinion on why Healy and Wohlforth maintained such a discreet silence for almost *two years* after Gerry Foley drew attention to the unprincipled nature of the bloc with Lora.—J.H.

Lora thus admits to what we had accused him of. Never really fighting to overthrow Torres, he had, along with the Stalinists, counted on one section of the bourgeoisie to arm the working class for the overthrow of the bourgeoisie as a whole! Lora thus was carrying out the very same policy he carried out with Pablo in 1952. At no point did he raise the slogan 'Down with Torres'. This was, of course, Lenin's policy in the 'April Theses', while Lora stands with Stalin and the 'old Bolsheviks'.

Even after the defeat, Lora is unable to draw any lessons at all. He openly defends his reformist position in the pages of the OCI's *Informations Ouvrières*:

> The ultra-lefts and the Pabloites forget the teachings of Lenin and Trotsky: they draw up their "documents" in a simple-minded way and place Torres and Ovando-Banzer on the same level. These people refuse to understand the various shades that bourgeois nationalism can take in underdeveloped countries.
>
> Since they are removed from the class struggle they do not understand the difference between bourgois-democratic demands of Torres and the methods of the fascists; that is the difference between going to prison legally or getting killed by a bullet in the back of the neck.
>
> Revolutionary tactics must begin with this difference. It is not a question of supporting Torres, but of crushing fascism to impose a workers' government.

Revolutionary strategy does not begin with the differences between left and right wings of the military, but from the perspective of the overthrow of the whole bourgeois order. It does not base its policy on a bloc with the left bourgeoisie against the fascist threat, but on the understanding that there is no way to stop fascism without taking up the independent struggle for socialism.

Thus lessons which Trotsky repeated thousands of times, particularly in regard to Spain, are once again borne out in the paralysis and complicity of Torres in the right-wing military takeover and in the prostration of the working class before this takeover because of the misleadership of all the workers' parties, but especially the POR which claimed to be Trotskyist.[31] In the end the workers of Bolivia got both the bullet in the head and the jail.

The policy of the POR was consistently opportunist from beginning to end. Under conditions of a mass revolutionary situation it acted as the left cover for Stalinism and bourgeois-nationalism. Nowhere did it decisively break from the CP. In fact it put forward a common candidate for the presidency of the Popular Assembly with the CP.

The policy of Lora had nothing whatsoever to do with the policy of Bolshevism, or Trotskyism. The construction of the Trotskyist movement in Latin America, as elsewhere, requires a decisive break with the narrow national outlook and a return to internationalism and the struggle to develop Marxist theory. The POR and Lora repeat the policies of the POUM in Spain in 1935–1938 and are in no fundamental way different from them. Their relations with Torres and the COB parallels those of the POUM with the Republican Government and the CNT.[32] The OCI's support for the POR now

---

31. Attention should be called to the fact that there are two PORs in Bolivia. They are so well known there that they are continually referred to in the press as the "POR of Lora" and the "POR of Gonzalez." The two organizations have gone through unifications and splits. The POR led by Hugo Gonzalez Moscoso is the Bolivian section of the Fourth International. During the Ovando and Torres regimes, when the political atmosphere in Bolivia was relatively relaxed, the POR of Gonzalez repeatedly called for arming of the workers and placing no confidence in the government, no matter how radical its demagogy.

For a recent summary of the situation in Bolivia, see "Our Role in Battling Against the Military Coup" by Hugo Gonzalez M. in the November 1, 1971, issue of *Intercontinental Press*.

Gonzalez has been vilely slandered by Lora. The November 19, 1969, issue of *Informations Ouvrieres* published a letter from Lora stating that "serious suspicions exist today" that Gonzalez "is working in the pay of the Bolivian government."

This slander—in a slightly modified form—was repeated in the January 17, 1970, issue of *Workers Press*. (See "Healyites and Lambertists in Strange Company," in the March 2, 1970, issue of *Intercontinental Press*.)

To this day, neither the Healyites nor the Lambertists have retracted the slander, although the Healyites now profess to have known since 1952 that Lora was not to be trusted.—*J.H.*

32. "CNT." Confederacion Nacional del Trabajo (National Confederation of Labor). The rank and file of the CNT were

makes clear the political meaning of their bloc with the POUM at Essen.

7. The way forward

- The essence of the struggle of the International Committee since 1953, has been the conscious construction of independent revolutionary parties of the Fourth International. Revisionists have always attacked this fundamental conception. Pablo with his 'new reality', 'mass pressure' and 'the revolution in all its forms', the LSSP with its 'united left front'.

Now the OCI, using the formula, 'imminence of revolution', elaborating a schema of natural stages through which the working class passes on the road to power, distorting the tactic of united front of the working class, has taken the road of liquidationism laid down by these revisionists.

The split comes now, when the [they?] stand at the point of transition from one phase of the class struggle to a higher one, the stage in which Trotskyist parties are called upon to win leadership in the struggle for working-class power. In this transition it is inevitable that a decisive clash, and a split, becomes necessary with all those like the OCI who rejected the struggle for dialectical materialism and refused to break from the old propagandist conceptions. This hostility to theory always leads to centrism and opportunism.

The record shows clearly that on all the disputed questions, and above all on the importance of theoretical development and training, the Socialist Labour League and the IC majority tried patiently to correct the course of the OCI, and never proceeded precipitately or in such way as to provoke a split. The decision of the OCI to join the centrists at Essen against the International Committee and their manoeuvring and demagogy on Bolivia, constitute a decision to reject and oppose the struggle to build independent revolutionary parties of the Fourth International. We call upon all Trotskyists in every country to reject completely the OCI line and to fight on the principled positions of the International Committee.

The Fourth Conference of the International Committee will meet in the first weeks of 1972. There it will be necessary to make a balance-sheet of the struggle against revisionism and the fight to establish the Trotskyist cadre throughout the period since 1938. A new period opens up, a period in which the Fourth International is called upon to lead struggles for workers' power. The perspectives of this struggle in the advanced capitalist countries, in the colonial countries, and in the fight for the political revolution in E Europe, the Soviet Union and China, will be discussed and decided.

The draft resolution for this Conference is now complete, and the discussion now begins in all sections of the International Committee.

WORKERS' LEAGUE, USA
(sympathetic to the IC of the FI).

REVOLUTIONARY COMMUNIST LEAGUE OF CEYLON

WORKERS INTERNATIONALIST LEAGUE OF GREECE.

LEAGUE FOR A WORKERS' VANGUARD OF IRELAND

SOCIALIST LABOUR LEAGUE, BRITAIN.
OCTOBER 24, 1971.

---

exceptionally militant. However, the Anarchists were in control. Despite their opposition "in principle" to all forms of the state, the Anarchists ended up taking posts in the bourgeois government and thus helped pave the way for the triumph of Franco.

The POUM, seeking to avoid conflicts with the Anarchists, did not carry on any serious revolutionary work in the CNT. A fatal consequence of the policy of the POUM was the isolation of the revolutionary vanguard from the working class.—J.H.

Lambertist 'Reply to a Splitting Act'

The November 5, 1971, issue of *Workers Press*, the daily paper of the Socialist Labour League, and the November 8 issue of the *Bulletin*, the weekly of the "Workers League" in the USA, published a document entitled "Declaration of the International Committee of the Fourth International (Majority)."

This document was adopted on October 24 as the result of a meeting which, going by the signatures, was attended by representatives of the following organizations: the Socialist Labour League (Great Britain); Workers League (USA); the League for a Workers Vanguard (Ireland); the Internationalist Workers League (Greece); and a German group, the "Sozialistische Arbeiter Bund," made up of elements expelled from the German Trotskyist organization, the IAK, for their refusal to observe, in action, the discipline of the organization.[1]

The title of this document already was in itself a flagrant political falsification. There cannot be any "majority" in the International Committee, any more than there can be a "minority," because there has been no meeting of the International Committee.

The factional meeting October 24 was held in fact without the OCI, the LSRH [Ligue des Revolutionnaires Socialistes Hongrois—Hungarian Revolutionary Socialist League], the Bolivian POR [Partido Obrero Revolucionario—Revolutionary Workers party], or the Mexican LOM [Liga Obrera Marxista—Marxist Workers League] being informed of it. The document that came out of this meeting was not sent to the sections of the IC before being made public.

The aim of the document is to break the framework of the International Committee in order to forestall discussion; it was not intended to provide a basis for serious discussion. As such, consequently, it does not require a reply but a correction. And that is the objective of the present statement.

The fact remains that this document in itself is an element in the debate it was designed to prevent. In any case, the Central Committee of the OCI will shortly publish a document taking up all the questions posed by the present stage for the reconstruction of the Fourth International.

Intercontinental Press, January 17, 1972.

WHO IS IT THAT WANTS TO BREAK UP THE INTERNATIONAL COMMITTEE?

The first section of the document adopted October 24 has as its title "A New Period for the Trotskyist Movement."

That is a grandiloquent designation for an attempt, by contemptible means, to break up the International Committee founded in 1953 to defend Trotskyism and the program of the Fourth International against the liquidators.

The whole argument of this first section is dictated by its conclusion:

> There is the International Committee of the Fourth International, resting on the foundation laid down by Trotsky in 1938, the first four Congresses of the Third International, and all the work of the IC since 1953, particularly the decisions of the 1966 Conference. And there is the bogus "IC for the reconstruction of the Fourth International", represented by the OCI and the Hungarian section, who want to regroup with centrists *against* the Fourth International. This split, and not the Bolivian revolution and the Bolivian POR, is the basic issue.

To believe the authors of this document, the OCI and the LSRH precipitated the split by joining with Lora (whose organization is not supposed to be affiliated to the IC) in publicly attacking the SLL and the Workers League, by holding a meeting where Comrade Stephane Just wrongfully appropriated the title of secretary of the IC, and so forth. All this is alleged to have been done to avoid discussing the "fundamental question." What crimes!

Let us suppose for an instant that there were a basis for the formal pretexts raised by the signers of the October 24 statement, that the OCI and the LSRH committed splitting acts against the International Committee. What, then, was the duty of the other sections, especially the largest, such as

---

1. It should be noted that this German group is listed among the signers only in the *Bulletin*. It is omitted in *Workers Press*.

the SLL? Their duty was to propose that a plenum of the International Committee meet as soon as possible, to demand that those endangering the unity of the International Committee face up to their responsibilities, to force them to retreat, or else to break on the basis of a clear difference. The line to follow was certainly not to hold a meeting kept secret from four sections of the International Committee in order to try to claim later that it was these four sections that initiated the split.

But this illogic is only apparent. The curious method used by the leadership of the SLL, which prompted the October 24 meeting, is explained by the inanity of the pretexts raised and a helter-skelter flight from the "fundamental discussion."

Let us get the facts straight. This is the best way to bring out the political questions.

For close to two years—and in particular since the preconference of the International Committee in July 1970—the leadership of the Socialist Labour League has tried repeatedly to block all discussion on the "fundamental question," that is, a discussion on the concrete content of the present stage in the struggle to reconstruct the Fourth International.

In September 1969, the OCI presented for discussion a political document entitled "Pour la reconstruction de la IVe Internationale" [For the Reconstruction of the Fourth International"].[2] In July 1970 the sections of the IC and the groups associated with it met in a preconference, which was a stage in preparing an international conference to bring together the organizations, groups, and militants standing on the ground of the Transitional Program.

The OCI document was the only one submitted for discussion. The SLL delegation began by stating that the nub of the question was "Marxist philosophy." Next it said that the OCI document was correct in its general line but that it required amending. Then it declared that the document was unacceptable. Finally it asked, "because of a lack of preparation" (although the document before it had been in its hands for nine months!), that the vote be postponed to a second session of the preconference. It proposed that this session take place in October.

Fighting to preserve and strengthen the International Committee, the OCI delegation made allowances for the political difficulties of the sections and accepted this report. But—on a joint proposal of the OCI and the SLL—a document was voted defining the framework for continuing the discussion. This resolution characterized the document presented by the OCI as a basis for discussion in conformity with the principles of the Fourth International.

Since July 1970 the SLL leadership has opposed convening a second session of the preconference. On the other hand, it turned to the leading center of the liquidators of the Fourth International, to the "United Secretariat" of Handel and Co., to propose a joint conference in terms not only contradicting the decisions of the preconference but contrary to the meaning of the entire struggle of the International Committee. This overture was testified to by an article by the general secretary of the SLL, Gerry Healy, in *Workers Press* of September 8, 1970.

A clear and quick response from the Central Committee of the OCI at the time stopped this dangerous tendency from going any further. But the fact that such a tendency could take hold to this degree indicated the gravity of the SLL leadership's oscillations and opened the way to the turn now taken by the SLL, in its October 24 document, to make itself the spokesman for conceptions so close to those of the Pabloites that the latter have been quick to disseminate them as widely as possible

Following this episode, the SLL leadership took a hardened obstructive attitude, from which it has shifted only to launch a deliberate offensive against the unity of the International Committee in the form of a dishonorable and slanderous attack against the Bolivian POR. This assault took place as early as August 30 in the form of an article by Tim Wohlforth published in the *Bulletin* of that date. The article was reprinted in the September 8 *Workers Press*. In the October 24 document it has become "Our Statement on Bolivia."

To this public offensive, the OCI responded publicly, giving its assessment of the revolutionary struggle in Bolivia (in a statement by the CC of the OCI dated September 17), without mentioning the SLL or the Workers League.

Then, after Comrade Lora had written to the sections of the IC asking that a meeting of this body be held as soon as possible to discuss the report

---

2. Published in *La Verite*, No. 545 of October 1967.

EDITORIAL NOTE—

The split in the "International Committee" would now appear to be irreparable, judging from the organizational moves being taken by each side. Yet the issues in dispute continue to remain rather obscure, despite increasingly bitter polemics. It is not yet possible to determine even the point of origin of the conflict.

The Healyites took the initiative in deciding to wash the dirty linen of the International Committee in public. This was done in an article in the August 30, 1971, issue of the *Bulletin*, the newspaper of the Workers League, an American grouping that shares the viewpoint of the Socialist Labour League in Britain. (See "Disaster in Bolivia for Healy-Lambert-Wohlforth" in the September 27, 1971, issue of *Intercontinental Press*, p. 816.)

The Organisation Communiste Internationaliste, the French-based component of the International Committee headed by Pierre Lambert, replied in the September 29 issue of their paper, *Informations Ouvrières*. (For a translation of this document, see "The Lambertist View of the Bolivian Events" in the October 18 issue of *Intercontinental Press*, p. 894.)

The OCI followed this up with a more detailed reply entitled "Declaration," which was distributed in thousands of copies in Paris. This called for a plenary meeting of the International Committee. (For a translation see "Lambertist 'Declaration' on Socialist Labour League" in the November 1 issue of *Intercontinental Press*, p. 942.)

To this the SLL responded with a statement, purportedly signed October 24 by the "International Committee of the Fourth International (Majority)." The statement appeared in the November 5 issue of *Workers Press*, the newspaper of the Central Committee of the SLL. (The full text was republished under the title "The Healyite Case Against the Lambertists" in the November 22 issue of *Intercontinental Press*, p. 1015.)

The response of the OCI, which we are publishing in an English translation here, appeared in a special issue of *Informations Ouvrières* dated November 24. The original title runs as follows: "Declaration of the Central Committee of the Internationalist Communist Organization (for the reconstruction of the Fourth International). Reply to a splitting act: For the defense of the International Committee! For the reconstruction of the Fourth International! (Concerning the document published November 5 by *Workers Press*, organ of the SLL.)"

The special issue included a French translation of the November 5 document.

For revolutionary Marxists, the main interest in this dispute comes from the fact that the SLL and the OCI were the largest organizations claiming to be Trotskyist that refused to join in the reunification of the overwhelming majority of the world Trotskyist movement in 1963.

In opposing the reunification and remaining outside of the reunited Fourth International, the SLL and OCI leaders declared that they and they alone represented Trotskyism.

Although the "International Committee" was only a rump formation, the majority of the original International Committee having participated in the reunification of the Fourth International, the SLL leaders held that the rump "International Committee" (more particularly the SLL) represented the living continuity of the Fourth International. The somewhat different OCI view was that the Fourth International had to be completely "reconstructed."

As to the real nature of the "International Committee," this should become much clearer as the polemic develops. Already the disputants have revealed a number of interesting facts on how the bloc functioned, and, more importantly, on how it evolved in face of the challenge of creating a world organization in a revolutionary epoch.

To understand the OCI document better, it must be remembered that the authors—like their Healyite opponents—use the term Trotskyist to refer to only their own ideas and allies. For instance, when the OCI document mentions the Bolivian POR, it means the POR led by Guillermo Lora, and not the POR led by Hugo González, which is a section of the Fourth International.

In the same way, the authors refuse to recognize the existence of the Fourth International, holding that it was shattered long ago.

Again, in speaking of the French presidential elections of 1969, the authors do not once mention the Trotskyist candidate, Alain Krivine of the Ligue Communiste, the French section of the Fourth International.

We have not commented on inconsistencies and errors in the text, partly because of its length and partly because a good deal would be repetition of comments already made in previous issues of *Intercontinental Press* in connection with the Healyite-Lambertist polemic.—*IP*

prepared by the POR leadership, Comrades Lambert (OCI), Nagy (LSRH), and Lora (POR) signed a statement later made public, which said, notably:

> What is more natural than that all the difficult problems of the whole international class struggle should be reflected and concentrated within it [the IC]? What is more natural than that the stake in a gigantic world combat should be translated into the crises of the Fourth International as it is translated into the crisis of all the organizations of the working class?
>
> Today, the leadership of certain organizations of the International Committee, like the Socialist Labour League and the Workers League, lacking the necessary clarity with regard to the strategy for the conquest of power and the reconstruction of the Fourth International, have given way to the enormous pressures by attacking the POR.
>
> The three delegations, meeting in Paris, while holding that a discussion is legitimate, both between the sections adhering to the IC as well as within each of the sections, condemn the method utilized by the Workers League and the SLL which, without even having studied the reports issued by the leadership of the POR, have undertaken to publicly condemn the Bolivian section of the IC.
>
> That is why the delegations of the OCI and of the Committee for the Organization of the Countries of the East approve the demand made by Comrade G. Lora, insisting that the IC be convened in a plenary session in the shortest possible time in order to take a stand on the report on the Bolivian revolution and the tasks of reconstructing the Fourth International which the leadership of the POR has prepared.

No political reaction to the political problems raised, no response to the proposals advanced, no attempt to set a frame work for discussion came from the SLL. But suddenly on October 24 a split was declared by a factional meeting kept secret from four sections of the IC, by a grouping that illegitimately baptized itself the "majority of the IC."

In fact, aside from the fact that we cannot see how a majority could be formed in the International Committee without this body meeting, we must point out the curious way the SLL went about constructing its "majority."

As is known, the work of the IC, the work of reconstructing the Fourth International, led it to form new groups that did not automatically become members of the IC. On this question as on the others, the rule of unanimity prevailed. Thus, for example, the German Trotskyist organization, the IAK, is a sympathizing group but not a member of the IC. The International Committee is thus presently composed of the following eight sections: the OCI (France), the SLL (Great Britain), the LSRH (Hungary), the POR (Bolivia), the Revolutionary Communist Party (Ceylon), the Marxist Workers League (Mexico), the League for a Workers Vanguard (Ireland), and the Workers League (USA).[3]

There is at present no Greek section because the organization that participated in the 1966 conference broke up into two groups on the eve of the 1967 coup d'etat and conditions have not permitted a clarification of the reasons for this split or an assessment of the policy of either group. As a result, on the proposal of Comrade Slaughter, the IC decided to treat both groups as sympathizing organizations.

As regards the Revolutionary Workers party of Bolivia, the facts are clear. This is an old Trotskyist organization, a section of the Fourth International before the 1951–52 split. It was on the basis of its experience and its struggle against Pabloism in Bolivia itself that the POR joined the International Committee in 1970. Its adherence to the IC following an IC meeting in which Comrade Lora participated personally was, moreover, officially announced in *La Verite* (No. 547, March 1970, page 14) and was not denied.

The legitimate membership of the POR in the International Committee was so little questioned by the SLL itself that issue No. 545 of its daily paper *Workers Press*, dated August 28, 1971, in reporting the death of a Trotskyist student leader in La Paz during the fight against Banzer's troops, noted

---

3. This organization is in political solidarity with the International Committee and has the political status of a section. But it is not organizationally affiliated to the IC because of reactionary legislation in the United States.

that "the P. O. R. is the Bolivian section of the International Committee." It would be inconceivable to think that the POR is a member of the International Committee when its militants are being struck down by fascist bullets but stops being one when it comes to discussing the balance sheet of its policies. In any case, these are procedures alien to Trotskyism.

Thus, the SLL's efforts to manufacture a "majority" in the IC by rejecting some and adding others do not change the facts one whit. Only four member organizations appear among the signers of the October 24 document.

Moreover, on the question of "reconstructing the Fourth International," since the October 24 document alludes to the decisions of the 1966 conference, let us recall that the basic documents of this meeting (the draft political resolution, manifesto, and resolution on tasks) were drawn up primarily by the OCI and that politically they justify the use of the term "reconstruction."

The resolution on tasks (approved unanimously) was, moreover, entitled "Resolution on the Reconstruction of the Fourth International." Among other things, it specified:

> The international conference considers that through the fight to reconstruct the Fourth International, the Trotskyist movement must construct the centralized leadership of the world party of the socialist revolution in a struggle organically linked to the battle to build centralized revolutionary parties in every country that can provide leadership to the revolutionary combat of the masses. The construction of these parties and of the International must be conducted on the basis of the experience and pursuit of a constant battle against revisionism. . . .
>
> The IC is made up of delegates chosen by the sections to represent them. At the present stage, decisions by the IC must be made on the basis of the rule of unanimity. The IC is not at this point claiming to be the centralized leadership of the Fourth International, which is still to be constructed.

Finally, regarding the post of secretary of the IC, let us note that in view of the SLL's difficulties in filling this role (which was entrusted to Comrade Slaughter), it was agreed to establish a cosecretariat consisting of comrades Slaughter and Just.

If we have dwelt at length on aspects that may seem secondary or legalistic, it was to clear the ground for the political questions. We have tried also to show that the formal pretexts invoked have no reality but were only feeble sophisms designed to cover up an organizational split carried through without political discussion.

The essential thing is, of course, this "fundamental discussion" referred to, which naturally incorporates the experience of the revolutionary struggle of the Bolivian proletariat and the policy of the POR, since these subjects lie at the heart of the debate. This involves the meaning of "imminent revolution," the question of the struggle for power and, thus, the ways the working class may perceive this problem (the question of the united front, of a workers and peasants' government, of the institutions of dual power and the dictatorship of the proletariat).

For Trotskyists this discussion takes on meaning only from the standpoint of the problems of reconstructing the Fourth International, the problems of the SLL leadership is trying to avoid by an attempt to break the framework of the IC. This is the debate that is involved in a criticism of the October 24 document, over and above maneuvers, untruths, and amalgams.

SPLIT AT ESSEN?

"Split at Essen" was the dramatic title of the second section of the October 24 document. This split was supposed to have been shown by the fact the "representatives of the OCI, the Hungarian section and the Mexican LOM, voted along with centrists and even right-wing organizations [this refers to the National Student Association of the United States] against the amendment to the main resolution put by the representative of the SLL and supported by representatives of a majority of the IC sections (Ceylon, Ireland, Canada, Greece, SLL)." We have already explained about this "majority." But what did happen at Essen? First of all, let us think back on this meeting, since some people seem to have forgotten it. It was an international assembly of revolutionary youth including 5,000 participants and representatives of thirty-two countries. This rally was convened on the basis of a call drawn up by the Alliance des Jeunes pour le Socialisme [Alliance of Youth for Socialism] and adopted by the Young Socialists at their January 1971 congress in Scarborough. This appeal, which was initiated by the youth organizations working in liaison with the International Committee, was also signed from the start by youth organizations that did not claim to be Trotskyist, such as the JCI, the POUM's youth organization.

The unquestionable success of the Essen rally was a political achievement that only the International Committee and its organizations could have built through waging a political fight in the framework of the struggle for the construction of a Revolutionary Youth International. It was in this sense that Comrade Slaughter, speaking in the name of the SLL Central Committee, could justly hail the rally as "a step forward for proletarian internationalism."

The international meeting was preceded by a conference of delegates in the course of which a resolution was presented and unanimously adopted (including by the Young Socialist delegation) and ratified the next day by the 5,000 youth present.

In Essen itself, the International Committee met to set the framework of its political activity. Amendments were proposed—several introduced by the SLL were accepted.

During the conference, the SLL and Young Socialist delegates broke the agreement passed at the IC by presenting a new amendment, which the OCI delegates considered to be profoundly wrong.

In order to prevent the YS and SLL delegation from suffering an overwhelming political defeat, Comrade Berg, the reporter, proposed that this amendment be referred to the Liaison Committee elected by the Essen rally. This solution made it possible to take up the question again inside the IC sections before making the final decision, thus avoiding a public fight. The YS delegation refused. The majority of the conference accepted the motion of referral made by the AJS. It should be noted for the sake of historical truth that the NSA delegates had only the status of observers and did not take part in the vote.

But this is not the essential thing. There was not the hint of a political concession by the OCI, the LSRH, the LOM, or the POR to centrist elements. The fact remains that for the OCI the amendment was unacceptable. It read:

> There can be no revolutionary party without revolutionary theory. Behind every opportunist development in the history of the workers' movement, and Stalinism in particular, lies revisionism.
>
> The continuity of the struggle for revolutionary Marxist theory in the past, the struggle of the Fourth International and the International Committee, were the sole basis for the initiatives that led to this rally and for the fight to construct an international revolutionary youth movement.
>
> Everywhere revolutionary youth must devote itself first of all to the task of developing Marxist theory through a struggle against bourgeois ideology in all the forms it takes in the workers' movement. This is the only basis for fighting the dangers of adventurism, the superactivism and "pure" militancy by which the revisionists and Maoists disoriented the youth and which can only lead to historic defeats for the working class.

Why did the OCI oppose this amendment? Primarily because it represented going over to idealist positions, abandoning Marxism for the sake of an ideology dubbed "Marxist philosophy."

> When the French delegation at Essen opposed the SLL amendment on the struggle for Marxist theory, they set the seal on an opposition to dialectical materialism which was not at all new [the October 24 document tells us]. One year earlier, in June 1970, at the international preconference of the IC, these differences became explicit.

At the 1970 preconference, the OCI and LSRH delegations warned the SLL comrades about the grave political dangers involved in any tendency to transform dialectical materialism into an ideology (philosophy), a self-contained system of ideas breaking with the very essence of dialectical materialism—the unity of method, form, and content. These delegations stressed that a discussion on the Marxist method was a serious and vital one because it concerned the foundations of our program and that therefore such a discussion should be approached with due deliberation.

The correctness of these warnings was shown by the Essen amendment. This chatter about "Marxist philosophy" has ended, we repeat, in falling into ideology.

No, "behind" every development of opportunism in the workers' movement lies not "ideology" in the form of a revision (abandonment) of Marxism, but the reality of contending social forces, the class struggle expressing itself within the workers' movement itself, the battleground and stake in this struggle. It is these pressures that give rise to arguments to justify capitulations, taking the form of revisions of Marxism.

It was not Bernstein's "lack of understanding" of Marxism that was behind reformism; it was the practice of class collaboration, based on the position of the workers' aristocracy in the epoch of expanding imperialism, that brought with it the need for an ideological justification of this practice. This does not mean that Bernstein was only a "reflection." By his political activity he was both an expression and a factor of the battle waged within the workers' movement. At the same time, defending the class interests of the proletariat involves a "defense of Marxism" through implacable theoretical criticism of revisionist ideology, criticism which itself has been a constituent element in the class consciousness of the proletariat over the course of its organized struggle to emancipate itself.

Marx explained that it was necessary to move from the weapon of criticism to the criticism of weapons. But the weapon of criticism is itself a stage in the development of the class struggle and, in this sense, of the criticism of weapons. Thus, the theoretical struggle is always an expression of the class struggle; it does not stand outside it.

Nor was it Stalin's narrow-mindedness that lay "behind" the theory of "socialism in one country." This concept expressed the interests of the bureaucratic caste that seized political power. Is this to say that the theoretical struggle is "secondary"? No, to the contrary! Marxist theory is the distillation and generalization of all the determining factors in the struggle of the proletariat, in the historical working-class movement. And in this sense, the class struggle "does not excuse a single theoretical error." But the theory, the method of Marxism, is not a system of ideas detached from social reality; it is not a self-contained system that need only be "applied." The Marxist method exists only through its content, which incorporates all stages of the workers' struggle to emancipate themselves. In this sense, the program of the socialist revolution represents the quintessence of Marxism, and defending Marxist theory can only mean defending this program, that is, struggling to resolve the crisis of revolutionary leadership.

It is not by struggling against "bourgeois ideology" in itself, on an ideological battleground, that the international, revolutionary parties, and, of course, a revolutionary youth organization can be built. It is by organizing youth on a battleground of political struggle for the benefit of the proletarian revolution and under the political leadership of the proletariat.

The formulation of the astonishing Essen amendment signifies that a youth organization is a substitute for a party and not part of the struggle to construct one. Theoretical elaboration proceeds from the program, and thus from the party. And the necessary link between theory and constructing a youth organization is training young communist cadres, a task that combines learning the program with political struggle.

PROGRAM, CONSCIOUSNESS, REVOLUTIONARY PARTY

But the Essen amendment goes further. By smuggling in the issue, since only youth organizations were being discussed, it makes ideological struggle the basis for constructing revolutionary parties.

"Revolutionary youth," we learn, "must devote themselves first of all to the task of developing Marxist theory."

At this point we are entitled to ask ourselves the following question. Is, or is not, the Transitional Program of the Fourth International the highest expression of Marxism, i.e., the theoretical generalization based on the Marxist method of the experiences, struggles, and acquisitions of the world proletariat, of the working-class movement as a whole?

On this point at least, the October 24 document is absolutely clear. The answer is No, and the content of the Essen amendment is thus fully illuminated.

Let us quote:

> What was most essential in the preparation of the sections was to develop dialectical materialism in a struggle to understand and to transform the consciousness of the working class in the changing objective conditions. This means the understanding and development of dialectical materialism as the theory of knowledge of Marxism.
>
> Reflecting the attacks on dialectical materialism by the petty-bourgeois intelligentsia of the advanced capitalist countries, especially France and Germany, and of E. Europe, the OCI and Hungarian delegations declared that dialectical materialism was not a theory of knowledge and took up the position that only programme was the basis of the building of parties. Here is the very essence of revisionism which prepares the way for liquidating the party into centrism.

You say so!

Innocents that we were, we thought that the method of the Transitional Program was to mobilize the working class on a revolutionary basis, starting from their present level of consciousness, against the bourgeois state, a task indissolubly linked to organizing the workers. We thought that the advance of the workers toward fulfilling their historical tasks depended on their consciousness, or as Marx and Engels said in *The German Ideology:*

> Both for the production on a mass scale of this communist consciousness, and for the success of the cause itself, the alteration of men on a mass scale is necessary, an alteration which can only take place in a practical movement, a *revolution;* this revolution is necessary, therefore, not only because the ruling class cannot be overthrown in any other way, but also because the class *overthrowing* it can only in a revolution succeed in ridding itself of all the muck of ages and become fitted to found society anew.

But, this is not so, the SLL says—"transforming" the consciousness of the working class is a specific task which becomes possible once you have "understood" this consciousness. And such understanding can be gained on the condition that you "develop" dialectical materialism. (What does that mean exactly? While we can understand how you can develop a muscle by special exercises, it is hard to conceive of "developing" dialectical materialism.)

What it means, in any case, is that the program is not enough. There is also supposed to be something higher, up in the sky, to tell the truth. This is supposed to exist as an independent force, whose "development" doubtless depends on the intellectual gymnastics of the SLL's thinkers—Marxist philosophy as "the theory of knowledge of Marxism." But what then is the program, if it is not the fullest expression of dialectical materialism in our epoch? A list of recipes?

This discussion must indeed be carried through to a conclusion, and preemptive "ruptures" justified by phony majorities are not going to stop it.

Deep disagreements appeared at Essen. Did they by themselves constitute a "split"? The proof that they did not was provided by the SLL leadership, who, after Essen, invited Comrade Lambert to give the concluding lecture at the SLL educational camp—a lecture on dialectical materialism!

FORM AND CONTENT— THE REVOLUTIONARY STRUGGLE OF THE BOLIVIAN PROLETARIAT, THE POLICY OF THE POR, AND THE DETERMINATION TO BREAK UP THE INTERNATIONAL COMMITTEE

It was not a sudden ideological vertigo that caused the SLL leadership's backsliding into ideology and putting forward fundamentally idealist positions.

The fog of this bogus Marxist "philosophy" descended over the SLL's political landscape at a precise moment and in response to precise political problems.

It is on the central question of reconstructing the Fourth International that the SLL leadership has oscillated most dangerously. It proclaims its disagreement with the decisions of the 1966 conference, which it had nonetheless accepted. The Fourth International does not have to be "reconstructed"; it is immutable, immobile, and incarnate in the International Committee.

In other words, the SLL leadership confounds preserving the continuity of the Fourth International and defending its program against an attempt at liquidation—as has been accomplished by the activity of the IC and its organizations—with the existence of political conditions, of relations between the Trotskyist organizations and the class, of conditions for selecting out an international leadership on the road toward forming a centralized international leadership.

This attitude is reinforced by a refusal to go all the way in analyzing the crisis of the Fourth International, by the tendency to see this crisis as merely an episode. But the Fourth International, reconstituted after the war, was shattered as an organization centralized on the basis of the Transitional Program—by the capitulation of the overwhelming majority of its leaders. And the origins of this capitulation must be traced if we are to conduct an effective struggle against revisionism.

There is no reason to reconstruct the Fourth International; it suffices to build the revolutionary party in every country. This in fact means constructing the Fourth International in every country. Thus, we find the correct assertion that the struggle for building the revolutionary party in every country is an international task reduced to a hollow formula, inasmuch as there is no longer any international dimension to this struggle in practice, that is, to the concrete work of reconstructing the Fourth International.

This is not a mere academic position. It has led the leadership of the SLL first to ignore and then, for all practical purposes, to oppose any initiatives taken in the process of reconstructing the Fourth International.

No Trotskyist organization can be built outside of the struggle for reconstructing the Fourth International. To the extent that this false orientation is pursued, the SLL's activity as a whole cannot fail to be affected. The ever expanding place occupied by "ideology" corresponds to the tightening impasse in which the SLL leadership is trapped.

From this standpoint, Essen marked an important stage. The oscillations of the SLL leadership were reflected in their refusal to participate in the Essen rally and then by their letting themselves be dragged into it without mobilizing their organization. They thus found themselves in an awkward position at this rally, and their "ideological" offensive was the expression of their political hostility toward this advance on the road of reconstructing the Fourth International which forced the SLL, as all the organizations of the IC, to face up to its responsibilities.

Unless you start off from the political contradictions in which the SLL leadership finds itself and its refusal to see them unraveled by discussion within the ranks of its organization, you cannot understand the astonishing bad faith and criminal light-mindedness with which it has approached the problems of the revolution in Bolivia and the policy of the POR. These are not moral failings but the results of an orientation that is leading the SLL down the road of abandoning the program of the Fourth International.

In all seriousness, the SLL leadership explains that Bolivia was only a pretext seized on by the OCI to precipitate a rupture and thus avoid a discussion.

The same relationship exists between the actual political developments in the IC and the SLL's claims as between the negative and positive of a photograph. You have to reverse their claims to find out the truth.

It was the SLL leadership and its spokesman in New York who seized on the problems of the Bolivian revolution, not as an occasion for political clarification, but as a pretext for presenting the other organizations of the IC with the accomplished fact of a brutal public offensive against the POR. It is the SLL leadership that is running away from a general discussion under cover of a public rupture on the Bolivian question and which, at the same time, is running away from a discussion on Bolivia.

But the form cannot be separated from the content. The pretext chosen is at the same time a question of crucial importance, since it touches directly on the proletarian revolution.

The revolutionary process in Bolivia marked the political high-point of the working-class upsurge throughout all of Latin America, and it was distinguished by the role played in the struggle by a Trotskyist party, a section of the IC.

What in fact deserves serious discussion is making a thorough account of the results of the POR's policy, learning the lessons of the struggle. To this extent, discussing the line followed at each stage by the POR is legitimate. For its part, the OCI did not wait for its hand to be forced by the events. Within the framework of the IC, among the organizations basing their activity on the same program, it already conducted a discussion with the POR. (See *La Verite*, No. 550, October 1970.)

What is criminal on the part of the Workers League and the SLL is that their deliberate attempt to take advantage of the victory of the August 1971 fascist coup to break the unity of the International Committee has led them to reject such serious discussion, to repeat the grossest slanders hurled against the POR by the enemies of Trotskyism and the proletarian revolution, without even trying to learn the facts. The coup d'etat took place on August 20. On August 30, while communications were cut off, Tim Wohlforth published an article singling out the POR as the section of the workers' movement mainly responsible for the victory of the fascist coup. In this article, on which the SLL quickly put its official stamp by publishing it in *Workers Press*, and in which there is not the slightest reference to solidarity in the fight against the class enemy or the least allusion to the role of American imperialism, Wohlforth went still further. He equated the POR's position with that of the LSSP in Ceylon. That is an amalgam comparable to the kind forged by the Stalinists. Even if you considered Wohlforth's attacks against the POR's policy to be correct, what relation is there between the LSSP renegades, sitting in a bourgeois government and covering up a bloody repression, and the POR fighters who rose with their class against the counterrevolution?

The attempt to treat the Bolivian question without any regard for the real positions of the POR but as a "ready-made weapon" against the unity of the IC is apparent again in the October 24 document.

> The POR and Lora repeat the policies of the POUM in Spain in 1935–1938 and are in no fundamental way different from them. Their relations with Torres and the COB parallel those of the POUM with the Republican Government and the CNT. The OCI's support for the POR now makes clear the political meaning of their bloc with the POUM at Essen.

This little paragraph is a concentration of untruths and a good example of an amalgam. Pages could be written on it alone. Let us limit ourselves to two observations. The first and crucial one "clarifies" the political crookedness of this false argument. One of the characteristic features of the POUM's policy was entering the Catalonian Generalidad (a bourgeois government). What characterized the policy of the POR was its refusal to collaborate with the Torres government, its preserving the political independence of the proletariat.

The second observation concerns the light-mindedness with which the SLL treats the problems of the history of the workers' movement. On the parallel between the CNT and the COB—the CNT was in the hands of a political faction, the anarchists. The POUM activists had been expelled and Trotsky chided them precisely for accepting this situation and founding their own trade-union organizations. The COB was an all-inclusive federation embracing all currents in the Bolivian working class. And, although the POR comrades were not in the leadership of it, they did play a considerable role, including at the level of the central leading bodies. Where is the parallel?

But there is better to come. In his interview with *Informations Ouvrieres*, Comrade Lora explained:

> The ultralefts and the Pabloites forget the teachings of Lenin and Trotsky: they draw up their "documents" in a simple-minded way and place Torres and Ovando-Banzer on the same level. These people refuse to understand the various shades that bourgeois nationalism can take in underdeveloped countries.
>
> Since they are removed from the class struggle, they do not understand the difference between the bourgeois-democratic methods of the Torres government and the methods of the fascists; that is, the difference between going to prison legally or getting killed by a bullet in the back of the neck.
>
> Revolutionary tactics must begin with this difference It is not a question of supporting Torres, but of crushing fascism in order to impose a workers' government.

This passage gets the following comment in the October 24 document:

Revolutionary strategy does not begin with the differences between left and right wings of the military, but from the perspective of the overthrow of the whole bourgeois order.

Where Lora spoke of tactics, the authors of the October 24 document substitute the term strategy. But the SLL has habitually made a practically absolute distinction between tactics and strategy. In discussing the united class front (we will come to this question), strategy and tactics are presented as totally distinct categories leading parallel existences in a metaphysical firmament. When it comes to attacking the policy of the POR, on the other hand, strategy and tactics become interchangeable terms.

When we read, moreover, that the SLL's critique of the POR's line was founded on the need for building "the Fourth International on the basis of political principle and complete honesty," we seem to find an unintentionally comic note in an otherwise sinister enough document.

But once again we must go to the root of the matter. The October 24 document, which proclaims Wohlforth's article "our public statement," has no more than this article itself to say about the Popular Assembly.

This, however, is the most important question, the basis on which the OCI first determined its position, the basis on which it made its assessment of the POR's line.

Therefore, it is this question that must be discussed first. But from reading the October 24 document, you will learn only that the OCI talks about an "overall process" embodied in "something" like the Popular Assembly.

In its September 17 statement, the CC of the OCI stressed that the POR had been

> the inspirer and driving force of the People's Assembly, i.e., the organ that incarnated the struggle of the Bolivian people to create their own government and which was opening the way toward a dictatorship of the proletariat in Bolivia.

Yes or no, was the Popular Assembly, whose origins lay in the united response of the Bolivian masses and their organizations to the October 1970 coup d'etat, an organ in which proletarian hegemony asserted itself from top to bottom?

Yes or no, did the Popular Assembly become, through the intervention of the POR, an organ of dual power opening up the way concretely for a workers' government? Did it, or did it not, deserve the label, pinned on it by its enemies, of the first soviet in Latin America?

Was it or was it not the correct strategy to take this reality created by the struggle of the masses themselves as a starting point? Was it or was it not correct to pose the question of power by linking an attempt to rally the masses around the Popular Assembly, as the organization expressing their will, to a struggle inside the assembly itself to open up the way concretely for the slogan "All Power to the Popular Assembly"?

Could such a struggle have been conducted without regard for the dangers of isolating the vanguard in Bolivia from the revolutionary development of the masses themselves, without regard for the position of the Bolivian revolution with respect to revolutionary developments in Latin America as a whole?

The OCI gave an answer to these questions. The anti-Trotskyist center of Mandel and Co., in the midst of confusion, gave its own. What is the answer of the SLL and the other groups that signed the October 24 statement?

This is also a discussion that cannot be avoided by any organizational maneuver, because it lies at the heart of the problems posed by the present stage of the class struggle. The period of the "imminence of revolution"—and thus also of imminent counterrevolution—is one of class confrontations raising the question of power. How can the masses perceive, grasp the question of power concretely?

This is a problem of institutions of dual power, of the working-class united front, of slogans dealing with the form of political rule. These are, of course, concrete questions, as the October 24 document notes. But this concreteness would only be a dead abstraction were it not the expression of a "general" principle, which is that the period we are living in is one when the march of the international working class toward power is taking form.

This is not, as we see it, an abstraction of which the revolutionary party should be a passive expression. This way of understanding the problems posed shows clearly the SLL's profound misconception of the dialectic. To the contrary, this advance is a concrete reality in which the revolutionary party, the fight to build the revolutionary party nationally and internationally, is the decisive element.

ON SOME ATTACKS AGAINST THE OCI

There is an implacable logic to political conflicts. The SLL's evolution could only lead it to attack the line of the OCI and to attack what is central to it—the very method of building the revolutionary party, the question of the working-class united front as the means and expression of mass mobilization, the essential factor in building the party.

But politics does not take place in a void. If you attack the OCI's line, you have to propose another. And for this purpose the SLL has had to go to the arsenal of Pabloism. Thus, its attacks against the OCI's line culminate in this conclusion:

> ... the OCI's position on the "united class front" becomes a complete liquidation of the party and its subordination to the Stalinist and social democratic parties and union apparatus.

But to come to this result, the SLL leadership thought itself obliged to attribute a "spontaneist" position to the OCI, which it made up of whole cloth with the help of vague terms. The SLL leadership felt it necessary to launch a flurry of attacks so exaggerated as to be meaningless to anyone who has observed the policy of the OCI and which—if they contained a grain of truth—would make it impossible to understand how the OCI and the SLL could have collaborated in the International Committee.

For our part, we seek political clarity, not to create an effect that can only fool those who want to be fooled. The SLL has not gone from good to bad overnight We will confine ourselves to pointing out the contradictions in which its leadership is entangling it and to showing that, if continued, the present orientation would lead to abandoning the program of the Fourth International and thus to the breakup of the SLL.

We want to draw attention to just two of the SLL's attacks.

First of all, the October 24 document dares claim that on the eve of 1968, Comrade Charles Berg had taken an openly *abstentionist* position on Vietnam. What this means in plain language is that he equated the actions of the imperialists and the revolutionary war of the Vietnamese people, in other words, that he had an openly counterrevolutionary position. This is an infamous lie. Not even the Stalinists have dared go to such lengths. So far only the illustrious Weber of the Ligue Communiste has talked about the OCI having a "defeatist" position.

Never in any way has any activist or any publication reflecting the views of the OCI equivocated on this question. To the contrary, and in contrast to some others (such as Comrade Banda who has seen in the party of Ho Chi Minh, the party that murdered the Indochinese Trotskyists, a reincarnation of the Bolsheviks), we have never confused unconditional support for the Vietnamese revolution with political support for the petty-bourgeois and Stalinist leaderships.

Having said this, if we dwell on this contemptible accusation, it is because at this time, owing to the growth of the AJS, Comrade Berg is the target of concentrated attacks from the bourgeoisie, the Stalinists, and the Pabloites. The fact that the SLL leadership has chosen this time to add its voice to the chorus is worthy of being noted.

The second attack that merits comment by us is the following. In its eagerness to find reasons for a rupture, the SLL leadership has gone digging into the past, as is its right. It has vehemently denounced the French Trotskyist organization's line toward the Algerian revolution. It has said that the Pabloites supported one petty-bourgeois nationalist faction and the French Trotskyists another. This is a bit oversimplified; it would be convincing only if the SLL were making its own self-criticism on this matter. In fact, if there was no difference between the FLN and the MNA, why did it, as it explains, give its support to the MNA? This support, we learn, was "critical," which doubtless makes everything all right.

The fact remains that the policy of the Trotskyist organization was wrong because it abandoned "the fight to select out a Trotskyist vanguard." There is no revelation in this. The above quotation is taken from the pamphlet *Quelques enseignements de notre histoire* ["Some Lessons From Our History"], published in May 1970.

We would express only one wish, and all the more so since the SLL thinks it useful to accuse the Lora POR of having been a pillar of Pabloism in Latin America—which is untrue—while failing to note, on the other hand, that in the early stage its own general secretary was the Pabloites' hatchet-man in Western Europe. Our wish is that the SLL would condescend, for the edification of the vanguard in Great Britain and throughout the world, to draw some lessons from its own history.

THE OFFENSIVE AGAINST THE UNITED CLASS FRONT AND ITS MEANING

The SLL's trumped-up charges against the OCI's line culminate in a general offensive against the united class front.

The question of the united class front has already occasioned differences between the OCI and the SLL in the IC. But for the SLL these differences seem to boil down to one point (which is raised again in the October 24 document), that is, the united front is a "tactic" and the OCI is making it a "strategy."

Counterposing strategy and tactics as absolutes means ignoring the dialectic involved. Of course, these terms are not identical; they refer to different levels of revolutionary politics. But strategy exists only through tactics, which express it, and at the same time every tactical operation has meaning only as it enters into a general strategy.

When we speak, in Marxist terms, of a strategic slogan, we are describing a slogan that in various forms (tactics) is a constant in revolutionary struggle. One example is the need for defending the social gains of the proletariat won by the October revolution and its extensions, which are today controlled and threatened by the bureaucracy. But strategy and tactics are relative terms for Marxists. Inasmuch as we can say that the strategic line of the Fourth International comes down to struggling for the proletarian revolution, the defense of the USSR is only a tactic flowing from this objective. Thus Trotsky could say the following about the defense of the USSR (while pointing out at the same time that this task was a major expression of the program of the Fourth International and a matter of principle):

> The defense of the USSR coincides for us with the preparation of world revolution. Only those methods are permissible which do not conflict with the interests of the revolution. The defense of the USSR is related to the world socialist revolution as a tactical task is related to a strategic one. A tactic is subordinated to a strategic goal and in no case can be in contradiction to the latter.

In this sense, in relation to the socialist revolution for which, as a means of mobilizing the proletariat, it prepares the way, the united class front is a tactic. It is a strategic line insofar as it is always (that is, without regard to the circumstances, the relationship of forces, or tactical factors in the strict sense of the term) *present* in a revolutionary policy. It is present, to be sure, in various tactical forms. Otherwise, it would be only an illusion. (The forms it takes are the slogan for "a government by the united working-class organizations" in France today; the battle for "a labor party based on the unions" in the United States; the slogan of "a Labour government on a program of defending the workers" in Great Britain; the slogan of "end the coalition and establish a purely Social Democratic government" in Germany.)

It will be seen, then, that it was not quarreling over definitions that brought the OCI into conflict with the implicit line now made explicit by the SLL in its October 24 document.

No, the united front is not, as the SLL says, only "a relationship between mass workers' parties of a temporary character for the purpose of winning the masses to the Communist Party." Reducing the united class front to this is not, as the SLL leadership falsely claims, the conception of Lenin and Trotsky. At best it was the one held by Zinoviev, or rather the current caricature of it based on the weaknesses in the way Zinoviev explained the policy of the Communist International.

The axis of the Transitional Program is to mobilize the workers to overthrow the bourgeoisie. It is in this sense that the united front, a "slogan" raised by this program, also lies at its center because it involves rallying the entire class and uniting it on the basis of political independence, against the common enemy. This is the translation into the concrete of the primary principle of every revolutionary policy since the *Communist Manifesto* in 1847—class against class. And where the working class is under the leadership and control of separate organizations, this policy takes the form of a united front of all the organizations of the class.

This is the way the document advanced by the OCI in September 1969 put it:

> The policy of class struggling against class represents the strategic line of the united class front of workers' parties and organizations. It is alien to "peaceful coexistence" between the traditional working-class parties and organizations and the revolutionary vanguard building the revolutionary party. Unless a policy is defined concretely, at every stage, counterposing the working class as a class to the bourgeoisie, its state, and its government, it is impossible to build the revolutionary party. Unless you build the revolutionary party, it is impossible to fight for a united class front, for a workers and peasants' government, for the destruction of the bourgeois state and for workers' power.

This conclusion recapitulates perfectly the conception of the united front brought to the fore by Trotsky in dealing with Germany, fascism, and France at the time of the working-class upsurge initiated by the united demonstration of February 12, 1934:

> First of all they [the usual formal definitions of soviets] do not explain why, in the struggle for power, precisely the soviets are necessary. The answer to this question is: just as the trade union is the rudimentary form of united front in the economic struggle, *the soviet is the highest form of the united front* under the conditions in which the proletariat enters the epoch of fighting for power.
>
> [And again] The natural mechanism of the united front in the days of combat is working-class representation, delegates from the factories and workshops, from working-class neighborhoods and unions—soviets.

It is this conception the SLL leadership is objecting to when it criticizes the OCI's line at the time of the 1968 general strike.

The October 24 document includes this sentence, which deserves being passed on to posterity.

> . . . the OCI leaders tail-ended the working class and restricted the political scope of the strike by demanding a central strike committee. This was a complete evasion of the *political* responsibilities of revolutionary leadership.

Thus, for the "deep-thinking" dialecticians of the SLL, the question of a national central strike committee was not a political one. This is an admission that points up the meaning of several things, such as: their hostile indifference toward the Popular Assembly in Bolivia; the absence, in a document purporting to be based on international developments in the class struggle, of any reference to the formation of workers' councils in Gdansk in December 1970; as well as the significance of the disparaging quotation marks placed around *Irbid soviet*.

Were the strike committees, thus, "economic" bodies? If so, then the general strike itself was an "economic strike," inasmuch as no "formula" was injected into it calling for a change in the government. No, a general strike, "one of the most acute forms of class struggle," as Leon Trotsky said, shows precisely the "impossibility of divorcing the economic element from the political one," as anyone knows who has taken the time to study Marxism since Rosa Luxemburg set down this precept in 1905. The general strike immediately assumed a *political* character both because the demands advanced led directly into struggling against the capitalist government and because the extent and form of the mass mobilization posed the question of working-class power. As a political struggle, the general strike was destined to prove incapable of achieving its objectives unless the illusion was outgrown that the economic action in itself could be victorious—unless an outlet could be opened leading into a struggle for power, a means of pushing for an alternative form of government.

It was such an outlet that was blocked by all the apparatuses linked to the bourgeoisie. The struggle for a national central strike committee was at the heart of the general strike. It was a political struggle par excellence because its objective was to open this outlet by centralizing the power of the working class *in struggle* against the bourgeois state.

This was to take place "in struggle," it must not be forgotten. This was why giving a centralized structure to the strike committees born out of this struggle—which was a stage on the road leading to workers' councils as the constituent elements of a united class front—was the concrete form that shaped up for projecting the perspective of a workers' government, a government of united workers' organizations.

But the SLL leadership, not satisfied with showing its utter ignorance of the dialectic of mobilizing the masses in general strikes, offers another formula for an alternative government, a CP-CGT [Confederation Generale du Travail—General Confederation of Labor, the CP-controlled union federation], and not a workers' government. Or rather, if the formula of a CP-CGT government could be considered synonymous with a "workers' government," it would mean that the Socialist party, the CGT-FO [Force Ouvriere—Labor Power, the federation produced by a Social Democratic-led split after the CP gained control of the CGT as a whole], and FEN [Federation de l'Education Nationale—National Teachers' Federation] were not working-class organizations. So far the SLL has never said this in writing. But what then is the meaning of this preference for the Stalinist bureaucracy over the reformist bureaucracy? Haven't both gone over to the side of the bourgeois order? Or is this a new analysis of Stalinism? Not such a new one, because it has already been set forth in the theory and practice of the Pablos and the Mandels. This attitude holds that—no matter what its crimes and its counterrevolutionary aspects—the Stalinist movement is the only political "representation" the workers have on an international scale.

This question also must be discussed. It is linked to a number of the SLL's political oscillations, such as the following: Its idealization of the North Vietnamese Communist party leadership and the NLF; its grave doubts about the political revolution in Czechoslovakia, apprehensions which led it, in assessing the situation just after the country was invaded by the tanks of the bureaucracy, to give equal weight to the need for struggling against capitalist restoration and to the demand for the withdrawal of Warsaw Pact troops; its discretion about the developments in the political revolution in Poland; and its refusal to comprehend the unity of the workers' struggle in the USSR, China, and East Europe against the bureaucracy and the struggle in the countries under the capitalist yoke.

Such a discussion will also clarify the meaning of the SLL's criticism—which may seem minor and tactical in nature—of the slogan of "one candidate representing the working-class organizations" at the time of the presidential elections. Once again, the form of this criticism shows the SLL's lack of concern for the facts. Thus, the OCI is scolded for failing to denounce the Social Democracy which refused to vote for Duclos in the second round. The French working class has enough well-founded accusations to raise against this reformist leadership. It does not need to invent any. Duclos was eliminated in the first round. This said, and so that things will be clear—because this again involves a tactical application of the strategic line of the united front—here is the position the Trotskyists took at the time of the presidential elections:

> In the wake of de Gaulle's fall, the perspective of a working-class alternative to the government and to the regime dominated the development of the great struggles of the proletariat. Such an alternative could arise only from a united front of the trade-union and political organizations that called for a No vote in the referendum. A single candidate representing the workers' organizations meant that these organizations were posing the alternative of a government of united workers' organizations against the bourgeois parties. Immediately, all the leaderships of the workers' organizations, especially the Socialist party and PCF leaders, maneuvered furiously to break the unity of the front brought together by the No vote in the referendum. Defferre's candidacy—supported by Mendes-France—was produced like a rabbit out of a hat. Before putting forward Duclos as a candidate, the PCF demanded the "formulation of a common program," as a condition for agreeing on a joint "left" candidate This worrying about program by the PCF, which in 1965 supported the bourgeois candidate Mitterrand without requiring any "common program,"

was designed to prevent one candidate from being put up by the workers' organizations and not by the "left." Developing a political campaign on the theme of running one candidate of the workers' organizations against the candidates of the bourgeoisie meant fighting for a united class front, a working-class front, against the divisions in the proletariat willfully and deliberately imposed by the Socialist party and the PCF. . . .

But what about program? Didn't a single candidate put up by the workers' organizations need a program? What was it developing into? In these specific circumstances, the development of a program for a government of the united workers' organizations derived from this joint campaign. By fighting for the defeat of the candidates of the bourgeoisie, the working class would have given a class content to the united campaign of the workers' organizations. And it was the job of the revolutionary organizations to develop this campaign. (Stephane Just, *Defense du Trotskysme* ["In Defense of Trotskyism"].)

IN CONCLUSION

We are coming to the end of this correction. Its objective has been to clarify—over and above the petty maneuvers, outrageous untruths, and verbal terrorism of the SLL—the real differences that divide us from this organization.

These differences are grave ones, deep ones. They demand a discussion out in the open. And the OCI has no fear of conducting such a debate publicly, in full view of the international workers' vanguard.

As one of the concluding points in its indictment of the OCI, the SLL leadership claims that the capitulation to spontaneism reached such a point in this organization that—it didn't even have a general secretary!

What should we say about the shamelessness and the depth of capitulation to spontaneism reached by a party like the Bolsheviks, who dared to lead the proletarian revolution to victory witout a general secretary and without even a political bureau?

This seems merely ridiculous. It is obvious that, while democratic centralism is part of the revolutionary program, the ways in which a leadership is organized are not a matter of principle, and the existence or nonexistence of general secretaries is no guarantee. But this charge is related to something deeper. For in the same paragraph the OCI is reproached for its erroneous notion "that the Fourth International does not really exist." This is a tendentious way of attacking the position held by the OCI, which is that we must fight to reconstruct the Fourth International, which was shattered as a politically centralized force on an international scale by the Pabloite liquidators.

There is, then, on the one hand, the revolutionary party, sufficient unto itself, an immutable metaphysical category awaiting its encounter with the class struggle. Its existence as a party depends on whether or not it is proclaimed to be so, on whether or not it has attributes arbitrarily determined to belong to it (such as a general secretary, for example).

On the other hand, there is the proletariat, its "objective" struggle, its general strikes which are not supposed to be "political." In its defense of the Essen amendment, the October 24 document pinpoints that

> only a basic struggle for dialectical materialism against all enemies of Marxism and carried forward in struggle *against* the spontaneous consciousness of the working class, can equip the youth for building of the Fourth International.

The dialectic has been decidedly mishandled here. Independently of the fact that the concept of a spontaneous "pure" working-class consciousness is strictly an arbitrary abstraction—proletarian class consciousness always being a product of history—this sentence sums up an entire, profoundly false, conception of the relationship between the revolutionary party (because this is what the struggle for dialectical materialism is!) and the movement of the class.

The revolutionary party is not parallel to or in opposition to the working-class movement. The construction of the revolutionary party proceeds from the overall development of the class struggle. It is based on the class struggle although not automatically produced by it. It can only exist and grow as conscious activity.

Marxism is "the conscious expression of an unconscious process." The revolutionary party is the organized form this conscious expression takes in the class struggle, but the conditions themselves of the proletarian revolution assign it a decisive role in accomplishing the historic tasks of the class.

Marxism, the method of the proletarian revolution, taking form as the unity of theory and practice in the construction of the revolutionary party and thus expressing the historic interests of the proletariat, stands in opposition to every limited stage in the formation of the class consciousness of the proletariat as a class in bourgeois society. But it rises above these limited stages by unifying the overall process of the formation of proletarian consciousness in which it is the ultimate determinant. This truth has been known since the *Communist Manifesto;* except on this basis Trotsky's phrase about "the proletariat's instinctive tendency to reconstruct society on communist foundations" would be only a utopian formula.

As S. Just noted in his *Defense du Trotskysme:*

> Considered as a historic and organic process, the development of the proletariat's class consciousness arises, then, out of an analysis of the progress of the class struggle. So let us have an end to these metaphysical discussions about whether or not class consciousness is brought in from the outside, as well as the ones about whether or not a vanguard is self-appointed.

The dualism the SLL leadership introduces between the party and the class lies at the root of its failure to understand the period in which we are living, the dynamic of the march of the world proletariat toward the socialist revolution, which was revealed concretely in the May–June 1968 general strike, in the political revolution in Czechoslovakia, in the formation of the Irbid soviet, in the formation of the Baltic workers' councils, and in the formation of the Popular Assembly.

The SLL's extreme subjectivism is thus inevitably accompanied by a mechanical objectivism. Thus, we learn that the years of the "postwar boom" were unfavorable to the development of Marxist theory (we wonder how the Transitional Program could have been formulated in years marked by profound setbacks and about the meaning of Trotsky's statement that the Fourth International was born out of the deepest defeats!), but that the "new conditions" are favorable to us.

Subjectivism and objectivism indissolubly linked were the methodological roots of the development of Pabloism within the Fourth International. The SLL leadership is paying the price today for its refusal to make a real accounting of Pabloism and its origins, which could not be done without analyzing its own history, without linking the problems of reconstructing the Fourth International with those of constructing the revolutionary party in Great Britain.

But there is nothing automatic about this. It is in connection with the specific political problems pushed to the fore by the struggle of the working class, the problems of the struggle for power itself, the precise timing of the struggle to reconstruct the Fourth International, that these features of the SLL are developing today into a policy whose logic, through the SLL's rupture with the International Committee, is leading to the abandonment of the program of the Fourth International.

In a responsible way, we appeal to all organizations and militants affiliated to the International Committee. In particular, we appeal to the SLL, its leadership and its ranks, because of this organization's special place in the formation of the International Committee

We say in a responsible way that the SLL is at a crossroads. The role of an organization and its political character do not depend on subjective intentions. No organization can exist without a definite political character. The SLL has won the place that it occupies in the class struggle in Great Britain as a Trotskyist organization. By setting out on the dangerous road of a rupture with the International Committee, the SLL is proceeding toward a break with Trotskyism—which has no existence outside the Fourth International, that is, in today's terms, outside the struggle to reconstruct the Fourth International. The SLL is thus setting out on the road that leads to its own destruction.

In any case, because the struggle for the reconstruction of the Fourth International is an international process organically linked to the world struggle of the proletariat, the conscious struggle for the construction of the revolutionary party will find expression in Great Britain in the resistance within the SLL's own ranks to its liquidation as a Trotskyist organization. But, we firmly declare, the path indicated by the interests of the Fourth International, by the need for defending its program, is one of political clarification.

A plenum of the International Committee must be convened as soon as possible, with the participation of all the member organizations. This is necessary, in particular, in response to Comrade G. Lora's legitimate request.

False pretexts for evading the political problems and genuine flight from them, amalgams, crass maneuvers—all this cannot go very far. We must end the false idolization of leaders, who, while doing positive work, have, like everybody else, made political mistakes. No section of the International Committee can run away from discussing the whole range of questions that the Trotskyist movement is compelled by the class struggle to settle.

We say, in any case, that this discussion will take place. No one has the power to prevent it.

In any case, the achievement represented by the International Committee, the continuity of the Fourth International and of its program will be preserved through the struggle for the reconstruction of the Fourth International and through the preparation of the fourth international conference initiated by the International Committee, which, on the basis of the decisions of the 1966 conference, will bring together all the organizations and groups fighting for the program of the socialist revolution.

We repeat. For all those who want to defend the program of the Fourth International, there is one demand. The International Committee must meet at the earliest possible date.

The Central Committee of the OCI
(for the reconstruction of the Fourth International)
NOVEMBER 21, 1971

'Construct' or 'Reconstruct' the Fourth International?
By Pierre Frank

The following is a translation of an article scheduled for publication in *Quatrième Internationale*.

For many years the stability of the large traditional workers' organizations and the monolithic character of the Communist parties gave rise to comments, often not very intelligent, on the contrast to the numerous splits among the Trotskyists. Many people, especially centrists who engaged in vain exertions to construct mass organizations, claimed that these splits expressed an inherent defect in Trotskyism.

In the last few years, the picture has changed considerably. It is rather hard to keep track of the splits in the various Maoist, spontanéist, etc., groups in the world, while the sections of the Fourth International have been registering substantial progress. Furthermore, since the Sino-Soviet dispute, Stalinist monolithism has been shattered beyond any possible repair. We have seen serious convulsions in some Communist parties in power (Czechoslovakia, Poland, Yugoslavia), even open splits in many other CPs (Spain, Greece, etc.).

Splits, therefore, no longer appear as the exclusive vice of the Trotskyists. In truth, the history of the workers' movement shows it to be, among other things, an incessant struggle of tendencies and groupings, entailing splits and reunifications. In fact, if there was ever anything that had hitherto been unknown in the workers' movement, it was the monolithic character imposed on workers' formations by the power of a bureaucratized workers state.

If the struggles of tendencies, splits, and regroupments have a varying importance on the

---

Intercontinental Press, March 6, 1972.

general level of the struggle of the masses, they are rarely without some political significance that ought to be examined. This holds true likewise for the break that has just taken place between the French OCI-AJS [Organisation Communiste Internationaliste-Alliance des Jeunes pour Socialisme—Internationalist Communist Organization-Alliance of Youth for Socialism] on the one hand and the British SLL [Socialist Labour League] on the other. These two organizations[1] constituted the main components of an "International Committee" whose objective was the "reconstruction" of the Fourth International, which had, according to their account, been destroyed by "Pabloism."

On various occasions we have explained[2] that at the end of the second world war, immense new problems were posed; that differing responses to them on the part of revolutionary Marxists, combined with the effects of considerable centrifugal forces, had precipitated a period of splits within the Fourth International; that this period ended in 1963, when the principal Trotskyist organizations in the world wound up advancing identical answers to these new problems and reuniting. Some groups refused to take part in this reunification, thus enabling some people to claim that there were four international organizations, all asserting their right to the name of the Fourth International.

That the Stalinists indulge in amalgamating these diverse formations in order to fight Trotskyism is not surprising. But for other, politically experienced people to commit such an error betrays a lack of common sense.

In point of fact, it suffices to see things as they really are:

As far as the "Posadistas" are concerned, it is impossible, even displaying much good will, to consider them to be anything more than a screwball sect of no political interest.

The "Pabloites," who are numerically small but politically well-defined, have nothing at all in common with the Fourth International. They renounced it implicitly upon splitting, when they said they were leaving the "hardened champions of a dead past without a future." (This is the basic reason they did not want to remain in the reunified international.) Today, they implicitly recognize this in preparing to eliminate mention of the Fourth International from their name.

On the international scale, outside the Fourth International, there was only Lambert and Healy's joint "committee," consisting of two national organizations of some size, asserting adherence to Trotskyism, waging a fierce, virulent battle against the existing Fourth International, and claiming to be constructing, or reconstructing, one that would have absolutely nothing in common with "Pabloism." Crash! The "International Committee" is now split wide open, and Lambert and Healy are denouncing each other in terms no less virulent than those they used against the Fourth International; each even finding that the other has become infected with "Pabloism."

The public documents of this struggle issued up to now are as follows: a declaration signed by Lambert, Lora, etc., last October 12; a declaration of the SLL, etc., October 24; a reply by Lambert November 21.[3] These documents do not provide complete clarity on the origins and basis of the break, but just the same they enable us to see, at least in part, what united Healy and Lambert and what led them to separate.

What united them

For a long time their unity was cemented by a common hostility—which neither of them has lost, toward the Fourth International. But what is the source of this hostility? As Trotskyists both of them recognize in principle the necessity of a revolutionary Marxist international, functioning on the basis of international democratic centralism.

But for them, this is an abstract concept; and between this concept and what they actually do, there is a big gap. Each has a national domain in which he operates politically because they think above all in terms of tactics. They accept general analyses on a world scale only so long as these do

---

1. For the sake of convenience, I will use the names of Healy and Lambert to designate these organizations.

2. See, among others, chapter six of my book *la Quatrieme Internationale*.

3. Lambert and Lora's October 12 declaration was printed in *Intercontinental Press*, November 1, 1971, p. 942. The SLL's October 24 declaration can be found in *Intercontinental Press*, November 22, 1971, p. 1015. Lambert's response of November 21 was printed in *Intercontinental Press*, January 17, 1972, p. 46.—IP

not upset the policies they decide on on a national scale. This trait, already observable in them when they were still members of the Fourth International, could only become worse after their break with the latter in 1952–53.

This trait received formal status at their 1966 international conference, where they passed a motion according to which their committee was bound only by unanimous decisions.[4]

They could not accept the reunification (in 1963), because they would have been in a minority. Not wanting to admit this openly, they concealed their fundamental hostility to a world party capable of interfering in their "national" affairs by denouncing the Fourth International as a "Pabloite" organization.

This became more and more ridiculous as time went on, for while they continually attacked Mandel, Maitan, Frank, Tariq Ali, Hansen, Krivine, etc., as "Pabloites," they never said a word about Pablo's current positions. The farce has reached the slapstick stage, now that they have discovered "Pabloism" in each other. Among them, this term no longer has any political content whatsoever. A Pabloite is any person who claims to be a Trotskyist but disagrees with them.

Along with this "national" trait, they both follow the same concept as to how to build an organization. Both of them are constantly cooking up gimmicks designed for no other aim but to recruit.[5] Hence the slogans often having no direct relation to development of the class struggle at any given moment, but advanced in ways to pull in new members. One of the consequences of this style of operating, to take the Lambertists as an example, is that since May 1968 (in which they floundered completely) they have let the mass demonstrations go by—in the demonstrations of solidarity with the Vietnamese people, they have not shown up; in the Burgos demonstrations they appeared belatedly after the Communist party was constrained to do something following the demonstrations of the far left; in the demonstrations of high-school students around the Guyot affair, they were not to be seen . . .

What divides them

There were frequent disagreements between the Lambertists and the Healyites, especially in 1966, but they remained united. There was no split when Healy refused to defend the Lambertist dogma according to which the productive forces continued to stagnate following the second world war. What was the origin then of the crisis that led to an open split?

According to Lambert's November 21 document, the disagreements allegedly began in 1969, when they decided to prepare an international conference of their committee. These disagreements are said to have intensified during 1970, about the time Healy went to the Fourth International to ask that a discussion be opened with the perspective of possible reunification.[6]

It was on the occasion of their rally at Essen (at the beginning of July 1971) that the conflict became public. Lambert rejected an amendment advanced at the rally by Healy. About three months later, the position taken by Lora during the Bolivian events precipitated the open break.

On the Bolivian question, Healy—aside from his usual excesses, such as comparing Lora with the Ceylonese Lanka Sama Samaja party ministers who participated in the repression in their country—criticized Lora for having followed a Menshevik policy in hoping, as he had himself written, that General Torres would arm the workers against the other generals. Lambert answered that the Popular Assembly had "become, through the intervention of Lora's POR, an organ of dual power," "an organism in which the hegemony of the proletariat is affirmed from top to bottom." How could a few speeches, which did not even call upon the workers to arm themselves, have created dual power?

On the other hand, after the split, Lambert condemned Healy for giving "critical support" to "the bourgeois Indian government"[7] for its military intervention in Bangladesh. One can see

---

4. Were there already differences between them? In any case, once outside the Fourth International, they showed the true nature of their "internationalism."

5. On this point, see H. Weber's pamphlet *Qu'est-ce que l'A.J.S.?*

6. See *Quatrieme Internationale,* No 45 (September 1970). Proposing possible reunification undermined their whole struggle against "Pabloism." In his November 21 document Lambert takes Healy to task for this maneuver, but at the time Lambert did not publicly disavow it.

7. *Workers Press,* December 6, 1971.

that Healy and Lambert bounce the ball back at each other, trading charges of opportunism. Each sees the faults of the other. But for our "national Trotskyists," neither Bangladesh nor Bolivia is the determining factor in the split.

Although the causes are also not to be found in Lambert's policies in France, it is fitting to mention the criticism Healy advanced in his October 24 document and the defense made by Lambert in his November 21 reply to Healy. Here the opportunist politics of the OCI emerge in full clarity.

In the first place, Healy accuses Lambert of having drawn such pessimistic conclusions from de Gaulle's rise to power that he was incapable of preparing for May 1968 and that as a result he tail-ended during the events themselves.

> May–June 1968, with the French workers on General Strike, themselves striving for an alternative government, was the greatest testing time for the OCI. But what did the strike reveal?
>
> It revealed the theoretical bankruptcy and political impotence of the OCI whose leadership—guided by a superficial impressionist analysis of de Gaulle's coup in 1958—had exaggerated the strength and viability of the Fifth Republic, abandoned its revolutionary perspective and written off the revolutionary capacities of the French working class.
>
> This defeatist conception, which extended even to the Vietnam war, was summed up in the rationalization of Lambert that the French working class was "decisively defeated in 1958". This pessimistic and essentially middle-class outlook expressed itself in all the organizational and agitational work of the OCI and the AJS before and after 1968. It is an undeniable fact that at no time during the General Strike did the OCI leadership advance a socialist programme. Nor did it attempt to undermine the political credibility of the Stalinist leadership by critically supporting the demand of the Renault workers for a "popular government" by advancing the demand of a CP-CGT government. Instead the OCI leaders tail-ended the working class and restricted the political scope of the strike by demanding a central strike committee.

This was a complete evasion of the *political* responsibilities of revolutionary leadership.

This same tail-ending tendency, Healy said, was shown in the 1969 presidential election. In practice the Lambertists split, some voting for Duclos, others for Defferre, and still others, like Lambert himself, abstaining.

> Even from this 1968 experience the lessons were not learned. In fact the abstentionist methods and omissions of the General Strike period were continued into the presidential elections of 1969.
>
> In the referendum in March of the same year, the OCI had correctly campaigned for a vote against de Gaulle, in contrast to the abstentionism of the Pabloites. However, the gains from this correct turn were lost in the presidential elections, the class character of which was ignored by the OCI. Basing themselves on their fraudulent theory of the "United Class Front", the OCI leaders used the failure of the CP and Socialist Party to agree on a single candidate as a pretext for not supporting the CP candidate, Duclos, against Pompidou.
>
> The task of revolutionaries was to raise the consciousness of Stalinist rank and file by critically supporting Duclos and pointing out that the main enemy was Pompidou. The OCI should have campaigned throughout the labour movement to demand that the CP candidate be pledged to a socialist policy against the banks and monopolies. To carry forward this fight, while calling for a massive vote for Duclos, was the best way to exposing the Stalinists and their programme of "advanced democracy" and fighting for alternative revolutionary leadership. Any other course leaves the Stalinist control undisturbed. It was also necessary to expose the SP candidate whose party refused to vote for Duclos in the second ballot and supported the bourgeois candidate, Poher.
>
> The OCI leaders did none of these things. Some members voted for Duclos, others for Deferre (SP) and others, including comrade Lambert, abstained. What was worse, the

OCI attacked the Stalinists for having dared to stand a candidate in the elections despite the fact that the Stalinists in the previous presidential elections in 1965 did not do so and instead supported Mitterrand, a bourgeois politician.

In Healy's opinion, these were not accidental errors, because Lambert has oriented not toward the workers influenced by the Stalinists but toward the more backward ones following the Social Democrats:

> At no time has the OCI been able consistently to put forward a policy and programme to bring it close to the mass of the French workers who vote for the Stalinists and are organized around the Stalinist-led CGT. Instead they have orientated towards those sections still supporting the social-democrats, primarily in the older industries.

This orientation toward the Social Democracy has recently been intensified. After all, isn't it necessary to "save" the Socialist party from Mitterrand?

After long denying all revolutionary perspectives, Lambert has now discovered "the imminence of revolution." This turn, which to my knowledge was made without any serious explanation, has not changed the Lambertist policy. As before, this policy still consists in calling for a "united class front." Healy denounces this as abandoning the perspective of building a revolutionary party:

> Now the OCI, using the formula, "imminence of revolution", elaborating a schema of natural stages through which the working class passes on the road to power, distorting the tactic of united front of the working class, has taken the road of liquidationism laid down by these revisionists.

Earlier in the document, Healy says:

> Within this framework the OCI's position on the "united class front" becomes a complete liquidation of the party and its subordination to the Stalinist and social democratic parties and union apparatus. Lenin and Trotsky saw the united front as a *tactic* and not a strategy as the OCI claim. They saw it as a relationship between mass workers' parties of a temporary character for the purpose of winning the masses to the Communist Party. The OCI has transformed this into an overall "unity" of the class achieved on the basis of its present leadership, without the participation in the united front of our party. This "united class front" more and more, in their theorizing and practice, takes over the role of the revolutionary party itself.

In his November 21 reply Lambert ducks questions such as his having oriented his activities toward the backward sections of the French working class by asking Healy if the PS [Parti Socialiste] and Force Ouvrière are not "workers' organizations," and leaving the impression that Healy's "preference" is the Stalinist bureaucracy—which would be a manifestation of "Pabloism."

Lambert displays his opportunism with notable clearness when in opposition to Healy he argues for his "united class front." This policy, he writes,

> is a strategic line insofar as it is always (that is, without regard to the circumstances, the relationship of forces, or tactical factors in the strict sense of the term) *present* in a revolutionary policy. [He specifies further on] And where the working class is under the leadership and control of separate organizations, this policy takes the form of a united front of all the organizations of the class.

In other words, where the workers are organized and led by reformist organizations, a revolutionary policy would always include a united front of these organizations, "without regard to the circumstances, the relationship of forces, or tactical factors." This is monstrous! It means quite simply jumping on the bandwagon of these organizations when they are engaging in betrayals, for example in time of war or of movements like May 1968, without mentioning lesser occasions when the united front of these organizations is carried out in practice at the expense of the workers.

We will perhaps be told: you exaggerate; Lambert may have expressed himself badly; he has not forgotten the program. Let's see. He deals in his document with the May 1969 presidential campaign in France, forgetting quite like Healy the Trotskyist candidacy of Alain Krivine and overlooking the differences within the OCI on the vote (Defferre, Duclos, or abstention), but he cites and stresses these words by Just:

> But what about program? Didn't a single candidate put up by the workers' organizations need a program? What was it developing into? In these specific circumstances, the development of a program for a government of the united workers' organizations derived from this joint campaign.

In other words, through his campaign the single candidate would have given expression to this program. A program emerging from an electoral campaign!

Healy and Lambert had denounced Krivine's candidacy in the presidential election as being, among other things, a diversion from the "united front." Haven't they ever read Trotsky's pamphlet *What Next?*, written in January 1932 in powerful defense of the united front of Communists and Socialists against the mounting Hitlerite danger? In this pamphlet Trotsky denounced all the various centrists who proposed that the Communists and Socialists present a single presidential candidate. Here is how Trotsky expressed himself (the reader should bear in mind that at the time Trotskyists still considered themselves a *faction* of the Communist International and its sections):

> . . . in the sphere of propaganda . . . a bloc is out of the question. Propaganda must lean upon clear-cut principles and on a definite program. March separately, strike together. A bloc is solely for practical mass actions. Deals arranged from above which lack a basis in principle will bring nothing except confusion.
> The idea of nominating a candidate for president on the part of the united workers' front is at its root a false one. A candidate can be nominated only on the grounds of a definite program. The party has no right to sacrifice during elections the mobilization of its supporters and the census of its strength. The party candidacy, in opposition to all other candidates, can in no instance conflict with any agreement made with other organizations for immediate aims of struggle. Communists, whether official members of the party or not, will support Thaelmann's candidacy to their utmost. What we are concerned with is not Thaelmann but the banner of Communism. We shall defend it against all other parties. Breaking down the prejudices with which the rank and file of the Communists have been inoculated by the Stalinist bureaucracy, the Left Opposition will clear the road into their consciousness for itself.[8]

No comment is required on these lines.

The basis of the divisions that led to the Healy-Lambert split probably lie in the amendment Healy raised at Essen:

> There can be no revolutionary party without revolutionary theory. Behind every opportunist development in the history of the workers' movement, and especially of Stalinism, has been the revision of Marxist theory. The continuity of the struggle for revolutionary Marxist theory in the past, the struggle of the Fourth International and the International Committee, was the only basis for the initiatives which led to this rally and for the struggle to build the international revolutionary youth movement. Revolutionary youth everywhere must devote themselves above all to the task of developing Marxist theory through the struggle against bourgeois ideology in all the forms it takes in the workers' movement. This is the only basis for combatting the dangers of adventurism, activism and "pure" militancy with which revisionists and Maoists mislead the youth, and which can only lead to historic defeats for the working class.

Lambert's refusal to vote for this amendment provoked two remarks from Healy. In the first place, this refusal showed that Lambert was guilty

---

8. *The Struggle Against Fascism in Germany*, [Pathfinder, 1971], p. 265–66 [2014 printing]

of underestimating, or renouncing, dialectical materialism. On this point we are faced with one of Healy's customs. Every time he engages in a tendency or faction struggle he believes it necessary to introduce the question of dialectical materialism. Why? Well because Trotsky dealt with this question in the struggle against Burnham and Shachtman in 1939. Trotsky did this because the question was introduced by his opponents, one totally denying dialectical materialism, the other declaring that it had no practical political importance. Trotsky conducted many tendency struggles without introducing this question; but that matters little for Healy. For him, every internal struggle cannot help but pose the question of dialectical materialism. And if no one else is inclined to raise it, he will never hesitate to do so.

Must we add that when Healy indulges in this bizarre idiosyncrasy, he succeeds most often in making himself look ridiculous?

Healy's other comment is politically more serious. For him, the "International Committee" must be considered the embodiment of the "continuity" of the Fourth International. It is therefore around him (with the help of dialectical materialism) that the Fourth International must be "constructed."

For Lambert, the Fourth International has already been destroyed as a centralized organization. It must therefore be "reconstructed." This necessitates beginning by joining with all sorts of groups, forming a "youth international," fronts, etc.

Here, a certain rigidity on Healy's part and Lambert's unbridled opportunism appear to clash. It would not be surprising if the source of this clash lies in the internal situation in the two organizations and in the relation of forces between them.

At one time Healy carried more weight than Lambert in the "International Committee." Now it seems to be the other way around. Also, Healy's organization may be losing some of its steam. In that case, his rigidity could be explained as a means of halting this development. Lambert's document alludes to this fact: "Unless you start off from the political contradictions in which the SLL leadership finds itself and its refusal to see them unraveled by discussion within the ranks of its organization. . . ." Since both organizations are quite empirical, capable of making sudden political flip-flops, their documents do not allow us to probe more deeply into the question at the moment.

The Healy-Lambert split and the Fourth International

Healy and Lambert will each continue, as the case may be, to "construct" or "reconstruct" the Fourth International. Up to now they have counterposed their joint committee to the Fourth International. Today, thanks to Healy and Lambert, instead of one "committee" we have a "Committee of the Fourth International" and a "Committee for the Reconstruction of the Fourth International." The defunct "committee" was able to deceive some people about what it really represented. The two present committees will more than ever appear as inventions of the OCI or the SLL, designed to give these groups a facade of international affiliation. The split between Healy and Lambert is not a new split in the Fourth International, but a split among its opponents. To divert attention from their split they will not fail—of this we can be sure—to redouble their crass attacks on the Fourth International. But from now on they will be even more incapable than in the past of blocking its progress.

JANUARY 23, 1972

SECTION XVIII: HEALYITE REVISION OF MARXIST ECONOMIC THEORY

Contradictory Nature of the Postwar Prosperity
By Dick Roberts

The March 19, 1973, issue of the *Bulletin*, weekly organ of the Workers League, takes up an article by Ernest Mandel that appeared in *Intercontinental Press* January 29.

Mandel stated in his article:

> The international capitalist recession seems to have ended. All the imperialist countries, except Italy, foresee accelerated growth in 1973. The three key countries of the international capitalist economy—the United States, West Germany, and Japan—are experiencing a clearly ascending phase in industrial production.

This is "utterly wrong" according to the *Bulletin*.

> The dollar has been devalued, the price of gold has hit $95 an ounce, the system of fixed exchange rates has all but collapsed as every major European currency is floating, foreign exchange markets have been shut down for the second time in less than a month and are not due to open until next week and the stock market has fallen nearly 100 points.
>
> [The *Bulletin* editors ask:] . . . how was it possible for Ernest Mandel, the author of two fat volumes on economics, to be so utterly wrong in his assessment of the economic trends? Why did he have such extraordinary confidence in the future of capitalism just days before the entire system was plunged into financial chaos?
>
> . . . [And they answer:] Mandel decisively broke from Marxism 20 years ago. He rejected dialectical materialism in favor of the crudest empiricism and abandoned the struggle for an understanding of capitalist society from the standpoint of contradiction. Blinded by the superficial characteristics of the post-war boom, Mandel concluded that Lenin's assessment of imperialism as the highest stage of capitalism was incorrect. Through a revision of every basic tenet of Marxism, he arrived at the theory of neocapitalism which seeks to wipe contradiction out of the capitalist system.

With little alteration, the Workers League and its parent organization, the British Socialist Labour League, have been repeating these charges against Mandel for the last four years.

Did Mandel actually "seek to wipe contradiction out of the capitalist system" in the *Intercontinental Press* article under consideration? No. In his article Mandel asked whether the recovery from the 1969–72 recession of the major capitalist powers had resolved the contradictions that brought the recession about. He answered that the contradictions were not resolved. "As is always the case during an international capitalist recession, interimperialist contradictions were exacerbated," Mandel stated.

Looking to the future, he wrote,

> The prospects for the international capitalist economy are . . . hardly optimistic. . . . Mon-

---

Intercontinental Press, May 7, 1973.

etary, financial, and industrial difficulties will combine with the growing social tensions to make the 1970s as a whole a decade of slowdown of economic expansion and of multiplication of the class struggle.

The *Bulletin* editors' assertions are clearly false as regards the *Intercontinental Press* article. It will be seen that their charges fare no better against any other article by Mandel. In fact the charges of the Healy-Wohlforth tendency against Mandel's analysis of post-World War II capitalist economic developments are fraudulent from start to finish.[1]

The leaders of the Workers League and their mentors in Britain must be asked once again why they repeatedly lie about Ernest Mandel's economic analyses. Why do they attempt to interject into the socialist movement the smear and slander techniques of the bourgeoisie and the Stalinists? Does their own economic line square with reality and help to further the struggle against imperialism?

A closer look at postwar capitalism, Ernest Mandel's economic theory, and the efforts of the Healy-Wohlforth group to explain capitalism's survival into the 1970s will shed light on these matters. The crisis of world capitalism that is everywhere impelling the bourgeoisie to intensify attacks on workers' living standards makes these questions of utmost significance.

Postwar capitalism

> What was it that converted capitalism from the cataclysmic failure which it appeared to be in the 1930s into the great engine of prosperity of the postwar Western world?

The question is raised by the British bourgeois economist Andrew Shonfield in *Modern Capitalism: The Changing Balance of Public and Private Power* (1965). Not only do bourgeois economists ask the question, but Marxists themselves have been compelled to consider it. To dismiss this postwar "prosperity" as "superficial," as the Healyites are wont to do, is to preclude any possibility of concretely understanding the diverse forms the class struggle has assumed during the last quarter century and of anticipating and preparing for the forms they are likely to assume in the near future.

Shonfield, who uses terms like "modern capitalism" and "new capitalism" to describe postwar imperialism, notes:

> From 1901 to 1913 industrial production in the advanced countries of Western Europe increased by almost half from the start of the century. From 1950 to 1962 the aggregate industrial output had doubled.

The postwar boom and relative class peace that prevailed in the advanced capitalist countries in the beginning of the 1960s produced a massive flight from Marxist economic theory, even among radicals. Typical of the American New Left was C. Wright Mills's categorical assertion in *The Marxists* (1962):

> There is now no substantial reason to believe that Marxist revolutions will come about in the foreseeable future in any major advanced capitalist society. In fact, the revolutionary potential—whatever the phrase may reasonably mean—of wageworkers, labor unions and political parties, is feeble.

British Labour party right-winger C. A. R. Crosland spelled out the glories of the "new capitalism" from the House of Commons in the late 1950s and early 1960s.

> The belief that 'inner contradictions' of capitalism would lead ... ultimately to the collapse of the whole system, has by now been rather obviously disproved.[2]

---

1. Mandel explicitly rejects the term "neocapitalism" in the sense the Healyites attribute to him. In "Workers Under Neo-Capitalism" (1968) he declared, "I do not care very much for the term 'neo-capitalism' which is ambiguous, to say the least.... Some European politicians and sociologists speak about 'neo-capitalism' in the senses that society has shed some of the basic characteristics of capitalism. I deny this most categorically, and therefore attach to the term 'neo-capitalism' the opposite connotation: a society which has all the basic elements of classical capitalism."

2. *The Future of Socialism* (1963). The first edition of this book appeared in 1957.

> One cannot imagine to-day a deliberate offensive alliance between Government and employers against the Unions on the 1921 or 1925–6 or 1927 model, with all the brutal paraphernalia of wage-cuts, national lockouts, and anti-Union legislation. . . .
>
> . . . in my view Marx has little or nothing to offer the contemporary socialist, either in respect of practical policy, or of the correct analysis of our society, or even of the right conceptual tools or framework. His prophecies have been almost without exception falsified, and his conceptual tools are now quite inappropriate.

Terms like neocapitalism were not an invention of Mandel's but of myopic reformists like Crosland.

> It . . . seems misleading to continue talking about 'capitalism' in Britain, as though the lines of battle were essentially the same as a generation ago [said Crosland]. . . . I believe that our present society is sufficiently defined, and distinct from classical capitalism, to require a different name.

Keynesianism

These apologists for capitalism believed that increasing state intervention in the economy could provide nearly permanent economic stability by moderating the business cycle. They represented this development as a shift of power away from the ruling class towards the people.

The loss of power by the "business class" to the state

> is largely a consequence of the explicit acceptance by governments of responsibility for full employment, the rate of growth, the balance of payments, and the distribution of incomes, [said Crosland.] The main instrument for exercising this responsibility is fiscal policy. Acting mainly through the Budget, though with the aid of other instruments, the government can exert any influence it likes on income-distribution, and can also determine within broad limits the division of the total output between consumption, investment, exports and expenditures.

Professor Shonfield declared:

> . . . control over the business cycle, which owes so much to Keynes's work, has been one of the decisive factors in establishing the dynamic and prosperous capitalism of the postwar era. Indeed, it is probably the single most important factor in this change.

Mandel's 'Marxist Economic Theory'

Mandel's two-volume *Marxist Economic Theory*, published in 1962,[3] provided a comprehensive refutation of these reformist theories and a reaffirmation of Marxist economics. It supplied new proofs of the main laws of capitalism that Marx had discovered. Where Marx had presented these laws in a logical order in *Capital*, Mandel showed their historical genesis and then their application to all sectors of world economics today.

Drawing on the Left Opposition's analysis of the degeneration of the Russian revolution, Mandel extended his historic study to postcapitalist societies and concluded it with a discussion of socialist economy. The two volumes are an outstanding contribution to revolutionary literature and are unquestionably the most important work in Marxist economics to appear in the postwar period.

Under capitalism—all capitalism—production of social surplus is also production and appropriation of *surplus value*, which can be created only by living labor. Thus capitalism faces the ever deepening contradiction that only living labor produces surplus value, yet competition more and more forces the capitalists to increase the proportion of "dead labor" in production (raw materials, plant, machinery, etc.). The smaller the proportion of invested capital going into wages, the greater the threat to capitalist profits. Thus the rate of profit tends to decline. Marx described this law as the opposite side of the coin of capitalist accumulation.

The situation must arise in which new investment cannot maintain sufficient profit rates. The

---

3. Citations from the English translation (New York: Monthly Review Press, 1970).

capitalists hold back. Production is cut and a crisis ensues.

In the fifth chapter of *Marxist Economic Theory* (entitled "The Contradictions of Capitalism") Mandel wrote:

> The increase in the social surplus product in relation to the necessary product does not lead to a tremendous increase in well-being and comfort for society as a whole, but to an increase *in the surplus labour appropriated by the possessing classes*, in a growth in the degree of exploitation of the working class. The decrease in the ratio between the new wealth created each year and accumulated social wealth does not mean that mankind can live more and more exclusively on this accumulated wealth, it does not mean a constant increase in leisure, but becomes, on the contrary, a periodical source of convulsions, crises and unemployment. The growth in the mass of dead labour in relation to living labour does not mean an ever-greater saving of human labour, but the creation of a vast industrial reserve army, under the pressure of which consumption by the producers remains restricted to the necessary product, and their physical effort is lengthened or intensified. This antogonistic form which is taken by the tendencies of the development of the capitalist system is what makes its destruction inevitable (pp. 169–70).

Yet the Healyites assert that Mandel, "through a revision of every basic tenet of Marxism . . . arrived at the theory of neocapitalism which seeks to wipe contradiction out of the capitalist system"!

State intervention

It is precisely because of the inevitability of crisis under capitalism that the state *must intervene more and more.* This does not change the fundamental character of capitalist society. Mandel stated:

> Monopoly capitalism turns more and more to the state, in order to secure by state intervention in the economy what the normal working of the latter can no longer secure for it. *The bourgeois state becomes the essential guarantor of monopoly profits* (pp. 501–2).

This is not a handing of power from the ruling class to the state, as the apologists for neocapitalism assert.

> . . . it expresses the submission of the state to the monopolies, through increasing personal links between the leading figures in the state and the heads of the big monopolies in person (p. 507).

The question remains as to the degree to which the capitalist state can moderate the fluctuations of the business cycle. *What are the contradictions of state intervention itself?* Mandel stressed that neocapitalist state intervention runs into an insuperable contradiction: the *"permanent tendency to currency inflation."* Government expenditure, above all on arms,

> increases the amount of purchasing power in circulation without creating on the market a corresponding additional supply of *goods*, as counter-value. Even when this increased purchasing power brings about the re-employment of previously idle machinery and men, it causes inflation eventually (p. 527).

Every effort to prolong the cycle through increased government expenditures will increase inflation. But the dollar is also the main currency in *international finance*. Thus, continued inflation threatens to wreck the international monetary system. Mandel pinpointed the economic arena in which the contradictions of neocapitalism would first manifest themselves: the international monetary system.

He wrote:

> Capitalism will . . . choose to employ the 'anti-cyclical' techniques. But it will do this hesitatingly, with many misgivings, and, finally, it will not prevent inflation from getting worse. The capacity of the currency to resist—which, by definition, is limited in time—thus appears as the insurmountable barrier against which, in the long run, the moderating intervention of the state is brought up short. The contradiction between the dollar as an anti-cyclical device in the United States and the dollar as money of account on the world market has already become insurmountable. It finds expression in a

tendency to deficit in the United States' balance of payments (pp. 532–3).

The development of "stop-go" cyclical policies in the Nixon administration since 1969 is the most recent confirmation of this analysis. Washington followed recessionary policies in 1969–71 in order to shore up the dollar and dampen inflation; but this threatened to create massive unemployment—and on the eve of national elections. In 1971–72 Washington was following expansionary policies, but as soon as industrial production turned up, inflation got out of hand again. Today the swing is back towards monetary restraint with talk about recession in 1974 while unemployment levels remain at near highs.

In comparison with Mandel's thoroughgoing and insightful analysis of postwar capitalism, the efforts of the Healy-Wohlforth tendency do not amount to much. What may not be so well known, however, is that the SLL's economic analysis deteriorated under the impact of blind factionalism. Prior to 1963, a start was made towards analyzing the postwar boom. This appeared in a series of articles by Tom Kemp published in *Labour Review.*

Kemp recognized in the late 1950s that capitalism had experienced unprecedented growth following the war and that Marxists should attempt to explain it. "Faith in capitalism has been strengthened by the great expansion and full employment of this last decade," Kemp wrote in the May–June 1957 *Labour Review.* In the September–October 1957 issue, he declared:

> British workers have experienced a decade and a half of full employment following a period of prolonged unemployment. Not only has it enabled the trade unions to improve wage levels and win other concessions, but it has made an immeasurable difference to many working-class families.

Kemp also recognized the basis for this unprecedented expansion.

> . . . (1) government-sponsored investment, especially in housing; (2) arms expenditures; (3) the technological spurt; and (4) world market expansion . . . have been sufficiently powerful to eliminate unemployment over twelve years and to bring about a fairly sustained upsurge in the economy of Britain and other countries, [he wrote in the July–August 1957 *Labour Review.*]

In the same article Kemp stressed that inflation could become a major problem.

> Inflation appears to have become inherent in the economy and the pound has steadily lost value since 1939; the ever-present risk that this so far 'surpassed' inflation should assume a runaway character, which would mean social chaos and breakdown, can hardly be associated with a healthy organism.

Missed the point

When it came to pulling all these observations together and analyzing the contradictions of the postwar expansion, Kemp faltered. He seems to have felt that the expansion would somehow run out of steam. The factors causing the expansion, "far from being the sort of built-in factors which are self-perpetuating, may well be simply using themselves up without prospect of renewal and becoming less and less significant," Kemp wrote in 1957; but he never explained why, when, and how this would happen.[4]

This was because he *failed to analyze the specific contradictions of the new aspects of imperialism*—so insistent was he on the theme that nothing had changed. Most striking was his failure to see the

---

4. That the SLL theoreticians realized the inadequacy of their analysis is evident from a number of remarks:

". . . it is certainly true that Marxists have not yet analyzed carefully enough, nor adequately explained, the present crisis of capitalism. . . .

"It is clear that the whole question of the role of government in modern capitalism needs further analysis." (Tom Kemp, *Labour Review,* 1957.)

"All these and related questions need fundamental examination in the light of Marxism and it will be our task to undertake this in the coming year." (Tom Kemp, *Labour Review,* 1960.)

"Marxists have yet to make any all-round analysis of the new developments in world economics and politics since Lenin wrote *Imperialism* in 1916." (Peter Jeffries, *Labour Review,* 1962)

". . . the whole process is of the most complex kind which permits of infinite variation in its practical working out." (Tom Kemp, *Labour Review,* 1963.)

contradictions of the war budget itself, that biggest of all government levers in the postwar period.

> Of course the level of arms budgets in the major capitalist countries has been considerably higher than in previous periods of peace. [Kemp wrote in "What Is Imperialism?" in the Autumn 1962 *Labour Review*.]
>
> Admittedly the demand from the state for arms has provided capitalism with a means of realizing surplus value.... But the devotion of such a high proportion of national output to arms production has been imposed by necessity—the pressure of an antagonistic world system threatening the position of... imperialism. To see the high arms production as the sign of a new stage, superseding imperialism, is to misunderstand the nature of the epoch in which we live: the epoch of decaying capitalism which, capable of prolonged bursts of economic expansion, is nonetheless fighting for its life.... Necessarily, the level of arms production has important economic results, as well as influence on the superstructure of capitalist society, but the dominating laws of capitalism have not been overcome.[5]

It is true that the United States, as the main police force of world imperialism, required a global military apparatus and that this has kept war permanently on the agenda as the "powderkegs" of imperialist oppression have continued to explode. All Trotskyists from 1944 on have stressed this.

But arms production also provides the "replacement market" that Keynes called for. It does so, however, only at the cost of permanent inflation and the ultimate wreckage of the international monetary system. This "important economic result" Kemp failed to see.

As late as 1964, the point still was missed by the SLL leadership. Peter Jeffries went so far as to suggest that war production might even be decreased in the United States.

> It is obvious that the vast programme of military expenditures carried out by the United States is now a burden upon the whole economy and is responsible in part for the slow rate of growth of the economy and the high level of taxation which hinders recovery and the attempt to reduce the level of unemployment, [Jeffries declared in the Summer 1964 *Fourth International*.]
>
> ... there is little prospect of a permanent and decisive upswing in the American economy. But without such an upswing there can be no rapid expansion of trade between the metropolitan countries; their future increasingly depends upon the position inside the United States.

But in the period when this article was written, the Kennedy-Johnson administrations decided to cut taxes, run huge government deficits, and launch a major war in Southeast Asia. War spending spiraled upwards and the U. S. economy was propelled into its biggest and longest boom in history. World trade expanded as never before.

At the same time, however, the U. S. economy encountered severe inflation *primed by the war;* the U. S. balance of payments position deteriorated sharply, and the international monetary system entered into severe and semi-permanent crisis.

Interestingly, the Jeffries article bears the name "The Crisis of Post-War Capitalism." *The Socialist Register 1964* published an article by Mandel entitled "The Economics of Neo-Capitalism" in which Mandel wrote:

> But if neo-capitalism's successes certainly shine bright, in view of results obtained during the past ten years, its inner contradictions—which superimpose themselves, so to speak, on the general contradictions of the capitalist mode of production, which have not been eliminated in any way whatsoever—are also coming to the forefront....
>
> Creeping inflation is one of the basic contradictions of neo-capitalism and of welfare-statism in general.... In the long run, this creeping inflation erodes the purchasing power of the

---

5. Kemp is here polemicizing against state capitalists like Michael Kidron. For reasons that have never been explained, the Healyite attack on Mandel's economic theory did not open until 1969—that is, seven years after the appearance of *Marxist Economic Theory* and long after the SLL, had opened its slander campaign against Mandel on a number of other points.

main currencies, disorganizes long-term investment operations, stimulates speculation of every kind. . . . Any attempts to come to grips with inflation through deflationary measures only throttles economic growth as such, and leads to stagnation, as Tory Britain (and in a certain sense the U. S. A. under Eisenhower) have learned to their cost: the cure is deadlier than the illness.

These contradictions of neo-capitalism are not only of theoretical importance inasmuch as they prove that the system remains fundamentally what it has always been. They also lead to the conclusion, that the present rate of growth cannot be kept up; that the Common Market countries will also witness recessions; and that the long wave of increased growth will probably come to an end during the 'sixties. (Emphasis added.)

Mandel's prediction proved to be correct. The second half of the 1960s saw the emergence of an international recession. It signified that postwar expansion had reached a turning point. It opened a new stage of intensified interimperialist competition and the escalated attacks on wages that inevitably accompany the "redivision of world markets."

This plunging of capitalism into crisis had not been foreseen and explained by the Healyites. But instead of modifying their theory in accordance with developing reality, they opened a smear campaign against Ernest Mandel.

Healyites Vs. Karl Marx on Gold and Inflation
By Dick Roberts

This is the second article of a three-part series on the economic theories of the Socialist Labour League, a sectarian British organization led by Gerry Healy, and its U.S. supporters, the Workers League, led by Tim Wohlforth. The first part of the series appeared in the May 7 issue of *Intercontinental Press*.

The tentative promises of the Socialist Labour League's economic expert Tom Kemp to analyze postwar capitalism and its contradictions in a comprehensive way were never carried out. Instead, the SLL leaders' interest in economic theory withered away, except insofar as theory could be applied in the field of sectarian warfare.[6]

The November 1964 monetary crisis, in which Harold Wilson's Labour government pursued deflationary policies to bolster the pound was reflected in the Healyite press in themes that have altered little in the intervening years. "Not since 1931 have we seen anything comparable to the present intervention by foreign banks," declared the November 25, 1964, *Newsletter*.

Labour MPs . . . were startled when they were suddenly told by government spokesmen that there would be no increase for old age pensioners at Christmas because of pressure from outside financial interests.

• September 18, 1965: "The future of sterling and the world crisis" by Peter Jeffries.

No loan from America, no reorganization of the institutions of world finance, no expansion of liquidity and credit or a moratorium on debt payment can solve the present crisis of British capitalism.

• March 19, 1966: "Sterling crisis worsens" by John Crawford.

---

6. Since 1963 the Socialist Labour League has been campaigning against the Fourth International as well as the Socialist Workers party, which, although one of the founding members of the Fourth International, is today barred by reactionary legislation from affiliating with the World Party of the Socialist Revolution. For details on the SLL's sectarian arguments and methods see *Marxism Vs. Ultraleftism: Key Issues in Healy's Challenge to the Fourth International* (1967) by Ernest Germain.

Intercontinental Press, May 14, 1973.

- June 25, 1966: "Sterling on the slide" by John Crawford.
- August 13, 1966: G. Healy writes: "World imperialism is drifting rapidly towards its most severe economic crisis since the end of the second world war."
- September 2, 1967: "Wilson reflates but . . . New crisis ahead."
- January 6, 1968: "United States cuts back, World recession looms."
- March 19, 1968: "World capitalism—1968, Crisis, panic, crash, Marxism vindicated" by G. Healy. The closing of British banks marks "a new stage of the world capitalist crisis. ". . . it has become impossible for the capitalist class and their representatives to halt the present crisis." "As the capitalist system staggers into the unknown . . ." "It is now plain that the present crisis can virtually dry up the international credit system. . . ."
- December 7, 1968: "Gold reserves slump, Crisis days in front" by the editors.

And so on down to the present day. Every report on U. S. or British trade or payments balances, or stock market swings, or gold-price changes (whether up or down), receives the same treatment until the word "crisis" becomes virtually meaningless. The editors of the *Newsletter* (and of the *Bulletin*, perhaps even more so) ought to recall Tom Kemp's admonition in 1957: ". . . the term 'crisis' has been on all our lips so frequently as to depreciate somewhat its meaning." That was 16 years ago.

Gold and inflation

Peter Jeffries appears to be the originator of an economic theory centering on the role of gold that has become one of the distinguishing features of Healyism. In the March 23, 1968, issue of The *Newsletter* in an article titled "Guide to the crisis," Jeffries asked a searching question: Why does the crisis take place?

> Look at the facts: America now holds only around 10 billion dollars of gold compared with nearly 25 billion 20 years ago. Yet the value of dollars now circulating in the rest of the capitalist world—in the hands of governments, banks or private individuals—now total around 30 billion dollars.

> In other words if all holders of dollars tried to exchange them for gold . . . the Americans would have to break their agreement which has kept the world financial system going since the war.

Jeffries continued in the March 30, 1968, issue:

> The operation of the law of value has . . . been 'suspended' or 'avoided' throughout much of the boom period.
>
> The Americans were able to do this through a combination of credit manipulation and by running down their reserves at Fort Knox while they got on with the job of exporting capital, buying up European industry, and piling up inflated profits.
>
> Now this has come to an end. With two-thirds of their massive gold supply gone and with a collapse of confidence in the entire post-war money system the day of reckoning has arrived.

And this sturdy opponent of empiricism exclaimed: "It is now clear for all to see: the dollar is an inflationary currency, which is completely out of line with the value of gold."[7]

An unsigned book review in the August 1968 *Fourth International* entitled "The boom . . . that was" adds,

> No economist or financial expert, however eminent, could get away from the reality of capitalism, that it involved the exchange of products of labour and that gold was the universal commodity in the background of all international transactions.
>
> This remained the limit on the boom and, somewhere along the line, the expansion of trade had to run into this contradiction. The fall in the rate of profit could be evaded only up to this point by means of investment in Europe and state purchases of armaments.

---

7. For the Healyite attack on Mandel's supposedly "empirical" methodology see "A Malignant Case of Sectarianism in Philosophy" and "Healyite Revisionism in the Field of Philosophy" by George Novack, in *Intercontinental Press*, 1972, pp.771 ff. and 1020 ff

There are certain elements of truth in this argument—noted long before by Mandel and others—notably the inflationary impact of government intervention in the economy and the important role this played in the postwar boom. But Jeffries's conceptions about gold and monetary crisis are way off base.

Jeffries, of course, is not voicing an individual opinion. A February 24, 1973, draft resolution of the Central Committee of the Socialist Labour League published in the February 24, 1973, *Workers Press* said

> In the early 1960s, gold constituted around 60 per cent of total world 'liquidity' (that is gold plus foreign exchange); today the figure has fallen to a little over a third. In other words, roughly two-thirds of world trading assets no longer have any value because they are no longer convertible to gold. . . .
>
> The most decisive turning point in the whole crisis came with Nixon's August 15, 1971, announcement that the dollar-gold link was broken for all time. . . .
>
> From this point onwards a vast pool of money was in circulation outside the United States, with no gold backing. Estimates now place this pool of paper at around $70 billion.

In reading these paragraphs anyone familiar with Marxist economics will note certain problems. In 1968 the "crisis" was caused by the fact that U. S. gold holdings of $10,000 million corresponded to foreign claims against U. S. reserves equal to $30,000 million. Today, according to the *Workers Press*, successor to the *Newsletter*, the "crisis" is caused by the fact that there is no gold backing for an outstanding $70,000 million. And this figure could be corrected. It stood at around $70,000 million in August 1971 when Nixon inaugurated the "New Economic Policy." When the February 24 *Workers Press* article was written, the figure had risen to about $80,000 million.

Doesn't this indicate that there is more to the monetary crisis than the relationship between the U. S. gold in Fort Knox and the volume of dollars held abroad? As a matter of historical fact, the volume of gold in the central banking system has barely changed since the introduction of the "two-tier" system in March 1968. But the value of dollars held abroad has nearly tripled.

The world capitalist powers have been in and out of an international recession since 1968. The dollar has been twice devalued. Major world currencies are floating today, a situation ruled out by central bankers in 1968. But the volume of U. S. dollars abroad continues to expand; world trade and finance continues, and it continues to be conducted largely in dollars.

Surely it would have been more in order for the February 1973 SLL draft resolution on world economics *to drop* Jeffries's arguments. Events have long since demonstrated that they don't explain anything.

But the logic of sectarianism goes the other way. The more a line is shown to be out of keeping with reality, the more shrilly is it repeated.

> With gold now supporting perhaps only 10 per cent of the value of world trade, [the February SLL resolution states,] the implications of the crisis must be a collapse of much of the other 90 per cent. For no matter how much the revisionists sneered at the analysis of the monetary crisis made by the SLL, gold and commodities are tied together inseparably. This was the whole purpose of Marx's analysis in 'Capital', a work which all these gentlemen said was now 'out of date'.

Marx and gold

The Healyites' appeals to Marx are often without justification. Marx's treatment of gold is a case in point. For in the third volume of *Capital* Marx discussed precisely the question under consideration, namely the relationship between the flow of gold in international finance and economic crisis.

Marx polemicized against British central bankers who believed that they could control economic development by regulating the supply of gold and manipulating interest rates.

In a brilliant analysis of the crises of 1847 and 1857, Marx showed that the origins of these crises must be traced to disruptions of production (in 1847, for example, to the collapse of British-India trade). Marx demonstrated that there is no exact correspondence between interest rates or gold supplies and the general direction of the economy.

Only in times of crisis, Marx emphasized, does gold play a role by taking on special qualities. Losing sight of this can lead to erroneous currency theories. "... even a very considerable drain of gold is relatively ineffective if it does not occur in the critical period of the industrial cycle."[8]

Then, in a famous passage Marx stated,

> A certain quantity of metal, insignificant compared with the total production, is admitted to be the pivotal point of the system. ... So long as enlightened economy treats 'of capital' *ex professo*, it looks down upon gold and silver with the greatest disdain, considering them the most indifferent and useless form of capital. But as soon as it treats of the banking system, everything is reversed, and gold and silver become capital *par excellence*, for whose preservation every other form of capital and labour is sacrificed. But how are gold and silver distinguished from other forms of wealth? Not by the magnitude of their value, for this is determined by the quantity of labour incorporated in them; but by the fact that they represent independent incarnations, expressions of the *social character of wealth*. ... This social existence of wealth therefore assumes the aspect of a world beyond, of a thing, matter, commodity, alongside of and external to the real elements of social wealth. So long as production is in a state of flux this is forgotten. Credit, likewise a social form of wealth, crowds out money and usurps its place. It is faith in the social character of production which allows the money-form of products to assume the aspect of something only evanescent and ideal, something merely imaginative. But as soon as credit is shaken—and this phase of necessity always appears in the modern industrial cycle—all the real wealth is to be actually and suddenly transformed into money, into gold and silver—a mad demand, which, however, grows necessarily out of the system itself. And all the gold and silver which is supposed to satisfy these enormous demands amounts to but a few millions in the vaults of the Bank (pp. 560–1).

Marx made a number of points in this remarkable passage. How is it possible, he asked, that gold, which is always insignificant in value compared to total production, plays such a big role in central banking? Does this refute the theory presented in the first volume of *Capital* that the essential character of capitalism is to be discovered in the production process and not in the process of circulation?

It is precisely because of production crises that gold maintains its special role, Marx answered. For in the panic there is a mad rush to dump "evanescent" paper values for the real value stored in gold.

But this does not mean that gold has a special effect on production generally. For the crisis originates in the "real elements of social wealth," that is, in production. So long as production is expanding, money and credit operations are mere paperwork, "evanescent and ideal." But crises inevitably flow from capitalist production ("the modern industrial cycle"). The credit system is shaken and there is a rush for gold—even for "a few millions." (Note that the short supply of gold did not begin in the 1960s; Marx discussed it here in the 1860s.)

According to Jeffries,

> Marx showed that ... the more the volume of credit was expanded on a narrower gold base, the greater the possibility of a collapse of the entire superstructure of credit" (*Workers Press*, October 30, 1969).

Jeffries seems to attribute to Marx a very profound explanation of credit crises! In fact, what he attributes to Marx is a tautology and Marx was not given to passing off tautology as explanation.

According to Marx—and he was speaking of the reality—credit *always* expands more rapidly than its gold base during the upswing of a capitalist cycle, unless, completely by accident, an increase in gold production happens to keep pace with the increased monetary requirements of the boom. But the further the system advances

---

8. References are to the Foreign Languages Publishing House (Moscow, 1962) edition.

into the upswing of the cycle, the closer it approaches the point of crisis, which must bring with it a contraction of credit and the possibility of collapse.

But the *explanation* of the collapse is not to be found in the ratio between credit and gold; it is to be found in the dialectical totality of the elements that determine the motion of the economic system, most fundamentally, the organic composition of capitals, rates of exploitation, rates of profit and physical productivity, and the uneven development of these rates between industrial and geographical sectors. The quantity of gold and the mass of credit neither cause nor prevent collapse.

Jeffries confuses tautology with explanation because he confuses appearance with reality. He repeats the error of the City of London in the 1840s and 1850s which Marx polemicized against.

Gold and inflation again

Marx, however, did not rule out crises being exacerbated by mistaken central banking policies. The Bank Act of 1844 rigidly tied the volume of pound notes in circulation to the gold reserves of the Bank of England. And from the standpoint of the Bank of England (and the SLL), this would seem to be sound monetary policy.

Marx explained:

> The Bank Act of 1844 thus directly induces the entire commercial world forthwith to hoard a reserve fund of bank-notes at the outbreak of a crisis; in other words, to accelerate and intensify the crisis. By such artificial intensification of demand for money accommodation, that is, for means of payment at the decisive moment, and the simultaneous restriction of the supply the Bank Act drives the rate of interest to a hitherto unknown height during a crisis. Hence, instead of eliminating crises, the Act, on the contrary, intensifies them (p. 542).

The truth of these remarks has long been known to British central bankers. From the 1870s onward they increasingly abandoned rigid money controls and resorted to inflationary deficits when the need arose.

Under the stress of the world crisis of the 1930s and the prodding of Keynes, capitalist central banking took another step in this direction. It abandoned the gold standard.

This, the Healyites believe, is the main error and one of these days the gold standard will be reasserted, wiping out "the other 90 per cent" of the value of world trade. Interestingly enough, leading sectors of French capitalism have been urging a return to the gold standard since 1965. Moreover, it is hardly a coincidence that readers of the *Newsletter* in 1965 would get the impression that General de Gaulle's advice to go back to gold was taken seriously.

"In fact," Ernest Mandel wrote in the February 19, 1965, *World Outlook* (the former name of *Intercontinental Press*), "only Pravda declared with a straight face that [de Gaulle's proposal] sounded 'reasonable.'"[9]

In this article, entitled "De Gaulle Doesn't Know It But the Golden Days of Capitalism Are Over," Mandel declared,

> there is not the slightest chance that de Gaulle's proposal will be taken up. It would be suicide for capitalism to return to a rigid system of money and credit controlled automatically by the supply of gold. Such a system could lead only to a major depression.
>
> Those who advocate returning to the gold standard score a good point when they argue that the present monetary system leads to increasing inflation. This is completely correct. But increasing inflation is the only means by which a capitalist economy can convert grave depressions into 'minor' recessions. What capitalist government in the United States, for instance, would risk having fifteen or twenty million unemployed for the sake of 'fighting inflation' or 'going back to the gold standard'?

This does not mean that gold will be ousted from central banking. On the contrary it will continue to play a central role, for the reasons Marx explained— because it is an "independent incarnation" of social

---

9. This article and a number of Mandel's writings on the international monetary crisis are collected in *Decline of the Dollar* (New York: Pathfinder Press, 1972).

wealth. The sharper the rivalry between competing bastions of world imperialism, the greater the instability of the rates of exchange of international currencies and the more will gold be prized.

Further, the price of gold in dollars will continue to rise as it already has with the two devaluations of the dollar. This expresses inflation without eliminating its basic causes in any way. Technology in the gold industry has lagged far behind the remainder of world industry. It means that the socially necessary labor required to mine gold is relatively greater than that required to produce other commodities.

The decline in the value of commodities—relative to that of gold—*would therefore be expressed in a sharp increase in their price,* [Mandel wrote in the March–April 1969 *International Socialist Review*:]

There is no better way of saying that the means of exchange—paper money—is being greatly inflated.[10]

Inflation, be it repeated, is the inevitable result of state intervention in the economy. It is caused by the massive increase in money (including credit) for which there are no countervalues on the market. This occurs independently of the quantity of gold in circulation.

(To be continued.)

---

10. See *Decline of the Dollar*, p. 99 ff.

Healyites Find That Capitalism Has Dropped Dead
By Dick Roberts

This is the third and final article of a series on the economic theories of the Socialist Labour League, a sectarian British organization led by Gerry Healy, and its U. S. supporters, the Workers League, led by Tim Wohlforth. The first part of the series appeared in the May 7 issue of *Intercontinental Press*.

Since the latter half of the 1960s world imperialism has been shaken by recurring and increasingly grave crises of the international monetary system. World trade warfare has escalated sharply with the increasing appearance of tariff and import-quota measures designed to protect national markets. Recessions began to appear in Europe and Japan and 1969–72 saw the first international recession in the postwar period.

This intensification of the economic problems of world imperialism has resulted in increasingly harsh measures against the wages and living standards of workers. An economic theory to provide a lucid explanation of the contradictions of imperialism is a key part of the revolutionary arsenal. But in the hands of the leaders of the Socialist Labour League and their followers in the United States, economic theory has been sacrificed in the interest of sectarian warfare against the world Trotskyist movement.

In fact, some of the key contributions first presented by Ernest Mandel have been picked up by the Healyites. But they have done this without the slightest acknowledgment and under cover of systematic falsification of Mandel's views.

The deep crisis of the monetary system compelled these indomitable opponents of pragmatism to finally notice that the inflation of the dollar is one of the consequences of deep-lying contradictions in international finance. Almost ten years after Mandel explained it in *Marxist Economic Theory*, Dennis O'Casey of the Workers League asserted that the "International Committee" was

> able to understand that the inflation of paper money by the United States agreed to at Bretton Woods in 1944 must serve at a certain point, through a reassertion of the law of value, to precipitate a world monetary crisis.

Intercontinental Press, May 21, 1973.

We were able to understand how this in turn would usher in a new period of revolutionary struggle.[11]

Then, in accordance with the usual Healyite way of covering up the source of their insights, O'Casey continued:

> Mandel could neither grasp the relationship between value and price nor how the abstraction, value, would assert itself against a mountain of concrete paper dollars. This is precisely the reason he could not anticipate this crisis. . . . the question of the world crisis building up under the surface of capitalism for the past 25 years never held any serious place in Mandel's analysis.

Production is central

It is one-sided and consequently incorrect to assert, as O'Casey and his mentors in London do, that the cause of postwar prosperity was simply the flooding of the capitalist world with dollars and currency inflation. This monetaristic concept turns reality and Marxism upside down.

In order to grasp the dynamics of postwar expansion we have to begin, with Marx, in the arena of *production*, not circulation. In the dialectical relation between production and circulation, production is the predominant category. This is the central theme of *Capital*. It is expressed in the logical structure of *Capital* which proceeds from the contradictions of production in the first volume to those of circulation in the second and third volumes.

Marx's labor theory of value is a theory of production relations. Marxism rejects all theories that, like modern marginalism, identify price and value, because they make it impossible to grasp the dynamics of capitalist production beneath the surface appearances in the sphere of circulation. What happens in the marketplace reflects and interacts with the conditions of production, but it does not determine them.

It was on this basis, as we have already seen, that Marx criticized English banking theory in the mid-nineteenth century. The source of capitalist crises is not to be found in the circulation of money, credit, and gold *isolated* from production. This central conception of Marxism is not overthrown by the actual history of imperialism in the postwar period.

On the contrary, to grasp the character of the postwar period, it is essential to begin with understanding that imperialism was able to undergo an unprecedented expansion of production following the holocaust of war. This was *different from* the period following World War I but it did not mean that imperialism had fundamentally changed its character.

Imperialism

For Marxists, the central contradiction of imperialism, monopoly capitalism in the twentieth century, is the *revolt of the forces of production against national boundaries*. Lenin and Trotsky constantly returned to this theme. In *Imperialism*, Lenin wrote:

> Capitalist monopolies occupy first place in economics and politics; the division of the world has been completed. On the other hand, instead of an undisputed monopoly by Great Britain, we see a few imperialist powers contending for the right to share in this monopoly, and this struggle is characteristic of the whole period of the beginning of the twentieth century.

The "division of world markets" completed at the beginning of this century impelled national capitalisms into fierce competition ultimately leading to World War I. But this bloody slaughter did not resolve the contradictions that brought it about. It re-created the basis for continued economic crisis and war.

In his far-sighted "Report on the World Economic Crisis and the New Tasks of the Communist International" (1921), Trotsky stated:

> At the given moment capitalism has entered a period of prolonged and profound depression. . . . the war lasted for too long, provoking not only an acute crisis but a protracted one; it destroyed completely Europe's capitalist economic apparatus, thereby accelerating America's feverish development. But after exhausting Europe, the war led in the long run

---

11. Ernest Mandel: *The Fraud of Neo-Capitalism* (1971).

to a great crisis in America, too. Once again we are witnessing that selfsame depression which they had sought to escape, but which has been intensified many-fold owing to Europe's impoverishment. . . .

It is quite obvious that America will have to suffer curtailment since the European war market is gone beyond recall.

The Healyites contend that the situation following the second world war was essentially the same.

World development has been characterized since the First World War not by the rise but by the decline of Europe. . . .

What Trotsky says of this relationship in his writings of 1922 and 1926 . . . remains essentially true today in spite of the further growth and development of this relationship and since its temporary and superficial reversal during the period of the boom, [O'Casey declared]. (*Fraud*, pp. 38–9).

But Trotsky least of all would hold that what he said after World War I could be applied to a different situation three and a half decades later. Marxism is ill served by the attempt to bend texts to preconceived notions. To understand the basis of postwar stability we must look at conditions in 1944 and after.

Four factors stand out:

1. In the advanced capitalist countries the crisis of leadership of the working classes had deepened, above all because of the strengthened grip of Stalinism. In a relatively brief period the Stalinist and Social Democratic betrayers quenched the revolutionary fires touched off by the war and marshaled workers back into the factories of capitalist recovery.

2. Nevertheless, the world revolution took giant strides beginning with Yugoslavia in 1943 right in the midst of the war. By 1949 the Red armies of China had driven Chiang Kai-shek off the mainland. A few years later, China, the most prized colonial possession of all, became a workers state. A third of the world's population lived in postcapitalist societies.

The permanent revolutionary ferment made the stabilizing and rebuilding of postwar capitalist societies a matter of urgent necessity to world imperialism. Whereas following the first world war, Washington had, in Trotsky's phrase put Europe on "rations," following the second it flooded Europe and Japan with dollars alongside its occupying NATO and SEATO military forces.

3. The United States was able to do this because it emerged from the war in a position of strength qualitatively superior to its situation following World War I. It commanded a worldwide police force and it opened world markets for U. S. goods and capital.

The physical destruction of Europe and Japan, coupled with the disorganization of the work force under a traitorous leadership, paved the way for massive investments and spectacular profits.

At Bretton Woods U. S. imperialism imposed a dollar-based system in international finance in order to open up the world to U. S. capital and credit. Washington was able to do this not because of the supply of gold in Ft. Knox but because of the military and economic might of U. S. capitalism and its success in the war. The gold supply resulted from this commanding position and reinforced it.

4. The ruling classes had learned some lessons from the economic and social crises of the 1930s and the war period itself. The market could not be left to its own devices. Capitalist governments would more and more intervene in the economy, along lines suggested by Keynes, in order to prevent downswings from becoming too deep. The social cost of severe unemployment outweighed its economic advantages. Inflationary policies were deemed less risky than stringent deflation.

The end result was not a repetition of the "prolonged and profound depression" that followed World War I. Moreover, it was not a "superficial reversal" as O'Casey asserts. It was the longest economic expansion in the advanced capitalist countries in the history of world imperialism.[12] It

---

12. I have limited this series of articles to the essential contradictions of the *advanced capitalist countries*, omitting the manifold contradictions of the economically oppressed capitalist countries and the contradictions between these two main sectors of world imperialism. This otherwise unwarranted simplification can be made because the Healyites,

saw unprecedented climbs in industrial production and real wages. Unemployment fell to historic lows in Europe and Japan.

But this prosperity did not resolve the fundamental contradictions of imperialism. It paved the way for subsequent crises.

Seeds of new crises

For it is precisely in the "division of world markets" that the seeds of new economic crises exist. This was the inevitable result of the postwar expansion, an expansion not only of U. S. monopoly but of the revived imperialisms of Europe and Japan.

Already by 1964, a record year's production of 10.0 million vehicles in the United States and Canada was surpassed by the production of 10.7 million cars and trucks outside of North America.

The 1960s saw a dramatic breaching of the U.S. monopoly of steel production. In 1963 the "Big Eight" U. S. steel companies outsold their eleven biggest foreign competitors by over 20 percent—$10,900 million as compared to $9,000 million. But in 1970, the number of foreign companies able to sell on the same scale as the "Big Eight" had grown from eleven to sixteen, and these sixteen outsold the eight U. S. firms by a margin of almost two to one—$28,900 million as compared to $15,000 million.[13]

The world oil industry, the industry *par excellence* of imperialism, has seen since the mid-1960s the emergence of unbridled competition for world sources and markets, a factor of immense and increasing importance in world politics.

A simple substitution serves to update the remark by Lenin cited above:

> Instead of the undisputed monopoly of the United States, we see a few imperialist powers contending for the right to share in this monopoly.

The United States has lost the absolute supremacy it held in the immediate postwar period but has retained its relative supremacy. This is the main feature of interimperialist relations today.[14]

This is the cause of the intensified struggle for markets in both the advanced and underdeveloped capitalist countries with its inevitable consequences: the tendency toward longer and deeper national and international recession; the intensified productivity drive in industry with increasing speedup and layoffs; the upward direction of unemployment levels even in times of recovery; the intensification of international inflation; and the increasingly grave shakeups of the international monetary system.

Factional frenzy

Here is how the *Bulletin* sizes up the most recent shake-up in international finance.

- February 12, 1973: "Crisis deflates Mandel."

> The bloated profits to which Mandel points are themselves the offspring of the unchecked inflation of the dollar. . . .
>
> The masses of worthless paper dollars which are contained within the mountains of capital invested by the capitalists in order to increase the rate of exploitation of the working class has driven the rate of profit produced by the working class below the level of zero percent.

- March 5, 1973: "Gold price soars to new heights" by David North.

> The most frantic gold rush in modern history—which last week drove the price of the precious metal up to $95 per ounce—is a warning to the working class that the lat-

---

in their sectarian attack on what they dub the "sectarianism" of the Trotkyist movement, themselves *entirely leave out* these pressing questions.

13. See "The World Crisis in Steel" by Dick Roberts, *International Socialist Review*, January 1972.

14. Mandel considers this at length in *Europe Versus America? Contradictions of Imperialism* (1968).

In Fraud, O'Casey asserts that "Mandel is completely steeped in the illusion of a rising Europe to the point in fact where it is the rise of Europe that will supposedly now shake America. The whole historical development of the last fifty years, dominated first by the decline of Europe and the rise of America and now the decline of both is turned upside down and inside out." This position of the Healyites, held for a number of years, is apparently being dropped, as usual without any explanation. The February 24, 1973, *Workers Press* states, "From November 1967 the Americans have had no choice but to prepare for economic and financial warfare against the rest of the capitalist world, and particularly against Europe."

est dollar devaluation is a direct prelude to the complete collapse of the world economic system.

- March 19, 1973: "Marx on the monetary crisis."

> Through the massive inflation of paper currency used to erect mountains of credit, the commodity can find no means to realize its exchange value....
>
> Because exchange value can no longer be realized the capitalists are forced to cease the production of commodities entirely.

The editors of the *Bulletin* may not know it, but the production of commodities hasn't ceased in the United States: It is on an upturn. In March 1973 Americans purchased 1.1 million cars, with dollars and on credit, the largest volume in the history of the country. Profits are at an all-time record. *Business Week* magazine described 1972 as "a spectacular year for profits" and with good reason predicted even higher profits for 1973. Unemployment remains very high, but more people are working in the United States than ever before.

The editors of the *Bulletin* outdo even themselves when they declare that the rate of profit has fallen "below the level of zero percent," especially when they say in the same sentence that inflation has "increased the rate of exploitation of the working class."

For it must be theoretically excluded that the rate of profit is below zero for U. S. imperialism at a time of increasing production and relatively low unemployment. Long before the rate of profit reaches zero, capitalist production is slowed. When they see no arena for profitable investment, except under extraordinary circumstances, capitalists do not invest. The result is curtailed production and increasing unemployment.

It is true that for a certain period in the economic crisis of the 1930s the rate of profit on investment fell below zero. But it should be unnecessary to point out that before this happened production had fallen off massively and unemployment stood at historic levels.

It is also true that despite the enormous mass of profit produced in the world capitalist economy, the rate of profit is under ever intensifying downward pressure as a result of the growing accumulation of unproductive capital, of surplus capital. But one function of the inflation has been to counteract the tendency of the rate of profit to decline, for, as the *Bulletin* rightly asserts, inflation has *increased* the rate of exploitation.

It is easy to see why Mandel's *Intercontinental Press* article "After the International Recession" so infuriated the Healyites. For if "the basis for the world monetary system has been knocked away,"[15] if "the means of converting ... commodities back into money ... has been destroyed,"[16] and if the rate of profit has fallen below zero, how can production be increasing? The answer is simple. It can't be. Under these circumstances there would be no production at all.

Economic recovery

The fact is that world imperialism did recover from the recession of 1969–72; and for those who take revolution seriously, this is not an event to be ignored, or worse still, wished out of existence. Mandel makes two important points in this "preliminary balance sheet."

First of all, the recovery depended on President Nixon's ability to "export inflation." Second, it depended on Washington's ability to increase the rate of exploitation.

> ... the American working class—under the pressure of the betrayal of the trade-union bureaucrats, who "went along" with the wage freeze imposed by Nixon—has allowed its standard of living to be reduced and has suffered massive unemployment.

But, Mandel emphasizes, this only heightens the contradictions of world imperialism. On one side of the Atlantic "exported inflation" has stepped up the militancy of the European working class all the more. On the other side of the ocean,

> with accelerated expansion, unemployment will no doubt decline in the United States. Then the workers will be able to take revenge

---

15. "'Recession seems to have ended' says Mandel" by Cliff Slaughter, *Workers Press*, February 17, 1973.

16. Ibid.

for the "lean years" imposed on them by Nixon. As soon as unemployment seriously drops, outbreaks of strikes can be expected.

The contradictions of world imperialism can be ameliorated only by stepping up the attack on workers. This is Mandel's point in the article on economic recovery and it is the central point of his analysis. These intensified attacks on workers do not resolve the contradictions of imperialism. They press the world working masses towards decisive confrontation with capitalist rule—and only the victory of workers can finally resolve the contradictions that impel them into revolutionary struggle.

Those who believe that Marxism is a science and not a religion do not pretend to be able to predict what is going to happen tomorrow or next week. We believe that such predictions, especially when carried to the point of factional frenzy, as in the pages of the Healyite press, can only end up by demoralizing some of the potential cadres of the impending revolutionary struggle.

It is certain, however, that the coming crises of capitalism will not exactly duplicate the crisis of the 1930s. The ruling classes learned certain lessons from that disaster and it is incumbent on revolutionists to do the same. As the economic contradictions deepen, governments will undertake quite different policies from those they tried in the 1930s. In the long run, however, even the most sophisticated policies will fail.

We have no doubt that capitalism with all its contradictions will ultimately be rejected by the vast majority of workers. For the socialist revolution to succeed, however, workers need a theory capable of correctly analyzing reality and a program that points the way to changing it. In this the Healyites have nothing to offer.

SECTION XIX: HEALYITE REVISION OF DIALECTICAL MATERIALISM

A Malignant Case of Sectarianism in Philosophy
By George Novack

The relation of philosophy to politics has been a subject of continual controversy within and around the socialist movement for over a century. Witness the criticisms of the utopian and "True" Socialists made by the creators of Marxism in the 1840's, Engels's pitiless dissection of Dühring notions, Plekhanov's refutations of the subjective method of the Populist ideologues, and Lenin's polemics against the partisans of empiriocriticism.

The most significant dispute of this kind in the history of Trotskyism was connected with the struggle waged by Trotsky, Cannon, and their associates in 1939–40 against the petty-bourgeois opposition led by Burnham, Shachtman, and Abern, who abjured the method of Marxism in their departure from the principles and positions of the Fourth International. The nature of dialectical materialism and its role in the practice of revolutionary politics was thoroughly illuminated in the course of that conflict.

Trotsky's contributions to the discussion are reprinted in the collection *In Defense of Marxism*. His views can be summarized in the following points. Dialectical materialism is the irreplaceable philosophic foundation of scientific socialism. Its mainspring is the dialectical method of thought whose laws and categories reflect the most general features of a changing world. This logic is especially useful in clarifying contradictory processes and complex problems of the class struggle. Rejection of dialectics under the pressure of nonproletarian forces is a telltale sign of revisionism and opportunism. Its abandonment opens the door for the intrusion of obsolescent, inadequate, and inferior modes of thought. These are evidenced in the intellectual productions as well as the political orientations and conduct of their adherents.

Trotsky documented these propositions by analyzing the specific errors committed by the unprincipled Burnham-Shachtman-Abern combination. It was imperative, he concluded, for the Socialist Workers party to uphold dialectical materialism and transmit its teachings to the younger generation in order to prevent infection by alien and incorrect theoretical tendencies and avoid aberrant habits of thought.

Trotsky primarily directed his arguments against the conception that philosophy in general, and dialectical materialism in particular, was of negligible use in dealing with political problems in the class struggle. This position was put forward by the chief theoretical inspirer of the opposition, James Burnham, who bluntly declared in *Science and Style*: "There is no sense *at all* in which dialectics ... is fundamental in politics, none at all." *In Defense of Marxism* [Pathfinder 1942, 1995], p. 323 [2015 printing]

Burnham was echoing the empiricists, positivists, and formalists, who divorce philosophy and logic in principle from sociology and politics, denying that they have any interconnection. The same opinion of their mutual irrelevance is held by diverse reformists who live from hand to mouth and from one crisis to the next without feeling the need for any theoretical grounding for their political activity or any consistent, thought-out perspective for the workers' movement.

In the course of time, dialectics teaches, everything is transformed into its opposite. This has

---

Intercontinental Press, July 3, 1972.

been the case with the controversies over the relation of philosophic method to political practice on the fringes of the Fourth International. They have been turned about. Whereas in 1939–40 we had to do battle against an aggressive rightward-moving tendency in order to ward off the dangers of skepticism about the dialectical method, now, a third of a century later, it's necessary to expose the errors and pretentions of sectarian phrasemongers represented by the Socialist Labour League in England and its satellite in the United States, the Workers League.*

The Healyite approach to this question is the converse of Burnham's and Shachtman's. Whereas Burnham asserted that dialectics had no value in politics, the SLL maintains that everything else is of subordinate importance. Whereas Shachtman was indifferent to the philosophical aspects and implications of Marxism, the SLL leaders are fanatically obsessed by them. They advertise themselves to the radical public as the exclusive custodians, prime exponents, and peerless practitioners of the dialectical method.

They unremittingly campaign in their press and publications for "the understanding and development of dialectical materialism as the theory of knowledge of Marxism." This, they reiterate, is the most essential task of the revolutionary vanguard today.

Whoever questions this order of priorities or their misinterpretations of Marxism is condemned forthwith as a revisionist, liquidator, centrist, and "capitulator to the vendors of bourgeois idealist philosophy." These labels are culled from indictments of their erstwhile French, Hungarian, and Bolivian comrades in the International Committee with whom they have recently broken, ostensibly over this very issue. (The editor and contributing editors of *Intercontinental Press* have been targets of similar accusations for a much longer time.)

The French Internationalist Communist Organization (OCI) had for its own reasons refused to ratify the SLL's injunction that "Everywhere revolutionary youth must devote itself *first of all* (our emphasis) to the task of developing Marxist theory through a struggle against bourgeois ideology in all the forms it takes in the workers movement." American radicals will understand why. They have become familiar with this kind of diversionary politics based on resolutions and declamations against one or another aspect of "bourgeois ideology." Ultralefts such as Progressive Labor, sometimes joined by opportunists like the CP, are accustomed to counterpose campaigns inveighing against "racism" and "sexism" in the abstract to the organization of mass actions on specific issues such as the struggle for Black control of the schools in the Black communities or for the repeal of laws restricting women's right of abortion. And when these groups encounter resistance from serious militants, they, like the Healyites, invariably hurl unrestrained epithets against their opponents for lack of political arguments.

Healy, Slaughter, Banda, and their overseas disciples fall into the category of sectarian dogmatists in philosophy as in politics. Ideologues of this type seize upon a correct idea and twist it into a caricature that has little correspondence with reality. What they lack above all is a sense of proportion. This unrealism runs through all their positions from their appraisals of the state of the class struggle to their perversion of dialectical materialism.

There are persons who appear to talk quite sensibly until we notice that they have one-track minds and are consumed by a single subject. The Healyite evangelists are like that. They are monomaniacs on the subject of the dialectical method. To them everything else in working-class politics is directly and unconditionally hooked up with their crusade on behalf of the dialectical gospel.

Having learned from Trotsky that a correct philosophical doctrine is indispensable for revolutionary politics, they inflate this truth beyond measure and apply it in the most exaggerated,

---

* In a series of articles entitled "The Liberal Philosophy of George Novack" Alex Steiner insinuates that I stayed on the sidelines in that struggle, ignoring a direct request from Trotsky for me to intervene. "There is no indication," he writes, "that Novack took any active part in the discussion, which was so crucial to the theoretical development of the SWP." (*Bulletin*, March 6, 1972.)

For the record, John G. Wright and I were assigned by the majority leadership to take responsibility for the education of the membership in Marxist theory both during and after the struggle. In the climactic debate between the contending factions in New York, Cannon presented the majority position on the political questions while I answered Burnham on the philosophical issues. But facts carry little weight in the Healy-Wohlforth Academy of Detraction and Distortion.

indiscriminate, and absolutistic manner. From a sound premise they draw the illegitimate conclusion that dialectical materialism is the central element in the political life of the revolutionary vanguard. This is not so.

Theory is united with practice in Marxist politics. The living link between them in the proletarian struggle for power is the revolutionary party. The basis of the party is its principles and program, not its philosophic method. Although the program of revolutionary socialism has been worked out and is refined with the aid of dialectical materialism, it does not coincide with it.

The distinction between the two is expressed, among other places, in the requirements for party membership. Whoever agrees with the programmatic positions and perspectives of the party and acts in a disciplined way to implement them is eligible to join its ranks.

The sectarians are not content with these standards. They demand in addition that all their members and collaborators swear by the teachings of dialectics as they misconstrue them. This criterion is erected into the supreme test of loyalty to the movement.

A scientific socialist party guided by materialist principles cannot exact any such philosophical loyalty test from its militants. It is not a religious denomination but a combat organization dedicated to transforming society. It judges people by where they stand and what they do in the arena of anticapitalist action, not by what they profess or believe in the field of philosophy.

Each and every adherent to the vanguard party cannot be expected or obliged to subscribe, hand on heart, to its philosophic outlook. This prescription would exclude all nondialecticians and nonmaterialists from its ranks. Of course, it is incumbent upon the Marxist party to educate its members in the ideas and spirit of dialectical materialism and counter the influence of antiscientific tendencies inside and outside its organization. But this is a pedagogical and propagandistic task dependent upon rational persuasion leading to conviction in free discussion.

Ideas, and still less philosophical systems and their theories of knowledge, cannot be imposed upon people's minds; and a genuine Marxist party would not bring organizational pressure to bear upon individual members to conform to official opinion in these matters.

The SLL, on the other hand, insists upon total compliance, at least outwardly, with its eccentric version of Marxist theory. The Workers League, its echo chamber in the United States, has, we have heard, expelled critics for the dereliction of "idealism." What this accusation really means is that the hapless individual has dared question some policy or action of the national leaders who, in the name of defending the Holy Grail, crack down on anyone who steps out of line.

This bureaucratic practice does not belong to the Marxist tradition. It is borrowed from Stalinism, which commands all the faithful to pay obeisance to scholasticized "diamat" on penalty of expulsion. Purely ideological dissent or nonconformity is ipso facto branded as disloyalty.

The Healyites rightly regard Trotsky as a high authority in these matters and their misappropriation of his mantle deceives some people. But Trotsky had a different conception of the place of dialectical materialism in the totality of party life. During his most vigorous defense of Marxist philosophy against its detractors, he stated: "To demand that every party member occupy himself with the philosophy of dialectics naturally would be lifeless pedantry." (Ibid. p111.) This is precisely what the Healyites call for. They are the "lifeless pedants" Trotsky warned against.

All members of the revolutionary party must accept, try to understand, and apply to the best of their capacity its principles, program, and perspectives. But such a demand cannot be extended to include the philosophy of dialectics. This is a voluntary, not a mandatory, aspect of party activity and personal development.

In 1940 Trotsky was willing to reserve room in the leadership of the SWP and also the Fourth International for individuals and groupings that rejected dialectical materialism or depreciated its importance, provided they abided by the stated program. This policy did not signify that he undervalued the Marxist method of thought in any respect. It was a realistic recognition that the struggle for philosophical ideas and the doctrine which constitutes the foundation of the revolutionary program does not override at all times other, more pressing tasks and objectives.

Trotsky engaged in hundreds of controversies over forty years. Many of his polemical writings contain valuable observations on the use and abuse of the Marxist method. But in only a few of these did he bring the role of dialectical reasoning to the fore. He did so when it was appropriate and urgent, as in the 1939–40 dispute over the fundamentals of Marxism. When in their flight from Trotskyism the leaders of the petty-bourgeois opposition disclaimed and disparaged the logical method of scientific socialism, Trotsky took up the challenge and probed the question to the bottom for the education of the party cadres. He knew how to invoke and apply its ideas when the issues at stake warranted. But he did not make an ikon out of this logical instrument or treat it as an end in itself.

The Healyites for their part make a fetish out of the dialectical method. They convert it into a hollow abstraction which they beat like a drum. For them it is a shibboleth around which the devotees must gather. They resemble idealistic thinkers in their reverential attitude toward a self-subsistent method detached from social reality.

The lifestream of materialist dialectics flows from its indissoluble merging with the facts of the real world. This is the source of the concrete content that makes its concepts meaningful and the method fruitful.

The Healyites, however, scornfully dismiss as a pragmatist or empiricist anyone who gives primacy to the facts. Here again they stand in opposition to Trotsky's position. In 1934 he told one of Healy's precursors, the Belgian sectarian Vereecken: "But we Marxists are interested, above all, in facts." *Writings of Leon Trotsky, 1934-35* [Pathfinder 1971, 1974], p. 329 [2011 printing]

By their criteria, such a statement would classify Trotsky as a dangerous petty-bourgeois empiricist who had to be fought tooth and nail. Actually Trotsky was voicing the mandate of materialism that facts, not ideas or personal opinions, determine what is so and not so, what is true and what is false, what is effective and what is misleading in action.

The SLL dogmatists, who shout so loudly about the struggle for the materialist dialectic in general, usually abstain from resorting to its procedures when it comes to concrete cases. These champion swimmers do not like to get wet.

Let us dwell upon two pertinent examples of their barrenness. Dialectical logic should enable competent Marxist thinkers to comprehend and cope with objective contradictions in all sectors of reality, and especially to analyze complex political phenomena.

The 1959 Cuban revolution traversed an extremely unusual path of development that diverged in salient respects from the pattern of the October 1917 revolution. In overthrowing Batista, the insurrectionary guerrilla forces proceeded from the rural areas to the cities and the capital while the armed struggle was led, not by a party with a Marxist program, but by a band of humanistic revolutionaries in the July 26 Movement. Yet in two years Castro and his followers went forward from demolishing the military dictatorship to expropriating the native and foreign capitalists and converting Cuba into a workers state. No one had foreseen this eventuality, its principal authors included.

These unexpected and anomalous developments offered, it would seem, a splendid opportunity for self-proclaimed masters of the Marxist method to display their skill. Moreover, it would have been seemly for would-be supporters of Trotsky to recognize that the Cuban events strikingly confirmed the unfolding of the permanent revolution in a colonial country fighting against imperialism for its national independence and social liberation. Historical realization is, after all, the supreme test of the truth of a theory that teaches the inseparable interdependence of the democratic and socialist objectives in our epoch.

What did the best minds of the SLL come up with? Confronted with the unlikely features that characterized the revolutionary process, they ran away from its objective contradictions and buried their heads in the sand. They simply refused to acknowledge fundamental facts known to the whole world.

Capitalist relations, they continue to assert to this day, have remained intact in Cuba; and Castro, like Batista, they say, heads a capitalist regime. These absurdities demonstrate how strident proclamations of undying fidelity to dialectical materialism can mask an incapacity to use its principles in making a correct assessment of so epoch-making an event as the first socialist revolution in the Americas.

The Healyites are not totally bereft of dialectical sense. They have recognized that under certain exceptional conditions capitalism could be abolished by Stalinist parties, as happened in Eastern Europe and China. But they balked when this was done without the benefit of the Soviet army through a non-Stalinist—and a non-Trotskyist—leadership. Such a contradictory state of affairs was beyond their limited comprehension. So they shut their eyes and their minds to what really happened.

But, as Trotsky observed, when dialectics goes out the door, other modes of thought come in the window. In order to file everything in familiar pigeonholes in their minds, the Healyites classify Cuba as state capitalist. There is a name for this sort of thinking that proceeds in defiance of the facts. It is formalistic and schematic, not dialectical; unrealistic, not materialistic.

A common appraisal of the Cuban revolution and its results promoted the reunification of the divided forces of the Fourth International in 1963. A rump organization called the International Committee, consisting of the SLL in England and the OCI of France, stayed by itself for the next eight years.

Although the OCI did not agree with the SLL's bizarre position on Cuba, the two managed to coexist under the same tent during that time. Then all of a sudden at the end of 1971 they openly split, exploding the pretension that the International Committee was a viable alternative to the Fourth International.

Since Paris is closer to London than Havana, it should be an easier chore for the SLL participants to give a clear, coherent, and convincing explanation of the split along dialectical lines. So far their statements have had a purely empirical character, being limited to listing a set of specific differences that cropped up over the past two years between them and the OCI. But why did these differences evolve to the point of irreconcilable antagonism and come to a head so abruptly? They do not tell us what the root causes of the rupture were.

Their explanation remains superficial because they do not know what they themselves really are as a political-theoretical current. To understand what is behind the breakup of the IC, it is necessary to understand the essential political character and direction of the disputants.

As the record shows, the Healyites are sectarians in theory and practice (which does not preclude an occasional opportunistic sortie.) The Lambertists of the OCI are opportunistic by inclination, as evidenced in their trade-union orientation, electoral policies, and international alignments. After the reunification of the Fourth International in 1963, the pair could get along in a loose alliance because of their common hostility to the organization, positions, and perspectives of the authentic Trotskyists in the Fourth International.

This cement began to crumble as the two groups kept pulling in divergent directions in their respective countries and on questions of world politics. It only remained for one of the partners to find a convenient occasion to part company with the other. Differences over the conduct of the Lora group in Bolivia seemingly precipitated the split.

But Healy, true to form, has a more "profound" rationalization for it. He claims that the French OCI did not see the urgency of inculcating the ideas of dialectical materialism in the youth. That was the OCI's unpardonable offense. Just as Wohlforth expels dissidents for "idealism," so Healy casts out Lambert over philosophic divergences.

This lame excuse still does not add up to a dialectical analysis which would have to set forth the nature of the contradictory factors and the course of their development that led to the split.

The truth is that the rump International Committee set up by Healy in 1963 has been an abortive combination of sectarians and opportunists who formed an unprincipled bloc against Trotskyism. Once its dissimilar components clashed, their ephemeral coalition was shattered. That is a correct accounting of the logic that underlay the split and rendered it inevitable.

Healy, however, dispenses with applying any such dialectical acumen to this unpleasant episode in his international maneuverings. To do so would cut the ground from under his feet. He would gain more credence if he lectured on dialectics less and utilized it more.

Systematized sectarianism is one of the worst varieties of that virulent political disease. In the mouths of the Healyites, dialectics is nothing but an incantation, a form of mumbo-jumbo.

The bombast and bluster of these phrasemongers may impress some inexperienced and credulous people who have still to deepen their knowledge of the essentials of Marxism and absorb the traditions of Trotskyism. It would not be the first counterfeit to temporarily pass for good coin.

But reiteration of formulas cannot be a satisfactory substitute for the real thing in philosophy or politics. Such a sterile approach has nothing in common with fruitful and creative application of the method of scientific socialism.

JUNE 15, 1972

Healyite Revisionism in the Field of Philosophy

The July 3 issue of *Intercontinental Press* published an article by George Novack, "A Malignant Case of Sectarianism in Philosophy," dealing with the abuses of dialectical materialism committed by Gerry Healy and Cliff Slaughter of the Socialist Labour League in Britain and their disciples of the Workers League in the United States.

A reader wrote in to raise some further questions. His letter and Novack's reply follow.

Have they turned Marxism upside down?

Editor:

I read George Novack's piece on sectarianism in philosophy; and while I liked everything he said, I was disappointed that he didn't say more. It is true that the way the Healyites relate dialectical materialism to revolutionary politics is wrong. But it seems to me that there is also something wrong with their brand of dialectical materialism. It would have been interesting and worthwhile to take up the content of their "philosophy."

Am I mistaken in concluding that in their all-out war on "empiricism" they have gone overboard and now stand for a type of "dialectics" so far divorced from empirical data, i.e., from material reality, that it can only be called a speculative, that is, idealist philosophy?

The materialist, as against the speculative concept of totality, which is of course basic to materialist dialectics, cannot be the mere result of intuition. It requires a prior full and all-sided study of empirical data. That, at least, is the way Marx and Engels always presented their method. Haven't the Healyites implicitly, if not explicitly,

Intercontinental Press, September 25, 1972.

reversed the sequence of phases in the process of knowledge by doing away completely with the first phase? Haven't they reduced the process from three phases to two phases? Is it possible to produce abstract categories otherwise than from a study of the concrete?

Novack's comments on these questions would be of considerable interest.

A Reader

How Healyites depart from Marxist method

My article focused on the relation of Gerry Healy and Cliff Slaughter's philosophy to revolutionary politics because this side of the matter most concerns revolutionists who run into these sectarians in discussions. However, I agree that much more could and should be said about their method.

I stressed their disregard for the facts. Mendacious distortions of the views of others is one expression of this. They will blithely accuse opponents of holding the opposite of their real positions. There is a method in this consistent misrepresentation. It is a manifestation of their departure from materialist objectivity.

Genuine empiricism at least has the merit of giving an accurate, if not the most comprehensive and deep-going, report of the facts. The Healyites do not even comply with that elementary criterion of empirical knowledge. They not only twist facts but cook them up to suit their factional needs.

Here is a fresh illustration. A front-page editorial in Wohlforth's *Bulletin* of August 28 entitled "McGovern, the Communist Party and Marxist Philosophy" polemicizes, in a matrix of pseudo-philosophizing, against the support offered by the

Stalinists to the Democratic candidate. It is a fact that the American Communist party, in its customary devious fashion, supports McGovern.

To smear the Socialist Workers party with the same brush, the author then goes on to assert that I, as well as the Stalinists, "create an identity between materialism and empiricism." This is a gross falsification as anyone who will turn to my book *Empiricism and Its Evolution* can readily verify.

This work expounds the thesis that the empirical philosophy in its heyday was closely associated with materialism in the struggle against medievalism and idealism but in its subsequent development shed more and more of its materialist ties and aspects until "the two schools of thought now stand arrayed against each other in fields extending from method in natural science to sociology and politics." (p. 138.)

This historical appraisal concurs with that given by Engels in his introduction to *Socialism, Utopian and Scientific*. In describing the British origin of modern materialism, he wrote:

> Bacon, Hobbes and Locke are the fathers of that brilliant school of French materialists which make the eighteenth century, in spite of all battles on land and sea won over Frenchmen by Germans and Englishmen, a preeminently French century.

The most qualified Marxist thinkers have not made empiricism into the absolute antithesis of materialism as the Healyites (and many empiricists themselves) do. In the philosophical classics of Marxism that place is allotted to idealism.

Empiricism occupied an intermediate position in the spectrum of philosophic schools and methods. It was a composite, a hybrid, of semimaterialist and semimetaphysical ideas in proportions that varied greatly from one thinker to another and from one stage of its evolution to another.

As Engels pointed out, the empirical theory of cognition, in opposition to idealism, shared with materialism the cardinal proposition that all human knowledge was derived from sensation. Materialism alone, however, applied this sensationalist principle in a consistent way, ridding philosophy of all religious prejudices and metaphysical errors.

To say that the two philosophies had or have certain elements in common does not mean that they are essentially the same. If I say that Hegel and Marx were both dialectical logicians, that does not entail the view that their philosophies were identical. To conclude otherwise would be to fall into the simple logical fallacy that stands out in Wohlforth's amalgam.

The Healyite approach to empiricism as a historical reality deviates in fundamental respects from that of dialectical materialism. Ernest Mandel correctly writes in the introduction to *Marxist Economic Theory* that the Marxist method "must . . . be genetico-evolutionary, critical, materialistic and dialectical." (p. 18.)

In philosophy as in politics the Healy-Wohlforth school ignores all these requirements. They do not view empiricism as a trend of thought that, like capitalism itself, has passed through various stages of growth and decadence from the age of bourgeois revolution to the age of socialist revolution and evolved, under pressure of its inner contradictions and the growing gap between its conceptions and the world around it, into something quite different from its original expression. As a result of the colossal socio-economic, scientific, and philosophical advances from the seventeenth to the twentieth centuries, empiricism has become transformed from a vigorous, innovative, fruitful mode of thought and set of ideas into an increasingly stale, skeptical, feeble, and sterile one. As its essential characteristics and contradictory nature have been defined and disclosed, the relations of empiricism with materialism have switched from ally to adversary. This has been the dialectic of its development.

The Healyites take a static, nondialectical, rather than a dynamic, approach to this philosophy. They do not grasp or set forth the inner contradictions that provide the driving forces of its specific course of development and account for its logic of motion. They do not correctly appraise the changing and complex connections it has had with rival schools of thought, including materialism itself in its progress from mechanical to dialectical materialism. They do not explain the reasons for the conversion of empiricism from a revolutionizing to a retrogressive mode of thought. They fix their gaze exclusively upon the end product, the final phase, of its evolution and palm it off for the whole.

This sort of rigid, narrow, unhistorical thinking that disregards the stages, transitions, and mediations characterizing the development of philosophic tendencies, like all other processes, is proper to a metaphysical outlook and method, not to dialectical materialism. Reality is variegated and multicolored but these color-blind sectarians see everything as either pure white or coal black.

Their polemics against "empiricism" are actually a shamefaced way of contesting Marxist materialism and its theory of knowledge. In disparaging the priority and importance of empirical data, Healy and his disciple Tim Wohlforth not only break with dialectical materialism but with scientific method in general. Consideration of the objective facts as given in experience is the elementary condition of any scientific inquiry or branch of knowledge.

They are disdainful of the history of scientific thought and the first principle of scientific practice. The practice of medicine, for example, first acquired a scientific character with the Hippocratic school of Ionia, which combined acute observation of the "empirical data" with reflective analysis in a harmonious synthesis of empiricism and rationalism. Whereas a quack or a witch doctor proceeds from arbitrary and a priori assumptions, a skilled physician bases his diagnosis on observable symptoms that indicate the probable type and cause of the disease and suggest its cure.

Scientific socialism and its method of knowledge likewise rest upon the primacy of empirical data. The objects encountered in the world are what thought reflects and concepts denote. The given facts are the basis for the origin, content, evolution, and verification of all ideas.

Epistemologists have set forth two opposing lines of explanation of the origin of ideas. One holds that ideas come from some inner source through intuition or revelation ultimately leading to divine inspiration; the other that they are derived from external reality mediated by sense-experience. The first conception has been upheld by idealists through the ages. Ready examples are the British neo-Platonists and Leibniz in Locke's time. The second is the materialistic view which was defended by Locke in his devastating criticism of innate ideas.

The origin of ideas in sensation and perception, refined by reflection, was the common premise of both the materialist and the classical empirical thinkers who were closely allied during the rise of bourgeois civilization and the formation of its culture (viz., Bacon, Hobbes, and Locke). Marxism adheres to this position. Where do ideas come from if not from the testimony of the senses reacting to natural and social conditions?

Anyone who in any way gives existential priority to concepts and abstractions over empirical data, as Healy, Slaughter, and Wohlforth do, is making impermissible concessions to the primacy of the subjective over the objective elements in the process of acquiring knowledge.

The essential content of all our thoughts, however complex or fantastic, is likewise ultimately derived from the features of the external world in its historical development.

This is confirmed by the observable fact that ideas have changed and evolved throughout history in accord with objective changes in economic activities and social relations that have given rise to expanded and deepened insight into the world around us.

True ideas are discriminated from false ones through their correspondence—or lack of it—with the empirical facts as these are disclosed and tested in practice, by experiment, or by industry.

Thus all aspects of intellectual activity and its results are shaped and controlled by objective factors.

The primacy of the objective over the subjective, of things over consciousness and concepts, is exhibited in the process of learning about the world. Three fundamental factors are at work in the process of knowledge: sensory perception of the phenomena in the environment, increasing penetration into the essence of things by means of theoretical thought, and the verification in practice of the correspondence of our conceptions with the objective regularities of the world.

Empiricism emphasized the first phase of this process and slighted the second; rationalism concentrated upon the role of the second to the detriment of the first. Dialectical materialism overcame the one-sidedness of these earlier philosophical schools by seeing the organic coordination of all three of these phases in the process of cognition.

Where do Healy, Slaughter, and their pupils

stand in the light of these principles of dialectical materialism?

They invert materialism and approach idealism by converting facts into abstractions and abstractions into realities under cover of exposing empiricism. The priests of their cult perform this act of transubstantiation as zealously as the Catholic priesthood converts the wafer and wine into the body and blood of Christ. Theirs is a real revision of Marxism.

For example, Dennis O'Casey in his fraudulent *The Fraud of Neo-Capitalism* objects to Ernest Mandel's including the "empirical grasping of facts" in his definition of Marxist method. He informs us on page 5 what a fact is as he sees it. It is simply and solely an appearance.

For materialists a genuine fact is something manifestly real. To say it is nothing but an appearance is to deprive fact of its objective material content. In fact, as Hegel knew, though O'Casey does not, every appearance is a manifestation of its essence. There are no real essences apart from their factual embodiments.

O'Casey tries to cover up his abandonment of the materialist position by bringing in Marx's notion of the "imaginary concrete" from the introduction to the *Critique of Political Economy*. He misuses this formulation by exalting the adjective and obliterating the noun. Marx did not at all intend to deny the objectivity of the concrete (indeed, he writes that "it is the real starting point . . . of both observation and conception"). Marx's point was that the phenomenal manifestation of the given facts lacks adequate definition and is only the beginning and not the conclusion of scientific analysis in political economy. Every fact or factor must be viewed in the wealth of its connections, in its contradictory historical development, in the sequence of its specific determinations.

O'Casey would have us believe that Marx is asserting that the concrete is, in and of itself, "imaginary"—not fact but fiction.

Similarly, Alex Steiner tells us (*Bulletin*, March 27, 1972) that "Marx noted that in this whole cognition process it is necessary to proceed from the concrete appearance, which is actually an extremely complex number of abstractions called 'facts,' to simple essential abstractions." Steiner matches O'Casey in clarity. Facts to him are really sets of abstractions, not bits of objective reality.

These wizards next transmogrify abstractions into realities. O'Casey writes in his pamphlet: ". . . abstractions are, as Lenin points out in the *Philosophic Notebooks*, more real than the so-called facts." (p. 6.) Further, theoretical abstractions in men's minds are "in fact, more real and express reality in a more fundamental way than any factual statement however quantitatively precise about surface, concrete, phenomena." (p. 10.)

In the passage Steiner cites, Lenin was discussing degrees of truth and not the essential difference between facts and ideas. He contrasted scientific generalizations and laws to observations and impressions that rest on the phenomenological surface of reality and do not penetrate to the essential connections and driving forces of things (e.g., the fluctuation of prices versus their regulation by the law of value). He was not saying that abstractions drawn from the facts have more reality than the facts themselves. That was what the medieval Realists maintained. Even the Nominalists, the forerunners of the materialists and the empiricists, knew better than that!

O'Casey's misinterpretation of the nature of value illustrates his mode of thought. He announces that "In point of fact, however, value is an abstraction." (p. 10.) To be sure, the *concept* of value and the *theory* of surplus value are (scientific) abstractions. But value is more than its conceptual expression as a category. Value is first of all a social property that is the product of the expenditure of labor power and the application of socially necessary labor of a definite magnitude. If value is nothing but an abstraction, then so is surplus value and its subdivisions—profits, rents, and interest. It follows from this point of view that capitalists exploit their workers and fight among themselves over these "abstractions." An odd propensity for so pragmatic a class!

The nonmaterialist bent of Healyite thinking is also exemplified in their conception of what a law is. In defense of Slaughter against me, Steiner writes: "But the law of uneven and combined development is not an empirical generalization from which we can project certain trends developing in the future as they have in the past." What is it? "Rather, it expressed a fundamental property of dialectical development as applied to sociology.

The discovery of this law is dependent on the development of dialectical materialism emerging as the culmination of all previous philosophy." (*Bulletin*, March 20, 1972.)

We understand the law as a formulation of certain fundamental and universal features of social and historical development discovered by Trotsky through his dialectical insight into the objective facts. The Healyites construe it as simply a product of autonomous advances in dialectical thinking about social phenomena, leaving out the factual basis that makes the law true, relevant, and fruitful.

Marx's own procedure is the best refutation of the disparagement and disqualification of empirical observation by O'Casey and his cothinkers. How does *Capital* in fact begin? It opens with an empirical statement of fact about the capitalist system as it immediately presents itself to an acute observer. "The wealth of societies in which the capitalist method of production prevails, takes the form of 'an immense accumulation of commodities,' wherein individual commodities are the elementary units." This is an empirical observation, is it not? Ricardo's *Principles of Political Economy*, on the other hand, begins on a different footing with a definition or explanation of what value consists of or depends on.

However, Marx is not a vulgar empiricist and he does not proceed in an empirical manner. He is a more scientific thinker equipped with the superior dialectical method. In the course of his work he moves from the phenomenal forms to the essential connections and inner laws of the mode of production under examination.

Dialectical materialism does not ignore or deny what is valid in the empirical approach—such as the collection, observation, and comparison of data—and its respect for facts provided by experience and tested by experiment. Bacon, the pioneer of the empirical method of studying reality, ushered in a new era in scientific and philosophic thought by insisting that correct conclusions can be arrived at only on the basis of facts that have been collected and critically studied.

Marxists part company with the empiricists by considering facts, not as isolated, fixed, and self-sustained entities, but as changing historical products that appear in concrete contexts and special forms and that have to be taken in their interconnections and interactions.

The empirical *fact* that the products of labor necessarily acquire the commodity form under capitalist conditions was what Marx felt called upon to explain and what he took so many pages to clarify in all its ramifications and results. O'Casey's approach would expunge the reference to the empirical facts that underlies the entire course of Marx's exposition. O'Casey scoffs at Ernest Mandel's efforts in his two-volume *Marxist Economic Theory* to present empirical verification of the laws of scientific political economy. This is consistent with Steiner's denial that the law of uneven and combined development is rooted in the facts of history, reflects them, and is validated by them. Laws of political economy and history that could not be empirically verified would have neither validity nor use value.

As one would expect, these sectarians have a one-sided view of the process of negation. Dialectical negation not only breaks up and breaks with the preceding stage and form of being out of which it emanates but preserves in a superior synthesis the positive, viable, enduring elements in it.

> Not empty negation, [wrote Lenin] not futile negation, not *sceptical* negation, vacillation and doubt is characteristic and essential in dialectics ... but negation as a moment of connection, as a moment of development, retaining the positive, i.e., without any vacillations, without any eclecticism. (*Collected Works*, Vol. 38, p. 226.)

The Healyites apply "empty negation" to intellectual and political phenomena and processes, admitting the destruction and discontinuity but not the continuity in successive phases of dialectical development. There would be no progress from lower to higher unless something was transmitted as well as transmuted and transcended.

To prove I am a liberal lamb masquerading in Marxist costume, Alex Steiner argues in his three-part series *The Liberal Philosophy of George Novack* as though there could be no elements of continuity whatsoever between bourgeois and proletarian democracy. What, then, makes them two successive forms of the same political type? We know they are irreconcilable because they have essentially antagonistic class foundations. But at the same time whatever rights of the people have been wrested from the propertied classes by struggle are to be preserved, protected, extended, and perfected under workers' rule.

In the eyes of this absolutist, not only formal democracy but formal logic is "completely reactionary." "... while formal logic was a progressive mode of thought in Ancient Greece," he says, "it is today completely reactionary.... To compromise with formal logic is to compromise with the bourgeoisie." (*Bulletin*, March 6, 1972.)

Admittedly, formal logic is inferior to and more limited than dialectical thinking. But Steiner aims to convey the idea that it is currently useless, utterly outmoded and inapplicable. How can a form of logic that everyone uses all the time be "completely reactionary"? Formal logic is no more reactionary in itself that Newton's laws of motion; and its fruitfulness is far from exhausted even today.

One of the foremost innovations in contemporary technology, the computer, is based upon binary numbers which are an expression of formal logical categories. Two mutually exclusive entities—0 and 1—operate in its system. There are no third values in ordinary computer logic.

Moreover, Steiner himself cannot avoid using formal logic. Here are the steps in his argument from major premise to conclusion: (a) To compromise with formal logic is to compromise with the bourgeoisie, (b) Novack compromises with formal logic. (c) Therefore Novack compromises with the bourgeoisie.

But Steiner's own tail is easily caught in this kind of fallacious reasoning. Because, if he has compromised with formal logic by using it, he himself is guilty of compromising with the bourgeoisie.

In rejecting empiricism in toto, the Healyites are equally unhistorical and undialectical. Dialectical materialism does not deny or discard everything in the empirical tradition. It has incorporated into its own doctrines whatever was innovative, true, and enduring in the contributions of empiricism to the progress of human thought, above all its insistence on the observation and ordering of the empirical data in the acquisition of genuine knowledge about the real world.

Though the Healyite habit of inventing facts and substituting them for realities is alien to Marxism, it can be found among religious folk in the form of miracle-making. What their desires crave and imagination projects becomes more real to them than the mundane facts. Such is the semireligious feature of the egocentric outlook and subjective method of this sect.

George Novack

A Travesty of Marxist Method
by George Novack

I spoke on December 1 at the Militant Labor Forum in New York City on the relevance of philosophy to politics. In the course of this wide-ranging talk I made the following points.

1. Philosophical theorizing and practical politics are almost totally divorced from each other in the United States today. The dominant schools among the professorial specialists in philosophy see no organic connection between their speculations and the practice of politics, while the officeholders and contenders for power in the Republican and Democratic parties have no use for philosophy.

2. This mutual estrangement of philosophy and politics is a sign of the degradation of American thought, not of its advancement and elevation.

3. In periods of intense class struggle there has as a rule been much closer collaboration between these two aspects of human activity. I cited as il-

Intercontinental Press, January 15, 1973.

lustrations the reasonings of the classical idealists, Plato and Aristotle, in regard to the revolutions and reactions that agitated the advanced city-states in ancient Greece; John Locke, the theorist of the consummation of the bourgeois revolution in England who wrote equally well and influentially on the empirical conception of knowledge and the issues of bourgeois parliamentarism; Ethan Allen, Tom Paine, Jefferson, Franklin, "and even Washington," leaders of the Patriot cause, nonchurchgoers who "turned away from orthodox systems of faith as well as against the sanctity of the British Crown"; John Dewey, whose instrumentalism provided a philosophic rationale for the middle-class reform movement of Progressivism and liberalism; and, last but not least, the Bolsheviks who headed the October revolution.

4. I concluded that the partnership of generalized thought and political action was indispensable for any genuine revolutionary movement against capitalism in our time and that the estrangement of philosophy and politics could best be overcome and their reunification effected through dialectical materialism, the theoretical foundation of Marxism.

Not everyone present agreed with all these propositions. The December 18, 1972, *Bulletin*, weekly organ of the Workers League, carried a full-page account of this talk; written by Alex Steiner, it was captioned "George Novack's Crusade for Philosophical Tolerance." Like so much of the material issued by these pseudo Trotskyists, it is crammed with misrepresentations and sheer stupidities.

I shall discuss as a sample only that part of the piece dealing with questions of American history, to show how the factional malice acquired in the Healy-Wohlforth School of Detraction and Distortion propels its author beyond the bounds of Marxism and how students of dialectical materialism can be misled if they mistake such views for the genuine article.

Though this section is only five paragraphs long, it contains that many errors.

> Novack [Steiner writes] was forced to revise history itself, in the course of the lecture. He stated that the American Revolution of 1776 was led by people who had assimilated the highest developments in philosophy of their time. Novack even went so far as to say that the American Revolution represented a closer unity of philosophy and politics than the French Revolution, because in the former, the "philosophers" such as Sam Adams and Tom Paine were actually men of action, while the French *philosophes* were not.

The reporter, who listened with only one ear and a prejudiced mind, missed what was actually stated. I observed that philosophizing and politics were more closely associated during the First American Revolution than at any other time in this country's history and that this fusion of theory and action was worth imitating. Second, that, while the "philosophes" of the Enlightenment from Voltaire to Diderot and Rousseau heralded the French revolution and prepared certain ideological prerequisites for its advent, their contemporaries, the leaders of our War of Independence, did more. The latter organized their revolution and led it to victory. This example of combining theorizing with participation in the revolutionary process was an admirable precedent for us to follow.

My critic, however, is concerned with neither the main facts of the historical situation nor the lessons they can convey to American revolutionists today. He protests that the ideologists of 1776 engaged in "the most shallow borrowing of the ideas of Locke and the *philosophes*."

The textbooks teach that they did indeed take many of their ideas on philosophy and politics from England and France. What Steiner disregards is the fact that they further developed and deepened these ideas and, above all, applied them to the problems at hand more radically and thoroughly than their mentors. Locke was not an antimonarchist, and he did not propose to disestablish the official Church of England.

The Patriot leaders took his doctrine of popular sovereignty so seriously that they booted out King George III and did not replace him with any native monarchy. They separated church from state. They embodied their bourgeois-democratic principles in enduring political institutions by creating a federal republic which was the freest in the world at that time.

To those who have understood what Marx meant when he declared: "The philosophers have only *interpreted* the world in various ways; the point is, to *change* it," this side of their activities is most decisive. Paine, Jefferson, Franklin, and their associates changed America along revolutionary lines. Steiner's failure to appreciate the national and world-historical significance of their deeds shows what a pedantic approach he takes to American history and how inadequately and ineptly he applies the method of Marxism to one of its outstanding events.

The rebellious American colonists were the Vietnamese of the eighteenth century. They waged the first triumphant colonial uprising of modern times against the mightiest of oppressive overseas powers. A young people that bred a Sam Adams, a Jefferson, and a Franklin, and adopted Tom Paine before Robespierre and Marat appeared on the scene were not inferior in revolutionary fervor, fortitude, or foresight to their transatlantic counterparts. Sam Adams was the ablest organizer of revolutionary forces, and Tom Paine the most influential propagandist for revolutionary ideas among the masses in American history. The many-sided Franklin and Jefferson had as much culture and capability as the Europeans among whom they diplomatized.

To say that these founding fathers were interested in nothing but "Locke's defense of the right of the bourgeoisie to private property as a 'natural' and 'inalienable' right," as Steiner does, is a vulgarized, one-sided interpretation of their role that is proper to sophomoric "debunkers" but does not come from the Marxist school of historical science.

Since they were *bourgeois* revolutionists, all of them, whether of high or low estate, they defended the rights of private property in principle and in practice. But, in order to secure and strengthen these rights for themselves and the classes they represented, they had to summon the masses to struggle and to arm themselves, wage a revolutionary war, topple crown rule, drive out royalists and loyalists, uproot feudalists, and in the process promote a measure of democracy as the price of victory.

This would-be exponent of the materialist dialectic completely overlooks the *contradictory* character of all the great revolutions from the sixteenth to the nineteenth centuries. These were both bourgeois and democratic. In order to defend and extend the powers and specific private-property interests of the native possessing classes, large and small, their more radical representatives had to institute rights previously denied to the people by monarchical, clerical, and aristocratic regimes. (See my *Democracy and Revolution* for an explanation of this dialectical process.)

In 1918, in "A Letter to American Workers," Lenin wrote:

> The history of modern civilized America opens with one of those great, really emancipatory, really revolutionary wars of which there have been so few compared with the numerous predatory wars which, like the present imperialist war, were caused by quarrels among kings, landlords, and capitalists over the division of usurped lands and stolen profits.

Note the marked difference between this laudatory appraisal of our War of Independence and Steiner's attempt to downgrade its leadership. The authentic Marxist speaks one way, the sectarian another.

This stern schoolmaster points an accusatory finger at me for defending

> the likes of George Washington as a great revolutionary of his time, as if this opportunist slave-owner had an ounce of the revolutionary spirit and elan of the great revolutionaries of France such as Robespierre or Danton!

It is true that Washington, like Jefferson, and others, was a slaveholding planter, just as Hancock, the first signer of the Declaration of Independence, was the richest merchant of the colonies. It is also true that he directly represented the patrician upper crust in the Patriot camp rather than its plebeian ranks. But surely he must have had at least "an ounce of revolutionary spirit and elan" to risk his life and his possessions by taking command of the Continental armies and keeping them in the field for seven years until they beat the British and won independence.

In fact, Washington's role in the eighteenth-century American revolution was comparable to that played by William of Orange in the Dutch War of Independence of the sixteenth century and by Cromwell in the English civil war of the mid-seventeenth century. These commanders in chief were all landed proprietors. But they exhibited enough courage, stamina, and initiative to battle and defeat the forces arrayed by the old regimes against their rebellions.

In discussing England's revolutionary traditions, Trotsky had this to say about Cromwell:

> We need not waste a single word to prove that Oliver Cromwell was the pioneer of *bourgeois* society, and not of *socialist* society. This great revolutionary bourgeois was opposed to the universal suffrage right, for he saw in it a danger to private property. [But, Trotsky went on,] Cromwell was the great revolutionary of his time, who learned to *hesitate at nothing* to defend the interests of the new bourgeois social order against the old aristocratic order ... We may say with a certain justification that Lenin is the proletarian Cromwell of the twentieth century. (*Whither England?*, pp. 131–33.)

Through this characterization, Trotsky was not intent on exalting Cromwell any more than I was intent on idealizing Washington. He had other aims in view. He wanted to indicate with scientific objectivity the work accomplished by this central figure in the revolution of his time and place and thereby recall to the English workers the audacity in action displayed by their revolutionary forebears so they might be inspired to emulate that example in their own struggles.

Steiner, who claims to be a true disciple of Trotsky as against the imposter Novack, does neither of these things. In order to deal an unmerited blow against a political opponent (a purely pragmatic purpose!), he is compelled to belittle and disfigure the national revolutionary traditions of the American people and to avoid bringing them forward as precedents for the workers to follow. This double default is the result of his departure from the scientific objectivity of Marxism.

He derogates the Patriot leaders for their "pragmatic, piecemeal borrowing from the philosophers of England and France." What they did, as I pointed out, was to assimilate the best ideas from the most progressive trends of thought available to them (empiricism bordering on materialism and the radical rationalism of the Enlightenment) and put these into practice to solve their most pressing social and political problems. And they did so with tremendous success.

As a diversion, Steiner throws in a comment from Engels on the theoretical backwardness of Americans in general and the workers in particular in the 1880s. However, Engels was not contrasting our bourgeois-democratic revolutionists of the eighteenth century with their forerunners or their contemporaries in Europe, as Steiner implies. He was doing something different. He was unfavorably comparing the mentality of the industrial workers here in the late nineteenth century with their European brothers and sisters.

This deficiency has persisted to the present day. The American workers are far less advanced in their ideology and politics, as everyone knows, than their counterparts in other major industrialized countries—and even in many less economically developed ones.

It does not occur to our critic that two centuries after 1776 American revolutionists face a similar situation and have comparable tasks to perform on a far higher historical level. Just as our forefathers borrowed and learned from their European predecessors, so contemporary Marxists in this country have to borrow the ideas of scientific socialism from our German and Russian predecessors and use them as a guide to practice.

If the current generation can carry out this job as effectively as Paine, Adams, Jefferson, and even Washington did theirs, we shall have discharged our duties well. Our tasks are greater and our adversary at home more formidable. But we have the advantage of the examples given by Marx and the Bolsheviks and the knowledge derived from the revolutionary experiences since their time incorporated in the teachings and program of the Trotskyist movement.

However, those who aspire to impart the philosophical and political doctrines of Marxism to others should first educate themselves in the ideas and methods of dialectical materialism and then apply them with a scrupulous care for scientific objectivity. Steiner and his mentors fail to meet these elementary qualifications. Steiner's tendentious assertions on philosophy, history, and politics are a sectarian travesty of the Marxist method.

DECEMBER 27, 1972

Facts Are Stubborn Things
By George Novack

The Healyite organ, *Labour Press*, saluted my arrival on a speaking tour of Australia in May 1973 with a four-page special supplement headed "An Open Letter to George Novack." In addition to the well-worn diatribes against the scarecrow of "Pabloism" and slanders against Trotskyist organizations from Ceylon to the United States, this salvo zeroed in on my philosophic works.

As they pursued this campaign during the discussion periods following my public talks in the principal cities, the Healyites put forward some opinions of their own. After my exposition of Marxism as a revolutionary materialist humanism, the national secretary of the Socialist Labour League, Jim Mulgrew, asserted that Marxism had nothing to do with humanism of any kind.

This denial breaks with the teachings and traditions of scientific socialism and places these sectarians in the same camp as the Maoists and the French Communist philosopher Althusser, who contend in similar ways that Marxism is antihumanistic.

Mulgrew also insisted that dialectical materialism cannot be twisted in a sectarian manner; only opportunistic revisionist adaptations to non-Marxist currents of philosophy exist (Lenin *dixit*). If your trousers are caught on a hook, try to extricate yourself by denying that any hook exists.

The Healyites conveniently overlook the precedent set by the brand of dialectical materialism sponsored by the Stalinists. Theirs was a falsified, dogmatic—extremely sectarian—perversion of Marxist thought. This deformation and degradation in philosophy corresponded to the bureaucratic degeneration of the Russian revolution and was an integral ideological component of it.

Stalin's "Red Professors" screened from the history of philosophy innovative contributions to thought that did not conform to the arbitrary criteria of a straight and narrow road of materialist development from the Milesians to the mastermind in the Kremlin. In 1947, at Stalin's behest, his watchdog on the cultural front, Zhdanov, indicted the *History of West European Philosophy* by the unlucky G.F. Alexandrov, who saw something good in the works of Kant, Hegel and Fourier.

Stalin himself expunged the law of the negation of the negation from his presentation of dialectical materialism. Throughout the Soviet bloc the slightest manifestations of independent thinking in this field were suspect or suppressed. Anyone who did not parrot the formulas sanctioned by the official doctrinaires was condemned out of hand as a dangerous "revisionist."

Although the Healyite approach to the dialectical method has a different basis, it exhibits certain traits of dogmatic rigidity characteristic of the Stalinist mode of philosophizing. Like children in a classroom under a strict teacher, the Healyites monotonously intone the same points in the same stereotyped phrases from individual to individual and from one country to another, without making the least effort to exercise critical thought about the material data and problems under consideration.

Like the Stalinist school, they demand unconditional and unquestioning submission to their peculiar misinterpretations and misapplications of Marxist philosophy. Whoever doubts or denies these shibboleths is subject to excommunication from the chapel and to the curses of the band of true believers. Thus, for their doubts and denials Healy broke with his erstwhile French partners in the International Committee. (See "A Malignant Case of Sectarianism in Philosophy," *Intercontinental Press*, July 3, 1972.)

Sectarianism in philosophy or politics is marked by disregard of objective realities. This was strikingly evidenced in the Australian "Open Letter" assailing my views.

Its signatory, Adrian Falk, presented in an introduction to the "Open Letter" the following pearls of wisdom on Cuba.

> On the basis of a completely empiricist evaluation of the 'facts' of the Cuban revolution (Nationalisation of industries, etc), the SWP

Intercontinental Press, July 23 1973.

concluded that Cuba had become a workers state.

The point at issue is not what are the facts, but the method with which "facts" are approached and grasped. The empiricist takes the so-called facts as an ultimate court of appeal, and sees them as having some fixed significance which they impose on consciousness. Marxists, on the contrary, see facts as partial abstractions, to be comprehended only in the practical struggle to change the world.

Thus in the case of Cuba, the point is not to contemplatively enumerate abstract criteria of a workers state, but to understand the political developments there through grappling with problems which can only be confronted in the struggle to lead the working class against every form of petty bourgeois opportunism (including Castroism).

To begin with, what are the "abstract criteria of a workers state" that Trotsky enumerated these many times in his writings from 1923 to 1940, and most forcefully in the 1939–40 polemic against Burnham and Shachtman reprinted in *In Defense of Marxism*? The most decisive are nationalization of the means of production, monopoly of foreign trade, and a planned economy.

What are the facts in this case? All three of these requisites have been instituted and developed in Cuba as the result of its socialist revolution.

Regardless of their attitude toward them, a host of other forces in the world, from the U.S. imperialists to the Cuban people, along with most tendencies on the left, have recognized these basic facts about the revolutionary reconstruction of Cuban society. Everyone—except these pseudo-Trotskyists. The Healyites acknowledge that the USSR under Brezhnev, the Chinese People's Republic under Mao, and even Albania conform to "the abstract criteria" of a workers state. Yet they adamantly insist that Cuba is capitalist and stands in the same socioeconomic category as Australia and New Zealand.

That is what Falk, who is an instructor in sociology at the University of New South Wales in Sydney, teaches us. He certainly didn't learn this kind of sociology in the school of Trotskyism.

What is the worth of a group that pretends to lead the world revolutionary vanguard but is incapable of recognizing a socialist overturn and assessing its results correctly when it actually happens? And thereafter sticks to its dogmatic error despite a decade of accumulated facts?

Falk has a theoretical justification for this purblindness. This Healyite wise man informs us that facts are not "the point at issue" in judging the state of affairs in Cuba. He makes the crude mistake of confusing materialism with empiricism because both take their point of departure from the facts. On this score any empiricist who is at least concerned about the facts is closer to materialism than our critic. Indeed, the Healyite dismissal of the importance of facts makes them less realistic than anyone guided by plain common sense!

According to Falk, "the so-called facts" (aren't there any real facts?) cannot be taken "as an ultimate court of appeal." He fails to inform us what in his view the ultimate arbiter of the truth of any idea or proposition is. Marxism teaches that objective reality, which is made up of facts in their development, is decisive in determining what is and what is not the case in all questions from the physical nature of the universe to the sociological nature of a given country like Cuba. This has been a cardinal principle of all materialisms from ancient times to the present and serves as a directive of its method. However, Falk does not acknowledge this elementary truth of dialectical materialism any more than he does the particular facts in regard to Cuba.

When he nonchalantly remarks that facts have no "fixed significance which they impose on consciousness," he is unaware that this viewpoint is the breeding ground of subjectivism and idealism, methods that are contrary to materialism as well as to scientific procedures. To hold that the facts of capitalism impose no fixed significance on the consciousness of its subjects would, for one thing, destroy the foundation of the Marxist explanation of the genesis and development of the consciousness of its constituent classes.

In connection with this problem, let me cite an example from the history of astronomy that is so simple that even the mind of a pupil of Healy's might grasp it. People once believed that the sun went around the earth, which was the center of the universe. Since Copernicus, whose five hundredth anniversary was commemorated this year, we know that the earth moves around the sun. What imposed this scientific truth upon the consciousness of humanity and exposed the earlier misconception as false? Was it not the objectively existing structural relations among the bodies of our solar system, that is, the discovery of the true physical facts about them?

In the body of the "Open Letter" itself Falk takes exception to a passage from my article "A Malignant Case of Sectarianism" that reads:

> The lifestream of materialist dialectics flows from its indissoluble merging with the facts of the real world. This is the source of the concrete content that makes its concepts meaningful and the method fruitful.

He tries to refute this as follows:

> This is a pragmatist formulation which attempts to smooth over the essential clash between knowledge and the developing world. By starting from the primacy of the facts and deriving the significance of dialectics from them, you actually deny the dialectical character of knowledge and its development.

Before dealing with "the essential clash" between knowledge and the external world, i.e., the unavoidable discrepancy between ideas and reality, a materialist has first to recognize and account for the *correspondence* between our valid knowledge and the developing world. This is to be found in the essential unity between what we know and what objectively exists. However, according to Falk, "starting from the primacy of the facts" has nothing to do with materialism or its dialectics but is the procedure of pragmatism!

Engels long ago pointed out in *Anti-Dühring* that the dialectical character of knowledge and its development is derived from the dialectical characteristics of matter in motion, including the contradictory course of human history and the dialectics of nature. Thus the dialectics of knowledge is rooted in the objective facts of society and nature as these are disclosed through practice by scientific knowledge of them.

"Dialectics," as Trotsky wrote, "cannot be imposed upon facts; it has to be deduced from facts, from their nature and development." *Problems of Everyday Life*, [Pathfinder, 1973], p. 306 [2014 printing]

In a personal encounter with me after I spoke at the university where he teaches, Falk contended that facts are nothing but "appearances." Actually facts are pieces of the objective world that have essential structural properties as well as apparent characteristics. In defining what a fact is in fact, our subjectivist leaves out of account its material objectivity in time and space that exists apart from human beings—unless the facts pertain to our species.

Facts, he writes in the "Open Letter," are no more than "partial abstractions." To be sure, no single fact exists by and for itself. Taken as such in everyday life or in the process of inquiry, the fact acquires a more abstract quality than is warranted by its actual embedding in the rest of reality. Nonetheless, this role in the knowing process does not deprive any fact of its concrete existence as an objective entity. In itself, and not for us, any given fact is essentially, substantively, a part or particle, a finite fragment, of the material world.

Our fumbling epistemologist does not comprehend or properly present either the difference between the concrete and the abstract or the relation of these correlative terms to objective reality.

The assertion "This man is George Novack" is a statement of concrete fact—unless a mistaken identity is involved.

The assertion "George Novack is a man" is a more abstract statement about the same factual entity, in which a particular individual is included in a general class.

The assertion "All humans originate from primate stock" is a much more abstract and generalized statement.

Not so, argues Falk. These are all nothing but "partial abstractions"; that they are statements of fact is irrelevant and immaterial.

Facts, however, are stubborn things. Order them out the door and they come creeping in through the basement or windows. No sectarian sophistry can banish them from reality or deprive them of their role as the ultimate determinant of the truth or the worth of all assertions and abstractions. That is primordial in the materialist theory of knowledge.

We now come to the most unexpected aspect of the position of our critic. Because I stand by the facts, he accuses me of being an empiricist who follows "the pragmatism of William James." The doctrines of James were highly influential during the 1920s at Harvard, where I received my initial education in philosophy. There I learned from his professorial associates what the pragmatic theory of knowledge was all about. Upon becoming a Marxist after the stock market crash of 1929, I consciously rejected its premises and conclusions along with the liberalism it rationalized.

This is more than my uninformed adversary in Australia has managed to do. What is the essential opposition between the Marxist and pragmatic theories of knowledge? Dialectical materialism regards truth as the correspondence, and error as the lack of correspondence, between an idea, a judgment, or a theory and the reality to which they refer. This objective linkage, or absence of linkage, constitutes the basis of the materialist epistemology. The practical activities of human beings do not *create* this correlation between things and any statements about them; they *disclose* and *verify*, i.e., substantiate it.

The pragmatism of William James (Dewey's instrumentalism is a different variant) contends that practical usefulness does more than ascertain the occurrence or nonoccurrence of knowledge and truth. Practice *creates* what is true or not true for us. For pragmatism the usefulness of ideas to humans defines the truth, which is brought to birth through their acting upon this or that idea. In Marxist theory the usefulness of ideas is derived from their correct reflections of the external world. The true or false content of our mental abstractions is brought to light and tested by our actions.

These two conceptions of truth are incompatible. One of them strives to report the relations, properties, and processes of objective reality as accurately and fully as possible. The other is content with the purely instrumental functions of ideas that presumably satisfy human needs (other than the urge to know what the foundations of truth really are!). Pragmatism does not insist that our ideas really harmonize with the facts.

Now hearken to the Healyite. "Far from being 'indissolubly merged' with the real world [as I had maintained], our concepts are brought into unity with objective reality only in the practical struggle to change this reality." Such a one-sided version of the interaction between reality and our concepts leaves out their preexisting material unity and makes knowledge depend, not upon the content common to ideas and facts, but only upon the practical activities that disclose and demonstrate the truth or nontruth of our ideas. *It is not I but my critic who follows in the track of the pioneer pragmatist William James!*

Falk goes on to argue: "Your undialectical approach to the Marxist method leads you into the empiricist [!] view that concepts are meaningful in virtue of some static relationship to 'the facts.'" Let us set aside the adjective "static," which is dragged in to obscure the issue. Whether facts are in motion or at rest, whether they are undergoing more change or less, concepts—even the most imaginary—have meaning only by virtue of some relationship to facts.

What other source could the meaning of ideas have, from the point of view of a materialist? Falk does not bother to tell us.

Despite his pretentions, the Healyite reasoner is really neither materialist nor dialectical in his approach to the problems of philosophy and politics. His erroneous objections to my views inexorably land him in the company of the pragmatists and idealists. Such is the ironic dialectical outcome of the debate between us.

Falk pejoratively describes me as "a middle class intellectual" trained in philosophy and excoriates me for betraying the task Trotsky entrusted to me in 1940 of defending and disseminating the logical method of Marxism. When I challenged several Healyites to name one other person in the English-speaking countries who has written more and worked harder to popularize the doctrines of dialectical materialism in the decades since Trotsky's death, they could only cite Cliff Slaughter, Healy's penman.

Since not only Novack, but Slaughter and Falk, happen to be middle-class intellectuals by origin, there can be no purely sociological distinction between us. On the political and theoretical levels the *quantity* of my philosophical production considerably outweighs that of my two opponents. To my knowledge Falk has written little else than his assigned attack upon my views; and Slaughter's output over the past fifteen years consists of a few pamphlets. I am willing to leave any judgment about the *quality* of our works to unprejudiced readers.

Thereby hangs a tale that deserves to be told. During the late fifties, when we were still political collaborators, Gerry Healy held a different estimate of my merits as a Marxist theoretician. During a meeting with him at Toronto he talked to me with some anxiety about the intellectuals such as Slaughter and others in England who had been won over to Trotskyism from the CP after Khrushchev's revelations and after the Kremlin had put down the proletarian uprising in Hungary.

Healy urged me to write a series of articles on Marxist method to help counteract the theoretical miseducation they had received under Stalinist auspices. He wanted to ensure that they would be guided by Marxist principles, not by shortsighted empirical considerations.

I agreed to fulfill the request and Healy subsequently published several early chapters of my book on *Empiricism and Its Evolution* in his theoretical magazine, *Labour Review*. At that time he had no inkling that I had departed from dialectical materialism or let Trotsky down. (I didn't even let him down!) He discovered these heinous faults in me only after he disagreed with the SWP on the necessity for reunifying the divided forces of the Fourth International.

Every sect must have its pontiff (Healy), its fetish (his peculiar distortion of the dialectic method), and villainous iconoclasts who refuse to accept its dogmas and must be defamed at all costs. Heading Healy's list are Joseph Hansen as a political analyst, Ernest Mandel as an economist, and myself as a philosopher. But the real target of the Healyite frenzy and fury is the genuine teachings of Trotskyism as these are implemented by the Fourth International. They resort to the most flagrant falsifications in pursuit of this unworthy aim.

Sectarians know no restraint. They compensate for their disdain of reality by being spiteful and vindictive toward their revolutionary opponents. These are bad traits in politics. Such subjectivism violates the objectivity demanded by Marxist materialism.

According to Lenin, "objectivity of consideration" is the first requirement of the dialectical method. (See: *Collected Works*, Vol. 38, Philosophical Notebooks, p. 221.) The Healyite disregard for the facts flouts this injunction at every step. Their ultrafactionalism, exemplified afresh by the Australian "Open Letter," precludes any objective and accurate examination by them of the real situation in economics, politics, or philosophy. These braggarts about dialectics cannot employ its method in any truthful or productive way.

JULY 2, 1973

THE CUBAN REVOLUTION AND WORLD POLITICS

October 1962
The 'Missile' Crisis as Seen from Cuba
TOMÁS DIEZ ACOSTA

In October 1962 Washington pushed the world to the edge of nuclear war. Here the full story of that historic moment is told from the perspective of the Cuban people, whose determination to defend their sovereignty and their socialist revolution blocked US plans for a devastating military assault. $17

Red Zone
Cuba and the Battle against Ebola in West Africa
ENRIQUE UBIETA GÓMEZ

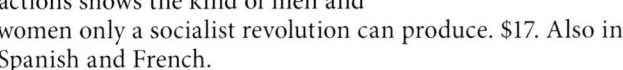

When three African countries were hit in 2014–15 by the Ebola epidemic, Cuba's revolutionary government sent what no other country even pretended to provide: more than 250 volunteer doctors, nurses, and other medical workers. This firsthand account of their actions shows the kind of men and women only a socialist revolution can produce. $17. Also in Spanish and French.

The First and Second Declarations of Havana

Nowhere are the questions of revolutionary strategy that today confront men and women on the front lines of struggles in the Americas addressed with greater truthfulness and clarity than in these uncompromising indictments of imperialist plunder and "the exploitation of man by man." Adopted by million-strong assemblies of the Cuban people in 1960 and 1962. $10. Also in Spanish, French, Farsi, Arabic, and Greek.

The Inevitable Battle
From the Bay of Pigs to Playa Girón
JUAN CARLOS RODRÍGUEZ

The rout of US-organized and -financed forces at Girón Beach on Cuba's Bay of Pigs in April 1961 was Washington's greatest military defeat in the Americas. It has marked the course of history for the last sixty years. $20. Also in Spanish.

Our History Is Still Being Written
The Story of Three Chinese Cuban Generals in the Cuban Revolution
ARMANDO CHOY, GUSTAVO CHUI, MOISÉS SÍO WONG, MARY-ALICE WATERS

"What was the key measure to uproot discrimination against Chinese and blacks in Cuba? It was the socialist revolution itself." New edition sheds light on Chinese Cubans' involvement in Cuba's internationalist course, including in Africa and Latin America. $15. Also in Spanish, French, Farsi, Greek, and Chinese.

Cuba and the Coming American Revolution
JACK BARNES

This is a book about the struggles of working people in the imperialist heartland, the youth attracted to them, and the example set by the Cuban people that revolution is not only necessary—it can be made. It is about the class struggle in the US, where the revolutionary capacities of workers and farmers are today as utterly discounted by the ruling powers as were those of the Cuban toilers. And just as wrongly. $10. Also in Spanish, French, and Farsi.

Cuba and Angola: The War for Freedom
HARRY VILLEGAS ("POMBO")

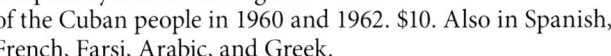

The story of Cuba's unparalleled contribution to the fight to free Africa from the scourge of apartheid. And how, in the doing, Cuba's socialist revolution was strengthened. $10. Also in Spanish, Farsi, and Greek.

Che Guevara Talks to Young People

Guevara challenges the youth of Cuba and the world to work. To become disciplined. To join the vanguard on the front lines of struggles, small and large. To become a different kind of human being as they fight together with working people of all lands to transform the world. $12. Also in Spanish and Greek.

WWW.PATHFINDERPRESS.COM

EXPAND YOUR REVOLUTIONARY LIBRARY

Labor, Nature, and the Evolution of Humanity
The Long View of History
FREDERICK ENGELS, KARL MARX, GEORGE NOVACK, MARY-ALICE WATERS

Without understanding that social labor, transforming nature, has driven humanity's evolution for millions of years, working people are unable to see beyond the capitalist epoch of class exploitation that warps all human relations, ideas, and values. Only the revolutionary conquest of state power by the working class can open the door to a world free of capitalist exploitation, degradation of nature, subjugation of women, racism, and war. A world built on human solidarity. A socialist world. $12. Also in Spanish and French.

Women in Cuba: The Making of a Revolution Within the Revolution
VILMA ESPÍN, ASELA DE LOS SANTOS, YOLANDA FERRER

The integration of women in the ranks and leadership of the Cuban Revolution was intertwined with the proletarian course of the leadership of the revolution from the start. This is the story of that revolution and how it transformed the women and men who made it. $17. Also in Spanish, Farsi, and Greek.

Their Trotsky and Ours
JACK BARNES

To lead the working class in a successful revolution, a mass proletarian party is needed whose cadres, well beforehand, have absorbed a world communist program, are proletarian in life and work, derive deep satisfaction from doing politics, and have forged a leadership with an acute sense of what to do next. This book is about building such a party. $12. Also in Spanish, French, and Farsi.

Is Socialist Revolution in the US Possible?
A Necessary Debate among Working People
MARY-ALICE WATERS

An unhesitating "Yes"—that's the answer given here. Possible—but not inevitable. That depends on what working people do. $7. Also in Spanish, French, and Farsi.

The Jewish Question
A Marxist Interpretation
ABRAM LEON

Why is Jew-hatred still raising its ugly head? What are its class roots—from antiquity through feudalism, to capitalism's rise and current crises? Why is there no solution under capitalism? The author, Abram Leon, was killed in the Nazi gas chambers. Revised translation, new introduction, and 40 pages of illustrations and maps. $17. Also in Spanish and French.

Are They Rich Because They're Smart?
Class, Privilege, and Learning under Capitalism
JACK BARNES

In battles forced on us by the capitalists, workers will begin to transform our attitudes toward life, work, and each other. We'll discover our worth, denied by the rulers and upper middle classes who insist they're rich because they're smart. We'll learn in struggle what we're capable of becoming. $10. Also in Spanish, French, Farsi, and Arabic.

The Clintons' Anti-Working-Class Record
Why Washington Fears Working People
JACK BARNES

What working people need to know about the profit-driven course of Democrats and Republicans alike over the last three decades. And the political awakening of workers seeking to understand and resist the capitalist rulers' assaults. $10. Also in Spanish, French, Farsi, and Greek.

Teamster Rebellion
FARRELL DOBBS

The 1934 strikes that won union recognition for truckers and warehouse workers in Minneapolis and helped pave the way for the working-class social movement that built the industrial unions. The first of four volumes by a central leader of these battles. $16. Also in Spanish, French, Farsi, and Greek.

Malcolm X Talks to Young People

"The young generation of whites, Blacks, browns, whatever else—you're living at a time of revolution," said Malcolm in 1964. "And I for one will join with anyone, I don't care what color you are, as long as you want to change this miserable condition that exists on this earth." Four talks and an interview in the last months of Malcolm's life. $12. Also in Spanish, French, Farsi, and Greek.

The History of the Russian Revolution
LEON TROTSKY

How, under Lenin's leadership, the Bolshevik Party led millions of workers and farmers to overthrow the state power of the landlords and capitalists in 1917 and bring to power a government that advanced their class interests at home and worldwide. Unabridged, 3 vols. in one. Written by one of the central leaders of that socialist revolution. $30. Also in French and Russian.

Imperialism's March toward Fascism and War
JACK BARNES

"There will be new Hitlers, new Mussolinis. That is inevitable. What is not inevitable is that they will triumph. The working-class vanguard will organize our class to fight back against the devastating toll we are made to pay for the capitalist crisis. The future of humanity will be decided in the contest between these contending class forces." In *New International* no. 10. $14. Also in Spanish, French, Farsi, and Greek.

Problems of Women's Liberation
EVELYN REED

Explores the social and economic roots of women's oppression from prehistoric society to modern capitalism and points the road forward to emancipation. $12. Also in Farsi, Arabic, and Greek.

Lenin's Final Fight
Speeches and Writings, 1922–23
V.I. LENIN

In 1922 and 1923, V.I. Lenin, central leader of the world's first socialist revolution, waged what was to be his last political battle—one that was lost following his death. At stake was whether that revolution, and the international communist movement it led, would remain on the revolutionary proletarian course that brought workers and peasants to power in October 1917. $17. Also in Spanish, Farsi, and Greek.

The Transitional Program for Socialist Revolution
LEON TROTSKY

The Socialist Workers Party program, drafted by Trotsky in 1938, still guides the SWP and communists the world over. The party "uncompromisingly gives battle to all political groupings tied to the apron strings of the bourgeoisie. Its task— the abolition of capitalism's domination. Its aim—socialism. Its method—the proletarian revolution." $17. Also in Farsi.

The Communist Manifesto
KARL MARX AND FREDERICK ENGELS

Communism, say the founding leaders of the revolutionary workers movement, is not a set of ideas or preconceived "principles" but workers' line of march to power, springing from a "movement going on under our very eyes." $5. Also in Spanish, French, Farsi, and Arabic.

Socialism on Trial
Testimony at Minneapolis Sedition Trial
JAMES P. CANNON

The revolutionary program of the working class, presented in response to frame-up charges of "seditious conspiracy" in 1941, on the eve of US entry into World War II. The defendants were leaders of the Minneapolis labor movement and the Socialist Workers Party. $15. Also in Spanish, French, and Farsi.

WWW.PATHFINDERPRESS.COM

In Defense of the US Working Class
MARY-ALICE WATERS

Drawing on the fighting traditions of the oppressed and exploited of all colors and national origins, in 2018 tens of thousands of teachers and other working people in West Virginia, Oklahoma, and other states waged victorious strikes. They fought for dignity and respect for themselves, their families, and for all working people. $7. Also in Spanish, French, Farsi, and Greek.

50 Years of Covert Operations in the US
Washington's Political Police and the American Working Class
LARRY SEIGLE, FARRELL DOBBS, STEVE CLARK

How class-conscious workers have fought against the drive to build the "national security" state essential to maintaining capitalist rule. $10. Also in Spanish and Farsi.

The Struggle for a Proletarian Party
JAMES P. CANNON

"The workers of America have power enough to topple the structure of capitalism at home and to lift the whole world with them when they rise," Cannon asserts. On the eve of World War II, a founder of the communist movement in the US and leader of the Communist International in Lenin's time defends the program and party-building norms of Bolshevism. $20. Also in Spanish and Farsi.

Dynamics of the Cuban Revolution
A Marxist Appreciation
JOSEPH HANSEN

How did the Cuban Revolution unfold? Why is it an "unbearable challenge" to US imperialism? Why are its lessons important to working people everywhere?

In "Cuba—The acid test: A reply to ultraleft sectarians," one of more than 20 articles here, Hansen starts with facts—not doctrine pretending to be theory—to examine the class struggle unfolding in Cuba in the 1960s. He refutes the political blindness of leftists who denied the dialectical richness of the socialist revolution and communist leadership developing before their eyes. $23

U.S. Imperialism Has Lost the Cold War
JACK BARNES

The collapse of regimes across Eastern Europe and the USSR claiming to be communist did not mean workers and farmers there had been crushed. In today's sharpening capitalist conflicts and wars, these toilers are joining working people the world over in the class struggle against exploitation. In *New International* no. 11. $14. Also in Spanish, French, Farsi, and Greek.

In Defense of Marxism
Against the Petty-Bourgeois Opposition in the Socialist Workers Party
LEON TROTSKY

A reply to those in the revolutionary workers movement in the late 1930s bending to bourgeois patriotism during Washington's buildup to enter World War II. Trotsky explains why only a party fighting to bring workers into its ranks and leadership can steer a communist course. In the process, he defends the materialist and dialectical foundations of Marxism. $17. Also in Spanish.

FBI on Trial
The Victory in the Socialist Workers Party Suit against Government Spying
MARGARET JAYKO

The record of an historic victory in the fight for political rights, including the 1986 federal court ruling against government spying and excerpts from trial testimony by SWP leaders Farrell Dobbs and Jack Barnes. $17

We Are Heirs of the World's Revolutions
Speeches from the Burkina Faso Revolution, 1983–87
THOMAS SANKARA

How peasants and workers in this West African country established a popular revolutionary government and began to fight hunger, illiteracy, and economic backwardness imposed by imperialist domination. They set an example not only for workers and small farmers in Africa, but their class brothers and sisters the world over. $10. Also in Spanish, French, and Farsi.